Chapter 6

Gross Wages *pp. 153, 154, 162*

$$\text{Gross earnings (salary)} = \frac{\text{Annual earnings}}{\text{Number of pay periods per year}}$$

$$\text{Gross earnings (commissions)} = \text{Net sales} \times \text{Commission rate}$$

$$\text{Gross earnings (wages)} = \text{Rate per hour} \times \text{Number of hours worked}$$

Bank Statement Reconciliation *p. 206*

To the Bank Balance

1. Add the total of all unrecorded deposits.
2. Subtract the total of all outstanding checks.

To the Checkbook Balance

1. Subtract the total of
   a. All previously deposited overdrafts.
   b. All miscellaneous charges.
2. Add the total of all interest and miscellaneous credit.

Chapter 7

Financial Ratios *pp. 234–237*

$$\text{Current ratio} = \frac{\text{Current assets}}{\text{Current liabilities}}$$

$$\text{Gross profit margin} = \frac{\text{Net sales} - \text{Cost of goods sold}}{\text{Net sales}}$$

$$\text{Acid-test ratio} = \frac{\text{Cash} + \text{Receivables}}{\text{Current liabilities}}$$

$$\text{Operating ratio} = \frac{\text{Cost of goods sold} + \text{Operating expenses}}{\text{Net sales}}$$

$$\text{Stockholders' equity ratio} = \frac{\text{Owners' equity}}{\text{Total assets}}$$

$$\text{Debt-equity ratio} = \frac{\text{Current liabilities} + \text{Long-term liabilities}}{\text{Owners' equity}}$$

Pre-1981 Depreciation Methods *pp. 255–257*

The Straight-Line Method

$$d = \frac{c - s}{n}$$

where d = depreciation amount per year, c = cost of asset, s = salvage value, and n = years of useful life.

The Declining-Balance Method

$$d = b \times r$$

where d = depreciation amount per year, b = book value of the preceding year, and r = depreciation rate.

The Sum-of-the-Year

$d =$

where r is a fraction determined as follows: The denominator is the sum of the digits representing the useful life of the asset, and the numerator is the number of years of useful life remaining at the beginning of the year for which the computation is made.

Chapter 8

Property Tax Calculations *p. 282*

$$\text{Tax rate} = \frac{\text{Total taxes to be raised}}{\text{Total assessments}}$$

Chapter 9

Time Calculations *p. 306*

Exact Interest

$$t = \frac{\text{Exact time}}{365}$$

Ordinary Interest

$$t = \frac{\text{Exact time}}{360}$$

Interest Calculations *pp. 299, 312*

$$I = Prt \qquad A = P(1 + rt)$$

where I = interest, P = principal (the amount of money borrowed or invested), r = annual rate, t = the length of time (in years) the principal is borrowed or invested, A = maturity value.

Chapter 10

Simple Discount Calculations *pp. 319, 324, 325*

$$D = Adt \qquad A = \frac{D}{dt} \qquad d = \frac{D}{At} \qquad t = \frac{D}{Ad} \qquad P = A(1 - dt)$$

where D = amount of discount, A = maturity value, d = discount percent, t = term of the loan in years, P = proceeds.

Simple Interest vs. Simple Discount *p. 333*

$$r = \frac{d}{1 - dt} \qquad d = \frac{r}{1 + rt}$$

where r = simple interest rate, d = discount percent.

FUNDAMENTALS OF BUSINESS MATHEMATICS

FUNDAMENTALS OF BUSINESS MATHEMATICS

Fifth Edition

Walter E. Williams
University of South Florida

James H. Reed
University of South Florida

Wm. C. Brown Publishers

Book Team

Editor *Earl McPeek*
Developmental Editor *Janette S. Stecki*
Production Editor *Reneê A. Menne*
Designer *Laurie J. Entringer*
Art Editor *Gayle A. Salow*
Photo Editor *Michelle Oberhoffer*
Visuals Processor *Joyce E. Watters*

Wm. C. Brown Publishers

President *G. Franklin Lewis*
Vice President, Publisher *George Wm. Bergquist*
Vice President, Publisher *Thomas E. Doran*
Vice President, Operations and Production *Beverly Kolz*
National Sales Manager *Virginia S. Moffat*
Advertising Manager *Ann M. Knepper*
Marketing Manager *David Horwitz*
Editor-in-Chief *Edward G. Jaffe*
Production Editorial Manager *Colleen A. Yonda*
Production Editorial Manager *Julie A. Kennedy*
Publishing Services Manager *Karen J. Slaght*
Manager of Visuals and Design *Faye M. Schilling*

Library of Congress Catalog Card Number: 89–061105

ISBN 0–697–06429–8

Printed in the United States of America by Wm. C. Brown Publishers, 2460 Kerper Boulevard, Dubuque, IA 52001

10 9 8 7 6 5 4 3 2 1

To Elizabeth and June

Contents

Part 4
Selected Topics *457*

Preface

The fifth edition of *Fundamentals of Business Mathematics* retains the format and style that made the previous editions popular. The book continues to provide basic skills in business mathematics and is written for the first-year community college or university student. While the book is intended for students who plan to major in business, the topics in the book remain pertinent to consumers as well as employers. For this reason, the text is also appropriate for a core course in basic mathematics.

The only prerequisite for the text is standard high school mathematics. In fact, the opening chapters provide a review of basic arithmetic for those students who need to solidify their arithmetic foundations before applying these skills to business situations.

About this book

The philosophy of the text continues to be **learning by doing,** and the pedagogy follows the successful formula of **explanation-example-exercise.** New material is immediately reinforced by examples and exercise sets relating to business situations. **Word problems** continue to be a key feature of the text and are valuable training for actual business operations. Additional learning aids in each chapter include **learning objectives,** a **glossary of key terms,** and **review tests.**

Another feature retained in the text is **flexibility.** Once the student masters the material in Part I, the instructor may choose any set of topics from the remaining chapters. This enables the book to be used successfully in courses ranging from one term to a full year.

The book is divided into the following parts.

Part 1—Basics. This part presents the foundation material of the book. Students review basic arithmetic, examine equations, and study in detail the fundamental formula of business mathematics $P = B \cdot R$.

Part 2—Retailing/Accounting. In addition to presenting the fundamentals of buying and selling and inventory control, chapters in this part cover fundamentals of record keeping with respect to payrolls, banking, accounting statements, budgeting, depreciation, and taxes.

Part 3—Finance. The principles of basic finance from the viewpoint of both the consumer and the businessperson are examined in this part. Topics include simple and compound interest, credit, stocks and bonds, annuities, and amortization.

Part 4—Selected Topics. Insurance is a business necessity, and the chapter on insurance includes detailed coverage of four forms of business insurance: life insurance, group insurance, fire insurance, and automobile insurance. Statistics and graphs have become vital decision tools for management, and businesses are rapidly converting to metric measurements. Chapters in this part examine these topics.

New to this edition

Changes in the fifth edition reflect comments from instructors and reviewers from around the nation. These changes include the following:

1. To get students more quickly into the business topics, the material on graphs has been combined with the material on statistics in chapter 17.
2. A revised and updated section on depreciation that covers the MACRS depreciation method.
3. Updated examples and exercises to reflect current changes in wages, interest rates, prices, and FICA and federal income tax tables.
4. A revision of the section on federal income taxes that reflects recent changes in tax reform legislation.
5. A revision of some formulas on pricing to make them easier to learn.
6. Additional examples and problems in the insurance chapter to include the payment of claims.
7. A revision of the metric chapter to make metric conversions more intuitive.
8. Revised and updated problems in most sections.
9. Updated chapter objectives, glossaries, and chapter review tests.

Supplements

In addition to the changes in the text, a number of improvements have been made in the instructor's manual. Along with complete solutions to all problems in the text, the manual features sections on the purpose of each chapter and includes valuable instructional tips and derivations of important formulas. At the end of each chapter there are six chapter examinations that may be used for in-class testing. These examinations now include multiple-choice tests. Answers to these examinations and to all workbook problems are provided. For those instructors who use overhead projectors in the classroom, a set of 38 transparency masters is provided at the end of the manual. An additional file of 118 two- and four-color acetate transparencies is available from WCB at no charge to qualifying adoptors of the textbook.

The optional student workbook has also been updated and revised. The workbook is designed for those students who need additional practice in solving problems similar to those found in the text.

Two optional computer packages are new to this edition. To provide instructors with additional flexibility in creating examinations, a test package has been prepared that allows instructors to select examination problems from three levels of difficulty. The second computer package features programs that match many key topics in the text and is designed for student use in a computer laboratory setting. These packages are on computer disks for either an IBM or Apple personal computer.

Many improvements in the text are due to our reviewers, and we would like to thank the following people for carefully reviewing our materials and providing many invaluable suggestions: A. Bruce Wadsworth, Fulton-Montgomery Community College; Maryann Birdsall, Ocean County College; J. David Felt, Northern Virginia Community College; Dorothy Terwilligar, Baker College; Rhosan Stryker, Delta College; Richard Miller, Arizona Western College; Ned W. Schillow, Lehigh County Community College; Ray E. Collings, Tri-County Technical College; and William O. Rider, Westmoreland County Community College.

We would also like to express our appreciation to the editors and staff at Wm. C. Brown Publishers. Their expertise and cooperation are unexcelled. Finally, we wish to thank our wives and children for their encouragement and support.

PART 1

Basics

The essential techniques necessary to successfully master the subject of business mathematics are presented in this part. The topics include a review of basic arithmetic, a discussion of the elementary principles involved in the use of equations and formulas, and a detailed study of the fundamental percentage formula $P = BR$.

CHAPTER 1

Review of Arithmetic

Chapter Objectives

I. Learn the meaning of the following terms:

Whole numbers, 4
Addend and sum, 4
Minuend, subtrahend, and difference, 7
Multiplicand, multiplier, factor, partial product, and product, 10, 11
Dividend, divisor, quotient, and remainder, 12, 13

II. Understand the principles of:

Positional notation, 4
Carrying and borrowing, 4, 7

III. Compute:

Sums of whole numbers, 4–6
Differences of whole numbers, 7–8
Products of whole numbers, 11–12
Quotients of whole numbers, 13

Student's self-examination for chapter 1

This test will help determine individual strengths and weaknesses in the basic arithmetic skills discussed in chapter 1. The answers are provided in appendix L.

In problems 1–8, perform the indicated operations.

1. $\begin{array}{r} 57{,}973 \\ +\underline{86{,}718} \end{array}$

2. $\begin{array}{r} 3{,}619 \\ 26{,}451 \\ 714 \\ +\underline{31{,}837} \end{array}$

3. $\begin{array}{r} 34{,}514 \\ -\underline{27{,}638} \end{array}$

4. $\begin{array}{r} 7{,}005 \\ -\underline{6{,}239} \end{array}$

5. $\begin{array}{r} 2{,}746 \\ \times\underline{374} \end{array}$

6. $\begin{array}{r} 9{,}503 \\ \times\underline{705} \end{array}$

7. $63\overline{)33{,}012}$

8. $354\overline{)182{,}310}$

Solve

9. Find the quotient and remainder for 453 ÷ 7.
10. Find the quotient and remainder for 2,803 ÷ 326.
11. A number added to 2,797 gives 17,423. What is the number?
12. A number divided by 23 is 47. What is the number?
13. When a number is subtracted from 5,617, the result is 1,998. Find the number.
14. A number multiplied by 409 is 15,133. What is the number?
15. When a number is divided by 73, the quotient is 23 and the remainder is 8. Find the number.
16. A video recorder is on sale for $213. If the regular price is $402, how much would be saved by buying the recorder on sale?
17. A local clothing store paid invoices of $23,792, $3,475, and $7,526. What was the total expenditure for the invoices?
18. Last week, a sales representative sold 63 units of product A at $14 each, 19 units of product B at $223 each, and 37 units of product C at $172 each. Find the total sales income for the week.
19. A sporting goods store sold 237 rowing machines for a total profit of $11,613. What profit was made on each machine?
20. A manufacturer filled an order for 57 units of an item at a total cost of $399. Then a second order was filled for 34 units of the same item. What was the cost of the second order?

Section 1.1 Introduction

The foundation of business mathematics is the ten **digits** of the decimal system: 0, 1, 2, 3, 4, 5, 6, 7, 8, 9. All numbers are written with these ten digits—a remarkable feat considering that the set of numbers is infinite. This is possible because of the Hindu-Arabic positional notation that emphasizes the position of the digits.* For example, 467 and 764 have the same three digits, but the position of each digit with respect to the other digits distinguishes 467 and 764 as different numbers. The same distinction is used in written language. The words *teach* and *cheat* contain the same letters, but the arrangement of the letters creates two different words.

Hundred thousands	Ten thousands	Thousands	Hundreds	Tens	Ones
			4	6	7
		5	0	2	9

Figure 1.1
Hindu-Arabic positional notation

In the decimal system, each position represents a product of tens, as shown in figure 1.1.

The notation in figure 1.1 indicates that 467 means 4 hundreds (400) plus 6 tens (60) plus 7 ones (7), or 400 + 60 + 7, and 5,029 means 5 thousands (5,000) plus 0 hundreds (0) plus 2 tens (20) plus 9 ones (9), or 5,000 + 20 + 9.

The numbers 0, 1, 2, 3, 4, 5, 6, 7, 8, 9, 10, 11, . . . are called **whole numbers.** In the sections that follow, we review the **operations** of whole numbers: addition, subtraction, multiplication, and division.

Section 1.2 Addition and subtraction

Addition

The Hindu-Arabic positional notation is more than just an efficient method for writing numbers. It also lends itself to an **algorithm** (a step-by-step process for performing a calculation) for the shortcut method of counting called addition. We add two or more numbers by adding the digits in each positional column separately, beginning with the ones column. If the sum of the digits in a column results in a two-digit number, the first digit of that number is "carried" to the next column and added with the digits in that column. Any of the numbers that are to be added are called **addends,** and the result of adding two or more numbers is called the **sum.** The addition algorithm is illustrated in example 1.

Example 1

Find: a. $\begin{array}{r} 427 \\ +\underline{\ 62} \end{array}$ b. $\begin{array}{r} 14 \\ 53 \\ +\underline{96} \end{array}$

Solution

a.

427	Addend
+ 62	Addend
489	Sum

b.

14	Addend
53	Addend
+ 96	Addend
163	Sum

*This notation is named after the Hindus, who invented it, and the Arabs, who refined it and exported it to the Western world.

In (a) of example 1, the sum of the digits in the ones column is 2 + 7 = 9, in the tens column is 6 + 2 = 8, and in the hundreds column is 0 + 4 = 4; hence, 427 + 62 = 489. In (b), the sum of the digits in the ones column is 6 + 3 + 4 = 13. Because 13 is a two-digit number, the 1 is carried to the tens column and added with the other digits in that column, or 9 + 5 + 1 + 1 = 16. Thus, 14 + 53 + 96 = 163.

The electronic calculator has eliminated much of the need for manual addition, but instances arise in which columns of numbers must be added by hand and the sum checked. In such instances, addition is often simplified by grouping combinations of digits whose sum is 10. For instance. in the problem

$$\begin{array}{r} 8 \\ 6 \\ 2 \\ +\underline{4} \end{array}$$

the sum is found more quickly by combining 8 + 2 = 10 and 6 + 4 = 10; then 10 + 10 = 20.

Example 2 Find:

$$\begin{array}{r} 86 \\ 68 \\ 42 \\ 35 \\ +\underline{14} \end{array}$$

Solution

$$\begin{array}{r} 2 \\ 86 \\ 68 \\ 42 \\ 35 \\ +\underline{\ 14} \\ 245 \end{array}$$

6 + 4 = 10, 8 + 2 = 10, 10 + 10 + 5 = 25; write 5, carry 2.

2 + 8 = 10, 6 + 4 = 10, 10 + 10 + 3 + 1 = 24; write 24.

For particularly long columns of numbers, it may be simpler to split the problem into two or more problems and then add the subtotals.

Example 3 Find:

```
  407
  939
  701
  463
  442
  565
+ 848
```

Solution

```
  407
  939
  701
+ 463    2,510   Subtotal
  442
  565
+ 848    1,855   Subtotal
         4,365   Total
```

Checking addition

Several methods exist for checking addition. Reversing the order of the addition is one method. That is, add beginning from the top of the column instead of the bottom (or vice versa). A second method is to re-add using the grouping technique illustrated in example 3.

With either method, if re-adding results in the same sum, odds are that the solution is correct.

Horizontal and vertical addition

Examples 1 through 3 illustrated addition of numbers in vertical columns. Numbers can also be added horizontally if we continue to observe the positional place of the digits. A number of business situations occur in which both horizontal and vertical addition are required.

By adding the sales information in the following table horizontally and vertically, we can determine both the sales of a particular brand and the total sales of all brands on a given day:

	Monday	Tuesday	Wednesday	Thursday	Friday	Total
Brand A	10	9	14	11	14	58
Brand B	17	22	19	15	23	96
Brand C	8	6	9	5	10	38
Total	35	37	42	31	47	192

The addition is checked by adding the totals to obtain the grand total of 192.

Figure 1.2
Productivity report

PRODUCTIVITY REPORT (IN DOLLARS)

	MON	TUES	WED	THURS	FRI	SAT	SUN	TOTAL
7 A.M.	108	117	112	110	107	116	129	799
8 A.M.	123	132	129	126	119	121	133	883
9 A.M.	134	139	140	129	131	137	142	952
10 A.M.	147	149	152	147	147	148	159	1,049
11 A.M.	159	164	162	159	161	173	183	1,161
OR 11:30 A.M.								
SUBTOTAL	671	701	695	671	665	695	746	4844

The productivity report in figure 1.2 is another example of horizontal and vertical addition. The horizontal totals indicate hourly production over a week, while the vertical totals indicate daily production for morning hours.

Subtraction The operations of addition and subtraction are closely related. For example, if 8 is the sum of 5 plus 3 ($8 = 5 + 3$), then 8 subtract 5 equals 3 ($8 - 5 = 3$). That is, to subtract 5 from 8, we seek that number that when added to 5 equals 8.

In a subtraction problem, the number from which another number is subtracted is called the **minuend,** while the number that is subtracted is called the **subtrahend.** The result of subtracting one number from another is called the **difference.**

When subtracting, we observe the same positional rules used in addition.

Example 4 Find: a. $49 - 28$ b. $44 - 18$

Solution

a.
$$\begin{array}{rl} 49 & \text{Minuend} \\ -\underline{28} & \text{Subtrahend} \\ 21 & \text{Difference} \end{array}$$

b.
$$\begin{array}{rl} \overset{3}{\not{4}}4 & \text{Minuend} \\ -\underline{18} & \text{Subtrahend} \\ 26 & \text{Difference} \end{array}$$

In the ones column of problem (b), there is no positive number that added to 8 equals 4. This difficulty is overcome by borrowing. Borrowing involves a rearrangement of the positional notation of the minuend to permit subtraction. The number 44 means 4 tens plus 4 ones in the positional notation. To facilitate subtraction, we write 44 as 3 tens plus 14 ones. That is,

$$\begin{array}{rl} 44 = & 3\text{ tens} + 14\text{ ones} \\ -\underline{18} = & \underline{1\text{ ten} + \ \ 8\text{ ones}} \\ & 2\text{ tens} + \ \ 6\text{ ones} = 26 \end{array}$$

Borrowing may be necessary in any positional column when subtracting one number from another.

Checking subtraction

The relationship between subtraction and addition provides a means for checking the answer to a subtraction problem. The answer (difference) is added to the subtrahend. If the result is the minuend, the subtraction was correctly performed.

Example 5 Find and check your answer: $834 - 263$

Solution

$$\begin{array}{r} 7 \\ \not{8}34 \\ -263 \\ \hline 571 \end{array} \qquad \begin{array}{r} \textit{Check:} \\ 263 \\ +571 \\ \hline 834 \end{array}$$

Exercises for Section 1.2

In problems 1–12, find the indicated sums.

1. $\begin{array}{r} 351 \\ +322 \\ \hline \end{array}$

2. $\begin{array}{r} 274 \\ +715 \\ \hline \end{array}$

3. $\begin{array}{r} 529 \\ +311 \\ \hline \end{array}$

4. $\begin{array}{r} 273 \\ +417 \\ \hline \end{array}$

5. $\begin{array}{r} 7{,}435{,}758 \\ +\ 947{,}762 \\ \hline \end{array}$

6. $\begin{array}{r} 4{,}539{,}743 \\ +\ 842{,}051 \\ \hline \end{array}$

7. $\begin{array}{r} 746 \\ 259 \\ +782 \\ \hline \end{array}$

8. $\begin{array}{r} 514 \\ 655 \\ +927 \\ \hline \end{array}$

9. $\begin{array}{r} 2{,}476 \\ 472 \\ +\ 231 \\ \hline \end{array}$

10. $\begin{array}{r} 2{,}721 \\ 3{,}273 \\ +4{,}529 \\ \hline \end{array}$

11. $\begin{array}{r} 7{,}423 \\ 8{,}291 \\ 4{,}726 \\ +1{,}429 \\ \hline \end{array}$

12. $\begin{array}{r} 4{,}271 \\ 7{,}214 \\ 2{,}143 \\ +9{,}526 \\ \hline \end{array}$

In problems 13–24, perform the indicated subtraction and check your results.

13. $\begin{array}{r} 743 \\ -\ 21 \\ \hline \end{array}$

14. $\begin{array}{r} 785 \\ -\ 43 \\ \hline \end{array}$

15. $\begin{array}{r} 5{,}496 \\ -\ 273 \\ \hline \end{array}$

16. $\begin{array}{r} 7{,}687 \\ -\ 376 \\ \hline \end{array}$

17. $\begin{array}{r} 741 \\ -\ 27 \\ \hline \end{array}$

18. $\begin{array}{r} 543 \\ -\ 39 \\ \hline \end{array}$

19. $\begin{array}{r} 5{,}601 \\ -\ 78 \\ \hline \end{array}$

20. $\begin{array}{r} 3{,}705 \\ -\ 76 \\ \hline \end{array}$

21. $\begin{array}{r} 3{,}251 \\ -\ 172 \\ \hline \end{array}$

22. $\begin{array}{r} 4{,}536 \\ -\ 347 \\ \hline \end{array}$

23. $\begin{array}{r} 14{,}732 \\ -\ 5{,}457 \\ \hline \end{array}$

24. $\begin{array}{r} 34{,}867 \\ -\ 778 \\ \hline \end{array}$

25. The Corner Grocery paid invoices to wholesalers in the following amounts: bakery items, \$74; dairy products, \$219; produce, \$198; meat products, \$1,723. What was the total expenditure for the invoices?

26. The monthly payroll of the ABC Machine Shop is summarized as follows: machinists, $17,829; draftspeople, $8,587; maintenance people, $3,720; executives, $25,280; consultants, $3,240. Find the total monthly payroll.

27. Owners' equity in a business is the total assets minus the total liabilities. Belcher's Bakery has total assets of $342,793 and total liabilities of $99,275. Find the owners' equity.

28. A recent balance sheet for a small restaurant listed total assets of $227,492 and total liabilities of $83,745. What is the owners' equity? (See problem 27.)

29. During the first week in September, an inspector at a manufacturing plant rejected 793 items on Monday, 1,021 items on Tuesday, 821 items on Wednesday, 1,129 items on Thursday, and 998 items on Friday. How many items did this inspector reject during the week?

30. A three-story warehouse is offered for lease. The warehouse has 5,427 square feet of storage space on the first floor, 5,272 square feet on the second floor, and 2,742 square feet on the third floor. Find the total storage space in the warehouse.

31. Mary Mackey wishes to buy a new house. The cost of the house is $167,750, and she agrees to a down payment of $59,250. Find the amount she will owe on the house.

32. The Furniture Mart purchased some used furniture for $2,314. The furniture was then sold for $2,703. How much profit was realized?

33. An apartment building contains four types of apartments: efficiency, one-bedroom, two-bedroom, and three-bedroom. The rental income per month from the efficiencies is $2,842; from the one-bedroom apartments is $7,423; from the two-bedroom apartments is $5,243; and from the three-bedroom apartments is $1,422. How much rental income does the building produce?

34. The Atlas Manufacturing Company is divided into five departments. During the month of January, the operating expenses for each department were as follows: department A, $672; department B, $7,422; department C, $927; department D, $4,898; department E, $2,747. What was the company's total operating expense for the month?

35. During the month of January, a small business had total sales of $93,492 of which $24,593 were for cash. Find the credit sales for the month.

36. It cost $47,217 to stock the shelves of the Corner Drug Store. The sales value of the stock is $73,291. If the stock is sold at sales value, what is the profit?

37. A department store offers to sell a dining-room set at a sale price of $763. If the regular price of the set was $819, how much would be saved by buying the set on sale?

38. A contractor built four houses at a total cost of $287,543. He sold them for a total of $342,722. How much profit did he realize?

39. Use horizontal and vertical addition to fill in the missing entries in the following chart showing the daily sales of each department at Waldo's Grocery during the first week in April:

	Mon.	Tues.	Wed.	Thurs.	Fri.	Sat.	Total
Bakery	$ 420	$ 360	$ 540	$ 490	$ 585	$ 310	____
Meats	760	840	910	429	719	554	____
Produce	510	485	547	493	604	641	____
Dairy products	314	219	337	408	373	381	____
Grocery items	2,342	2,719	1,921	2,567	2,681	2,501	____
Total	____	____	____	____	____	____	____

40. The following chart shows the departmental operating expenses at Orion, Inc., during the first six months of last year. Use horizontal and vertical addition to fill in the missing entries in the chart.

	Jan.	Feb.	Mar.	Apr.	May	June	Total
Office	$2,132	$1,814	$1,701	$2,147	$2,211	$1,982	____
Showroom	714	841	902	893	721	746	____
Sales	3,142	3,015	3,257	3,419	3,221	3,657	____
Storage	517	631	597	551	492	481	____
Total	____	____	____	____	____	____	____

Section 1.3 Multiplication and division

Multiplication

Multiplication began as a shortcut for repeated addition. For example, $3 \times 5 = 5 + 5 + 5 = 15$, and $4 \times 7 = 7 + 7 + 7 + 7 = 28$. The multiplication table is a listing of these products, and our first training in multiplication is to memorize a portion of this table. However, we soon are taught an efficient algorithm for multiplying two numbers. The process involves multiplying each digit in the **multiplicand** (the number that is multiplied by another) by each digit in the **multiplier** (the number by which another number is multiplied) to obtain a **partial product.** The **product** is the sum of the partial products, as shown in example 1.

Example 1 Find: 24×7

Solution

$$\begin{array}{rl} 24 & \text{Multiplicand or } \textbf{factor} \\ \times \underline{\ \ 7} & \text{Multiplier or } \textbf{factor} \\ 28 & \text{Partial product } (7 \times 4 = 28) \\ \underline{140} & \text{Partial product } (7 \times 2 \text{ tens} = 14 \text{ tens} = 140) \\ 168 & \text{Product (sum of the partial products)} \end{array}$$

With practice, we learn to condense the example 1 solution by employing the carrying device:

$$\begin{array}{r} 2 \\ 24 \\ \times \underline{\ \ 7} \\ 168 \end{array}$$

The reasoning is $7 \times 4 = 28$; write 8, carry 2. $7 \times 2 = 14$, $14 + 2 = 16$; write 16.

Example 2 Find: 36×18

Solution

$$\begin{array}{rl} 36 & \text{Multiplicand} \\ \times \underline{18} & \text{Multiplier} \\ 48 & \text{Partial product } (8 \times 6 = 48) \\ 240 & \text{Partial product } (8 \times 3 \text{ tens} = 24 \text{ tens} = 240) \\ 60 & \text{Partial product } (1 \text{ ten} \times 6 = 6 \text{ tens} = 60) \\ \underline{300} & \text{Partial product } (1 \text{ ten} \times 3 \text{ tens} = 10 \times 30 = 300) \\ 648 & \text{Product} \end{array}$$

The example 2 problem can also be solved by carrying:

$$\begin{array}{rl} 36 & \text{Multiplicand} \\ \times \underline{18} & \text{Multiplier} \\ 288 & \text{Partial product } (8 \times 6 = 48\text{; write 8, carry 4.} \\ & \qquad 8 \times 3 = 24,\ 24 + 4 = 28\text{; write 28.)} \\ \underline{360} & \text{Partial product } (10 \times 36 = 360) \\ 648 & \end{array}$$

Checking multiplication

One method of checking multiplication involves transposing the multiplicand and multiplier as follows:

Solution:	*Check:*
53	28
× 28	× 53
424	84
106	140
1,484	1,484

Multiplication shortcuts

Several mathematical shortcuts exist when either the multiplicand or multiplier contains zeros. The simplest case is when the multiplier is a product of tens, that is, 10, 100, 1,000, and so on. The product is found by appending to the multiplicand the number of zeros in the multiplier. For example,

$$21 \times 10 = 210$$
$$433 \times 100 = 43{,}300$$
$$91 \times 1{,}000 = 91{,}000$$

Other multipliers ending in zero are handled as shown in example 3.

Example 3 Find: a. 74 × 80 b. 5,300 × 76

Solution

a. *Long Method*	*Shortcut*	b. *Long Method*	*Shortcut*
74	74	5,300	5,300
× 80	× 80	× 76	× 76
00	592	31,800	318
5,920		371,000	3,710
5,920	5,920	402,800	4,028
			402,800

Division Just as subtraction "reverses" the operation of addition, division reverses the operation of multiplication. That is, if 3 × 12 = 36, then 36 ÷ 12 = 3.

In a division problem, the number that is divided by another is called the **dividend,** and the number by which another number is divided is called the **divisor.**

As with the other operations, there is an algorithm for division. In the division problem 504 ÷ 6, the algorithm is illustrated in the following steps:

Step 1	*Step 2*	*Step 3*	*Step 4*
8 (8×6 = 48)	8	84 (4×6 = 24)	84—Quotient
6) 504	6) 504	6) 504	6) 504
48	−48↓	48	48
	24	24	24
Dividend (504)		24	− 24
Divisor (6)			0—Remainder

Steps in the division algorithm are repeated until all of the digits in the dividend are used and the subtraction step yields a number less than the divisor. The solution is called the **quotient,** and the number left over is called the **remainder.** In the preceding problem, the quotient is 84 with remainder 0. When the remainder is 0, the divisor is said to divide the dividend evenly.

Checking division

The relationship between multiplication and division furnishes a method for checking division problems. The procedure is to multiply the divisor by the quotient and add the remainder; the result should equal the dividend. That is,

(Divisor × Quotient) + Remainder = Dividend

Example 4 Find and check your result: 7,329 ÷ 24

Solution

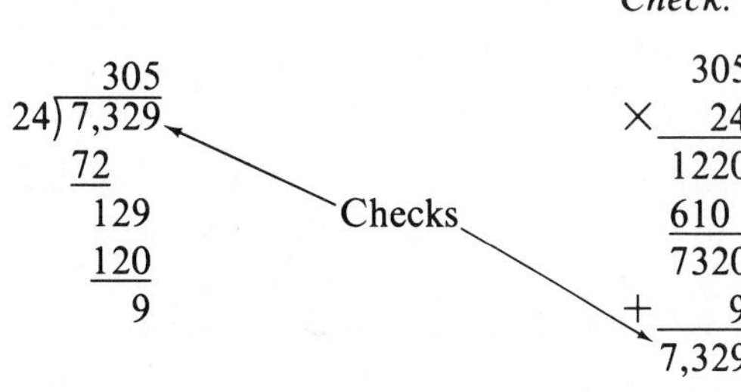

Exercises for Section 1.3 In problems 1–14, perform the indicated multiplication and check each answer by transposing the multiplicand and multiplier.

1. 14 × 6
2. 21 × 4
3. 376 × 5
4. 457 × 6
5. 679 × 76
6. 766 × 78

7. $\begin{array}{r} 905 \\ \times \underline{319} \end{array}$

8. $\begin{array}{r} 872 \\ \times \underline{407} \end{array}$

9. $\begin{array}{r} 51{,}273 \\ \times \underline{\quad 37} \end{array}$

10. $\begin{array}{r} 63{,}192 \\ \times \underline{\quad 74} \end{array}$

11. $\begin{array}{r} 7{,}893 \\ \times \underline{2{,}471} \end{array}$

12. $\begin{array}{r} 9{,}356 \\ \times \underline{3{,}271} \end{array}$

13. $\begin{array}{r} 7{,}283 \\ \times \underline{2{,}406} \end{array}$

14. $\begin{array}{r} 8{,}173 \\ \times \underline{4{,}057} \end{array}$

In problems 15–30, find the quotient and remainder and check your result.

15. 609 ÷ 7
16. 522 ÷ 9
17. 756 ÷ 54
18. 986 ÷ 34
19. 3,053 ÷ 43
20. 3,230 ÷ 34
21. 23,968 ÷ 428
22. 16,864 ÷ 248
23. 310,648 ÷ 412
24. 380,304 ÷ 684
25. 3,068 ÷ 75
26. 5,569 ÷ 64
27. 2,214 ÷ 34
28. 4,188 ÷ 57
29. 7,897 ÷ 83
30. 3,967 ÷ 48

31. A shipping clerk dispatched 127 packages averaging 43 pounds each. Find the total weight of the packages.

32. A small office building contains 14 offices, each renting for $523 per month. What is the total rental income from the building per month?

33. A university charges tuition at the rate of $34 per credit. If a student decides to take 17 credits of course work, how much tuition will she pay?

34. The A.B.C. Clothing Outlet purchased 225 men's suits from the manufacturer for $14,625. Find the cost of each suit.

35. A businessman decides to construct an office building containing 26 offices. He plans to rent each office at the same monthly rate, and he wants a total rental income (at full occupancy) per month of $16,172. How much rent per month should he charge for each office?

36. A lathe operator in a machine shop produces 37 units per day. Each unit sells for $24. Find the daily income from the operation of the lathe.

37. A discount store purchased 132 television sets at a wholesale cost of $322 per set. How much did the store pay for the sets?

38. The Mighty-Mite Manufacturing Company received a purchase order for 996 units of its best-quality electric shaver motors. The company computed the cost of the order to be $7,968. Find the price per unit that the buyer paid for the motors.

39. A business executive had carpeting installed in her conference room for a total cost of $1,445. If 85 square yards of carpeting were required, what did she pay per square yard?

40. A manufacturing plant produced 4,297 golf carts in one month. The production cost for the carts was $77,346. How much did it cost to produce one cart?

41. A machine shop received an order for 1,562 units of a part to be used in the construction of jet engines. The tooling costs required to fill the order amounted to $46,860. Find the tooling cost per unit.

42. A trucking company hauls citrus at the rate of $13 per mile per truckload. A citrus grower estimates his crops to be 572 truckloads, and he wishes to ship 327 truckloads to packing plant A and the remainder of his crop to packing plant B. If the distance to packing plant A is 123 miles and the distance to packing plant B is 67 miles, what will be the total shipping charge?

43. The M & M Motel has a total of 137 rooms, 93 of which are double occupancy and the remainder are single occupancy. If the doubles rent for $77 per day and the singles rent for $63 per day, what is the total rental income per day at full occupancy?

44. Fiberglass Industries manufactures canoes, and all of its canoes sell for the same price. The total sales for the month of April amounted to $20,516 for 92 units. What was the selling price per unit?

45. The owner of a small 12-unit apartment building received a total rental income of $46,080 in 1989. Due to increasing overhead expenses, the owner needed to receive $49,968 in 1990 to make a satisfactory profit. How much was the rent of each unit per month increased? (Assume full occupancy.)

46. A company filled a purchase order for 1,472 of its economy model electronic computers at a total cost of $401,856. The company then filled a second purchase order for 927 of the computers at the same price per unit. Find the cost of the second purchase order.

Glossary

Addend Any of the numbers that are to be added.
Algorithm A step-by-step process for performing a calculation.
Difference The result of subtracting one number from another.
Digit Any of the numbers 0, 1, 2, 3, 4, 5, 6, 7, 8, 9. All numbers may be written using these ten digits.
Dividend In a division problem, the number that is divided by another.
Divisor In a division problem, the number by which another number is divided.
Factor Any of the numbers that are to be multiplied in a multiplication problem.
Minuend In a subtraction problem, the number from which another number is subtracted.
Multiplicand In a multiplication problem, the number that is multiplied by another; the first or top number in the problem.
Multiplier In a multiplication problem, the number by which another number is multiplied; the second or bottom number in the problem.
Operation Any of the processes of addition, subtraction, multiplication, or division.
Partial product In a multiplication problem, the result of multiplying the multiplicand by one of the digits in the multiplier.
Product The result of multiplying two or more numbers (the sum of the partial products).
Quotient The result of dividing one number by another.
Remainder In a division problem, the number remaining at the bottom after the last step of the division process. The sum of the remainder with the product of the divisor times the quotient is equal to the dividend.
Subtrahend In a subtraction problem, the number that is subtracted from another.
Sum The result of adding two or more numbers.
Whole number Any of the numbers 0, 1, 2, 3, 4, 5, 6, 7, 8, 9, 10, 11. . . .

Review Test

In problems 1–10, perform the indicated operations.

1. $\begin{array}{r} 78{,}548 \\ +\ \underline{4{,}427} \end{array}$

2. $\begin{array}{r} 62{,}203 \\ -\ \underline{9{,}648} \end{array}$

3. $\begin{array}{r} 7{,}241 \\ 15{,}896 \\ 8{,}248 \\ 79{,}972 \\ +\underline{61{,}241} \end{array}$

4. $\begin{array}{r} 9{,}427 \\ \times\ \underline{257} \end{array}$

5. $\begin{array}{r} 115{,}225 \\ -\ \underline{7{,}336} \end{array}$

6. $\begin{array}{r} 83{,}576 \\ \times\ \underline{427} \end{array}$

7. $13{,}172 \div 37$

8. $34{,}398 \div 49$

9. $40{,}372 \div 71$

10. $47{,}242 \div 591$

11. An assembly-line worker assembled 137 units on Monday, 144 units on Tuesday, and 134 units on Wednesday. How many units were assembled during the three days?

12. A pet supply store purchased 48 cases of dog food for \$528. What was the cost per case?

13. For their home, the Smiths purchased new carpeting on sale for \$1,847. The regular price for the carpeting was \$2,031. How much did the Smiths save by purchasing the carpet on sale?

14. Julie Adams sells real estate. During the month of May, she received commissions of \$542, \$273, \$312, \$341, and \$428. What was her total commission for the month?

15. Bill Jacobs wrote checks for $112, $49, and $232. The balance in his account before writing the checks was $847. Find the balance in his account after writing the three checks.

16. Atlas Industries manufactures aluminum storage sheds. For the month of March, the total sales of the company amounted to $107,271 for 137 sheds. All of the storage sheds have the same selling price. Find the selling price of each shed.

17. An apartment complex contains 12 one-bedroom apartments and 8 two-bedroom apartments. The one-bedroom apartments rent for $346 per month, and the two-bedroom apartments rent for $432 per month. At full occupancy, what is the total rental income per month from the complex?

18. Use horizontal and vertical addition to fill in the missing entries on the following chart, which shows the daily sales of each salesperson at the Tri-County Furniture Outlet:

	Mon.	**Tues.**	**Wed.**	**Thurs.**	**Fri.**	**Total**
J. Beeson	$ 4,271	$8,279	$2,413	$3,892	$ 4,721	______
M. Pruitt	10,114	3,420	4,611	743	3,995	______
P. Baker	2,421	6,744	5,546	2,109	1,815	______
S. Rae	943	5,219	4,428	3,456	11,423	______
Q. Ramirez	6,711	3,978	2,119	5,827	7,319	______
Total	______	______	______	______	______	______

CHAPTER 2

Review of Fractions

Chapter Objectives

I. Learn the meaning of the following terms:

Numerator and denominator of a fraction, 20
Proper, improper, and complex fractions, 20
Greatest common divisor, 21
Least common denominator, 27
Mixed number, 32
Decimal point, 38

II. Understand:

The four interpretations of a fraction, 20
The concept of equal fractions, 20
The procedure for reducing fractions to lowest terms, 22
The procedure for adding and subtracting fractions, 27–29
The procedure for multiplying and dividing fractions, 31–32
The technique of canceling, 31–32
The procedure for adding, subtracting, multiplying, and dividing mixed numbers, 34
The procedure for rounding numbers, 41

III. Compute:

Sums, differences, products, and quotients of fractions, 27–29, 31–32
Sums, differences, products, and quotients of mixed numbers, 33–34
Sums, differences, products, and quotients of decimal fractions, 38–41

Student's self-examination for chapter 2

This test will help determine individual strengths and weaknesses in the basic arithmetic skills discussed in chapter 2. The answers are provided in appendix L.

In problems 1–8, perform the indicated operations and express your answer as a mixed number or a proper fraction reduced to lowest terms.

1. $\frac{1}{3} + \frac{12}{30}$
2. $\frac{14}{8} - \frac{32}{40}$
3. $\frac{5}{12} \times \frac{18}{35}$
4. $\frac{12}{21} \div \frac{10}{14}$
5. $2\frac{2}{15} + 1\frac{1}{5}$
6. $8\frac{3}{4} - 4\frac{1}{8}$
7. $2\frac{1}{3} \times 1\frac{1}{4}$
8. $5\frac{2}{3} \div 2\frac{1}{6}$

Solve

9. $\begin{array}{r} 3{,}713.42 \\ 144.57 \\ +\ \underline{266.98} \end{array}$

10. $\begin{array}{r} 2{,}487.62 \\ -\underline{1{,}996.87} \end{array}$

11. $\begin{array}{r} 12.43 \\ \times\ \underline{0.26} \end{array}$

12. $123.84 \div 51.6$

13. $34.119 \div 2.55$

14. Round 27.492 to (a) the nearest tenth and (b) the nearest whole number.

15. Round 4.84675 to (a) the nearest thousandth and (b) the nearest hundredth.

16. A contractor purchased 42 acres and subdivided it into $1\frac{1}{2}$ acre lots. How many lots did he have?

17. A job pays $7.80 per hour for a forty-hour week. Overtime hours are paid at $1\frac{1}{2}$ times $7.80. Find the overtime hourly pay.

18. Sara has three apple trees in her backyard. The yield of the first tree was $1\frac{3}{4}$ bushels of apples, the second tree yielded $2\frac{1}{8}$ bushels, and the third tree yielded $1\frac{1}{2}$ bushels. How many total bushels of apples did Sara get from the trees?

19. A salesperson is paid a commission on net sales (total sales less returns). Last week the salesperson had sales of $446.85, $1,268.40, $2,988.69, and $668.75, and returns of $88.25 and $226.50. Find the salesperson's net sales for the week.

20. While modernizing its factory, a company laid off $\frac{1}{6}$ of its 420 workers. Of those laid off, $\frac{1}{7}$ found other jobs. Of the remaining laid-off workers, $\frac{1}{4}$ were retrained for new jobs in the company. How many workers were retrained for new jobs?

Section 2.1 Introduction

A **fraction** consists of two numbers separated by a horizontal or slanting bar; for example, the fraction one-sixth may be written $\frac{1}{6}$ or 1/6. In either event, the number to the top or left of the bar is called the **numerator,** while the number below or to the right of the bar is called the **denominator.***

There are at least four different interpretations for a number like $\frac{1}{6}$:

1. **A part of a whole** If one pie is cut into six equal slices, then a slice is $\frac{1}{6}$ of the whole pie.
2. **A part of a group** One-sixth of 36 bottles is 6 bottles, or 1 six-pack out of 6 six-packs.
3. **Division of two numbers** The number $\frac{1}{6}$ can mean $1 \div 6$. In this sense, the bar is just another symbol for the division sign ($\div$).
4. **Ratio of two numbers** If during a baseball game a player gets one hit in six times at bat, then we can say that he or she hit $\frac{1}{6}$ of the time. Here the fraction implies a comparison between the numbers 1 and 6.

There are three different kinds of fractions:

1. A **proper fraction** is a fraction with a numerator less than the denominator. Examples of proper fractions are $\frac{1}{6}$, $\frac{3}{8}$, and $\frac{5}{7}$.
2. An **improper fraction** is a fraction with a numerator greater than or equal to the denominator. Examples of improper fractions are $\frac{9}{7}$, $\frac{8}{3}$, and $\frac{7}{7}$.
3. A **complex fraction** is a fraction consisting of a fractional numerator, a fractional denominator, or both. Examples of complex fractions are $\dfrac{\frac{6}{7}}{14}$, $\dfrac{15}{\frac{2}{3}}$, and $\dfrac{\frac{1}{2}}{\frac{3}{4}}$.

Section 2.2 Equality of fractions

The two fractions $\frac{a}{b}$ and $\frac{c}{d}$ are said to be *equal* if $a \times d = b \times c$. The products $a \times d$ and $b \times c$ are called **cross products.** Thus, two fractions are equal if their cross products are equal.

Example 1

Show that a. $\dfrac{4}{7} = \dfrac{12}{21}$ b. $\dfrac{2}{5} = \dfrac{6}{15}$

Solution

a. Since $4 \times 21 = 84$, $7 \times 12 = 84$, $\dfrac{4}{7} = \dfrac{12}{21}$

b. Since $2 \times 15 = 30$, $5 \times 6 = 30$, $\dfrac{2}{5} = \dfrac{6}{15}$

*The denominator cannot be zero.

The definition of equality of fractions leads to an important application. For a nonzero number n,

$$\frac{a \times n}{b \times n} = \frac{a}{b} \qquad (2\text{–}1)$$

because $a \times n \times b = b \times n \times a$.* For example, since

$$\frac{16}{40} = \frac{2 \times 8}{5 \times 8}$$

then from equation 2–1,

$$\frac{16}{40} = \frac{2}{5}$$

This process is called **reducing a fraction.**

Example 2

Reduce: a. $\frac{27}{36}$ b. $\frac{28}{40}$

Solution

Using equation 2–1,

a. $\frac{27}{36} = \frac{3 \times 9}{4 \times 9} = \frac{3}{4}$ b. $\frac{28}{40} = \frac{7 \times 4}{10 \times 4} = \frac{7}{10}$

In reducing fractions, the largest number n that evenly divides both the numerator and the denominator is called the **greatest common divisor.** Frequently, the greatest common divisor (GCD) can be determined by inspection. However, if this is not feasible, the GCD can always be found by utilizing the prime factorizations of the numerator and the denominator. A **prime** is a whole number larger than 1 that is evenly divisible only by itself and 1. The first nine primes are 2, 3, 5, 7, 11, 13, 17, 19, and 23. It is known that every whole number larger than 1 is either itself a prime or can be expressed as a product of primes. This product is called the **prime factorization** of the number. For example, the prime factorization of $60 = 2 \times 2 \times 3 \times 5$ can be found by repeated division by prime divisors as follows:

$$\begin{array}{r|l} 2 & 60 \\ \hline 2 & 30 \\ \hline 3 & 15 \\ \hline & 5 \end{array}$$

*$a \times n \times b = b \times n \times a$ because of the commutative property of multiplication, which states that a product of two or more numbers is not affected by a rearrangement of the numbers. For example, $2 \times 3 \times 4 = 4 \times 3 \times 2$.

To find the GCD of a fraction, find the prime factorization of the numerator and the denominator, then form columns so that only identical primes are in each column. The GCD is the product of the primes that have a pairing. This process is illustrated in the next example.

Example 3 Find the greatest common divisor of a. 96 and 180 b. 75 and 210.

Solution

a. The prime factorizations are $96 = 2 \times 2 \times 2 \times 2 \times 2 \times 3$ and $180 = 2 \times 2 \times 3 \times 3 \times 5$. Forming columns,

2	2	2	2	2	3		
2	2				3	3	5

the GCD is the product of the paired primes or $2 \times 2 \times 3 = 12$.

b. The prime factorizations are $75 = 3 \times 5 \times 5$ and $210 = 2 \times 3 \times 5 \times 7$. Forming columns,

	3	5	5	
2	3	5		7

the GCD is the product of the paired primes or $3 \times 5 = 15$.

When a fraction is reduced using the GCD of the numerator and the denominator, the fraction is said to be reduced to **lowest terms.**

Example 4 Reduce to lowest terms: a. $\frac{24}{30}$ b. $\frac{70}{105}$

Solution

a. The GCD of 24 and 30 is 6. Hence, using equation 2–1,

$$\frac{24}{30} = \frac{4 \times 6}{5 \times 6} = \frac{4}{5}$$

b. The GCD of 105 and 70 is 35. Hence, using equation 2–1,

$$\frac{70}{105} = \frac{2 \times 35}{3 \times 35} = \frac{2}{3}$$

Equation 2–1 can also be used to construct a fraction equal to a given fraction by multiplying the numerator and denominator of the given fraction by the same nonzero number. For instance,

$$\frac{2}{5} = \frac{2 \times 3}{5 \times 3} = \frac{6}{15}$$

Multiplying the numerator and denominator of $\frac{2}{5}$ by 2, 3, 4, 5, . . . produces an infinite number of fractions that are equal to the given fraction; that is, $\frac{2}{5} = \frac{4}{10} = \frac{6}{15} = \frac{8}{20} = \frac{10}{25} = \cdots$

Example 5 Find a fraction with denominator 48 that is equal to the fraction $\frac{5}{6}$.

Solution

In symbols, the problem is $\frac{5}{6} = \frac{?}{48}$. Since $48 \div 6 = 8$, we multiply the numerator and denominator of $\frac{5}{6}$ by 8 to get

$$\frac{5}{6} = \frac{5 \times 8}{6 \times 8} = \frac{40}{48}$$

As indicated in section 2.1, a fraction like $\frac{9}{3}$ may be interpreted as a ratio of 9 to 3. An alternative notation for this ratio is 9:3 (read 9 to 3). The ratio interpretation of a fraction is used primarily for comparison. When the denominator of a ratio is 1, it is said to be a **comparison to 1.** Thus, since $9 \div 3 = 3$, each of the following notations represent the same fraction:

$$\frac{9}{3}, \quad \frac{3}{1}, \quad 9:3, \quad 3:1$$

Many business ratios are written as comparisons to 1.

Example 6 A company employs 120 union employees and 15 management personnel. The annual payroll is $2,250,000 for the union employees and $750,000 for management personnel. Find as a comparison to 1 (a) the ratio of union employees to management personnel, and (b) the ratio of the union payroll to that of management.

Solution:

a. $\frac{120}{15} = 8 = \frac{8}{1}$

The ratio of union employees to management personnel is 8:1.

b. $\frac{\$2,250,000}{\$750,000} = 3 = \frac{3}{1}$

The ratio of the union payroll to the management payroll is 3:1.

Exercises for Section 2.2

In problems 1–10, find three fractions that are equal to the given fraction.

1. $\frac{1}{4}$
2. $\frac{5}{7}$
3. $\frac{3}{5}$
4. $\frac{7}{15}$
5. $\frac{5}{6}$
6. $\frac{1}{3}$
7. $\frac{5}{8}$
8. $\frac{7}{20}$
9. $\frac{5}{14}$
10. $\frac{21}{43}$

In problems 11–16, find a fraction with denominator 60 equal to the given fraction.

11. $\frac{1}{6}$
12. $\frac{5}{12}$
13. $\frac{2}{5}$
14. $\frac{7}{15}$
15. $\frac{17}{30}$
16. $\frac{3}{4}$

In problems 17–22, find a fraction with denominator 90 equal to the given fraction.

17. $\frac{4}{5}$
18. $\frac{14}{15}$
19. $\frac{5}{9}$
20. $\frac{2}{3}$
21. $\frac{11}{45}$
22. $\frac{13}{30}$

In problems 23–30, use cross multiplication to decide whether or not the two given fractions are equal.

23. $\frac{3}{4}$ and $\frac{15}{20}$
24. $\frac{5}{7}$ and $\frac{25}{35}$
25. $\frac{5}{6}$ and $\frac{39}{42}$
26. $\frac{7}{8}$ and $\frac{14}{15}$
27. $\frac{27}{28}$ and $\frac{81}{94}$
28. $\frac{17}{21}$ and $\frac{68}{84}$
29. $\frac{13}{41}$ and $\frac{65}{205}$
30. $\frac{32}{33}$ and $\frac{192}{198}$

In problems 31–36, find the greatest common divisor of the given numbers.

31. 30 and 36
32. 90 and 105
33. 42 and 735
34. 154 and 770
35. 78 and 546
36. 182 and 195

In problems 37–50, reduce the given fraction to lowest terms.

37. $\frac{7}{14}$
38. $\frac{15}{30}$
39. $\frac{21}{28}$
40. $\frac{24}{36}$
41. $\frac{8}{12}$
42. $\frac{21}{28}$
43. $\frac{95}{100}$
44. $\frac{118}{124}$
45. $\frac{63}{90}$

46. $\frac{36}{54}$

47. $\frac{24}{120}$

48. $\frac{48}{168}$

49. $\frac{88}{396}$

50. $\frac{54}{180}$

Express the answers to problems 51–62 as fractions reduced to lowest terms.

51. Sunshine Hardware received a shipment of 64 chain saws and sold 24 of them in one week. Find the fraction of the shipment that was sold during the week.

52. A restaurant's receipts for one day totaled $810. Of this amount, $90 was for the sale of liquor. Find the fraction of the total receipts that was due to liquor sales.

53. A warehouse contains 28,000 square feet of floor space. Of the total floor space, 2,000 square feet is used for offices, and the rest is used for storage. What fraction of the total floor space is used for offices? What fraction is used for storage?

54. A contractor maintains a fleet of 275 trucks, of which 240, on the average, are in service at any given time. Find the fraction of the total fleet that is not in service (on the average) at any given time.

55. Kirby Electronics specializes in used television sets. Recently, John Kirby bought a color set for $112 and sold it for $164. What fraction of the selling price was his profit?

56. W. L. Mercer bought 575 shares of stock in a land development company. A year later, she sold 252 shares of the stock. Find the fraction of stock that was sold.

57. Arlin Lackey inherited $266,000 and used $210,000 to pay off his creditors. What fraction of his original inheritance did he have left after paying off his debts?

58. Sally Smith and Dr. Denton entered into a joint business venture from which they realized a profit of $48,000. Because Sally initially put more money into the venture than Dr. Denton, they agreed that Sally would receive $32,000 and that Dr. Denton would receive $16,000. Find the fraction of the total profit that Sally received.

59. A shoe store carries 12 different styles of boy's shoes, 22 different styles of girl's shoes, 16 different styles of men's shoes, and 34 different styles of women's shoes. What fraction of the total shoe styles is for females?

60. According to the personnel officer, 20 employees of the company are single or divorced with no children, 18 are divorced with children, 12 are married with no children, and 32 are married with children. What fraction of the employees has no children? What fraction of the employees is married?

61. A check of shopping records at a supermarket revealed the following data:

Number of Shoppers	Total of Purchases
20	Less than $10
120	$10 but less than $40
95	$40 or more

What fraction of the shoppers spent less than $40? What fraction of the shoppers spent $10 or more?

62. Of the 120 cars sold by an automobile dealer last month, optional air conditioning orders were as follows:

	2-Door	4-Door	Sports Coupe
Air Conditioning	28	26	24
No Air Conditioning	12	4	26

What fraction of the cars was ordered with air conditioning? What fraction of the Sports Coupes was ordered with no air conditioning? What fraction of cars sold was 2-Door or 4-Door models?

63. The current inventory of a shoe outlet store shows 5,201 pairs of ladies' shoes and 743 pairs of men's shoes. Express the ratio of ladies' shoes to men's shoes as a comparison to 1.

64. The total sales of the Bartco Company were $3,771,250 last year as compared with $754,250 five years ago. Express the ratio of last year's sales to the sales of five years ago as a comparison to 1.

65. Stan Pantling and Will Holmes are business partners. Last year, Stan worked an average of 51 hours per week and Will worked an average of 17 hours per week. The total profit from the business was $81,450, of which Stan received $54,300 and Will received the rest. Find as a comparison to 1 (a) the ratio of Stan's average hours per week to Will's average hours per week, and (b) the ratio of Stan's share of the total profit to Will's share of the total profit.

66. A hospital employs 161 nurses and 23 physicians. The average salary for a nurse is $28,000 per year and the average salary for a physician is $84,000 per year. Find as a comparison to 1 (a) the ratio of nurses to physicians at the hospital, and (b) the ratio of the average salary for a physician to the average salary for a nurse.

Section 2.3 Addition and subtraction of fractions

Addition of fractions

To add fractions, we must consider two cases: (1) fractions with the same (common) denominator and (2) fractions with unlike denominators.

The sum of two fractions with a common denominator is a fraction with the same denominator and whose numerator is the sum of the numerators of the given fractions.

Example 1

Find: a. $\frac{3}{5} + \frac{1}{5}$ b. $\frac{8}{27} + \frac{19}{27}$

Solution

a. $\frac{3}{5} + \frac{1}{5} = \frac{3 + 1}{5} = \frac{4}{5}$ b. $\frac{8}{27} + \frac{19}{27} = \frac{8 + 19}{27} = \frac{27}{27} = 1$

Addition of fractions with unlike denominators is accomplished by using equation 2–1 to convert the given fractions to fractions with a common denominator. Then the method demonstrated in example 1 can be used to add the fractions.

One common denominator is the product of the denominators of the given fractions, but it is better to find the **least common denominator,** which is the smallest nonzero whole number divisible by the denominators of the given fractions. The least common denominator (LCD) is often determined by inspection. However, if this is not feasible, the LCD can always be found by utilizing the prime factorizations of the denominators. To find the LCD of two denominators, find the prime factorization of each denominator, then form columns so that only identical primes are in each column. The LCD is the product of the representative primes from each column. This process is illustrated in the next example.

Example 2

Find the least common denominator of a. 30 and 36 b. 35 and 50

Solution

a. The prime factorizations are $36 = 2 \times 2 \times 3 \times 3$ and $30 = 2 \times 3 \times 5$. Forming columns and selecting a representative from each column,

2	2	3	3	
2		3		5

the LCD is $2 \times 2 \times 3 \times 3 \times 5 = 180$

b. The prime factorizations are $35 = 5 \times 7$ and $50 = 2 \times 5 \times 5$. Forming columns and selecting a representative from each column,

	5		7
2	5	5	

the LCD is $2 \times 5 \times 5 \times 7 = 350$

Example 3 Add by finding the least common denominators:

a. $\frac{3}{4} + \frac{1}{6}$ b. $\frac{1}{3} + \frac{1}{15}$ c. $\frac{1}{4} + \frac{3}{5} + \frac{1}{8}$

Solution

a. The LCD of 4 and 6 is 12. Using equation 2–1,

$$\frac{3}{4} = \frac{3 \times 3}{4 \times 3} = \frac{9}{12} \quad \text{and} \quad \frac{1}{6} = \frac{1 \times 2}{6 \times 2} = \frac{2}{12}$$

$$\text{thus} \quad \frac{3}{4} + \frac{1}{6} = \frac{9}{12} + \frac{2}{12} = \frac{9 + 2}{12} = \frac{11}{12}$$

b. The LCD of 3 and 15 is 15. Using equation 2–1,

$$\frac{1}{3} = \frac{1 \times 5}{3 \times 5} = \frac{5}{15}$$

$$\text{thus} \quad \frac{1}{3} + \frac{1}{15} = \frac{5}{15} + \frac{1}{15} = \frac{5 + 1}{15} = \frac{6}{15}$$

This solution can be reduced to lowest terms by using equation 2–1 as follows:

$$\frac{6}{15} = \frac{2 \times 3}{5 \times 3} = \frac{2}{5}$$

Thus,

$$\frac{1}{3} + \frac{1}{15} = \frac{2}{5}$$

c. The LCD of 4, 5, and 8 is 40. Using equation 2–1,

$$\frac{1}{4} = \frac{1 \times 10}{4 \times 10} = \frac{10}{40}, \quad \frac{3}{5} = \frac{3 \times 8}{5 \times 8} = \frac{24}{40}, \quad \text{and}$$

$$\frac{1}{8} = \frac{1 \times 5}{8 \times 5} = \frac{5}{40}$$

$$\text{thus} \quad \frac{1}{4} + \frac{3}{5} + \frac{1}{8} = \frac{10}{40} + \frac{24}{40} + \frac{5}{40} = \frac{10 + 24 + 5}{40} = \frac{39}{40}$$

Subtraction of fractions

The method for subtracting fractions is similar to the method for adding fractions except for the replacement of a plus sign by a minus sign.

Example 4

Find: a. $\frac{13}{20} - \frac{9}{20}$ b. $\frac{3}{5} - \frac{1}{4}$ c. $\left(\frac{35}{16} - \frac{3}{2}\right) - \frac{1}{8}$

Solution

a. $\frac{13}{20} - \frac{9}{20} = \frac{13 - 9}{20} = \frac{4}{20} = \frac{1}{5}$

b. The LCD of 4 and 5 is 20. Using equation 2–1,

$$\frac{3}{5} = \frac{3 \times 4}{5 \times 4} = \frac{12}{20} \text{ and } \frac{1}{4} = \frac{1 \times 5}{4 \times 5} = \frac{5}{20}$$

$$\text{thus } \frac{3}{5} - \frac{1}{4} = \frac{12}{20} - \frac{5}{20} = \frac{12 - 5}{20} = \frac{7}{20}$$

c. The LCD of 16, 2, and 8 is 16. Using equation 2–1,

$$\frac{3}{2} = \frac{3 \times 8}{2 \times 8} = \frac{24}{16} \text{ and } \frac{1}{8} = \frac{1 \times 2}{8 \times 2} = \frac{2}{16}$$

$$\text{thus } \left(\frac{35}{16} - \frac{3}{2}\right) - \frac{1}{8} = \left(\frac{35}{16} - \frac{24}{16}\right) - \frac{2}{16} = \frac{(35 - 24) - 2}{16} = \frac{9}{16}$$

Exercises for Section 2.3

In problems 1–10, find the least common denominator of the given pair of fractions. Then add the fractions and express the sum as a fraction in lowest terms.

1. $\frac{1}{2}, \frac{1}{5}$
2. $\frac{2}{5}, \frac{1}{6}$
3. $\frac{1}{3}, \frac{1}{4}$
4. $\frac{2}{7}, \frac{1}{8}$
5. $\frac{2}{5}, \frac{3}{7}$
6. $\frac{5}{12}, \frac{1}{9}$
7. $\frac{3}{8}, \frac{9}{16}$
8. $\frac{1}{6}, \frac{7}{24}$
9. $\frac{9}{23}, \frac{8}{69}$
10. $\frac{7}{15}, \frac{9}{20}$

In problems 11–24, perform the indicated operation. Express your answer as a fraction reduced to lowest terms.

11. $\frac{3}{10} - \frac{1}{7}$
12. $\frac{1}{6} + \frac{3}{8}$
13. $\frac{7}{5} - \frac{7}{8}$
14. $\frac{2}{13} + \frac{4}{9}$
15. $\frac{3}{5} - \frac{5}{14}$
16. $\frac{1}{6} + \frac{9}{14}$
17. $\frac{17}{19} - \frac{2}{3}$
18. $\frac{9}{21} - \frac{13}{42}$
19. $\frac{11}{28} - \frac{5}{14}$

20. $\frac{8}{11} - \frac{5}{7}$

21. $\frac{1}{3} + \frac{1}{4} + \frac{3}{8}$

22. $\left(\frac{5}{6} - \frac{2}{9}\right) - \frac{5}{18}$

23. $\frac{3}{8} + \frac{7}{36} + \frac{5}{12}$

24. $\left(\frac{43}{39} - \frac{2}{13}\right) - \frac{5}{52}$

25. John Johnson's house is located on $\frac{2}{5}$ acre of land. He plans to buy an adjacent lot that contains $\frac{3}{8}$ acre. How much land will John own following the purchase?

26. A land developer deeded $\frac{1}{9}$ of a tract of land to the county for roads and $\frac{2}{7}$ of the tract to a creditor for payment of debts. Find the fraction of the tract that the developer had left.

27. Comtek had $\frac{1}{6}$ of its capital invested in merchandise, $\frac{3}{7}$ in equipment, $\frac{3}{8}$ in real estate, and the balance in cash. What fraction of the company's capital was invested in equipment and real estate? What fraction of the company's capital was cash?

28. Robison's Music Store received a shipment of record albums and sold $\frac{1}{5}$ of the shipment in one week. During the next week, $\frac{4}{9}$ of the shipment was sold, and $\frac{4}{15}$ of the shipment was sold in the third week. What fraction of the albums was sold during the three-week period?

29. Sybil's Flower and Gift Shop received a shipment of merchandise that was $\frac{1}{7}$ flowers, $\frac{2}{5}$ glassware, $\frac{3}{7}$ leather goods, and $\frac{1}{35}$ miscellaneous items. What fraction of the shipment was glassware and leather goods? What fraction was flowers and miscellaneous items?

30. Eastern Storage leases $\frac{2}{5}$ of the floor space of its Charlottesville warehouse to company A, $\frac{4}{15}$ of the floor space to company B, and $\frac{2}{9}$ of the floor space to company C. How much of the floor space is leased to company A and company B? How much is leased to all three companies?

31. The inventory of a sporting goods store is found to be $\frac{5}{9}$ sporting equipment, $\frac{2}{7}$ clothing, $\frac{2}{21}$ books, and the remainder miscellaneous merchandise. What fraction of the inventory is equipment and clothing? What fraction is miscellaneous merchandise?

32. A company found that $\frac{3}{7}$ of its total production cost for the year was for employees' wages, $\frac{4}{9}$ was for equipment and supplies, $\frac{2}{21}$ was for plant maintenance, and the remainder was for miscellaneous expenses. Find the fraction of the total production cost due to equipment, supplies, and wages. Find the fraction due to miscellaneous expenses.

33. The president of a company ordered a truckload of turkeys for Christmas and gave $\frac{2}{5}$ of the truckload as gifts to the employees, $\frac{1}{10}$ as gifts to the board of directors, $\frac{2}{7}$ to other business friends, and the remainder to charitable organizations. What fraction of the truckload was donated to charitable organizations?

Section 2.4 Multiplication, division, and mixed numbers

The product of two fractions is a fraction found by multiplying the numerators and multiplying the denominators of the given fractions. This is true whether the fractions are proper, improper, or complex.

Multiplication of fractions

Example 1

Find: a. $\frac{2}{7} \times \frac{5}{3}$ b. $\frac{4}{3} \times \frac{5}{9}$

Solution

a. $\frac{2}{7} \times \frac{5}{3} = \frac{2 \times 5}{7 \times 3} = \frac{10}{21}$ b. $\frac{4}{3} \times \frac{5}{9} = \frac{4 \times 5}{3 \times 9} = \frac{20}{27}$

The procedure of multiplying numerators and multiplying denominators also applies for the product of three or more fractions.

Example 2

Find: a. $\frac{1}{2} \times \frac{3}{4} \times \frac{7}{5}$ b. $\frac{1}{4} \times \frac{1}{7} \times \frac{11}{5} \times \frac{9}{2}$

Solution

a. $\frac{1}{2} \times \frac{3}{4} \times \frac{7}{5} = \frac{1 \times 3 \times 7}{2 \times 4 \times 5} = \frac{21}{40}$

b. $\frac{1}{4} \times \frac{1}{7} \times \frac{11}{5} \times \frac{9}{2} = \frac{1 \times 1 \times 11 \times 9}{4 \times 7 \times 5 \times 2} = \frac{99}{280}$

Multiplication by canceling

A modification of the technique for reducing fractions, called **cancellation,** provides a shortcut for finding the product of fractions. To illustrate:

$$\frac{9}{20} \times \frac{8}{27} = \frac{\overset{1}{\cancel{9}}}{\underset{5}{\cancel{20}}} \times \frac{\overset{2}{\cancel{8}}}{\underset{3}{\cancel{27}}} = \frac{1}{5} \times \frac{2}{3} = \frac{2}{15}$$

The canceled numbers represent dividing 20 and 8 by 4, and dividing 27 and 9 by 9.

Example 3 Using cancellation wherever possible, find: $\frac{6}{25} \times \frac{10}{3}$

Solution

$$\frac{6}{25} \times \frac{10}{3} = \frac{\overset{2}{\cancel{6}}}{\underset{5}{\cancel{25}}} \times \frac{\overset{2}{\cancel{10}}}{\underset{1}{\cancel{3}}} = \frac{2}{5} \times \frac{2}{1} = \frac{4}{5}$$

Division of fractions

Division by a fraction involves the reciprocal of the dividing fraction. The **reciprocal** of a fraction is found by interchanging the numerator and the denominator. Thus, the reciprocal of $\frac{3}{4}$ is $\frac{4}{3}$, and the reciprocal of $\frac{1}{6}$ is $\frac{6}{1} = 6$.

To divide a number by a nonzero fraction, multiply the number by the reciprocal of the fraction.

Example 4 Find: a. $\frac{3}{17} \div \frac{1}{4}$ b. $12 \div \frac{1}{3}$ c. $\frac{3}{8} \div \frac{8}{5}$ d. $\frac{5}{7} \div 9$

Solution

a. $\frac{3}{17} \div \frac{1}{4} = \frac{3}{17} \times \frac{4}{1} = \frac{12}{17}$

b. $12 \div \frac{1}{3} = \frac{12}{1} \div \frac{1}{3} = \frac{12}{1} \times \frac{3}{1} = \frac{36}{1} = 36$

c. $\frac{3}{8} \div \frac{8}{5} = \frac{3}{8} \times \frac{5}{8} = \frac{15}{64}$

d. $\frac{5}{7} \div 9 = \frac{5}{7} \div \frac{9}{1} = \frac{5}{7} \times \frac{1}{9} = \frac{5}{63}$

Mixed numbers

A **mixed number** is the sum of an integer and a fraction, written as one number. For example, $6 + \frac{3}{4}$ is written $6\frac{3}{4}$. But

$$6 + \frac{3}{4} = \frac{6}{1} + \frac{3}{4} = \left(\frac{6}{1} \times \frac{4}{4}\right) + \frac{3}{4} = \frac{24}{4} + \frac{3}{4} = \frac{27}{4}$$

Hence, we have $6\frac{3}{4} = \frac{27}{4}$.

The number 27 comes from the three numbers found in the mixed number $6\frac{3}{4}$:

$27 = (4 \times 6) + 3$

This suggests a shortcut for converting mixed numbers to improper fractions. Observe that

$2\frac{3}{5} = \frac{13}{5}$, where $13 = (5 \times 2) + 3$, and

$8\frac{1}{2} = \frac{17}{2}$, where $17 = (2 \times 8) + 1$.

Example 5

Convert to improper fractions: a. $1\frac{2}{3}$ b. $4\frac{7}{8}$

Solution

a. $(3 \times 1) + 2 = 5$. Hence, $1\frac{2}{3} = \frac{5}{3}$.

Check: $1 + \frac{2}{3} = \frac{3}{3} + \frac{2}{3} = \frac{5}{3}$

b. $(8 \times 4) + 7 = 39$. Hence, $4\frac{7}{8} = \frac{39}{8}$.

Check: $4 + \frac{7}{8} = \left(\frac{4}{1} \times \frac{8}{8}\right) + \frac{7}{8} = \frac{32}{8} + \frac{7}{8} = \frac{39}{8}$

The reverse process—converting an improper fraction to a mixed number—can be accomplished by dividing the numerator by the denominator. (See interpretation 3 for a fraction on page 20.) Given the improper fractions in example 5:

a. $\frac{5}{3} = 5 \div 3 = 1$ with remainder 2. Hence, $\frac{5}{3} = 1 + \frac{2}{3} = 1\frac{2}{3}$.

b. $\frac{39}{8} = 39 \div 8 = 4$ with remainder 7. Hence, $\frac{39}{8} = 4 + \frac{7}{8} = 4\frac{7}{8}$.

Example 6

Convert to mixed numbers: a. $\frac{9}{4}$ b. $\frac{26}{3}$

Solution

a. $9 \div 4 = 2$ with remainder 1. Hence, $\frac{9}{4} = 2\frac{1}{4}$.

b. $26 \div 3 = 8$ with remainder 2. Hence, $\frac{26}{3} = 8\frac{2}{3}$.

Example 7

Find: a. $3\frac{5}{8} + 1\frac{7}{12}$ b. $9\frac{5}{9} - 7\frac{3}{4}$

Solution

a.
$$\begin{aligned} 3\frac{5}{8} + 1\frac{7}{12} &= \frac{29}{8} + \frac{19}{12} \\ &= \left(\frac{29}{8} \times \frac{3}{3}\right) + \left(\frac{19}{12} \times \frac{2}{2}\right) \\ &= \frac{87}{24} + \frac{38}{24} \\ &= \frac{125}{24} \text{ or } 5\frac{5}{24} \end{aligned}$$

b.
$$\begin{aligned} 9\frac{5}{9} - 7\frac{3}{4} &= \frac{86}{9} - \frac{31}{4} \\ &= \left(\frac{86}{9} \times \frac{4}{4}\right) - \left(\frac{31}{4} \times \frac{9}{9}\right) \\ &= \frac{344}{36} - \frac{279}{36} \\ &= \frac{344 - 279}{36} \\ &= \frac{65}{36} \text{ or } 1\frac{29}{36} \end{aligned}$$

Example 8

Find: a. $2\frac{1}{6} \times 3\frac{2}{5}$ b. $4\frac{2}{3} \div 1\frac{7}{8}$

Solution

a.
$$\begin{aligned} 2\frac{1}{6} \times 3\frac{2}{5} &= \frac{13}{6} \times \frac{17}{5} \\ &= \frac{221}{30} \text{ or } 7\frac{11}{30} \end{aligned}$$

b.
$$\begin{aligned} 4\frac{2}{3} \div 1\frac{7}{8} &= \frac{14}{3} \div \frac{15}{8} \\ &= \frac{14}{3} \times \frac{8}{15} \\ &= \frac{112}{45} \text{ or } 2\frac{22}{45} \end{aligned}$$

Exercises for Section 2.4

In problems 1–12, use cancellation when possible and compute the products of the given fractions. Express the answer as either a mixed number or as a proper fraction reduced to lowest terms.

1. $\frac{1}{2} \times \frac{1}{3}$
2. $\frac{1}{4} \times \frac{1}{3}$
3. $\frac{7}{9} \times \frac{45}{21}$
4. $\frac{39}{48} \times \frac{12}{13}$
5. $\frac{24}{35} \times \frac{7}{12}$
6. $\frac{27}{35} \times \frac{70}{81}$
7. $\frac{1}{2} \times \frac{2}{3} \times \frac{4}{5}$
8. $\frac{4}{9} \times \frac{3}{7} \times \frac{1}{3}$
9. $\frac{24}{40} \times \frac{16}{22} \times \frac{10}{64}$
10. $\frac{33}{28} \times \frac{7}{11} \times \frac{12}{15}$
11. $\frac{2}{3} \times \frac{4}{5} \times \frac{1}{4} \times \frac{1}{2}$
12. $\frac{6}{5} \times \frac{3}{2} \times \frac{1}{3} \times \frac{4}{3}$

In problems 13–22, perform the indicated division and express the result as either a mixed number or as a proper fraction reduced to lowest terms.

13. $\frac{5}{7} \div \frac{3}{8}$
14. $\frac{3}{7} \div \frac{6}{5}$
15. $\frac{3}{2} \div \frac{39}{8}$
16. $\frac{5}{32} \div \frac{1}{16}$
17. $\frac{7}{12} \div \frac{7}{24}$
18. $\frac{5}{17} \div \frac{5}{28}$
19. $5 \div \frac{6}{54}$
20. $\frac{73}{13} \div 9$
21. $\frac{121}{110} \div \frac{11}{5}$
22. $\frac{143}{69} \div \frac{11}{23}$

In problems 23–28, express the given mixed number as an improper fraction.

23. $4\frac{2}{5}$
24. $5\frac{1}{4}$
25. $5\frac{3}{8}$
26. $4\frac{4}{5}$
27. $7\frac{3}{11}$
28. $9\frac{2}{7}$

In problems 29–34, express the given improper fraction as a mixed number.

29. $\frac{14}{9}$
30. $\frac{11}{4}$
31. $\frac{15}{6}$
32. $\frac{21}{4}$
33. $\frac{24}{15}$
34. $\frac{62}{7}$

In problems 35–50, convert the mixed numbers to improper fractions and perform the indicated operation. Express the answer as either a mixed number or as a proper fraction reduced to lowest terms.

35. $6\frac{2}{3} \times 4\frac{7}{8}$
36. $7\frac{2}{5} \times 11\frac{5}{9}$
37. $11\frac{1}{3} \div 12\frac{3}{4}$
38. $4\frac{2}{3} \div 8\frac{2}{3}$

39. $3\frac{5}{7} \times 6\frac{2}{3}$

40. $7\frac{4}{7} \times 9\frac{4}{9}$

41. $5\frac{7}{8} \div 3\frac{1}{4}$

42. $3\frac{5}{6} + 1\frac{2}{3}$

43. $4\frac{3}{5} - 4\frac{1}{10}$

44. $3\frac{2}{6} - 1\frac{1}{4}$

45. $9\frac{7}{8} + 3\frac{5}{6}$

46. $11\frac{3}{5} + 9\frac{2}{3}$

47. $7\frac{3}{7} + 4\frac{5}{21}$

48. $17\frac{2}{5} - 4\frac{1}{3}$

49. $7\frac{3}{8} + 5\frac{2}{5} + 2\frac{1}{10}$

50. $8\frac{2}{11} - 3\frac{5}{22} - 1\frac{43}{44}$

51. A produce dealer purchased $\frac{3}{4}$ of a truckload of watermelons and sold $\frac{7}{8}$ of it. He donated the rest of the watermelons to a church picnic. What fraction of a truckload did he sell?

52. A builder purchased $2\frac{1}{2}$ cubic yards of concrete to make a driveway, but he used only $\frac{4}{5}$ of it. How much concrete was used to make the driveway?

53. A farmer purchased $\frac{1}{4}$ ton of seed and planted $\frac{5}{6}$ of it. How much seed did he plant?

54. Apco Land Company purchased $\frac{4}{5}$ of an acre of land and divided it equally into four lots. How large was each lot?

55. Farmer Jones bought $\frac{3}{4}$ of a truckload of seed. If it requires $\frac{1}{8}$ of a truckload to plant one acre, how many acres can he plant?

56. A contractor estimates that $\frac{7}{8}$ of her fleet of trucks is in service at any given time. She also estimates that she needs $\frac{1}{16}$ of her fleet of trucks for each job she undertakes. How many jobs can the contractor undertake at any given time?

57. An office building is under construction in which $\frac{3}{5}$ of the total floor space is to be used for offices. If each office uses $\frac{1}{20}$ of the total floor space of the building, how many offices will the building contain?

58. Weber Enterprises presented a petition to the zoning commission to subdivide a $14\frac{2}{3}$ acre tract into 20 parcels of equal size. If the petition is approved, how many acres will each parcel contain?

59. Bender's Poultry Farm sold 1,500 pounds of chickens for $28\frac{1}{2}$¢ per pound. How much was received from the sale?

60. Delta Rock & Gravel Company purchased $3\frac{1}{2}$ truckloads of decorative gravel and sold $\frac{2}{5}$ of it the day it was delivered. The next day, $\frac{3}{8}$ of the original shipment was sold. Find the number of truckloads sold during the two days.

61. A warehouse is rented by an appliance dealer, who uses $\frac{3}{4}$ of the storage capacity of the warehouse to store a shipment of washing machines. When all but $\frac{1}{3}$ of the machines are sold, how much of the storage capacity of the warehouse will the dealer need to store the remaining machines?

62. A tract of land is to be planted in apple trees. If the tract is $\frac{5}{6}$ of an acre and if each tree occupies $\frac{1}{90}$ of an acre, how many trees can be planted on the tract?

63. Fancy Food processes $\frac{1}{12}$ truckload of potatoes each day. How many days will it take to process $1\frac{7}{8}$ truckloads?

64. A cable manufacturing company leases $\frac{3}{4}$ of the total floor space of a warehouse to store its cable. The company estimates that each hundred rolls of cable will occupy $\frac{1}{80}$ of the total floor space of the warehouse. How many hundreds of rolls of cable can the company store in the warehouse?

65. Luigi's Restaurant is being remodeled. Luigi plans to use $\frac{5}{6}$ of the total floor space for the dining area and the remainder of the space for the kitchen. He estimates that each table in the dining area will require $\frac{1}{24}$ of the total floor space of the restaurant. How many tables will the dining room contain?

66. A produce dealer received a shipment of 224 crates of grapes, which are to be repacked in boxes for retail sale. If each box holds $\frac{2}{5}$ of a crate, how many boxes of grapes can be packed?

67. Louisa's Dress Shop received a shipment of ladies' coats. Some of the coats were damaged and thus returned, but $\frac{4}{5}$ of the shipment was accepted. Louisa had estimated that she would sell $\frac{1}{10}$ of the number of coats in the original shipment per day. How many days will it take for the unreturned coats to be sold?

68. Don's Paint and Body Shop uses $\frac{4}{5}$ of the total floor space of the shop for the work area and the remainder for office space. A paint room occupies $\frac{1}{3}$ of the work area, and $\frac{1}{5}$ of the paint room is used to store paint. What fraction of the total floor space of the shop is used to store paint?

69. A citrus grower produced $112\frac{3}{4}$ tons of fruit from one grove and $97\frac{2}{3}$ tons of fruit from another. How much fruit was produced from the two groves? If $\frac{7}{8}$ of the fruit was sold to a packing house and the remainder was sold at roadside stands, how many tons of fruit were sold at roadside stands?

70. The J & J Lumber Company received an order for 324 feet of pressure-treated two-by-fours and 48 feet of pressure-treated two-by-sixes. If the two-by-fours cost $18\frac{1}{4}$¢ per foot and the two-by-sixes cost $49\frac{1}{2}$¢ per foot, what was the cost of the order?

71. A company has 40 cars, 112 light trucks, and 16 heavy trucks in its fleet. Of these, $\frac{1}{5}$ of the cars, $\frac{1}{4}$ of the light trucks, and all of the heavy trucks have diesel engines. The company plans to build a storage tank that will hold 300 gallons of diesel fuel for each diesel engine in the fleet. How many gallons should the tank hold?

Section 2.5

Decimal fractions and rounding

Decimal fractions

Decimal fractions are an extension of the Hindu-Arabic positional notation, as shown in figure 2.1. The dot or **decimal point** separates columns that are products of 10 from columns that are products of $\frac{1}{10}$. In this notation, 0.25 means 2 tenths ($\frac{2}{10}$) + 5 hundredths ($\frac{5}{100}$), or $\frac{2}{10} + \frac{5}{100} = \frac{25}{100}$.

There is an immediate relationship between decimal fractions and fractions:

$$0.1 = \frac{1}{10}$$

$$0.01 = \frac{1}{100}$$

$$0.001 = \frac{1}{1{,}000}$$

$$0.0001 = \frac{1}{10{,}000}$$

etc.

Hundreds	Tens	Ones	Tenths	Hundredths	Thousandths
		•	2	5	

Figure 2.1
Hindu-Arabic positional notation

Operations with decimal fractions use the same algorithms as whole numbers. In addition and subtraction of decimal fractions, positional notation is observed by aligning the numbers according to positional columns. The decimal point is a natural alignment guide.

Example 1 Find and check your answer: a. 1,204.685 + 322.96

b. 129.77 − 32.604

Solution

a.

		Check (Reversing Addends):
1,204.685	Addend	322.96
+ 322.96	Addend	+1,204.685
1,527.645	Sum	1,527.645

b.

		Check:
129.770	Minuend	32.604
− 32.604	Subtrahend	+ 97.166
97.166	Difference	129.770

Multiplication of decimal fractions requires a different technique. *If the multiplier is a product of tens, the solution is found by moving the decimal point in the multiplicand to the right one place for each zero in the multiplier.* For example,

1.865 × 10 = 18.65 (One zero; move decimal point one place.)

1.865 × 100 = 186.5 (Two zeros; move decimal point two places.)

1.865 × 1,000 = 1,865.0 (Three zeros; move decimal point three places.)

If the multiplier is a decimal fraction, the numbers are written and multiplied as if they were whole numbers; then the decimal point is inserted in the answer. *The product will contain digits to the right of the decimal point equal to the sum of the numbers of digits to the right of the decimal points in the factors.*

Example 2 Find: 2.63 × 5.7

Solution

2.63	Multiplicand or factor
× 5.7	Multiplier or factor
1841	
1315	
14.991	Product

There are 2 + 1 = 3 digits to the right of the decimal points in the factors; thus, the decimal point is located in the product so that there are 3 digits to its right.

Example 3 Find: 0.03 × 0.6

Solution

0.03	2 digits to right of decimal point
× 0.6	+ 1 digit to right of decimal point
0.018	3 digits to right of decimal point

A zero was inserted in the product to obtain the answer. Since

$$0.03 \times 0.6 = \frac{3}{100} \times \frac{6}{10} = \frac{18}{1{,}000}$$

this procedure is justified.

There are three cases to consider in the division of decimal fractions:

1. **The divisor is a product of tens.** If the divisor is a product of tens, the solution is found by moving the decimal point in the dividend to the *left* for each zero in the divisor. For example:

   $26.47 \div 10 = 2.647$ (One zero; move decimal point one place.)

   $26.47 \div 100 = 0.2647$ (Two zeros; move decimal point two places.)

   $26.47 \div 1{,}000 = 0.02647$ (Three zeros; move decimal point three places.)

2. **The divisor is a nonzero whole number.** If the divisor is a nonzero whole number, the decimal point in the quotient is located directly above its position in the dividend. Thus, to divide 704.96 by 32,

```
      22.03
 32)704.96
    64
     64
     64
       96
       96
        0
```

3. **The divisor is a decimal fraction.** If the divisor is a decimal fraction, convert it to a whole number by multiplying both the dividend and the divisor by a product of tens. Then divide as in case 2 above.

Example 4 Find and check your answer: a. $40.096 \div 1.79$ b. $3.9567 \div 1.635$

Solution

a. Multiplying both numbers by 100, $40.096 \div 1.79 = 4{,}009.6 \div 179$. Hence,

```
        22.4              Check:
 179)4,009.6                 1.79
     358                    ×22.4
      429                     716
      358                    358
       716                  358
       716                 40.096
         0
```

b. Multiplying both numbers by 1,000, 3.9567 ÷ 1.635 = 3,956.7 ÷ 1,635. Hence,

```
        2.42             Check:
1,635)3,956.70                1.635
      3270                  × 2.42
       6867                   3270
       6540                  6540
        3270                3270
        3270                3.95670
           0
```

Rounding Some calculations yield answers that are not practical. For example, suppose an employee earns \$5.37 per hour and works 38.75 hours during a particular week. Then the amount of money earned for the week is

\$5.37 × 38.75 = \$208.0875

But this result is not practical because it is an amount of money that cannot be paid in standard coinage.

In problems such as these, the answer is frequently "rounded" to obtain a practical result. To round a number, first locate the digit to the right of the decimal place to which the number is to be rounded. This is the test digit. The number is then rounded according to table 2.1.

Table 2.1 Rounding Rules

	Test Digit Is Located to the Right of the Decimal Point.	**Test Digit Is Located to the Left of the Decimal Point.**
Test Digit Is Four or Smaller.	Delete the test digit and all digits to its right.	Change to zero the test digit and all digits to the decimal point; delete all digits to the right of the decimal point.
Test Digit Is Five or Larger.	Delete the test digit and all digits to its right. Add one to the digit preceding the test digit.	Change to zero the test digit and all digits to the decimal point; delete all digits to the right of the decimal point. Add one to the digit preceding the test digit.

Using table 2.1 to round \$208.08⑦5 to the nearest hundredth, the test digit is the circled digit 7, which is larger than 5 and located to the right of the decimal point. Thus, \$208.0875 rounds to \$208.09, and this is the amount that the employee should be paid for the week's work.

Example 5 Round to hundredths: a. 35.1426 b. 35.1476

Solution

The circled digit is the test digit.

a. 35.14②6 rounds to 35.14

b. 35.14⑦6 rounds to 35.15

Example 6 Round 1.72546 to the (a) thousandths place, (b) hundredths place, (c) tenths place, and (d) ones place.

Solution

The circled digit is the test digit.

a. 1.725④6 rounds to 1.725

b. 1.72⑤46 rounds to 1.73

c. 1.7②546 rounds to 1.7

d. 1.⑦2546 rounds to 2

Example 7 Round 8,671.56 to (a) hundreds and (b) thousands.

Solution

The circled digit is the test digit.

a. 8,6⑦1.56 rounds to 8,700

b. 8,⑥71.56 rounds to 9,000

For the remainder of this text, answers to problems should be rounded to two decimal places (hundredths) unless otherwise indicated.

Fractions, decimal fractions, and calculators

Many of the problems in this textbook are suitable for solution using a hand-held calculator. In operations involving fractions, should the fraction or its decimal representation be used? Recall that every fraction has a decimal representation found by dividing the numerator by the denominator. This decimal representation will be either terminating or infinitely repeating. For example, the following fractions have terminating decimal representations:

$$\frac{1}{2} = 0.5$$

$$\frac{5}{4} = 1.25$$

$$\frac{375}{1{,}000} = 0.375$$

On the other hand, some fractions that have infinitely repeating decimal representations are:

$\frac{1}{3} = 0.33333\ldots$ (the 3s repeat infinitely)

$\frac{4}{9} = 0.4444\ldots$ (the 4s repeat infinitely)

$\frac{1}{6} = 0.1666\ldots$ (the 6s repeat infinitely)

$\frac{5}{11} = 0.454545\ldots$ (the pair of digits 45 repeats infinitely)

On a typical hand-held calculator, the register will display a decimal number up to seven decimal places. Hence, a fraction with an infinitely repeating decimal representation can be approximated at best only to the seventh decimal place. Approximating an infinite decimal introduces a certain amount of error into the calculation. The rougher the approximation, the greater is the error. This is particularly true in multiplication and division problems. To see this, consider the following calculations involving the fraction $\frac{4}{9} = 0.444\ldots$ that were performed on a calculator with a register display up to the seventh decimal place.

Product	*Answer*	*Error*
$710{,}550 \times \frac{4}{9}$	315,800	0
710,550 × 0.4444444	315,799.96	0.04
710,550 × 0.444444	315,799.68	0.32
710,550 × 0.44444	315,796.84	3.16
710,550 × 0.4444	315,768.42	31.58
710,550 × 0.444	315,484.20	315.8
710,550 × 0.44	312,642	3,158
710,550 × 0.4	284,220	31,580

In this text, multiplication and division involving fractions with infinitely repeating decimal expansions will be performed using the fraction instead of a decimal approximation. The final answer will then be rounded to the desired accuracy. If the fraction has a terminating decimal representation, the decimal representation will ordinarily be used.

Exercises for Section 2.5

In problems 1–32, perform the indicated operation. Do not round answers.

1. $27.4 + 32.3$
2. $42.7 + 53.2$
3. $219.6 + 34.7$
4. $21.9 + 34.4$
5. $21.93 + 34.71$
6. $43.71 + 23.28$
7. $189.349 + 272.58 + 357.152$
8. $498.31 + 217.576 + 929.915$
9. $542.075 - 396.477$
10. $872.054 - 425.947$
11. $974.3 - 27.91$
12. $547.86 - 29.476$
13. $471.6 - 52.854$
14. $429.8 - 47.726$
15. $492.83 - 74.2$
16. $72.95 - 1.4$
17. $85.006 - 19.0172$
18. $49.239 - 7.9459$
19. 4.015×6.14
20. 7.107×4.67
21. 41.07×8.15
22. 57.62×2.73
23. 80.02×46.07
24. 70.09×61.07
25. 4.7856×3.726
26. 7.6543×2.097
27. $72.696 \div 2.33$
28. $45.752 \div 6.88$
29. $99.2712 \div 4.56$
30. $96.2885 \div 6.71$
31. $543.5279 \div 6.43$
32. $745.5156 \div 9.58$

Money answers resulting from computations in mathematics of finance are rounded to values that can be paid in standard coinage. In problems 33–40, round the money values accordingly.

33. Dr. Denton's electric bill was computed from the meter reading in March to be $87.3252. For what amount was she actually billed?

34. Professor Porter's salary for teaching summer school was to be 28.2% of his nine-month salary. On this basis, he computed the amount he would be paid for the summer and arrived at the figure $5,721.54731. How much was he actually paid?

35. Salesperson Sam Smooth receives 23.7% of his total monthly sales as commission. In September, his computed commission was $3,533.45831. What commission was he paid?

36. A retail firm determined that the selling price of its product should be $37.7152 per unit. What will be the actual price per unit?

37. A businesswoman is given a travel allowance based on the number of miles traveled and the number of days spent en route. For a recent trip, her travel allowance was $97.2992. How much did she receive?

38. A city council decided to spend 12.3% of the city's receipts from parking meters on the development of parks and recreation areas, which yielded the figure $56,723.72514. How much money can the city spend on parks?

39. Professor Porter computed his deduction for home office space for his income tax and arrived at the figure $407.6952. What amount will he deduct?

40. A real estate salesperson is allowed a depreciation on an automobile for tax purposes since the automobile is essential to the occupation. Last year, the depreciation was computed at $1,801.247. What figure did the salesperson use on the tax return?

In problems 41–50, round the given numbers to (a) ones, (b) tenths, and (c) hundredths.

41. 23.713
42. 46.341
43. 217.483
44. 548.872
45. 4,219.785
46. 7,429.867
47. 217,499.981
48. 456,799.974
49. 23,452.899
50. 97,876.979

In problems 51–60, round the given numbers to (a) thousands, (b) hundreds, and (c) hundredths.

51. 4,872.576
52. 3,729.049
53. 6,974.997
54. 9,294.372
55. 19,942.193
56. 17,596.991
57. 927,399.954
58. 743,899.639
59. 149,891.691
60. 199,996.797

61. A citrus grower operates five groves. During the past year, the income from the crops of each of the groves was as follows: grove A, $11,293.14; grove B, $22,492.36; grove C, $9,403.26; grove D, $17,413.19; and grove E, $14,297.93. How much income did the grower receive from the five groves?

62. Belcher's Bakery leases space in a warehouse to store supplies. The monthly charge for storage depends on the amount of goods stored. The storage fees for the past six months were $219.72, $413.39, $327.72, $523.78, $319.47, and $209.42. Find the amount paid for storage during the six months.

63. Dr. Denton purchased new equipment for her office with $1,000.00 down and twelve payments of $972.31 each for a total cost of $12,667.72. If the cash price of the equipment was $10,727.35, what was the difference in the cash price and the amount she paid?

64. W. L. Mercer purchased 183.43 acres of land at $1,525.00 per acre for a total cost of $279,730.75. She then sold 172.85 acres for a total price of $288,572.81. How many acres of land did she have left? How much cash profit did she realize from the transaction?

65. A small manufacturing business has total sales of $76,728.72 for one year. The operating expenses for the same year are as follows: rent, $8,723.42; labor, $21,742.41; machinery, $12,242.79; supplies, $13,742.57; and incidentals, $5,429.73. Compute the profit for the year.

66. An apartment complex has 178 units, each unit providing rental income of $433.50 per month. Assuming all units are rented, what is the total rental income of the complex per month?

67. A citrus grower has 2,743.47 acres of groves. He estimates the gross income from the year's crop to be $476 per acre. How much income will he realize from his citrus?

68. A storage warehouse agrees to store 7,263 barrels of salt at the rate of 7¢ per barrel per month. Find the total storage fee for the salt in dollars per month.

69. The owner of a restaurant decides to have 572 square yards of carpeting installed. The carpet he selects is $9.23 per square yard, and it will cost $1.19 per square yard for padding and $0.99 per square yard for installation. How much will he have to pay for carpet, pad, and installation?

70. The inventory of men's suits in a department store was as follows: 27 suits (grade A) at $320.50 per suit; 32 suits (grade B) at $257.25 per suit; 63 suits (grade C) at $122.50 per suit. What was the total value of the suits?

71. A discount store purchases 273 refrigerators at a cost of $353.00 per unit. The regular retail price per unit is $625.50. The store plans to offer the refrigerators on sale at $469.95 each. If all the refrigerators were sold at the sale price, what would be the total profit? How much more profit could the store make if all the refrigerators were sold at the regular price?

72. A firm manufactures steel cable that it sells for 92.5¢ a foot. A construction company purchases some of the cable for a total price of $573.50. How many feet of the cable were purchased?

73. An estate of $737,281.20 was to be equally divided among five heirs. A sixth heir was then found who also was entitled to an equal share of the estate. How much less did each of the original five heirs receive?

74. A produce dealer paid a farmer $2,113.75 for 2,742 crates of lettuce and $4,526.04 for 1,372 boxes of tomatoes. The farmer's profit on the lettuce was $825.01 and on the tomatoes was $1,987.84. How much did it cost the farmer to grow a crate of lettuce? To grow a box of tomatoes?

Glossary

Cancellation Dividing one of the numerators and one of the denominators in the product of fractions by the same nonzero number.

Complex fraction A fraction with either a fractional numerator, a fractional denominator, or both.

Cross products Given fractions $\frac{a}{b}$ and $\frac{c}{d}$, the cross products are $a \times d$ and $b \times c$.

Decimal point A dot used to separate positional columns that are products of 10 from positional columns that are products of $\frac{1}{10}$.

Denominator That part of a fraction that is below the line signifying division.

Fraction A numerical representation of the quotient of two numbers where the indicated division is represented by a horizontal or slanting line.

Greatest common divisor (GCD) The largest number that evenly divides two or more given numbers.

Improper fraction A fraction in which the numerator is a number that is greater than or equal to the denominator.

Least common denominator (LCD) For two or more fractions, the smallest nonzero whole number that is evenly divisible by the denominators of the given fractions.

Lowest terms A phrase applied to a fraction for which the largest common divisor of the numerator and the denominator is 1.

Mixed number The sum of a whole number and a proper fraction, written as one number.

Numerator That part of a fraction that is above the line signifying division.

Prime A whole number larger than 1 that is evenly divisible only by itself and 1.

Prime factorization The expression of a whole number larger than 1 as a product of primes.

Proper fraction A fraction in which the numerator is a number that is smaller than the denominator.

Reciprocal A fraction formed from a given fraction by interchanging the numerator and the denominator.

Reducing a fraction Dividing the numerator and the denominator of a fraction by the same number.

Review Test

In problems 1–12, perform the indicated operations and write the answer as either a mixed number or as a proper fraction reduced to lowest terms.

1. $\frac{2}{5} \times \frac{25}{7}$
2. $\frac{12}{13} \times \frac{6}{24}$
3. $\frac{5}{4} - \frac{6}{9}$
4. $\frac{7}{8} - \frac{9}{24}$
5. $\frac{2}{3} + \frac{1}{12}$
6. $\frac{7}{30} + \frac{7}{12}$
7. $1\frac{3}{7} - \frac{15}{35}$
8. $\frac{7}{11} \div \frac{21}{55}$
9. $\frac{3}{7} \div \frac{3}{21}$
10. $2\frac{8}{9} - \frac{5}{6}$
11. $\frac{2}{3} \div 4\frac{2}{3}$
12. $1\frac{1}{24} + \frac{5}{16}$

In problems 13–16, perform the indicated operations and round the answer to the nearest hundredth.

13. $24.838 + 16.557$
14. $122.936 - 57.78$
15. 9.54×3.7
16. $1271.808 \div 62.1$

17. Waldo's Supermarket received a shipment of 32 cases of cornmeal, 4 of which were later discovered to be infested with insects. What fraction of the shipment was undamaged?

18. A sporting goods store reported monthly sales for the six months of January through June as follows: January, \$6,482.35; February, \$8,749.87; March, \$11,493.73; April, \$13,473.71; May, \$14,973.71; and June, \$12,372.42. Find the total sales for the six-month period.

19. A building contains 4,075 square feet of floor space, of which $\frac{3}{5}$ is used for equipment storage. Of the remaining space, $\frac{1}{3}$ is used for offices. How many square feet are used for offices?

20. One lathe in the M & M Machine Shop can produce $9\frac{3}{5}$ units of a certain item per hour. How many lathes will be required to produce $67\frac{1}{5}$ units per hour?

Equations and Formulas

Chapter Objectives

I. Learn the meaning of the following terms:

Equation, 50
Variable, 50
Identity, 51
Conditional equation, 51
Proportion, 58
Formula, 62

II. Understand the concepts of:

A *solution* to a conditional equation, 51

Restructuring a conditional equation, 51–52

Using and restructuring formulas, 62–65

III. Learn to:

Use a conditional equation to solve a word problem, 56–58

Use a proportion to solve a word problem, 59

Solve a formula for any one of its variables, 63

Section 3.1 Introduction

Many ideas in business are expressed as formulas: interest, bank discounts, annuities, and installment accounting are familiar examples. To use formulas effectively in business decisions, it is necessary to understand the basic properties of equations. This chapter begins with a discussion of these properties.

Section 3.2 Equations and variables

An **equation** expresses the equality of two quantities. The equation

$$6 = 4 + 2 \tag{3–1}$$

means that 6 and 4 + 2 are symbols for the same number.

One fundamental property of an equation is that the equality is preserved if the same number is added to both sides of the equation. Thus, if 5 is added to both sides of equation 3–1, we have

$$6 + 5 = (4 + 2) + 5 \tag{3–2}$$

Since each side equals 11, the equality is preserved.

This property is inherently nonrestrictive; that is, *any* number added to both sides of an equation preserves the equality. To emphasize this, we write

$$6 + x = (4 + 2) + x \tag{3–3}$$

The letter x in equation 3–3 acts as a placeholder for any number. Such a placeholder is called a **variable.**

Variables are an important concept in mathematics. The purpose of a variable is to act as a placeholder for numbers. In equation 3–3, if the variable x were replaced by 10, $\frac{3}{2}$, and 0.75 respectively, the equations would be

$$6 + 10 = (4 + 2) + 10 \tag{3–4}$$

$$6 + \tfrac{3}{2} = (4 + 2) + \tfrac{3}{2} \tag{3–5}$$

$$6 + 0.75 = (4 + 2) + 0.75 \tag{3–6}$$

Equation 3–3 is an example of an equation with one variable. The equation

$$x + y = y + x \tag{3–7}$$

is an example of an equation with two variables, where both letters are placeholders for numbers. For particular values of x and y, say 5 for x and 2 for y, equation 3–7 becomes

$$5 + 2 = 2 + 5 \tag{3–8}$$

Similarly, if $x = 4$ and $y = 6$, we have

$$4 + 6 = 6 + 4 \tag{3–9}$$

Equations 3–3 and 3–7 are examples of identities. An **identity** is an equation in which the left side equals the right side for any substitution of the variable(s). However, most equations are of another type, called conditional equations. A **conditional equation** is an equation in which the left side does *not* equal the right side for all substitutions of the variable(s). The equation

(3–10) $$x = 7$$

is a conditional equation. The variable in this equation is x, but only one replacement for x (namely 7) will cause the left side of the equation to equal the right side. All other substitutions fail to produce an equality. Other examples of conditional equations are*

(3–11) $$4 \cdot x = 24$$

(3–12) $$3 \cdot x + 8 = 17$$

The left side is equal to the right side for only one substitution of x, 6 in equation 3–11 and 3 in equation 3–12.

Section 3.3 Solving conditional equations

A **solution to a conditional equation** is any numerical substitution for the variable(s) that results in equality between the left side of the equation and the right side. Thus, 7 is a solution to equation 3–10, 6 is a solution to equation 3–11, and 3 is a solution to equation 3–12. This section is devoted to techniques for finding solutions to conditional equations.

It is easy to see that the solution to equation 3–10 is 7, but the solutions to equations 3–11 and 3–12 are less obvious. However, if these equations could be restructured to a form similar to that of equation 3–10, then their solutions would also be obvious. This is precisely what is done in solving conditional equations.

One set of tools needed to restructure a conditional equation is the arithmetic of chapter 1, because every conditional equation is composed of numbers and placeholders for numbers. The following four properties of equations also are needed. An equality is preserved if:

Property 1 The same number is added to both sides of the equation.
Property 2 The same number is subtracted from both sides of the equation.
Property 3 Both sides of the equation are multiplied by the same number.
Property 4 Both sides of the equation are divided by the same nonzero number.

*To avoid possible confusion between the variable x and the cross ($\times$) for multiplication, it is customary to use a dot ($\cdot$) as the symbol for multiplication or to omit the symbol entirely. Thus, $4 \times x = 24$, $4 \cdot x = 24$, and $4x = 24$ all have the same meaning.

Other tools frequently used to restructure a conditional equation are the following identities:

(3–13) $x + y = y + x$ Commutative property of addition

(3–14) $x \cdot y = y \cdot x$ Commutative property of multiplication

(3–15) $\left.\begin{array}{l} x \cdot z + y \cdot z = (x + y) \cdot z \\ x \cdot z - y \cdot z = (x - y) \cdot z \end{array}\right\}$ Distributive properties

We illustrate the use of these tools with a series of examples. In each of these examples, the object is to restructure the equation so that the variable x is alone on the left side. In general, the procedure is

Step 1 Use property 1 or 2 or both to restructure the equation so that all terms containing the variable are on the left and all constants are on the right.

Step 2 Combine the terms on the left using equation 3–15, and combine the constants on the right.

Step 3 Use property 3 or 4 to multiply or divide both sides of the equation by the appropriate number that will leave x alone on the left.

Example 1 Solve: $4x = 20$

Solution

Steps 1 and 2 of the restructuring procedure do not apply here, so we go directly to step 3. Dividing both sides of the equation by 4, we obtain

(Step 3) $\frac{4x}{4} = \frac{20}{4}$ (Property 4)

Since $\frac{4x}{4} = \frac{4}{4} \cdot \frac{x}{1} = 1 \cdot x = x$, and $\frac{20}{4} = 5$, we have

$x = 5$

Check: $4 \cdot 5 = 20$; hence, 5 is the correct solution to $4x = 20$.

EXAMPLE 2 Solve: $3x + 8 = 17$

Solution

(Step 1) Subtract 8 from both sides.

$3x + 8 - 8 = 17 - 8$ (Property 2)

(Step 2) $3x + 0 = 9$ $(8 - 8 = 0, 17 - 8 = 9)$

$3x = 9$ $(3x + 0 = 3x)$

(Step 3) Divide both sides of the equation by 3.

$$\frac{3x}{3} = \frac{9}{3} \qquad \text{(Property 4)}$$

Since $\frac{3x}{3} = \frac{3}{3} \cdot \frac{x}{1} = 1 \cdot x = x$, and $\frac{9}{3} = 3$, we have

$x = 3$

Check: $3 \cdot 3 + 8 = 17$; hence, 3 is the solution.

Example 3 Solve: $\frac{1}{2}x - 6 = 8$

Solution

We eliminate 6 and $\frac{1}{2}$ from the left side by adding 6 to both sides and then multiplying both sides by 2.

(Step 1) $\frac{1}{2}x - 6 + 6 = 8 + 6$ (Property 1)

(Step 2) $\frac{1}{2}x + 0 = 14$ $(6 - 6 = 0, 8 + 6 = 14)$

$\frac{1}{2}x = 14$ $(\frac{1}{2}x + 0 = \frac{1}{2}x)$

(Step 3) $2 \cdot \frac{1}{2}x = 2 \cdot 14$ (Property 3)

Since $2 \cdot \frac{1}{2}x = 2 \cdot \frac{1}{2} \cdot x = 1 \cdot x = x$, and $2 \cdot 14 = 28$, we have

$x = 28$

Check: $\frac{1}{2} \cdot 28 - 6 = 8$; hence, 28 is the solution.

Example 4 Solve: $5y + y = 30$

Solution

Step 1 does not apply here, so we go to step 2.

(Step 2) $5y + y = 5 \cdot y + 1 \cdot y$, and by equation 3–15,

$5 \cdot y + 1 \cdot y = (5 + 1) \cdot y = 6y$; hence,

$6y = 30$

(Step 3) $\frac{6y}{6} = \frac{30}{6}$ (Property 4)

Since $\frac{6y}{6} = y$, and $\frac{30}{6} = 5$, we have

$y = 5$

Check: $5 \cdot 5 + 5 = 30$; hence, 5 is the solution.

Example 5 Solve: $10z + 7 = 3z + 56$

Solution

First 7, then $3z$ is subtracted from both sides.

(Step 1) $10z + 7 - 7 = 3z + 56 - 7$ (Property 2)

$10z + 0 = 3z + 49$ $(7 - 7 = 0,$ $56 - 7 = 49)$

$10z = 3z + 49$ $(10z + 0 = 10z)$

$10z - 3z = 3z - 3z + 49$ (Property 2)

(Step 2)

By equation 3–15,

$10z - 3z = (10 - 3) \cdot z$ and

$3z - 3z = (3 - 3) \cdot z$; hence,

$7z = 0 \cdot z + 49$ $(10 - 3 = 7, 3 - 3 = 0)$

$7z = 49$ $(0 \cdot z = 0)$

(Step 3) $\frac{7z}{7} = \frac{49}{7}$ (Property 4)

$z = 7$

Check: Replacing z by 7 in the original equation, we have

$10 \cdot 7 + 7 = 3 \cdot 7 + 56$

$77 = 77$

Exercises for Sections 3.2 and 3.3

In problems 1–43, solve the given conditional equations.

1. $4x = 12$
2. $6x = 24$
3. $3x + 2 = 14$
4. $7 + 4x = 31$
5. $4x - 10 = 6$
6. $3x - 3 = 45$
7. $11 + 3z = 44$
8. $5 + 9y = 32$
9. $3x + 2x = 30$
10. $7x + 2x = 18$
11. $5y - 2y = 60$
12. $8z - z = 56$
13. $3x + 2x + 45 = 250$
14. $6x + 3x + 7 = 88$
15. $z + 2 + 3z = 22$
16. $3y - y - 1 = 19$
17. $6x - 4 - 3x = 11$
18. $7 + 4x = 17 - x$
19. $15 + 3w = 43 - w$
20. $5z = 42 - 2z$
21. $3y + 1 = 25 + y$
22. $9x - 3x = 12 + 2x$
23. $20x + 4x = 14x + 110$
24. $4 + 9w = 7w + 48$
25. $6z + z = 33 + 2z$
26. $7y - 4y = 32 - y$
27. $\frac{1}{2}x = 5$
28. $\frac{1}{4}x = 3$
29. $\frac{2}{5}z = 8$
30. $\frac{2}{7}w = 4$
31. $3x = \frac{9}{2}$
32. $5x = \frac{10}{3}$
33. $5x + \frac{2}{3} = 4$
34. $4x - \frac{2}{5} = 2$
35. $\frac{2}{5}z + z = 210$
36. $\frac{3}{4}w + 3w = 40$
37. $3y + \frac{3}{2}y - 6 = 114$
38. $5z - \frac{5}{6}z + 18 = 293$
39. $\frac{7}{9}p - \frac{1}{2} = \frac{3}{4}$
40. $\frac{4}{5}w + \frac{2}{3} = \frac{7}{9}$
41. $\frac{5}{9}s + \frac{1}{3}s = \frac{1}{2}$
42. $\frac{3}{4}p - 2 = \frac{4}{5} - \frac{1}{5}p$
43. $\frac{2}{5}q + 3 = \frac{7}{2} + \frac{1}{3}q$
44. Does the equation $2x = 2(x + 4)$ have a solution? Explain your answer.

17) $6x - 4 - 3x = 11$
$+4 \quad\quad +4$
0
$6x - 3x = 15$
$3x = 15$
$x = 5$

Section 3.4 Conditional equations and word problems

The Grayson Wholesale Plumbing Company has outlets in Atlanta and Knoxville. During April, the sales of the Atlanta office were three times the sales of the Knoxville office. Together, their sales totaled \$24,000. What were the sales of each outlet?

Word problems such as this one have two parts to the solution: (1) expressing the problem as a conditional equation and (2) solving the conditional equation.

While no algorithm exists for converting a word problem to a conditional equation, four steps are often helpful:

1. Read the problem carefully to ascertain the known and unknown information.
2. Denote one item of the unknown information by a variable; then express the remaining unknown items in terms of this variable.†
3. Write a conditional equation that combines the known and unknown information.
4. Solve the equation for the variable and check your answer.

For the plumbing company problem cited above, these steps are as follows:

1a. Unknown information

(1) The April sales of the Atlanta office
(2) The April sales of the Knoxville office

b. Known information

(1) Total sales = \$24,000
(2) Total sales = Atlanta sales + Knoxville sales
(3) Atlanta sales = 3 times Knoxville sales

2. Let x = April sales of the Knoxville office
$3x$ = April sales of the Atlanta office

3. $x + 3x = \$24{,}000$
$4x = \$24{,}000$ (Equation 3–15)

4. $\dfrac{4x}{4} = \dfrac{\$24{,}000}{4}$ (Property 4)

$x = \$6{,}000$

$3x = 3 \cdot \$6{,}000 = \$18{,}000$

Check: $x + 3x = \$6{,}000 + \$18{,}000 = \$24{,}000$

Thus, for the month of April, the Knoxville sales were \$6,000 and the Atlanta sales were \$18,000.

†In many word problems, more than one variable may be required, but such problems are beyond the scope of this text.

Example 1 The Toast-Eze Company sells its economy toaster for $\frac{6}{5}$ of the production cost plus \$3. If the selling price of the toaster is \$27, what is the production cost per unit?

Solution

1a. Unknown information

(1) The production cost per unit

b. Known information

(1) Selling price for one unit = \$27
(2) Selling price per unit = $\frac{6}{5}$ of production cost plus \$3

2. Let x = the production cost per unit

3.
$$27 = \left(\frac{6}{5}\right)x + 3$$

$$27 - 3 = \left(\frac{6}{5}\right)x + 3 - 3 \qquad \text{(Property 2)}$$

$$24 = \left(\frac{6}{5}\right)x$$

$$5 \cdot 24 = (5)\left(\frac{6}{5}\right)x \qquad \text{(Property 3)}$$

Since $5 \cdot \left(\frac{6}{5}\right) = 6$, we have

$$120 = 6x$$

Thus, $$\frac{120}{6} = \frac{6x}{6} \qquad \text{(Property 4)}$$

and $$20 = x$$

Check: Substituting $x = 20$ into the equation, we have

$$27 = \left(\frac{6}{5}\right)(20) + 3$$

$$27 = 24 + 3$$

$$27 = 27$$

Thus, the production cost per unit is \$20.

Example 2 Walker's Produce Market received a shipment of tomatoes and avocados. The cost of the tomatoes was \$7.50 a box, and the avocados cost \$12.00 a box. The total cost of the shipment was \$360.00, and there were 36 boxes in the shipment. Find the number of boxes of tomatoes and the number of boxes of avocados in the shipment.

Solution

1a. Unknown information

(1) The number of boxes of tomatoes
(2) The number of boxes of avocados

b. Known information

(1) Total number of boxes in the shipment = 36
(2) Total cost of shipment = \$360.00
(3) Cost of tomatoes per box = \$7.50
(4) Cost of avocados per box = \$12.00
(5) Total cost of avocados plus total cost of tomatoes = \$360.00

2. If x = number of boxes of avocados, then $36 - x$ = number of boxes of tomatoes.

3. $12x + (7.5)(36 - x) = 360$

4.
$$12x + (36 - x)(7.5) = 360 \quad \text{(Equation 3–14)}$$
$$12x + 36(7.5) - x(7.5) = 360 \quad \text{(Equation 3–15)}$$
$$12x - (7.5)x + 36(7.5) = 360$$
$$(12 - 7.5)x + 270 = 360 \quad \text{(Equation 3–15)}$$
$$(4.5)x + 270 - 270 = 360 - 270 \quad \text{(Property 2)}$$
$$(4.5)x = 90$$
$$\frac{(4.5)x}{4.5} = \frac{90}{4.5} \quad \text{(Property 4)}$$
$$x = 20$$
$$36 - x = 16$$

Check: $12(20) + (7.5)(16) = 360$

Thus, 20 boxes of avocados and 16 boxes of tomatoes were in the shipment.

As discussed in chapter 2, a ratio is one interpretation for a fraction. The equality of two ratios is called a **proportion.** Thus, $\frac{2}{5} = \frac{10}{25}$ is a proportion and may be written 2:5 = 10:25 (read 2 is to 5 as 10 is to 25). The numbers 2 and 25 are called the *extremes* of this proportion and the numbers 5 and 10 are called the *means*. Thus, from the rule for the equality of fractions, *the product of the means equals the product of the extremes*. The next example demonstrates how a proportion may be used to obtain the solution to a problem.

Example 3 Last year a homeowner paid \$1,200 in taxes on property appraised at \$90,000. This year the property was appraised at \$105,000. Assuming the ratio of appraised value to taxes paid will be the same for this year as last, how much will the homeowner pay in taxes this year?

Solution:

1a. Unknown information

(1) The property taxes for this year

b. Known information

(1) The property taxes for last year = \$1,200
(2) The property appraisal for last year = \$90,000
(3) The property appraisal for this year = \$105,000

(4) $\frac{\text{This year appraisal}}{\text{This year taxes}} = \frac{\text{Last year appraisal}}{\text{Last year taxes}}$

2. Let x = property taxes for this year

3. $\frac{105{,}000}{x} = \frac{90{,}000}{1{,}200}$

4. $90{,}000x = 126{,}000{,}000$ (Equality of fractions)

$x = 1{,}400$ (Property 3)

Check: $\frac{\$105{,}000}{\$1{,}400} = \frac{\$90{,}000}{\$1{,}200}$ since $\$105{,}000 \times \$1{,}200 = \$90{,}000 \times \$1{,}400$

Thus, the property taxes for this year are \$1,400.

Exercises for Section 3.4

Express the given problem as a conditional equation in one variable and solve.

1. The C and J Appliance Store sold 135 refrigerators during a recent five-day sale. If the same number of refrigerators were sold each day of the sale, how many were sold each day?

2. One-fifth of the sales of the Fit-N-Trim Sporting Goods Store are charges. Find the total sales of the store on a day when charges total \$265.

3. A television set is on sale for \$323, which is $\frac{5}{6}$ of the regular price. What is the regular price?

4. A supermarket chain purchased two tracts of land on which to build new stores. Tract A cost $3,000 more than tract B, and the two tracts together cost $147,500. How much did each tract cost?

5. Professor Porter's salary is $172 a month less than Professor Smith's. If their combined salary is $5,750 per month, what is the monthly salary of each?

6. An apartment complex contains only one- and two-bedroom units, and there are twice as many one-bedroom units as two-bedroom units. If there are a total of 120 units, how many one-bedroom units are there?

7. Sam Smooth's commission for February was $415 more than half his commission for March, and his total commission for the two months was $4,633. Find his commission for each month.

8. The number of administrative employees at a plant is $\frac{1}{14}$ the number of assembly-line workers. If the company employs 240 people in administrative and assembly-line work, how many are administrators? How many are assembly-line workers?

9. Elsie's Restaurant spent 3.2 times as much for television advertising last year as for all other types of advertising. If the total amount spent on advertising for the year was $9,240, how much was spent on television advertising? How much was spent on other types of advertising?

10. Cool Pool built 539 swimming pools last year. If they build $4\frac{1}{2}$ times as many rectangular pools as nonrectangular pools, find the number of rectangular pools constructed. How many nonrectangular pools were built?

11. J. W. Masterson, a building contractor, purchased sand and gravel for a construction project. He bought $3\frac{1}{4}$ times as much sand as gravel, and the total amount of sand and gravel purchased was 42 tons. Find the number of tons of sand and the number of tons of gravel that he bought.

12. An estate is valued at $225,000 and is to be distributed to a son and a daughter so that the daughter receives four times as much as the son. What is the son's share of the estate? What is the daughter's share?

13. A warehouse contains 440,000 square feet of storage space. Company A leases three times as much space as company B. How much space does each company lease if together they lease the entire warehouse?

14. The Brite-Lite Company produces 1,100 reading lamps a day when it operates on two shifts. The first shift produces only $\frac{5}{6}$ as many lamps as the second shift. Find the number of lamps that each shift produces per day.

15. The inventory of the Comfort-Step Shoe Store totaled $56,000. If the inventory for ladies' shoes was $2\frac{1}{2}$ times the inventory for men's shoes, what was the inventory for men's shoes?

16. Bud's Hardware Store makes a profit of $3 on each economy model electric hand drill it sells, and it makes a $4 profit on each deluxe drill sold. In one week, the store made $289 profit from the sale of drills. If four more deluxe drills were sold than economy drills, how many drills of each type were sold during the week?

17. Two more than $\frac{1}{5}$ of the employees of a company have 20 years or more of service. If 15 employees have 20 or more years of service, find the number of people employed by the company.

18. The Bargain Furniture Store pays $242 a unit for one type of office desk and $65 a unit for the matching file cabinet. A recent shipment of 22 units of the office furniture cost the store $3,731. How many desks and how many file cabinets were in the shipment?

19. A manufacturing company finds that to produce one unit of its product, it costs $140 for labor and $230 for material. The total cost for labor and material during the month of January was $14,060. How many units did the company produce in January?

20. Bob's Farm Store received a shipment of electric- and gasoline-powered hedge trimmers. The electric trimmers cost $57.92 each, and the gasoline trimmers cost $84.68 each. The entire shipment contained 28 trimmers, and the total cost of the shipment was $1,942.88. How many of each of the two kinds of trimmers were in the shipment?

21. The Corner Grocery makes a profit of $0.37 on each gallon of vitamin D milk sold. The profit on each gallon of lowfat milk sold is $0.05 less. Last week, the store sold $2\frac{1}{2}$ times as many gallons of vitamin D milk as it did lowfat milk, and the total profit from the sale of both kinds of milk for the week was $522.90. How many gallons of each kind of milk were sold during the week?

22. Last year a clothing company used 7,788 yards of denim to manufacture 9,735 pairs of jeans. This year, the company plans to manufacture 12,000 pairs of jeans. How many yards of denim will be required?

23. A company uses 2.3 pounds of a certain chemical to manufacture 240 pounds of its product. How many pounds of this chemical will be required to manufacture 2,000 pounds of the product?

24. The Freeman Company employs salespeople and production people in the ratio of 7:2. If 84 production people are employed, how large is the sales force?

25. Smythe and Wessen are business partners. When they first formed their partnership, they agreed to divide all profits in the ratio of 5:3, with the larger portion going to Smythe. Last year, Smythe's share of the profits was $91,400. What was Wessen's share?

Section 3.5 Formulas

A conditional equation may contain more than one variable. Conditional equations with more than one variable are sometimes called **formulas.** The equations

(3–16) $$y = 3x + 7$$

(3–17) $$P = B \cdot R$$

(3–18) $$I = Prt$$

are formulas. Generally, formulas have one variable on the left side of the equation and the remaining variables on the right side of the equation.

Primarily, formulas are used to evaluate the variable on the left side for given substitutions of the variables on the right side.

Example 1 In formula 3–16, evaluate y if: a. $x = 4$ b. $x = 7$

Solution

a. If $x = 4$, then $y = 3 \cdot 4 + 7$

$y = 19$

b. If $x = 7$, then $y = 3 \cdot 7 + 7$

$y = 28$

Example 2 In formula 3–17, evaluate P if:

a. $B = 16$ and $R = 12$ b. $B = 480$ and $R = \frac{3}{4}$

Solution

a. $P = BR$

$P = 16 \cdot 12$

$P = 192$

b. $P = BR$

$P = 480 \cdot \frac{3}{4}$

$P = 360$

Example 3 In formula 3–18, evaluate I if:

a. $P = 14, r = 6, t = 8$ b. $P = 25, r = 14, t = \frac{3}{4}$

Solution

a. $I = Prt$

$I = 14 \cdot 6 \cdot 8$

$I = 672$

b. $I = Prt$

$I = 25 \cdot 14 \cdot \frac{3}{4}$

$I = 262\frac{1}{2}$

Since formulas are equations, it is possible to restructure formulas using the properties of equations. For example, to solve formula 3–16 for x in terms of y,

$$y = 3x + 7$$

$$3x + 7 = y$$

$$3x = y - 7 \qquad \text{(Property 2)}$$

$$x = \frac{y - 7}{3} \qquad \text{(Property 4)}$$

Example 4

a. Solve formula 3–17 for R.

b. Find R if $P = 3{,}460$ and $B = 20$.

Solution

a.

$$P = BR$$

$$BR = P$$

$$R = \frac{P}{B} \qquad \text{(Property 4)}$$

b.

$$R = \frac{P}{B}$$

$$R = \frac{3{,}460}{20}$$

$$R = 173$$

Example 5

a. Solve formula 3–18 for t.

b. Find t if $I = 540$, $r = 0.045$, $P = 6{,}000$.

Solution

a.

$$I = Prt$$

$$Prt = I$$

$$t = \frac{I}{Pr} \qquad \text{(Property 4)}$$

b.

$$t = \frac{I}{Pr}$$

$$t = \frac{540}{6{,}000 \times 0.045}$$

$$t = 2$$

Example 6 The H & N Candy Company has determined that the demand for their deluxe box of Valentine candy is

$$x = 18{,}000 - \frac{8{,}000p}{3}$$

where p is the selling price per box to dealers and x is the number of boxes that can be sold. Find the number of boxes that can be sold if

a. $p = \$1.95$ b. $p = \$2.85$ c. $p = \$4.50$

Solution

a.
$$\begin{aligned} x &= 18{,}000 - \frac{8{,}000p}{3} \\ &= 18{,}000 - \frac{8{,}000 \times 1.95}{3} \\ &= 18{,}000 - \left(8{,}000 \times \frac{1.95}{3}\right) \\ &= 18{,}000 - 5{,}200 \\ &= 12{,}800 \end{aligned}$$

b.
$$\begin{aligned} x &= 18{,}000 - \frac{8{,}000p}{3} \\ &= 18{,}000 - \frac{8{,}000 \times 2.85}{3} \\ &= 18{,}000 - \left(8{,}000 \times \frac{2.85}{3}\right) \\ &= 18{,}000 - 7{,}600 \\ &= 10{,}400 \end{aligned}$$

c.
$$\begin{aligned} x &= 18{,}000 - \frac{8{,}000p}{3} \\ &= 18{,}000 - \frac{8{,}000 \times 4.50}{3} \\ &= 18{,}000 - \left(8{,}000 \times \frac{4.50}{3}\right) \\ &= 18{,}000 - 12{,}000 \\ &= 6{,}000 \end{aligned}$$

Example 7 The formula for gross sales is $G = np$, where G = gross sales, n = number of items sold, and p = price per item. Which of the prices in example 6 produces the largest gross sales?

Solution

a. $G = np$

$= 12{,}800 \times \$1.95$

$= \$24{,}960$

b. $G = np$

$= 10{,}400 \times \$2.85$

$= \$29{,}640$

c. $G = np$

$= 6{,}000 \times \$4.50$

$= \$27{,}000$

Thus, a price of \$2.85 produces the largest gross sales.

Exercises for Section 3.5

In problems 1–8, evaluate the variable on the left side of the given formula when the variables on the right side of the formula are given the indicated values.

1. $y = x + 2z$; $x = 2$, $z = 12$
2. $P = 2l + 2w$; $l = 4$, $w = 5$
3. $V = lwh$; $l = 3$, $w = 7$, $h = 2$
4. $A = (bh)/2$; $b = 8$, $h = 3$
5. $I = Prt$; $P = 2{,}000$, $r = 0.05$, $t = 3$
6. $R = (abc)/(4K)$; $a = 2$, $b = 1$, $c = 3$, $K = \frac{1}{2}$
7. $K = [(a + b)h]/2$; $a = 3$, $b = 1$, $h = 0.5$
8. $V = (\frac{1}{6})h(b + B + 4M)$; $M = 3$, $B = 9$, $b = 3$, $h = 1$
9. Solve the formula in problem 1 for z. Find z if $y = 8$ and $x = 2$.
10. Solve the formula in problem 2 for l. Find l if $P = 20$ and $w = 5$.
11. Solve the formula in problem 6 for c. Find c if $R = 2$, $K = 4$, $a = 1$, and $b = 4$.
12. Solve the formula in problem 8 for B. Find B if $V = 12$, $h = 3$, $b = 4$, and $M = 2$.

In problems 13–20, solve the given formula for x and find the value of x when y and z are given the indicated values.

13. $z = xyz - 2y;\ y = 2,\ z = 3$

14. $y = (z - 4)/(xz);\ y = 3,\ z = 8$

15. $y = xz + yz - z;\ y = 1,\ z = 6$

16. $z = (yx + y)/(y + 1);\ y = 2,\ z = 6$

17. $z = (x/y) - 5;\ y = 2,\ z = 7$

18. $z = [x/(zy)] - y;\ y = 4,\ z = 8$

19. $y = [1/(xyz)] - 2z;\ y = 2,\ z = 3$

20. $z = (xyz)/(y + z);\ y = 4,\ z = 5$

21. The formula $G = np$ is used to compute the gross sales G from the sale of n units of a product at a selling price of p dollars per unit. Solve this formula for n. If a product is sold for \$8 per unit and the gross sales are \$3,696, how many units are sold?

22. Simple interest is computed by the formula $I = Prt$, where I = interest, P = principal, r = rate of interest, and t = time. Find the interest paid on \$2,000 invested for two years at rate $r = 0.05$.

23. Solve the formula $I = Prt$ for r in terms of I, P, and t. Find the value of r if a principal of \$4,000 earns \$1,440 interest over a period of four years. (See problem 22.)

24. The formula $N = G - C$ is used to compute the net profit N, where G is gross profit and C is production cost. Solve this formula for C and find the production cost if the gross profit is \$280,520 and the net profit is \$42,520.

25. The checking accounts at the West End Bank are subject to a monthly charge of C dollars, where C is given by the formula $C = 1 + (0.01)x$ and x is the number of checks written during the month. Find the charge C for a month in which (a) 25 checks are written, (b) 30 checks are written, and (c) 40 checks are written.

26. The amount S of Sam Smooth's weekly paycheck is given by the formula $S = 425 + (x/10)$, where x is the amount of his sales during the week (in dollars). Find the amount of Sam's paycheck for a week in which he sells (a) \$700 worth of merchandise, (b) \$950 worth of merchandise, and (c) \$1,200 worth of merchandise.

27. A company estimates that its production cost C to produce x units of its product is given by the formula $C = 5x + 1,000$. Find C when (a) 1,000 units are produced, (b) 1,200 units are produced, and (c) 2,000 units are produced.

28. The Sporty Shirt Company finds that the amount S of its weekly gross sales is given by the formula $S = 1{,}500 + 100x$, where x is the number of 30-second television commercials per week. Find the weekly gross sales if (a) 8 commercials are run, (b) 15 commercials are run, and (c) 20 commercials are run.

29. The cost S (in dollars) of an order of x pounds of premium grade fertilizer from the Gro-Green Fertilizer Company is given by the formula $S = (0.6)x + 1$. Find the cost of an order of (a) 60 pounds, (b) 100 pounds, and (c) 120 pounds.

30. Magnum Corporation determines the retail price p for its product by using the formula $p = 18 - (x/250)$, where x is the number of units produced by the company. Determine the price p if the company produces (a) 250 units, (b) 750 units, and (c) 1,000 units.

31. The Drill-Rite Company determines that the demand x for their deluxe electric drill is given by the formula $x = 3{,}000 - (200/3)p$, where p is the selling price per drill to dealers and x is the number of drills that can be sold. How many drills can be sold if the price p is (a) \$12, (b) \$15, and (c) \$18?

32. Use the formula $G = np$, where G = gross sales, n = number of units sold, and p = price per unit, to determine which of the prices in problem 31 yields the maximum gross sales.

33. Budget Beans estimates that the demand x for their small-size can of baked beans is given by the formula $x = 58{,}000 - 1{,}250p$, where p is the selling price (in cents) per can and x is the number of cans that can be sold. Find the number of cans that can be sold if the price p is (a) 20¢, (b) 23¢, and (c) 27¢.

34. Use the formula $G = np$, where G = gross sales, n = number of units sold, and p = price per unit, to determine which of the prices in problem 33 yields the maximum gross sales.

Glossary

Conditional equation An equation for which the asserted equality is not true for all numerical replacements of the variable(s).
Equation A mathematical assertion that two expressions or quantities are equal.
Formula A conditional equation containing more than one variable.
Identity An equation for which the asserted equality is true for all numerical replacements of the variable(s).
Proportion The equality of two ratios.
Solution to a conditional equation Any numerical replacement(s) for the variable(s) that makes the asserted equality true.
Variable A letter or symbol used to represent or act as a placeholder for numbers.

Review test

1. Classify each of the following equations as either (1) an identity or (2) a conditional equation.

   a. $3x - 9 = 0$

   b. $x + 5x = 6x$

   c. $5(x + 1) = 10$

   d. $10x + 4y = 2(5x + 2y)$

In problems 2–11, solve each of the equations.

2. $5x - 3 = 17$
3. $7x + 4x = 88$
4. $4z + 11z - 5 = 115$
5. $14x - 11x = x + 500$
6. $10 + 3z = 59 - 4z$
7. $4w + 5w - 21 = 3w + 9$
8. $\frac{2}{5}w + 4 = 12$
9. $5x - \frac{2}{3} = 10$
10. $\frac{3}{2}x + 14 = \frac{1}{2}x + 42$
11. $\frac{4}{5}w + \frac{1}{3}w = \frac{2}{5}$
12. Solve the formula $I = Prt$ for t in terms of P, r, and I. Find the value of t if $P =$ \$15,000, $r = 0.08$, and $I =$ \$6,000.

In problems 13–15, express the given information as a conditional equation in one variable and solve.

13. John Chambliss purchased two delivery trucks for his building supply store. The larger truck cost \$2,000 more than the smaller, and the two trucks together cost \$24,500. How much did each truck cost?
14. A manufacturing plant employs twice as many women as men. If 258 people are employed at the plant, how many are men? How many are women?
15. This week, Betty Perkins earned \$200 more than half of the amount that she earned last week. Her total earnings for the last two weeks are \$1,340. How much did she earn during each of the last two weeks?

CHAPTER 4

Percent, Base, and Percentage

Chapter Objectives

I. Learn the meaning of the following terms:

Percent, 70

Base, 74

Percentage, 74–75

II. Understand:

The relationship between percent, base, and percentage, 74–75

The variations of the basic percentage formula, 81, 83, 84

III. Learn to:

Convert percents to decimal numbers and fractions, 70–71

Convert decimal numbers and fractions to percents, 71–73

Solve word problems using the basic percentage formula, 75–77

Use variations of the basic percentage formula, 81–84

Section 4.1 Introduction

Progress is measured by comparison with a predetermined base. For example, we compare this week's production with last week's production, this month's sales with last month's sales, this year's earnings with last year's earnings. Whether an increase or decrease, these changes are frequently measured in percent.

Salespeople are often paid according to the dollar amount of their sales. A portion of the total amount is paid in commissions and bonuses. The unit of measurement for these payments is percent.

Banks and savings and loan companies pay investors and charge borrowers according to fixed rates. Again, the unit of measurement for these rates is percent.

Section 4.2 The meaning of percent

Percent is an important business term. In fact, no other word dominates the quantitative language of business as does *percent*. The word stems from the Latin *per centum,* meaning "by the hundred." Over time, the phrase was shortened to *per cent,* and now it appears as the single word *percent.*

Because our number system is the decimal system and because our monetary system is decimal based, it is natural to subdivide units into hundredths. In business, these hundredths are called percent.

The symbol for percent is %. Thus, 5% means 5 hundredths, and 75% means 75 hundredths. From chapter 2, we conclude that

$$5\% = \frac{5}{100} = 0.05$$

and $$75\% = \frac{75}{100} = 0.75$$

The following examples demonstrate simple methods for converting percents to fractions or decimal numbers and vice versa.

Example 1 Convert the following percents to decimal numbers:

a. 2% c. 6.5% e. $\frac{1}{2}\%$

b. 47% d. $12\frac{3}{4}\%$ f. 130%

Solution

a. $2\% = \frac{2}{100} = 0.02$

b. $47\% = \frac{47}{100} = 0.47$

c. $6.5\% = \frac{6.5}{100} = 0.065$

d. $12\frac{3}{4}\% = 12.75\% = \frac{12.75}{100} = 0.1275$

e. $\frac{1}{2}\% = 0.5\% = \frac{0.5}{100} = 0.005$

f. $130\% = \frac{130}{100} = 1.30$

Example 1 shows that a shortcut method for converting a percent to a decimal number is to move the decimal point two places to the left and drop the percent symbol.

Example 2 Convert the following decimal numbers to percents:

a. 0.03 c. 0.045 e. 0.00075

b. 0.1 d. 0.8525 f. 1.25

Solution

a. $0.03 = \frac{3}{100} = 3\%$

b. $0.1 = 0.10 = \frac{10}{100} = 10\%$

c. $0.045 = \frac{4.5}{100} = 4.5\%$ (or $4\frac{1}{2}\%$)

d. $0.8525 = \frac{85.25}{100} = 85.25\%$ (or $85\frac{1}{4}\%$)

e. $0.00075 = \frac{0.075}{100} = 0.075\% \left(\text{or } \frac{75}{1000}\% \text{ or } \frac{3}{40}\%\right)$

f. $1.25 = \frac{125}{100} = 125\%$

Thus, a shortcut method for converting a decimal number to a percent is to move the decimal point two places to the right and affix the % symbol.

Example 3 Convert the following percents to fractions:

a. 20% c. $\frac{3}{4}\%$ e. $\frac{9}{4}\%$

b. 45% d. 0.5% f. 110%

Solution

a. $20\% = \frac{20}{100} = \frac{1}{5}$

b. $45\% = \frac{45}{100} = \frac{9}{20}$

c. $\frac{3}{4}\% = \frac{3/4}{100} = \frac{3}{400}$

d. $0.5\% = \frac{1}{2}\% = \frac{1/2}{100} = \frac{1}{200}$

e. $\frac{9}{4}\% = \frac{9/4}{100} = \frac{9}{400}$

f. $110\% = \frac{110}{100} = \frac{11}{10}$

Examples 4–7 illustrate how to convert fractions to percents. To convert a fraction to a percent, divide the numerator of the fraction by the denominator for two places to the right of the decimal point; the percent consists of the digits of the quotient plus the fraction whose numerator is the remainder and whose denominator is the divisor.

Example 4

Find the percent equal to $\frac{1}{8}$.

Solution

$$\begin{array}{r} 0.12 \\ 8\overline{)1.00} \\ \underline{8} \\ 20 \\ \underline{16} \\ 4 \end{array}$$

Thus, $\frac{1}{8} = 12\frac{4}{8}\% = 12\frac{1}{2}\%$.

Example 5

Find the percent equal to $\frac{3}{20}$.

Solution

$$\begin{array}{r} 0.15 \\ 20\overline{)3.00} \\ \underline{2\,0} \\ 1\,00 \\ \underline{1\,00} \\ 0 \end{array}$$

$\frac{3}{20} = 15\%$

Example 6

Find the percent equal to $\frac{1}{3}$.

Solution

$$\begin{array}{r} 0.33 \\ 3\overline{)1.00} \\ \underline{9} \\ 10 \\ \underline{9} \\ 1 \end{array}$$

$\frac{1}{3} = 33\frac{1}{3}\%$

Example 7

Find the percent equal to $\frac{7}{5}$.

Solution

$$\begin{array}{r} 1.40 \\ 5\overline{)7.00} \\ \underline{5} \\ 2\,0 \\ \underline{2\,0} \\ 0 \\ \underline{0} \end{array}$$

$$\frac{7}{5} = 1.40 = \frac{140}{100} = 140\%$$

Certain percents occur frequently in business because they are equivalent to simple fractions, which facilitates computations. For example, $33\frac{1}{3}\% = \frac{1}{3}$, $50\% = \frac{1}{2}$, and so on. Table 4.1 shows some of the more common percents and their equivalent fractions.

Table 4.1 Common Percents and Equivalent Fractions

$\frac{1}{2}=50\%$	$\frac{1}{3}=33\frac{1}{3}\%$	$\frac{1}{4}=25\%$	$\frac{1}{5}=20\%$	$\frac{1}{6}=16\frac{2}{3}\%$	$\frac{1}{8}=12\frac{1}{2}\%$	$\frac{1}{12}=8\frac{1}{3}\%$
	$\frac{2}{3}=66\frac{2}{3}\%$	$\frac{3}{4}=75\%$	$\frac{2}{5}=40\%$	$\frac{5}{6}=83\frac{1}{3}\%$	$\frac{3}{8}=37\frac{1}{2}\%$	$\frac{5}{12}=41\frac{2}{3}\%$
			$\frac{3}{5}=60\%$		$\frac{5}{8}=62\frac{1}{2}\%$	$\frac{7}{12}=58\frac{1}{3}\%$
			$\frac{4}{5}=80\%$		$\frac{7}{8}=87\frac{1}{2}\%$	$\frac{11}{12}=91\frac{2}{3}\%$

Note: An aliquot part of 100 is any number that divides 100 evenly. Each of the percents in line 1 of the table represents an aliquot part of 100.

Exercises for Section 4.2

In problems 1–18, convert the given percents to decimal numbers.

1. 4%
2. 9%
3. 58%
4. 43%
5. 92.6%
6. 87.4%
7. 7.81%
8. 5.39%
9. 92.42%
10. 61.37%
11. $14\frac{1}{2}\%$
12. $4\frac{3}{4}\%$
13. $\frac{1}{4}\%$
14. $\frac{3}{4}\%$
15. 123%
16. 142%
17. 172.5%
18. 349.3%

In problems 19–36, convert the given decimal numbers to percents.

19. 0.01
20. 0.04
21. 0.53
22. 0.76
23. 0.7
24. 0.9
25. 0.053
26. 0.018
27. 0.5934
28. 0.6421
29. 0.0032
30. 0.0047
31. 4.32
32. 5.17
33. 7.246
34. 8.992
35. 7.0263
36. 8.5752

In problems 37–60, convert the given percents to fractions reduced to lowest terms.

37. 12%
38. 28%
39. 35%
40. 82%
41. 0.2%
42. 0.6%
43. 0.25%
44. 0.75%
45. 0.44%
46. 0.68%
47. $\frac{7}{8}\%$
48. $\frac{5}{6}\%$
49. $\frac{3}{5}\%$
50. $\frac{5}{12}\%$
51. $\frac{7}{4}\%$
52. $\frac{8}{5}\%$
53. 102%
54. 225%
55. 152%
56. 340%
57. 98.4%
58. 72.6%
59. 155.5%
60. 148.2%

In problems 61–76, convert each of the given fractions to percents.

61. $\frac{1}{4}$
62. $\frac{1}{5}$
63. $\frac{3}{4}$
64. $\frac{4}{5}$
65. $\frac{9}{20}$
66. $\frac{7}{20}$
67. $\frac{7}{8}$
68. $\frac{5}{8}$
69. $\frac{15}{16}$
70. $\frac{24}{25}$
71. $\frac{9}{11}$
72. $\frac{7}{9}$
73. $\frac{4}{15}$
74. $\frac{8}{5}$
75. $\frac{9}{4}$
76. $\frac{15}{8}$

Section 4.3 Base and percentage

Percent is related to two other quantities: base and percentage. The sentence

$95 is 25% of $380

illustrates the relationship. The **base** is a quantity one calculates a percent "of"; in the preceding sentence, the base is $380. The **percentage** is a portion of the base; in the preceding sentence, \$95 is 25% (a one-fourth portion) of \$380. The relationship between percent, base, and percentage is summarized by the formula

■ (4–1) $$P = B \cdot R$$

where P = percentage (portion), B = base, and R = rate (percent).

Because the words *percent* and *percentage* are similar, they are frequently used incorrectly. Many times *percent* is used in conversation by someone who is actually discussing *percentage,* or vice versa. Formula 4–1 clarifies the distinction between the two words: Percentage is a quantity determined by multiplying the base quantity by the percent.

When the base and percent are known, formula 4–1 is used to find the percentage. When the percent and percentage are known, a formula for finding the base is derived by dividing both sides of formula 4–1 by R to obtain

■ (4–2) $$B = \frac{P}{R}$$

When the percentage and base are the given quantities, a formula for finding the percent is derived by dividing both sides of formula 4–1 by B to obtain

■ (4–3) $$R = \frac{P}{B}$$

Many problems that involve percent, percentage, or base can be solved using formulas 4–1, 4–2, and 4–3. Choosing the correct formula for a given problem involves correctly identifying the known and unknown quantities. The rate is easily identified by the word *percent* or by the percent sign (%). To distinguish between percentage and base, keep in mind that the base is the quantity that we find the percent "of." Thus, the base is usually the quantity or phrase following the word "of."

Example 1 What amount is 5% of \$3,000?

Solution

The quantity following "of" is \$3,000, hence this is the base. Thus, $P = ?$, $B = \$3{,}000$, $R = 5\% = 0.05$. Using formula 4–1,

$$P = B \cdot R$$

$$= \$3{,}000 \times 0.05$$

$$= \$150$$

Five percent of \$3,000 is \$150.

Example 2 Twenty-five percent of what number is 30?

Solution

Following "of" is "what number," hence the base is the unknown. Thus, $P = 30$, $B = ?$, $R = 25\% = 0.25$. Using formula 4–2,

$$B = \frac{P}{R}$$

$$= \frac{30}{0.25}$$

$$= 120$$

Twenty-five percent of 120 is 30.

Example 3 This month's inventory of 248 cases is 80% of last month's inventory. What was last month's inventory?

Solution

The word "of" is used twice in this problem, "of 248" and "80% of last month's inventory." Since last month's inventory is the quantity we are finding a percent of, it is the base. Thus $P = 248$, $B = ?$, $R = 80\% = 0.80$. Using formula 4–2,

$$B = \frac{P}{R}$$

$$= \frac{248}{0.80}$$

$$= 310$$

Last month's inventory was 310 cases.

Example 4 If the commission on a sale of \$42.00 is \$3.78, what percent commission is paid?

Solution

Following "of" is \$42.00, hence this is the base. Thus, $P = \$3.78$, $B = \$42.00$, $R = ?$. Using formula 4–3,

$$R = \frac{P}{B}$$

$$= \frac{3.78}{42}$$

$$= 0.09$$

$$= 9\%$$

A common application of formulas 4–1, 4–2, and 4–3 is the sales tax levied on retail sales. In problems involving sales tax, P = amount of the sales tax, B = purchase price, and R = tax rate. The next examples illustrate this application. (Sales taxes will be discussed in greater detail in chapter 9.)

Example 5 The selling price of an item is \$58.95. If the sales tax rate is 5%, find the amount of the sales tax.

Solution

P = ?, B = \$58.95, R = 5% = 0.05. Using formula 4–1,

$$\begin{aligned} P &= B \cdot R \\ &= \$58.95 \times 0.05 \\ &= \$2.9475 \\ &= \$2.95 \end{aligned}$$

Example 6 The sales tax on an item was \$13.27. If the sales tax rate is 6.25%, what was the selling price of the item?

Solution

P = \$13.27, B = ?, R = 6.25% = 0.0625. Using formula 4–2,

$$\begin{aligned} B &= \frac{P}{R} \\ &= \frac{13.27}{0.0625} \\ &= \$212.32 \end{aligned}$$

Example 7 The sales tax on an item priced at \$140.66 was \$5.63. To the nearest percent, find the sales tax rate.

Solution

P = \$5.63, B = \$140.66, R = ?. Using formula 4–3,

$$\begin{aligned} R &= \frac{P}{B} \\ &= \frac{5.63}{140.66} \\ &= 0.0400255 \\ &= 4\% \end{aligned}$$

Exercises for Section 4.3

In problems 1–32, find the indicated amounts.

1. 6% of 300 is what amount?
2. 8% of 600 is what amount?
3. 54 is 15% of what amount?
4. 132 is 11% of what amount?
5. What percent of 320 is 48?
6. What percent of 810 is 162?
7. 12% of 40 is what amount?
8. 16% of 120 is what amount?
9. 50.4 is 8.4% of what amount?
10. 62.16 is 14.8% of what amount?
11. 48.6 is what percent of 216?
12. 60.84 is what percent of 585?
13. 48% of 76 is what amount?
14. 36% of 43 is what amount?
15. What percent of 364 is 30.94?
16. 12 is 5% of what amount?
17. 14 is 12% of what amount?
18. What percent of 250 is 15?
19. What percent of 120 is 18?
20. 20.88 is 14.4% of what amount?
21. 18.432 is 18% of what amount?
22. 6.5541 is 21% of what amount?
23. 28.2% of 612 is what amount?
24. 32.3% of 1,540 is what amount?
25. 8.7796 is 47% of what amount?
26. What percent of 96 is 2.88?
27. 136.94 is 16.7% of what amount?
28. 97.24 is 14.3% of what amount?

29. What percent of 112 is 10.08?

30. What percent of 75.2 is 5.264?

31. 8.9% of 2,620 is what amount?

32. 10.845 is 15% of what amount?

33. A salesperson's commission was 18% of $972. What was the amount of the commission?

34. The sales tax on an item that sells for $14.50 was $0.87. Find the sales tax rate.

35. A corporation paid income taxes of $49,588 on gross profits of $225,400. What was the income tax rate?

36. A stock dividend of $58.80 is 6% of the original investment. What was the original investment?

37. A worker earning $22,500 received a bonus of $1,125. What percent of the salary was the bonus?

38. A video recorder is on sale for $249.50. If the sales tax is 5.75% of the sale price, what is the total purchase price of the recorder?

39. The sales tax on an item priced at $140.80 is $7.04. Find the sales tax rate.

40. Bob Martin ordered a stereo cassette player from a catalog. If the sales tax was $4.03 and the sales tax rate was 6.25% of the catalog price, what was the price listed in the catalog?

41. Find the amount of the sales tax on an item priced at $318.20 if the sales tax rate is 5.25%.

42. Out of 1,840 items manufactured by a machine, 2.5% were defective. Find the number of defective items.

43. The sales force of a company made 450 calls last month. Eighteen percent of those calls resulted in sales. How many sales were made?

44. A real estate commission of $8,430 represented 6% of the selling price. Find the selling price.

45. Find the amount of sales tax on $68.80 if the sales tax rate is 4%.

46. A professional quarterback received a bonus of $1,000 for completing 68.18% of the passes he threw in a game. If he completed 30 passes, how many did he attempt?

47. Mary Mackey purchased a new barbecue grill priced at \$275. She made a down payment of 15% of the price. Find the amount of the down payment.

48. Pete's Pet Shop spent \$1,825 for advertising this year. Last year, the store spent 82% of this amount. How much was spent on advertising last year?

49. The Quality-Wise Furniture Store recorded total sales of \$21,000 for January, of which \$4,200 were charges. What percent of the sales were charges?

50. Barb Fox had a total income of \$31,362.00 for the year and paid \$6,586.02 in taxes. Find the percent of her income that she paid in taxes.

51. Sam Smooth earned \$94 commission on the sale of an exercise set. If the commission rate is 8%, find the selling price of the set.

52. The annual dividend return from an investment in preferred stock is \$450. If this return is 9% of the investment, how much did the stock cost?

53. Northwest Motors accepted 160 used cars as trade-ins during February. Of these, 25% were wholesaled to a used car dealer, and 5% were sold as junk. The remaining cars were reconditioned and sold through the company's used car division. How many cars were reconditioned? How many cars were sold as junk?

54. Cameron Industries employs 580 people, of which 493 are union members. What percent of the company's work force are union members?

55. Peabody & Sons reduced its monthly office expense by 5% after consulting efficiency experts. If the monthly office expense was \$3,200 before the efficiency study, how much per month did the company save?

56. Paxton Products reported a profit of \$17,500 for the month of January, which was 5.4% of the company's sales for that month. Find the amount of the company's January sales.

57. Last year Murdock Industries paid \$5,184 in property taxes on their office building. If the building was assessed at \$216,000, find the property tax rate.

58. The Eltek Corporation reported profits of \$26,730 in April on sales of \$356,400. What percent of the company's April sales are its profits?

59. William Martin bought corporate stock for \$7,400 and sold it for \$7,992. What percent of his original investment was his profit?

60. During a recent sale at Stan's Music Store, the profit made on Regal transistor radios was 5% of the sale price. If the profit on each radio was 75¢, find the sale price of the radios.

61. The manager of the men's department decides to close out a certain line of sport coats, so he reduces the price of the coats from $180 to $135. What percent of the original price is the reduced price?

62. Lotus Industries reported that, due to rising expenses, the development of one of its new products cost 20% more than originally projected. If it cost $12,000 more than projected to develop the product, find the original estimate of the cost.

63. Frances Thomas purchased the Children's Apparel Shop. At the end of the first year, she had $21,200 invested in the shop. If the net income from the shop was $9,200 for the year, what percent of the investment did she receive as income? (Round to the nearest percent.)

64. The Fairview Meat Market pays 3% of its monthly net sales to the landlord for rent. In February, the market's net sales were $39,472.40. How much rent did the market pay for February? (Round to the nearest cent.)

65. Jan Foster paid $13,765.78 in federal income taxes based on an adjusted gross income of $47,468.20. What percent of her adjusted gross income did she pay in taxes? (Round to the nearest percent.)

66. Bill Curtis has $62.60 deducted from his monthly check for health insurance, which is 2.9% of his gross pay. What is Bill's monthly gross pay? (Round to the nearest cent.)

67. A salesman sold $885 worth of fittings. At a commission rate of 12% of sales, how much commission will he receive?

68. Barb Snyder purchased a new stereo system for a total price of $734.50. If the sales tax was $23.50, what percent of the total price was sales tax? (Round to the nearest percent.)

Section 4.4 Variations of the percentage formula

At the beginning of this chapter, it was pointed out that percents are often used to describe increases or decreases. In this section, we discuss formulas used to solve problems of this type. The first problems involve finding the percent increase or decrease in the base. The formula is

$$R = \frac{\text{Increase (or decrease) in base}}{\text{Base}}. \qquad (4\text{–}4)$$

The base in formula 4–4 is the original quantity before the increase or decrease is realized.

Example 1 The sale price of a man's jacket is \$25.95, compared to the regular price of \$33.95. By what percent was the price reduced on the jacket?

Solution

The new base of \$25.95 is a decrease from the initial base of \$33.95. Using formula 4–4,

$$
\begin{aligned}
R &= \frac{\text{Decrease in base}}{\text{Base}} \\
&= \frac{\$33.95 - \$25.95}{\$33.95} \\
&= \frac{\$8.00}{\$33.95} \\
&= 0.2356 \\
&= 23.56\%
\end{aligned}
$$

The price of the jacket was reduced by 23.56%.

Example 2 During a recent fiscal year, revenue for the 100 largest U.S. agricultural cooperatives increased from \$50.3 billion to \$57.8 billion. Calculate the percent increase in revenue.

Solution

Using formula 4–4,

$$
\begin{aligned}
R &= \frac{\text{Increase in base}}{\text{Base}} \\
&= \frac{57.8 - 50.3}{50.3} \\
&= \frac{7.5}{50.3} \\
&= 0.1491 \\
&= 14.91\%
\end{aligned}
$$

Revenue increased 14.91% during the fiscal year.

Example 3 Retail gasoline sales of independent gasoline dealers declined from 11.8 billion gallons in 1988 to 11.6 billion gallons in 1989. Calculate the percent decrease in sales for the one-year period.

Solution

$$R = \frac{11.8 - 11.6}{11.8} \quad \text{(Decrease in base)}$$

$$= \frac{0.2}{11.8}$$

$$= 0.0169$$

$$= 1.69\%$$

Gasoline sales of independent gasoline dealers declined 1.69% from 1988 to 1989.

A second variation of the percentage formula occurs in situations where the base is increased or decreased by a known percent. If the base B is increased or decreased by the rate R to the quantity B_1, the formula is

$$B_1 = (1.00 \pm R) \times B \tag{4–5}$$

The symbol $\pm$ means "plus or minus." Only one of the signs is used in a given problem. The plus sign is used if the base is increased; the minus sign is used if the base is decreased.

Example 4 The Addison Appliance Company has decided to raise its retail prices on home freezers by 5%. One of the freezers currently sells for \$320. What is the new retail price of the freezer?

Solution

$R_1 = 5\% = 0.05$, and $B = \$320$. The base is increased; hence,

$$B_1 = (1.00 + R) \times B$$

$$= (1.00 + 0.05) \times \$320$$

$$= 1.05 \times \$320$$

$$= \$336$$

The new retail price of the freezer is \$336.

Example 5 The Dixon Corporation reported that profits for the year 1989 had declined by 7% to \$102,500. To the nearest dollar, calculate the 1988 profits.

Solution

$R = 0.07$, and $B_1 = \$102{,}500$. The base B has decreased; hence,

$$B_1 = (1.00 - R) \times B$$

$$\$102{,}500 = (1.00 - 0.07) \times B$$

$$\$102{,}500 = 0.93\ B$$

$$\frac{\$102{,}500}{0.93} = B$$

$$\$110{,}215 = B$$

Profits in 1988 were \$110,215.

Example 6 Over a period of two years, the average hourly wage of a group of manufacturing workers rose 17%. If the hourly wage at the beginning of the period was \$6.20, what was the hourly wage after two years?

Solution

$R = 0.17$, and $B = \$6.20$; hence,

$$\begin{aligned} B_1 &= (1.00 + R) \times B \\ &= (1.00 + 0.17) \times \$6.20 \\ &= 1.17 \times \$6.20 \\ &= \$7.254 \\ &= \$7.25 \end{aligned}$$

After two years, the hourly wage was \$7.25.

An alternate way of writing formula 4–5 is

$$B_1 = B \pm BR$$

Using this form of the formula, example 6 could have been solved as follows:

$$\begin{aligned} B_1 &= B + BR \\ &= \$6.20 + \$6.20(0.17) \\ &= \$6.20 + \$1.054 \\ &= \$7.254 \\ &= \$7.25 \end{aligned}$$

Exercises for Section 4.4

In problems 1–10, compute the percent increase or decrease of the given base B.

1. B = $40 to $60
2. B = 400 employees to 380 employees
3. B = 52 lbs. to 65 lbs.
4. B = $84 to $105
5. B = $136 to $145.52
6. B = $472 to $401.20
7. B = 14.2 tons to 18.46 tons
8. B = 52.05 kilograms to 114.51 kilograms
9. B = $4,752 to $4,134.24
10. B = $8,628.02 to $12,942.03

In problems 11–20, compute the value B_1 obtained by increasing or decreasing the given value B by the given percent.

11. B = 86 kilograms, increased by 50%
12. B = 108 shares of stock, decreased by 25%
13. B = 154 grams, increased by 13%
14. B = 65.6 pounds, increased by 110%
15. B = 147 liters, increased by 31%
16. B = 474.8 pounds, decreased by 80%
17. B = $86.40, increased by 17.5%
18. B = $4,612.24, increased by 14.2%.
19. B = 205.5 gallons, decreased by 14.8%
20. B = $17,462.80, decreased by 21.7%
21. Smithfield Enterprises normally employs 420 full-time employees. During a recent recession, the company cut its work force to 357 people. Find the percent decrease in the company's work force.
22. Southern Auto Company increased the base price of its automobiles by 4%. What is the new selling price of a car that previously sold for $12,100?
23. The cosmetics department lost $324 of its inventory last month due to theft. This month, $420 worth of merchandise was stolen. Find the percent increase in stolen goods. (Round to the nearest percent.)

24. The sales at Lambert's Delicatessen increased this month by 3% over last month's sales. If last month's sales were $1,240, what were this month's sales?

25. The manager of Mom's Restaurant discovered that supplies that cost $350.00 a year ago now cost $409.50 because of rising prices. What is the percent increase in the cost of supplies?

26. Chuck's Marine Equipment cut the price on outboard motors by 6% for a special sale. Find the sale price of a motor that regularly sells for $979.50.

27. Bernard Bonds owns a pet shop. Last year, the gross sales were $68,420.00 as compared to $75,946.20 for this year. What is the percent increase in sales?

28. The manager of the ladies' apparel department increased the price of a certain line of blouses by 7.5%. Find the new price of a blouse that originally sold for $24.

29. The office expenses at J & B Enterprises were reduced from $1,420 last month to $1,290 this month. Find the percent decrease. (Round to the nearest percent.)

30. This month, the retail value of the stock on hand at Simon's Pharmaceuticals is 28% less than last month's value of $46,484. What is the retail value of the stock on hand this month?

31. Ray Richards purchased an air conditioner for his automobile at a sale price of $829.75. If the regular price was $892.50, what percent of the regular price did he save? (Round to the nearest percent.)

32. The value of the inventory in the sporting goods section of a large department store increased from $124,400 to $139,950 during the first quarter of the year. Find the percent increase.

33. The J and J Construction Company estimates that a building that cost $315,000 to construct three years ago costs $385,000 to construct today. What is the percent increase in the construction cost? (Round to the nearest percent.)

34. A truckload of apples arrived at the Super Sweet Cannery. If 15% of the apples were spoiled, and if there were 1,250 pounds of apples in the shipment, how many pounds of apples were usable?

35. A university had 8,420 students in attendance last year. This year, the enrollment has increased to 9,240. Find the percent increase in enrollment. (Round to the nearest percent.)

36. B and D Hardware sells its lighting fixtures for 32% more than cost. Find the selling price of a fixture with a cost price of $104.50.

37. The operating expenses at the Pick-A-Pair shoe store were $540 a week last year. This year, the operating expenses have been reduced to $520 a week. What percent reduction is this? (Round to the nearest percent.)

38. Built-Well Furniture sold a living-room suite for $540, which was $80 less than the regular price. What percent of the regular price did the customer save? (Round to the nearest percent.)

39. Wanda Phillips recently purchased a gas grill for $182.64, including the sales tax. If the sales tax rate was 6%, find the price of the grill, excluding the sales tax.

40. Susan Prentice purchased a new stereo sound system for a total price of $724.42, including the sales tax. If the sales tax rate was 5.5%, what was the price of the stereo system, excluding the sales tax?

41. The selling price of a motorcycle at Sol's Scooter Shack is 18% more than the wholesale cost. Find the wholesale cost of a motorcycle that sells for $2,450.

42. The inventory of 520 sacks of fertilizer at Larry's Lawn and Garden Shop was 15% short of the amount required. Find the required number of sacks. (Round to the nearest whole number.)

43. The sales at Henry's Harness & Feed Store were $1,824 this month, which was 4% less than last month's sales. Find the sales for last month.

44. Jean Prentice wishes to sell her house, so she lists the house with a real estate agency. If she wishes to receive $67,500 for the house and the realtor's fee is 8% of the selling price, find the price at which the realtor will advertise the house. (Round your answer to the nearest hundred dollars.)

45. Peerless Products installed new equipment that reduced the production cost per unit of its product by 12%. If the new production cost per unit is $120, what was the old cost? (Round your answer to the nearest cent.)

Glossary

Base A quantity one calculates a percent "of"; the number that is multiplied by a percent.

Percent Means "by the hundred" or "hundredths"; the quotient of the percentage and the base, expressed as hundredths; also called the *rate*.

Percentage The product of the base and the percent; a portion of the base.

Rate See *percent*.

Review test

1. Convert to decimal numbers: (a) 43%, (b) $19\frac{1}{2}$%.
2. Convert to percents: (a) 0.73, (b) 0.024.
3. Find: (a) 18% of 400, (b) 12% of 780.
4. Express as percents: (a) $\frac{3}{5}$, (b) $\frac{7}{25}$.
5. Express 65% as a fraction reduced to lowest terms.
6. Express $\frac{7}{20}$ as (a) a percent, (b) a decimal.
7. Twelve percent of what amount is 42?
8. What percent of 72.9 is 29.16?
9. What is the percent increase of 78 to 107.64?
10. What is the percent decrease of 125 to 50?
11. Express the percent increase from 55 to 88 as a fraction reduced to lowest terms.
12. If 430 is increased by 30% to B_1, what is B_1?
13. If 75 is decreased by 20% to B_1, what is B_1?
14. A worker paid 27% of her adjusted gross income of $36,000 in federal income taxes. How much did she pay in taxes?
15. An automobile insurance claim amounted to 44% of the value of the car, which was $3,800. How much was the claim?
16. Sales at a retail store increased from $3,200 to $4,320 in one month. What was the percent increase in sales?
17. A merchant had to raise the price on an item selling for $68 by 8%. What was the new selling price?
18. During a day's trading, the price of a share of stock decreased from $46.00 to $40.25. What was the percent decrease?
19. A corporation reduced its quarterly dividend from $5.40 per share to $3.80 per share. To the nearest percent, what percent was the dividend reduced?
20. An employee was given a wage increase of 7.5%. If she was earning $12.40 per hour before her raise, what is her new hourly rate?

PART 2

Retailing/Accounting

■

In addition to presenting the fundamentals of buying and selling and inventory control, chapters in this part cover the essentials of record keeping with respect to payrolls, banking, accounting statements, budgeting, depreciation, and taxes.

CHAPTER 5

Retailing Decisions

Chapter Objectives

I. Learn the meaning of the following terms:

List price, 91
Cost price, 91
Selling price, 91
Net price, 91
Discount, 91
Billing price, 91

Overhead, 91
Markon, 91
Net profit, 91
Markdown, 127
Inventory control, 134

Perpetual inventory, 134
Periodic inventory, 135
Inventory turnover, 145
Average inventory, 145

II. Understand the concepts of:

Trade discount, 91
Complement of the discount, 93
Chain discounts, 96
Quantity discounts, 102
Cash discounts, 107
Ordinary dating, 112
End of the month dating, 112
Receipt of goods dating, 112

Extra dating, 113
Installment dating, 113
Anticipation dating, 114
The basic markon equation, 116
Markon of perishables and irregulars, 120–121
Conversion of the markon base, 122
Operating loss, 130
Gross loss, 130

Inventory valuation using the methods of:
Specific identification, 136–137
Average cost, 137–138
FIFO, 138
LIFO, 138–139
Inventory value estimation using:
Gross profit method, 143
Retail method, 144

III. Learn to use:

The basic percentage formula $P = BR$ to calculate discounts and markdown, 93–94, 102, 127

The formulas for markon based on selling or cost price to calculate selling price, 117–119

The formulas to convert from one markon base to the other, 122–123
The formulas for calculating inventory turnover, 145–146

Section 5.1 Introduction

The retail store is the final step of the marketing process that begins with raw materials and ends with a product for purchase by the public. Retail stores may be large or small, may be independently owned or part of a nationwide chain, but they have one thing in common: Their managers are engaged in buying merchandise for resale to the public. Approximately 13% of the country's work force is engaged in some aspect of retailing, and annual sales of retail stores now exceed $700 billion. The basic mathematics of retailing is the subject of this chapter.

A number of special terms are required for the discussion of retail mathematics:

The **list price** or **suggested retail price** is the catalog price or the price on a price list or price tag.

A **discount** is a percentage reduction from the list price.

The **net price** is the list price less any discounts.

The **billing price** is the net price plus freight or transportation charges.

The **cost price** is the billing price plus any other charges (for example, storage charges).

The **selling price** of an item is the amount of money a vendor receives in exchange for the product.

Markon is the difference between the selling price and the cost price. Markon is also known as gross profit or margin.

Overhead is the expense of operation, including rent, taxes, salaries, utilities, insurance, and so on.

Net profit is markon less overhead.

Section 5.2 Trade discounts

A **trade discount** is a percentage reduction from the list price offered to certain categories of customers by the seller. Often, the manufacturer's list price is approximately the resale price of the retailer. Therefore, if the retailer is to sell at the suggested price, the merchandise must be bought at a discount if the retailer is to cover his or her overhead and earn a net profit.

An invoice illustrating a trade discount is shown in figure 5.1. Note that the trade discount of 50% reduces the list price of $436 by $218. Thus, the net price is $436 − $218 = $218.

Figure 5.1
Invoice with trade discount

PRINCE GARDNER
Manufacturers of Fine Personal Leather Goods
1234 SOUTH KINGSHIGHWAY BOULEVARD
ST. LOUIS, MISSOURI 63110
TELEPHONE (314) 535-9500 D-U-N-S 628-6215

INVOICE DATE

INVOICE NUMBER A-337069 — PLEASE REFER TO THIS INVOICE NUMBER IN ALL CORRESPONDENCE — PAGE 1

ATTENTION	OUR ORDER NUMBER	DEPT.	STORE NO.	SHIP DATE	ACCOUNT NO.
	500367	333			0001030

INVOICE NUMBER	CUSTOMER ORDER NO.	SHIPPED VIA	TRADE DISCOUNT (EXCEPT AS NOTED BY*)	TERMS	DIV/SLSM.
A-337069	9742736	UPSP	50 %	2% 10 DAYS E.O.M. NET THEREAFTER NO ANTICIPATION ALLOWED	000

SHIP TO:
THE LEATHER SHOP
1644 BROADWAY
BALLWIN MO 63011

PRPD
Z-4

SOLD TO:
THE LEATHER SHOP
1644 BROADWAY
BALLWIN MO 63011

PRINCE GARDNER LOT NUMBER	DESCRIPTION OR CUSTOMER LOT NO.	RETAIL PRICE	BLACK 1	BROWN 2	GREEN 3	TAN 4	RED 5	BLUE 6	YELLOW 7	WHITE 8	ORANGE 9	PINK 0	TOTAL UNITS	UNIT COST	COST EXTENSION
000-3006	ACCESSORY M	.80										5	5	.40	2.00
035-0101	REGISTRAR M	10.00	12	6									18	5.00	90.00
020-0502	CR/PHOTO M	6.00	1				1						2	3.00	6.00
044-0412	THREE-FOLD M	8.00	3	3									6	4.00	24.00
002-0103	REGISTRAR M	15.00	1	1									2	7.50	15.00
058-0943	CIG CASE L	5.00			1	1	1						3	2.50	7.50
058-2242	GIFT SET L	11.50			2	4	5						11	5.75	63.25
096-0551	I D CASE L	4.50								1			1	2.25	2.25
025-0142	REGISTRAR L	8.00						2					2	4.00	8.00

SHIPPED FROM	1 = COMPLETE, 2 = BACK ORDER	APPROX. WEIGHT (LBS)	RETAIL VALUE	TRADE DISCOUNT	TOTAL UNITS	MDSE. TOTAL COST
ST.LOUIS	1	18.7	436.00	218.00	50	218.00

ALL AGREEMENTS ARE CONTINGENT UPON STRIKES, ACCIDENTS, DELAYS OF CARRIERS, OR OTHER CAUSES BEYOND OUR CONTROL. NO CLAIMS OF ANY KIND ALLOWED UNLESS REPORTED WITHIN 5 DAYS UPON RECEIPT OF GOODS. PRICES SUBJECT TO CHANGE WITHOUT NOTICE.

PRINCE 042776 GSC-A

SEE ORDER

WEIGHT CHGS IF ANY,ON LAST INVOICE

INVOICE AMOUNT
GRAND TOTAL ▶ $ 218.00

A-337069

PLEASE REMIT DIRECTLY FROM THIS INVOICE; WE DO NOT SEND STATEMENTS—ORIGINAL INVOICE

Example 1 The Appleton Company buys refrigerators from a wholesale appliance dealer. The list price of one model is \$678 with a trade discount of 40%. Find the amount of the trade discount and the net price.

Solution

The amount of a discount is just an application of the basic percentage formula $P = BR$, where P = trade discount, B = list price, and R = discount percent. In this problem, $P = ?$, $B = \$678$, and $R = 40\%$.

$$P = BR$$
$$= \$678 \times 0.40$$
$$= \$271.20$$

\$678.00	List price
− 271.20	Trade discount
\$406.80	Net price

Example 2 A wholesale hardware company lists a water heater at \$246 with a trade discount of 30%. Find the net price.

Solution

\$246.00	List price
− 73.80	Trade discount (\$246 × 0.30)
\$172.20	Net price

In example 2, a trade discount of 30% means that the net price is 70% (100% − 30%) of the list price. Multiplying the list price by 0.70 yields

\$246.00	List price
× 0.70	
\$172.20	Net price

Relative to the 30% discount, 70% is called the **complement of the discount** or the **net price percent.** A discount and its complement are related by the formula

■ (5–1) $$100\% - D = C$$

where D = discount percent and C = complement of the discount (net price percent).

Thus, an alternate method of calculating the net price is to multiply the list price by the net price percent.

Example 3 A dining-room suite with a list price of $1,268.00 carries a trade discount of 70%. The freight charges are $94.60. Find the net price using the complement of the discount and then find the billing price.

Solution

	$1,268.00	List price
×	0.30	Net price percent (complement of the discount)
	$ 380.40	Net price
+	94.60	Freight charges
	$ 475.00	Billing price

Frequently, discounts are in fractional percents, such as $16\frac{2}{3}\%$, $33\frac{1}{3}\%$, and so on. In such instances, it may be simpler to multiply the list price by the fractional equivalent of the discount percent. Recall from section 4.2 that

$$16\frac{2}{3}\% = \frac{16\ 2/3}{100} = \frac{50}{3} \times \frac{1}{100} = \frac{1}{6}$$

$$33\frac{1}{3}\% = \frac{33\ 1/3}{100} = \frac{100}{3} \times \frac{1}{100} = \frac{1}{3}$$

The complement of the discount is found by subtracting the fractional equivalent of the discount percent from 1.

$$100\% - 16\frac{2}{3}\% = 83\frac{1}{3}\% \qquad 100\% - 33\frac{1}{3}\% = 66\frac{2}{3}\%$$

$$1 - \frac{1}{6} = \frac{5}{6} \qquad 1 - \frac{1}{3} = \frac{2}{3}$$

Example 4 A load of fertilizer with a list price of $880 carries a trade discount of $12\frac{1}{2}\%$. Find the net price using the complement of the discount.

Solution

$$12\frac{1}{2}\% = \frac{12\ 1/2}{100} = \frac{25}{2} \times \frac{1}{100} = \frac{1}{8}$$

$$100\% - 12\frac{1}{2}\% = 87\frac{1}{2}\%$$

$$1 - \frac{1}{8} = \frac{7}{8}$$

List price → $\$880 \times \frac{7}{8} = \$770$ Net price

Complement of the discount (net price percent) → $\frac{7}{8}$

Exercises for Section 5.2

1. Century Electronics Company buys its television sets from a wholesale appliance dealer. One model has a list price of $575 with a trade discount of 32%. Find the amount of the trade discount and the net price.

2. If a wholesale appliance dealer lists an air-conditioning unit at $428 with a trade discount of 38%, find the net price of the unit.

3. Walt's Water Conditioning Service buys water softeners from a wholesaler at a list price of $620 with a trade discount of 38%. Find the amount of the trade discount and the net price.

4. What is the net price of a washing machine that lists for $424 with a trade discount of 32%?

5. A set of bedroom furniture with a list price of $2,420.00 carries a trade discount of 65%. If the freight charges are $62.70, find (a) the net price using the complement of the discount and (b) the billing price.

6. A furniture wholesaler lists a living-room suite at $1,840.00 with a trade discount of 54%. Find the net price using the complement of the discount. If the freight charges are $47.30, what is the billing price?

7. The net price of a self-cleaning oven at a wholesale outlet is $382.20. If the list price is $490.00, what percent is the trade discount? What is the complement of the trade discount?

8. The list price of a refrigerator is $630.00, and the net price is $415.80. Find the trade discount percent and the complement of the trade discount.

9. The Quality Appliance Company recently purchased a shipment of vacuum cleaners from a wholesaler. Each unit had a list price of $219 with a trade discount of $33\frac{1}{3}\%$. Find the amount of the trade discount and the net price for each unit.

10. An appliance wholesaler lists a color television set at $525.00 with a trade discount of $16\frac{2}{3}\%$. Find the net price using the complement of the discount. If the freight charges are $12.23, what is the billing price?

11. A building supply store purchased a load of lumber for a net price of $892.50. If the lumber was purchased at a trade discount of 15%, what was the list price?

12. Find the list price of a set of office furniture that was purchased at a net price of $680.40 if the trade discount was 58%.

13. Find the list price of a fur coat that was purchased at a net price of $841 if the trade discount was $8\frac{1}{3}\%$.

Section 5.3 Chain discounts

Changes in market conditions may affect the price of an already discounted product. Improved technology, reduction in the price of raw materials, or wholesale price adjustments may necessitate a price change to maintain a competitive position. Rather than changing the entire price structure, the seller may add an additional trade discount. For example, the price of an item may be quoted at \$100 less 40% less 20%. This means that the list price is discounted 40% and that the result is then discounted an additional 20% to obtain the net price. Two or more discounts on a single item are called series discounts or **chain discounts.**

Example 1 A load of paneling has a list price of \$684 less 30% less 15%. What is the net price?

Solution

\$684.00	List price
− 205.20	First discount (\$684 × 0.30)
\$478.80	
− 71.82	Second discount (\$478.80 × 0.15)
\$406.98	Net price

Example 2 What is the net price of a musical instrument with a list price of \$500 less 60% less 30% less 10%?

Solution

\$500.00	List price
− 300.00	First discount (\$500 × 0.60)
\$200.00	
− 60.00	Second discount (\$200 × 0.30)
\$140.00	
− 14.00	Third discount (\$140 × 0.10)
\$126.00	Net price

The chain discount percents should *not* be added to obtain a single discount percent. Had this been done in example 2, the single discount percent would have been 60% + 30% + 10% = 100%, and the net price would have been:

\$500.00	List price
− 500.00	Trade discount (\$500 × 1.00)
\$ 0.00	Net price

A vendor using this kind of mathematics would have a difficult time making a profit!

To correctly determine a single discount percent equivalent to the chain discounts in example 2, the *complements* of the chain discounts are used. In example 2, the complement of 60% is 40%, the complement of 30% is 70%, and the complement of 10% is 90%. The product of these complements is:

$0.40 \times 0.70 \times 0.90 = 0.252$

Multiplying the list price by this product gives us

$500.00	List price
× 0.252	Product of the complements
$126.00	Net price

Thus, an alternative method for solving example 2 is to multiply the list price by the product of the complements of the chain discounts. This means that the product of the complements is the complement of the equivalent single discount. *Thus, to find the single discount percent equivalent to a chain discount, the product of the complements is subtracted from 100%*. In example 2,

$100\% - 25.2\% = 74.8\% \qquad (0.252 = 25.2\%)$

This is the correct single discount percent because

$500.00	List price
− 374.00	Discount ($500 × 0.748)
$126.00	Net price

Example 3 A stereophonic tape recorder listing at $495 has trade discounts of $33\frac{1}{3}/16\frac{2}{3}$ (list less $33\frac{1}{3}\%$ less $16\frac{2}{3}\%$). Find the net price using (a) the product of the complements and (b) the single discount percent equivalent to the chain discount.

Solution

a. In fractions, the discounts are $\frac{1}{3}$ and $\frac{1}{6}$ (see table 4.1, p. 73). Hence, the product of the complements is $\frac{2}{3} \times \frac{5}{6} = \frac{5}{9}$.

$\$495 \times \frac{5}{9} = \$275$ Net price

b. A fractional equivalent to the single discount percent is found by subtracting the product of the complements from 1; that is,

$$1 - \frac{5}{9} = \frac{4}{9}$$

Thus,

$495.00	List price
− 220.00	Trade discount $\left(\$495 \times \frac{4}{9}\right)$
$275.00	Net price

Example 4 Complete the following invoice.

INVOICE
NO 287402
DATE 8/2
YOUR ORDER NO 4749

SOLD TO Eagle Construction Company
1816 High Street
Madison, Wisconsin

SHIPPED TO
4618 Chestnut Street
Watertown, Wisconsin

OUR ORDER NO.	SALESMAN	TERMS	F.O.B.	DATE SHIPPED	SHIPPED VIA
K4711	J.D.	Net		7/31	Greyhound

QUANTITY ORDERED	QUANTITY SHIPPED	STOCK NUMBER/DESCRIPTION	PRICE		UNIT	AMOUNT	
1	1	106 - 8490 Home Intercom System	199	90	ea.		
2	2	107 - 8490 Room Stations	21	99	ea.		
		Total List					
		Less 40% less 10%					
		Net					
		Prepaid freight				3	88
		Grand Total					

ORIGINAL

Solution

The product of the complements of the chain discounts is $0.60 \times 0.90 = 0.54$, thus the single discount percent equivalent to the chain discounts is $1 - 0.54 = 0.46$. The invoice is completed as follows.

$199.90	
+ 43.98	($21.99 × 2)
$243.88	Total of list prices
− 112.18	Chain discounts ($243.88 × 0.46)
$131.70	Net price
+ 3.88	Freight charges
$135.58	Grand total (Billing price)

Example 5 Chieftan Camping offers a camping tent with a list price of \$290 and a trade discount of 40%. Chieftan learned that a competitor is selling a similar size tent for a net price of \$147.90. What additional trade discount must Chieftan use to match the competitor's price?

Solution

\$290.00	List price
− 116.00	Discount (\$290 × 0.40)
\$174.00	Net price with one trade discount

To match the competitor, the amount of the additional discount is \$174.00 − \$147.90 = \$26.10.

$P = \$26.10,\ B = \$174.00,\ R = ?$

$$R = \frac{P}{B}$$

$$= \frac{\$26.10}{\$174.00}$$

$$= 0.15 = 15\%$$

Thus, Chieftan can match the competition with a list price of \$290 and chain discounts of 40/15.

Exercises for Section 5.3

1. A stereo amplifier has a list price of \$360 less 20% less 15%. What is the net price?
2. If a platform rocker has a list price of \$240 less 12% less 5%, what is the net price?
3. Find the net price of a camera listed at \$340 less 30% less 4%.
4. What is the net price of a washer-dryer combination with a list price of \$800 less 30% less 20% less 10%?
5. A pocket calculator has a list price of \$60 less 15% less 10% less 8%. What is the net price?
6. A home entertainment center has a list price of \$720 less $16\frac{2}{3}\%$ less $8\frac{1}{3}\%$. What is the net price?
7. An executive office desk has a list price of \$943 less $33\frac{1}{3}\%$ less $16\frac{2}{3}\%$. Find the net price of the desk.
8. A home heating system listing at \$950 has trade discounts of 30/20/10. Find the net price using the product of the complements.

9. Some bedroom furniture is listed at $2,200 with trade discounts of 40/20/20. Find the net price using the product of the complements.

10. Use the product of the complements to find the net price of some office furniture listed at $1,600 with trade discounts of 60/50/30.

11. Find the net price of a piece of furniture listed at $900 with discounts of 40/10/5.

12. Some display cases for a jewelry store are listed at $1,140 each with trade discounts of 20/10/5. What is the net price of each case?

13. A living-room suite is listed at $2,450 with trade discounts of $33\frac{1}{3}/16\frac{2}{3}$. Find the net price using the product of the complements.

14. Find the net price of a home freezer listed at $480 with discounts of $16\frac{2}{3}/8\frac{1}{3}/3\frac{1}{3}$.

15. Find the single discount percent equivalent to the following chain discounts. (Round to the nearest tenth of a percent.)

    a. 50%, 20%, 10%
    b. 70%, 40%, 20%
    c. 40%, 20%, 10%
    d. 30%, 15%, 5%

16. Find the single discount percent equivalent to the following chain discounts. (Round to the nearest tenth of a percent.)

    a. $66\frac{2}{3}\%$, $33\frac{1}{3}\%$
    b. $33\frac{1}{3}\%$, $16\frac{2}{3}\%$
    c. $16\frac{2}{3}\%$, $8\frac{1}{3}\%$, $3\frac{1}{3}\%$
    d. $66\frac{2}{3}\%$, $16\frac{2}{3}\%$, $8\frac{1}{3}\%$

17. The list price of an industrial cleaner is $9.90 per gallon with trade discounts of 20/10/10. Find the net price per gallon using the single discount percent equivalent to the chain discounts.

18. A cordless telephone with a list price of $108 has trade discounts of 30/30/10. Find the net price using the single discount percent equivalent to the chain discounts.

19. A set of beverage glasses with a list price of $59.99 carries trade discounts of 40/10/5. Using the single discount percent equivalent to the chain discounts, find the net price.

20. A case (24 bottles) of multivitamins with a list price of $110.40 carries trade discounts of 65/15. To the nearest cent, what is the net price per bottle?

21. Which of the following chain discounts yields the highest single discount percent equivalent to the chain discounts?

    a. 30%, 20%, 10% or 40%, 15%, 15%
    b. 60%, 10%, 10% or 50%, 20%, 10%

22. A merchant can place a $1,500 order with company A, which offers chain discounts of 30/10/5, or company B, which offers chain discounts of 20/20/5. Which company should she choose?

23. Complete the following invoice.

INVOICE
NO. 874
DATE 5/7
YOUR ORDER NO. 10623

SOLD TO City Auto Supply
777 Main Street
Concord, N.H.

SHIPPED TO

OUR ORDER NO.	SALESMAN	TERMS	F.O.B.	DATE SHIPPED	SHIPPED VIA
	Louis	Net		5/5	Delivery

QUANTITY ORDERED	QUANTITY SHIPPED	STOCK NUMBER/DESCRIPTION	PRICE	UNIT	AMOUNT
4	4	A-6356-A Chrome-plated steel wheels	83 90	ea.	
		Less 30% less 5%			
		Net			

ORIGINAL

24. Complete the following invoice.

INVOICE
NO. 404
DATE 2/17
YOUR ORDER NO. 10411

SOLD TO Parsons Department Store
2128 Ryder Road
Lakewood, N.J.

SHIPPED TO Parsons Dept. Store
2128 Ryder Road
Lakewood, N.J.

OUR ORDER NO.	SALESMAN	TERMS	F.O.B.	DATE SHIPPED	SHIPPED VIA
4275	B.L.	Net		2/16	U.P.S.

QUANTITY ORDERED	QUANTITY SHIPPED	STOCK NUMBER/DESCRIPTION	PRICE	UNIT	AMOUNT
4 ctns	1 ctn	6830A Mirror tiles	14 80	ctn	
2 ctns	2 ctns	9943A Mirror tiles	18 10	ctn	
		Total list			
		Less 20/10			
		Prepaid freight			14 20
		Total			

ORIGINAL

25. The Koolpool Company offers an above-ground pool and accessories with a list price of $2,000 and a trade discount of 40%. A competitor offers a similar pool for a net price of $960. What additional trade discount must Koolpool offer if it intends to match the competition?

26. The Atherton Company sells a heavy-duty utility trailer for $610.00 with a trade discount of 25%. What additional trade discount must be offered to meet a competitor's net price of $430.05?

Section 5.4 Quantity discounts

A **quantity discount** is a reduction in price because of the amount purchased. Quantity discounts may be based on:

1. The number of units purchased
2. The dollar value of the entire order
3. The size of the package purchased

Example 1

The list prices of a manufacturer are subject to the following discounts:

Units	Discount from List Price
1–24	40%
25–49	43%
50 or more	46%

If an item has a list price of $25, what is the net price on an order of 30 units?

Solution

Quantity discounts are also an application of the basic percentage formula $P = BR$, where P = quantity discount, B = list price, and R = discount percent. Thus,

$750.00	List price ($25 × 30)
− 322.50	Quantity discount ($750 × 0.43)
$427.50	Net price

The solution also could have been found by using the complement of the discount:

$750.00	List price ($25 × 30)
× 0.57	Complement of the discount (100% − 43%)
$427.50	Net price

Example 2 An invoice of the Olympic Sports Company contains the following at the bottom of the page:

Quantity	Discount Allowed
$100 to $499.99	3%
$500 to $899.99	5%
$900 and over	7%

Find the billing price for an order totaling $750.88 if transportation charges are $9.65.

Solution

	$750.88	List price
−	37.54	Quantity discount ($750.88 × 0.05)
	$713.34	Net price
+	9.65	Transportation charges
	$722.99	Billing price

Example 3 A brand of toothpaste with a list price of $8 per dozen tubes has a trade discount of $33\frac{1}{3}$%. An additional 2% discount is offered for orders by the case (a case contains 12 dozen tubes). What is the net price on an order of two cases?

Solution

	$192.00	List price ($8 × 24)
−	64.00	Trade discount ($192 × $\frac{1}{3}$)
	$128.00	
−	2.56	Quantity discount ($128 × 0.02)
	$125.44	Net price

Quantity discounts are offered to induce customers to purchase in larger quantities and are possible because of certain economies realized by the seller. On large orders, there may be a reduction in the salesperson's expenses or in packaging, accounting, or transportation costs. In fact, federal regulations require this. Quantity discounts are subject to the Robinson-Patman Act of 1936, which prohibits lower prices for large orders unless such prices reflect a reduction in the cost of doing business or are needed to meet the prices of a competitor. The purpose of the Robinson-Patman Act is to preserve competition and to prevent the creation of monopolies.

Exercises for Section 5.4

1. The list prices of a manufacturer are subject to the following discounts:

Units	Discount from List Price
1–49	30%
50–99	35%
100 or more	40%

If each unit has a list price of $22, what is the net price of an order of 70 units?

2. The following discounts apply to merchandise purchased at Ralph's Wholesale Plumbing Supply:

Quantity	Discount Allowed
$500 to $999.99	5%
$1,000 to $1,499.99	7%
$1,500 and over	10%

Find the net price for an order totaling $964.75.

3. Merchandise purchased at Universal Hardware Supply is subject to the following discounts:

Quantity	Discount Allowed
$100 to $299.99	2%
$300 to $599.99	5%
$600 to $999.99	8%
$1,000 and over	10%

Find the billing price for an order totaling $678.25 if freight charges are $14.78.

4. A wholesale distributor of appliances offers the following discounts on built-in dishwashers:

Units	Discount from List Price
1–10	20%
11–20	$33\frac{1}{3}$%
21 or more	60%

If each dishwasher has a list price of $325, what is the net price of an order for 12 dishwashers?

5. Stone's Building Products offers the following discounts:

Quantity	Discount Allowed
$400 to $599.99	10%
$600 to $999.99	12%
$1,000 to $1,399.99	$16\frac{2}{3}$%
$1,400 and over	18%

Find the billing price for an order totaling $1,238.00 if transportation charges are $73.52.

6. The following discounts apply to refrigerators purchased at Atlas Appliance Wholesalers:

Units	Discount from List Price
1–5	20%
6–15	$33\frac{1}{3}$%
16–25	40%
26 and over	45%

If each refrigerator has a list price of $423, what is the net price of an order for 40 refrigerators?

7. Trim-Eze Hair Clippers list at $23 each with a trade discount of 26%. An additional $8\frac{1}{3}$% discount is offered for orders of a shipping case of 20 clippers. What is the net price of an order of five cases?

8. Electric carving knives list at $32.00 each with a trade discount of 34%. An additional 4% discount is offered for orders of a shipping case of 12 knives. Find the billing price for an order of six cases if freight charges are $41.61.

9. Complete the following invoice.

INVOICE
NO. 87409
DATE 7/16
YOUR ORDER NO. 473

SOLD TO Jackson Lighting Company
1220 Belair Road
Baltimore, MD

SHIPPED TO Same

OUR ORDER NO.	SALESMAN	TERMS	F.O.B.	DATE SHIPPED	SHIPPED VIA
K411	B.J.	Net		7/14	

QUANTITY ORDERED	QUANTITY SHIPPED	STOCK NUMBER/DESCRIPTION	PRICE	UNIT	AMOUNT
6	6	52" Ceiling fan #488	140 00	ea.	
		Quantity discount 15%			
		Net			
		Freight charges			28 30
		Total			

ORIGINAL

10. Complete the following invoice.

INVOICE
NO. 740
DATE 3/22
YOUR ORDER NO. 1027

SOLD TO Brenda's Boutique
12638 W. 6th Avenue
Denver, Colorado

SHIPPED TO
12638 W. 6th Avenue
Denver, Colorado

OUR ORDER NO.	SALESMAN	TERMS	F.O.B.	DATE SHIPPED	SHIPPED VIA
7041	107	Net		3/21	

QUANTITY ORDERED	QUANTITY SHIPPED	STOCK NUMBER/DESCRIPTION	PRICE	UNIT	AMOUNT
24	24	Sport separates, styles A42, B16, D18	19 00	ea.	
		Quantity discount 10%			
		Net			
		Shipping charges			16 64
		Total			

ORIGINAL

Section 5.5 Credit terms

The majority of sales by manufacturers or wholesalers to retailers are on credit; that is, retailers are permitted a period of time following the sale before payment must be made. Credit sales have become widespread because they permit retailers to carry a larger assortment of merchandise. This means a potential increase in sales, an advantage to both retailers and suppliers.

Credit terms are shown on the invoice, usually in an abbreviated notation. The most common credit period is 30 days and appears on an invoice as "net 30 days" or "n/30." This notation means that the buyer has 30 days after the date on the invoice to make payment. If the bill is not paid within 30 days, it is considered overdue and may be subject to penalty charges.

Similarly, the notations "n/60" or "n/90" mean that the credit period is 60 days and 90 days, respectively, after the date of the invoice.

If credit is not extended by the seller, the invoice contains the notation "**C.O.D.**," which stands for **cash on delivery.**

Section 5.6 Cash discounts

While credit may be a competitive necessity, the delay in payment can be costly to the seller. With prompt payment, the seller could reinvest the money or use it to pay bills. (A delay in payment may be even more costly to the buyer, as we will see in sections 9.4 and 10.4.) As a result, it is a common practice to offer buyers an inducement, in the form of an additional discount called a cash discount, to pay promptly. A **cash discount** is a percentage reduction in price for payment within a specified time. Cash discounts usually range from 1% to 3% and are indicated on the invoice along with the credit period, as follows:

The cash discount percent (2%) ⟶ 2/10, n/30

The exact number of days after the invoice date during which the cash discount is applicable (→ 10)

The exact number of days after the invoice date before the bill is overdue (→ 30)

If the preceding notation is on an invoice dated May 1, then the following dates apply:

May 2–11	2% cash discount applicable
May 12–31	Net price applicable
June 1	Bill is overdue

Cash discounts are calculated in the same manner as trade discounts and quantity discounts except that cash discounts are taken after all other discounts have been applied. Cash discounts are not applicable to freight charges.

Example 1 The list price on an invoice dated November 1 is \$195.50, with terms of 2/10, n/30. How much should be remitted if the bill is paid on (a) November 10 or (b) November 30?

Solution

a. November 10 falls within the cash discount period of 10 days following November 1. Hence,

\$195.50	List price
− 3.91	Cash discount (\$195.50 × 0.02)
\$191.59	Amount to be remitted

b. November 30 is in the period of the eleventh through the thirtieth day after the invoice date. Thus, the amount to be remitted is the list price of \$195.50.

Example 2 The invoice that follows shows the following information: office desk—list, \$478.90; trade discounts, 70/10; freight charges, \$12.68; and terms, 2/30, n/60. If the bill is paid on May 10, how much should be remitted?

SHIP TO: Britton Office Supply, 2824 Dennison Boulevard, Detroit, Michigan

SOLD TO: Britton Office Supply, 2824 Dennison Boulevard, Detroit, Michigan

STORE NO.	CUSTOMER DEPT.	CUSTOMER ORDER NO.
12		11378

INVOICE DATE	TERMS (NO ANTICIPATION ALLOWED)
4/20	2/30, n/60

ROUTING INSTRUCTIONS

NO. OF CNTS.	WGT.	OUR REFERENCE NO.	INVOICE NO.
1	236	21823	67021

DESCRIPTION

STORE USE	STYLE OR LOT	DESCRIPTION	PCS	PRICE	EXTENDED AMOUNT
	113-M	Desk, Executive	1	478.90	478.90

SALESMAN	PAGE NO.	TOTAL NUMBER OF UNIT →	SHIPMENT COMPLETE	SHIPMENT PARTIAL	SUB TOTAL MDSE. AMOUNT	478.90

Less 70% Less 10%	−349.60
net	129.30
FRT. CHARGES	12.68
GRAND TOTAL	141.98

Solution

May 10 is well within the cash discount period. Hence, both the trade discounts and the cash discount are to be taken.

$478.90	List price
− 349.60	Total trade discounts
$129.30	
− 2.59	Cash discount ($129.30 × 0.02)
$126.71	
+ 12.68	Freight charges
$139.39	Amount to be remitted

More than one cash discount may be offered on a given sale. The notation 3/15, 1/30, n/60 on an invoice dated June 10 means:

June 11–June 25	3% cash discount applicable
June 26–July 10	1% cash discount applicable
July 11–August 9	Billing price due
August 10	Bill overdue

Example 3 An invoice for floor coverings shows a billing price of $659.82, including freight charges of $42.16. If the invoice is dated July 16 and indicates terms of 5/15, 4/45, n/60, what amount should be remitted if the bill is paid on August 30?

Solution

Since freight charges are not subject to cash discounts, they must be deducted from the billing price and then re-added after the cash discount is taken.

$659.82	Billing price
− 42.16	Freight charges
$617.66	
− 24.71	Cash discount ($617.66 × 0.04)
$592.95	
+ 42.16	Freight charges
$635.11	Amount to be remitted

Exercises for Sections 5.5 and 5.6

1. The list price on an invoice dated June 12 is $872.60, with terms of 3/10, n/30. How much should be remitted if the bill is paid on (a) June 19, (b) July 11?

2. If the list price on an invoice is $747.42 and if the terms of the invoice are 4/15, n/60, what amount should be remitted on March 26 if the date of the invoice is March 12?

3. An invoice dated September 5 contains the following information: plumbing supplies—list, $1,142.00; trade discounts, 20/5; freight charges, $75.40; terms, 3/30, n/60. If the bill is paid on October 2, how much should be remitted?

4. Find the amount to be remitted for an invoice dated January 7 and paid on February 20 if the terms of the invoice are as follows: list price, $973.38; trade discounts, 30/10; freight charges, $62.50; terms, 4/45, n/90.

5. An invoice for draperies is dated April 5 and shows a list price of $1,489. If the terms are 5/10, 3/30, n/60, how much should be remitted if the bill is paid on (a) April 15, (b) May 1, (c) June 3?

6. An invoice for lighting fixtures is dated December 8 and contains the following information: list price, $793.62; terms, 4/15, 3/30, n/60. How much should be remitted if the bill is paid on (a) December 22, (b) January 5, (c) February 5?

7. Find the amount to be remitted for an invoice dated August 27 and paid on September 21 if the terms of the invoice are as follows: list price, $2,279.60; trade discounts, 20/5; freight charges, $112.40; terms, 3/30, 2/60, n/90. How much should be remitted if the bill is paid on October 25?

8. The list price on an invoice for electronic equipment is $1,972.32. The invoice is dated May 17 and contains the following information: trade discounts, 30/15; freight charges, $37.20; terms, 5/10, 4/30, n/60. How much should be remitted if the bill is paid on May 25? If it is paid on June 14?

9. The list price of an invoice dated November 11 is $827.93. If the freight charges are $11.24 and if the terms of the bill are 5/15, 4/30, n/60, how much should be remitted if the bill is paid on November 24? If it is paid on December 5?

10. An invoice for optical equipment is dated March 19 and shows a list price of $1,826.12 plus freight charges of $78.46. The invoice contains the following information: trade discounts, 25/10; terms, 6/10, 4/30, n/45. How much should be remitted if the bill is paid on March 28? If it is paid on April 15?

11. Complete the following invoice and determine the amount to be remitted if the invoice is paid on June 15.

INVOICE

NO 2874

DATE 6/12

YOUR ORDER NO. 11338

SOLD TO Le Bathtique
714 4th Street
New Orleans, LA

SHIPPED TO Same

OUR ORDER NO.	SALESMAN	TERMS	FOR	DATE SHIPPED	SHIPPED VIA
7010	L.R.	4/15,n/30	Dest.	6/12	Overland

QUANTITY ORDERED	QUANTITY SHIPPED	STOCK NUMBER/DESCRIPTION	PRICE		UNIT	AMOUNT	
24	24	FH 1399 Bath Towels	15	50	ea.		
24	24	FH 3027 Hand Towels	9	00	ea.		
24	24	FH 3215 Washcloths	6	00	ea.		
		Less 20% less 5%					
		Net					

12. Complete the following invoice and determine the amount to be remitted if the invoice is paid on July 25.

INVOICE

NO 7406

DATE 7/18

YOUR ORDER NO. 23047

SOLD TO Atlas Plumbing
12016 Airport Road
St. Louis, MO

SHIPPED TO Atlas Plumbing
12016 Airport Road
St. Louis, MO

OUR ORDER NO.	SALESMAN	TERMS	F.O.B.	DATE SHIPPED	SHIPPED VIA
1104	Art	5/10,n/30		7/17	Stimson Freight

QUANTITY ORDERED	QUANTITY SHIPPED	STOCK NUMBER/DESCRIPTION	PRICE		UNIT	AMOUNT	
8	6	B-0858 Faucet-Dual Handle	52	50	ea.		
8	8	B-0841 Faucet-Single Handle	62	50	ea.		
		Less 40% less 20%					
		Freight Charges				6	38
		Total					

Section 5.7 Dating

The terms of payment in the previous examples are called **ordinary dating.** Other forms of dating are used in conjunction with cash discounts, some of which are discussed here.

End of month dating

End of month dating, also called **proximo dating,** means that the cash discount period begins the first day of the following month and that the bill becomes overdue 20 days after the expiration of the cash discount period. Thus, an invoice dated October 12 with terms 2/10, n/30, **E.O.M. (end of month)** or **Prox. (proximo)** means

October 12	Invoice date
November 1–10	Cash discount period
November 11–30	Billing price due
December 1	Bill is overdue

An exception to the meaning of these terms occurs when the invoice date is after the twenty-fifth day of a month. Then the cash discount period begins the first day of the second month after the month of the invoice date. Thus, for an invoice dated October 29,

October 29	Invoice date
December 1–10	Cash discount period
December 11–30	Billing price due
December 31	Bill is overdue

E.O.M. terms are commonly stated without a net credit period, such as 2/10, E.O.M. When this notation is used, it is understood that the buyer has 20 days following the discount period to pay the full amount of the invoice. This is done on the assumption that E.O.M. terms are simply an extension of n/30 terms.

E.O.M. dating is a convenience to retailers who make frequent purchases from the same supplier in that it permits a single payment for all purchases made during the month.

Receipt of goods dating

Receipt of goods (R.O.G.) dating is used when the transport time is relatively long. In this case, the cash discount period begins upon receipt of the merchandise by the buyer. Suppose, for example, that an invoice is dated April 16 and marked 3/10, n/30, R.O.G. If the merchandise is received by the buyer on May 12, then

April 16	Invoice date
May 13–22	Cash discount period
May 23–June 11	Billing price due (20 days)
June 12	Bill is overdue

These terms can also be written 3/10, R.O.G. As with E.O.M. dating, if the net credit period is not indicated, it is understood that the billing price becomes due 20 days after the last day of the discount period.

R.O.G. dating permits a vendor located a considerable distance from a retailer to be competitive with local vendors offering ordinary dating. It also allows for inspection of the merchandise before the cash discount period begins.

Extra dating

In **extra dating,** the seller allows an added number of days before the cash discount period ends. Thus, an invoice dated July 7 with terms 2/10, 30X, net 60 means

July 7	Invoice date
July 8–August 16	Cash discount period (10 days + 30 extra days)
August 17–September 5	Billing price due
September 6	Bill is overdue

Extra dating is used most frequently in the sale of seasonal items in advance of the peak market demand. For example, air conditioners may be sold in the winter in anticipation of summer sales. For the supplier, the sales effected by extra dating help to stabilize production and to eliminate storage costs.

Example 1

An invoice for $196.13 is dated March 12, and the merchandise is delivered on April 2. What is the last day of the cash discount if the invoice terms are (a) 2/10, n/30; (b) 2/10, E.O.M.; (c) 2/10, R.O.G.; and (d) 2/10, 60X?

Solution

a. Ten days after March 12 is March 22.

b. Ten days after March 31 is April 10.

c. Ten days after April 2 is April 12.

d. Seventy days after March 12 is May 21.

The extension of credit in future datings, such as R.O.G. or extra dating, presents retailers with an opportunity to turn at least a part of the purchases into cash before payment is due. This is an advantage particularly for retailers handling slow-selling merchandise or for small retailers with limited finances.

Other forms of dating

A recent innovation in terms of payment is **installment dating.** In this form of dating, the invoice is paid in two installments over a 60-day period. A cash discount is offered if a specified percent of the total invoice amount is paid within 30 days. A second cash discount is offered if the remaining balance is paid within 60 days. The next example illustrates this form of dating.

Example 2 An invoice dated April 20 for $368.44 contains the following information. A 2% discount is offered if 80% of the invoice amount is paid within 30 days, and another 2% discount is offered if the remaining 20% of the invoice amount is paid within 60 days. To take advantage of the two discounts, find the amount to be remitted on May 10 and June 5.

Solution

May 10 payment

$294.75	($368.44 × 0.80)
− 7.37	Cash discount ($368.44 × 0.02)
$287.38	Amount to be remitted

June 5 payment

$ 73.69	($368.44 − $294.75)
− 1.47	Cash discount ($73.69 × 0.02)
$ 72.22	Amount to be remitted

Most buyers choose to pay for merchandise at the end of the discount period, since this allows them the maximum time to use their money. To encourage payment before the last day of the discount period, some vendors offer a form of dating called **anticipation dating.** If an invoice is paid prior to the expiration of the cash discount period, the buyer can deduct an amount determined by the current bank interest rate for the number of days of early payment. Compared to other cash discounts, the amount of this discount is small; but for retail organizations that make a large number of purchases during a year, the savings can be significant. Calculations used in anticipation dating are covered in chapter 10, and examples of anticipation dating are included in that chapter.

Exercises for Section 5.7

1. An invoice for $477.56 is dated April 22 with terms of 4/10, E.O.M. How much should be remitted if the bill is paid on May 9? If it is paid on May 27? When does the bill become overdue?
2. If an invoice dated July 27 has a list price of $966.70 with terms of 5/10, Prox., how much should be remitted if the bill is paid on September 8? If it is paid on September 19? When does the bill become overdue?
3. An invoice dated October 17 is marked 4/10, R.O.G., and the merchandise is received by the buyer on November 21. If the list price on the invoice is $572.50, how much should be remitted if the bill is paid (a) on November 30, (b) on December 10?
4. Find the amount that should be remitted for a $473.60 invoice dated January 10 and marked 5/10, R.O.G. if the merchandise is received on February 14 and the invoice is paid on February 20.

5. The invoice for a shipment of swimming pool chemicals is marked 3/15, 20X, net 60. The invoice is dated March 6, and the list price is \$844.50. How much should be remitted if the bill is paid on April 18?

6. Find the amount to be remitted on August 10 for an invoice dated July 2 with list price \$1,822.72 and terms of 3/10, 30X, net 60.

7. An invoice for \$824.75 is dated May 6, and the merchandise is delivered on May 23. Find the amount to be remitted on June 2 if the terms are (a) 3/10, n/30; (b) 3/10, E.O.M.; (c) 5/10, R.O.G.; (d) 4/10, 20X, net 60.

8. Find the amount to be remitted on December 12 for an invoice for \$679.20 dated November 15 if the merchandise is delivered on November 22 and the terms of the invoice are (a) 4/10, 2/60, n/90; (b) 2/10, Prox.; (c) 3/10, R.O.G.; (d) 3/10, 30X, net 60.

9. An invoice dated July 7 for \$842.20 offers the following installment dating. A 3% discount is offered if 70% of the invoice amount is paid within 30 days, and another 2% discount is offered if the remaining 30% of the invoice amount is paid within 60 days. To take advantage of the two discounts, find the amount to be remitted on August 2 and September 3.

10. Find the amount to be remitted on February 14 and March 9 for an invoice dated January 19 with a billing price of \$658.26 that offers the following installment terms. A 5% discount is offered if 60% of the invoice amount is paid within 30 days, and another 3% discount is offered if the remaining 40% of the invoice amount is paid within 60 days.

11. Complete the following invoice and determine the amount to be remitted if the invoice is paid on June 10.

INVOICE
NO 287
DATE 5/7
YOUR ORDER NO. 7003

SOLD TO Crafts N'Things
106 71st Street
Indianapolis, IN

SHIPPED TO Crafts N'Things
106 71st Street
Indianapolis, IN

OUR ORDER NO.	SALESMAN	TERMS	F.O.B.	DATE SHIPPED	SHIPPED VIA
A 205	John	3/10 EOM		5/7	P. Post

QUANTITY ORDERED	QUANTITY SHIPPED	STOCK NUMBER/DESCRIPTION	PRICE	UNIT	AMOUNT
2 dz	2 dz	5-Piece Scissor Set	480 00	dz	
		Discount 20/5/5			
		Prepaid freight			7 29
		Total			

ORIGINAL

12. Complete the following invoice and determine the amount to be remitted if the invoice is paid on March 10.

INVOICE

NO. 7410

DATE 1/6

YOUR ORDER NO. 7123

SOLD TO Wallpaper Unlimited
3813 Elm Street
Spartanburg, SC

SHIPPED TO Wallpaper Unlimited
3813 Elm Street
Spartanburg, SC

OUR ORDER NO.	SALESMAN	TERMS	F.O.B.	DATE SHIPPED	SHIPPED VIA
141B	Bill	3/10,60X		1/4	Rodeway

QUANTITY ORDERED	QUANTITY SHIPPED	STOCK NUMBER/DESCRIPTION	PRICE		UNIT	AMOUNT	
10	10	Vinyl-coated wallpaper - pattern 03	12	00	Roll		
10	10	Vinyl-coated wallpaper - pattern 04	12	00	Roll		
10	10	Vinyl-coated wallpaper - pattern 07	16	00	Roll		
10	10	Vinyl-coated wallpaper - pattern 10	16	00	Roll		
		Less 35% less 5%					
		Prepaid freight				12	82
		Total					

ORIGINAL

Section 5.8 The basic markon equation

To be successful, retailers must sell merchandise at a price higher than the cost price. This difference, called markon, must be sufficient to cover overhead and provide a net profit. Judicious pricing is one of the keys to any successful retail operation. If the price is too high, sales are reduced or lost to a competitor. If the price is too low, the markon may not be sufficient to cover operating expenses and earn a reasonable net profit. For these reasons, pricing is as much an art as it is a science and requires experience coupled with sound judgment.

The selling price of an item is equal to the cost price plus the markon. This fundamental concept can be expressed by the equation

■ (5–2) $$C + M = S$$

where C = cost, M = markon, and S = selling price. Markon is usually a percentage of either the cost price or the selling price.*

*The terms *markon* and *markup* are often used interchangeably in this equation, but in modern terminology, the term *markup* is reserved for an increase in an original selling price.

Markon based on cost price

Small retail businesses frequently express markon as a percentage of the cost price. To calculate the selling price S when markon is a percentage of the cost price C, the following formula is used:

■ (5–3) $$S = C \times (100\% + \text{Markon \% of Cost price})$$

Example 1

What is the selling price of an article if the cost price is \$42 and the markon is 30% of the cost price?

Solution

Using formula 5–3,

$$\begin{aligned} S &= C \times (100\% + \text{Markon \% of Cost price}) \\ &= \$42 \times (100\% + 30\%) \\ &= \$42 \times (130\%) \\ &= \$42 \times 1.3 \\ &= \$54.60 \end{aligned}$$

Example 2

The invoice for a group of furniture pieces indicates a list price of \$528.60, a trade discount of 40%, and transportation charges of \$9.25. The retailer determines a markon of 60% of the cost price. What should be the selling price of the furniture?

Solution

\$528.60	List price
− 211.44	Trade discount (\$528.60 × 0.40)
\$317.16	Net price
+ 9.25	Transportation charges
\$326.41	Cost price

Using formula 5–3,

$$\begin{aligned} S &= C \times (100\% + \text{Markon \% of Cost price}) \\ &= \$326.41 \times (100\% + 60\%) \\ &= \$326.41 \times (160\%) \\ &= \$326.41 \times 1.6 \\ &= \$522.26 \end{aligned}$$

Formula 5–3 may also be used to solve for cost price or markon percent as shown in the next examples.

Example 3 A lamp that sells for \$50 cost the retailer \$20. What is the markon percent based on cost price?

Solution

Using formula 5–3,

$$S = C \times (100\% + \text{Markon \% of Cost price})$$
$$\$50 = \$20 \times (100\% + \text{Markon \% of Cost price})$$
$$\frac{\$50}{\$20} = 100\% + \text{Markon \% of Cost price}$$
$$2.5 = 1.0 + \text{Markon \% of Cost price}$$
$$1.5 = \text{Markon \% of Cost price}$$
$$150\% = \text{Markon \% of Cost price}$$

Example 4 A patio set sells for \$220, which includes a markon of 58% of the cost price. Find the cost price.

Solution

Using formula 5–3,

$$S = C \times (100\% + \text{Markon \% of Cost price})$$
$$\$220 = \text{Cost price} \times (100\% + 58\%)$$
$$\$220 = \text{Cost price} \times (158\%)$$
$$\$220 = \text{Cost price} \times 1.58$$
$$\frac{\$220}{1.58} = \text{Cost price}$$
$$\$139.24 = \text{Cost price}$$

Markon based on selling price

Most large retail establishments base markon on the selling price. There are several reasons for this: Sales data are more available than cost data; trade statistics are expressed using a sales base; and a number of internal operations, such as sales commissions, taxes, and advertising, are based on sales.

The formula for computing the selling price when the markon is based on the selling price is:

■ (5–4)
$$S = \frac{C}{100\% - \text{Markon \% of Selling price}}$$

Example 5 A hardware item that costs \$4.60 is to have a markon of $33\frac{1}{3}\%$ of the selling price. Find the selling price.

Solution

With a markon of $33\frac{1}{3}\%$, calculations are simplified using the fraction $\frac{1}{3}$.* Using formula 5–4,

$$S = \frac{C}{100\% - \text{Markon \% of Selling price}}$$

$$= \frac{\$4.60}{100\% - 33\frac{1}{3}\%}$$

$$= \frac{\$4.60}{1 - \frac{1}{3}}$$

$$= \frac{\$4.60}{\frac{2}{3}}$$

$$= \$4.60 \times \frac{3}{2}$$

$$= \$6.90$$

Example 6 An item that sells for \$61.50 carries a markon of 16% of the selling price. What is the cost price?

Solution

Using formula 5–4,

$$S = \frac{C}{100\% - \text{Markon \% of Selling price}}$$

$$\$61.50 = \frac{C}{100\% - 16\%}$$

$$\$61.50 = \frac{C}{84\%}$$

$$\$61.50 = \frac{C}{0.84}$$

$$\$61.50 \times 0.84 = C$$

$$\$51.66 = C$$

*See example 6 of section 4.2.

Example 7 After examining a brand of tennis rackets, a sporting goods retailer estimates that she could sell the rackets for $70 each. If she must maintain a markon of 40% of the selling price, what is the top price the retailer can afford to pay and still sell the rackets at $70 each?

Solution

Using formula 5–4,

$$S = \frac{C}{100\% - \text{Markon \% of Selling price}}$$

$$\$70 = \frac{C}{100\% - 40\%}$$

$$\$70 = \frac{C}{60\%}$$

$$\$70 = \frac{C}{0.60}$$

$$\$70 \times 0.60 = C$$

$$\$42 = C$$

Markon of Perishables and Irregulars

In the previous examples, the markon was calculated per item, because it was assumed that each item in stock was saleable. For some products, however, this is not the case. Vendors of perishable items such as fruit, produce, dairy products, bakery products, and flowers recognize that because of spoilage some items cannot be sold at the regular price, or perhaps not at all. As a consequence, the selling price of the saleable items must be adjusted to provide the desired markon percent for the entire stock. This is accomplished by calculating the selling price of the entire stock, then dividing the result by the number of saleable items. The technique is illustrated in the next example.

Example 8 A grocer purchased 500 lbs. of ripe peaches at $0.20 per pound. The grocer anticipates that 20% of the peaches will spoil and will have to be discarded. What is the selling price per pound if the markon is 40% of the cost price?

Solution

$$\text{The price per pound} = \frac{\text{Selling price of entire stock}}{\text{Pounds of saleable peaches}}$$

The total cost of the peaches was $0.20 × 500 = $100.00.

Using formula 5–3,

$$
\begin{aligned}
S &= C \times (100\% + \text{Markon \% of Cost price}) \\
&= \$100(140\%) \\
&= \$100(1.40) \\
&= \$140
\end{aligned}
$$

A spoilage rate of 20% means 100% − 20% = 80% of the peaches will be saleable.

Using the basic percentage equation with P = ?, B = 500 and R = 0.80:

$$
\begin{aligned}
P &= BR \\
&= 500 \times 0.80 \\
&= 400 \text{ pounds of saleable peaches}
\end{aligned}
$$

$$
\begin{aligned}
\text{The price per pound} &= \frac{\$140}{400} \\
&= \$0.35 \text{ per pound}
\end{aligned}
$$

Had all the peaches been saleable in the previous example, a markon of 40% of the cost price would have meant a selling price of $0.20 × (1.40) = $0.28 per pound and the grocer would have received $0.28 × 500 = $140 for the peaches. With only 400 pounds of saleable peaches, it takes a selling price of $0.35 per pound for the grocer to receive $0.35 × 400 = $140.

Manufacturers may produce some items that cannot be sold at the regular selling price because of defects or blemishes in manufacture. If the defects or blemishes are minor, these irregular items may be sold to retailers at a reduced price. Again, the selling price per item of merchandise must be adjusted to obtain the desired markon percent. This is illustrated in the next example.

Example 9 The Keystone Clothing Company manufactures a brand of women's blouses at a cost of $12 per unit. The company anticipates that 7% of the blouses will contain defects and must be sold as irregulars at $16 each. Find the selling price per unit on the manufacture of 2,200 blouses if the markon is 45% of the selling price.

Solution

$$
\text{Price per item} = \frac{\text{Selling price of entire stock} - \text{Income from sale of irregulars}}{\text{Number of regular items}}
$$

The total cost of the blouses is $12 × 2,200 = $26,400.

Using formula 5–4,

$$S = \frac{C}{100\% - \text{Markon \% of Selling price}}$$
$$= \frac{\$26{,}400}{100\% - 45\%}$$
$$= \frac{\$26{,}400}{1 - 0.45}$$
$$= \frac{\$26{,}400}{0.55}$$
$$= \$48{,}000 \quad \text{Selling price of entire stock}$$

The number of irregulars is found by an application of the basic percentage equation with $P = ?$, $B = 2{,}200$, $R = 0.07$:

$$P = BR$$
$$= 2{,}200 \times 0.07$$
$$= 154 \text{ irregular items}$$

The income from the sale of the irregulars is $16 × 154 = $2,464. With 154 irregular items there are 2,200 − 154 = 2,046 regular items. Thus,

$$\text{The price per item} = \frac{\$48{,}000 - \$2{,}464}{2{,}046}$$
$$= \frac{\$45{,}536}{2{,}046}$$
$$= \$22.256$$
$$= \$22.26$$

Thus, a regular selling price of $22.26 per blouse will provide the manufacturer with the desired markon even with part of the stock sold at a reduced price.

Section 5.9

Conversion of the markon base

If an item costs $10 and sells for $15, the markon of $5 is 50% of the cost price and $33\frac{1}{3}\%$ of the selling price. The markon based on selling price appears to be smaller, another reason that this base is used to determine markon. Under certain conditions, it is desirable to convert from one markon base to the other. The formulas used for this conversion are:

■ (5–5) $$\text{Markon \% of Cost price} = \frac{\text{Markon \% of Selling price}}{100\% - \text{Markon \% of Selling price}}$$

■ (5–6) $$\text{Markon \% of Selling price} = \frac{\text{Markon \% of Cost price}}{100\% + \text{Markon \% of Cost price}}$$

Example 1 The markon on an item is 40% of the selling price. What is the markon percent of the cost price?

Solution

Using formula 5–5,

$$\text{Markon \% of Cost price} = \frac{\text{Markon \% of Selling price}}{100\% - \text{Markon \% of Selling price}}$$
$$= \frac{40\%}{100\% - 40\%}$$
$$= \frac{0.40}{1 - 0.40}$$
$$= \frac{0.40}{0.60}$$
$$= 0.666...$$
$$= 66\frac{2}{3}\%$$

Example 2 The markon on an item is 20% of the cost price. What is the markon percent of the selling price?

Solution

Using formula 5–6,

$$\text{Markon \% of Selling price} = \frac{\text{Markon \% of Cost price}}{100\% + \text{Markon \% of Cost price}}$$
$$= \frac{20\%}{100\% + 20\%}$$
$$= \frac{0.20}{1 + 0.20}$$
$$= \frac{0.20}{1.20}$$
$$= 0.1666...$$
$$= 16\frac{2}{3}\%$$

Exercises for Sections 5.8 and 5.9

In problems 1–12, find the selling price from the given information.

	Cost Price	*Markon Percent*	*Markon Base*
1.	\$ 28.00	20%	Cost Price
2.	\$ 36.00	30%	Cost Price
3.	\$144.00	42%	Selling Price
4.	\$162.00	38%	Selling Price
5.	\$238.50	52%	Cost Price
6.	\$194.57	60%	Cost Price
7.	\$336.60	70%	Selling Price
8.	\$504.25	35%	Selling Price
9.	\$185.95	$33\frac{1}{3}\%$	Cost Price
10.	\$328.30	46%	Cost Price
11.	\$405.75	$66\frac{2}{3}\%$	Selling Price
12.	\$684.90	38%	Selling Price

13. A pair of golf shoes is to have a markon of 40% of the cost price of \$28.50. Find the selling price.

14. An infant walker is to have a markon of 38% of the selling price. If the cost price is \$42, find the selling price.

15. An article of clothing with a cost price of \$47.50 is to have a markon of 51% of the selling price. Find the selling price.

16. A pool table with a cost price of \$674 is to have a markon of 86% of the cost price. What is the selling price?

17. The manager of Atlas Building Supplies decides on a markon of 32% of the selling price for a workbench. If the cost price of the workbench is \$120.70, what is the selling price?

18. Find the selling price of an article of clothing if the cost price is \$47 and the markon is (a) 60% of the cost price and (b) 62% of the cost price.

19. If the cost price of a digital clock radio is \$22.50, find the selling price if the markon is (a) 25% of the cost price and (b) 32% of the cost price.

20. The cost price for a piece of electronic equipment is \$82.32. What is the selling price if the markon is 45% of the selling price?

21. What is the selling price of a set of drapes with a cost price of \$80 and a markon of (a) 68% and (b) 72% of the cost price?

22. The cost price of a certain lighting fixture is $79. What is the selling price if the markon is (a) 40% of the cost price, (b) 35% of the selling price?

23. The cost price of an adjustable exercise bench is $129. What is the selling price if the markon is (a) 60% of the cost price, (b) 45% of the selling price?

24. The list price for a washing machine is $424.50. If the trade discount is 40% and freight charges are $34.70, find the cost price. If the markon is 55% of the cost price, what is the selling price of the washer?

25. An invoice for a color television set shows a list price of $724.24, a trade discount of 35%, and freight charges of $11.40. The retailer decides on a markon of 40% of the cost price. What should be the selling price for the television set?

26. The invoice for a photographic enlarger shows a list price of $324.50, a trade discount of 55%, and freight charges of $7.56. If the retailer decides on a markon of 60% of the cost price, what should be the selling price for the enlarger?

27. The selling price of an article is $72.00, which includes a markon of $14.40. What is the markon percent based on the cost price?

28. A box of stationery that sells for $5.97 costs the retailer $4.30. What is the markon percent based on cost price? (Round your answer to the nearest percent.)

29. A retailer buys blank cassette tapes at $42.00 per dozen and sells them at $4.48 each. Per cassette, what is the amount of markon and the markon percent based on cost price?

30. A mattress that sells for $140 carries a markon of 60% of the selling price. What is the cost price?

31. A retailer sells a line of glassware with a markon of 47% of the selling price of $16.00 per set. If transportation and handling charges average $1.80 per set, what is the net price the retailer paid for a set of glassware?

32. A buyer for a department store has found a line of junior dresses that should sell for $40 per dress. The store maintains a markon of 39% of the selling price in that department. At what cost price per dress could the buyer plan to purchase the dresses?

33. The owner of a shoe store has examined a new style of shoes that she believes she could sell at $52 a pair. Her standard markon is 42% of the selling price. At what cost price could she afford to buy the shoes?

34. A buyer can buy stuffed toy animals at $40.00 a dozen. He estimates that the toy animals could be sold at $4.95 each. If the markon on stuffed animals is 38% of the selling price, what trade discount (to the nearest percent) must the buyer seek to buy one dozen of the stuffed animals?

35. Val's Florist Shoppe purchased 100 dozen long stem roses at $10 per dozen. Val anticipates that 30% of the roses will have to be discarded because of spoilage. What is the selling price per dozen if the markon is 60% of the cost price?

36. A produce dealer purchased 400 pounds of apples at $0.40 per pound. If markon is 50% of cost price, and if the dealer expects 15% of the apples to spoil and be discarded, what is the selling price per pound?

37. A grocer anticipates that 25% of an order of 200 pounds of grapes will spoil. If the grapes cost the grocer $0.35 per pound, and if the markon is 50% of the selling price, what is the selling price of the grapes per pound?

38. A company manufactured 1,500 items of its product at a cost of $5.00 per item. If the markon is 40% of the selling price and if the company expects 15% of the items to be sold as irregulars at $6.00 each, find the selling price per item.

39. The Tifton Company manufactured 2,000 men's shirts at a cost of $8.00 per shirt. The company expects that 10% of the shirts will be defective and will be sold at $12 per shirt. Find the selling price per shirt if the markon is 60% of the selling price.

40. A manufacturer uses a markon of 30% of the cost price. Find the selling price per unit if 3,000 units are manufactured at a cost of $14 each, and the company expects that 20% of the items will be sold as irregulars for $10 each.

41. The markon on an item is 25% of the selling price. Find the markon percent of the cost price.

42. If the markon on an item is 25% of the cost price, what is the markon percent of the selling price?

In problems 43–47, round all markon percents to the nearest percent.

43. A retailer decides on a markon of 42% of the cost price for one model of a microwave oven. What is the markon percent of the selling price?

44. Find the markon percent of the cost price if the markon percent of the selling price is (a) 30% and (b) 35%.

45. What is the markon percent of the selling price if the markon percent of the cost price is (a) 40% and (b) 30%?

46. A trash compactor has a markon of 38% of the selling price. What is the markon percent of the cost price? Using this result, if the cost price is \$142.50, what is the selling price?

47. Find the markon percent of the selling price for a lawn mower that has a markon percent of 48% of the cost price. Using this result, if the selling price is \$382.40, what is the cost price?

Section 5.10 Markdown

The dynamics of retailing require a continuous adjustment in pricing. Economic conditions and competition cause prices to fluctuate both upward and downward. Price adjustments include discounts to employees, markup (an additional markon), and the most significant of all, markdowns.

A **markdown** is a reduction in the selling price of an item, and it is one of the principal means by which retailers adjust inventory to internal and external conditions. Markdowns occur for a number of reasons: special sales and promotions, the need to meet competition, and the need to clear out merchandise that is obsolete, shopworn, unpopular, or part of broken assortments. Markdowns are ordinarily expressed as a percentage of the selling price and are calculated as a straight application of the percentage formula $P = BR$, with P = amount of markdown, B = selling price, and R = markdown percent.

Example 1 The price of a book was marked down from \$4.95 to \$3.95. To the nearest percent, what was the markdown percent?

Solution

The amount of the markdown P was \$4.95 − \$3.95 = \$1.00, B = \$4.95, and R = ?

$$R = \frac{P}{B}$$

$$= \frac{1.00}{4.95}$$

$$= 0.202$$

$$= 20\%$$

Example 2 A department store advertised women's blouses on sale at 20% off the regular price. If the blouses sold originally at \$35, what is the new selling price?

Solution

The new selling price is the original selling price less the markdown.

\$35.00	Original selling price
− 7.00	Markdown (\$35 × 0.20)
\$28.00	New selling price

Alternatively, a markdown of 20% means that the new selling price is 100% − 20% = 80% of the original selling price. By using this complement of the discount,

\$35.00	Original selling price
× 0.80	Complement of the discount
\$28.00	New selling price

Example 3 A large scratch was discovered on a dining-room table on display in a furniture store. The selling price of the table included a markon of 50% of the selling price. The retailer decided to mark down the table 30% of the selling price because of the scratch. If the cost price of the table was \$178, find (a) the original selling price and (b) the new selling price.

Solution

a. $S = \dfrac{C}{100\% - \text{Markon \% of Selling price}}$

$= \dfrac{\$178}{100\% - 50\%}$

$= \dfrac{\$178}{0.50}$

$= \$356$ Original selling price

b.

\$356.00	Original selling price
× 0.70	Complement of the markdown
\$249.20	New selling price

Section 5.11 Extent of markdown

The question of how much to mark down an item is as difficult to answer as the question of how much markon should be applied. The general rule is that the markdown must be sufficiently large to induce customers to purchase the merchandise. A dress reduced from $60.00 to $58.50 is not likely to attract attention, but a markdown to $46.00 may result in a quick sale. An old adage in retailing is, "The first markdown is the least expensive," meaning that efforts to clear out merchandise should be in one step rather than a series of successive markdowns.

While the markdown should be large enough to sell the merchandise, there are practical restraints to consider when making a markdown. These can be made clear by a reexamination of the price structure. From equation 5–2, the selling price equals the cost price plus markon. As previously mentioned, markon includes overhead plus net profit. Thus,

■ (5–2) $$S = C + M$$

and

■ (5–7) $$M = O + P$$

where O = overhead and P = net profit. Substituting,

■ (5–8) $$S = C + O + P$$

This formula is illustrated in figure 5.2.

Figure 5.2
The price structure

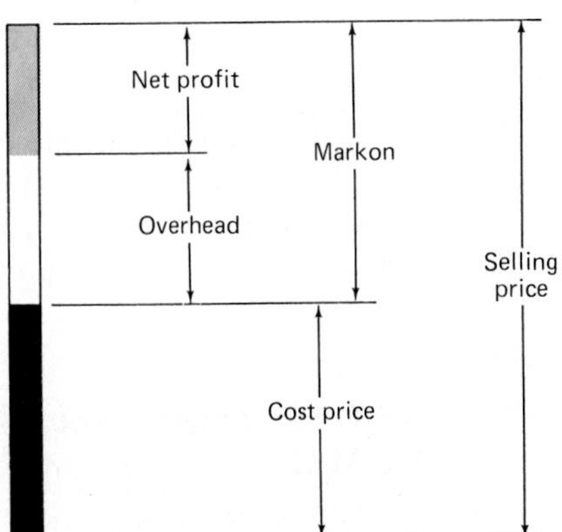

If possible, the markdown on an item should be confined to the net profit region. A markdown equal to the total net profit yields a reduced selling price called the **break-even point** because retailers recover the cost price and operating expenses. In this event, there is no profit, but neither is there a loss. If the price reduction falls into the overhead region, retailers are said to suffer an **operating loss.** If the markdown falls into the cost price, then the result is called a **gross loss.** This is illustrated in figure 5.3.

Expressed differently, if the markdown is less than the markon but exceeds the net profit, there is an operating loss; if the markdown exceeds the markon, there is a gross loss.

Figure 5.3
Break-even point

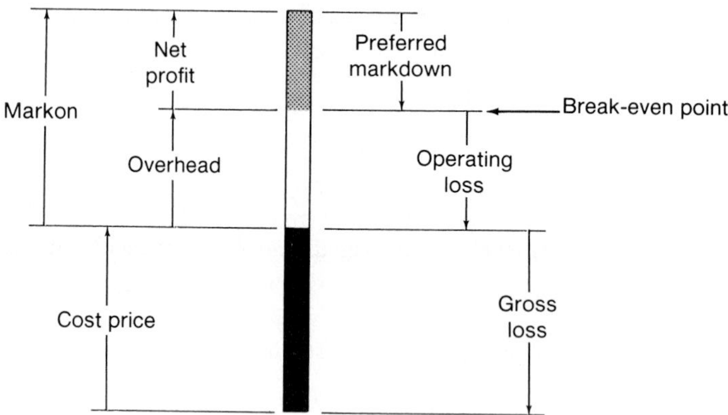

Example 1 The R. J. Taylor Department Store sells an item of toddler's wear at \$6.95. Included in this price is a markon of \$2.78. Estimated overhead on the item is \$2.08. During an end-of-season sale, the item was marked down to \$5.00. Determine if a sale results in a profit or a loss.

Solution

\$6.95	Original selling price
− 2.78	Markon
\$4.17	Cost price
+ 2.08	Overhead
\$6.25	Break-even point

\$6.25	Break-even point
− 5.00	Final selling price
\$1.25	Operating loss

Example 2 As part of a sales promotion, a stereo was advertised at $25.00 off the selling price of $369.95. The cost price is $231.84, and overhead is estimated at 40% of the cost price. Determine whether a sale results in a profit or loss.

Solution

	$231.84	Cost price
+	92.74	Overhead ($231.84 × 0.40)
	$324.58	Break-even point

	$369.95	Original selling price
−	25.00	Markdown
	$344.95	Final selling price
−	324.58	Break-even point
	$ 20.37	Profit

Example 3 A department store bought ten men's suits at a cost price of $108 per suit. Five of the suits sold at the selling price of $220 per suit, three of the suits sold after they were marked down to $160, and the remaining two suits sold after they were marked down again to $120. If the overhead is 18% of the cost price, determine if the store made a profit or a loss.

Solution

	$1,080.00	Total cost ($108 × 10)
+	194.40	Overhead ($1,080 × 0.18)
	$1,274.40	Break-even point

	$1,100.00	($220 × 5)
+	480.00	($160 × 3)
+	240.00	($120 × 2)
	$1,820.00	Total sales income
−	1,274.40	Break-even point
	$ 545.60	Net profit

Exercises for Sections 5.10 and 5.11

1. The price of an air-conditioning unit was marked down from $275.00 to $206.25. Find the markdown percent.

2. A pair of women's shoes with an original selling price of $60 is on sale for $48. Find the markdown percent.

3. Find the markdown percent on an item marked down from $182.50 to $131.40.

4. A woman's blouse that was damaged was marked down from $34 to $25. To the nearest percent, find the markdown percent.

5. A clothing store advertised men's suits on sale at 25% off the regular price. If the suits originally sold for $198, find the sale price.

6. An 18-horsepower lawn tractor was advertised at 30% off the selling price. If the original selling price was $1,500, find the sale price.

7. A boy's rain slicker was marked down 40% from the selling price of $16. Find the new selling price.

8. Find the new selling price of a child's car seat if the original selling price of $52 was marked down 20%.

9. A pair of boy's roller skates was marked down 18.14% from the original selling price of $21.99. Find the new selling price.

10. A video game system was marked down 61.6% from its original selling price of $129.95. What was the new selling price?

11. An air purifier with an original selling price of $250 was marked down 24%. When the purifier still did not sell, it was marked down 35% from its original selling price and sold. What was (a) the selling price after the first markdown and (b) the final selling price?

12. A man's jacket was marked down 20% from its original selling price of $65. When the jacket still did not sell, it was marked down 45% from its original selling price. What was (a) the selling price after the first markdown and (b) the final selling price?

13. A portable typewriter with an original selling price of $520 was marked down 12%. However, to meet the price of a competitive brand, it was necessary to mark down the typewriter 26% from the original selling price. What was (a) the selling price after the first markdown and (b) the final selling price?

14. To make room for spring fashions, a woman's wool suit was marked down 18% from its original selling price of $204. When the suit did not sell, it was marked down 32% from its original price. What was (a) the selling price after the first markdown and (b) the final selling price?

15. A department store had seven adjustable piano lamps in stock. Two lamps sold when the selling price of $45 was marked down 15%. When the lamps were marked down 25% from the original selling price, three lamps were sold. The remaining lamps did not sell until a third markdown of 40% of the original selling price. How much money was received from the sale of the seven lamps?

16. Four cutlery sets sold when the selling price of $90 was marked down 22%. When the cutlery sets were marked down 32% of the original selling price, five more sets sold. The three remaining sets sold when a third markdown of 48% of the original selling price was made. How much money was received from the sale of the cutlery sets?

17. A dent in the side of a washing machine dictated a markdown in the price of the machine by 30%. The cost price of the machine was $252, and the markon was 40% of the selling price. Find (a) the original selling price and (b) the new selling price.

18. A living-room easy chair was found to have a small tear in the fabric. The cost price of the chair was $140, and the markon was 60% of the cost price. The retailer decided to mark down the selling price of the chair by 25%. Find (a) the original selling price and (b) the new selling price.

19. A man's jacket at Quality Clothiers was originally priced at $78.00, but during a recent sale it was marked down to $65.00. The estimated overhead on the jacket was $4.75. If the markon was $28.00, determine whether selling the jacket at $65.00 will yield a profit or a loss.

20. A power saw at Hall's Hardware is priced at $55.00. The overhead on the saw is $7.70, and the markon is $14.00. If the saw is marked down to $48.50, will a sale result in a profit or a loss?

21. Frank's Furniture Store advertised a record cabinet for $49.95 during a recent sale. The cost price of the cabinet was $39.95, and overhead is estimated to be 20% of cost price. Will the sale of the cabinet at $49.95 result in a profit or a loss?

22. Samson's Stereo Shop marked down a tape recorder from $295.75 to $260.00. If the cost price of the recorder was $195.25 and overhead is 30% of cost, will a sale at $260.00 result in a profit or a loss?

23. A coffee table at Fred's Furnishings was originally priced at $79.95. The cost price of the table was $51.25, and overhead is estimated to be 40% of cost. What is the smallest sale price for the table that will not result in an operating loss?

24. Dempsey's Department Store sells an outdoor barbecue for $149.50. The cost price of the barbecue is $96.00, and the overhead is estimated to be 30% of cost. By how much can Dempsey's reduce the price of the barbecue and still not incur an operating loss?

25. A picnic table at Del's Discount Center is on sale at $117.30. The original price of the table was $138.00. What is the markdown percent? If the markdown is 20% of cost, what is the cost price of the table? If the overhead is estimated to be $10.20, will the sale of the table at $117.30 result in an operating loss?

26. A department store purchased 400 boxes of Christmas cards at a cost price of $2.90 per box. Of the 400 boxes, 250 were sold at the selling price of $4.95, 90 were sold after they were marked down to $3.95, and the remaining 60 were sold after Christmas at $2.00 per box. If the overhead is 22% of the cost price, determine if the store made a profit or a loss on the Christmas cards.

27. An appliance store purchased 12 AM-FM radios at a total cost of $216. Overhead is 40% of the cost price. The store sold two-thirds of the radios at the selling price of $30, three were sold after being marked down to $24, and one radio was stolen. What was the net profit or loss on the radios?

28. A bookstore owner purchased 50 copies of a book at a cost price of $6.25 per copy. The books were to retail at $9.95 a copy, but only 20 copies were sold at that selling price. If overhead is 38% of the cost price, how much can the owner mark down the remaining copies and not incur an operating loss?

Section 5.12 Inventory valuation

One key to successful business management is proper inventory control. **Inventory control** means the determination of how much merchandise is on hand, how much should be on hand, and the value of what is on hand.

To determine the amount of merchandise on hand, two methods are commonly used: (1) perpetual inventory and (2) periodic inventory.

Perpetual inventory is a system whereby a constant record is maintained of all inventory transactions. One recording method uses a perpetual inventory card such as shown in figure 5.4. The card indicates the quantity received, the quantity issued, the remaining balance, and a description of the item.

Inventory transactions may be posted manually as in figure 5.4 or by electronic data processing machines. With the latter, data from punched cards, price tickets, or cash registers are fed into computers that record transactions electronically and thus continuously monitor inventory.

Figure 5.4
Perpetual inventory card

ARTICLE | SIZE / UNIT | MAX. / MIN. | LOCATION | STOCK NO.

RECEIVED			ISSUED			BALANCE	RECEIVED			ISSUED			BALANCE
DATE	ORDER	QUAN.	DATE	ORDER	QUAN.		DATE	ORDER	QUAN.	DATE	ORDER	QUAN.	

TOPS FORM 490 LITHO IN U.S.A.

A **periodic inventory** is the physical count of all merchandise on hand. Most businesses conduct a periodic inventory at least once a year. One method of recording the merchandise count involves using a physical inventory sheet such as that shown in figure 5.5. The key items on the inventory sheet include the quantity inventoried, a description of the material, and the price per unit. A more sophisticated technique uses electronic recording equipment to store this information.

Even firms that maintain a perpetual inventory periodically conduct a physical count. The purpose of this periodic inventory is to reconcile the book inventory with the physical count. Discrepancies between the two figures are usually due to bookkeeping errors, but other factors, such as breakage, product deterioration, or theft, can also cause the counts to differ.

Figure 5.5
Physical inventory sheet

INVENTORY__________ PAGE_____

SHEET NO._____ PRICED BY_____

CALLED BY_____ DEPARTMENT_____ EXTENDED BY_____

ENTERED BY_____ LOCATION_____ EXAMINED BY_____

	CHECK	QUANTITY	DESCRIPTION	✓	PRICE	UNIT	EXTENSIONS
1							
2							
3							
4							
5							
6							
7							
8							
9							
10							
11							
12							
13							
14							
15							
16							
17							
18							
19							
20							
21							
22							
			AMOUNT FORWARD				

Figure 5.6
Sales and inventory data

Net sales		$100,000
Beginning inventory (cost)	$20,000	
+Purchases	72,000	
Merchandise available for sale	$92,000	
−Ending inventory (cost)	24,000	
Cost of goods sold		68,000
Gross profit (net sales less cost of goods)		$32,000

Once an inventory has been completed, its value must be determined. The importance of inventory valuation can be demonstrated by the data in figure 5.6. In this figure, if the ending inventory had been $5,000 higher, the gross profit entry would also have been $5,000 higher; if the ending inventory had been valued $5,000 lower, the gross profit entry would have been $5,000 lower. Thus the value of the inventory directly affects the gross profit entry.

A number of inventory valuation methods have been approved by the Internal Revenue Service (IRS). Among these are

1. Specific identification
2. Average cost
3. First in, first out (FIFO)
4. Last in, first out (LIFO)

Specific identification

When the **specific identification** method of inventory valuation is used, each item in stock is specifically identified, counted, and listed.

Example 1

The A & T Electronics Company's inventory of television picture tubes is as follows:

	CHECK	QUANTITY	DESCRIPTION	√	PRICE	UNIT	EXTENSIONS
1		1	A 4301 TV Picture Tube		$120 00	ea.	120 00
2		2	K 2064 TV Picture Tube		$160 00	ea.	320 00
3		1	T 1062 TV Picture Tube		$ 95 00	ea.	95 00
4							
5							

Find the value of the inventory.

Solution

The value of the inventory is the sum of the extensions, or $535.

The specific identification method works well when the number of units is small and the exact cost of each unit is known. For example, automobile or farm implement dealers could easily use this method. However, if the number of units of merchandise on hand is large and if the unit cost of the merchandise is subject to change, it may be difficult or even impossible to use the specific identification method to find the value of the inventory.

Average cost The **average cost** method of inventory valuation involves finding the average cost of a unit of merchandise, which is the sum of the total costs divided by the total units available for sale during the period. The value of the inventory is the product of the average cost and the number of units on hand.

Example 2 Given the following inventory card from Jack's Hardware, use the average cost method to determine the December 30 inventory value of the outlet boxes:

ARTICLE: Single switch outlet box

SIZE:	MAX: 90	LOCATION:
UNIT: Each	MIN: 30	Bin 28-D

RECEIVED				ISSUED		CURRENT BALANCE
DATE	ORDER	QUAN.	UNIT COST	ORDER	QUAN.	
12-31	Beg. Inv.	40	$ 0.22			40
3-5				12073	12	28
3-20	1-4072	30	$0.24			58
4-9				13071	30	28
6-6	1-6073	60	$0.26			88
7-20				14043	24	64
8-12				15116	44	20
9-1	1-8840	30	$0.28			50
12-30	End. Inv.					50

Solution

$0.22 × 40 = $ 8.80
$0.24 × 30 = $ 7.20
$0.26 × 60 = $15.60
$0.28 × 30 = $ 8.40
160 $40.00 Sum of total costs

$40 ÷ 160 = $0.25 Average cost of one unit
$0.25 × 50 = $12.50 Inventory value

First in, first out (FIFO)

Most business people attempt to sell merchandise that they bought first before they sell their newer goods. This is sound management practice in that it keeps stocks fresh and merchandise new. The **first in, first out (FIFO)** inventory valuation method is based on the concept that the merchandise on hand is the newest and that the oldest merchandise has been sold.

Example 3 Given the inventory card from Jack's Hardware in example 2, use the FIFO method to find the December 30 inventory value of the outlet boxes.

Solution

Assuming that the 50 boxes in inventory are the latest purchased, then the 50 units include all of the September 1 purchase and 20 units of the June 6 purchase. Thus,

$0.28 × 30 = $ 8.40 September purchase
$0.26 × 20 = $ 5.20 June purchase
$13.60 Inventory value

FIFO is an advantage to a business when prices are decreasing but a disadvantage when prices are increasing. When prices are increasing, replacement costs tend to absorb profits that appear to exist but that in reality have been used to purchase higher-priced merchandise.

Last in, first out (LIFO)

Because of the inflationary economy that developed during World War II, the IRS approved the **last in, first out (LIFO)** inventory valuation method that assumes that the merchandise on hand is the oldest and that the merchandise sold was the latest purchased.

Example 4 Given the inventory card from Jack's Hardware in example 2, use the LIFO method to find the December 30 inventory value of the outlet boxes.

Solution

Assuming that the boxes in the December 30 inventory were the first purchased, then the 50 units include all of the December 31 beginning inventory and 10 units from the March 20 purchase. Thus,

$0.22 × 40 =	$ 8.80	December 31 beginning inventory
$0.24 × 10 =	$ 2.40	March purchase
	$11.20	Inventory value

In contrast to the FIFO inventory valuation method, LIFO is an advantage to a business if costs are increasing and a disadvantage if costs are decreasing. When costs are increasing, the LIFO method produces a lower inventory value and a lower profit figure, and therefore lower income taxes.

Exercises for Section 5.12

1. Apex Hardware Store's inventory of galvanized fencing is shown on the following inventory sheet:

	CHECK	QUANTITY	DESCRIPTION	PRICE	UNIT	EXTENSIONS
1		15	100-foot rolls	$ 59 00	Each	
2		12	50-foot rolls	$ 31 00	Each	
3		9	25-foot rolls	$ 17 00	Each	
4						
5						

Fill in the blanks on the sheet and use the specific identification method to find the value of the inventory.

2. The inventory of tropical-fish aquariums at the Sea World Shop is shown on the following inventory sheet:

	CHECK	QUANTITY	DESCRIPTION	PRICE	UNIT	EXTENSIONS
1		8	10-gallon	$ 9 85	Each	
2		13	20-gallon	$ 17 59	Each	
3		3	30-gallon	$ 24 39	Each	
4		7	50-gallon	$ 41 79	Each	
5		2	60-gallon	$ 63 29	Each	

Fill in the missing entries on the sheet and use the specific identification method to find the value of the inventory.

In problems 3–5, use the information shown on the following perpetual inventory card:

ARTICLE:
Model 114-S pocket calculator

SIZE:	MAX: 80	LOCATION:
UNIT: Each	MIN: 10	Shelf C-3

RECEIVED				ISSUED		CURRENT BALANCE
DATE	ORDER	QUAN.	UNIT COST	ORDER	QUAN.	
12-31-88	Beg. Inv.	15	$ 8.40			15
1-5-89	A-2071	40	$ 9.20			55
2-11-89				B-411	15	40
4-28-89				B-517	22	18
6-2-89	A 5713	60	$9.60			78
9-17-89				B-771	30	48
10-20-89				B-901	38	10
11-6-89	A-7621	45	$10.00			55
12-30-89	End. Inv.					55

3. Use the average cost method to find the December 30, 1989, inventory value of the pocket calculators.

4. What is the December 30, 1989, inventory value of the pocket calculators using the FIFO method?

5. Use the LIFO method to find the December 30, 1989, inventory value of the pocket calculators.

In problems 6–8, use the information shown on the following perpetual inventory card:

ARTICLE: AM-FM radio-tape player 214D						
SIZE:		MAX: 60		LOCATION:		
UNIT: Each		MIN: 15		Shelf 210		

	RECEIVED			ISSUED		CURRENT BALANCE
DATE	ORDER	QUAN.	UNIT COST	ORDER	QUAN.	
12-31-88	Beg. Inv.	23	$41.50			23
2-10-89				25107	18	5
2-16-89	4-111	40	$43.00			45
3-8-89				27810	15	30
5-7-89				31642	20	10
6-1-89	4-714	42	$45.25			52
7-4-89				33872	15	37
10-11-89				37412	20	17
11-15-89				41062	15	2
11-20-89	4-992	45	$49.20			47
12-30-89	End. Inv.					47

6. What is the December 30, 1989, inventory value of the radio-tape players using the average cost method?
7. Use the FIFO method to find the December 30, 1989, inventory value of the radio-tape players.
8. Use the LIFO method to find the December 30, 1989, inventory value of the radio-tape players.

In problems 9–11, use the information shown on the following perpetual inventory card:

ARTICLE: Video cassette tape TR120						
SIZE: 6-hour		MAX: 150		LOCATION: Shelf 142		
UNIT: Each		MIN: 40				
RECEIVED				ISSUED		CURRENT BALANCE
DATE	ORDER	QUAN.	UNIT COST	ORDER	QUAN.	
12-31-88	Beg. Inv.	55	$ 9.24			55
1-27-89				B-513	20	35
2-15-89	A-273	100	$ 9.78			135
3-20-89				B-601	50	85
4-5-89				B-692	30	55
6-2-89				B-748	50	5
6-15-89	A-814	150	$10.40			155
7-23-89				B-920	30	125
8-14-89				B-1102	40	85
10-10-89				B-1310	20	65
11-18-89				B-1408	50	15
11-30-89	A-1022	125	$11.20			140
12-30-89	End. Inv.					140

9. What is the December 30, 1989, inventory value of the video tapes using the average cost method?

10. Use the FIFO method to find the December 30, 1989, inventory value of the video tapes.

11. Use the LIFO method to find the December 30, 1989, inventory value of the video tapes.

Section 5–13

Inventory value estimation and inventory turnover

Inventory value estimation

Because it is time consuming and expensive, a periodic inventory may be conducted only once or twice a year. But businesses often need to monitor their financial status more frequently than this. Thus, methods have been developed to approximate inventory values. Two popular methods for estimating the value of an inventory are (1) the gross profit method and (2) the retail method.

To understand the **gross profit method** of estimating the value of inventory, refer again to figure 5.6 on page 136. Note that while

Merchandise available for sale − Ending inventory = Cost of goods sold,

it is also true that

Merchandise available for sale − Cost of goods sold = Ending inventory.

That is,

	Beginning inventory (at cost)
+	Purchases (at cost)
	Merchandise available for sale (at cost)
−	Cost of goods sold
	Ending inventory (at cost)

Except for cost of goods sold, the preceding entries are available from current records. Cost of goods sold can be calculated from formula 5–4 on page 118 solved for C.

Example 1

The December 31 inventory value of a company was $148,000. Through March 31, the company recorded purchases of $125,000 and net sales of $200,000. Estimate the value of the inventory on March 31 if the company uses a markon rate of 35% of the retail price.

Solution

First, we calculate the cost of goods sold. Using formula 5–4, with

$S = \$200{,}000$ and markon % of selling price = 35%,

$$\begin{aligned} C &= S \times (100\% - \text{Markon \% of Selling price}) \\ &= \$200{,}000 \times (100\% - 35\%) \\ &= \$200{,}000 \times (1 - 0.35) \\ &= \$200{,}000 \times (0.65) \\ &= \$130{,}000 \end{aligned}$$

	$148,000	Beginning inventory (December 31)
+	125,000	Purchases
	$273,000	Merchandise available for sale
−	130,000	Cost of goods sold
	$143,000	Ending inventory (March 31)

The second method for estimating inventory value is called the **retail method** because it requires a company to maintain records of all purchases at both cost and retail prices. The retail method utilizes the same format as the gross profit method except that all entries are recorded at retail price. This means that net sales must be used instead of cost of goods sold. That is,

	Beginning inventory (at retail)
+	Purchases (at retail)
	Merchandise available for sale (at retail)
−	Net sales
	Ending inventory (at retail)

The ending inventory value at retail is then converted to an estimated value at cost by multiplying it by the ratio of the merchandise available for sale (at cost) to the merchandise available for sale (at retail). The retail method assumes that this ratio is equal to that of the ending inventory (at cost) divided by the ending inventory (at retail).

Example 2 The December 31 inventory of the Stocton Corporation was valued at $6,000 (cost), $10,000 (retail). During the next three months, the company made purchases totaling $30,000 (cost), $50,000 (retail) and had net sales of $48,000. Estimate the value of the inventory at cost as of March 31.

Solution

	Cost	*Retail*
Previous inventory	$ 6,000	$10,000
+ Purchases	+ 30,000	+ 50,000
Merchandise available for sale	$36,000	$60,000
− Net sales		− 48,000
March 31 inventory (at retail)		$12,000

$\frac{\$36,000}{\$60,000} = 0.60$ Ratio of merchandise available for sale at cost to merchandise available for sale at retail

$\$12,000 \times 0.60 = \$7,200$ Estimated value at cost of March 31 inventory

Estimation of the inventory value by the retail method is a paper figure. When physical inventories are conducted, these paper figures must be adjusted to reflect actual conditions.

The primary advantage of the retail method is that gross profits can be determined more quickly than by any other valuation method. The chief disadvantage of the retail method is the extensive bookkeeping required because records must be maintained at both cost and retail prices.

Inventory turnover

Another important part of inventory control is inventory turnover. **Inventory turnover** (also known as *stock turnover* or *stockturn*) is the number of times during a given period that the average inventory on hand is sold and replaced. Inventory turnover varies according to the type of business. For example, inventory turnover for food markets is about once a month; for hardware stores, it is about twice a year.

The first step in calculating inventory turnover is finding the average inventory. The **average inventory** is the sum of the values of the inventories during the period divided by the number of inventories.

Example 3

A company recorded the following inventories, each valued at retail: January 1, \$26,300; July 1, \$18,500; December 31, \$25,700. Determine the average retail inventory.

Solution

$$\text{Average retail inventory} = \frac{\text{Sum of the retail inventory values}}{\text{Number of inventories}}$$

$$= \frac{\$26{,}300 + \$18{,}500 + \$25{,}700}{3}$$

$$= \$23{,}500$$

The inventory turnover may be computed on the basis of cost or retail, depending on the inventory control method used by the business. The formulas are:

■ (5–9) $$\text{Inventory turnover (retail)} = \frac{\text{Net sales}}{\text{Average inventory (at retail)}}$$

■ (5–10) $$\text{Inventory turnover (cost)} = \frac{\text{Cost of goods sold}}{\text{Average inventory (at cost)}}$$

Example 4

The Kotton Kandy Company had annual net sales of \$46,000. Find the inventory turnover (rounded to the nearest tenth) if the average inventory (at retail) for the year was \$3,400.

Solution

Using formula 5–9,

$$\text{Inventory turnover} = \frac{\$46{,}000}{\$3{,}400}$$

$$= 13.5 \text{ (Rounded)}$$

Thus, the company sold and replaced its average inventory on hand 13.5 times during the year.

Example 5 For a six-month period, the cost of goods sold of an appliance store was \$64,000. Find the inventory turnover if the average inventory (at cost) for the same period was \$25,600.

Solution

Using formula 5–10,

$$\text{Inventory turnover} = \frac{\$64{,}000}{\$25{,}600}$$

$$= 2.5$$

The inventory turnover figure in itself has little meaning; it becomes significant only in comparison with some other standard. Trade associations and business research bureaus furnish statistics on turnover rates for different kinds of businesses, but it is also desirable to compare current figures with those of previous periods. A decrease in inventory turnover is a warning that corrective action may be needed.

In general, it is desirable to increase the rate of inventory turnover, provided that the increase does not adversely affect profits. Some of the benefits of increased stock turnover are

1. Stocks are fresher, thus reducing markdowns and losses due to deterioration or obsolescence.
2. Less capital is tied up in current inventory; thus, more funds are available to take advantage of manufacturers' closeouts and special purchases.
3. Storage space is reduced, thus reducing insurance costs and property taxes.

It is possible for inventory turnover to be excessive. When this happens, profits are reduced because

1. Sales may suffer because of reduced customer selection.
2. Quantities shipped in small lots may result in higher transportation costs. In addition, quantity discounts may be lost.
3. Operating expenses may increase as a result of the additional paperwork and manpower required to process a greater number of shipments.

From the preceding, it is clear that inventory turnover is complex and requires careful attention. Maintaining adequate stock turnover while maintaining adequate stock margins is a central task of retailing management.

Exercises for Section 5.13

1. Use the gross profit method to estimate the value of the ending inventory at cost for a company if the beginning inventory at cost is $57,000, purchases at cost total $32,000, net sales total $68,000, and the company uses a markon rate of 38% of the retail price.

2. For the first quarter of last year, the beginning inventory at cost of the Carver Company was $322,000. During the quarter, the company recorded purchases of $281,000 and net sales of $405,000. If the company uses a markon rate of 34% of the retail price, estimate the value of the inventory at the end of the quarter using the gross profit method.

3. The March 31 inventory value at cost of Zimmer laboratories was $96,250. Through June 30, the company recorded purchases of $34,140 and $47,720. The net sales over the same three-month period were $135,410. Use the gross profit method to estimate the value of the inventory on June 30 if the company uses a markon rate of 28% of the retail price.

4. Autotron Industries recorded a beginning inventory at cost of $424,000. Through the next quarter the company had purchases of $122,720, $213,040, and $209,120. The company uses a markon rate of 30% of the retail price. Use the gross profit method to estimate the value of the inventory at the end of the quarter if net sales during the quarter were $694,520.

5. The net sales of the Brister Company for the first six months were $712,200. The beginning inventory at cost was $326,800 and the company had purchases of $110,460, $80,640, and $174,400. If the company uses a markon rate of 36% of the retail price, use the gross profit method to estimate the value of the inventory at the end of the six-month period.

6. Use the retail inventory method to estimate the current inventory value at cost from the following records of the Mountain Manor Gift Shop:

	Cost	*Retail*
Previous inventory	$14,220	$19,800
Purchases	26,210	42,400
Total merchandise available for sale	$40,430	$62,200
Less: Net sales		37,400
Current inventory (retail)		$24,800

7. From the following records of Western Leather Products, Inc., estimate the current inventory value at cost using the retail inventory method:

	Cost	*Retail*
Previous inventory	$18,200	$ 33,480
Purchases	39,180	73,020
Total merchandise available for sale	$57,380	$106,500
Less: Net sales		78,650
Current inventory (retail)		$ 27,850

8. The June 30 inventory of Fairwell Industries was valued at $24,400 (cost), $35,900 (retail). During the next three months, the company made purchases totaling $52,100 (cost), $76,600 (retail), and had net sales of $62,300. Use the retail inventory method to estimate the value of the inventory at cost as of September 30.

9. Estimate the value of the inventory at cost as of June 30, 1989, for the Meredith Corporation, using the retail inventory method and the following information: March 31 inventory was valued at $28,411 (cost), $50,740 (retail); purchases made between March 31 and June 30 totaled $78,465 (cost), $140,110 (retail); the company had net sales of $84,680 during the three-month period.

10. Quik-Fix Hardware Supplies recorded retail inventories of $22,400, $18,700, and $29,700 for the first three months of 1989. Find the average retail inventory for the three-month period.

11. Spencer's Hobby Shop recorded four inventories (at cost) last year. They were: $16,750, $20,180, $14,010, and $19,420. What was the average inventory (at cost) for the year?

12. Federal Food Distributors had annual net sales of $246,675. Find the inventory turnover if the average inventory (at retail) for the year was $17,250.

13. The average inventory (at cost) of an office supply store over a six-month period was $34,200. During the same period, the cost of goods sold at the store was $54,720. Find the inventory turnover during the six months.

14. The Cover-Glo Paint Company recorded three inventories (at retail) last year: $8,420, $12,780, and $7,405. If the company had annual net sales of $26,698, what was the inventory turnover for the year?

15. The net sales at Lawton's Products last year were $392,490. The company took inventory (at retail) four times during the year, recording amounts of $80,210, $106,530, $70,820, and $116,240. Find the inventory turnover for the year.

16. The cost of goods sold by a company during the past year was $1,201,750. The company took inventory (at cost) three times during the year, recording amounts of $182,250, $310,810, and $162,440. Find the inventory turnover for the year.

17. Pearson's Poultry Products took inventory (at cost) four times during the year, recording figures of $28,400, $42,300, $37,600, and $31,100. The cost of goods sold during the year was $581,995. Find the inventory turnover for the year.

Glossary

Anticipation dating Terms of sale allowing the buyer to deduct an amount determined by the current bank interest rate for the number of days remaining in the cash discount period.

Average cost For a unit of merchandise, the sum of the total costs divided by the total units available for sale during the period; used in the average cost inventory valuation method.

Average inventory The sum of the inventories during a period divided by the number of inventories.

Billing price The net price plus freight or transportation charges.

Break-even point When the selling price of an item equals the cost price plus operating expenses.

Cash discount A percentage reduction in price for payment within a specified time.

Cash on delivery (C.O.D.) When payment is required upon receipt of goods.

Chain discounts Two or more discounts on a single item of merchandise.

Complement of the discount Also called net price percent. The difference between 100% and a discount expressed in percent.

Cost price The billing price plus any additional charges.

Discount A percentage reduction from the list price.

End of month (E.O.M.) dating Also called proximo (Prox.) dating. Terms of sale providing a cash discount period beginning the first day of the month following the month of the invoice date.

Extra dating An extension of the ordinary dating period for a specified number of days.

First in, first out (FIFO) An inventory valuation method that assumes that the merchandise on hand is the newest and that the oldest merchandise has been sold.

Gross loss When the markdown on an item exceeds the markon.

Gross profit method A procedure for estimating the value of an inventory using the formula:

Ending inventory (at cost) = Beginning inventory (at cost) + Purchases (at cost) − Cost of goods sold

Installment dating Terms of sale providing for a cash discount if a specified percent of the total invoice amount is paid within 30 days, and a second cash discount if the remaining balance is paid within 60 days.

Inventory control The determination of how much merchandise is on hand, how much should be on hand, and the value of what is on hand.

Inventory turnover The number of times during a given period that the average inventory on hand is sold and replaced.

Last in, first out (LIFO) An inventory valuation method that assumes that the merchandise on hand is the oldest and that the newest merchandise has been sold.

List price The catalog price of an item or the price on a price list or price tag.

Markdown A reduction in the selling price of an item.

Markon The difference between the selling price and the cost price.

Net price The list price of an item less any discounts.

Net price percent See complement of the discount.

Net profit Markon less overhead.

Operating loss When the markdown exceeds the net profit but is less than the net profit plus operating expenses.

Ordinary dating Terms of sale that provide a cash discount period beginning with the date of the invoice.

Overhead The expense of operation, including rent, taxes, salaries, utilities, and so on. Also called operating expenses.

Periodic inventory The physical count of all merchandise on hand.

Perpetual inventory A system whereby a constant record is maintained of all inventory transactions.

Proximo dating See end of month (E.O.M.) dating.

Quantity discount A reduction in price because of the quantity of merchandise purchased.

Receipt of goods (R.O.G.) dating Terms of sale providing a cash discount period beginning on the day the merchandise is received.

Retail method A procedure for estimating the value of an inventory using the formula:

Ending inventory (at retail) = Beginning inventory (at retail) + Purchases (at retail) − Net sales

Selling price The amount of money a vendor receives in exchange for a product.

Specific identification An inventory valuation method wherein each item in stock is specifically identified, counted, and listed.

Trade discount A percentage reduction from the list price offered to certain categories of customers by the seller.

Review test

1. The ________________________ is the catalog price or the price on a price list or price tag.
2. The expense of operation, such as rent, taxes, and salaries, is called ____________________.
3. A reduction in list price offered to certain categories of customers by the seller is called ____________________.
4. The complement of a 45% trade discount is __________ %.
5. A reduction in the selling price of an item is called ________________________.
6. A lawn fertilizer spreader carries a list price of $25 with a trade discount of 40%. Find the net price.
7. What is the net price of an electric clock with a list price of $48.40 less 25% less 10%?
8. An invoice dated May 17 carries a billing price of $614.30 including freight charges of $16.30. What amount should be remitted on June 1 if the terms are 5/10, 4/15, n/30?
9. An invoice dated September 11 is dated 2/10, 30X, net 60. What is the last day of the cash discount?
10. What is the selling price of an article if the cost price is $63 and the markon is 46% of the cost price?
11. The markon of an item is 30% of the cost price. What is the markon percent of the selling price? (Round to the nearest percent.)
12. The price of a dress is marked down from $78.95 to $56.00. What is the markdown percent? (Round to the nearest percent.)
13. A Chippendale style curio with a selling price of $229 was advertised at $129. The cost price is $78, and overhead is estimated at 45% of the cost price. Determine whether a sale results in a profit or a loss.
14. A merchant's beginning inventory was 10 bottles of antacid valued at $2.00 per bottle. Purchases were 24, 12, and 24 bottles at cost prices of $2.12, $2.15, and $2.05, respectively. If the ending inventory was 30 bottles, find the value of the ending inventory using (a) the LIFO method and (b) the FIFO method.
15. A company recorded the following data: previous inventory: $30,100 (cost), $36,120 (retail); purchases: $45,832 (cost), $56,480 (retail); net sales at retail: $50,100. Estimate the value of the inventory using the retail method.
16. During one year, a company had the following inventories, each valued at retail: $18,200, $24,650, $19,240, and $21,060. Find the inventory turnover (rounded to the nearest tenth) if net sales for the year were $88,452.

Payrolls and Banking

Chapter Objectives

I. Learn the meaning of the following terms:

Gross earnings, 152
Net earnings, 152
Salary, 153
Commissions, 154
Wages, 162
Piecework, 163
Overtime, 169
Withholding allowance, 179–180
Bank statement reconciliation, 206

II. Understand:

The concept of payroll deductions, 152
The purpose of employer contributions, 196
The information required on payroll records, 199
The process of reconciling a checking account, 206

III. Learn to:

Compute gross earnings for:
Salaries, 153
Commissions, 155–158
Wages, 163–164

Compute overtime for:
Salaries, 170
Commissions, 171
Wages, 171–172

Calculate payroll deductions, 179–193

Section 6.1 Introduction

Payment for services rendered is the most fundamental of employer-employee relationships. The record of these payments is the company payroll.

Fifty years ago, the company payroll may have consisted of little more than a simple entry in a paybook; today, payroll clerks record an array of items, such as hours worked, regular and overtime rates, federal income and social security taxes, hospitalization insurance, union dues, and pledges to the United Way fund. Much of the complexity of the payroll is due to social legislation and labor laws enacted by the federal government, while other items are the result of union contracts or trade competition.

Today, keeping payroll records requires specialized knowledge. Accuracy is essential; not only are mistakes damaging to employee morale, but penalties may be imposed by governmental agencies for incorrect reports.

Since employees are paid at specified intervals called pay periods, the payroll is a recurring responsibility. Most pay periods are either weekly, biweekly, or monthly.

The basic structure of the payroll is contained in the meanings of the terms *gross earnings* and *net earnings*. The term **gross earnings** refers to the total earnings of an employee within a pay period. **Net earnings** are gross earnings less deductions; that is, gross earnings less amounts withheld from the employee's pay. The payroll department is responsible for calculating gross earnings, withholding deductions, and remitting net earnings. The actions of the payroll department are summarized in figure 6.1.

Figure 6.1
Actions of the payroll department

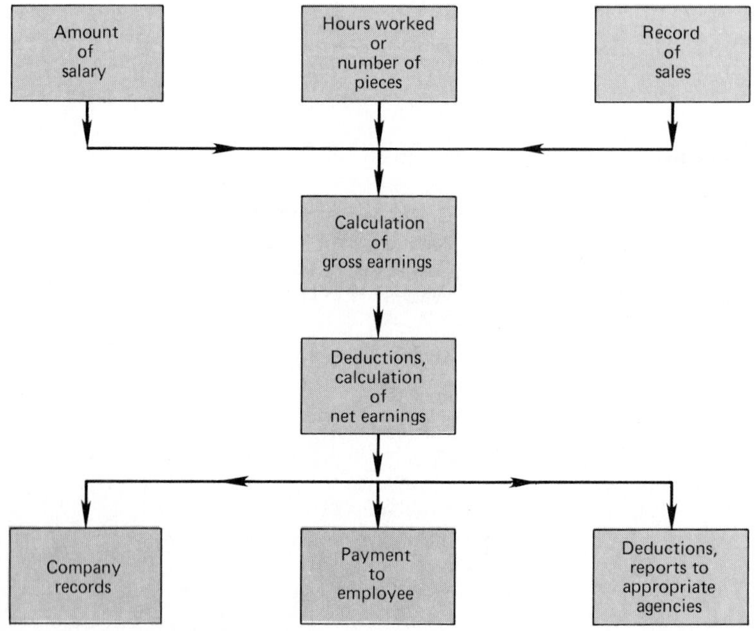

Section 6.2 Gross earnings

There are three forms of gross earnings: salaries, commissions, and wages.

A. Salaries

The word **salary** is used to describe earnings of executives, supervisors, office personnel, and others who are paid according to a specified period of employment. A salary is independent of both production and working time.

The gross earnings of salaried employees are calculated by dividing the annual earnings by the number of pay periods per year:

$$\text{(6–1)} \quad \text{Gross earnings (salary)} = \frac{\text{Annual earnings}}{\text{Number of pay periods per year}}$$

Example 1 The president of the Triton Manufacturing Company earns a salary of \$60,000 per year. The salary of his private secretary is \$1,200 per month. If the company pay period is biweekly, calculate the gross earnings per pay period of (a) the president and (b) his private secretary.

Solution

There are 26 pay periods per year when the pay period is biweekly. Thus,

a. $\text{Gross earnings} = \frac{\$60{,}000}{26} = \$2{,}307.69 \text{ per pay period}$

b. The annual earnings of the secretary are \$1,200 × 12 = \$14,400.

$\text{Gross earnings} = \frac{\$14{,}400}{26} = \$553.85 \text{ per pay period}$

Exercises for Section 6.2A

Round all answers to the nearest cent.

1. Leon Allen earns an annual salary of \$22,000 at S.M.C. Industries, where the pay period is biweekly. Find his gross earnings per pay period.
2. Wendy Miller is a computer programmer at the Coughlin Corporation, where she earns \$1,650 per month. If the company's pay period is weekly, find her gross earnings per pay period.
3. The Britton Company pays draftspeople a beginning salary of \$21,400 per year. If the pay period at Britton is biweekly, find the gross earnings of a beginning draftsperson per pay period.
4. John Elliot earns \$1,240 per month at Wellington Motors, where the pay period is biweekly. Compute his gross earnings per pay period.
5. The Carter Chemical Company pays its vice-president a salary of \$96,000 per year. If the pay period is biweekly, compute the vice-president's gross earnings per pay period.

6. Find the gross earnings per pay period of an employee who earns $1,124 per month at the Atlas Manufacturing Company, where the pay period is weekly.

7. The president of Union Mills is paid $82,000 a year. Find her gross earnings per pay period if the pay period is weekly.

8. Ed Mason receives a monthly salary of $1,460 as a bookkeeper for the Barrett Construction Company. Compute his gross earnings per pay period if the pay period is biweekly.

9. Judy Hill is an office manager at Ampek Enterprises. She earns a salary of $1,470 per month, and the pay period is weekly. Find her gross earnings per pay period.

10. Grace Johnson is the senior vice-president of Sutton Foodstores. Her annual salary is $78,000, and the pay period is biweekly. Find her gross earnings per pay period.

11. The Bookshire Company is presently operating on a weekly pay period. James Richards, an employee, has gross earnings of $340 per pay period. Next year, the company will switch to a monthly pay period. What will his gross earnings be after the switch? (Hint: First compute his annual salary.)

12. The biweekly gross earnings of Patricia Cook at the Lakeside Loan Agency currently amount to $656. When the company converts to a monthly pay period next January, what will Patricia's gross earnings be per month? (Hint: First compute her annual salary.)

13. Find the monthly salary of an employee whose weekly gross earnings amount to $285. (Hint: First compute the annual salary.)

14. Jack Pharr has biweekly gross earnings of $424 at the Preston Clothing Outlet. Compute his monthly salary. (Hint: First compute his annual salary.)

B. Commissions

Commissions are the earnings of sales personnel. Three common commission plans are (1) straight commission, (2) graduated commissions, and (3) salary and commission.

Straight commission

Salespeople on straight commission earn according to the amount of their **net sales** (total sales less returns and cancellations). This may be a set amount per item sold, but more often it is a percentage of the dollar amount of their net sales. Thus, calculation of gross earnings is simply an application of the percentage formula $P = BR$. The commission (percentage) equals the net sales (base) times the rate of commission (percent):

■ (6–2) Gross earnings (commissions) = Net sales × Commission rate

Example 2 Herbert Wesley is paid a straight commission of 12% on his net sales. During April, his net sales totaled \$8,600. Find his gross earnings for the month.

Solution

Using formula 6–2,

$$\text{Gross earnings} = \$8{,}600 \times 0.12$$
$$= \$1{,}032$$

Example 3 Charles Schultz submitted orders for \$16,450 worth of machinery during the month of September. During the same month, the company received cancellation of two orders from one of Schultz's customers totaling \$1,220. At a straight commission rate of 8%, calculate Schultz's gross earnings for the month.

Solution

The net sales are \$16,450 − \$1,220 = \$15,230. Using formula 6–2,

$$\text{Gross earnings} = \$15{,}230 \times 0.08$$
$$= \$1{,}218.40$$

Figure 6.2 Salesperson advertisement

SALES **Commission Sales**

MASON CITY and FORT DODGE AREAS

If you have some (outside) sales experience, a way with people, the desire to advance your income . . . and your career, we can help you reach your career potential and accelerate your professional growth in an environment that thrives on personal achievement.

We are the nation's largest supplier of equipment, furnishings and supplies for hotels, restaurants and institutions, and have an immediate opening in an established territory. We offer excellent commissions, where your earnings are in direct relation to your efforts. Compensation is based on a \$200 a week draw against commission. Our average salespeople earn annually

\$22,000

(based SOLELY on commission)

Everything is up to you . . . you must have your own car and take care of your own expenses . . . but we'll take care of the rest. If you have the confidence it takes, let us hear from you.

Please write in confidence, including education, experience and current or last salary, to the attention of:

Bob Denker
Personnel Department

EDWARD DON & CO.

2500 S. Harlem Avenue
North Riverside, Ill. 60546
an equal opportunity employer

The advantage of the straight commission plan is its simplicity. However, because sales tend to vary from month to month, the income of a sales representative also fluctuates. In addition, new or inexperienced sales personnel initially may not produce sufficient volume to earn a reasonable income. To offset these disadvantages, a company may augment a straight commission plan with a drawing account. A **drawing account** is essentially an advance on future commissions; it is repaid from future commissions. The ad in figure 6.2 is for a salesperson to work on straight commission with a drawing account.

Example 4 During her first four months of employment with the Glover Company, sales representative Carol Cook had sales of $2,800, $3,800, $4,500, and $3,400. Carol receives a straight commission of $12\frac{1}{2}\%$ of net sales with a draw of $450 per month. Calculate Carol's gross earnings for the four-month period.

Solution

Using formula 6–2, the commissions for the four months are $350.00, $475.00, $562.50, and $425.00, respectively. Her earnings are calculated as follows:

Sales	Earned Commissions	Draw Advance	Draw Deficit Brought Fwd.	Gross Earnings	Draw Deficit Carried Fwd.
$2,800	$350.00	$100.00	—	$450.00	$100.00
3,800	475.00	—	$100.00	450.00	75.00
4,500	562.50	—	75.00	487.50	—
3,400	425.00	25.00	—	450.00	25.00

As a result of her drawing account, Carol would receive $450.00, $450.00, $487.50, and $450.00, respectively, as gross earnings for each of the four months.

Graduated commissions

As an additional incentive, commissions may be established on a graduated scale. In other words, the commission rate increases as sales volume increases. Companies offer a **graduated commission** plan because travel, meals, and other sales expenses absorbed by the company remain relatively constant regardless of the sales volume.

Example 5 The Shelby Corporation pays its sales personnel monthly according to the following graduated scale:

6% of the first $5,000 in net sales
$7\frac{1}{4}$% of the next $5,000 in net sales
8% of all net sales over $10,000

Last month, Travis Clark had net sales of $14,750. Calculate his gross earnings.

Solution

Sales		*Commissions*
$5,000 × 0.06	=	$300.00
$5,000 × 0.0725	=	362.50
$4,750 × 0.08	=	380.00
$14,750		$1,042.50

Salary and commission

Sales personnel under a salary and commission plan receive a salary plus a percentage of net sales. Since the sales representative receives a guaranteed salary, the commission rate is usually less than a straight commission rate.

Example 6 During a week that Harry Carson sold $1,630 worth of supplies, the company had returns of $208 from one of his customers. Harry receives a salary of $240 a week plus a commission of 3% of his net sales. Calculate his gross earnings for the weekly pay period.

Solution

Gross sales	=	$1,630.00	Commission	=	$ 42.66 ($1,422 × 0.03)
Returns	=	− 208.00	Salary	=	+240.00
Net sales	=	$1,422.00	Gross earnings	=	$282.66

Retail stores commonly offer a salary and commission plan wherein a commission is paid only when sales exceed a specified quota.

Example 7 Nancy Sherman, Sharon Blake, and Sarah Brennan are salesclerks in the women's wear section of a large department store. Each is paid a weekly salary of $228 for a 35-hour workweek, plus a commission of 4% of net sales in excess of $800 per week. Calculate their gross earnings during a week when Nancy recorded sales of $960, Sharon's sales were $880, and Sarah's sales were $840.

Solution

	Nancy Sherman	*Sharon Blake*	*Sarah Brennan*
Salary	$228.00	$228.00	$228.00
Commission	6.40 ($160 × 0.04)	3.20 ($80 × 0.04)	1.60 ($40 × 0.04)
Gross earnings	$234.40	$231.20	$229.60

Department heads or sales managers often are paid a commission that is a percentage of the net sales of the people they supervise. This type of commission is called an **override.**

Example 8 Joan Littlefield heads the women's wear section of the department store in example 7. In addition to her weekly salary of $250, she receives a commission of 4% of her personal net sales in excess of $800, plus an override of $\frac{1}{2}$% of the net sales of the three clerks in her section. Using the information in example 7, calculate her gross earnings if her personal sales for the week were $1,140.

Solution

Salary	$250.00
Commission	13.60 ($340 × 0.04)
Override	13.40 ($2,680 × 0.005)
Gross earnings	= $277.00

Exercises for Section 6.2B

1. Joe Prentice is paid a straight commission of 11% on his net sales. During March, his net sales totaled $12,350. Find his gross earnings for the month.

2. In September, Marcia Peters sold $14,720 worth of merchandise. At a straight commission rate of 9%, how much were her gross earnings for the month?

3. During the month of January, Bob Reynolds submitted orders for $18,472 worth of fittings. Two of the orders, totaling $3,250, were subsequently cancelled. Calculate his gross earnings for the month if he is paid a straight commission of 7%.

4. Yvonne Parker is paid a straight commission of 6% on net sales. In May, her sales were $21,420 with returns and cancellations totaling $3,942. What was her commission for the month?

5. Last month, Walter Lewis sold $15,314 worth of furniture, with returns and cancelled orders totaling $1,323. If he is paid a straight commission rate of 9% of net sales, find his gross earnings for the month.

6. Jack Randall sells plumbing fixtures on a straight commission of 8% of net sales. Find his gross earnings for a month during which he submitted orders totaling $16,316 and cancellations amounted to $4,115.

7. Marla Davis is paid a straight commission of 4% of her net sales. During the past week, she had sales of $770 on Monday, $511 on Tuesday, $637 on Wednesday, $792 on Thursday, and $606 on Friday. Returned merchandise for the week totaled $51. What are her gross earnings for the week?

8. Joan Nichols sold $273 worth of merchandise on Monday, $314 on Tuesday, $342 on Wednesday, $290 on Thursday, and $315 on Friday. If returned merchandise for the week totaled $104, find her gross earnings for the week at a straight commission rate of 11%.

9. Conway Higgins, a stockbroker, received a commission of $69.30 for purchasing some stock for one of his customers. The sale price of the stock was $9,240. If he is paid a straight commission on the sale price, what is his commission rate?

10. Real estate salesperson Mary Burke received a commission of $4,290 on the sale of a home. If her commission rate is 6% of the selling price, how much did the home sell for?

11. Glenn Chapman recently accepted a position as a salesperson with Hoffman Industries, where he receives a straight commission of 9% of net sales with a draw of $575 per month. Complete the following record of his monthly gross earnings for his first three months with the company:

Month	Net Sales	Commission	Draw Advance	Draw Deficit Brought Fwd.	Gross Earnings	Draw Deficit Carried Fwd.
Jan.	$5,200	$468.00	$107.00	$ 0.00	$575.00	$107.00
Feb.	6,850			107.00		65.50
Mar.	8,450					0.00

12. Fashion Flair, a wholesale clothing firm, pays its sales personnel 7% of net sales with a draw of $520 per month. Complete the following record of the monthly gross earnings for sales representative Patricia Wolfe:

Month	Net Sales	Commission	Draw Advance	Draw Deficit Brought Fwd.	Gross Earnings	Draw Deficit Carried Fwd.
Sept.	$5,650			$ 71.50		$196.00
Oct.	8,225			196.00		140.25
Nov.	8,140					

13. Redmund Industries pays salesperson Martin Wells a straight commission of 6% with a monthly draw of $550. Complete the following record of his monthly gross earnings:

Month	Net Sales	Commission	Draw Advance	Draw Deficit Brought Fwd.	Gross Earnings	Draw Deficit Carried Fwd.
April	$ 8,842			$70.00		
May	11,540					
June	12,760					

14. Shirley Jenkins is paid a straight commission of 12% with a draw of $500 per month. Complete the following record of her monthly gross earnings:

Month	Net Sales	Commission	Draw Advance	Draw Deficit Brought Fwd.	Gross Earnings	Draw Deficit Carried Fwd.
Aug.	$4,225			$44.00		
Sept.	4,850					
Oct.	4,975					

15. Donald Ross is paid a monthly graduated commission of 5% of the first $5,000 in net sales and 6.5% of net sales over $5,000. Last month, he had net sales of $9,420. Find his gross earnings for the month.

16. The Shelby Corporation pays its sales personnel a monthly graduated commission of 7% of the first $3,000 in net sales and 9% of net sales over $3,000. Compute the gross earnings of one of the company's salespersons for a month during which the salesperson's net sales were $6,250.

17. Pickwick Products pays its sales personnel a monthly graduated commission of 6% of the first $4,000 in net sales, 6.75% of the next $3,000, and 7.5% of net sales in excess of $7,000. In January, salesperson Bill Walker reported net sales of $8,124. What were his gross earnings for the month?

18. Leslie Maynard is paid a weekly graduated commission of 8% of the first $1,000 of net sales, 9.25% of the next $500, and 10.5% of net sales in excess of $1,500. Find her gross earnings for a week during which her net sales total $1,622.

19. During the month of October, salesperson Jerry Roberts submitted orders totaling $25,483. Jerry is paid a monthly graduated commission of 5% of the first $10,000 in net sales, 6.5% of the next $8,000, and 7% of net sales over $18,000. Compute Jerry's gross earnings for the month if $4,120 worth of his orders were subsequently cancelled.

20. Lisa Taylor submitted orders totaling $17,563 in February, with cancellations totaling $2,657. Lisa is paid a monthly graduated commission of 5.5% of the first $9,000 in net sales, 6.5% of the next $4,000, and 7.25% of net sales in excess of $13,000. What were Lisa's gross earnings for the month?

21. Linda Roberts is employed as a salesclerk in the sporting goods department of a large store. She is paid a salary of $335 a week plus a commission of 3.25% of her weekly net sales. Find her gross earnings for a week during which she sold $1,242 worth of merchandise and returns totaled $165.

22. Patton's Home Improvement Center pays salesperson Mark Watson $360 per week plus a commission of 2.75% of net sales. Last week, Mark sold $2,720 worth of supplies, with returns totaling $323. What were his gross earnings for the week?

23. Dennis Putnam is paid a monthly salary of $950 plus a commission of 5% of net sales in excess of $5,500. During the past month, he sold $11,424 worth of goods, with cancellations totaling $2,720. How much were his gross earnings for the month?

24. Laura Lindsey is employed by Griffin's Gift Shoppe, where she is paid a weekly salary of $232 plus a commission of 3.25% of net sales in excess of $1,200. Find her gross earnings for a week during which she sells $1,572 worth of merchandise with returns of $117.

25. Tom Weber is the manager of the men's wear section in a department store. He is paid a salary of $330 a week plus a commission of 4% of net sales over $800 and an override of 0.75% of the net sales of the clerks working under him. His sales last week totaled $2,300 with returns of $143. The people working under him had sales of $7,240 with returns of $619. What were his gross earnings for the week?

26. Michele Turner manages the Hillside branch of S. Bentley, a women's clothing chain. She receives a salary of $345 a week plus a commission of 3.5% of net sales over $500 and an override of 0.5% of the net sales of the people working in her store. Find her gross earnings for a week when she sold $3,125 worth of merchandise with returns of $217 and her employees sold $12,420 worth of merchandise with returns of $757.

27. The following payroll record gives the net sales, commission rate, quota, amount of returns, and salary for each of the five salespeople employed at Sam's Style Shoppe. Find the gross earnings of each of the salespeople for the week.

Sam's Style Shoppe — *Week Ending 4/6/89*

Name	Sales	Returns	Net Sales	Quota	Commission	Salary	Gross Earnings
Mazurek, S.	$2,452	$47	____	$ 800	6.5%	$245	____
Reese, S.	3,187	63	____	—	4.0	255	____
Taylor, J.	2,740	18	____	1,200	7.0	250	____
Velasco, R.	3,416	27	____	—	5.5	240	____
Williams, P.	3,141	36	____	1,000	5.75	260	____

28. Frieda's Card & Gift Shop employs five salespeople. Complete the following payroll record for the week ending June 7, 1989:

Frieda's Card & Gift Shop — *Week Ending 6/7/89*

Name	Sales	Returns	Net Sales	Quota	Commission	Salary	Gross Earnings
Darke, L.	$1,720	$102	____	$500	8%	$250	____
Hargraves, E.	1,542	182	____	600	8.5	255	____
Lynam, J.	1,912	94	____	—	4.5	240	____
Robinson, M.	2,004	114	____	—	5.25	235	____
Ullrich, J.	1,643	83	____	700	9	260	____

C. Wages

The majority of American workers are paid according to actual time at work. Their earnings are called **wages** and are calculated on a per hour basis. Gross earnings for hourly workers are found by multiplying the hourly rate by the number of hours worked per pay period; that is,

■ (6–3) Gross earnings (wages) = Rate per hour × Number of hours worked

Example 9 A baker earns $8.06 per hour. Calculate his gross earnings for a 40-hour workweek.

Solution

Using formula 6–3,

Gross earnings = $8.06 × 40

= $322.40

Example 10 An electrician wiring apartments in a new complex works the following hours in a two-week period:

	Sun.	Mon.	Tues.	Wed.	Thurs.	Fri.	Sat.
Week 1	0	8	6	4	8	8	4
Week 2	0	8	8	8	8	4	4

At an hourly rate of $7.56, calculate his gross earnings for the biweekly pay period.

Solution

The electrician worked 38 hours in week 1 and 40 hours in week 2 for a total of 78 hours.

Gross earnings = $7.56 × 78

= $589.68

In addition to the hourly rate, the term *wages* also refers to compensation based on production. The oldest form of production wages is called **piecework** or **piece-rate.** Workers under this payment plan earn according to the number of units produced.

Example 11 A plastics company pays a worker $0.68 for each load of sheets fed into a baking press. Calculate the gross earnings of the worker on a day that she feeds 92 loads of sheets into the press.

Solution

The gross earnings are found by multiplying the number of loads by the rate per load; that is,

Gross earnings = $0.68 × 92

= $62.56

Piecework of this kind is called *straight piece-rate.* Prior to World War II, piecework was used more than any other wage plan, but since that time its popularity has declined rapidly. Part of this is due to requirements imposed by the Federal Labor Standards Act (discussed in section 6.3), but the primary reason is union dissatisfaction.

Piecework rewards the fast, efficient worker who can exceed the average production, but it penalizes the slower, below-average worker. Today there is considerable pressure to guarantee a minimum wage to the pieceworker regardless of production. These minimum wages are set near a "standard," a production requirement per unit of work time established by work measurement methods.

Example 12 shows how a straight piece-rate plan can be coupled with a minimum wage. The worker is paid the higher of the piece-rate or the minimum wage.

Example 12 A lathe operator is paid $0.45 for each part machined and has a guaranteed weekly wage of $240.00. His production for the week was as follows:

Sun.	Mon.	Tues.	Wed.	Thurs.	Fri.	Sat.
0	100	107	106	110	102	0

Calculate his gross earnings for the week.

Solution

The worker turned out a total of 525 pieces during the week. His piece-rate is:

Piece-rate = Number of pieces × Rate per piece

= 525 × $0.45

= $236.25

Since this is less than the guaranteed rate, his weekly gross earnings are $240.00.

A popular wage plan today is called the **standard hour plan.** This is also a form of compensation based on production. In the standard hour plan, a worker is paid an hourly rate based on a "standard" number of units produced per hour and a piece-rate. For instance, suppose that the lathe operator in example 12 normally machines 13 parts per hour. At a piece-rate of $0.45 per part, the hourly wage is

$$\begin{aligned}\text{Hourly wage} &= \text{Number of pieces per hour} \times \text{Piece-rate}\\ &= 13 \times \$0.45\\ &= \$5.85\end{aligned}$$

Thus, an hourly wage of $5.85 per hour is equivalent to a piece-rate of $0.45 per piece at a "standard" production level of 13 pieces per hour. In an era when hourly wage equivalents are required by the federal government, this simplifies the clerical work of the payroll department.

The "standard" production level per hour is the basis for a guaranteed minimum wage in the standard hour plan. Production exceeding standards is rewarded in the form of an "incentive bonus."

Example 13 A worker in a company manufacturing electrical devices normally can assemble 340 units in a week's time (40 hours). At an hourly rate of $5.50, calculate the gross earnings in a week when 374 units were assembled.

Solution

A production of 374 units is 34 units above the weekly standard. This is an efficiency of $\frac{374}{340} = 110\%$. Accordingly, the worker receives the regular wage plus a 10% incentive bonus.

$$\begin{aligned}\text{Regular pay} &= \$5.50 \times 40 &&= \$220.00\\ \text{Incentive bonus} &= \$220.00 \times 0.10 &&= \underline{22.00}\\ \text{Gross earnings} & &&= \$242.00\end{aligned}$$

Production plans such as piecework or the standard hour plan fall under the general category of **incentive wage plans.** For workers engaged in production, it has long been evident that extra or sustained effort is possible only if some incentive exists. Numerous incentive wage plans have been developed, ranging from piecework to the profit-sharing plans of today. Some of the plans are discussed in the exercises.

The appropriate wage plan for a given institution depends upon a number of factors, including size, type of business, unionization of the work force, and competitive practices. Wage plans are continually changing, and this evolutionary process will continue as long as the free enterprise system exists.

Exercises for Section 6.2C

1. Max Goddard earns $6.35 per hour as a mechanic. Compute his gross earnings for a week in which he worked 36 hours.

2. Last week, Elsie Davis worked 32 hours, and the previous week she worked 28 hours. At a wage rate of $5.56 per hour, find her gross earnings for the two-week period.

3. Fred Geiger, a carpenter, worked the following hours during the past two weeks:

	Sun.	Mon.	Tues.	Wed.	Thurs.	Fri.	Sat.
Week 1	0	8	6	5	7.5	8	0
Week 2	0	6	6.5	4	8	8	0

Find his gross earnings for the two-week period if he earns $7.15 per hour.

4. John Killian earns $8.23 per hour working for a local air-conditioning contractor. Calculate his gross earnings for a two-week period during which he worked the following hours:

	Sun.	Mon.	Tues.	Wed.	Thurs.	Fri.	Sat.
Week 1	0	7	5.5	8	4.5	7	0
Week 2	0	6.5	4	7	8	2	0

5. Nell Phillips assembles electrical components at Mohawk Industries. She is paid on a straight piecework basis of $0.72 per component assembled. Find her gross earnings for a day during which she assembles 84 components.

6. Eugene Maycroft is paid on a straight piecework basis of $0.87 per piece. What are his gross earnings for a day during which his production is 47 pieces?

7. The Chandon Company employs Louise Reeves to operate a machine that produces components for electric motors. Louise is paid $0.58 per unit produced, with a guaranteed weekly wage of $260.00. Find her gross earnings for a week during which her production is as follows:

Sun.	Mon.	Tues.	Wed.	Thurs.	Fri.	Sat.
0	88	89	94	90	85	0

8. Dandy Draperies pays Ruby Nesbit, a sewing machine operator, $0.87 per unit produced, with a guaranteed weekly wage of $215.00. Calculate her gross earnings for a week during which her production rate is as follows:

Sun.	Mon.	Tues.	Wed.	Thurs.	Fri.	Sat.
0	50	52	47	51	48	0

9. Wilma Hogue is a packer for Wellington Industries. She is paid $0.19 per item packed for shipping with a guaranteed wage of $250.00 per week. Last week, she packed the following number of items each day:

Sun.	Mon.	Tues.	Wed.	Thurs.	Fri.	Sat.
0	257	265	261	259	255	0

Compute her gross earnings for the week.

10. Theresa Dinsmore is an assembler at the Merritt Company. She receives $0.77 per unit assembled, with a guaranteed wage of $225.00 per week. Find her gross earnings for a week during which she assembled the following number of units per day:

Sun.	Mon.	Tues.	Wed.	Thurs.	Fri.	Sat.
0	62	59	57	63	59	0

11. In problem 7, suppose the Chandon Company decides to convert to the standard hour plan and sets Louise Reeves's standard level of production at 480 units per week (40 hours). Using her piecework rate of $0.58 per unit produced, find her hourly wage.

12. In problem 8, calculate Ruby Nesbit's hourly wage (using her piecework rate of $0.87 per unit produced) if the company converts to the standard hour plan and sets Ruby's weekly (40 hours) production level at 245 units per week.

13. Clyde Shaw is an assembler in a manufacturing company that uses the standard hour plan. Clyde is paid $6.40 per hour, and his standard production level is 200 units per 40-hour workweek. Find his gross earnings for a week during which he produces 215 units.

14. Sally Greer is paid according to the standard hour plan. Her production level is 280 units per week (40 hours), and her hourly wage is $5.30. What are her gross earnings for a week during which she produces 294 units?

15. In problem 9, if Wellington Industries converts to the standard hour wage plan and sets Wilma Hogue's weekly (40-hour) production level at 1,400 units, find her gross earnings for a week during which she produces 1,390 units. (Hint: First find her hourly wage, using her piecework rate of $0.19 per unit.)

16. In problem 10, the Merritt Company converts to the standard hour wage plan and sets Theresa Dinsmore's weekly (40-hour) production level at 320 units. What are her gross earnings for a week during which she produces 352 units? (Hint: First find her hourly wage, using her piecework rate of $0.77 per unit.)

A common variation of the straight piecework wage plan is a method of wage compensation called **differential piecework.** This plan offers additional production incentive by providing two different piece-rates, one for all units up to a specified standard and a second (higher) one for all units if the worker's production exceeds the standard. For example, a worker might be paid $0.25 a unit if production is 100 units or less and $0.27 a unit if production exceeds 100 units. Thus, for 100 units, the worker receives $25.00, and for 101 units he or she receives $27.27.

17. Carol Rhodes is employed by Western Textiles, where she operates a knitting machine to produce infant footwear. She is paid under a differential piecework plan as follows: She receives $0.34 a unit on a day when her production is 120 units or less and $0.38 a unit for a day when her production exceeds 120 units. Find her gross earnings for a week during which her daily production is as follows:

Sun.	Mon.	Tues.	Wed.	Thurs.	Fri.	Sat.
0	125	116	117	130	120	0

18. Ken Methi is paid on a differential piecework basis of $0.40 per unit on a day when his production is 100 units or less and $0.43 per unit on a day when his production exceeds 100 units. Calculate his gross earnings for a week during which his daily production is as follows:

Sun.	Mon.	Tues.	Wed.	Thurs.	Fri.	Sat.
0	101	98	100	102	99	0

The *efficient production bonus* plan is another piecework incentive plan. Under this system, if a worker's production is less than or equal to a set standard, only a guaranteed hourly wage is paid. However, if the worker's production exceeds the standard, the hourly wage is increased by a predetermined percentage. For example, a worker might be paid \$6.10 per hour for a day when production is less than or equal to 25 units and 10% more per hour (\$6.71 per hour) for a day when production exceeds 25 units.

19. Ruth Goodnik operates a machine that assembles a component part used in the production of vacuum cleaners. She is paid \$4.80 an hour for an eight-hour day during which she produces 56 units or less. If her production exceeds 56 units, her hourly wage for the day is increased by 18%. Compute her gross earnings for a day during which she produces (a) 54 units and (b) 59 units.

20. Joe Gentner receives \$5.40 an hour for an eight-hour day during which he produces 35 units or less. If he produces more than 35 units, his hourly wage for the day is increased by 15%. Find his gross earnings for a day during which he produces (a) 34 units and (b) 36 units.

Section 6.3 Overtime

For some 47 million workers in the United States covered by the **Fair Labor Standards Act,** hours on the job must be separated into two categories: regular and overtime. First passed by Congress in 1938, this act (also known as the Federal Wage and Hour Law) establishes minimum wages, overtime pay, and other labor standards for every employee engaged in interstate or foreign commerce or in the production of goods for such commerce. Under the latest amendment to the act, regular hours consist of a workweek of 40 hours. Hours worked in excess of 40 hours during a workweek constitute **overtime** hours. The act specifies the rate of pay for overtime to be $1\frac{1}{2}$ times the rate for regular hours.

While the act is aimed primarily at wage earners, its overtime provisions also apply to certain categories of salaried and commissioned employees. For the latter, it is standard practice to convert their earnings to an hourly wage equivalent, and then compute regular and overtime wages.

Salaries

If a salary is paid to an employee for a specified number of hours to be worked per week, then the employee is covered by the Fair Labor Standards Act and must be paid the overtime rate for hours in excess of the specified workweek. An hourly rate of pay for salaried workers is determined by dividing the weekly salary (or the monthly salary reduced to a weekly basis) by the specified weekly hours.

Example 1 Vivian Moore is employed as a secretary. Her salary is \$208.80 for a specified workweek of 40 hours. Calculate her gross earnings for a week during which she worked 46 hours.

Solution

A salary of \$208.80 for a 40-hour workweek amounts to a regular hourly rate of $\frac{\$208.80}{40}$ = \$5.22 per hour. The overtime rate is $\$5.22 \times 1\frac{1}{2}$ = \$7.83 per hour. Thus,

$$\begin{aligned}
\text{Regular pay} &= \$5.22 \times 40 = \$208.80 \\
\text{Overtime pay} &= \$7.83 \times 6 = \underline{46.98} \\
\text{Gross earnings} &= \$255.78
\end{aligned}$$

Example 2 The Spring Pure Water Company pays one of its office workers a salary of \$728 per month. The salary is paid for a workweek of 40 hours, but during a two-week period, the following hours were worked:

	Sun.	Mon.	Tues.	Wed.	Thurs.	Fri.	Sat.
Week 1	0	10	7	10	8	8	4
Week 2	0	7	9	8	9	7	4

Calculate the gross earnings of the office worker if the pay period is biweekly.

Solution

The monthly salary is converted to an hourly rate in two steps:

$$\begin{aligned}
\text{Weekly salary} &= \$728 \times \tfrac{12}{52} = \$168.00 \\
\text{Hourly rate} &= \$168 \div 40 = \$\ \ 4.20 \\
\text{Overtime rate} &= \$4.20 \times 1\tfrac{1}{2} = \$\ \ 6.30
\end{aligned}$$

Week 1	Regular pay = \$4.20 × 40 =	\$168.00	
	Overtime pay = \$6.30 × 7 =	44.10	
	Subtotal		\$212.10
Week 2	Regular pay = \$4.20 × 40 =	\$168.00	
	Overtime pay = \$6.30 × 4 =	25.20	
	Subtotal		193.20
	Gross earnings		\$405.30

Commissions

"Outside" sales personnel (that is, sales representatives who spend most of their time away from their employer's place of business) are exempt from the Fair Labor Standards Act. However, "inside" sales personnel are covered by the act, and their commissions must be considered when calculating overtime pay. This is true whether the commissions are a percentage of total sales or sales in excess of a quota.

Example 3

A salesclerk for Gilbert's Department Store is paid \$176 a week for a 40-hour week and 3% of her sales in excess of \$700. Calculate her gross earnings for a week during which she worked 44 hours and recorded sales of \$1,844.

Solution

This is an inside sales position; hence, the employee is entitled to four hours overtime pay. To determine the overtime pay, we first calculate a regular hourly rate for both the salary and the commission, then multiply by $1\frac{1}{2}$. For the salary, the regular rate is $\frac{\$176}{40} = \$4.40$ per hour, and the overtime rate is $\$4.40 \times 1\frac{1}{2} = \$6.60$ per hour. The total commission for the week is $\$1{,}144 \times 0.03 = \$34.32$; thus, the "regular commission rate" is $\frac{\$34.32}{44} = \$0.78$, and the "overtime commission rate" is $\$0.78 \times 1\frac{1}{2} = \$1.17$.

Regular weekly pay	= \$4.40 × 40	= \$176.00	
Overtime weekly pay	= \$6.60 × 4	= 26.40	
Subtotal			\$202.40
Regular commission	= \$0.78 × 40	= \$ 31.20	
Overtime commission	= \$1.17 × 4	= 4.68	
Subtotal			35.88
Gross earnings			\$238.28

Wages

Overtime for employees paid an hourly wage is $1\frac{1}{2}$ times the hourly rate for hours in excess of a 40-hour workweek.

Example 4

A switchboard operator for a metropolitan telephone company earns \$3.66 an hour for a 40-hour workweek. Calculate her gross earnings for a week during which she worked 48 hours.

Solution

The overtime rate is $\$3.66 \times 1\frac{1}{2} = \$5.49$. Thus,

Regular wages	= \$3.66 × 40	= \$146.40
Overtime wages	= \$5.49 × 8	= 43.92
Gross earnings		= \$190.32

Many payroll employees compute the overtime wages of example 4 by multiplying the number of overtime hours by $1\frac{1}{2}$ instead of the hourly rate by $1\frac{1}{2}$. The result is the same.* For example,

Regular wages	= \$3.66 × 40 =	\$146.40
Overtime wages	= \$3.66 × 12 =	43.92 ($12 = 8 \times 1\frac{1}{2}$)
Gross earnings	=	\$190.32

Since employees are paid a higher rate for overtime, it is important that the employer keep accurate records of the hours worked. Most employers accomplish this by means of individual time sheets or by time clock cards. An example of a time card is shown in figure 6.3. A more sophisticated procedure utilizes an individual plastic card that is inserted into a timing device directly linked to a computer. The computer records and stores the time worked and during the payroll-run calculates the regular and overtime wages.

Figure 6.3
Time card

WEEKLY TIME CARD FROM .... TO ....
(DATE) (DATE)

(Notice-This card must be turned in to the proper authority before payment can be made)

EMPLOYEE'S NAME________ S.S. ACCT. NO.________

ADDRESS________

POSITION________ DEPT.________ BADGE NO.________

NAME OF EMPLOYER________

	A. M.		P. M.		Overtime		Total Hours	
	IN	OUT	IN	OUT	IN	OUT	REGULAR	OVERTIME
MONDAY								
TUESDAY								
WEDNESDAY								
THURSDAY								
FRIDAY								
SATURDAY								
SUNDAY								
I, the undersigned, certify that this is a true and accurate record of my working time for the period above mentioned.					WEEKLY TOTAL			

SIGNATURE________

Form W.T.C. Redi-Record Payroll Systems Inc. Oceanside, N.Y.

*This is an immediate consequence of the associative law of multiplication, which states that for any numbers a, b, and c,

$(a \times b) \times c = a \times (b \times c)$

In the regular calculation of overtime, we multiply: (Hourly rate × $1\frac{1}{2}$) × Hours worked.

However, by the associative law this is equivalent to: Hourly rate × ($1\frac{1}{2}$ × Hours worked).

Example 5 George Welch earns \$6.20 an hour for a 40-hour workweek. Calculate his gross earnings for the week using the information on the following time card.

WEEKLY TIME CARD FROM 3/7 (DATE) TO 3/13 (DATE)

(Notice-This card must be turned in to the proper authority before payment can be made)

Form W.T.C. Redi-Record Payroll Systems Inc. Oceanside, N.Y.

EMPLOYEE'S NAME George C. Welch S.S. ACCT. No. 321-54-9876

ADDRESS 110 Oak Street

POSITION ______ DEPT. Production BADGE No. 10479

NAME OF EMPLOYER ______

	A. M. IN	A. M. OUT	P. M. IN	P. M. OUT	Overtime IN	Overtime OUT	Total Hours REGULAR	Total Hours OVERTIME
MONDAY	8:00	12.01	12:30	4:30			8	
TUESDAY	8:02	12.00	12:30	4:30	6:00	9:30	8	3 1/2
WEDNESDAY	8:01	12.01	12:30	4:32	4:32	8:00	8	3 1/2
THURSDAY	8:00	12:00	12:31	4:31			8	
FRIDAY	8:00	12:05	12:35	4:30			8	
SATURDAY								
SUNDAY								
						WEEKLY TOTAL	40	7

I, the undersigned, certify that this is a true and accurate record of my working time for the period above mentioned.

SIGNATURE George C. Welch

Solution

The overtime rate is \$6.20 $\times$ $1\frac{1}{2}$ = \$9.30 per hour.

Regular wages = \$6.20 $\times$ 40 = \$248.00
Overtime wages = \$9.30 $\times$ 7 = 65.10
Gross earnings = \$313.10

While the wage and hour law defines overtime as work in excess of 40 hours per workweek, some wage agreements recognize other forms of overtime as well. "Time and a half" ($1\frac{1}{2}$ times the regular rate) may be paid for hours in excess of 8 hours per day, and "double time" (2 times the regular rate) is often paid for work on Sundays or holidays. Hours for which an employee receives time-and-a-half or double-time pay are still counted as part of the 40-hour workweek used to determine overtime wages.

Example 6 The time card of an employee indicated the following hours worked during the week of Sunday, June 30, through Saturday, July 6:

6/30	7/1	7/2	7/3	7/4	7/5	7/6
8	0	$8\frac{1}{2}$	8	$4\frac{1}{2}$	8	8

The regular hourly rate for the employee is $5.40, and he receives time and a half for work in excess of 8 hours a day or 40 hours per week, plus double time for Sundays or holidays. Find his gross earnings for the week.

Solution

The hours worked are distributed as regular (R), overtime or time and a half (OT), and double time (DT).

	6/30	7/1	7/2	7/3	7/4	7/5	7/6	Total Hours	Rate	Total Wages
R			8	8		8	3	27	$ 5.40	$145.80
OT			$\frac{1}{2}$				5	$5\frac{1}{2}$	8.10	44.55
DT	8				$4\frac{1}{2}$			$12\frac{1}{2}$	10.80	135.00
								Gross earnings		$325.35

Note that the $4\frac{1}{2}$ double-time hours on 7/4 are because of a holiday, and that only 3 of the 8 hours worked on 7/6 are regular hours since the employee has already worked 37 hours of the 40-hour workweek during the preceding six days.

Employees on piecework also receive overtime pay for work in excess of a 40-hour workweek. To calculate overtime pay, the total wages earned by piecework first must be converted to an hourly rate; the overtime rate is $1\frac{1}{2}$ times the hourly equivalent.

Example 7 An employee on piecework earns \$0.87 per piece. What are his gross earnings for a week during which he works 50 hours and his production is 400 pieces?

Solution

The total amount earned by piecework during the week is $\$0.87 \times 400 = \$348.00$. Thus, the regular hourly rate is $\frac{\$348.00}{50} = \$6.96$ per hour, and the overtime rate is $\$6.96 \times 1\frac{1}{2} = \$10.44$ per hour.

Regular wages	= \$ 6.96 × 40	= \$278.40
Overtime wages	= \$10.44 × 10	= \$104.40
Gross earnings		= \$382.80

Example 8 Donna Appleton is paid a piece-rate of \$0.32 with a guaranteed weekly wage of \$280.00. She produced 850 pieces during a week that she worked 44 hours. Calculate Donna's gross earnings for the week.

Solution

The guaranteed weekly wage amounts to $\frac{\$280.00}{40} = \$7.00$ per hour. The total amount earned by piecework is $\$0.32 \times 850 = \$272.00$, which converts to only $\frac{\$272.00}{44} = \$6.18$ per hour. Since this is less than the guaranteed wage of \$7.00 per hour, she is paid the guaranteed wage. The overtime rate is $\$7.00 \times 1\frac{1}{2} = \$10.50$.

Regular wages	= \$7 × 40	= \$280
Overtime wages	= \$10.50 × 4	= 42
Gross earnings		= \$322

Exercises for Section 6.3

1. John James is paid a salary of \$234.40 per 40-hour workweek. Calculate his gross earnings for a week during which he works 44 hours.

2. Diane Mathis is a salaried employee at the Decker Company, where she earns \$236.80 per 40-hour workweek. Find her gross earnings for a week during which she works 46 hours.

3. Frank Larkin is an office manager at the Bissett Paint Company. He is paid a monthly salary of $1,976 for a workweek of 40 hours. The pay period at the Bissett Company is biweekly, and during the last two-week period Frank worked the following hours:

	Sun.	Mon.	Tues.	Wed.	Thurs.	Fri.	Sat.
Week 1	0	8	6	7	6	8	6
Week 2	0	7	8	8	8	7	5

Compute Frank's gross earnings for this two-week period.

4. The Amazon Marine Equipment Company pays one of its office workers a monthly salary of $1,456 for a workweek of 40 hours. If the pay period at Amazon is biweekly, find the worker's gross earnings for the following two-week period:

	Sun.	Mon.	Tues.	Wed.	Thurs.	Fri.	Sat.
Week 1	0	7	8	6	7	8	6
Week 2	0	8	8	8	8	6	6

5. Robinson's Metal Works pays Joan Schyler an annual salary of $11,648. The workweek at Robinson's is 40 hours, and the pay period is biweekly. Find Joan's gross earnings for a pay period during which she worked the following hours:

	Sun.	Mon.	Tues.	Wed.	Thurs.	Fri.	Sat.
Week 1	0	8	8	6	8	7	7
Week 2	0	8	8	7	7	6	6

6. Hallamore Industries pays one of its branch office managers an annual salary of $37,856 for a 40-hour workweek. The pay period at Hallamore is biweekly, and during the last two weeks the manager worked the following hours:

	Sun.	Mon.	Tues.	Wed.	Thurs.	Fri.	Sat.
Week 1	0	8	8	7	7	7	8
Week 2	0	8	7	7	6	8	7

Calculate his gross earnings for this two-week period.

7. Vernon Kyle works in the sporting goods section of a department store. He is paid a salary of $340 for a 40-hour workweek, plus a commission of 4% of sales in excess of $1,500. Find his gross earnings for a week during which he works 50 hours and sells $1,725 worth of merchandise.

8. Isabel Keene sells leisure wear at the Fun-N-Frolic Shoppe. She receives a salary of $328 per 40-hour workweek, plus a commission of 2.5% of sales in excess of $600. Calculate her gross earnings for a week during which she works 45 hours and records sales of $1,176.

9. The sales personnel at Apple's Appliance Store are paid $184 per 40-hour workweek, plus a commission of 2.5% of sales in excess of $2,000. What are the gross earnings of a sales representative for a week during which the representative works 43 hours and sells $2,688 worth of merchandise?

10. Ed Alexander worked 42 hours last week at the Futura Furniture Store. He is paid a salary of $180 per 40-hour workweek, plus a commission of 3% of sales in excess of $1,800. If he recorded sales for the week totaling $2,668, what were his gross earnings?

11. If Bruce Jackson is paid $4.80 per hour for a 40-hour workweek, what are his gross earnings for a week during which he works 48 hours?

12. Find Camille Jordan's gross earnings for a week during which she works 43 hours, if she receives $5.40 per hour for a specified 40-hour workweek.

13. Doug Johnson earns $6.60 per hour for a 40-hour workweek. Calculate his gross earnings for a week when his time report is as follows:

TIME REPORT							
Week Beginning 7/15						Week Ending 7/21	
Day of Week	*Time Worked*						*Total Hours*
	Start	*Stop*	*Start*	*Stop*	*Start*	*Stop*	
Sunday							
Monday	7:00	11:30	12:30	3:00			
Tuesday	7:00	11:30	12:30	3:00			
Wednesday	7:00	11:30	12:30	3:00	3:00	7:00	
Thursday	7:00	11:30	12:30	3:00	3:00	4:30	
Friday	7:00	11:30	12:30	3:00			
Saturday	7:00	11:30					
Name: Johnson, Douglas M.						Total	
I hereby certify that the above is correct. Employee Signature: Douglas M. Johnson							

14. Diane Gaskins filed the following time report for the week of April 15 through April 21. If she is paid $8.20 per hour for a 40-hour workweek, compute her gross earnings for the week.

TIME REPORT							
Week Beginning 4/15						Week Ending 4/21	
Day of Week	*Time Worked*						*Total Hours*
	Start	*Stop*	*Start*	*Stop*	*Start*	*Stop*	
Sunday							
Monday	8:00	12:02	1:15	5:15	7:00	8:30	
Tuesday	8:02	12:04	1:00	5:00			
Wednesday	8:00	12:00	1:00	5:00	7:00	8:00	
Thursday	8:00	12:00	1:10	5:10	7:00	9:00	
Friday	9:04	12:05	2:00	6:00			
Saturday	9:00	12:00	1:00	3:00			
Name: Gaskins, Diane P.						Total	
I hereby certify that the above is correct. Employee Signature: *Diane P. Gaskins*							

15. The Buckline Company pays its employees time and a half for work in excess of 8 hours a day or 40 hours a week plus double time for Sundays and holidays. Richard Sneyd, an accountant at Buckline, is paid $5.80 per hour. Compute his gross earnings for the week of Sunday, December 30, through Saturday, January 5, during which he worked the following hours:

	12/30	12/31	1/1	1/2	1/3	1/4	1/5
Hours	4	4	6	$7\frac{1}{2}$	9	$8\frac{1}{2}$	4

16. Julia Mays is employed at the Fulwood Company, where she receives $4.40 per hour with time and a half for work in excess of 8 hours per day or 40 hours per week and double time for Sundays and holidays. Find her gross earnings for the week of Sunday, July 1, through Saturday, July 7, during which she worked the following hours:

	7/1	7/2	7/3	7/4	7/5	7/6	7/7
Hours	3	6	$8\frac{1}{2}$	5	$9\frac{1}{2}$	4	0

17. Gene Walters is an assembler at Fairline Industries, where he is paid on a piecework basis of $0.48 per part assembled. Last week, he worked 48 hours and assembled 558 units. Calculate his gross earnings for the week.

18. An employee at the Brookwood Company is paid a piecework rate of $0.75 per piece. Find the gross earnings for a week during which the person worked 45 hours and produced 408 units.

19. Lillian Brink is paid a piece-rate of $0.85 per piece with a guaranteed weekly wage of $312.00. What are her gross earnings for a week during which she works 46 hours and produces 420 pieces?

20. The Waterford Company pays its employees in the shipping department $0.94 per unit packed for shipment, with a guaranteed weekly wage of $220.00. Compute the gross earnings of an employee for a week during which he works 47 hours and packs 278 units.

21. Maude Richardson is paid a piece-rate of $0.80 per piece with a guaranteed weekly wage of $222.00. Find her gross earnings for a week during which she works 42 hours and produces 294 pieces.

22. John Lopez works for the Winters Company, where he is paid a piece-rate of $0.48 per piece with a guaranteed weekly wage of $148.00. Calculate his gross earnings for a week during which he works 45 hours and produces 344 pieces.

Section 6.4 Net earnings

Following the computation of gross earnings, the next step in preparation of the payroll is the calculation of net earnings. As previously stated, net earnings are gross earnings less deductions. Deductions are amounts that the employer withholds from the employee's earnings. The payroll department subtracts deductions from gross earnings and remits the difference, or net earnings, to the employee. A record is maintained of all deductions, and periodically, these sums are sent to the appropriate agency.

Deductions may be voluntary or required by law. We examine the latter category first.

Federal income tax

The federal government has authorized employers to withhold a percentage of the employee's gross earnings each payday as advance payment of the employee's **federal income tax.**

The percentage subtracted from gross earnings depends on three factors: (1) gross earnings, (2) marital status, and (3) number of withholding allowances. A **withholding allowance*** reduces the amount of tax withheld from the employee's earnings. The government grants one withholding allowance for

*Formerly called a "withholding exemption." Form W-4 now uses the term "withholding allowance". See figure 6.4.

each person supported by the employee and additional allowances on the basis of certain special circumstances. At the time of employment, each employee is required to complete an Employee's Withholding Allowance Certificate (Form W-4) on which the employee declares the number of allowances he or she wishes to claim (see figure 6.4). A person with a spouse and two children may claim four allowances, one for the employee and one for each of the other family members. If both spouses work, then the couple may split the allowances as they see fit.

A detailed discussion of withholding allowances and eligible dependents is beyond the scope of this text, but it should be noted that an employee may claim fewer allowances than the number to which he or she is entitled. Since the amount of tax withheld is only an approximation, the employee may owe additional taxes on April 15, the deadline for filing income tax returns. By claiming fewer allowances, a greater amount is withheld, thus reducing the likelihood of owing additional tax upon filing the return. The government refunds any amount in excess of the taxes the employee owes.

To assist the payroll clerk in computing the amount of income tax to be withheld, the Internal Revenue Service has prepared tables. The table most frequently used is the Wage Bracket Table. This table categorizes employees by the three factors previously mentioned: marital status, gross earnings, and number of withholding allowances. Portions of this table are shown in tables 6.1 through 6.3 (pp. 184–189).

To illustrate the use of these tables, consider a married employee claiming four withholding allowances who is paid weekly a salary of $325. To determine the tax to be withheld, we locate the table entitled Married Persons—Weekly Payroll (table 6.2) and find the employee's wage bracket in the left column headed "And the wages are."* A weekly salary of $325 falls in the wage bracket "at least $320 but less than $330." We then proceed to the right along this line until we reach the column for four allowances. The amount to be withheld is $16.00.

*As used in this table, wages means all forms of compensation, including salaries and commissions.

Figure 6.4
Employee's Withholding Allowance Certificate (Form W-4)

1989 Form W-4

Department of the Treasury
Internal Revenue Service

Purpose. Complete Form W-4 so that your employer can withhold the correct amount of Federal income tax from your pay.

Exemption From Withholding. Read line 6 of the certificate below to see if you can claim exempt status. If exempt, only complete the certificate; but do not complete lines 4 and 5. No Federal income tax will be withheld from your pay.

Basic Instructions. Employees who are not exempt should complete the Personal Allowances Worksheet. Additional worksheets are provided on page 2 for employees to adjust their withholding allowances based on itemized deductions, adjustments to income, or two-earner/two-job situations. Complete all worksheets that apply to your situation. The worksheets will help you figure the number of withholding allowances you are entitled to claim. However, you may claim fewer allowances than this.

Head of Household. Generally, you may claim head of household filing status on your tax return only if you are unmarried and pay more than 50% of the costs of keeping up a home for yourself and your dependent(s) or other qualifying individuals.

Nonwage Income. If you have a large amount of nonwage income, such as interest or dividends, you should consider making estimated tax payments using Form 1040-ES. Otherwise, you may find that you owe additional tax at the end of the year.

Two-Earner/Two-Jobs. If you have a working spouse or more than one job, figure the total number of allowances you are entitled to claim on all jobs using worksheets from only one Form W-4. This total should be divided among all jobs. Your withholding will usually be most accurate when all allowances are claimed on the W-4 filed for the highest paying job and zero allowances are claimed for the others.

Advance Earned Income Credit. If you are eligible for this credit, you can receive it added to your paycheck throughout the year. For details, obtain Form W-5 from your employer.

Check Your Withholding. After your W-4 takes effect, you can use **Publication 919,** Is My Withholding Correct for 1989?, to see how the dollar amount you are having withheld compares to your estimated total annual tax. Call 1-800-424-3676 (in Hawaii and Alaska, check your local telephone directory) to obtain this publication.

Personal Allowances Worksheet

A Enter "1" for **yourself** if no one else can claim you as a dependent . . . . . A ______

B Enter "1" if:
1. You are single and have only one job; or
2. You are married, have only one job, and your spouse does not work; or
3. Your wages from a second job or your spouse's wages (or the total of both) are $2,500 or less.

. . . . . B ______

C Enter "1" for your **spouse.** But, you may choose to enter "0" if you are married and have either a working spouse or more than one job (this may help you avoid having too little tax withheld) . . . . . C ______

D Enter number of **dependents** (other than your spouse or yourself) whom you will claim on your tax return . . . . . D ______

E Enter "1" if you will file as a **head of household** on your tax return (see conditions under "Head of Household," above) . . E ______

F Enter "1" if you have at least $1,500 of **child or dependent care expenses** for which you plan to claim a credit . . . . F ______

G Add lines A through F and enter total here . . . . . ▶ G ______

For accuracy, do all worksheets that apply.

- If you plan to **itemize or claim adjustments to income** and want to reduce your withholding, turn to the Deductions and Adjustments Worksheet on page 2.
- If you are **single** and have **more than one job** and your combined earnings from all jobs exceed $25,000 OR if you are **married** and have a **working spouse or more than one job,** and the combined earnings from all jobs exceed $40,000, then turn to the Two-Earner/Two-Job Worksheet on page 2 if you want to avoid having too little tax withheld.
- If **neither** of the above situations applies to you, **stop here** and enter the number from line G on line 4 of Form W-4 below.

----- **Cut here and give the certificate to your employer. Keep the top portion for your records.** -----

Form **W-4**
Department of the Treasury
Internal Revenue Service

Employee's Withholding Allowance Certificate

▶ **For Privacy Act and Paperwork Reduction Act Notice, see reverse.**

OMB No. 1545-0010
1989

1 Type or print your first name and middle initial | Last name | 2 Your social security number

Home address (number and street or rural route)

City or town, state, and ZIP code

3 Marital Status: ☐ Single ☐ Married ☐ Married, but withhold at higher Single rate.
Note: *If married, but legally separated, or spouse is a nonresident alien, check the Single box.*

4 Total number of allowances you are claiming (from line G above or from the Worksheets on back if they apply) . . . | 4 |

5 Additional amount, if any, you want deducted from each pay . . . . . | 5 | $

6 I claim exemption from withholding and I certify that I meet **ALL** of the following conditions for exemption:
- Last year I had a right to a refund of **ALL** Federal income tax withheld because I had **NO** tax liability; **AND**
- This year I expect a refund of **ALL** Federal income tax withheld because I expect to have **NO** tax liability; **AND**
- This year if my income exceeds $500 and includes nonwage income, another person cannot claim me as a dependent.

If you meet all of the above conditions, enter the year effective and "EXEMPT" here . . . . . ▶ | 6 | 19

7 Are you a full-time student? **(Note:** *Full-time students are not automatically exempt.)* . . . . . | 7 | ☐**Yes** ☐**No**

Under penalties of perjury, I certify that I am entitled to the number of withholding allowances claimed on this certificate or entitled to claim exempt status.

Employee's signature ▶ **Date ▶** , 198

8 Employer's name and address **(Employer:** Complete 8 and 10 **only if sending to IRS)** | 9 Office code (optional) | **10** Employer identification number

Figure 6.4
(continued)

Form W-4 (1989)

Deductions and Adjustments Worksheet

Note: *Use this worksheet only if you plan to itemize deductions or claim adjustments to income on your 1989 tax return.*

1	Enter an estimate of your 1989 itemized deductions. These include: qualifying home mortgage interest, 20% of personal interest, charitable contributions, state and local taxes (but not sales taxes), medical expenses in excess of 7.5% of your income, and miscellaneous deductions (most miscellaneous deductions are now deductible only in excess of 2% of your income)	1	$
2	Enter: { $5,200 if married filing jointly or qualifying widow(er); $4,550 if head of household; $3,100 if single; $2,600 if married filing separately }	2	$
3	**Subtract** line 2 from line 1. If line 2 is greater than line 1, enter zero	3	$
4	Enter an estimate of your 1989 adjustments to income. These include alimony paid and deductible IRA contributions	4	$
5	**Add** lines 3 and 4 and enter the total	5	$
6	Enter an estimate of your 1989 nonwage income (such as dividends or interest income)	6	$
7	**Subtract** line 6 from line 5. Enter the result, but not less than zero	7	$
8	**Divide** the amount on line 7 by $2,000 and enter the result here. Drop any fraction	8	
9	Enter the number from Personal Allowances Worksheet, line G, on page 1	9	
10	**Add** lines 8 and 9 and enter the total here. If you plan to use the Two-Earner/Two-Job Worksheet, also enter the total on line 1, below. Otherwise, **stop here** and enter this total on Form W-4, line 4 on page 1	10	

Two-Earner/Two-Job Worksheet

Note: *Use this worksheet only if the instructions at line G on page 1 direct you here.*

1	Enter the number from line G on page 1 (or from line 10 above if you used the Deductions and Adjustments Worksheet)	1	
2	Find the number in **Table 1** below that applies to the **LOWEST** paying job and enter it here	2	
3	If line 1 is **GREATER THAN OR EQUAL TO** line 2, subtract line 2 from line 1. Enter the result here (if zero, enter "0") and on Form W-4, line 4, on page 1. **DO NOT** use the rest of this worksheet.	3	

Note: *If line 1 is **LESS THAN** line 2, enter "0" on Form W-4, line 4, on page 1. Complete lines 4–9 to calculate the additional dollar withholding necessary to avoid a year-end tax bill.*

4	Enter the number from line 2 of this worksheet	4	
5	Enter the number from line 1 of this worksheet	5	
6	**Subtract** line 5 from line 4	6	
7	Find the amount in **Table 2** below that applies to the **HIGHEST** paying job and enter it here	7	$
8	**Multiply** line 7 by line 6 and enter the result here. This is the additional annual withholding amount needed	8	$
9	Divide line 8 by the number of pay periods each year. (For example, divide by 26 if you are paid every other week.) Enter the result here and on Form W-4, line 5, page 1. This is the additional amount to be withheld from each paycheck	9	$

Table 1: Two-Earner/Two-Job Worksheet

Married Filing Jointly		All Others	
If wages from **LOWEST** paying job are—	Enter on line 2 above	If wages from **LOWEST** paying job are—	Enter on line 2 above
0 - $4,000	0	0 - $4,000	0
4,001 - 8,000	1	4,001 - 8,000	1
8,001 - 18,000	2	8,001 - 13,000	2
18,001 - 21,000	3	13,001 - 15,000	3
21,001 - 23,000	4	15,001 - 19,000	4
23,001 - 25,000	5	19,001 and over	5
25,001 - 27,000	6		
27,001 - 32,000	7		
32,001 - 38,000	8		
38,001 - 42,000	9		
42,001 and over	10		

Table 2: Two-Earner/Two-Job Worksheet

Married Filing Jointly		All Others	
If wages from **HIGHEST** paying job are—	Enter on line 7 above	If wages from **HIGHEST** paying job are—	Enter on line 7 above
0 - $40,000	$300	0 - $23,000	$300
40,001 - 84,000	560	23,001 - 50,000	560
84,001 and over	660	50,001 and over	660

Privacy Act and Paperwork Reduction Act Notice.—We ask for this information to carry out the Internal Revenue laws of the United States. We may give the information to the Department of Justice for civil or criminal litigation and to cities, states, and the District of Columbia for use in administering their tax laws. You are required to give this information to your employer.

Example 1 Derek Tracy is single and claims one withholding allowance (S-1). His job at the Carson Publishing Company pays \$12.22 per hour for a 40-hour workweek. Because of a broken press, he worked 56 hours during one workweek. How much income tax was withheld for that weekly pay period?

Solution

The tax to be withheld is found in table 6.1, Single Persons—Weekly Payroll Period, but first we must calculate Derek's gross earnings for the week to determine the appropriate wage bracket. The regular rate is \$12.22, and the overtime rate is $\$12.22 \times 1\frac{1}{2} = \$18.33$ per hour; hence,

Regular wages	= \$12.22 × 40	= \$488.80
Overtime wages	= \$18.33 × 16	= 293.28
Gross earnings		= \$782.08

The gross earnings lie in the wage bracket of "at least \$780 but less than \$790." The tax for one allowance is \$157.00.

Example 2 Perry Watson sells chemical products on a straight commission of 30%. During the last biweekly pay period, his sales were \$748 for the first week and \$1,232 for the second week. Perry's wife works in an office, and they have one child. How much tax should be deducted from Perry's gross earnings if he claims two allowances on his W-4 form?

Solution

Perry's total sales for the pay period are \$1,980.

Commissions = \$1,980 × 0.30 = \$594

In the table entitled Married Persons—Biweekly Payroll Period (table 6.3), Perry's tax bracket is "at least \$580 but less than \$600." His tax for two allowances is \$47.00.

Social Security The economic depression of the 1930s spawned a number of emergency measures and legislation. Perhaps the most significant of these was the **Federal Insurance Contributions Act (FICA)** of 1937. Better known as the Social Security Act, it established a fund to provide monthly benefits to retired or disabled workers and to pay burial and survivors' benefits to the surviving family of a deceased worker. A recent amendment to the act provides health insurance benefits under the Medicare Program.

Table 6.1 Single Persons—Weekly Payroll Period

And the wages are–		And the number of withholding allowances claimed is–										
At least	But less than-	0	1	2	3	4	5	6	7	8	9	10
		The amount of income tax to be withheld shall be–										
$0	$25	$0	$0	$0	$0	$0	$0	$0	$0	$0	$0	$0
25	30	1	0	0	0	0	0	0	0	0	0	0
30	35	2	0	0	0	0	0	0	0	0	0	0
35	40	2	0	0	0	0	0	0	0	0	0	0
40	45	3	0	0	0	0	0	0	0	0	0	0
45	50	4	0	0	0	0	0	0	0	0	0	0
50	55	5	0	0	0	0	0	0	0	0	0	0
55	60	5	0	0	0	0	0	0	0	0	0	0
60	65	6	0	0	0	0	0	0	0	0	0	0
65	70	7	1	0	0	0	0	0	0	0	0	0
70	75	8	2	0	0	0	0	0	0	0	0	0
75	80	8	3	0	0	0	0	0	0	0	0	0
80	85	9	3	0	0	0	0	0	0	0	0	0
85	90	10	4	0	0	0	0	0	0	0	0	0
90	95	11	5	0	0	0	0	0	0	0	0	0
95	100	11	6	0	0	0	0	0	0	0	0	0
100	105	12	6	1	0	0	0	0	0	0	0	0
105	110	13	7	1	0	0	0	0	0	0	0	0
110	115	14	8	2	0	0	0	0	0	0	0	0
115	120	14	9	3	0	0	0	0	0	0	0	0
120	125	15	9	4	0	0	0	0	0	0	0	0
125	130	16	10	4	0	0	0	0	0	0	0	0
130	135	17	11	5	0	0	0	0	0	0	0	0
135	140	17	12	6	0	0	0	0	0	0	0	0
140	145	18	12	7	1	0	0	0	0	0	0	0
145	150	19	13	7	2	0	0	0	0	0	0	0
150	155	20	14	8	2	0	0	0	0	0	0	0
155	160	20	15	9	3	0	0	0	0	0	0	0
160	165	21	15	10	4	0	0	0	0	0	0	0
165	170	22	16	10	5	0	0	0	0	0	0	0
170	175	23	17	11	5	0	0	0	0	0	0	0
175	180	23	18	12	6	0	0	0	0	0	0	0
180	185	24	18	13	7	1	0	0	0	0	0	0
185	190	25	19	13	8	2	0	0	0	0	0	0
190	195	26	20	14	8	3	0	0	0	0	0	0
195	200	26	21	15	9	3	0	0	0	0	0	0
200	210	28	22	16	10	5	0	0	0	0	0	0
210	220	29	23	18	12	6	0	0	0	0	0	0
220	230	31	25	19	13	8	2	0	0	0	0	0
230	240	32	26	21	15	9	3	0	0	0	0	0
240	250	34	28	22	16	11	5	0	0	0	0	0
250	260	35	29	24	18	12	6	0	0	0	0	0
260	270	37	31	25	19	14	8	2	0	0	0	0
270	280	38	32	27	21	15	9	3	0	0	0	0
280	290	40	34	28	22	17	11	5	0	0	0	0
290	300	41	35	30	24	18	12	6	1	0	0	0
300	310	43	37	31	25	20	14	8	2	0	0	0
310	320	44	38	33	27	21	15	9	4	0	0	0
320	330	46	40	34	28	23	17	11	5	0	0	0
330	340	47	41	36	30	24	18	12	7	1	0	0
340	350	49	43	37	31	26	20	14	8	2	0	0
350	360	50	44	39	33	27	21	15	10	4	0	0
360	370	52	46	40	34	29	23	17	11	5	0	0
370	380	53	47	42	36	30	24	18	13	7	1	0
380	390	56	49	43	37	32	26	20	14	8	3	0
390	400	58	50	45	39	33	27	21	16	10	4	0
400	410	61	52	46	40	35	29	23	17	11	6	0
410	420	64	53	48	42	36	30	24	19	13	7	1
420	430	67	56	49	43	38	32	26	20	14	9	3
430	440	70	59	51	45	39	33	27	22	16	10	4
440	450	72	62	52	46	41	35	29	23	17	12	6
450	460	75	64	54	48	42	36	30	25	19	13	7
460	470	78	67	56	49	44	38	32	26	20	15	9
470	480	81	70	59	51	45	39	33	28	22	16	10
480	490	84	73	62	52	47	41	35	29	23	18	12
490	500	86	76	65	54	48	42	36	31	25	19	13
500	510	89	78	68	57	50	44	38	32	26	21	15
510	520	92	81	70	60	51	45	39	34	28	22	16
520	530	95	84	73	62	53	47	41	35	29	24	18
530	540	98	87	76	65	54	48	42	37	31	25	19

Table 6.1 *(continued)*

And the wages are–		And the number of withholding allowances claimed is–										
At least	But less than	0	1	2	3	4	5	6	7	8	9	10
		The amount of income tax to be withheld shall be–										
$540	$550	$100	$90	$79	$68	$57	$50	$44	$38	$32	$27	$21
550	560	103	92	82	71	60	51	45	40	34	28	22
560	570	106	95	84	74	63	53	47	41	35	30	24
570	580	109	98	87	76	66	55	48	43	37	31	25
580	590	112	101	90	79	68	58	50	44	38	33	27
590	600	114	104	93	82	71	60	51	46	40	34	28
600	610	117	106	96	85	74	63	53	47	41	36	30
610	620	120	109	98	88	77	66	55	49	43	37	31
620	630	123	112	101	90	80	69	58	50	44	39	33
630	640	126	115	104	93	82	72	61	52	46	40	34
640	650	128	118	107	96	85	74	64	53	47	42	36
650	660	131	120	110	99	88	77	66	56	49	43	37
660	670	134	123	112	102	91	80	69	59	50	45	39
670	680	137	126	115	104	94	83	72	61	52	46	40
680	690	140	129	118	107	96	86	75	64	53	48	42
690	700	142	132	121	110	99	88	78	67	56	49	43
700	710	145	134	124	113	102	91	80	70	59	51	45
710	720	148	137	126	116	105	94	83	73	62	52	46
720	730	151	140	129	118	108	97	86	75	65	54	48
730	740	154	143	132	121	110	100	89	78	67	57	49
740	750	156	146	135	124	113	102	92	81	70	59	51
750	760	159	148	138	127	116	105	94	84	73	62	52
760	770	162	151	140	130	119	108	97	87	76	65	54
770	780	165	154	143	132	122	111	100	89	79	68	57
780	790	168	157	146	135	124	114	103	92	81	71	60
790	800	170	160	149	138	127	116	106	95	84	73	63
800	810	173	162	152	141	130	119	108	98	87	76	65
810	820	176	165	154	144	133	122	111	101	90	79	68
820	830	179	168	157	146	136	125	114	103	93	82	71
830	840	182	171	160	149	138	128	117	106	95	85	74
840	850	184	174	163	152	141	130	120	109	98	87	77
850	860	187	176	166	155	144	133	122	112	101	90	79
860	870	190	179	168	158	147	136	125	115	104	93	82
870	880	193	182	171	160	150	139	128	117	107	96	85
880	890	196	185	174	163	152	142	131	120	109	99	88
890	900	199	188	177	166	155	144	134	123	112	101	91
900	910	202	190	180	169	158	147	136	126	115	104	93
910	920	205	193	182	172	161	150	139	129	118	107	96
920	930	209	196	185	174	164	153	142	131	121	110	99
930	940	212	199	188	177	166	156	145	134	123	113	102
940	950	215	203	191	180	169	158	148	137	126	115	105
950	960	219	206	194	183	172	161	150	140	129	118	107
960	970	222	209	197	186	175	164	153	143	132	121	110
970	980	225	213	200	188	178	167	156	145	135	124	113
980	990	229	216	203	191	180	170	159	148	137	127	116
990	1,000	232	219	206	194	183	172	162	151	140	129	119
1,000	1,010	235	222	210	197	186	175	164	154	143	132	121
1,010	1,020	238	226	213	200	189	178	167	157	146	135	124
1,020	1,030	242	229	216	204	192	181	170	159	149	138	127
1,030	1,040	245	232	220	207	194	184	173	162	151	141	130
1,040	1,050	248	236	223	210	198	186	176	165	154	143	133
1,050	1,060	252	239	226	214	201	189	178	168	157	146	135
1,060	1,070	255	242	230	217	204	192	181	171	160	149	138
1,070	1,080	258	246	233	220	207	195	184	173	163	152	141
1,080	1,090	262	249	236	223	211	198	187	176	165	155	144
1,090	1,100	265	252	239	227	214	201	190	179	168	157	147
1,100	1,110	268	255	243	230	217	205	192	182	171	160	149
1,110	1,120	271	259	246	233	221	208	195	185	174	163	152
1,120	1,130	275	262	249	237	224	211	199	187	177	166	155
1,130	1,140	278	265	253	240	227	215	202	190	179	169	158
1,140	1,150	281	269	256	243	231	218	205	193	182	171	161
1,150	1,160	285	272	259	247	234	221	208	196	185	174	163
1,160	1,170	288	275	263	250	237	224	212	199	188	177	166
1,170	1,180	291	279	266	253	240	228	215	202	191	180	169
1,180	1,190	295	282	269	256	244	231	218	206	193	183	172
1,190	1,200	298	285	272	260	247	234	222	209	196	185	175
$1,200 and over		Other IRS tables, not included in this text, must be used.										

Table 6.2 Married Persons—Weekly Payroll Period

And the wages are–		And the number of withholding allowances claimed is–										
At least	But less than	0	1	2	3	4	5	6	7	8	9	10
		The amount of income tax to be withheld shall be–										
$0	$65	$0	$0	$0	$0	$0	$0	$0	$0	$0	$0	$0
65	70	1	0	0	0	0	0	0	0	0	0	0
70	75	2	0	0	0	0	0	0	0	0	0	0
75	80	2	0	0	0	0	0	0	0	0	0	0
80	85	3	0	0	0	0	0	0	0	0	0	0
85	90	4	0	0	0	0	0	0	0	0	0	0
90	95	5	0	0	0	0	0	0	0	0	0	0
95	100	5	0	0	0	0	0	0	0	0	0	0
100	105	6	0	0	0	0	0	0	0	0	0	0
105	110	7	1	0	0	0	0	0	0	0	0	0
110	115	8	2	0	0	0	0	0	0	0	0	0
115	120	8	3	0	0	0	0	0	0	0	0	0
120	125	9	3	0	0	0	0	0	0	0	0	0
125	130	10	4	0	0	0	0	0	0	0	0	0
130	135	11	5	0	0	0	0	0	0	0	0	0
135	140	11	6	0	0	0	0	0	0	0	0	0
140	145	12	6	1	0	0	0	0	0	0	0	0
145	150	13	7	1	0	0	0	0	0	0	0	0
150	155	14	8	2	0	0	0	0	0	0	0	0
155	160	14	9	3	0	0	0	0	0	0	0	0
160	165	15	9	4	0	0	0	0	0	0	0	0
165	170	16	10	4	0	0	0	0	0	0	0	0
170	175	17	11	5	0	0	0	0	0	0	0	0
175	180	17	12	6	0	0	0	0	0	0	0	0
180	185	18	12	7	1	0	0	0	0	0	0	0
185	190	19	13	7	2	0	0	0	0	0	0	0
190	195	20	14	8	2	0	0	0	0	0	0	0
195	200	20	15	9	3	0	0	0	0	0	0	0
200	210	22	16	10	4	0	0	0	0	0	0	0
210	220	23	17	11	6	0	0	0	0	0	0	0
220	230	25	19	13	7	1	0	0	0	0	0	0
230	240	26	20	14	9	3	0	0	0	0	0	0
240	250	28	22	16	10	4	0	0	0	0	0	0
250	260	29	23	17	12	6	0	0	0	0	0	0
260	270	31	25	19	13	7	2	0	0	0	0	0
270	280	32	26	20	15	9	3	0	0	0	0	0
280	290	34	28	22	16	10	5	0	0	0	0	0
290	300	35	29	23	18	12	6	0	0	0	0	0
300	310	37	31	25	19	13	8	2	0	0	0	0
310	320	38	32	26	21	15	9	3	0	0	0	0
320	330	40	34	28	22	16	11	5	0	0	0	0
330	340	41	35	29	24	18	12	6	1	0	0	0
340	350	43	37	31	25	19	14	8	2	0	0	0
350	360	44	38	32	27	21	15	9	4	0	0	0
360	370	46	40	34	28	22	17	11	5	0	0	0
370	380	47	41	35	30	24	18	12	7	1	0	0
380	390	49	43	37	31	25	20	14	8	2	0	0
390	400	50	44	38	33	27	21	15	10	4	0	0
400	410	52	46	40	34	28	23	17	11	5	0	0
410	420	53	47	41	36	30	24	18	13	7	1	0
420	430	55	49	43	37	31	26	20	14	8	3	0
430	440	56	50	44	39	33	27	21	16	10	4	0
440	450	58	52	46	40	34	29	23	17	11	6	0
450	460	59	53	47	42	36	30	24	19	13	7	1
460	470	61	55	49	43	37	32	26	20	14	9	3
470	480	62	56	50	45	39	33	27	22	16	10	4
480	490	64	58	52	46	40	35	29	23	17	12	6
490	500	65	59	53	48	42	36	30	25	19	13	7
500	510	67	61	55	49	43	38	32	26	20	15	9
510	520	68	62	56	51	45	39	33	28	22	16	10
520	530	70	64	58	52	46	41	35	29	23	18	12
530	540	71	65	59	54	48	42	36	31	25	19	13
540	550	73	67	61	55	49	44	38	32	26	21	15
550	560	74	68	62	57	51	45	39	34	28	22	16
560	570	76	70	64	58	52	47	41	35	29	24	18
570	580	77	71	65	60	54	48	42	37	31	25	19
580	590	79	73	67	61	55	50	44	38	32	27	21
590	600	80	74	68	63	57	51	45	40	34	28	22
600	610	82	76	70	64	58	53	47	41	35	30	24
610	620	83	77	71	66	60	54	48	43	37	31	25

Table 6.2 *(continued)*

And the wages are–		And the number of withholding allowances claimed is–										
At least	But less than	0	1	2	3	4	5	6	7	8	9	10
		The amount of income tax to be withheld shall be–										
$620	$630	$85	$79	$73	$67	$61	$56	$50	$44	$38	$33	$27
630	640	86	80	74	69	63	57	51	46	40	34	28
640	650	88	82	76	70	64	59	53	47	41	36	30
650	660	89	83	77	72	66	60	54	49	43	37	31
660	670	92	85	79	73	67	62	56	50	44	39	33
670	680	94	86	80	75	69	63	57	52	46	40	34
680	690	97	88	82	76	70	65	59	53	47	42	36
690	700	100	89	83	78	72	66	60	55	49	43	37
700	710	103	92	85	79	73	68	62	56	50	45	39
710	720	106	95	86	81	75	69	63	58	52	46	40
720	730	108	98	88	82	76	71	65	59	53	48	42
730	740	111	100	90	84	78	72	66	61	55	49	43
740	750	114	103	92	85	79	74	68	62	56	51	45
750	760	117	106	95	87	81	75	69	64	58	52	46
760	770	120	109	98	88	82	77	71	65	59	54	48
770	780	122	112	101	90	84	78	72	67	61	55	49
780	790	125	114	104	93	85	80	74	68	62	57	51
790	800	128	117	106	96	87	81	75	70	64	58	52
800	810	131	120	109	98	88	83	77	71	65	60	54
810	820	134	123	112	101	91	84	78	73	67	61	55
820	830	136	126	115	104	93	86	80	74	68	63	57
830	840	139	128	118	107	96	87	81	76	70	64	58
840	850	142	131	120	110	99	89	83	77	71	66	60
850	860	145	134	123	112	102	91	84	79	73	67	61
860	870	148	137	126	115	105	94	86	80	74	69	63
870	880	150	140	129	118	107	97	87	82	76	70	64
880	890	153	142	132	121	110	99	89	83	77	72	66
890	900	156	145	134	124	113	102	91	85	79	73	67
900	910	159	148	137	126	116	105	94	86	80	75	69
910	920	162	151	140	129	119	108	97	88	82	76	70
920	930	164	154	143	132	121	111	100	89	83	78	72
930	940	167	156	146	135	124	113	103	92	85	79	73
940	950	170	159	148	138	127	116	105	95	86	81	75
950	960	173	162	151	140	130	119	108	97	88	82	76
960	970	176	165	154	143	133	122	111	100	89	84	78
970	980	178	168	157	146	135	125	114	103	92	85	79
980	990	181	170	160	149	138	127	117	106	95	87	81
990	1,000	184	173	162	152	141	130	119	109	98	88	82
1,000	1,010	187	176	165	154	144	133	122	111	101	90	84
1,010	1,020	190	179	168	157	147	136	125	114	103	93	85
1,020	1,030	192	182	171	160	149	139	128	117	106	95	87
1,030	1,040	195	184	174	163	152	141	131	120	109	98	88
1,040	1,050	198	187	176	166	155	144	133	123	112	101	90
1,050	1,060	201	190	179	168	158	147	136	125	115	104	93
1,060	1,070	204	193	182	171	161	150	139	128	117	107	96
1,070	1,080	206	196	185	174	163	153	142	131	120	109	99
1,080	1,090	209	198	188	177	166	155	145	134	123	112	102
1,090	1,100	212	201	190	180	169	158	147	137	126	115	104
1,100	1,110	215	204	193	182	172	161	150	139	129	118	107
1,110	1,120	218	207	196	185	175	164	153	142	131	121	110
1,120	1,130	220	210	199	188	177	167	156	145	134	123	113
1,130	1,140	223	212	202	191	180	169	159	148	137	126	116
1,140	1,150	226	215	204	194	183	172	161	151	140	129	118
1,150	1,160	229	218	207	196	186	175	164	153	143	132	121
1,160	1,170	232	221	210	199	189	178	167	156	145	135	124
1,170	1,180	234	224	213	202	191	181	170	159	148	137	127
1,180	1,190	237	226	216	205	194	183	173	162	151	140	130
1,190	1,200	240	229	218	208	197	186	175	165	154	143	132
1,200	1,210	243	232	221	210	200	189	178	167	157	146	135
1,210	1,220	246	235	224	213	203	192	181	170	159	149	138
1,220	1,230	248	238	227	216	205	195	184	173	162	151	141
1,230	1,240	251	240	230	219	208	197	187	176	165	154	144
1,240	1,250	254	243	232	222	211	200	189	179	168	157	146
1,250	1,260	257	246	235	224	214	203	192	181	171	160	149
1,260	1,270	260	249	238	227	217	206	195	184	173	163	152
1,270	1,280	262	252	241	230	219	209	198	187	176	165	155

$1,280 and over — Other IRS tables, not included in this text, must be used.

Table 6.3 Married Persons—Biweekly Payroll Period

And the wages are–		And the number of withholding allowances claimed is–										
At least	But less than	0	1	2	3	4	5	6	7	8	9	10
		The amount of income tax to be withheld shall be–										
$0	$125	$0	$0	$0	$0	$0	$0	$0	$0	$0	$0	$0
125	130	1	0	0	0	0	0	0	0	0	0	0
130	135	1	0	0	0	0	0	0	0	0	0	0
135	140	2	0	0	0	0	0	0	0	0	0	0
140	145	3	0	0	0	0	0	0	0	0	0	0
145	150	4	0	0	0	0	0	0	0	0	0	0
150	155	4	0	0	0	0	0	0	0	0	0	0
155	160	5	0	0	0	0	0	0	0	0	0	0
160	165	6	0	0	0	0	0	0	0	0	0	0
165	170	7	0	0	0	0	0	0	0	0	0	0
170	175	7	0	0	0	0	0	0	0	0	0	0
175	180	8	0	0	0	0	0	0	0	0	0	0
180	185	9	0	0	0	0	0	0	0	0	0	0
185	190	10	0	0	0	0	0	0	0	0	0	0
190	195	10	0	0	0	0	0	0	0	0	0	0
195	200	11	0	0	0	0	0	0	0	0	0	0
200	205	12	0	0	0	0	0	0	0	0	0	0
205	210	13	1	0	0	0	0	0	0	0	0	0
210	215	13	2	0	0	0	0	0	0	0	0	0
215	220	14	3	0	0	0	0	0	0	0	0	0
220	225	15	3	0	0	0	0	0	0	0	0	0
225	230	16	4	0	0	0	0	0	0	0	0	0
230	235	16	5	0	0	0	0	0	0	0	0	0
235	240	17	6	0	0	0	0	0	0	0	0	0
240	245	18	6	0	0	0	0	0	0	0	0	0
245	250	19	7	0	0	0	0	0	0	0	0	0
250	260	20	8	0	0	0	0	0	0	0	0	0
260	270	21	10	0	0	0	0	0	0	0	0	0
270	280	23	11	0	0	0	0	0	0	0	0	0
280	290	24	13	1	0	0	0	0	0	0	0	0
290	300	26	14	3	0	0	0	0	0	0	0	0
300	310	27	16	4	0	0	0	0	0	0	0	0
310	320	29	17	6	0	0	0	0	0	0	0	0
320	330	30	19	7	0	0	0	0	0	0	0	0
330	340	32	20	9	0	0	0	0	0	0	0	0
340	350	33	22	10	0	0	0	0	0	0	0	0
350	360	35	23	12	0	0	0	0	0	0	0	0
360	370	36	25	13	2	0	0	0	0	0	0	0
370	380	38	26	15	3	0	0	0	0	0	0	0
380	390	39	28	16	5	0	0	0	0	0	0	0
390	400	41	29	18	6	0	0	0	0	0	0	0
400	410	42	31	19	8	0	0	0	0	0	0	0
410	420	44	32	21	9	0	0	0	0	0	0	0
420	430	45	34	22	11	0	0	0	0	0	0	0
430	440	47	35	24	12	1	0	0	0	0	0	0
440	450	48	37	25	14	2	0	0	0	0	0	0
450	460	50	38	27	15	4	0	0	0	0	0	0
460	470	51	40	28	17	5	0	0	0	0	0	0
470	480	53	41	30	18	7	0	0	0	0	0	0
480	490	54	43	31	20	8	0	0	0	0	0	0
490	500	56	44	33	21	10	0	0	0	0	0	0
500	520	58	47	35	23	12	0	0	0	0	0	0
520	540	61	50	38	26	15	3	0	0	0	0	0
540	560	64	53	41	29	18	6	0	0	0	0	0
560	580	67	56	44	32	21	9	0	0	0	0	0
580	600	70	59	47	35	24	12	1	0	0	0	0
600	620	73	62	50	38	27	15	4	0	0	0	0
620	640	76	65	53	41	30	18	7	0	0	0	0
640	660	79	68	56	44	33	21	10	0	0	0	0
660	680	82	71	59	47	36	24	13	1	0	0	0
680	700	85	74	62	50	39	27	16	4	0	0	0
700	720	88	77	65	53	42	30	19	7	0	0	0
720	740	91	80	68	56	45	33	22	10	0	0	0
740	760	94	83	71	59	48	36	25	13	2	0	0
760	780	97	86	74	62	51	39	28	16	5	0	0
780	800	100	89	77	65	54	42	31	19	8	0	0
800	820	103	92	80	68	57	45	34	22	11	0	0
820	840	106	95	83	71	60	48	37	25	14	2	0
840	860	109	98	86	74	63	51	40	28	17	5	0
860	880	112	101	89	77	66	54	43	31	20	8	0

Table 6.3 *(continued)*

And the wages are–		And the number of withholding allowances claimed is–										
At least	But less than	0	1	2	3	4	5	6	7	8	9	10
		The amount of income tax to be withheld shall be–										
$880	$900	$115	$104	$92	$80	$69	$57	$46	$34	$23	$11	$0
900	920	118	107	95	83	72	60	49	37	26	14	3
920	940	121	110	98	86	75	63	52	40	29	17	6
940	960	124	113	101	89	78	66	55	43	32	20	9
960	980	127	116	104	92	81	69	58	46	35	23	12
980	1,000	130	119	107	95	84	72	61	49	38	26	15
1,000	1,020	133	122	110	98	87	75	64	52	41	29	18
1,020	1,040	136	125	113	101	90	78	67	55	44	32	21
1,040	1,060	139	128	116	104	93	81	70	58	47	35	24
1,060	1,080	142	131	119	107	96	84	73	61	50	38	27
1,080	1,100	145	134	122	110	99	87	76	64	53	41	30
1,100	1,120	148	137	125	113	102	90	79	67	56	44	33
1,120	1,140	151	140	128	116	105	93	82	70	59	47	36
1,140	1,160	154	143	131	119	108	96	85	73	62	50	39
1,160	1,180	157	146	134	122	111	99	88	76	65	53	42
1,180	1,200	160	149	137	125	114	102	91	79	68	56	45
1,200	1,220	163	152	140	128	117	105	94	82	71	59	48
1,220	1,240	166	155	143	131	120	108	97	85	74	62	51
1,240	1,260	169	158	146	134	123	111	100	88	77	65	54
1,260	1,280	172	161	149	137	126	114	103	91	80	68	57
1,280	1,300	175	164	152	140	129	117	106	94	83	71	60
1,300	1,320	178	167	155	143	132	120	109	97	86	74	63
1,320	1,340	183	170	158	146	135	123	112	100	89	77	66
1,340	1,360	189	173	161	149	138	126	115	103	92	80	69
1,360	1,380	194	176	164	152	141	129	118	106	95	83	72
1,380	1,400	200	179	167	155	144	132	121	109	98	86	75
1,400	1,420	206	184	170	158	147	135	124	112	101	89	78
1,420	1,440	211	190	173	161	150	138	127	115	104	92	81
1,440	1,460	217	195	176	164	153	141	130	118	107	95	84
1,460	1,480	222	201	179	167	156	144	133	121	110	98	87
1,480	1,500	228	206	185	170	159	147	136	124	113	101	90
1,500	1,520	234	212	191	173	162	150	139	127	116	104	93
1,520	1,540	239	218	196	176	165	153	142	130	119	107	96
1,540	1,560	245	223	202	180	168	156	145	133	122	110	99
1,560	1,580	250	229	207	186	171	159	148	136	125	113	102
1,580	1,600	256	234	213	191	174	162	151	139	128	116	105
1,600	1,620	262	240	219	197	177	165	154	142	131	119	108
1,620	1,640	267	246	224	203	181	168	157	145	134	122	111
1,640	1,660	273	251	230	208	187	171	160	148	137	125	114
1,660	1,680	278	257	235	214	192	174	163	151	140	128	117
1,680	1,700	284	262	241	219	198	177	166	154	143	131	120
1,700	1,720	290	268	247	225	203	182	169	157	146	134	123
1,720	1,740	295	274	252	231	209	187	172	160	149	137	126
1,740	1,760	301	279	258	236	215	193	175	163	152	140	129
1,760	1,780	306	285	263	242	220	199	178	166	155	143	132
1,780	1,800	312	290	269	247	226	204	183	169	158	146	135
1,800	1,820	318	296	275	253	231	210	188	172	161	149	138
1,820	1,840	323	302	280	259	237	215	194	175	164	152	141
1,840	1,860	329	307	286	264	243	221	200	178	167	155	144
1,860	1,880	334	313	291	270	248	227	205	184	170	158	147
1,880	1,900	340	318	297	275	254	232	211	189	173	161	150
1,900	1,920	346	324	303	281	259	238	216	195	176	164	153
1,920	1,940	351	330	308	287	265	243	222	200	179	167	156
1,940	1,960	357	335	314	292	271	249	228	206	184	170	159
1,960	1,980	362	341	319	298	276	255	233	212	190	173	162
1,980	2,000	368	346	325	303	282	260	239	217	196	176	165
2,000	2,020	374	352	331	309	287	266	244	223	201	180	168
2,020	2,040	379	358	336	315	293	271	250	228	207	185	171
2,040	2,060	385	363	342	320	299	277	256	234	212	191	174
2,060	2,080	390	369	347	326	304	283	261	240	218	197	177
2,080	2,100	396	374	353	331	310	288	267	245	224	202	181
2,100	2,120	402	380	359	337	315	294	272	251	229	208	186
2,120	2,140	407	386	364	343	321	299	278	256	235	213	192
2,140	2,160	413	391	370	348	327	305	284	262	240	219	197
2,160	2,180	418	397	375	354	332	311	289	268	246	225	203

$2,180 and over — Other IRS tables, not included in this text, must be used.

More a compulsory insurance program than a tax, the act requires employers to withhold a percentage of the employee's gross earnings as contributions to the benefit fund. These contributions are matched by the employer until the total annual contribution reaches a maximum established by the act. Both the contribution percent and the maximum to be withheld are amended by Congress periodically to liberalize benefits. This is necessary because of the rise in the cost of living and inflation. Table 6.4 shows the contribution percent and the maximum gross earnings taxed for each of the years 1985–1989. The contributions of the employee are matched by the employer, and periodically, these sums are deposited with a bank authorized to accept FICA taxes.

Tax tables for FICA are furnished by the Internal Revenue Service, or the tax may be computed by multiplying the employee's gross earnings by the appropriate percent given in table 6.4. In this text, the 1989 rate of 7.51% of the first $48,000 of gross earnings, or $3,604.80, is used to compute FICA taxes.

Table 6.4 FICA Taxes (1985–1989)

Employee Contributions

	Worker's Maximum Annual Pay Taxed	Tax Rate	Maximum Tax per Worker
1985	$39,600	7.05%	$2,791.80
1986	42,000	7.15%	3,003.00
1987	43,800	7.15%	3,131.70
1988	45,000	7.51%	3,379.50
1989	48,000	7.51%	3,604.80

Example 3 Juan Hernandez earns a salary of $245.25 per week. How much is deducted for FICA taxes?

Solution

The amount deducted for FICA taxes is

$\$245.25 \times 0.0751 = \$18.42$

At the end of a year, Juan will have contributed a total of $\$18.42 \times 52 = \$957.84$ in FICA taxes.

Example 4 In 1989, the comptroller of the Barrett Corporation was paid a salary of \$54,000. How much was deducted each monthly pay period for FICA taxes?

Solution

An annual salary of \$54,000 amounts to gross earnings of $\$54,000 \div 12 = \$4,500$ per month. The comptroller's FICA tax per month was

$\$4,500 \times 0.0751 = \$337.95$

After ten months, the comptroller had contributed \$3,379.50; hence, the contribution for the eleventh month was $\$3,604.80 - \$3,379.50 = \$225.30$. No further deductions were made for the rest of the year.

Example 5 Wade Taylor is a salesperson whose commission rate is 18% of net sales with a guaranteed draw of \$400 per week. Last week, his sales were \$2,100. How much FICA tax should be deducted?

Solution

The earned commission for the week is $\$2,100 \times 0.18 = \$378$; hence, Wade's gross earnings for the week will be the draw of \$400. The FICA tax on this amount is:

$\$400 \times 0.0751 = \$30.04$

Other deductions Deductions for Social Security and federal income tax are the main required payroll deductions. Some states may have compulsory deductions for state income tax or disability insurance. Additionally, there may be voluntary deductions made by the employer as a service to the employee. Group insurance premiums, union dues, United States Savings Bonds, credit union loan payments, or contributions to charitable organizations are examples of such deductions. Figure 6.5 shows a sample paycheck stub with deductions listed.

Figure 6.5
Sample paycheck stub

STATEMENT OF EARNINGS AND DEDUCTIONS

CHECK NO.	DEPT.	EMPLOYEE NO.	EMPLOYEE NAME	PERIOD ENDING
13942	0005	01199		

CHECK NO.

YEAR TO DATE	GROSS EARNINGS	FED WITHHOLDING	FICA	STATE AND/OR CITY	
	7700.00	869.00	578.27	460.46	700.00

CURRENT PAY PERIOD

REG HOURS	OT OR OTHER HRS	REG EARNINGS	OT OR OTHER EARN	FED WITHHOLDINGS	FICA	STATE AND OR CITY	FIRST NET
		700.00		79.00	52.57	41.86	526.57

DEDUCTIONS

1	2	3	4	5
			89.10	

6	7	8	9
	28.00		

NET PAY
409.47

Example 6 Harrison Keely is a single die maker earning \$6.15 per hour for a 40-hour workweek. In addition to deductions for federal income tax (S-1) and Social Security, union dues of \$3.25 per month are also withheld from his pay. Find Keely's net earnings for a 40-hour workweek if the company pay period is weekly.

Solution

Gross earnings = \$6.15 × 40		= \$246.00
Income tax	= \$28.00	
FICA	= 18.47	
Union dues (\$3.25 × $\frac{12}{52}$)	= 0.75	
Total deductions		= \$ 47.22
Net earnings		= \$198.78

Example 7 Charles Patton is paid weekly and earns \$4.40 per hour for a 40-hour workweek. He has joined the payroll savings plan and purchases a bond a month for \$25.00. He also participates in the company group insurance plan, which costs him \$35.10 a month. He is classified M-4. Calculate his net earnings for a week during which he worked 42 hours.

Solution

The overtime rate is \$4.40 × $1\frac{1}{2}$ = \$6.60 per hour.

Regular wages	= \$4.40 × 40	= \$176.00	
Overtime wages	= \$6.60 × 2	= 13.20	
Gross earnings			= \$189.20
Federal income tax		= \$ 0.00	
FICA		= 14.21	
Savings bond	= (\$25.00 × $\frac{12}{52}$)	= 5.77	
Group insurance	= (\$35.10 × $\frac{12}{52}$)	= 8.10	
Total deductions			= \$ 28.08
Net earnings			= \$161.12

Example 8 Virginia Krisloff sells cosmetics. She receives a salary of $200.00 per week, plus 5% of all sales in excess of $1,500.00. During the last biweekly pay period, her weekly sales were $1,800.00 and $1,600.00. Virginia is married and claims three allowances for income tax purposes. In addition to Social Security, she contributes $12.20 per month to the company retirement plan. To insure her family under the group insurance plans costs $37.00 per month, and Virginia has agreed to a deduction of $1.00 per month as a pledge to the United Fund. What are her net earnings for the last pay period?

Solution

The commission for the pay period is $400 × 0.05 = $20; hence,

Salary	= $200 × 2	= $400.00	
Commissions		= 20.00	
Gross earnings			= $420.00
Income tax (M-3)		= $ 11.00	
FICA	= $420 × 7.51%	= 31.54	
Retirement	= $12.20 × $\frac{12}{26}$	= 5.63	
Group insurance	= $37 × $\frac{12}{26}$	= 17.08	
United Fund	= $1 × $\frac{12}{26}$	= 0.46	
Total deductions			= $ 65.71
Net earnings			= $354.29

Exercises for Section 6.4

1. Tony Di Salvo is married, has three children, and claims three withholding allowances. His weekly salary is $314. How much income tax is withheld from his weekly gross earnings?

2. Find the income tax withheld from the biweekly gross earnings of an employee who is married, claims two allowances, and is paid a monthly salary of $920.

3. Joanne McMannis is an office manager at the Carleton Company, where she receives a salary of $18,450 per year. She is married with two children, and she claims all four allowances. If the pay period at Carleton is biweekly, how much income tax is withheld from her biweekly gross earnings?

4. Ray Baker earns $6.80 an hour for a 40-hour workweek at the Calvert Manufacturing Company. He is single, claims one allowance, and is paid weekly. Find the amount of income tax withheld for a week during which he works 47 hours.

5. Accutex Scientific Equipment operates on a biweekly pay period. Richard Thaxton, an employee at Accutex, is married with four children and claims three allowances. He is paid $4.20 per hour for a 40-hour workweek. How much income tax is withheld from his gross earnings for a pay period during which he works 43 hours the first week and 47 hours the second week?

6. Glenn Darnell sells office furniture on a straight commission of 11% of net sales. He is married with one child and claims three allowances. How much income tax was withheld from his last biweekly gross earnings if he sold $2,340 worth of merchandise the first week and $2,984 the second week?

7. Beverly Morrow is employed by Cory Products Company, where she is paid weekly a straight commission of 14% of her net sales. She is single and claims one allowance. Find the amount of income tax withheld from her gross earnings for a week during which she sells $2,142.60 worth of merchandise, with returns of $211.40.

8. Cecil Beamon is paid a biweekly graduated commission of 6% of the first $3,500.00 in net sales and 7.5% of net sales in excess of $3,500.00. He is married with two children and claims four allowances. How much income tax is withheld from his gross earnings for a pay period in which he sells $9,842.40 worth of merchandise, with cancellations and returns of $622.50?

9. The Doyle Company pays its sales personnel a weekly graduated commission of 7% of the first $1,500.00 in net sales and 9% of net sales in excess of $1,500.00. Find the income tax withheld from the gross earnings of a married salesperson claiming two allowances for a week during which sales total $3,240.00, with returns of $519.20.

10. Judy Roberts receives a salary of $230.00 per week, plus a commission of 3.25% of net sales. Judy is married but claims only one allowance. How much income tax is withheld from her gross earnings for a week during which she has sales of $2,140.51, with returns of $291.72?

11. Nelson's Computer Supplies pays its salespeople $325 a week, plus 4.25% of weekly net sales in excess of $500. If the pay period is biweekly, find the income tax withheld from the gross earnings of a married salesperson claiming three allowances who reports the following sales:

	Total Sales	Returns
Week 1	$1,142.41	$203.72
Week 2	$1,003.39	$114.78

In the following problems, use the 1989 FICA contribution rate of 7.51% of the first $48,000 in gross earnings when calculating FICA deductions.

12. Ted Lee is paid $379.42 per week. How much is deducted from his gross earnings for FICA taxes each biweekly pay period? How much will Ted have contributed in FICA taxes in a year?

13. Julia Tibbetts is a department manager for the Drexel Company and is paid an annual salary of $50,000. How much is deducted each biweekly pay period from her gross earnings for FICA taxes? For how many pay periods of the year will she contribute to FICA?

14. David Bland, a salesperson, receives a commission of 16% of net sales with a guaranteed draw of $210.00 per week. How much FICA tax is deducted from his gross earnings for a week during which his net sales total $1,242.50?

15. Nancy Miller sells cookware on a biweekly commission basis of 14.5% of net sales with a guaranteed biweekly draw of $375. During the last two-week period, she reported the following sales:

	Total Sales	**Returns and Cancellations**
Week 1	$1,352.63	$72.41
Week 2	$1,411.71	$53.69

How much was deducted for FICA taxes this pay period?

16. Morehouse Metal Works employs Charles McDonald as a machinist. He receives $9.20 per hour for a 40-hour workweek. In addition to deductions for federal income tax (his classification is S-2) and Social Security, he also has deducted from his weekly gross earnings (a) union dues of $5.90 per month and (b) a group insurance payment of $32.14 per month. Find his net earnings for a week during which he works 43 hours.

17. John Ritch is paid biweekly at Timsco Industries. He is paid $3.90 per hour for a 40-hour workweek. His group insurance payment is $37.42 per month, his union dues are $10.11 per month, and he has $50.00 per pay period deducted from his earnings and deposited with the company credit union. His classification is M-3. Compute his net earnings for the last two-week period, during which he worked 47 hours the first week and 40 hours the second week.

18. Madison's Department Store employs Cheryl Watts as a salesclerk. She is paid biweekly a salary of $160.00 per week, plus a commission of 4.75% of weekly sales in excess of $1,200.00. She is classified M-2. In addition to FICA, she contributes $13.75 per month to the company retirement plan. She also has $32.14 per month for insurance, $5.00 per month for the United Fund, and $3.72 per month for union dues deducted from her earnings. Calculate her net earnings for a pay period during which she sold $1,432.71 worth of merchandise the first week and $1,563.42 the second week.

19. Terry Gilbreath is paid weekly a salary of $225.00, plus a commission of 7.5% of net sales in excess of $1,400.00. He is classified M-3, and in addition to FICA, he contributes $22.72 per month to the company retirement plan. He also has deductions to cover (a) his union dues of $8.43 per month, (b) his group insurance payment of $47.15 per month, (c) his credit union payment of $50.00 per month, and (d) his United Fund contribution of $10.00 per month. Find his net earnings for a week during which he sells $1,873.17 worth of merchandise, with returns and cancellations totaling $94.12.

20. Ben Darlington earns $14,720.00 per year as a supervisor at the Busbee Corporation. He is classified M-1, and in addition to FICA, he contributes $19.31 per month to the company retirement plan. He also has deductions for (a) $14.42 per month union dues, (b) $41.17 per month group insurance, and (c) $18.75 per month for savings bonds. If the pay period at Busbee is biweekly, find his net earnings for the first pay period in February.

21. The vice-president of Holstrum Enterprises is paid $65,500.00 per year. She is classified M-3. She has deductions from her weekly earnings to cover (a) $87.21 per month for the company retirement plan, in addition to FICA; (b) $56.25 per month for savings bonds; (c) $200.00 per month for savings in the credit union; and (d) $56.82 per month for group insurance. If the pay period at Holstrum is weekly, what are her net earnings for the first week in March? What are her net earnings for the last week in November?

Section 6.5 Employer contributions, records, and reports

Except for income tax, most payroll deductions are payments for employee benefits. Ordinarily, the employee pays only a portion of the total cost of these benefits; the remainder is paid by the employer. Some employer contributions are required by law, while others are voluntary in the form of fringe benefits to the employee.

Social Security The employer is required to match the FICA contributions of the employee.

Example 1 An employee had gross earnings of $536.42 for a weekly pay period. Find the total amount to be deposited for FICA.

Solution

Employee FICA deductions	= $536.42 × 0.0751	= $40.29
Employer FICA contributions		= 40.29
Total FICA tax		$80.58

Federal unemployment tax

Employees who lose their jobs or who are temporarily laid off may receive limited compensation through a provision of the FICA. A fund called the Federal Unemployment Trust Fund has been established from taxes on industry. From this fund, payments are made to unemployed workers either for a limited time period or until reemployment, whichever comes first.

The **federal unemployment tax** is currently 6.2% of the first $7,000 of the employee's gross earnings and is paid entirely by the employer. However, most states also have unemployment tax laws, and an employer can credit state unemployment taxes against the federal tax up to a maximum of 5.4% of the first $7,000. In other words, if the state tax exceeds 5.4% of the first $7,000, the employer pays the state tax plus a federal tax of 0.8%. If the state tax is less than 5.4% of the first $7,000, then the combined federal and state tax paid by the employer is 6.2% of the first $7,000. Each state sets its own tax rate. In many states, the lower the company's unemployment rate, the lower the tax.

Example 2 The K & C Company is located in a state that has a standard unemployment tax of 6.3% of the first $7,000 of gross earnings of each employee. However, as a result of favorable employment experience, the current tax rate for the K & C Company is 5.7%. If the company employed 36 people last year and all 36 employees earned in excess of $7,000, calculate the total unemployment taxes paid by the employer.

Solution

The state tax is $7,000 × 0.057 = $399 per person. Since the state tax is more than 5.4% of $7,000 per person, the employer must pay the state tax plus a federal tax of 0.8% of $7,000 = $56 per person.

State tax	= $399 × 36	= $14,364
Federal tax	= $ 56 × 36	= 2,016
Total unemployment tax		= $16,380

Group life and health insurance

A common employee fringe benefit is **group insurance.** Under a master policy issued to the company, employees may be insured for life insurance, hospitalization, surgery, and other medical expenses. In addition, most policies extend the health benefits to the employee's family, if the employee wishes to contract for this option. Group insurance is usually available without medical examination and is less expensive than individual insurance for two reasons: First, the policy is sold to a group, thus reducing paperwork and administrative expenses, and second, it is customary for the employer to pay a portion of the cost.

The employer's share of the insurance premium varies from company to company. Some employers pay the entire premium; others pay a percentage, say 50%. A common arrangement is for the employer to pay the employee's premium while the employee, in turn, pays the cost of insuring his or her family. Group insurance is discussed again in chapter 16.

Example 3 The Bradford Dry Goods Company has a group insurance plan whereby each employee is covered under a major medical health plan. In addition, each employee is insured for $5,000 term life insurance except the officers of the company, who are insured for $12,000. The premiums are as follows:

Life insurance	$0.68 per $1,000.00 per month
Major medical	
Employee only	$15.42 per month
Dependents only	$36.15 per month

The company has agreed to pay for the cost of the employee benefits; the employee must pay for any dependents. If the company has 42 employees and 4 officers, and if 24 of the 28 married employees elect to insure their families, what is (a) the total monthly premium and (b) the cost to the employer?

Solution

The life insurance costs $0.68 × 5 = $3.40 per month for $5,000 insurance and $0.68 × 12 = $8.16 for $12,000 of coverage.

Life insurance premiums		
Officers ($8.16 × 4)	$ 32.64	
Other employees ($3.40 × 42)	142.80	
Subtotal		$ 175.44
Major medical premium		
Employee ($15.42 × 46)	$709.32	
Dependents ($36.15 × 24)	867.60	
Subtotal		$1,576.92
Total monthly premium		$1,752.36
Cost to the employer ($709.32 + $175.44)		$ 884.76

Records and reports

Employers are required by the Fair Labor Standards Act to keep accurate employee records that include the following information:

Identifying information Employee's full name, address, Social Security number, birth date, sex, and occupation

Hours (wage earners) Time and day of week when the workweek begins, hours worked each day, total hours worked each workweek

Earnings Basis on which earnings are paid, regular hourly rate, total regular earnings, total overtime earnings, all additions to or deductions from the employee's earnings for each pay period

One method of recording this information is an employee earnings record. A sample earnings record is shown in figure 6.6. Often, this form has quarterly totals because quarterly reports are required by federal and state governments. The calendar quarters of a year are January 1 to March 31, April 1 to June 30, July 1 to September 30, and October 1 to December 31.

The Employer's Quarterly Tax Return (Form 941) is an example of a quarterly report required by the federal government. (See figure 6.7.) Deductions for both FICA and federal income tax are reported on this form. Also, the employer must remit to the United States Treasury Department (through a Federal Reserve Bank or any commercial bank authorized to receive federal taxes) the FICA tax levied on him or her as an employer, the FICA tax withheld from employees' wages, and the federal income tax deducted from employees' wages. The frequency of these deposits depends on the amount of taxes withheld. The rules for deposits are given in the instructions for Form 941.

Figure 6.6
Employee earnings record

–RECAPITULATION BY QUARTERS–

QTR	EARNINGS	DEDUCTIONS: F I C A	FED WHLDG	STATE WHLDG	INS	UNION DUES	NET PAID
1st	3272 –	245 73	178 00		136 50	24 –	2687 77
2nd							
3rd							
4th							
TOT							

EMPLOYEE RECORD

NAME *James Harvard Lyon* EXEMPTIONS *M-3*
ADDRESS *201 Debra Lane* PHONE *622-1212*
S S ACC'T NO. *987-65-4321* SEX *M* SINGLE ☐ MARRIED ☒
CLOCK NO. *123* POSITION *Welder* DATE BORN *8-1-50*
HRS. PER DAY ____ PER WEEK ____ DATE EMPLOYED *6/84* TERMINATED ____
REMARKS ____
RATE OF PAY: DATE *7/87* $ *6.20* PER *HR* DATE ____ $ ____ PER ____

FIRST QUARTER—19*88*

	PAYROLL PERIOD	REGULAR TIME: TIME	RATE	OVERTIME: HRS	RATE	TOTAL EARNINGS	NON-TAXABLE SICK PAY ETC.	AM'T TAXABLE	DEDUCTIONS: F.I.C.A.	FED WHLDG	STATE WHLDG	DISA-BILITY	INS	UNION DUES	NET EARNINGS: AMOUNT	DATE PAID
JAN.	12/30-1/3	40	6.20	8	12.40	347 20			26 07	25 –			10.50	8.00	277 63	1-10
	6-10	40		8	9.30	322 40			24 21	22 –			10.50		265 69	1-17
	13-17	40		8	9.30	322 40			24 21	22 –			10.50		265 69	1-24
	20-24	40				248 –			18 62	10			10.50		208 88	1-31
	27-31	40				248 –			18 62	10			10.50		208 88	2-7
FEB.	2-7	32				198 40			14 90	3			10.50	8.00	162 –	2-14
	10-14	32				198 40			14 90	3			10.50		170 –	2-21
	17-21	40				248 –			18 62	10			10.50		208 88	2-28
	TOTAL 1ST QTR.															

Figure 6.7
Employer's Quarterly Federal Tax Return (Form 941)

Form **941** (Rev. January 1989) Department of the Treasury Internal Revenue Service

Employer's Quarterly Federal Tax Return

4141 ▶ **For Paperwork Reduction Act Notice, see page 2.**

Please type or print.

OMB No. 1545-0029 Expires: 5-31-91

Type or print your name, address, employer identification number, and calendar quarter of return as shown on original. ▶

Name (as distinguished from trade name) | Date quarter ended

Trade name, if any | Employer identification number

Address and ZIP code

If you do not have to file returns in the future, check here . . . ▶ ☐ Date final wages paid . . . . ▶

If you are a seasonal employer, see **Seasonal employer** on page 2 and check here . . . ▶ ☐

1a	Number of employees (except household) employed in the pay period that includes March 12th ▶	1a	
b	If you are a subsidiary corporation AND your parent corporation files a consolidated Form 1120, enter parent corporation employer identification number (EIN) . . ▶ 1b –		
2	Total wages and tips subject to withholding, plus other compensation . . . ▶	2	
3	Total income tax withheld from wages, tips, pensions, annuities, sick pay, gambling, etc. ▶	3	
4	Adjustment of withheld income tax for preceding quarters of calendar year (see instructions) ▶	4	
5	Adjusted total of income tax withheld (see instructions)	5	
6	Taxable social security wages paid . . . $ ______ × 15.02% (.1502)	6	
7a	Taxable tips reported . . . $ ______ × 15.02% (.1502)	7a	
b	Taxable hospital insurance wages paid . . . $ ______ × 2.9% (.029)	7b	
8	Total social security taxes (add lines 6, 7a, and 7b)	8	
9	Adjustment of social security taxes (see instructions for required explanation)	9	
10	Adjusted total of social security taxes (see instructions) ▶	10	
11	Backup withholding (see instructions)	11	
12	Adjustment of backup withholding tax for preceding quarters of calendar year ▶	12	
13	Adjusted total of backup withholding	13	
14	Total taxes (add lines 5, 10, and 13)	14	
15	Advance earned income credit (EIC) payments, if any ▶	15	
16	Net taxes (subtract line 15 from line 14). **This must equal line IV below** (plus line IV of Schedule A (Form 941) if you have treated backup withholding as a separate liability)	16	
17	Total deposits for quarter, including overpayment applied from a prior quarter, from your records ▶	17	
18	Balance due (subtract line 17 from line 16). This should be less than $500. Pay to IRS ▶	18	
19	If line 17 is more than line 16, enter overpayment here ▶ $ ______ and check if to be: ☐ Applied to next return **OR** ☐ Refunded.		

Record of Federal Tax Liability (Complete if line 16 is $500 or more.) See the instructions on page 4 for details before checking these boxes.

Check only if you made eighth-monthly deposits using the 95% rule ▶ ☐ Check only if you are a first time 3-banking-day depositor ▶ ☐

Do NOT Show Federal Tax Deposits Here

Date wages paid	Show tax liability here, **not deposits.** IRS gets deposit data from FTD coupons.					
	First month of quarter		Second month of quarter		Third month of quarter	
1st through 3rd	A		I		Q	
4th through 7th	B		J		R	
8th through 11th	C		K		S	
12th through 15th	D		L		T	
16th through 19th	E		M		U	
20th through 22nd	F		N		V	
23rd through 25th	G		O		W	
26th through the last	H		P		X	
Total liability for month	*I*		*II*		*III*	
▶ *IV* Total for quarter (add lines *I*, *II*, and *III*). **This must equal line 16 above** ▶						

Sign Here Under penalties of perjury, I declare that I have examined this return, including accompanying schedules and statements, and to the best of my knowledge and belief, it is true, correct, and complete.

Signature ▶ Title ▶ Date ▶

Exercises for Section 6.5

Use the 1989 FICA contribution rate of 7.51% of the first $48,000 in gross earnings when calculating FICA deductions.

1. Thelma Baxter earns a weekly salary of $386.42. How much total FICA tax per week (employee deduction plus employer contribution) will be deposited for FICA? What total amount will be deposited for FICA in one year?

2. An employee has gross earnings of $29,450 per year. How much total FICA tax per biweekly pay period (employee deduction plus employer contribution) is deposited for FICA? What total amount is deposited for FICA in one year?

3. Everett Hawkins earns $72,800 per year as the vice-president of Alco, Inc. Find the total FICA tax per week (employee deduction plus employer contribution) to be deposited for FICA during February. How much total FICA tax will be deposited for the year?

4. Carol Paige is a branch manager at Pittman Industries. She is paid $58,500 per year, and the pay period is biweekly. Find the total FICA tax per pay period (employee deduction plus employer contribution) deposited for FICA during March. How much total FICA tax will be deposited for the year?

5. Sterling Imports is located in a state that has a standard unemployment tax of 5.2% of the first $7,000 of gross earnings of each employee. Because of favorable employment experience, the state tax rate for Sterling is 4.2%. The company employs 43 people, and all of the employees earn more than $7,000 per year. Find the total unemployment taxes paid by the company.

6. Superior Plastics pays a state unemployment tax of 5.9% of the first $7,000 of gross earnings of each employee. The company employs 57 people, and all 57 employees earn in excess of $7,000 per year. How much total unemployment tax does Superior pay?

7. Find the total federal unemployment tax paid by a company that has 23 employees, each earning more than $7,000 per year, if the state unemployment tax is 4.4% of the first $7,000 earned by each employee.

8. The Drewfield Company employs 18 people, and each employee earns more than $7,000 per year. Last year, the company paid a total of $5,670 in federal unemployment tax. How much total state unemployment tax was paid?

9. The Simpson Machinery Company provides group insurance plans for its employees. Each employee is insured for $10,000 of term life insurance at a cost of $0.72 per $1,000 per month, and each officer of the company is insured for an additional $10,000 at the same rate. Also, each employee is covered under a health insurance plan that costs $21.54 per month for the employee only, plus $47.20 per month for dependents. The company has 37 employees, 3 of whom are officers, and 24 employees elect to insure dependents. If the company pays only for the cost of employee benefits, find (a) the total monthly insurance premium and (b) the monthly cost to the employer.

10. A company has group insurance plans for its employees for life insurance, medical insurance, and disability insurance. Each officer of the company receives $15,000 of life insurance, and all other employees receive a $10,000 policy. Every employee is provided disability insurance, and each employee is covered under a medical plan that costs $18.15 per month for the employee only, plus $35.60 per month for dependents. The cost of the life insurance is $0.92 per $1,000 per month, and each disability policy costs the company $8.82 per month. If there are 78 employees, 7 of whom are officers, and 56 employees elect to cover dependents on the medical plan, find the monthly cost to the employer if the employer pays for (a) all life insurance, 50% of all disability insurance, and all medical insurance for each employee, excluding dependent coverage; and (b) all disability insurance, all life insurance, all medical insurance for each employee, and 50% of the cost of dependent medical coverage.

Section 6.6 Bank statement reconciliation

Most businesses and individuals prefer to pay their obligations by check. There are two reasons for this: (1) checks are safer than cash, and (2) checks provide written legal receipts of transactions.

A **checking account** is a service provided by a bank whereby funds of a business, institution, or an individual are placed in a bank for safekeeping and for future use. The owner of a checking account is called the **depositor.** A **check** is a written order directing the bank to pay a specified amount of money to a specified party, called the **payee.** A typical check is shown in figure 6.8.

The act of placing funds in a checking account is called a **deposit.** Deposits are accompanied by a deposit slip, which classifies the deposit funds according to coin, currency, or checks. Checks are usually listed on the deposit slip according to bank number, an identification number located in the upper right corner of the check. An example of a completed deposit slip is shown in figure 6.9.

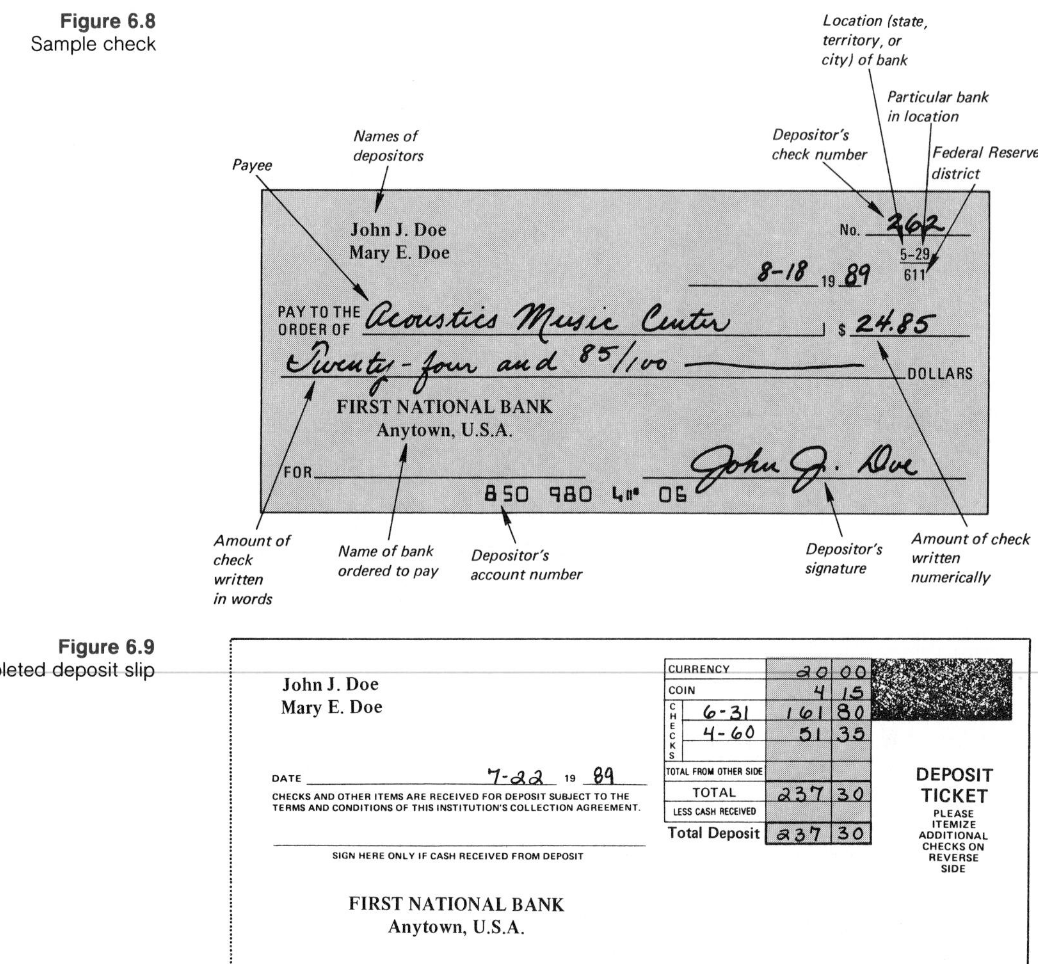

Figure 6.8
Sample check

Figure 6.9
Completed deposit slip

Before the payee can cash or deposit a check, it should be endorsed. An **endorsement** provides written instructions for the disposition of the funds. An endorsement can direct the bank to (1) pay the amount of the check to the payee (a blank endorsement), (2) deposit the amount of the check in the payee's checking account (restrictive endorsement), or (3) pay the amount of the check to a third party (special endorsement). These kinds of endorsements are illustrated in figure 6.10. The blank endorsement should not be executed until the payee is ready to cash the check because a check with a blank endorsement that is lost or stolen can be cashed by another person, who simply endorses the check below the payee's signature.

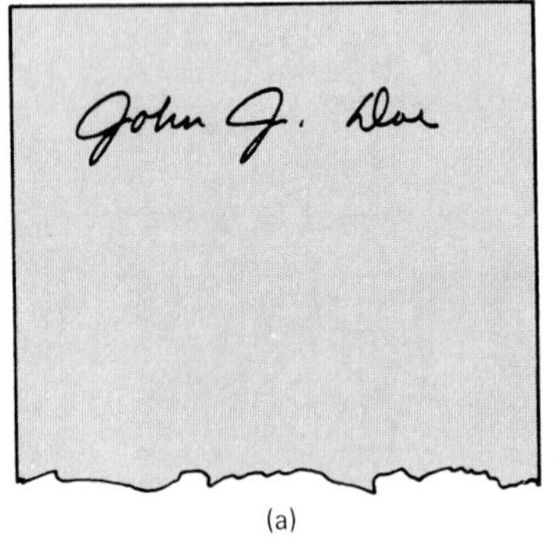

(a)

Pay to the order of the
First National Bank
For deposit only
John J. Doe

(b)

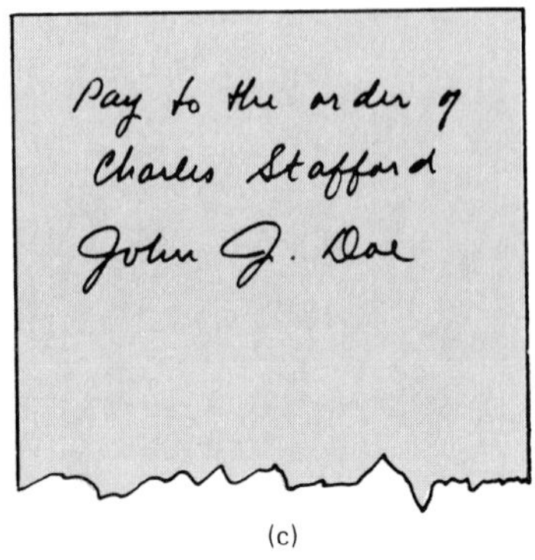

(c)

Figure 6.10
The three types of endorsements

PLEASE BE SURE TO DEDUCT ANY PER CHECK CHARGES OR SERVICE CHARGES THAT MAY APPLY TO YOUR ACCOUNT

CHECK NUMBER	DATE	CHECKS ISSUED TO OR DESCRIPTION OF DEPOSIT	(−) AMOUNT OF CHECK	√ T	(−) CHECK FEE (If any)	(+) AMOUNT OF DEPOSIT	BALANCE
							1216 47
415	5/30	TO/FOR City Electric Co.	185 16				BAL 1031 31
	6/1	TO/FOR Deposit				973 80	BAL 2005 11
416	6/10	TO/FOR Brooks Wholesale Plumbing	216 75				BAL 1788 36
417	6/10	TO/FOR Stinson's Sheet Metal Co.	101 40				BAL 1686 96
		TO/FOR					BAL
		TO/FOR					BAL

Figure 6.11
Check register

Both the depositor and the bank keep a record of all transactions (checks written, deposits made, etc.) within the account. The record maintained by the depositor is on a **check stub** or **check register.** (See figure 6.11.) Beginning with the current amount of money in the checking account, called the **balance,** deposits are added to the balance, and written checks are subtracted from the balance.

Example 1 As of February 19, the Reffitt Company had a balance of $4,692.17 in its bank checking account. On February 20, a deposit of $316.40 was made, and a check was written in the amount of $172.95. What was the balance in the company checking account as of February 20?

Solution

	$4,692.17	Balance on February 19
+	316.40	Deposit on February 20
	5,008.57	Total
−	172.95	Check written on February 20
	$4,835.62	Balance as of February 20

The record of checks and deposits maintained by the bank is the **bank statement.** Periodically (usually monthly), a copy of the bank statement is sent to the depositor. The bank statement indicates the balance at the beginning of the period; provides an account of deposits, checks, fees, and miscellaneous credits recorded by the bank for the period; and gives the balance in the account at the end of the period. A typical bank statement is shown in figure 6.12.

Figure 6.12
Typical bank statement

Johnson Drug Store
101 Main Street
Anytown, U.S.A.

ACCOUNT NUMBER 1-01138
7-20-89 STATEMENT DATE

BALANCE LAST STATEMENT	CHECKS		DEPOSITS		SERVICE CHARGE	BALANCE THIS STATEMENT
	NO	TOTAL AMOUNT	NO	TOTAL AMOUNT		
942.81	13	2,044.85	4	2,226.70	2.75	1,121.91

DATE	CHECKS AND DEBIT CHARGES				DEPOSITS & CREDITS	BALANCE
	CHECK NO.	AMOUNT	CHECK NO.	AMOUNT		
6-23	111	14.65	109	38.40	623.17	1,512.93
6-25	112	101.60				1,411.33
7-1		28.75 RT			402.70	1,785.28
7-8	115	33.50				1,751.78
7-9	108	472.70			602.20	1,881.28
7-12	114	114.78	110	192.80		1,573.70
7-12	102	321.40	116	50.00		1,202.30
7-15	117	66.80	119	73.40		1,062.10
7-16		2.75 SC	121	536.07	598.63	1,121.91

CODES			
CM-CREDIT MEMO DC-DEPOSIT CORRECTION	DM-DEBIT MEMO EC-ERROR CORRECTION	RT-RETURN CHECK SC-SERVICE CHARGE	RC-RETURN CHECK CHARGE

SHOULD FURTHER INFORMATION BE HELPFUL PLEASE REFER TO YOUR ACCOUNT NO. WHEN MAKING INQUIRIES.
PLEASE EXAMINE AT ONCE. IF NO ERROR IS REPORTED IN TEN DAYS THE ACCOUNT WILL BE CONSIDERED CORRECT.

The balance on the bank statement (the bank balance) at the end of a period seldom agrees with the balance shown on the check stub or check register (the checkbook balance). This may be due to an arithmetic error by either party, but more often it is the result of one or more of the following:

1. **Outstanding checks** Checks written on the account and subtracted on the check stub or check register that have not yet been received by the bank and hence are not listed on the bank statement.
2. **Unrecorded deposits** Deposits that are added to the balance on the check register that have not yet been recorded on the bank statement.
3. **Overdrafts** Checks written on a checking account when there are insufficient funds in the account to pay the payee. If a depositor receives a check from a third party and submits it to the bank for deposit in his or her account, and if the bank is unable to collect the funds, then the amount is deducted from the depositor's account, and the check is returned to the depositor.
4. **Miscellaneous charges or credits** Credits or fees on the bank statement that are not recorded on the check register. Many banking institutions now pay interest on funds in a checking account, and this interest appears as a credit on the statement. Fees on the statement could include charges for providing the checking account service (service charges), charges for the printing of new checks, or corrections of previously undetected bank errors.

When the bank balance and the checkbook balance are not in agreement, the depositor should attempt to **reconcile** the account. This is accomplished as follows:

To the Bank Balance

1. Add the total of all unrecorded deposits.
2. Subtract the total of all outstanding checks.

To the Checkbook Balance

1. Subtract the total of
   a. All previously deposited overdrafts.
   b. All miscellaneous charges.
2. Add the total of all interest and miscellaneous credits.

The result of this arithmetic is an adjusted bank balance and an adjusted checkbook balance. These two balances will be identical, provided that all transactions were recorded correctly and that there were no mathematical

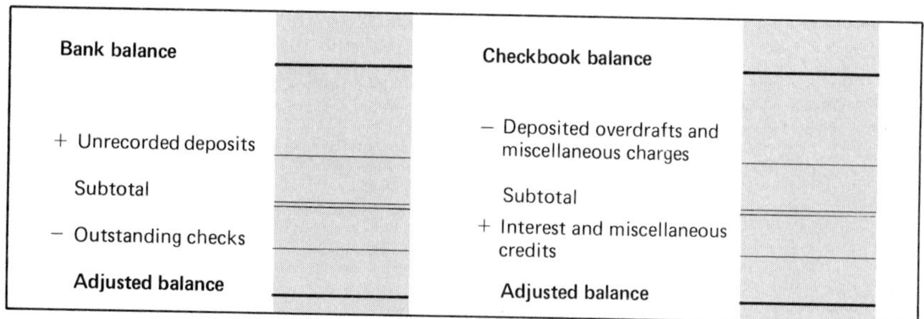

Bank balance
+ Unrecorded deposits
Subtotal
− Outstanding checks
Adjusted balance
Checkbook balance
− Deposited overdrafts and miscellaneous charges
Subtotal
+ Interest and miscellaneous credits
Adjusted balance

Figure 6.13 Format for bank statement reconciliation

errors. The adjusted balance represents the true balance in the checking account, and the check register should be corrected to reflect the adjusted balance.

A format for bank statement reconciliation is shown in figure 6.13.

Example 2 The bank statement of Dunn's Flower & Gift Shop indicated a balance of \$794.15. The shop's checkbook balance was \$945.60. For the preceding period, there was an unrecorded deposit of \$424.18, service charges of \$3.80, and outstanding checks of \$100.64, \$39.95, \$12.48, and \$123.46. Reconcile the checking account.

Solution

The total of the outstanding checks is \$276.53. Using the format of figure 6.13,

Bank balance	\$ 794.15	Checkbook balance	\$ 945.60
Unrecorded deposit	+ 424.18	Service charge	− 3.80
Subtotal	1,218.33	Subtotal	941.80
Outstanding checks	− 276.53	Interest and misc. credits	+ 0.00
Adjusted balance	\$ 941.80	Adjusted balance	\$ 941.80

If the adjusted balances fail to agree following a reconciliation attempt, there has been an error. This may be an error on the part of the bank, but more likely it is a mistake by the depositor. The most common errors include adding or subtracting incorrectly, copying numbers incorrectly, or failing to record a check or deposit. Checks, check stubs, and deposit slips should be examined for these errors, and a new reconciliation statement prepared. If, after repeated attempts, the account cannot be reconciled, the depositor should seek assistance from the bank.

Example 3 Reconcile the following checking account. Items on the register marked with a check (√) indicate items that appeared on the previous month's bank statement. (The code SC on the bank statement means "**service charge**"; the code RT means "**returned check,**" that is, a previously deposited overdraft; and the code INT means "**interest credited.**")

Bank Statement

Checks and Debits				Deposits	Date	Balance
Check No.	Amount	Check No.	Amount			
					9–30	924.16
613	64.46				10–2	859.70
616	124.30				10–11	735.40
615	58.70		74.36 RT		10–14	602.34
617	515.00			3.02 INT	10–15	90.36
				189.60	10–16	279.96
618	16.60		2.60 SC		10–24	260.76

Check Register

Date	Check No.	Check Issued to	Amount	√	Deposits	Balance
						1,095.16
9–24	612	J. R. Discon	43.20	√		1,051.96
9–26	613	Armis Co.	64.46			987.50
9–27	614	Security Alarms	127.80	√		859.70
10–8	615	Jackson Supply	58.70			801.00
10–10	616	Farmington Co.	124.30			676.70
10–11	617	Payroll	515.00		189.60	351.30
10–20	618	Terrell's Off. Supply	16.60			334.70
10–25	619	Lawson Lumber Co.	122.40			212.30

Solution

Bank balance	$260.76	Checkbook balance	$212.30
Outstanding check	−122.40	Returned check	− 74.36
		Service charge	− 2.60
		Interest	+ 3.02
Adjusted balance	$138.36	Adjusted balance	$138.36

Example 4 Mary Jo Reynolds was unable to reconcile her checking account. Her checkbook stubs, bank statement, and reconciliation attempt follow. What went wrong?

Mary's Check Stubs

145 IF TAX DEDUCTIBLE CHECK HERE ☐
$ 29.07
3-7 19 89
To Allied Dept. Store
For Bedspread

	DOLLARS	CENTS
BAL FWD	672	12
DEPOSIT		
DEPOSIT		
TOTAL	672	12
THIS ITEM	29	07
SUB-TOTAL		
OTHER DEDUCT. (IF ANY)		
BAL FWD	643	05

146 IF TAX DEDUCTIBLE CHECK HERE ☐
$ 92.16
3-10 19 89
To Saveway
For Groceries

	DOLLARS	CENTS
BAL FWD	643	05
DEPOSIT		
DEPOSIT		
TOTAL	643	05
THIS ITEM	92	16
SUB-TOTAL		
OTHER DEDUCT. (IF ANY)		
BAL FWD	551	89

147 IF TAX DEDUCTIBLE CHECK HERE ☐
$ 375.00
3-10 19 89
To Shady Villas Inc.
For Rent

	DOLLARS	CENTS
BAL FWD	551	89
DEPOSIT		
DEPOSIT		
TOTAL	551	89
THIS ITEM	375	00
SUB-TOTAL		
OTHER DEDUCT. (IF ANY)		
BAL FWD	176	89

148 IF TAX DEDUCTIBLE CHECK HERE ☐
$ 78.44
3-15 19 89
To Tallowondy Electric
For Feb. Electric Bill

	DOLLARS	CENTS
BAL FWD	176	89
DEPOSIT	1086	42
DEPOSIT		
TOTAL	1273	31
THIS ITEM	78	44
SUB-TOTAL		
OTHER DEDUCT. (IF ANY)		
BAL FWD	1194	87

Bank Statement (as of 3–16–89)

Checks and Debits: Check No.	Checks and Debits: Amount	Deposits	Date	Balance
				672.12
145	29.07		3–11	643.05
147	375.00		3–12	268.05
146	92.16	1,086.42	3–16	1,262.31
	2.60 SC		3–16	1,259.71

Mary's Reconciliation Statement

Bank balance	$1,239.71	Checkbook balance	$1,194.87
Outstanding check	− 78.44	Service charge	− 2.60
Adjusted balance	$1,161.27	Adjusted balance	$1,192.27

Solution

Mary Jo made three errors: a subtracting error on check stub 146, an adding error on check stub 148, and a copying error when writing the bank balance on her reconciliation statement. Once these errors are corrected, the adjusted bank balance and the adjusted checkbook balance is $1,181.27.

Exercises for Section 6.6

In problems 1–10, use the given information to find the balance in the account as of the indicated date.

1. April 6: Balance = \$1,352.14
   April 10: Check written for \$211.15
   April 12: Check written for \$947.20
   Balance as of April 12 = ?

2. September 8: Balance = \$4,721.42
   September 9: Check written for \$1,621.29
   September 14: Check written for \$2,142.41
   Balance as of September 14 = ?

3. January 28: Balance = \$3,431.78
   January 30: Deposit of \$1,620.71
   February 3: Check written for \$2,247.60
   Balance as of February 3 = ?

4. October 14: Balance = \$974.21
   October 15: Deposit of \$347.98
   October 17: Check written for \$211.19
   Balance as of October 17 = ?

5. May 8: Balance = \$1,213.78
   May 9: Check written for \$217.15
   May 11: Deposit of \$412.42
   May 15: Check written for \$709.39
   Balance as of May 15 = ?

6. November 21: Balance = \$2,142.08
   November 25: Check written for \$1,342.71
   November 26: Deposit of \$727.77
   November 27: Check written for \$942.31
   Balance as of November 27 = ?

7. June 28: Balance = \$3,217.11
   June 29: Deposit of \$426.07
   June 30: Checks written for \$7.11 and \$45.80
   July 2: Check written for \$1,247.12
   Balance as of July 2 = ?

8. August 2: Balance = \$1,742.13
   August 6: Checks written for \$143.12 and \$913.72
   August 10: Check written for \$547.08
   August 11: Deposit of \$322.27
   Balance as of August 11 = ?

9. October 17: Balance = \$1,194.37
   October 18: Deposit of \$398.14
   October 19: Checks written for \$177.43 and \$313.79
   October 23: Deposit of \$211.14
   October 25: Check written for \$97.14
   Balance as of October 25 = ?

10. February 16: Balance = \$1,427.63
    February 18: Deposit of \$619.17
    February 21: Check written for \$523.14
    February 26: Checks written for \$113.14 and \$422.73
    March 1: Deposit of \$241.47
    Balance as of March 1 = ?

11. Fill in the missing entries on the following check stubs, proceeding in numerical order and carrying each balance to the next stub:

No. 82	\$ 32.00
May 3, 1989	
To: J. Best	
For: Insurance	
Bal. Brt. Forward	947.10
Amt. Dep.	182.00
Total	
Amt. This Check	32.00
Bal. Car. Forward	

No. 83	\$ 157.21
May 7, 1989	
To: Fla. Power	
For: Elec. Bill	
Bal. Brt. Forward	
Amt. Dep.	0.00
Total	
Amt. This Check	157.21
Bal. Car. Forward	

No. 84	\$ 87.13
May 12, 1989	
To: S.F.U.W.	
For: Auto Repair	
Bal. Brt. Forward	
Amt. Dep.	431.82
Total	
Amt. This Check	
Bal. Car. Forward	

No. 85	\$ 221.37
May 13, 1989	
To: B. Gadsden	
For: Pump Service	
Bal. Brt. Forward	
Amt. Dep.	0.00
Total	
Amt. This Check	
Bal. Car. Forward	

No. 86	\$ 200.00
May 13, 1989	
To: Mastercharge	
For: Payment	
Bal. Brt. Forward	
Amt. Dep.	379.14
Total	
Amt. This Check	
Bal. Car. Forward	

No. 87	\$ 333.14
May 14, 1989	
To: Amer. Finance	
For: Loan Payment	
Bal. Brt. Forward	
Amt. Dep.	0.00
Total	
Amt. This Check	
Bal. Car. Forward	

12. Fill in the blanks on the following check register:

Check Register

Check No.	Date	Check Issued to or Description of Deposit	Amount of Check	√	Amount of Deposit	Balance
						782.15
354	5–13	Colony Shops	47.12			________
355	5–17	Dr. Cone	29.00			________
	5–23	Deposit			582.14	________
356	5–24	Daily Enterprise	12.50			________
357	5–26	Vol. Fire Dept.	12.20			________
358	5–26	Hecht Company	82.14			________
359	5–28	Sterling Savings & Loan	254.13			________
360	6–1	Mutual Life Ins.	74.32			________
	6–7	Deposit			241.72	________
361	6–9	W. P. Black	187.50			________

13. A checking account has a bank statement balance of $514.13, a checkbook balance of $385.09, outstanding checks of $12.14 and $120.15, and a service charge of $3.25. Use the format of figure 6.13 to reconcile the account.

14. The bank statement of El Dorado Auto Upholstery indicated a balance of $2,350.15, and the checkbook balance was $1,573.52. For the preceding period, there was an unrecorded deposit of $732.14, a service charge of $1.20, and outstanding checks of $302.64, $417.81, $306.02, and $483.50. Use the format of figure 6.13 to reconcile the account.

15. The latest bank statement received by Drummond Enterprises indicated a balance in the company's checking account of $3,114.27. The company's checkbook balance was $3,195.81. There were unrecorded deposits of $2,113.17 and $1,011.10, and outstanding checks of $742.14, $311.10, $108.82, $473.14, and $1,415.03. There was a charge of $7.50 on the account for printing new checks. Use the format of figure 6.13 to reconcile the account.

16. Using the format of figure 6.13, reconcile the following account: The bank statement balance was $4,321.19, and the checkbook balance was $5,249.61. There were unrecorded deposits of $1,517.12, $509.13, and $714.98. Outstanding checks were in the amounts of $444.45, $123.19, $1,509.23, $4.42, and $52.49. There was a charge of $8.50 on the account for printing new checks, and a check for $312.47 that was deposited was returned because of insufficient funds (an overdraft).

17. Use the format of figure 6.13 to reconcile the following account of the Dolby Company: The bank statement balance was $2,251.19, and the checkbook balance was $2,983.12. The unrecorded deposits were in the amounts of $237.15, $975.83, $1,214.58, $547.19, and $642.81. There

were outstanding checks of $171.46, $858.88, $619.92, $741.08, $1,106.41, $213.41, $109.29, and $19.17. There was a service charge of $2.15, and a charge for new checks of $9.27. Also, two checks in the amounts of $321.14 and $621.43 that had been deposited were returned because of insufficient funds.

18. The bank statement and check register for the account of Lory's Boutique follow. The items on the register marked with a check (√) indicate items that appeared on the previous month's bank statement. Fill in the missing entries on the check register, find the outstanding checks and unrecorded deposits, and reconcile the account. (The code SC on the bank statement means "service charge," the code RT means "returned check," and the code INT means "interest credited.")

Check Register

Check No.	Date	Check Issued to or Description of Dep.	Amount of Check	√	Amount of Deposit	Balance
						1,241.46
121	6–24	Pacific Light	112.46	√		1,129.00
122	6–26	Sizemore's Office Supply	41.14			1,087.86
123	6–27	Apex Fuel Company	82.24			1,005.62
124	6–27	Reese Wholesale	214.82	√		790.80
	6–29	Deposit			527.31	1,318.11
125	7–2	Global Imports	92.37			1,225.74
	7–4	Adjustment for Service Charge	2.75	√		1,222.99
126	7–9	Gerrell Fashions	153.91			________
	7–10	Deposit			417.84	________
127	7–16	Financial Trust	321.47			________
128	7–23	Ray-Mar Designs	472.14			________
129	7–27	J. T. Whittington	29.36			________
	7–30	Deposit			687.81	________

Bank Statement

Checks and Debits				Deposits	Date	Balance
Check No.	Amount	Check No.	Amount			
					6–30	911.43
123	82.24		317.81 RT		7–2	511.38
				527.31	7–3	1,038.69
125	92.37				7–9	946.32
				417.84	7–14	1,364.16
127	321.47	122	41.14	2.86 INT	7–21	1,004.41
128	472.14		1.50 SC		7–31	530.77

19. Fill in the missing entries on the following check register and bank statement. The items marked with a check (√) on the register appeared on the previous month's statement. Find the outstanding checks and unrecorded deposits and reconcile the account. (The codes INT, SC, RT, and DM on the bank statement mean, respectively, "interest credited," "service charge," "returned check," and "debit memo.")

Check Register

Check No.	Date	Check Issued to or Description of Dep.	Amount of Check	√	Amount of Deposit	Balance
						2,475.91
387	10–23	Cities Supply Co.	215.82	√		2,260.09
388	10–23	Martin Plumbing	83.14			2,176.95
	10–26	Deposit		√	485.30	2,662.25
389	10–26	Consolidated Elec.	138.41	√		2,523.84
390	10–30	Haynes Transport	47.18			2,476.66
391	11–2	Justin Construction	914.82			1,561.84
	11–4	Adjustment for SC	2.65	√		1,559.19
	11–6	Deposit			842.13	
392	11–9	Delta Engineering	1,417.10			
	11–15	Deposit			817.10	
393	11–16	Holiga Glass Co.	123.72			
394	11–20	Midwest Finance	782.37			
395	11–21	E. J. Reed	23.10			
396	11–27	Central Heating	214.02			
	11–28	Deposit			392.68	
397	11–29	Avco Tile	514.27			

Bank Statement

Checks and Debits				Deposits	Date	Balance
Check No.	Amount	Check No.	Amount			
					10–31	2,604.33
391	914.82				11–6	
				842.13	11–10	
388	83.14		121.13 RT	11.02 INT	11–14	
				817.10	11–18	
	224.15 RT				11–19	
392	1,417.10				11–20	
395	23.10		7.50 DM		11–23	
394	782.37				11–24	
	3.42 SC				11–30	

20. The bank statement and check register for the account of Warner's Hardware follow. Fill in the missing entries, find the outstanding checks and unrecorded deposits, and reconcile the account. Items marked with a check (√) on the register appeared on the previous month's statement. (The codes SC, RT, DM, CM, and INT on the bank statement mean, respectively, "service charge," "returned check," "debit memo," "credit memo," and "interest credited.")

Check Register

Check No.	Date	Check Issued to or Description of Dep.	Amount of Check	√	Amount of Deposit	Balance
						1,892.01
211	4–21	Lake City Supply	182.77	√		1,709.24
212	4–23	A. R. Robbins	86.13			1,623.11
	4–26	Deposit		√	1,478.04	3,101.15
213	4–26	Johnson Sheet Metal	287.12			2,814.03
214	4–27	Superior Rubber Products	513.21	√		2,300.82
215	5–1	Wood Products Inc.	918.42			1,382.40
	5–8	Adjustment for SC	2.25	√		1,380.15
	5–10	Deposit			914.22	______
216	5–14	Statewide Electric	192.14			______
217	5–17	Foster Tools	478.13			______
218	5–18	Amer. Whlsl. Supply	742.91			______
219	5–18	W. E. Williams	47.18			______
	5–19	Deposit			849.47	______
220	5–21	United Savings & Loan	271.17			______
221	5–23	Greenwell Fertilizer Co.	381.41			______
222	5–25	Perma-Plastics Inc.	172.10			______
	5–26	Deposit			1,724.29	______
223	5–27	T. R. Bascomb	14.81			______
224	5–27	Central Realty	92.36			______
225	5–29	Standard Sales Inc.	147.90			______
	5–30	Deposit			1,141.13	______

Bank Statement

Checks and Debits				Deposits	Date	Balance
Check No.	Amount	Check No.	Amount			
					4–30	2,671.82
213	287.12	215	918.42		5–4	______
	392.10 RT			9.64 INT	5–8	______
				914.22	5–14	______
216	192.14		83.10 RT		5–17	______
				849.47	5–22	______
220	271.17	218	742.91		5–23	______
219	47.18		15.20 DM		5–25	______
224	92.36			10.00 CM	5–28	______
221	381.41			1,724.29	5–29	______
	2.75 SC				5–31	______

Glossary

Balance The current amount of money in a checking account.

Bank statement A record of the transactions in a checking account (checks written, deposits made, fees charged, etc.) maintained by the bank.

Check A written order directing a bank to pay a specified amount of money from a checking account to a specified party.

Checking account A service provided by a bank whereby funds of a business, institution, or individual are placed in the bank for safekeeping and future use.

Check register or check stub A record maintained by the owner of a checking account of the checks and deposits in the account.

Commission Earnings of sales personnel based on the amount of items sold; usually a percentage of net sales.

Deposit The act of placing funds in a checking account.

Depositor The owner of a checking account.

Differential piecework An incentive wage plan that provides two different piece-rates, one for all units produced up to a specified standard and a second (higher) piece-rate for all units if the worker's production exceeds the standard.

Drawing account A fund from which salespeople may receive advances against future commissions.

Endorsement An inscription on the back of a check by the payee providing instructions for the disposition of the check.

Fair Labor Standards Act A federal law (also known as the Federal Wage and Hour Law) enacted in 1938 that establishes minimum wages, overtime pay, and other labor standards for all employees covered by the act.

Federal income tax A federal tax based on an employee's earnings, marital status, and number of withholding allowances.

Federal unemployment tax A federal tax used to support a fund to provide compensation to workers who are unable to find employment. The tax is paid entirely by the employer.

FICA tax Federal Insurance Contributions Act (Social Security) tax levied on a base amount of each employee's yearly gross earnings and matched by the employer. The tax supports a fund that provides monthly benefits to retired or disabled workers and to the surviving families of deceased workers.

Graduated commission Commissions that are based on a graduating scale; that is, the commission rate increases as sales volume increases.

Gross earnings The total earnings of an employee within a specified pay period, before any deductions are made.

Group insurance Insurance issued to a company that provides benefits for the employees.

Incentive wage plan Any method of computing wages for workers engaged in production that rewards extra or sustained effort (for example, piecework or standard hour plans).

Interest credited Interest paid on funds in a checking account and shown as a credit on a bank statement.

Net earnings The actual earnings paid to a worker after all deductions are made.

Net sales Total sales less returns and cancellations.

Outstanding check A check written on a checking account but not yet received by the bank and hence not entered on the bank statement.

Overdraft A check written on a checking account when there are insufficient funds in the account to pay the payee.

Override A commission paid to supervisory personnel based on the net sales of the people they supervise.

Overtime Hours worked in excess of a specified workweek (usually 40 hours, but sometimes less). The Fair Labor Standards Act specifies the rate of pay for overtime hours to be $1\frac{1}{2}$ times the rate for regular hours.

Payee The party named to receive the funds from a check.

Piecework or piece-rate Wage compensation based on the number of units produced by workers engaged in production.

Reconciliation Adjustments to the bank statement and the check register of a checking account to determine that both records of the account are in agreement.

Returned check A check returned to the party that deposited it because there are insufficient funds in the account on which the check was written.

Salary Gross earnings that are paid according to a specified period of employment. A salary is independent of both production and actual working time.

Service charge A fee charged by a bank for providing a checking account service.

Standard hour plan An incentive wage plan based on a standard production level of a specified number of units per hour.

Unrecorded deposit A deposit that has been added to the balance of a checking account on the check register but has not yet been listed on the bank statement.

Wages Gross earnings of workers that are paid according to actual time at work; usually calculated on a per hour basis as the rate per hour times the number of hours worked.

Withholding allowance Allowance granted by the federal government that reduces the amount of income tax withheld from gross earnings.

Review test

1. Jennifer Collins earns a salary of $2,240 per month. Compute her gross earnings per pay period if the pay period is biweekly.

2. Bob Richert sells lighting fixtures on a straight commission of 12% of net sales. During April, his sales were $21,417, with returns and cancellations totaling $1,742. Find his gross earnings for the month.

3. The Brooker Corporation pays Susan Wecksler a straight commission of 8% of net sales with a monthly draw of $800. Complete the following record of her monthly gross earnings:

4. In August, Pete Clark submitted orders totaling $23,420. Pete is paid a monthly graduated commission of 4% of the first $10,000 of net sales, 6% of the next $10,000, and 8.5% of net sales in excess of $20,000. Find his gross earnings for the month if returns and cancellations totaled $1,740.

Month	Net Sales	Commission	Draw Advance	Draw Deficit Brought Fwd.	Gross Earnings	Draw Deficit Carried Fwd.
Jan.	$ 9,422			$60.00		
Feb.	11,112					
Mar.	12,748					

5. Pam Stephens is employed as an assembler by a company that uses the standard hour plan. Pam is paid $4.60 per hour, and her standard production level is 140 units per 40-hour workweek. Find her gross earnings for a week during which she produces 161 units.

6. Richard Stringline earns $2,028 per month. His salary is based on a 40-hour workweek, but during the last two weeks he worked the following hours:

	Sun.	Mon.	Tues.	Wed.	Thurs.	Fri.	Sat.
Week 1	0	8	9	8	8	7	3
Week 2	0	8	8	10	8	7	4

Calculate Richard's gross earnings for this two-week period.

7. Brenda Sales is paid weekly and earns $5.60 per hour for a 40-hour workweek. In addition to deductions for federal income tax (M-2) and FICA, union dues of $8.60 per month and group insurance premiums of $28.10 per month are also withheld from her pay. Use table 6.2 and the 1989 FICA contribution rate of 7.51% of the first $48,000 in gross earnings and find Brenda's net earnings for a 40-hour workweek.

8. The McPherson Company pays a state unemployment tax of 6.1% of the first $7,000 of gross earnings of each employee. The company employs 34 people, and all 34 employees earn in excess of $7,000 per year. How much total (state and federal) unemployment tax does the company pay?

9. A checking account has a bank statement balance of $451.53, a checkbook balance of $330.74, outstanding checks totaling $242.81, unrecorded deposits of $116.22, and a service charge of $5.80. Reconcile the account.

10. Reconcile the following checking account: Bank balance, $1,417.40; checkbook balance, $917.32; returned check, $413.28; unrecorded deposits, $218.41 and $709.52; service charge, $5.40; outstanding checks, $311.81, $904.72, $622.14, and $8.02.

CHAPTER 7

Topics in Accounting

Chapter Objectives

I. Learn the meaning of the following terms:

Income statement, 220
Balance sheet, 222
Assets, 222
Liabilities, 222
Owners' equity, 222
Equities, 222
Cash budget, 239
Depreciation, 247
Real property, 247
Tangible personal property, 247
Recovery period, 247
Cost of an asset, 255
Useful life of an asset, 255
Salvage value, 255
Partnership, 264

II. Learn the principles of:

Income statement, 220
Balance sheet, 222
Vertical analysis, 224
Horizontal analysis, 225
Financial ratios, 233–237
Cash budget, 239–240
Depreciation schedule, 255–257
Overhead distribution, 261–263
Partnership distribution of profits and losses, 263–267

III. Calculate:

Current ratio, 234
Acid-test ratio, 235
Gross profit margin, 235
Operating ratio, 236
Stockholders' equity ratio, 236
Debt-equity ratio, 237
Depreciation using the MACRS and ACRS methods, 247–253
Straight-line depreciation, 255–256
Declining balance depreciation, 256
Sum-of-the-years-digits depreciation, 257
Units-of-production depreciation, 259

Section 7.1 Introduction

A requisite of efficient business operation is accurate data. The collection, summarization, and communication of accurate information are essential to sound planning. The kinds of information needed by management and analysts are records of past activities, data concerning current operating efficiency, and projections for future activities. These three items summarize the role of accounting in business. Accounting techniques are the most widely used means of describing and communicating business operations. This chapter examines some of the basic accounting procedures central to all businesses.

Section 7.2 The income statement

Periodically, a company must appraise its progress. Managers and owners need to check the financial health of the enterprise and note its economic activity. Two documents summarize this information: the income statement and the balance sheet.

The **income statement** is a report on the company income for a period of time, generally a month or a year. The income statement describes the general manner in which the income of the business is earned. There are two basic forms of the statement, the single-step and the multiple-step. The single-step income statement is illustrated in figure 7.1. The basic format of this statement is the fundamental business equation

■ (7–1) $$\text{Revenue} - \text{Expenses} = \text{Income}$$

where revenue is sales and gains, expenses are costs incurred to generate income, and income is net earnings. The single-step income statement has been adopted by many companies because of its simplicity and readability.

The multiple-step income statement is illustrated in figure 7.2. The basic format of this statement is the equation

■ (7–2) $$\text{Gross margin} - \text{Expenses} = \text{Income}$$

where gross margin is the difference between net sales and the cost of goods sold. Companies who favor the multiple-step income statement compare the gross margin with that of previous years and with national industry averages to evaluate operating results.

Income statements are used in an analysis of company operations. To management, the income statement is a report on the success or failure of the firm's activities; to owners, it is a measure of the efficiency of management.

Figure 7.1
Income statement—Meyer Company

Meyer Company
Income Statement for the Year Ended
December 31, 19__

Revenue	
Sales	$ 960,000
Gain from Sale of Land	46,000
Interest and Other	72,000
	$1,078,000
Expenses	
Cost of Merchandise Sold	$ 450,000
Operating Expenses	320,000
Interest Expenses	96,000
Federal and State Taxes	120,000
	$ 986,000
Net Income	$ 92,000

Figure 7.2
Income statement—Craft Industries

Craft Industries
Income Statement
For the Year Ended November 30, 19__

Sales		$9,250,000
Less Cost of Goods Sold		5,475,000
Gross Margin		$3,775,000
Less Operating Expenses		
Salaries and Commissions	$ 800,000	
Advertising	1,250,000	
Depreciation	225,000	
Income Taxes	650,000	
Other Expenses	230,000	$3,155,000
Income		$ 620,000

Section 7.3 The balance sheet

The **balance sheet** presents the financial condition of a firm at a given moment of time. It is developed from past activities of the company and involves the classification and valuation of the firm's resources.

The balance sheet is a representation of the basic accounting equation

■ (7–3) Assets = Liabilities + Owners' equity

Defined in a broad sense, the term **assets** refers to the dollar value of everything the company owns, the term **liabilities** means the dollar value of everything the company owes, and the difference between the two is **owners' equity.*** The term **equities** is used for the sum of liabilities plus owners' equity and represents the claims upon the assets if the business is dissolved.

Traditionally, assets are reported on the left-hand side of the balance sheet and equities on the right-hand side (account form). Alternatively, assets may be at the top of the report and equities at the bottom (report form). In either event,

Figure 7.3
Balance sheet—Vargas Company

THE VARGAS COMPANY
Balance Sheet
December 31, 19__

Assets		Equities	
Current Assets		Current Liabilities	
Cash	$ 4,500	Due to Bank	$ 3,000
Accounts Receivable	6,000	Notes Payable	4,500
Merchandise Inventory	4,700	Total Current Liabilities	$ 7,500
Prepayments	1,300		
Total Current Assets	$16,500	Long-Term Liabilities	
		Mortgage	$20,000
Plant and Equipment		Total Liabilities	$27,500
Equipment	$ 5,000		
Building	22,000	Owners' Equity	
Land	3,000	M. Vargas, Owner	$19,000
Total	$30,000		
Total Assets	$46,500	Total Equities	$46,500

*Assets can also be thought of as the location of investment, and liabilities can be thought of as the source of the funds.

since assets and equities are just two dimensions of the same investment, it follows that the two sides balance—hence, the name balance sheet.

The two forms of balance sheets are illustrated in figures 7.3 and 7.4. On a balance sheet, the general headings of assets and liabilities are subdivided according to short-term and long-term categories. Current assets and current liabilities are short-term transactions; noncurrent assets and long-term liabilities are long-term transactions. Traditionally, short-term categories consist of items that could be converted to cash or disposed of within a period of one year.

Figure 7.4
Balance sheet—Brown Corporation

The Brown Corporation

Statement of Financial Condition

At December 31, 19__

Assets	
Current Assets	
Cash	$ 16,288,000
Marketable Securities (at Cost)	60,883,000
Receivables	90,061,000
Inventory	109,758,000
	$276,990,000
Fixed Assets	
Investments in Foreign Branches	$ 50,310,000
Property, Plant, and Equipment	$130,964,000
	$181,274,000
Total Assets	$458,264,000
Liabilities and Stockholders' Equity	
Current Liabilities	
Payables and Accruals	$ 38,285,000
Accrued Taxes	26,270,000
Current Installments on Long-Term Debt	1,229,000
Dividends Payable	2,882,000
Customers' Deposits	2,005,000
Customers' Service Prepayments	22,917,000
	93,588,000
Long-Term Debt	123,187,000
Total Liabilities	$216,775,000
Stockholders' Equity	
Common Stock, 8,607,000 shares, $5 par value	$154,187,000
Earnings Retained for Use in the Business	87,302,000
Total Stockholders' Equity	$241,489,000
Total Liabilities and Stockholders' Equity	$458,264,000

Section 7.4 Vertical and horizontal analysis

As public statements, the income statement and the balance sheet describe the economic activities of a company. Properly analyzed, these two statements disclose a company's earning capability and its financial strength. In the short run, a company must have sufficient funds for current needs. In the long run, a company must have sufficient earning and borrowing capacity to provide for continued growth and productivity.

The measure of a company's financial health requires an assessment that is both qualitative and quantitative. Qualitative evaluation is subjective and requires good intuition coupled with sound judgment. Quantitative analysis uses the mathematics of percents and ratios. Thus, financial analysis is both an art and a science.

The two basic forms of quantitative analysis are vertical analysis and horizontal analysis. **Vertical analysis** expresses in percent form component parts in relation to a whole. The computations in vertical analysis are an application of the basic percentage equation solved for R:

$$R = \frac{P}{B}$$

On an income statement, the base B typically is the value of net sales. This relates all other entries in the statement to sales, as percents.

The example of vertical analysis in figure 7.5 answers the question, "Where did the sales dollar go?" In this instance, 89.3% of each dollar (89.3¢) went for cost of goods, 1.6% for depreciation (1.6¢), and so on.

Figure 7.5
Income statement—Turner Company

The Turner Company
Income Statement
For the Year Ended December 31, 19__

		Amount	Percent
Net Sales		$375,000	100.0
Less:			
Cost of Sales	$335,000		89.3
Depreciation	6,000		1.6
Maintenance and Repairs	4,200		1.1
Taxes (Other than Federal Income)	6,500		1.7
Total Cost and Operating Expenses		$351,700	93.8
Operating Income		23,300	6.3
Interest Expense		2,500	0.7
Federal Income Taxes		9,900	2.6
Net Income		$ 10,900	2.9

The second type of financial analysis, **horizontal analysis,** compares dollar amounts for different periods shown on the same line of a comparative statement.* Figure 7.6 illustrates horizontal analysis. The earlier year is the base for computing percent increase or decrease.

Horizontal analysis is applicable to income statements as well as to balance sheets. The primary advantage of horizontal analysis is in disclosing trends.

Figure 7.6
Comparative balance sheet—Troy Manufacturing Company, Inc.

Troy Manufacturing Co., Inc.
Comparative Balance Sheet
As of December 31, 1989, 1990

	1990	1989	Increase or (Decrease) Amount	Increase or (Decrease) Percent
Current Assets				
Cash	$ 250,000	$ 249,000	$ 1,000	0.4
Short-Term Investments	382,000	400,000	18,000	(4.5)
Accounts Receivable	237,000	175,000	62,000	35.4
Inventories	300,000	330,000	30,000	(9.1)
Unexpired Insurance	40,000	30,000	10,000	33.3
Total Current Assets	$1,209,000	$1,184,000	$25,000	2.1
Land, Buildings, and Equipment				
Land	$ 135,000	$ 130,000	$ 5,000	3.8
Buildings (Net)	370,000	340,000	30,000	8.8
Machinery and Equipment (Net)	180,000	186,000	6,000	(3.2)
Total	$ 685,000	$ 656,000	$29,000	4.4
Total Assets	$1,894,000	$1,840,000	$54,000	2.9
Liabilities				
Accounts Payable	$ 64,000	$ 70,000	$ 6,000	(8.6)
Bank Loans	100,000	85,000	15,000	17.6
Wages Payable	40,000	30,000	10,000	33.3
Federal Income Tax Payable	215,000	195,000	20,000	10.3
Bonds Payable	300,000	300,000	-0-	-0-
Total Liabilities	$ 719,000	$ 680,000	$39,000	5.7
Owners' Equity				
Common Stock	$ 850,000	$ 832,000	$18,000	2.2
Retained Earnings	325,000	328,000	3,000	0.9
Total Owners' Equity	$1,175,000	$1,160,000	$15,000	1.3
Total Liabilities and Owners' Equity	$1,894,000	$1,840,000	$54,000	2.9

*A comparative statement is one that provides financial data for more than one reporting period.

Exercises for Sections 7.2 through 7.4

1. Fill in the missing entries in the following income statement if the sales for the Topkin Company were $870,000 and the operating expenses were $122,000:

The Topkin Company Income Statement for the Year Ended December 31, 19__		
Revenue		
Sales		______
Rental Income		$ 73,500
Interest		17,400
	Total	______
Expenses		
Cost of Merchandise Sold		$642,500
Operating Expenses		______
Interest Expenses		7,200
Federal and State Taxes		97,000
	Total	______
Net Income		______

2. Fill in the missing entries in the following balance sheet for the Clinton Corporation if the current assets in cash are $10,200, assets in land are $7,300, and the long-term mortgage liability is $42,700:

The Clinton Corporation Balance Sheet December 31, 19__			
Assets		**Equities**	
Current Assets		**Current Liabilities**	
Cash	______	Due to Bank	$111,200
Accounts Receivable	$12,500	Notes Payable	18,800
Merchandise Inventory	72,300	Total Current Liabilities	______
Prepayments	3,200		
Total Current Assets	______	**Long-Term Liabilities**	
Plant and Equipment		Mortgage	______
Equipment	$58,000	Total Liabilities	______
Buildings	97,000		
Land	______	**Owners' Equity**	
Total	______	R. H. Clinton, Owner	______
Total Assets	______	Total Equities	______

3. Fill in the missing entries in the following income statement:

The Anderson Corporation Income Statement For the Year Ended December 31, 19__	
Sales	$1,500,000
Cost of Goods Sold	
Gross Margin	$ 600,000
Expenses	
Salaries	
Advertising	140,000
Administrative Expenses	94,000
Other Expenses	61,000
Total Expenses	510,000
Net Income	$

4. Fill in the missing entries in the following balance sheet for the Elkhorn Company if the current accounts receivable are $218,400, fixed assets in plant and equipment are $430,000, and long-term debts total $257,000:

The Elkhorn Company Balance Sheet December 31, 19__	
Assets	
Current Assets	
Cash	$ 47,500
Marketable Securities	82,000
Accounts Receivable	
Inventories	249,000
Total Current Assets	
Land, Plant, and Equipment	
Land	$ 98,000
Plant and Equipment	
Total Fixed Assets	
Total Assets	
Equities	
Current Liabilities	
Payables	$748,200
Accrued Taxes	37,400
Long-Term Liabilities	
Long-term Debts	
Owners' Equity	
P. H. Elkhorn, Owner	$ 82,300
Total Equities	

5. Fill in the missing entries and complete the vertical analysis of the following income statement, using net sales as the base for computing percents (to the nearest tenth):

The Hamilton Company Income Statement
Year Ended December 31, 19__

		Amount	Percent
Net Sales		$450,000	_____
Less:			
Cost of Sales	$375,000		_____
Depreciation	9,700		_____
Maintenance	6,300		_____
Total Cost and Operating Expenses		_____	_____
Operating Income		_____	_____
Interest Expense		4,500	_____
Federal Taxes		7,200	_____
Net Income		_____	_____

6. Fill in the missing entries and complete the vertical analysis of the following income statement, using net sales as the base for computing percents (to the nearest tenth):

Gehrig Brothers
Income Statement
For the Year Ended June 30, 19__

	Amount	Percent
Net Sales	$850,000	_____
Cost of Goods Sold	372,900	_____
Gross Margin	_____	_____
Expenses		
Selling Expense	155,800	_____
General and Administrative Expense	51,000	_____
Federal Income Tax	44,800	_____
State Income Tax	14,400	_____
Total Expenses	_____	_____
Income	_____	_____

7. Complete the vertical analysis of the following income statement, using total income as the base for computing percents (to the nearest tenth):

Houser Wholesalers Income Statement December 31, 19__		
	Amount	**Percent**
Revenue		
Sales	$730,000	______
Rentals	60,000	______
Interest	7,000	______
Total Income	______	______
Expenses		
Cost of Merchandise	$540,000	______
Operating Expenses	92,000	______
Interest Expenses	6,000	______
Taxes	46,000	______
Total Expenses	______	______
Net Income	______	______

8. Complete the vertical analysis of the following balance sheet, using total assets as the base for computing percents (to the nearest tenth):

William Mullins, Inc. Balance Sheet December 31, 19__		
Assets		
Current Assets	**Amount**	**Percent**
Cash	$105,000	______
Accounts Receivable	140,000	______
Inventory	350,000	______
Total Current Assets	______	______
Land, Plant, and Equipment		
Land	$ 75,000	______
Plant and Equipment	320,000	______
Total Fixed Assets	______	______
Total Assets	______	______
Equities		
Current Liabilities		
Payables	$720,000	______
Accrued Taxes	42,000	______
Long-Term Liabilities		
Long-Term Debts	$150,000	______
Owners' Equity		
W. E. Mullins, Owner	$ 78,000	______
Total Equities	______	______

9. Complete the vertical analysis of the following balance sheet, using total assets as the base for computing percents (to the nearest tenth):

Felicione & Sons Balance Sheet
December 31, 19__

Assets	Amount	Percent
Current Assets		
Cash	$ 61,000	______
Accounts Receivable	184,000	______
Inventory	______	______
Total Current Assets	475,000	______
Land and Equipment	345,000	______
Total Assets	$______	______
Equities		
Current Liabilities		
Accounts Payable	$180,000	______
Accrued Liabilities	26,000	______
Long-Term Liabilities		
Bonds Payable, 12%	90,000	______
Stockholders' Equity		
Common Stock	300,000	______
Retained Earnings	224,000	______
Total Equities	$______	______

10. Complete the vertical analysis of the following income statement (compute percents to the nearest tenth):

AAA Insulation Income Statement
for Years Ending December 31, 1989 and 1990

	1990	1989	Increase or (Decrease) Amount	Increase or (Decrease) Percent
Net Sales	$77,000	$60,000	______	______
Cost of Goods Sold	34,000	26,500	______	______
Gross Margin	43,000	33,500	______	______
Operating Expenses				
Selling Expense	13,200	9,600	______	______
Administrative Expense	10,500	8,400	______	______
Depreciation Expense	2,750	3,000	______	______
Total Operating Expenses	26,450	21,000	______	______
Net Income	16,550	12,500	______	______

11. Complete the horizontal analysis of the following income statement (compute percents to the nearest tenth):

Oswald Enterprises Income Statement
for Years Ending December 31, 1989 and 1990

	1990	1989	Increase or (Decrease) Amount	Increase or (Decrease) Percent
Net Sales	$450,000	$370,000	_____	_____
Less:				
Cost of Sales	310,000	240,000	_____	_____
Depreciation	8,000	6,200	_____	_____
Maintenance	5,200	4,800	_____	_____
Total Cost and Operating Expenses	323,200	251,000	_____	_____
Operating Income	126,800	119,000	_____	_____
Interest Expense	14,000	12,000	_____	_____
Federal Taxes	22,000	18,000	_____	_____
Net Income	90,800	89,000	_____	_____

12. Complete the horizontal analysis of the following balance sheet (compute percents to the nearest tenth):

J. W. Wall, Inc. Balance Sheet
for Years Ending December 31, 1989 and 1990

	1990	1989	Increase or (Decrease) Amount	Increase or (Decrease) Percent	Percent of Total Assets 1990	Percent of Total Assets 1989
Assets						
Cash	$ 92,000	$ 74,000	_____	_____	___	___
Accounts Receivable	260,000	240,000	_____	_____	___	___
Inventory	374,000	370,000	_____	_____	___	___
Total Current Assets	_____	684,000	_____	_____	___	___
Fixed Assets	420,000	470,000	_____	_____	___	___
Total Assets	_____	_____	_____	_____	___	___
Equities						
Payables	$816,000	$810,000	_____	_____	___	___
Accrued Taxes	57,000	51,000	_____	_____	___	___
Total Current Liabilities	_____	861,000	_____	_____	___	___
Long-Term Liabilities	170,000	190,000	_____	_____	___	___
Total Liabilities	_____	1,051,000	_____	_____	___	___
Owners' Equity	103,000	103,000	_____	_____	___	___
Total Equities	_____	_____	_____	_____	___	___

13. Complete the horizontal analysis of the following balance sheet (compute percents to the nearest tenth):

Brooker Enterprises
Balance Sheet for Years Ending
December 31, 1989 and 1990

			Increase or (Decrease)		Percent of Total Assets	
	1990	**1989**	**Amount**	**Percent**	**1990**	**1989**
Assets						
Cash	$ 3,220,000	$ 4,110,000	____	____	___	___
Marketable Securities	11,700,000	9,100,000	____	____	___	___
Accounts Receivable	8,756,000	8,386,000	____	____	___	___
Inventory	16,750,000	14,200,000	____	____	___	___
Total Current Assets	____	____	____	____	___	___
Plant and Equipment	110,000	70,000	____	____	___	___
Total Assets	____	____	____	____	___	___
Equities						
Payables	$15,700,000	$14,100,000	____	____	___	___
Accrued Taxes	2,700,000	2,200,000	____	____	___	___
Dividends Payable	4,100,000	3,476,000	____	____	___	___
Deposits	1,842,000	1,040,000	____	____	___	___
Total Current Liabilities	____	____	____	____	___	___
Long-Term Debt	6,214,000	5,470,000	____	____	___	___
Total Liabilities	____	____	____	____	___	___
Common Stock	$ 9,740,000	$ 8,840,000	____	____	___	___
Retained Earnings	240,000	740,000	____	____	___	___
Total Stockholders' Equity	____	____	____	____	___	___
Total Liabilities and Stockholders' Equity	____	____	____	____	___	___

Section 7.5 Financial ratios

A ratio is another name for a fraction. The fraction $\frac{5}{1}$ in ratio form is 5:1. The fraction $\frac{216}{648}$ can be expressed as $\frac{1}{3}$ or 1:3 by reduction of fractions, or $33\frac{1}{3}\%$ by division and conversion to percent.

In financial analysis, numerous ratios have been developed to interpret a company's economic activities. A select group of these are examined:

Ratios Measuring Liquidity

1. Current ratio
2. Acid-test ratio

Ratios Measuring Profitability

3. Gross profit margin
4. Operating ratio

Ratios Measuring Long-Term Financial Condition

5. Stockholders' equity ratio
6. Debt-equity ratio

The balance sheet and income statement of Space-Tronics, Inc., figures 7.7 and 7.8, are used to discuss these basic ratios.

Figure 7.7
Balance sheet—Space-Tronics, Inc.

Space-Tronics, Inc.
Balance Sheet
December 31, 19__

Current Assets		Current Liabilities	
Cash	$ 12,200	Accounts Payable	$ 13,400
Accounts Receivable	21,900	Notes Payable	4,700
Inventory	18,300	Wages Payable	1,400
Prepaid Insurance	1,200	Income Tax Payable	2,400
Total Current Assets	$ 53,600	Total Current Liabilities	$ 21,900
Fixed Assets		Long-Term Liabilities	
Plant and Machinery	$ 97,000	Bonds Payable	$ 12,000
Land	12,400	Stockholders' Equity	
		Capital Stock	$120,000
		Retained Earnings	9,100
Total Assets	$163,000	Total Liabilities and Stockholders' Equity	$163,000

Figure 7.8
Income statement—
Space-Tronics, Inc.

Space-Tronics, Inc. Income Statement December 31, 19__	
Sales	$250,000
Expenses	
Cost of Goods Sold	$150,000
Operating Expenses	75,000
Interest Charges	600
Common Stock Dividend	12,500
Total	$238,100
Net Income	$ 11,900

Liquidity is the ability of a company to convert assets into cash quickly without incurring a significant loss. The current ratio (also called the working capital ratio) offers a rough measure of whether a company can meet its liabilities in the near future as they come due. The **current ratio** is the ratio of current assets to current liabilities:

■ (7–4) $$\text{Current ratio} = \frac{\text{Current assets}}{\text{Current liabilities}}$$

Example 1 Find the current ratio for Space-Tronics, Inc.

Solution

$$\text{Current ratio} = \frac{53{,}600}{21{,}900}$$

$$= 2.4$$

The current ratio is 2.4 to 1.

The current ratio assumes that current assets could be used to pay current liabilities. Most creditors want more than just a 1:1 current ratio, and traditionally, a 2:1 current ratio is considered a minimum.

A variation of the current ratio is the acid-test ratio. The inference is that the real measure, or the "acid test," of liquidity is to eliminate inventories and prepaid expenses from current assets. Prepaid expenses is money already spent, and inventories, it is argued, require both sales and collection before cash can be obtained. Thus, the **acid-test ratio** is the ratio of cash and receivables to current liabilities.

■ (7–5) $$\text{Acid-test ratio} = \frac{\text{Cash} + \text{Receivables}}{\text{Current liabilities}}$$

Example 2 Find the acid-test ratio of Space-Tronics, Inc.

Solution

$$\text{Acid-test ratio} = \frac{\$12{,}200 + \$21{,}900}{\$21{,}900}$$

$$= 1.6$$

The acid-test ratio is 1.6 to 1.

An acid-test ratio of 1:1 is considered acceptable, but a more practical analysis involves comparing a company's acid-test ratio with the acid-test ratio of other companies in the specific trade or industry.

The difference between net sales and the cost of goods sold is called gross margin. Gross margin should be sufficient to cover all operating expenses, interest expense, and profit for the owners. The percent found by dividing gross margin by net sales is called the **gross profit margin,** and it shows the average spread between the cost of goods sold and the selling price:

■ (7–6) $$\text{Gross profit margin} = \frac{\text{Net sales} - \text{Cost of goods sold}}{\text{Net sales}}$$

Example 3 Find the gross profit margin of Space-Tronics, Inc.

Solution

$$\text{Gross profit margin} = \frac{\$250{,}000 - \$150{,}000}{\$250{,}000}$$

$$= 0.40$$

$$= 40\%$$

Diminishing earnings over a period of time may be explained by a corresponding decline in gross profit margin.

The **operating ratio** is the ratio of cost of goods sold plus operating expenses to net sales:

■ (7–7) $$\text{Operating ratio} = \frac{\text{Cost of goods sold} + \text{Operating expenses}}{\text{Net sales}}$$

Expressed as a percent, the operating ratio reflects the amount of sales dollars used to defray the cost of goods and administrative expenses. The higher the operating ratio, the less income to meet interest payments, dividends, and other financial obligations.

Example 4 Determine the operating ratio of Space-Tronics, Inc.

Solution

$$\text{Operating ratio} = \frac{\$150{,}000 + \$75{,}000}{\$250{,}000}$$

$$= 0.90$$

$$= 90\%$$

The ratio of owners' equity to total assets is called the **stockholders' equity ratio:**

■ (7–8) $$\text{Stockholders' equity ratio} = \frac{\text{Owners' equity}}{\text{Total assets}}$$

Expressed as a percent, this ratio indicates the investment in assets that is financed by the owners or stockholders.

Example 5 Find the stockholders' equity ratio of Space-Tronics, Inc.

Solution

$$\text{Stockholders' equity ratio} = \frac{\$120{,}000 + \$9{,}100}{\$163{,}000}$$

$$= 0.7920245$$

$$= 79\%$$

Creditors regard a high stockholders' equity ratio as favorable, since it indicates a large cushion of security.

Another safety indicator is the debt-equity ratio. The **debt-equity ratio** is the ratio of total debt to total ownership equity:

■ (7–9) $$\text{Debt-equity ratio} = \frac{\text{Current liabilities} + \text{Long-term liabilities}}{\text{Owners' equity}}$$

Example 6 Determine the debt-equity ratio of Space-Tronics, Inc.

Solution

$$\text{Debt-equity ratio} = \frac{\$21{,}900 + \$12{,}000}{\$120{,}000 + \$9{,}100}$$

$$= 0.2625871$$

$$= 26\%$$

A debt-equity ratio of 1:1 (100%) is considered acceptable for established manufacturing firms; for small firms, a 1:4 (25%) ratio may be the acceptable minimum.

Exercises for Section 7.5

Round current ratios and acid-test ratios to the nearest tenth. Round all other ratios to the nearest percent.

1. The Bilford Company lists current assets of $47,400 and current liabilities of $19,700. Find the current ratio.
2. In problem 1, if inventories and prepaid expenses total $24,300 of the company's current assets, find the acid-test ratio.
3. Find the current ratio and the acid-test ratio for the Sanderson Company, which reported current liabilities of $21,400 and current assets of $58,800. Inventories and prepaid expenses of the current assets total $29,100.
4. The Concord Company reported net sales of $174,000. Find the gross profit margin if the cost of the goods sold was $92,000.
5. Tamtek reported net sales of $324,000, with operating expenses of $120,000. If the cost of the goods sold was $190,000, find the gross profit margin and the operating ratio.
6. The net sales of Taylor Enterprises was $520,000, with operating expenses of $260,000. The cost of goods sold was $245,000. Find the gross profit margin and the operating ratio.

7. The owners' equity of the Lewis Company is $91,000, and last year's total assets were $130,000. Find the stockholders' equity ratio.

8. Lerch Enterprises reported current liabilities of $34,000, long-term liabilities of $11,400, and total assets of $210,000. If the owners' equity in the company is $142,000, find the stockholders' equity ratio and the debt-equity ratio.

9. The owners' equity of the Thresher Company is $109,000, and last year's total assets were $183,000. The current liabilities are $31,500, and long-term liabilities are $9,700. Find the stockholders' equity ratio and the debt-equity ratio.

10. The common stock outstanding in the Scott Corporation totals $120,000. Last year, the company retained $14,000 in earnings and reported total assets of $273,000. The current liabilities were $42,300, and the long-term liabilities were $13,200. Find the stockholders' equity ratio and the debt-equity ratio.

For problems 11–15, refer to the following balance sheet and income statement of the Brewster Company:

The Brewster Company
Balance Sheet
December 31, 19__

Current Assets		**Current Liabilities**	
Cash	$18,500	Accounts Payable	$ 15,400
Accounts Receivable	34,000	Notes Payable	5,200
Inventory	28,000	Wages Payable	2,100
Prepaid Insurance	1,750	Income Tax Payable	2,450
Total Current Assets	______	Total Current Liabilities	______
Plant, Equipment, and Land		**Long-Term Liabilities**	
Plant and Equipment	$82,500	Bonds Payable	$ 18,400
Land	______	**Stockholders' Equity**	
Total Assets	______	Capital Stock	$136,000
		Retained Earnings	______
		Total Liabilities and Stockholders' Equity	$184,450

The Brewster Company Income Statement December 31, 19__		
Sales		$324,000
Expenses		
Cost of Goods Sold		$182,000
Operating Expenses		92,400
Interest Charges		______
Common Stock Dividend		8,200
Total Expenses		$285,000
Net Income		______

11. Fill in the missing entries in the balance sheet and the income statement for the Brewster Company.
12. Find the current ratio for the Brewster Company. What is the acid-test ratio?
13. Compute the gross profit margin and the operating ratio for the Brewster Company.
14. Find the stockholders' equity ratio for the Brewster Company.
15. What is the debt-equity ratio for the Brewster Company?

Section 7.6 Cash budgets

Most people plan expenditures for food, clothing, and other needs on the basis of expected income. Along with these short-term plans, many individuals and families use income estimates to plan for long-term activities, such as college expenses, the purchase of a house, or travel upon retirement. This process of planning for the financial needs of the future is called budgeting. A budget, whether formal or informal, is a plan for utilization of anticipated resources.

The budget of a business serves much the same function as an individual or family budget. Like a personal or family budget, a business budget plans the expenditure of anticipated funds for immediate and long-term goals.

One budget common to both large and small businesses is called the cash budget. The **cash budget** is a detailed plan showing how cash resources will be acquired and used over a specified time period. For many companies, this time period is monthly for the first three months of the budget period, then quarterly for the remainder of the year. A typical cash budget is composed of four major sections:

1. *The receipts section* This section consists of the sum of the opening cash balance and estimated cash receipts for the budget period. For many firms, the major source of cash receipts is sales.

2. *The disbursements section* This section consists of all estimated cash payments for the budget period. Examples are payments for labor and materials, taxes, equipment purchases, and advertising.
3. *The cash excess or cash deficiency section* The entries in this section represent the difference between the totals of the receipts section and the disbursements section. If receipts are greater than disbursements, there is an excess of cash. If receipts are less than disbursements, there is a cash deficiency.
4. *The financing section* This section gives an account of any borrowing or loan repayments projected to take place during the budget period.

The following is an example of a cash budget.

The McQuade Company
Cash Budget

	January
Cash Balance, Beginning	$ 9,000
Receipts	
Cash Sales	14,000
Accounts Receivable Collections	12,000
Total Available Cash	35,000
Disbursements	
Materials	10,000
Labor	9,500
Selling and Administrative Expenses	9,300
Income Taxes	7,200
Total Disbursements	36,000
Excess (Deficiency) of Cash	(1,000)
Financing	
Borrowed Funds Needed	2,000
Repayment of Borrowed Funds	---
Interest (at 10% Per Annum)	---
Total Financing	2,000
Cash Balance, End of Month	1,000

While the cash budget is useful to all companies, it is especially helpful to small firms because management can exercise more control in matching income with disbursements, in negotiating loans with the most favorable interest rates and terms, and in planning investments when there is an excess of cash. Some of the effects of management decisions on the cash budget are illustrated in the next examples.

Example 1 For the month of February, the McQuade Company anticipates a decrease in cash sales and accounts receivable collections of 5%, an increase in material costs of 3%, and no payment for income taxes. Assuming there are no other changes in the disbursement section, prepare a cash budget for January and February if the company requires a minimum cash balance of $1,000.

Solution

The McQuade Company
Cash Budget

	January	February	
Cash Balance, Beginning	$ 9,000	$ 1,000	
Receipts			
Cash Sales	14,000	13,300	(14,000 × 0.95)
Accounts Receivable Collections	12,000	11,400	(12,000 × 0.95)
Total Available Cash	35,000	25,700	
Disbursements			
Materials	10,000	10,300	(10,000 × 1.03)
Labor	9,500	9,500	
Selling and Administrative Expenses	9,300	9,300	
Income Taxes	7,200	---	
Total Disbursements	36,000	29,100	
Excess (Deficiency) of Cash	(1,000)	(3,400)	
Financing			
Borrowed Funds Needed	2,000	4,400	
Repayment of Borrowed Funds	---	---	
Interest (at 10% Per Annum)	---	---	
Total Financing	2,000	4,400	
Cash Balance, End of Month	1,000	1,000	

Example 2 With spring approaching, March sales of the McQuade Company are expected to double those of February, and accounts receivable collections are expected to increase by 20%. The cost of materials is estimated at $14,100, anticipated labor costs are $10,000, and selling and administrative expenses are expected to be $9,600. There are no other changes in disbursements. If the January loan plus $35 in interest is repaid at the end of the month, complete the cash budget for the first three months of the year.

Solution

The McQuade Company
Cash Budget

	January	February	March
Cash Balance, Beginning	$ 9,000	$ 1,000	$ 1,000
Receipts			
Cash Sales	14,000	13,300	26,600
Accounts Receivable Collections	12,000	11,400	13,680
Total Available Cash	35,000	25,700	41,280
Disbursements			
Materials	10,000	10,300	14,100
Labor	9,500	9,500	10,000
Selling and Administrative Expenses	9,300	9,300	9,600
Income Taxes	7,200	---	---
Total Disbursements	36,000	29,100	33,700
Excess (Deficiency) of Cash	(1,000)	(3,400)	7,580
Financing			
Borrowed Funds Needed	2,000	4,400	---
Repayment of Borrowed Funds	---	---	(2,000)
Interest (at 10% Per Annum)	---	---	(35)
Total Financing	2,000	4,400	(2,035)
Cash Balance, End of Month	1,000	1,000	5,545

Exercises for Section 7.6

1. On December 31 of the current year, McGee and Sons expect to have a cash balance of $3,600. For January, they have made the following estimates: raw materials purchased, $24,000; cash sales, $22,000; direct labor costs, $24,000; supervision costs, $2,960; utilities, $6,000; insurance and taxes, $1,700; accounts receivable collections, $38,000. If company policy requires a minimum cash balance of $2,000, prepare a cash budget for January.

2. Using the data in problem 1, prepare a cash budget if disbursements include the purchase of a new machine for $5,000.

3. Repeat problem 1, changing the following data: cash sales, $20,000; accounts receivable collections, $35,000; utility costs, $5,500. All other entries remain the same.

4. Repeat problem 1, using the following data: cash sales, $18,000; labor costs, $28,000; new equipment purchase, $9,700. All other entries remain the same.

5. The Osbourne Company expects cash sales for January to be $28,000 and accounts receivable collections to be $80,400. The company estimates the following expenses: accounts payable, $70,000; taxes, $3,700; advertising, $2,000; merchandise purchases, $24,000; payroll, $12,000; rent, $2,800; insurance, $12,600; other expenses, $1,350. If the balance from the previous month was $20,000 and if the company maintains a minimum monthly cash balance of $15,000, prepare the cash budget for January.

6. Make the following changes in the data for problem 5 and prepare the budget: beginning cash balance, $25,000; insurance, $9,800; rent, $2,500; advertising, $1,500. All other entries remain the same.

7. Repeat problem 5, incorporating the following changes: accounts receivable collections, $75,600; accounts payable, $55,000; no insurance premium; machine purchase, $6,600. All other entries remain the same.

8. Repeat problem 5, using the following data: receipts include a state tax refund for $7,000; merchandise purchases, $27,550; other expenses, $1,500; payroll, $15,000. All other entries remain the same.

9. Complete the following cash budget if the corporation maintains a minimum cash balance of $2,500.

Peterson Corporation Cash Budget	2nd Quarter
Cash Balance, Beginning	$ 6,600
Receipts	
Cash Sales	16,000
Accounts Receivable Collections	30,000
Total Available Cash	____
Disbursements	
Materials Purchased	19,000
Payroll	23,900
Rent	2,100
Other Expenses	2,400
Equipment Purchase	9,000
Total Disbursements	____
Excess (Deficiency) of Cash	____
Financing	
Borrowed Funds Needed	____
Repayment of Borrowed Funds	---
Interest (at 8% Per Annum)	---
Total Financing	____
Cash Balance, End of Quarter	____

10. Note: This problem requires information from the solution to problem 9. In the third quarter, when the Peterson Corporation prepares for the Christmas season, the corporation estimates that, compared to the second quarter, cash sales will increase 10%, accounts receivable collections will decrease 5%, cost of materials purchased will double, payroll costs will be $40,000, other expenses will increase 40%, and there will be no equipment purchases. If there are no other changes in disbursements, if no borrowed funds are repaid, and if there are no interest payments, complete the cash budget for the third quarter.

11. Note: This problem requires information from the solution to problem 10. For the fourth quarter, the Peterson Corporation estimates that, compared to the second quarter, cash sales will increase by 30%, accounts receivable collections will increase by 90%, cost of materials

purchased will decrease by 60%, other expenses will increase by 5%, and the payroll will be $20,000. There are no equipment purchases planned, and no other changes in disbursements are anticipated. If both loans are repaid, along with $350 interest, complete the cash budget for the fourth quarter.

12. Complete the following cash budget if the company maintains a minimum cash balance of $1,000.

C. J. Tibbitts Company Cash Budget	
	January
Cash Balance, Beginning	$ 1,200
Receipts	
Cash Sales	14,000
Collection of Receivables	______
Collection of Notes Receivable	---
Total Available Cash	$27,200
Disbursements	
Manufacturing Expenses	19,000
Selling and Administrative Expenses	8,900
Equipment Purchase	---
Total Disbursements	______
Excess (Deficiency) of Cash	______
Financing	
Borrowed Funds Needed	______
Repayment of Borrowed Funds	---
Interest (at 9% Per Annum)	---
Total Financing	______
Cash Balance, End of Month	______

13. Note: This problem requires information from the solution to problem 12. For February, the Tibbitts Company expects cash sales, accounts receivable collections, and manufacturing expenses to increase $1,000 each. No repayment of borrowed money or interest is planned for the month. If selling and administrative expenses are estimated to be $11,100 and there are no other changes in the cash budget from the previous month, prepare the cash budget for February.

14. Note: This problem requires information from the solution to problem 13. For March, cash sales and the collection of receivables for the Tibbitts Company are expected to be $4,000 greater than the January estimates, and the collection of a $4,000 note is anticipated. The purchase of a new machine for $1,200 and manufacturing expenses of $20,600 are expected to result in total disbursements of $30,800. The company plans to repay the January and February loans and will budget $85 for the interest. Prepare the cash budget for March.

15. Complete the following cash budget if the organization maintains a minimum cash balance of $10,000.

Meyers Pharmacies
Cash Budget

	March
Cash Balance, Beginning	$ 16,500
Receipts	
Cash Sales	81,000
Accounts Receivable Collections	$147,500
Total Available Cash	
Disbursements	
Merchandise Purchases	$90,000
Payroll	25,500
Utilities	550
Advertising	16,000
Taxes	—
Other Expenses	2,400
Total Disbursements	
Excess (Deficiency) of Cash	
Financing	
Borrowed Funds Needed	
Repayment of Borrowed Funds	—
Interest (at 12% Per Annum)	—
Total Financing	
Cash Balance, End of Month	

16. Note: This problem requires information from the solution to problem 15. In April, the company anticipates a drop in cash sales of 10% and a decrease in merchandise purchases of 15%. Utilities will decrease $50 and the estimated federal income tax payment is $26,450. If all remaining entries are the same, prepare the April cash budget of Meyers Pharmacies.

17. Note: This problem requires information from the solution to problem 16. In May, the company anticipates total available cash of $158,250, of which $84,500 will be accounts receivable collections. Merchandise purchases are anticipated to be $84,000, utilities are expected to double because of air conditioning, and payroll and advertising expenses are expected to decline by 10% from the April estimates. If the loan from April is repaid plus $124 interest, prepare the cash budget for May.

Section 7.7 Depreciation: MACRS and ACRS

Depreciation is a means of partially recovering an investment in an asset. The Internal Revenue Service (IRS) recognizes certain items of property used to operate a business as business expenses and through a tax deduction permits a company to recover a portion of the cost of these items over a specified period of time. Examples of items that may be depreciated are machinery, motor vehicles, buildings, furniture, equipment, and computers.

In general, an asset is depreciable if it meets the following requirements:

1. It is used in the operation of a trade or business or held for the production of income.
2. It has a useful life of more than one year. Useful life is the period that the asset is functional or income producing.
3. It wears out, becomes obsolete, depletes, or loses value from natural causes.

There are several depreciation systems. The system used depends on when the asset was placed in service; that is, when it was operable or ready for use.

MACRS

The first system is called the **Modified Accelerated Cost Recovery System (MACRS)** and is used for assets placed in service in 1987 and thereafter. Property that can be depreciated under MACRS is divided into two primary categories: real property and tangible personal property. **Real property** is real estate; that is, anything erected on, attached to, or growing on land. Land by itself is not depreciable. **Tangible personal property** is depreciable property that is not real estate, such as vehicles, machinery, and equipment.

The IRS has assigned each item of depreciable property a **recovery period,** a length of time for which the property may be depreciated. For each year of the recovery period an asset may be depreciated at a specified percent, as shown in tables 7.1 and 7.2. Note that the assets are depreciated one year more than the recovery period length. This is because only a partial depreciation is allowed during the first year. The remaining depreciation amount is recovered one year after the last year of the recovery period.

Table 7.1 MACRS Depreciation Percents—Tangible Personal Property

	Recovery Period					
Year	3-yr	5-yr	7-yr	10-yr	15-yr	20-yr
1	33.33%	20.00%	14.29%	10.00%	5.00%	3.750%
2	44.45	32.00	24.49	18.00	9.50	7.219
3	14.81	19.20	17.49	14.40	8.55	6.677
4	7.41	11.52	12.49	11.52	7.70	6.177
5		11.52	8.93	9.22	6.93	5.713
6		5.76	8.92	7.37	6.23	5.285
7			8.93	6.55	5.90	4.888
8			4.46	6.55	5.90	4.522
9				6.56	5.91	4.462
10				6.55	5.90	4.461
11				3.28	5.91	4.462
12					5.90	4.461
13					5.91	4.462
14					5.90	4.461
15					5.91	4.462
16					2.95	4.461
17						4.462
18						4.461
19						4.462
20						4.461
21						2.231

For a given year, the depreciation amount is calculated using the basic percentage equation $P = B \cdot R$, where P = amount of depreciation, B = cost or purchase price, and R = depreciation percent from table 7.1 or table 7.2.

Table 7.2 MACRS Depreciation Percents—Real Estate*

Year	27.5-yr Period	31.5-yr Period	Year	27.5-yr Period	31.5-yr Period
1	3.485%	3.042%	17	3.636%	3.174%
2	3.636	3.175	18	3.637	3.175
3	3.636	3.175	19	3.636	3.174
4	3.636	3.175	20	3.637	3.175
5	3.636	3.175	21	3.636	3.174
6	3.636	3.175	22	3.637	3.175
7	3.636	3.175	23	3.636	3.174
8	3.636	3.175	24	3.637	3.175
9	3.636	3.174	25	3.636	3.174
10	3.637	3.175	26	3.637	3.175
11	3.636	3.174	27	3.636	3.174
12	3.637	3.175	28	1.970	3.175
13	3.636	3.174	29		3.174
14	3.637	3.175	30		3.175
15	3.636	3.174	31		3.174
16	3.637	3.175	32		1.720

*Table 7.2 assumes the asset was placed in service in January. For assets placed in service in other months, other tables apply.

Example 1 A company purchased three microcomputers at a cost of $5,000 each. Find the total amount of depreciation of the microcomputers for the fourth year of the recovery period.

Solution

Computers have a recovery period of five years. From table 7.1, the fourth year depreciation percent is 11.52%. Hence, with $P = ?$, $B = \$5,000$, and $R = 0.1152$

$$P = B \cdot R$$
$$= \$5,000 \times 0.1152$$
$$= \$576$$

For the fourth year, the total amount of depreciation was
$\$576 \times 3 = \$1,728$

Example 2 An automobile (5-year period) that cost $12,500* was purchased by the Scott Company for business use. Find (a) the amount of depreciation for each year, and (b) the total depreciation amount.

Solution

(a) Using table 7.1,

Year	Cost (B)	Rate (R)	Depreciation (P)
1	$12,500	0.20	$2,500
2	12,500	0.32	4,000
3	12,500	0.1920	2,400
4	12,500	0.1152	1,440
5	12,500	0.1152	1,440
6	12,500	0.0576	720
			$12,500

(b) The total depreciation amount is $12,500, the sum of the depreciation amounts in the last column in part (a).

*Special depreciation rules apply to automobiles that cost more than $12,760. These rules will not be discussed in this section.

Example 3 A building purchased for $550,000 had a recovery period of 31.5 years. Find (a) the amount of depreciation for the tenth year, and (b) the total depreciation amount.

Solution

(a) Using table 7.2,

$$P = B \cdot R$$
$$= \$550{,}000 \times 0.03175$$
$$= \$17{,}462.50$$

(b) Note from table 7.2 there are 12 years in the table for which the depreciation rate is 3.174% and 18 years for which the depreciation rate is 3.175%. Thus,

$ 16,731	Depreciation for year 1	($550,000 × 0.03042)
+209,484	Depreciation for 12 of the years	($550,000 × 0.03174 × 12)
+314,325	Depreciation for 18 of the years	($550,000 × 0.03175 × 18)
+ 9,460	Depreciation for year 32	($550,000 × 0.0172)
$550,000		

The total cost of $550,000 is depreciated if the asset is held for the entire recovery period.

ACRS MACRS is a modification of an earlier depreciation system called the **Accelerated Cost Recovery System (ACRS).** In general, ACRS is used for assets placed in service in the years 1981 through 1986. The primary difference between ACRS and MACRS is that MACRS has more recovery periods and most assets under ACRS were shifted to the next longer period under MACRS. Table 7.3 gives the recovery periods and depreciation percents for ACRS.

For a given year, depreciation under ACRS is calculated using the basic percentage equation in the same manner as MACRS.

Table 7.3 ACRS Depreciation Percents

	Recovery Period	Type of Property	Depreciation Percent By Year				
Tangible Personal Property	Three Years	Special tools, such as molds, jigs, dies	Year 1	Year 2	Year 3		
			25%	38%	37%		
	Five Years	Equipment; heavy, general purpose trucks; furniture; fixtures; computers	Year 1	Year 2	Years 3-5		
			15%	22%	21%		
	Ten Years	Manufactured homes, certain public utility property, railroad tank cars	Year 1	Year 2	Year 3	Years 4-6	Years 7-10
			8%	14%	12%	10%	9%

	Recovery Period	Type of Property	Year	Month Placed in Service											
				1	2	3	4	5	6	7	8	9	10	11	12
Real Property	Nineteen Years	Real estate	1st	8.8%	8.1%	7.3%	6.5%	5.8%	5.0%	4.2%	3.5%	2.7%	1.9%	1.1%	0.4%
			2nd	8.4	8.5	8.5	8.6	8.7	8.8	8.8	8.9	9.0	9.0	9.1	9.2
			3rd	7.6	7.7	7.7	7.8	7.9	7.9	8.0	8.1	8.1	8.2	8.3	8.3
			4th	6.9	7.0	7.0	7.1	7.1	7.2	7.3	7.3	7.4	7.4	7.5	7.6
			5th	6.3	6.3	6.4	6.4	6.5	6.5	6.6	6.6	6.7	6.8	6.8	6.9
			6th	5.7	5.7	5.8	5.9	5.9	5.9	6.0	6.0	6.1	6.1	6.2	6.2
			7th	5.2	5.2	5.3	5.3	5.3	5.4	5.4	5.5	5.5	5.6	5.6	5.6
			8th	4.7	4.7	4.8	4.8	4.8	4.9	4.9	5.0	5.0	5.1	5.1	5.1
			9th	4.2	4.3	4.3	4.4	4.4	4.5	4.5	4.5	4.5	4.6	4.6	4.7
			10-19th	4.2	4.2	4.2	4.2	4.2	4.2	4.2	4.2	4.2	4.2	4.2	4.2
			20th	0.2	0.5	0.9	1.2	1.6	1.9	2.3	2.6	3.0	3.3	3.7	4.0

Example 4 A toy company purchased molds for a new line of plastic toys. If the purchase price was $18,000 and the recovery period was three years, find the amount of depreciation allowed for each year.

Solution

From table 7.3 the depreciation percents for a 3-year recovery period are 25% (first year), 38% (second year), and 37% (third year).

First Year Depreciation Amount	*Second Year Depreciation Amount*	*Third Year Depreciation Amount*
$P = B \cdot R$	$P = B \cdot R$	$P = B \cdot R$
= \$18,000 × 0.25	= \$18,000 × 0.38	= \$18,000 × 0.37
= \$4,500	= \$6,840	= \$6,660

Note that \$4,500 + \$6,840 + \$6,660 = \$18,000. Thus, the entire investment is depreciated over the 3-year period.

Example 5 The M & H Construction Company purchased a used mobile home (10-year recovery period) for use as a field office. If the purchase price was $11,600, what was the depreciation amount for the second year?

Solution

From table 7.3, for a 10-year recovery period the second year depreciation percent is 14%. Hence, with $P = ?$, $B = \$11{,}600$, and $R = 0.14$,

$$\begin{aligned} P &= B \cdot R \\ &= \$11{,}600 \times 0.14 \\ &= \$1{,}624 \end{aligned}$$

Example 6 The Madison Corporation purchased a warehouse (19-year recovery period) for $288,000. Find the amount of the first year depreciation if the warehouse was placed in service on April 20.

Solution

From table 7.3, the depreciation percent for the first year is 6.5%, since the warehouse was placed in service in April. Hence, with $P = ?$, $B = \$288{,}000$, and $R = 0.065$,

$$\begin{aligned} P &= B \cdot R \\ &= \$288{,}000 \times 0.065 \\ &= \$18{,}720 \end{aligned}$$

Exercises for Section 7.7

1. Maple Industries spent $34,600 for special tools (5-year recovery period) to be used in a new branch manufacturing plant. Find the amount of depreciation for the first year using MACRS.

2. Dennison Industries purchased an automobile (5-year recovery period) for $8,700 to use in the company business. Find the amount of depreciation allowed for the first year of the recovery period using MACRS.

3. The Osborn Company purchased an automobile (5-year recovery period) for $9,250. The automobile is to be used entirely for company business. Find the amount of depreciation allowed for the first year and the third year of the recovery period using MACRS.

4. Hood and Hoenig bought a $10,200 light-duty truck (5-year recovery period) to be used in their surveying business. The partners depreciated the truck using the MACRS method. Find the amount of depreciation allowed for the first year and the fifth year of the recovery period using MACRS.

5. Shoreline Rail Freight acquired five new tank cars (7-year recovery period) for a total cost of $874,250. If Shoreline uses MACRS, how much depreciation can the company claim for (a) the first year of the recovery period, and (b) the sixth year of the recovery period?

6. Mabel Williams has her own consulting business. She purchased a copying machine (5-year recovery period) for $2,400, but kept it only 3 years. Find the total amount of depreciation she was allowed under MACRS.

7. Charles Campbell is an independent trucker. He recently bought a used tractor (3-year recovery period) for $9,500 and kept it for 4 years. Find the amount of depreciation allowed for each year using MACRS.

8. The Kalter Realty Company purchased an automobile (5-year recovery period) for $12,000 to be used in showing real estate to clients but traded the car after 3 years. The company depreciated the automobile using MACRS. Find the amount of depreciation allowed for each of the 3 years.

9. Derek Fastlane, president of a company, purchased a $4,500 desk (7-year recovery period) for his personal use in company business. Find the amount of depreciation allowed for each year using MACRS.

10. In 1984 Woodward Appliance Repair purchased a new welding machine (7-year recovery period) for $2,185. The machine was depreciated using MACRS. Find the amount of depreciation for each year.

11. In 1982, the accounting firm of Jason, Hancock, & Smith purchased four personal computers (5-year recovery period) at a cost of $5,300 each and depreciated them using ACRS. Find the amount of depreciation for each year of the recovery period.

12. Suncoast Sprinklers bought ditch-digging equipment (5-year recovery period) for $7,500 and depreciated it using ACRS. Find the amount of depreciation for each year of the recovery period.

13. Use ACRS to find the depreciation for each year of the recovery period on $8,460 worth of furniture (5-year recovery period) purchased by the Worthington Company.

14. In 1984, Bayside Concrete purchased a heavy-duty truck (5-year recovery period) for $46,500 and depreciated it using ACRS. Find the amount of depreciation allowed for each year.

15. Entel, Inc. purchased telephone switching equipment (10-year recovery period) for a central office at a cost of $3,870,000. Find the amount of depreciation allowed for (a) the first year and (b) the last year using ACRS.

16. James Jones is a building contractor, and in 1983 he purchased a mobile home (10-year recovery period) for $18,750 to use as a temporary office at construction sites. Jones depreciated the mobile home using ACRS. Find the amount of depreciation for (a) the first year and (b) the last year of the recovery period.

17. A prefabricated housing unit (10-year recovery period) that cost $46,800 was depreciated using ACRS. Find the depreciation for (a) the first year and (b) the eighth year.

18. A repair shop (19-year recovery period) was purchased for $420,000 by Overland Trucking Company and placed in service on October 12, 1981. If the company depreciated the shop using ACRS, (a) what was the amount of the first year depreciation and (b) what was the amount of the twelfth year depreciation?

19. Foster Frozen Foods purchased a cold storage building for $845,400 (31.5-year recovery period) adjacent to the main plant and placed it in service on January 25. Using MACRS, (a) how much was the first year depreciation, (b) how much was the fifth year depreciation, and (c) how much was the fourteenth year depreciation?

20. Using ACRS, find the amount of depreciation for each year of the recovery period for an office building (19-year property) that cost $642,000 and was placed in service in May.

Section 7.8 Depreciation: Other methods

Prior to 1981, the federal government did not specify a particular method of depreciating assets. The general rule was that any method or formula was acceptable, provided that it was logical, reasonable, and consistently applied.

While the IRS did not advocate any particular depreciation formula, it did accept three commonly used methods: (1) the straight-line method, (2) the declining-balance method, and (3) the sum-of-the-years-digits method. For federal tax purposes, these methods are applicable only for assets placed in service prior to 1981. However, for state income tax returns or for internal accounting procedures, these methods may still apply.

We will use the following information to illustrate these methods: The Scott Company purchased a forklift in 1979 for $7,500 (**cost of the asset**). It was estimated that after six years (the **useful life**) the forklift would be worth $1,200 in **trade-in value** (also called **salvage value**). The salvage value is the minimum value to which the asset can be depreciated.

The straight-line method

The simplest and most commonly used, the **straight-line method** spreads the depreciation uniformly over the useful life of the asset. The formula for the straight-line method is:

■ (7–10) $$d = \frac{c - s}{n}$$

where d = depreciation amount per year, c = cost of asset, s = salvage value, and n = years of useful life. For the Scott Company forklift

$$d = \frac{\$7,500 - \$1,200}{6}$$

$$= \$1,050$$

The depreciation amount is $1,050 per year. Note that this is at a constant rate of $16\frac{2}{3}\%$ per year ($\frac{1,050}{6,300} = 0.166\ldots$).

A **depreciation schedule** is used to keep track of the depreciation for each asset. A depreciation schedule for the previous computation is shown in table 7.4.

Table 7.4 Depreciation Schedule for the Straight-Line Method

Year	Annual Depreciation	Accumulated Depreciation	Book Value*
0	—	—	$7,500
1	$1,050	$1,050	6,450
2	1,050	2,100	5,400
3	1,050	3,150	4,350
4	1,050	4,200	3,300
5	1,050	5,250	2,250
6	1,050	6,300	1,200

*Book value is the current depreciated value of an asset. This is not necessarily the current market value.

The advantage of the straight-line method is its simplicity; a disadvantage is that it penalizes the later years, when repairs are heaviest.

The declining-balance method

The formula for the **declining-balance method** is

■ (7–11) $$d = b \times r$$

where d = depreciation amount per year, b = book value of the preceding year, and r = depreciation rate.

For new property, the depreciation rate may be any percent up to twice the straight-line rate (provided that the rate chosen does not depreciate the property below its salvage value); for used property, the maximum depreciation is $1\frac{1}{2}$ times the straight-line rate.*

If the Scott Company decided on a rate of 25%, a depreciation rate schedule for the company forklift would be as shown in table 7.5 (the formula calculations are shown in parentheses).

Table 7.5 Depreciation Schedule for the Declining-Balance Method

Year	Depreciation	Accumulated Depreciation	Book Value
0	—	—	$7,500.00
1	$1,875.00 ($7,500 × .25)	$1,875.00	5,625.00
2	1,406.25 ($5,625 × .25)	3,281.25	4,218.75
3	1,054.69 ($4,218.75 × .25)	4,335.94	3,164.06
4	791.02 ($3,164.06 × .25)	5,126.96	2,373.04
5	593.26 ($2,373.04 × .25)	5,720.22	1,779.78
6	444.95 ($1,779.78 × .25)	6,165.17	1,334.83

*The straight-line rate is the depreciation amount per year divided by the difference between the cost of the asset and the salvage value. It can be shown that this is the percent determined by $\frac{1}{n}$, where n is the number of years of useful life. Thus, the maximum possible depreciation rate under the declining-balance method is $\frac{2}{n}$ for new property and $\frac{3}{2n}$ for used property.

The declining-balance method results in high depreciation in the early life of the asset, an advantage for income tax purposes. A disadvantage is that the probable maintenance and repair costs will occur late in the life of the asset, when depreciation is low.

The sum-of-the-years-digits method

In the straight-line and declining-balance formulas, the rate per year remained constant. In the **sum-of-the-years-digits method,** the rate is different for each year. The formula for this method is

■ (7–12) $$d = (c - s) \times r$$

where r is a fraction determined as follows: The denominator is the sum of the digits representing the useful life of the asset, and the numerator is the number of years of useful life remaining at the beginning of the year for which the computation is made.*

To illustrate, the Scott Company forklift had a useful life of six years. Hence, the denominator is $1 + 2 + 3 + 4 + 5 + 6 = 21$. The number of years of useful life remaining at the beginning of each year was 6, 5, 4, 3, 2, 1. Hence, the fractions used are $\frac{6}{21}$, $\frac{5}{21}$, $\frac{4}{21}$, $\frac{3}{21}$, $\frac{2}{21}$, and $\frac{1}{21}$. The depreciation schedule is shown in table 7.6 (the formula calculations are in parentheses).

Table 7.6 Depreciation Schedule for the Sum-of-the-Years-Digits Method

Year	Depreciation	Accumulated Depreciation	Book Value
0	—	—	$7,500
1	$1,800 ($6,300 × $\frac{6}{21}$)	$1,800	5,700
2	1,500 ($6,300 × $\frac{5}{21}$)	3,300	4,200
3	1,200 ($6,300 × $\frac{4}{21}$)	4,500	3,000
4	900 ($6,300 × $\frac{3}{21}$)	5,400	2,100
5	600 ($6,300 × $\frac{2}{21}$)	6,000	1,500
6	300 ($6,300 × $\frac{1}{21}$)	6,300	1,200

The sum-of-the-years-digits method of depreciation has the same advantages and disadvantages as the declining-balance method.

*The denominator may also be found by using the formula $\frac{n(n+1)}{2}$, where n = number of years. This formula is useful when the useful life of the asset is a large number of years.

Comparison of the methods

The three methods can be visually compared by graphing their depreciation schedules on the same graph. (See figures 7.9 and 7.10.)

Figure 7.9
Comparison of depreciation amounts resulting from the three depreciation methods

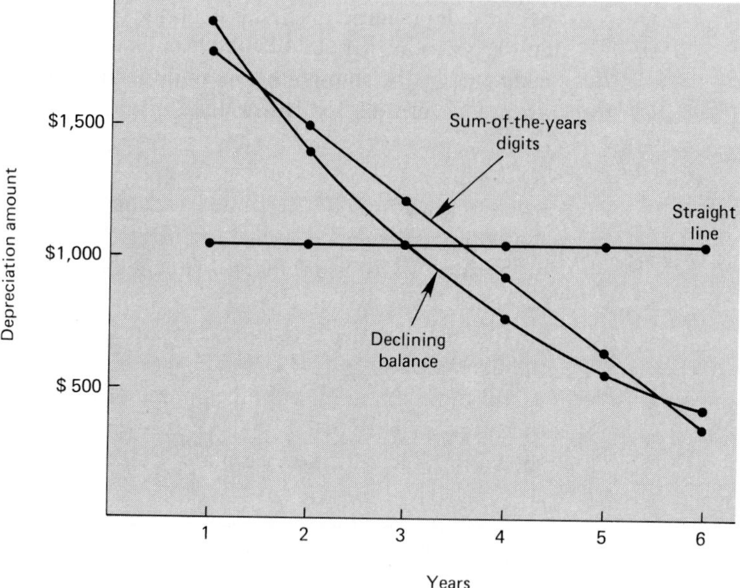

Figure 7.10
Comparison of book values resulting from the three depreciation methods

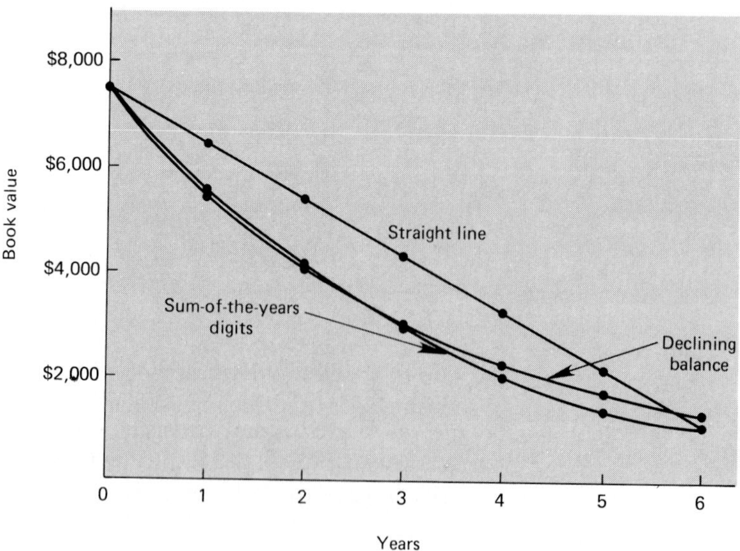

Units-of-production method

In the previous methods, the life of an asset was based on time. In another method of depreciation called **units-of-production,** the life of an asset is based on use. Use may be measured in items produced, miles traveled, hours of actual operation, etc. Calculation of depreciation using this method is in two parts. A per unit depreciation is first calculated, then this is used to calculate an annual depreciation amount.

For example, suppose a stamping machine that cost \$120,000 is expected to stamp 2,000,000 parts before being sold at its salvage value of \$20,000. The per unit depreciation is

$$\frac{\text{Cost} - \text{Salvage value}}{\text{Total units produced}} = \frac{\$120{,}000 - \$20{,}000}{2{,}000{,}000} = \$0.05$$

Thus, if during the first 2 years the actual number of parts stamped was 150,000 and 210,000, then:

First Year Depreciation	*Second Year Depreciation*
150,000 × \$0.05 = \$7,500	210,000 × \$0.05 = \$10,500

The units-of-production depreciation method has several shortcomings, among which is the difficulty of estimating in advance the useful life of a machine. Also, there is no depreciation when the machine is not in use, for example when the employees that operate the machine are on strike.

Exercises for Section 7.8

1. The Madison Manufacturing Company purchased a new conveyor for \$10,000. The useful life of the conveyor was 10 years, and its salvage value was \$1,000. Find the amount of depreciation per year using the straight-line method.

2. Prepare a depreciation schedule for the conveyor in problem 1 (see table 7.4).

3. Halpen Enterprises purchased some tooling equipment for \$23,500. The salvage value of the equipment was \$4,000, and its useful life was 8 years. Find the amount of depreciation per year using the straight-line method.

4. Prepare a depreciation schedule for the tooling equipment in problem 3 (see table 7.4).

5. Processing equipment at Central Food Packers had an initial purchase cost of \$18,000 and a useful life of 6 years. The equipment was depreciated at 20% per year using the declining-balance method. Prepare a depreciation schedule for the equipment (see table 7.5).

6. The Carson Company used the declining-balance method at a rate of 25% to depreciate its equipment. If the purchase price of the equipment was \$52,000 and the useful life was 8 years, prepare a depreciation schedule for the equipment (see table 7.5).

7. Nelson Meat Packers purchased new meat-cutting equipment for \$36,000. The useful life of the equipment was 8 years. Prepare a depreciation schedule for the equipment using a depreciation rate of 15% and the declining-balance method.

8. The Prescott Company purchased an automobile for \$6,000. The salvage value of the car was \$1,000, and its useful life was 5 years. Prepare a depreciation schedule for the car using the sum-of-the-years-digits method (see table 7.6).

9. A new platform loader at Holden Industries cost \$16,000 and had a useful life of 8 years. If the salvage value of the loader was \$2,000, prepare a depreciation schedule for the loader using the sum-of-the-years-digits method (see table 7.6).

10. Use the sum-of-the-years-digits method to prepare a depreciation schedule for a \$25,000 piece of machinery at Holden Industries if the machinery had a useful life of 6 years and a salvage value of \$5,000.

11. A packing machine cost \$10,000, had a salvage value of \$4,000, and a useful life of 5 years. Prepare depreciation schedules for the machine using (a) the straight-line method, (b) the declining-balance method with $r = 16\%$, and (c) the sum-of-the-years-digits method.

12. Repeat problem 11 for a piece of machinery that cost \$8,000, had a useful life of 4 years, and a salvage value of \$2,000. Use a depreciation rate of 28% in the declining-balance method.

13. A company car, purchased new for \$8,000, had a useful life of 5 years and a salvage value of \$600. Use the declining-balance method and the maximum depreciation rate to prepare a depreciation schedule. (Hint: The straight-line rate is $\frac{1}{n}$, where n is the number of years of useful life of the asset.)

14. Lake Scientific Laboratories purchased a new electron microscope for \$38,000. It had a useful life of 8 years and a salvage value of \$3,800. Use the declining-balance method and the maximum depreciation rate to prepare a depreciation schedule. (Hint: The straight-line rate is $\frac{1}{n}$, where n is the number of years of useful life of the asset.)

15. A crane purchased by the Decker Construction Company cost \$15,000 and had a useful life of 8 years. Its salvage value was \$5,000. Use the straight-line method to prepare a depreciation schedule for the crane.

16. Use the declining-balance method with $r = 11\%$ to prepare a depreciation schedule for the crane in problem 15.

17. Use the sum-of-the-years-digits method to prepare a depreciation schedule for the crane in problem 15.

18. The Jennings Company purchased new central air-conditioning equipment for $8,000. The useful life was 6 years, and the salvage value was $550. Use the declining-balance method and the maximum depreciation rate to prepare a depreciation schedule.

19. All-Occasion Florists purchased a delivery van for $11,000. The estimated useful life was 70,000 miles with a salvage value of $1,900. Using the units-of-production method, find the depreciation in a year the truck was driven (a) 18,000 miles, and (b) 22,000 miles.

20. Admiral Motors purchased a robot welding machine for $1,220,000. After its estimated life of 75,000 hours, the salvage value was $140,000. Using the units-of-production method, find the depreciation in a year the machine operated for (a) 7,100 hours, and (b) 8,000 hours.

21. The Schmidt Corporation bought a machine for manufacturing carriage bolts with a purchase price of $16,250 and a salvage value of $950 after manufacturing 900,000 boxes of bolts over its lifetime. (a) Using the units-of-production method, find the annual depreciation if 120,000 boxes were manufactured in the first year and 95,000 boxes were manufactured in the second year. (b) Find the book value at the end of the second year.

22. A machine with an estimated useful life of 3,500,000 units cost $410,000 with a salvage value of $32,000. The first year depreciation was $46,000. The second year production was 400,000 units. Using the units-of-production method, find the book value at the end of the second year.

Section 7.9 Distribution of overhead and profits and losses

Distribution of overhead

Overhead, as previously defined, is a general term for operating expenses, such as rent, utilities, maintenance, and so on. Since overhead contributes to the cost of doing business, it must be kept to a minimum. One mechanism for controlling overhead involves allocating a portion of the total amount of overhead to each department or subunit of the company. If this distribution is equitable, management has a standard for measuring the efficiency of each department or subunit. Two widely used methods of distribution are (1) allocation according to floor space and (2) allocation according to net sales.

Example 1 The Banning Corporation distributed its total overhead expense of $24,000 according to the square feet of floor space occupied by each department. Determine the distribution if the floor space of each department is as follows:

Department	*Floor Space*	*Ratio to Total Space*
Offices	1,500	$\frac{1{,}500}{30{,}000} = \frac{1}{20}$
Accounting	2,500	$\frac{2{,}500}{30{,}000} = \frac{1}{12}$
Production	14,000	$\frac{14{,}000}{30{,}000} = \frac{7}{15}$
Warehouse	12,000	$\frac{12{,}000}{30{,}000} = \frac{2}{5}$
Total	30,000	

Solution

The allocation is an application of the basic percentage equation $P = BR$, with P = allocation amount, B = \$24,000, and R = ratio of department space to total space.

$$\text{Office allocation} = \$24{,}000 \times \frac{1}{20} = \$1{,}200$$

$$\text{Accounting allocation} = \$24{,}000 \times \frac{1}{12} = \$2{,}000$$

$$\text{Production allocation} = \$24{,}000 \times \frac{7}{15} = \$11{,}200$$

$$\text{Warehouse allocation} = \$24{,}000 \times \frac{2}{5} = \$9{,}600$$

As a check, the sum of the departmental allocations should equal the total overhead expense:

$$\$1{,}200 + \$2{,}000 + \$11{,}200 + \$9{,}600 = \$24{,}000$$

A second method of distributing overhead is allocation according to net sales.

Example 2 The Lombard Company had monthly net sales in its departments as follows:

Department	*Net Sales*	*Ratio to Total Sales*
Appliances	$ 1,000	$\frac{1{,}000}{12{,}000} = \frac{1}{12}$
Automotive	2,800	$\frac{2{,}800}{12{,}000} = \frac{7}{30}$
Ladies' wear	6,200	$\frac{6{,}200}{12{,}000} = \frac{31}{60}$
Men's wear	1,200	$\frac{1{,}200}{12{,}000} = \frac{1}{10}$
Toys	800	$\frac{800}{12{,}000} = \frac{1}{15}$
Total	$12,000	

If the month's overhead of $2,400 was distributed according to net sales, what was the allocation to each department?

Solution

$P = ?$, $B = \$2{,}400$, $R =$ ratio to total net sales

Appliances allocation $= \$2{,}400 \times \frac{1}{12} = \$200$

Automotive allocation $= \$2{,}400 \times \frac{7}{30} = \$560$

Ladies' wear $= \$2{,}400 \times \frac{31}{60} = \$1{,}240$

Men's wear $= \$2{,}400 \times \frac{1}{10} = \$240$

Toys $= \$2{,}400 \times \frac{1}{15} = \$160$

Check: $200 + $560 + $1,240 + $240 + $160 = $2,400

Distribution of partnership profits and losses

The distribution of the profits or losses of a business depends on the type of business ownership. Three basic categories of business organization are (1) sole proprietorship, (2) corporation, and (3) partnership.

A sole proprietorship is a business owned by one individual who receives all of the profits (therefore, no distribution is necessary) but who must also bear all of the losses.

The owners of a corporation are its stockholders, but the distribution of profits or losses is the responsibility of a board of directors elected by the stockholders. Distribution of corporate profits is discussed in chapter 15.

The third type of business organization is a partnership. A **partnership** is formed when two or more individuals join in a business venture as co-owners. Like the sole proprietor, the co-owners are entitled to all profits of the business but must also absorb any losses. As a result, when establishing a partnership, it is advisable to draw up a written partnership agreement specifying the interest and responsibilities of each partner and how the profits or losses of the business are to be distributed. One method of distributing profits or losses is according to the amount of money invested in the business, as shown in the next example.

Example 3 Collins, Mills, and Tozer formed a business partnership. To start the business, Collins contributed \$15,000, Mills contributed \$9,000, and Tozer contributed \$6,000. During the first year of operation, the business lost \$1,280. How much did each partner share in the loss?

Solution

Each partner's share of the loss is the ratio of his or her investment to the total investment.

Partner	*Initial Investment*	*Ratio to Total Investment*
Collins	\$15,000	$\frac{15{,}000}{30{,}000} = \frac{1}{2} = 0.50$
Mills	9,000	$\frac{9{,}000}{30{,}000} = \frac{3}{10} = 0.30$
Tozer	6,000	$\frac{6{,}000}{30{,}000} = \frac{1}{5} = 0.20$
Total	\$30,000	

The allocation of the loss is an application of $P = BR$, with P = allocation amount, B = \$1,280, and R = ratio to total investment.

Collins $\$1{,}280 \times 0.50 = \$640$
Mills $\$1{,}280 \times 0.30 = \$384$
Tozer $\$1{,}280 \times 0.20 = \$256$

As a check, the sum of the allocation of the losses should equal the total loss:

$\$640 + \$384 + \$256 = \$1{,}280$

Another method of distributing profits or losses considers the time invested in the operation of the business.

Example 4 Jones, Barclay, Riddle, and Symanski formed a business partnership. It was agreed that, as manager of the business, Jones would receive 55% of the profits, with the other partners sharing the remaining profits equally. How much did each partner receive in a year when the total profit was $26,400?

Solution

If Jones receives 55%, the other partners each receive 45% ÷ 3 = 15%.

Jones	$26,400 × 0.55 = $14,520
Barclay	$26,400 × 0.15 = $3,960
Riddle	$26,400 × 0.15 = $3,960
Symanski	$26,400 × 0.15 = $3,960

Check: $14,520 + $3,960 + $3,960 + $3,960 = $26,400

A third way of distributing profits or losses is according to a fixed ratio.

Example 5 Smith, Jones, and Welch agreed to distribute the profits of their partnership according to a ratio of 3:4:5, respectively. Find the distribution if the profit was $60,000.

Solution

The agreed ratio means that the profit was split into 3 + 4 + 5 = 12 shares.

$\$60{,}000 \times \frac{3}{12} = \$15{,}000$ Smith's share

$\$60{,}000 \times \frac{4}{12} = \$20{,}000$ Jones's share

$\$60{,}000 \times \frac{5}{12} = \$25{,}000$ Welch's share

Check: $15,000 + $20,000 + $25,000 = $60,000

If a partner receives a salary from the business, the salary is deducted from profits before distribution.

Example 6 Crawford and Freeman are business partners. As a silent partner, Crawford has no part in the business other than his investment. However, Freeman runs the business, and it was agreed that she would receive an annual salary of \$20,000, with the remaining profits to be split evenly. In a year when the business had a \$45,000 profit, how much was paid to each partner?

Solution

After deducting Freeman's salary, the profit to be split is

\$45,000 − \$20,000 = \$25,000

Crawford is paid \$25,000 × $\frac{1}{2}$ = \$12,500. Freeman is paid \$12,500 (profit distribution) + \$20,000 (salary) = \$32,500.

Still another variation in the distribution of profits is for one or more partners to receive a specified percent of their investment prior to the distribution of any remaining profits.

Example 7 When Acton, Eads, and Nichols formed a partnership, they contributed \$20,000, \$25,000, and \$10,000, respectively, to start the business. The partnership agreement specified that annually the partners would receive 9% of their investment, that Nichols would receive a salary of \$18,000, and that any remaining profits would be shared equally. Find the distribution on profits of (a) \$30,000 and (b) \$6,000.

Solution

The amount paid before the distribution of any remaining profits is

	\$ 1,800	(\$20,000 × 0.09)
+	2,250	(\$25,000 × 0.09)
+	900	(\$10,000 × 0.09)
+	18,000	Salary
	\$22,950	Total

(a) \$30,000 − \$22,950 = \$7,050
\$7,050 ÷ 3 = \$2,350

The amount received by each partner is

Partner	*Return on investment*	*Salary*	*Share of profits*	*Total received*
Acton	\$1,800		+\$2,350	\$ 4,150
Eads	2,250		+ 2,350	4,600
Nichols	900	+\$18,000	+ 2,350	21,250

(b) $22,950 − $6,000 = $16,950 loss

$16,950 ÷ 3 = $5,650

The amount received by each partner is

Partner	*Return on investment*	*Salary*	*Share of loss*	*Total received or lost*
Acton	$1,800		−$5,650	−$ 3,850
Eads	2,250		− 5,650	− 3,400
Nichols	900	+$18,000	− 5,650	13,250

Exercises for Section 7.9

1. The Stratford Corporation distributed its overhead expense of $62,000 according to the floor space occupied by each department. Determine the distribution of overhead if the floor space (in square feet) of each department is as follows:

Department	*Floor Space*	*Ratio to Total Floor Space*
Offices	1,000	$\frac{1{,}000}{40{,}000} = \frac{1}{40}$
Accounting	3,000	$\frac{3{,}000}{40{,}000} = \frac{3}{40}$
Production	16,000	$\frac{16{,}000}{40{,}000} = \frac{2}{5}$
Warehouse	20,000	$\frac{20{,}000}{40{,}000} = \frac{1}{2}$
Total	40,000	

2. The floor space (in square feet) of the Nelson Company is distributed as follows:

Department	*Floor Space*	*Ratio to Total Floor Space*
Offices	1,400	$\frac{1{,}400}{8{,}000} = \frac{7}{40}$
Accounting	1,300	$\frac{1{,}300}{8{,}000} = \frac{13}{80}$
Showroom	2,200	$\frac{2{,}200}{8{,}000} = \frac{11}{40}$
Maintenance	900	$\frac{900}{8{,}000} = \frac{9}{80}$
Warehouse	2,200	$\frac{2{,}200}{8{,}000} = \frac{11}{40}$
Total	8,000	

Determine the distribution of the company's overhead of $28,000 if the overhead is distributed according to the floor space occupied by each department.

3. For the month of June, the departmental net sales at the Parker Company were as follows:

Department	*Net Sales*	*Ratio to Total Sales*
Clothing	$ 4,900	$\frac{4{,}900}{16{,}000} = \frac{49}{160}$
Hardware	2,500	$\frac{2{,}500}{16{,}000} = \frac{5}{32}$
Appliances	3,200	$\frac{3{,}200}{16{,}000} = \frac{1}{5}$
Toys	1,300	$\frac{1{,}300}{16{,}000} = \frac{13}{160}$
Home furnishings	4,100	$\frac{4{,}100}{16{,}000} = \frac{41}{160}$
Total	$16,000	

The total overhead for the month of June was $2,760. If the overhead is distributed according to net sales, find the allocation to each department.

4. The total overhead at Braxton Industries for the month of February was $4,850. The net sales for the month totaled $50,000 and were distributed among the departments as follows:

Department	*Net Sales*	*Ratio to Total Sales*
Garden supplies	$ 6,250	$\frac{6{,}250}{50{,}000} = \frac{1}{8}$
Glassware	8,450	$\frac{8{,}450}{50{,}000} = \frac{169}{1{,}000}$
Hardware	12,100	$\frac{12{,}100}{50{,}000} = \frac{121}{500}$
Carpets	16,200	$\frac{16{,}200}{50{,}000} = \frac{81}{250}$
Lighting	7,000	$\frac{7{,}000}{50{,}000} = \frac{7}{50}$
Total	$50,000	

If the month's overhead was distributed according to net sales, what was the allocation to each department?

5. The W. T. Southerd Company reported total overhead of $3,250 for the month of November. The net sales for November were $40,000 and were distributed as follows:

Department	*Net Sales*
Office supplies	$11,200
Furnishings	7,700
Floor coverings	5,200
Office machines	15,900
Total	$40,000

Find the overhead allocation to each department if the distribution is made according to net sales.

6. The floor space (in square feet) of Frederick's is distributed as follows:

Department	*Floor Space*
Offices	1,200
Accounting	1,600
Home furnishings	3,200
Hardware	2,100
Paints	1,800
Draperies	2,700
Carpets	2,400
Total	15,000

Determine the distribution of the company's overhead of $44,500 if the overhead is distributed according to the floor space occupied by each department.

7. Elco Enterprises reported total overhead of $5,620 for the month of June. The net sales for June were $65,000 and were distributed as follows: office equipment, $17,500; business forms, $3,500; furnishings, $23,200; art supplies, $4,700; and chemicals, $16,100. The month's overhead was distributed according to net sales. Prepare a table showing the ratio of the net sales of each department to total net sales and the allocation of overhead to each department.

8. The floor space (in square feet) at Prindles is distributed as follows: accounting, 1,400; offices, 900; men's clothing, 2,600; women's clothing, 3,600; children's wear, 1,800; and shoes, 1,000. Prepare a table showing the ratio of the floor space of each department to total floor space and the allocation of the company's overhead of $54,200 to each department if the overhead is distributed according to floor space.

9. Jackson, Peters, and Adams formed a business partnership. To start the business, Jackson contributed $15,000, Peters contributed $40,000, and Adams contributed $25,000. During the first year, the business lost $8,700. Based on the amount of money each partner invested in the business, how much did each partner share in the loss?

10. During the first year of operation, a new business formed by three partners earned a profit of $14,250. To form the business, partner A had invested $36,000, partner B had invested $30,000, and partner C had invested $54,000. Based on the amount that each partner initially invested in the business, determine the amount of profit that each partner received.

11. John Barrett formed a new business with three other partners. It was agreed that Barrett would receive 64% of the profits, since he would manage the business, and the other three partners would share the remaining profits equally. How much did Barrett and each of the other three partners receive in a year when the total profit earned by the business was $76,640?

12. Sheila Bishop and Ann Tucker started an investment counseling service. They formed a partnership with two other people, and it was agreed that Bishop and Tucker would each receive 32% of the profits and that the other two partners would equally share the remainder. Find the distribution of profits for a year when the total profit was $87,500.

13. Criswell, Davis, and Meyer agreed to distribute the profits of their partnership according to a ratio of 2:5:7, respectively. How much was each partner's profit for a year when the total profit was $185,000?

14. A business owned by four partners earned a total profit of $234,420 last year. Find the distribution of profits if the partners have agreed to distribute all profits and losses according to the ratio 3:5:6:10.

15. Foster, Thomas, Harvey, and Daniels distribute all profits and losses from their partnership according to the ratio 7:7:4:2, respectively. Determine each partner's loss for a year when the losses of the business totaled $14,350.

16. Alice Swenson, Joan Hefferman, and Jean Banks formed a partnership. Swenson and Hefferman run the business and receive annual salaries of $27,500 and $22,000, respectively. Banks is a silent partner and receives no salary, but the three partners divide all remaining profits (after salaries) equally. In a year when total profits were $101,190 (before salaries), how much did each partner receive?

17. A business owned by four partners earned a total profit of \$316,740 (before salaries) during its third year of operation. Two of the partners run the business, earning annual salaries of \$31,500 and \$29,500. Remaining profits (after salaries) are divided equally among the four partners. How much was paid to each partner during the third year of operation?

18. Harper, Taylor, Simmons, and Marshall formed a partnership. They agreed that Harper and Taylor would receive salaries of \$35,000 and \$24,000, respectively, and that remaining profits (after salaries) would be distributed among the four partners according to the ratio 3:3:5:6, respectively. Find the amount paid to each partner for a year when total profits were \$186,200 (before salaries).

19. The partnership agreement of Kessler and Schneider specifies that annually each partner will receive 8% on their investments in the business, \$50,400 and \$75,600 respectively, and that any remaining profits will be shared according to the ratio 2:3. Find the distribution of profits of (a) \$12,000 and (b) \$9,000.

20. To start a business, Buck, Hansley, and Reid contributed \$20,000, \$22,000, and \$15,000, respectively. The partnership agreement specifies that Buck will manage the business and that annually each partner will receive 8.5% of their investment, that Buck will receive a salary of \$25,000, and that any remaining profits will be shared equally. Find the distribution of profits of (a) \$33,490 and (b) \$28,885.

Glossary

Accelerated cost recovery system (ACRS) A method of depreciating assets placed in service after 1980 and before 1987.
Acid-test ratio A measure of a firm's ability to meet current liabilities; found by dividing cash plus receivables by current liabilities.
Assets Possessions owned by a business; money owed to a business.
Balance sheet A financial statement indicating the financial condition of a business at a given time.
Book value The current depreciated value of an asset.
Cash budget A detailed plan showing how cash resources will be acquired and used over a specified time period.
Cost of an asset The original purchase price of an asset.
Current ratio A measure of the ability of a firm to meet its debts promptly; found by dividing current assets by current liabilities.
Debt-equity ratio A measure of the security of a company; found by dividing current liabilities plus long-term liabilities by owners' equity.
Declining-balance method A depreciation method wherein an asset is depreciated at a constant rate using the formula $d = b \times r$, where d is the depreciation amount per year, b is the book value of the preceding year, and r is the depreciation rate.

Depreciation A tax deduction that permits a business to partially recover its investment in an asset.
Depreciation schedule A table showing the depreciation, accumulated depreciation, and book value per year.
Equities The claims upon the assets if a business is dissolved; liabilities plus owners' equity.
Gross profit margin A measure of the average spread between cost of goods sold and the selling price; found by dividing the difference between net sales and the cost of goods sold by net sales.
Horizontal analysis For entries on a balance sheet or an income statement, the comparison of dollar amounts for different periods of time.
Income statement A report on a company's income for a period of time, generally a month or a year.
Liabilities The dollar value of everything a company owes.
Liquidity The ability of a company to convert assets into cash quickly without incurring a significant loss.
Modified accelerated cost recovery system (MACRS) A method of depreciating assets placed in service in 1987 and thereafter.
Operating ratio A measure of the amount of sales dollars used to defray the cost of goods and administrative expenses; found by dividing the cost of goods sold plus operating expenses by net sales.
Overhead The operating expenses of a business, such as rent, utilities, salaries, supplies, advertising, and maintenance.
Owners' equity The owners' share of a firm's assets; the difference between total assets and total liabilities.
Partnership When two or more individuals join in a business venture as co-owners.
Real property For depreciation purposes, anything erected on, attached to, or growing on land.
Recovery period A length of time established by the Internal Revenue Service during which property may be depreciated.
Salvage value For assets placed in service prior to 1981, the value of an asset at the end of its useful life.
Stockholders' equity ratio A measure of the investment in assets financed by the owners or stockholders; found by dividing the owners' equity by total assets.
Straight-line method A depreciation method wherein an asset is depreciated a constant amount each year. The constant amount is determined by the formula $\frac{c - s}{n}$, where c is the cost of the asset, s is the salvage value, and n is the number of years the asset is depreciated.
Sum-of-the-years-digits method A depreciation method wherein an asset is depreciated at a decreasing rate. The formula for each year's depreciation is $(c - s) \times r$, where c is the cost of the asset, s is the salvage value, and r is a fraction whose denominator is the sum of the digits representing the useful life of the asset and the numerator is the number of years of useful life remaining at the beginning of the year.
Tangible personal property Depreciable property that is not real estate, such as vehicles, machinery, and equipment.
Trade-in value See salvage value.
Units of production method A depreciation method wherein an asset is depreciated at a constant rate. The constant rate is determined by the formula $\frac{c - s}{l}$, where c is the cost of the asset, s is the salvage value, and l is the useful life of the asset. The useful life of the asset may be in units other than time such as items produced, miles traveled, etc. The annual depreciation is the product of the annual usage and the constant rate.
Useful life For depreciation purposes, the period an asset is expected to be functional.
Vertical analysis Expressed as a percent, the ratio of entries on an income statement or a balance sheet to a particular entry, usually net sales or total assets.

Review test

1. Complete the missing items in the following balance sheet:

The Aztec Corporation Balance Sheet December 31, 19__			
Assets		**Equities**	
Current Assets		**Current Liabilities**	
Cash	$ 10,500	Due to Bank	$ 50,000
Accounts Receivable	________	Notes Payable	12,000
Merchandise Inventory	20,500	Total Current Liabilities	________
Total Current Assets	67,000		
Equipment, Buildings, and Land		**Long-Term Liabilities**	
Equipment	$159,000	Mortgage	$200,000
Buildings	240,000	Total Liabilities	________
Land	100,000	**Owners' Equity**	
Total Fixed Assets	________	A. J. Davis, Owner	$304,000
Total Assets	________	**Total Equities**	________

2. Find the acid-test ratio of the Aztec Corporation in problem 1.
3. Find the stockholders' equity ratio of the Aztec Corporation in problem 1.
4. Find the debt-equity ratio of the Aztec Corporation in problem 1.
5. The Aztec Corporation purchased a light-duty truck for $9,200 and used the ACRS method of depreciation. The depreciation rates for property with a 3-year recovery period are 25%, 38%, and 37%. Find the amount of depreciation for each year of the recovery period, if the maximum depreciation is $3,200 (year 1) and $4,800 (years 2 and 3).
6. A piece of equipment (5-year recovery period) that cost $142,550 was depreciated using MACRS. Find the depreciation for each year if the depreciation percents were 20%, 32%, 19.2%, 11.52%, and 5.76%.

7. The Aztec Corporation purchased a piece of tooling equipment for $12,000. After 5 years, the salvage value was $900. During the 5 years, the company depreciated the equipment using the maximum rate under the declining-balance method. What rate of depreciation did the company use?

8. The stockroom of the Aztec Corporation occupies 5,000 square feet of the total floor space of 160,000 square feet. How much of the company's overhead of $68,000 should be allocated to the stockroom if overhead is allocated according to floor space?

9. A finishing machine at the Aztec Corporation is valued at $15,000, with a useful life of 6 years. If the salvage value is $2,400, find the book value after three years using the sum-of-the-years-digits method of depreciation.

10. Lombardi and Berra are business partners. The partnership agreement calls for Lombardi to receive a monthly salary of $1,200, with the remaining profits to be distributed as follows: 45% to Lombardi, 55% to Berra. Find the distribution in a year when profits are $44,000.

11. If company policy requires a minimum cash balance of $1,500, complete a monthly cash budget from the following information. Accounts receivable collections, $12,500; total available cash, beginning of month, $29,700; material costs, $9,000; labor costs, $10,000; selling and administrative expenses, $8,400; taxes, $1,600; advertising, $1,000; beginning cash balance, $4,700.

CHAPTER 8

Taxes

Chapter Objectives

I. Learn the meaning of the following terms:

Assessed value, 281
Adjusted gross income, 288
Deductions, 289
Taxable income, 289

II. Understand:

Sales taxes, 276–279
Excise taxes, 279
Property tax rate, 282
Steps in computing Federal income tax, 286

III. Learn to:

Calculate sales taxes and excise taxes, 276–280
Calculate property taxes, 283–284
Compute income tax, 291–293

Section 8.1 Introduction

Revenue for federal, state, and local governments is obtained from three sources: taxation, borrowing, and service fees. Of these, taxation is the most important source of income. Taxes absorb some 30% of total income in the United States, which means that the average American works nearly four months out of every twelve to support federal, state, and local governments.

For these tax dollars, Americans receive a variety of services and benefits. Among these are education, health care, national defense, police and fire protection, public housing, streets and highways, recreation facilities, and parklands. While dislike of taxes is universal, most people probably would agree with Justice Oliver Wendell Holmes, Jr., who said that "Taxes are the price that we pay for civilization."

Sales and excise taxes, property tax, and income tax constitute the major source of revenue for federal, state, and local governments.

Section 8.2 Sales taxes

Sales tax is a primary source of revenue for state governments. Forty-five states have a sales tax, and these taxes generate an income of more than $46 billion dollars annually.

The **sales tax** is a percentage of retail sales, with rates ranging from 3% to $7\frac{1}{2}\%$. Some states also permit municipalities to impose a sales tax, but these local sales rates usually are less than the state percent. Retail merchants are responsible for collecting sales taxes and forwarding them to the appropriate governmental agency.

Calculation of the sales tax is an application of the basic percentage equation $P = B \cdot R$, where P = amount of the sales tax, B = purchase price, and R = tax rate. In retail stores with electronic cash registers, the tax is automatically calculated and added to the total selling price. Stores without electronic cash registers utilize a tax table that enables salesclerks to read the appropriate tax.

Example 1 The purchase price of a ceiling fan is $130. If the sales tax is 4%, find: (a) the amount of the sales tax and (b) the total price paid by the buyer.

Solution

a. $P = ?,\ B = \$130,\ R = 4\% = 0.04$

$$
\begin{aligned}
P &= B \cdot R \\
&= \$130 \times 0.04 \\
&= \$5.20
\end{aligned}
$$

b. The total price paid by the buyer is the purchase price plus the sales tax.

$130.00	Purchase price
+ 5.20	Sales tax
$135.20	Total price paid by the buyer

In some states, sales of less than one dollar are taxed according to tax brackets arbitrarily established by state or local taxing authorities. Table 8.1 illustrates sample tax brackets for a sales tax of 4% and 5%. Thus, with a 4% sales tax, an item that sells for $0.30 would be taxed $0.02; had the percentage equation been used to calculate the tax, the tax would have been $0.01.

Table 8.1 Sales Tax on Amounts Less Than One Dollar

4%		5%	
Sale Amount	*Tax*	*Sale Amount*	*Tax*
$0.01–$0.09	$0.00	$0.01–$0.10	$0.00
0.10– 0.25	0.01	0.11– 0.25	0.01
0.26– 0.50	0.02	0.26– 0.45	0.02
0.51– 0.75	0.03	0.46– 0.65	0.03
0.76– 0.99	0.04	0.66– 0.85	0.04
		0.86– 0.99	0.05

For sales involving dollars and cents, one method of computing the sales tax is to use the basic percentage equation to calculate the tax on the dollars and the tax brackets to find the tax on the cents.

Example 2 Using table 8.1, find the sales tax on a transistor radio priced at $19.29 if the tax rate is 4%.

Solution

$19.29 = $19.00 + $0.29

$0.76	($19.00 × 0.04)
+ 0.02	Table 8.1
$0.78	Total sales tax

In certain instances, the sales tax is not applicable. For example, sales taxes on interstate sales are prohibited by the United States Constitution, and local sales taxes normally are limited to the local taxing district. Thus, an item sold in a state with a state sales tax but outside the limits of a city with a municipal sales tax would be subject only to the state sales tax.

There may also be exemptions or exclusions from the sales tax. An exemption means that a specific item is not subject to the tax. Common exemptions are prescription drugs and home-consumed food items. An exclusion means that purchases by a particular organization are not taxed. Religious groups, charitable organizations, and nonprofit hospitals typically receive such exclusions.

Example 3 A state sales tax is 5% of retail sales, excluding food items. Use the basic percentage equation to find the amount of the sales tax on the following items purchased at a supermarket:

Meat	\$24.28
Vegetables	4.35
Shampoo	1.98
Laundry soap	4.70
Milk	2.35
Razor blades	0.79

Solution

The prices for the nonfood items (shampoo, soap, and razor blades) total \$7.47.

$$P = B \cdot R$$

$$= \$7.47 \times 0.05$$

$$= \$0.37$$

If both the total paid by the buyer and the sales tax rate are known, it is possible to find the purchase price using formula 4–5:

$$B_1 = (1.00 \pm R) \times B$$

where B_1 = total paid by the buyer, R = sales tax rate, and B = purchase price.

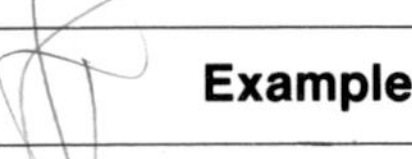

Example 4 In going over the daily sales, a store manager came upon a sales slip for \$23.10 that indicated only the total paid by the buyer. If the sales tax rate is 5%, find (a) the purchase price and (b) the amount of the sales tax.

Solution

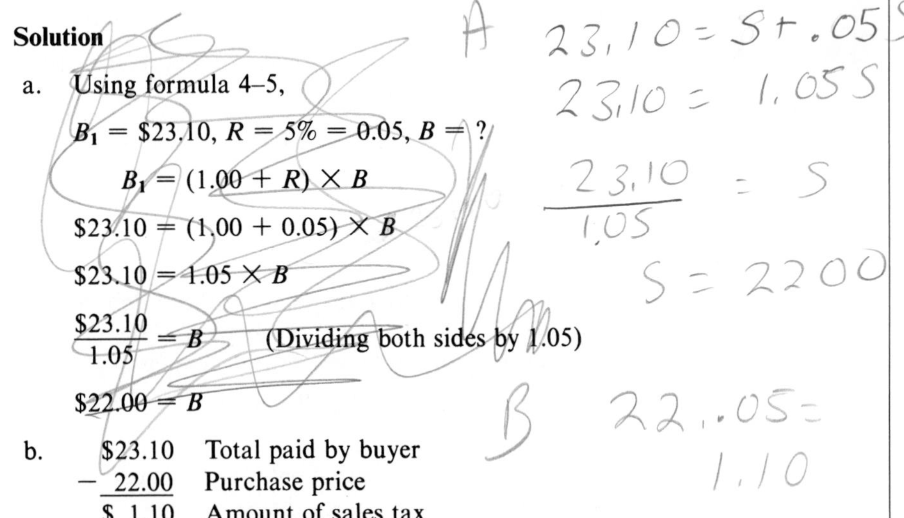

a. Using formula 4–5,

$B_1 = \$23.10,\ R = 5\% = 0.05,\ B = ?$

$$B_1 = (1.00 + R) \times B$$

$$\$23.10 = (1.00 + 0.05) \times B$$

$$\$23.10 = 1.05 \times B$$

$$\frac{\$23.10}{1.05} = B \quad \text{(Dividing both sides by 1.05)}$$

$$\$22.00 = B$$

b.

	\$23.10	Total paid by buyer
−	22.00	Purchase price
	\$ 1.10	Amount of sales tax

Section 8.3 Excise taxes

Excise taxes are taxes imposed upon particular commodities by governments at the federal, state, or local level. Whereas sales taxes are imposed on a wide range of products, excise taxes generally are levied on specific nonessential or luxury items. Commodities subject to excise taxes include alcoholic beverages, tobacco products, motor vehicles, firearms, fishing rods, and such luxury items as furs, jewelry, appliances, and photographic equipment. Examples of services subject to excise taxes include telephone service, entertainment, airline service, and highway construction and maintenance (via taxes on petroleum products).

Excise taxes may be a percentage of the manufacturer's selling price or a fixed amount per quantity sold. Excise taxes that are a percentage of the manufacturer's selling price are calculated using the basic percentage equation.

Example 1 A fishing rod on sale for $26 is subject to a sales tax of 4% and an excise tax of 10%. Find the total amount paid by the buyer.

Solution

$P = ?$, $B = \$26$, $R = 4\% = 0.04$ (sales tax), $R = 10\% = 0.10$ (excise tax)

$26.00	Sale price
+ 1.04	Sales tax ($26 × 0.04)
+ 2.60	Excise tax ($26 × 0.10)
$29.64	Total paid by the buyer

Exercises for Sections 8.2 and 8.3

1. The purchase price for some overhead lighting fixtures is $548.29. If the sales tax is 5%, find (a) the amount of the tax using only the basic percentage formula and (b) the amount of the tax using the percentage formula for the dollars and the tax brackets in table 8.1 for the cents.

2. A piece of china is priced at $37.79. If the sales tax is 4%, find (a) the amount of the tax using only the basic percentage formula and (b) the amount of the tax using the percentage formula for the dollars and the tax brackets in table 8.1 for the cents.

In problems 3–6, use the basic percentage formula for whole dollar amounts and the tax brackets in table 8.1 for cents to find the sales tax on the given items.

3. a. A man's suit priced at $348, 4% sales tax
   b. A figurine for $74.47, 5% sales tax

4. a. A pair of shoes priced at $87.60, 5% sales tax
   b. A utility building for $624.79, 4% sales tax

5. a. A piece of furniture for $671.35, 4% sales tax
   b. Draperies priced at $547.67, 5% sales tax

6. a. A watch priced at $78.28, 5% sales tax
   b. Carpeting for $947.32, 4% sales tax

In problems 7–14, use only the basic percentage formula to compute sales and excise taxes. Assume that food items are tax-exempt.

7. Find the total sales tax paid on the following items purchased in a state with a 6% sales tax:

Canned goods	$13.92
Produce	6.14
Paper goods	8.24
Toiletries	4.71
Meat	17.27

8. In a state with a sales tax rate of 5%, find the total tax paid on the following items:

Frozen food	$11.28
Bakery items	6.14
Toothpaste	2.39
Dog food	9.87
School supplies	4.71
Household cleaner	6.43

9. Myra Fleming paid a total of $691.06, including tax, for a new television set. If the sales tax rate is $4\frac{1}{2}$%, find the purchase price (excluding tax) and the amount of the sales tax.

10. Jim Clements purchased a new electric typewriter for a total of $587.95, including 5% sales tax. Find the purchase price (excluding tax) and the amount of the sales tax.

11. Find the amount of the sales tax paid on a home computer if the sales tax rate is 6% and the total amount paid, including tax, is $2,755.95. What was the purchase price of the computer, excluding tax?

12. A fur coat on sale for $495.99 is subject to a sales tax of 5% and an excise tax of 8%. Find the total amount paid by the buyer.

13. Find the total amount paid for a man's gold ring priced at $1,249.50 if the sales tax is 4% and the excise tax is 12%.

14. A camera is subject to a sales tax of 6% and an excise tax of 9%. Judy Phillips purchased the camera for a total price of $500.83, including taxes. Find the purchase price of the camera, excluding taxes.

Section 8.4 Property taxes

The primary source of revenue of county governments, municipalities, and school districts is the property tax. One reason for this is that the property tax can be most readily administered at the local level. Another reason is that property owners benefit more from community services and, therefore, pay more to support these services.

The word **property** in property tax can mean real property (land and the building improvements on it) as well as personal property (automobiles, furniture, jewelry, and so on). Property tax is a function of two factors: assessed valuation and the tax rate.

The **assessed value** is a percentage of the estimated market value of the property. For real property, the assessed value is determined by the tax assessor, a representative of the local governmental unit. Suppose, for example, that real property in Central City is assessed at 80% of the fair market value. Then an office building with a fair market value of \$220,000 would have an assessed value of

$$\$220,000 \times 0.80 = \$176,000$$

The **property tax rate** is the quotient obtained by dividing the total taxes to be raised by the total assessments. For example, if the annual budget of the Franklin County School District is \$1,760,000 and the total assessed value of the property in the school district is \$62,857,142, then the tax rate is

$$\text{Tax rate} = \frac{\text{Total taxes to be raised}}{\text{Total assessments}} = \frac{\$1,760,000}{\$62,857,142} = 0.028$$

This tax rate may be expressed in several ways: 2.8%, \$2.80 per \$100 of assessed value, or \$28 per \$1,000 of assessed value. Another way of expressing \$28 per \$1,000 of assessed value is 28 mills, where 1 **mill** $= \frac{1}{1,000}$ of a dollar.

The number of decimal places in the tax rate varies among taxing authorities. Rounding practices also vary. One method is to round the final digit up, regardless of the value of the next digit; mills are rounded up to the next whole mill. Thus, while normal rounding of 0.02423 as a percent to two decimal places would be 2.42%, for tax purposes, it is commonly rounded to 2.43%. Rounded to the next whole mill, this tax rate would be 25 mills.

Example 1 The annual budget of Central City is \$2,600,000, and the total of all assessed property is \$98,400,000. Find the tax rate in (a) percent rounded up to two decimal places, (b) dollars per \$100 of assessed value, (c) dollars per \$1,000 of assessed value, and (d) mills rounded up to the next whole mill.

Solution

$$\text{Tax rate} = \frac{\text{Total taxes to be raised}}{\text{Total of all assessments}} = \frac{\$2,600,000}{\$98,400,000} = 0.0264227$$

a. $0.0264227 = 0.0265 = 2.65\%$

b. $0.0265 \times \$100 = \$2.65$

c. $0.0265 \times \$1,000 = \$26.50$

d. $0.0265 \times 1,000 = 26.5 = 27$ mills

Calculation of the property tax is an application of the formula $P = B \cdot R$, where P = property tax, B = assessed value, and R = tax rate.

Example 2 Find the property tax on property with an assessed value of $234,000 if the tax rate is 2.12%.

Solution

$P = ?,\ B = \$234{,}000,\ R = 2.12\% = 0.0212$

$$
\begin{aligned}
P &= B \cdot R \\
&= \$234{,}000 \times 0.0212 \\
&= \$4{,}960.80
\end{aligned}
$$

Example 3 An office building has an assessed value of $380,000 in a city where property is taxed at a rate of $1.63 per $100 of assessed value. Find the property tax.

Solution

$P = ?,\ B = \$380{,}000,\ R = \frac{1.63}{100} = 0.0163$

$$
\begin{aligned}
P &= B \cdot R \\
&= \$380{,}000 \times 0.0163 \\
&= \$6{,}194
\end{aligned}
$$

Example 4 Property in Johnson County is assessed at 78% of its fair market value. If the tax rate is 34 mills, what is the property tax on property with a fair market value of $144,500?

Solution

The assessed value of the property is $144,500 × 0.78 = $112,710.

$P = ?,\ B = \$112{,}710,\ R = 34 \text{ mills} = \frac{34}{1{,}000} = 0.034$

$$
\begin{aligned}
P &= B \cdot R \\
&= \$112{,}710 \times 0.034 \\
&= \$3{,}832.14
\end{aligned}
$$

If the property tax and the tax rate are known, the assessed value can be found by using the formula

$$B = \frac{P}{R}$$

If the property tax and the assessed value are known, the tax rate can be found by using the formula

$$R = \frac{P}{B}$$

Example 5 The property tax on a building is \$1,602.54. If the tax rate is 1.74%, find the assessed value.

Solution

$P = \$1{,}602.54$, $B = ?$, $R = 1.74\% = 0.0174$

$$B = \frac{P}{R}$$

$$= \frac{\$1{,}602.54}{0.0174}$$

$$= \$92{,}100$$

Example 6 Property taxes on property with an assessed value of \$416,000 are \$8,569.60. Find the tax rate expressed in dollars per \$1,000 of assessed value.

Solution

$P = \$8{,}569.60$, $B = \$416{,}000$, $R = ?$

$$R = \frac{P}{B}$$

$$= \frac{\$8{,}569.60}{\$416{,}000}$$

$$= 0.0206$$

$$0.0206 \times \$1{,}000 = \$20.60$$

Exercises for Section 8.4

In problems 1–4, find the property tax rate in (a) percent rounded up to two decimal places, (b) dollars per \$1,000 of assessed value, and (c) mills rounded up to the next whole mill.

1. Taxes to be raised, \$3,400,000; total of all assessments, \$124,000,000
2. Taxes to be raised, \$1,750,000; total of all assessments, \$75,480,000

3. Taxes to be raised, $3,542,000; total of all assessments, $181,370,000

4. Taxes to be raised, $2,876,000; total of all assessments, $126,810,000

5. The annual budget of Midtown is $1,265,000, and the total of all assessed property is $58,300,000. Find the property tax rate expressed in (a) percent rounded up to two decimal places, (b) dollars per $100 of assessed value, (c) dollars per $1,000 of assessed value, and (d) mills rounded up to the next whole mill.

6. The total assessed property in the city of Bayview is $208,640,000. If the annual city budget is $4,031,000, find the property tax rate expressed in (a) percent rounded up to two decimal places, (b) dollars per $100 of assessed value, (c) dollars per $1,000 of assessed value, and (d) mills rounded up to the next whole mill.

7. Find the property tax on property assessed at $184,000 if the tax rate is (a) 2.43%, (b) 21 mills.

8. What is the property tax on a small shopping center assessed at $1,264,000 if the tax rate is (a) $1.78 per $100 of assessed value, (b) 18 mills?

9. Property in the city of Riverside is assessed at 72% of its fair market value. What is the tax on a building with a fair market value of $405,000 if the tax rate is (a) $24.40 per $1,000 of assessed value, (b) 32 mills?

10. If the property is assessed at 85% of its fair market value, find the property tax on some acreage with a fair market value of $820,000 when the tax rate is (a) $2.47 per $100 of assessed value, (b) 27 mills.

11. What is the assessed value of an office building if the property tax on the building is $12,870 and the tax rate is 1.98%?

12. Find the assessed value of a piece of property if the tax rate is 1.60% and the property tax is $2,126.

13. The assessed value of a home in Lincoln City is $182,000, and the property tax on the home is $3,276. Find the tax rate expressed in (a) percent and (b) mills.

14. If the assessed value of a building is $234,000 and the property tax is $5,616, find the tax rate expressed in (a) percent and (b) mills.

15. Property in Canyon County is assessed at 76% of its fair market value. Find the fair market value of a piece of property if the tax rate is 1.46% and the property tax is $721.24.

731.93

Section 8.5 Federal income tax

In 1913, ratification of the Sixteenth Amendment to the United States Constitution gave Congress the "power to lay and collect taxes on incomes, from whatever source derived." Since that time, the individual income tax has become the mainstay of the federal tax system, as shown in figure 8.1.

All citizens of the United States are required to file an income tax return if their income exceeds an amount determined by age and marital status. A tax return is filed on government form 1040 (or 1040A or 1040EZ) for income earned the previous calendar year and must be submitted before midnight on April 15th. The Internal Revenue Service (IRS) is the government agency responsible for collecting federal taxes.

The following are the basic steps in computing personal income tax:

1. Compute your *total income.*
2. Compute your *adjustments to income.*
3. Subtract your adjustments to income from your total income. The difference is your *adjusted gross income.*
4. Compute your itemized deductions. Reduce your adjusted gross income by this total provided it exceeds the *standard deduction;* otherwise reduce your adjusted gross income by the amount of the standard deduction. In 1989, the projected standard deduction amounts are

Filing Status	*Basic Standard Deduction*	*Elderly or Blind*
Single	$3,100	$3,850
Married filing jointly	5,200	5,800
Married filing separately	2,600	3,200
Head of household	4,550	5,300
Qualifying widow(er)	5,200	5,800

5. Multiply your total number of exemptions by $2,000 and subtract this from the amount obtained in step 4. This is your *taxable income.*
6. Compute your tax from the appropriate tax table according to your taxable income and *marital status.*

Total income

For most people, **total income** means the income from employment, from interest on savings or bonds, or from stock dividends. For income from employment, employers must furnish each employee with an IRS form W-2 Wage and Tax Statement that indicates the amount earned by the employee the previous calendar year (see figure 8.2). Annual income from interest or dividends is reported to the recipient on IRS form 1099 or a similar statement.

Figure 8.1
The budget dollar, fiscal year 1989 estimate

The Federal Government Dollar
Fiscal Year 1989 Estimate

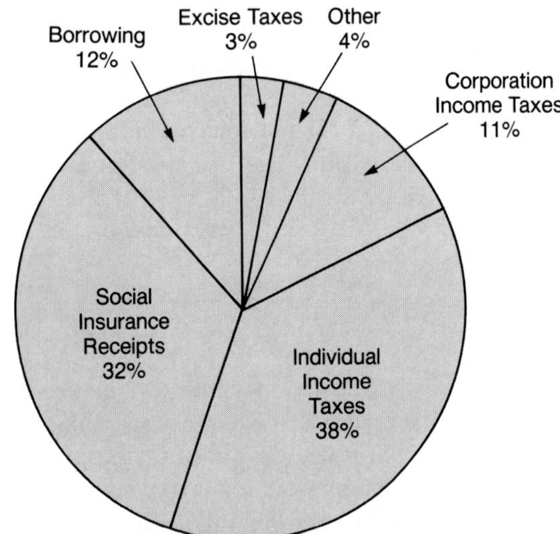

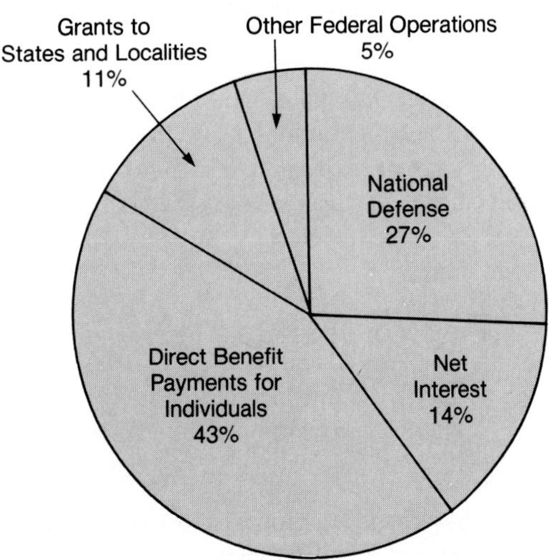

Source: Office of Management and Budget

Figure 8.2
Wage and Tax Statement (Form W-2)

1 Control number		OMB No 1545-0008	
2 Employer's name, address, and ZIP code The Conglomerate Corporation Industrial Park Anytown, USA 00000		3 Employer's identification number 241-2883	4 Employer's state I.D. number
		5 Statutory employee ☐ Deceased ☐ Pension plan ☐ Legal rep ☐	942 emp ☐ Subtotal ☐ Deferred compensation ☐ Void ☐
		6 Allocated tips	7 Advance EIC payment
8 Employee's social security number 123-45-6789	9 Federal income tax withheld 4,108	10 Wages, tips, other compensation 34,320.00	11 Social security tax withheld 2,577.43
12 Employee's name, address, and ZIP code John J. Doe 2824 Spring Street Anytown, USA 00000		13 Social security wages 34,320.00	14 Social security tips 0.00
		16	16a Fringe benefits incl. in Box 10
		17 State income tax / 18 State wages, tips, etc.	19 Name of state
		20 Local income tax / 21 Local wages, tips, etc.	22 Name of locality

Form **W-2 Wage and Tax Statement 1989**
This information is being furnished to the Internal Revenue Service.
Copy B To be filed with employee's FEDERAL tax return — Dept. of the Treasury—IRS

Adjustments to income

Adjustments to income are amounts that are subtracted from total income. Examples are deductions for reimbursed employee business expenses, penalties for early withdrawal of savings, alimony payments, contributions to a Keough pension plan, or for taxpayers not covered by a company pension plan, contributions to an individual retirement account.

Adjusted gross income

The **adjusted gross income** is found by subtracting the total adjustments to income from the total income.

Example 1

Julie Stone earned $34,000 last year as a computer programmer. During that year, she contributed $1,500 to a Keough pension plan. In addition to her salary, Julie earned $375 in stock dividends. Find Julie's adjusted gross income.

Solution

$34,000	Employment income
+ 375	Dividends
34,375	Total income
− 1,500	Adjustments to income
$32,875	Adjusted gross income

Deductions **Deductions** are expenses that reduce the amount of taxable income. Examples of such expenses are:

Medical and dental expenses in excess of a percent of the adjusted gross income as determined by the IRS
Mortgage interest
State and local income taxes
Real estate taxes
Contributions to charitable organizations
Dues to professional organizations

The government has calculated an average amount an individual or family is expected to incur in deductible expenses during a year, called the **standard deduction.** The taxpayer has the option of subtracting from the adjusted gross income either the standard deduction or the total of all itemized deductions, whichever is greater.

Exemptions In general, an **exemption** is the taxpayer or a relative who depends on the taxpayer for financial support. For example, a married taxpayer with two small children could claim four exemptions: the taxpayer, the taxpayer's spouse, and the two children. Exemptions are used to reduce the adjusted gross income. The reduction is $2,000 per exemption.

Taxable income The **taxable income** is the adjusted gross income minus the amount for exemptions and minus either (a) the total of itemized deductions, or (b) the standard deduction, whichever is greater.

Example 2 Joe Millins had an adjusted gross income last year of $51,500. After itemizing, his total deductions were $6,955, compared with a standard deduction of $5,200. Find his taxable income if he had four exemptions.

Solution

The total itemized deductions exceeds the standard deduction. Thus

$51,500	Adjusted gross income
− 6,955	Total of itemized deductions
− 8,000	Exemptions ($2,000 × 4)
$36,545	Taxable income

Example 3 Rita Wilson earned an adjusted gross income of $37,000 last year. Her deductible expenses (in excess of IRS exclusions) were as follows: medical and dental expenses, $290; interest charges, $330; real estate taxes, $1,200; contributions to charitable organizations, $940. Find her taxable income if she claims one exemption and the standard deduction is $3,100.

Solution

Itemizing Rita's deductions,

$ 290	Medical and dental expenses
330	Interest charges
1,200	Real estate taxes
940	Contributions to charitable organizations
$2,760	Total of deductions

Since her itemized deductions do not exceed the standard deduction, Rita should not itemize her deductions. Thus,

$37,000	Adjusted gross income
− 2,000	Exemption
− 3,100	Standard deduction
$31,900	Taxable income

Tax The amount of the tax depends on two components: the taxable income and the filing status of the taxpayer. Table 8.2 lists the projected 1989 tax rates.

Table 8.2 Tax Owed According to Taxable Income and Filing Status

Filing Status	**Portion of Taxable Income Taxed at:**		
	15%	*28%*	*Additional 5%*
Single	$0–$18,550	Over $18,550	From $44,900 to $93,130
Married filing jointly or Qualifying widow(er)	$0–$30,950	Over $30,950	From $74,850 to $155,320
Married filing separately	$0–$15,475	Over $15,475	From $37,425 to $117,895
Head of household	$0–$24,850	Over $24,850	From $64,200 to $128,810

Example 4 A married taxpayer filing a joint return had a taxable income of $15,630. Find the amount of the tax.

Solution

From table 8.2, the amount of the tax is $15,650 × 0.15 = $2,347.50.

Example 5 A single taxpayer had a taxable income of $98,000. Find the amount of the tax.

Solution

From table 8.2,

$ 2,782.50	$18,550 × 0.15
+ 22,246.00	($98,000 − 18,550) × 0.28
+ 2,411.50	($93,130 − 44,900) × 0.05
$27,440.00	Amount of Tax

Example 6 Joanna Sparks had an adjusted gross income of $39,450 and itemized deductions of $3,936. She is single but claims her mother as an exemption. Find the amount of her tax if she files as head of household.

Solution

$39,450	Adjusted gross income
− 3,936	Itemized deductions
− 4,000	Exemptions ($2,000 × 2)
$31,514	Taxable income

From table 8.2,

$3,727.50	$24,850 × 0.15
+ 1,865.92	($31,514 − 24,850) × 0.28
$5,593.42	Amount of tax

Example 7 Juan Garcia and his wife have a combined income of $58,900 and interest income of $500. They receive an adjustment to income of $1,450. Their deductible expenses (in excess of IRS exclusions) include doctor and dentist bills of $2,688, $163 in finance charges, $1,922 in state income taxes, $1,689 in real estate taxes, $485 in union dues, and charitable contributions of $1,056. The Garcias are filing a joint return claiming six exemptions. Find the amount of the tax if the standard deduction is $5,200.

Solution

$58,900	Employment income
+ 500	Interest income
$59,400	Total income
− 1,450	Adjustment to income
$57,950	Adjusted gross income
$2,688	Medical and dental expenses
163	Finance charges
1,922	State income taxes
1,689	Real estate taxes
485	Union dues
1,056	Contributions
$8,003	Total itemized deductions
$57,950	Adjusted gross income
− 8,003	Total itemized deductions
− 12,000	Exemptions ($2,000 × 6)
$37,947	Taxable income
$4,642.50	$30,950 × 0.15
+ 1,959.16	($37,947 − 30,950) × 0.28
$6,601.66	Amount of tax

The federal government has authorized employers to withhold a percentage of the employee's earnings each payday as advance payment on the employee's personal income tax. The percentage subtracted from the employee's earnings depends upon the employee's total earnings, marital status, and the number of withholding allowances (exemptions claimed by the employee). The total amount withheld is reported to the employee on government form W-2 (see figure 8.2).

Example 8 Charles Kirk had a taxable income of $16,290 last year. Charles is single and claimed one exemption. He is paid weekly, and $38 per week was withheld from his pay. Determine if at the end of the year Charles paid additional taxes or received a refund.

Solution

From table 8.2, Charles's tax was $2,443.50. The total withheld from his pay was $\$38 \times 52 = \$1{,}976$. Thus, Charles paid an additional amount of $\$2{,}443.50 - \$1{,}976 = \$467.50$.

Example 9 Last year, John Higgins earned $48,400. He also received $2,016 in interest on savings and made payments of $1,816 to a Keough pension plan. John is paid every two weeks and has $270 withheld each payday. In preparing his federal income tax return, John itemized deductions, and the total was $5,420. John is married with one child and files a joint return. Determine if John paid additional taxes or received a refund.

Solution

	Amount	
	$48,400	Employment income
+	2,016	Interest
	$50,416	Total income
−	1,816	Adjustments to income
	$48,600	Adjusted gross income
−	5,420	Deductions
−	6,000	Exemptions ($2,000 × 3)
	$37,180	Taxable income
	$ 6,386.90	Tax (table 8.2)
−	7,020.00	Withheld ($270 × 26)
	$ 633.10	Refunded to John

Exercises for Section 8.5

In problems 1–5, use the information given to find the adjusted gross income.

1. Earned income, $24,752; interest income, $257; adjustments to income, $782.
2. Earned income, $33,284; interest income, $792; dividend income, $147; payments to a Keough plan, $1,141; other adjustments to income, $857.
3. Earned income, $47,214; interest income, $1,214; dividend income, $392; payments to a Keough plan, $482; other adjustments to income, $700.
4. Earned income, $28,427; interest income, $108; dividend income, $210; payments to an IRA, $160 per month; other adjustments to income, $319.

5. Earned income, \$51,908; interest income, \$1,942; dividend income, \$4,249; payments to a Keough plan, \$410 per month; other adjustments to income, \$2,317.

In problems 6–11, find the taxable income using the given information. (Assume that the reduction for exemptions is \$2,000 per exemption.)

6. Adjusted gross income, \$36,214; total itemized deductions, \$5,287; head of household; two exemptions.
7. Adjusted gross income, \$41,902; total itemized deductions, \$6,142; married filing jointly; four exemptions.
8. Adjusted gross income, \$22,578. Deductions (in excess of IRS exclusions): medical expenses, \$312; interest charges, \$1,935; real estate taxes, \$841; charitable contributions, \$428. Single; one exemption.
9. Adjusted gross income, \$35,551. Deductions (in excess of IRS exclusions): interest charges, \$3,326; real estate taxes, \$1,918; charitable contributions, \$622; miscellaneous, \$326. Married filing jointly; three exemptions.
10. Earned income, \$40,201; interest income, \$821; adjustments to income, \$1,750. Deductions (in excess of IRS exclusions): medical expenses, \$578; interest charges, \$1,826; real estate taxes, \$1,226; charitable contributions, \$1,394; miscellaneous, \$418. Married filing jointly; four exemptions.
11. Earned income, \$31,802; interest income, \$278; adjustments to income, \$1,505. Deductions (in excess of IRS exclusions): interest charges, \$1,737; real estate taxes, \$1,892; charitable contributions, \$1,246; union dues, \$495. Married filing jointly; three exemptions.

In problems 12–21, use table 8.2 to find the amount of tax. (Assume that the reduction for exemptions is \$2,000 per exemption.)

12. Married taxpayer; filing separately; taxable income, \$29,200.
13. Married taxpayer; joint return; taxable income, \$32,480.
14. Single taxpayer; one exemption; adjusted gross income, \$21,014; total itemized deductions, \$2,842.
15. Single taxpayer; two exemptions; adjusted gross income, \$27,573; total itemized deductions, \$3,214.
16. Adjusted gross income, \$49,700. Deductible expenses (in excess of IRS exclusions): medical, dental, and drug expenses, \$470; mortgage interest, \$2,700; union dues, \$440; real estate taxes, \$1,850; charitable contributions, \$280. Married, filing jointly, three exemptions.

17. Adjusted gross income, $53,500. Deductible expenses (in excess of IRS exclusions): medical, dental, and drug expenses, $125; mortgage interest, $1,400; real estate taxes, $1,670; state income tax, $1,250; charitable contributions, $1,500. Head of household; two exemptions.

18. Income from employment, $57,800; interest income, $920; dividend income, $800. Deductible expenses (in excess of IRS exclusions): medical, dental, and drug expenses, $415; mortgage interest, $2,620; real estate taxes, $1,860; finance charges, $610; charitable contributions, $1,420. Married, filing jointly, five exemptions.

19. Income from employment, $68,600; interest income, $1,300; dividend income, $1,500. Deductible expenses (in excess of IRS exclusions): medical, dental, and drug expenses, none; mortgage interest, $2,900; state income tax, $1,200; real estate taxes, $1,100; finance charges, $320; charitable contributions, $1,000. Married filing jointly, three exemptions.

20. Bob and Jean Farrell have a combined income from their jobs of $92,000. They also have interest income of $1,800. Their deductible expenses (in excess of IRS exclusions) include medical, dental, and drug expenses of $235, finance charges of $210, state income taxes of $1,700, mortgage interest of $5,240, real estate taxes of $1,600, and charitable contributions of $1,500. If the Farrells file a joint return claiming four exemptions, how much federal income tax will they owe?

21. Last year, Pat and Jim Roberts had a combined income from employment of $57,500. They also had interest income of $600 and dividend income of $800. Their deductible expenses (in excess of IRS exclusions) for the year were: medical, dental, and drug expenses, $895; mortgage interest, $5,800; real estate taxes, $2,100; union dues, $840; charitable contributions, $1,200. The Roberts filed a joint return claiming five exemptions. Find the amount of federal income tax they owe.

Glossary

Adjusted gross income Total income less adjustments to income.

Adjustments to income Expenses that may be subtracted from total income to obtain adjusted gross income; includes such expenses as deductions for reimbursed employee business expenses, penalties for early withdrawal of savings, alimony payments, contributions to a Keough pension plan, or for taxpayers not covered by a company pension plan, contributions to an individual retirement account.

Assessed value A percentage of the estimated market value of property.

Deduction An expense that reduces the amount of taxable income.

Excise tax A tax imposed by federal, state, or local governments on specific nonessential or luxury items.

Exemption An allowance used to reduce the adjusted gross income. In general, an exemption is the taxpayer or any relative of the taxpayer who is dependent on the taxpayer for financial support.

Mill 1/1,000 of a dollar.
Property For tax purposes, this term can mean real property (land and the building improvements on the land) or personal property (automobiles, furniture, jewelry, and so on).
Property tax rate The quotient obtained by dividing the total taxes to be raised by the total assessments.
Sales tax A tax on retail sales imposed by state or local governments.
Standard deduction The average amount an individual or family is expected to incur in deductible expenses during a year.
Taxable income The adjusted gross income minus the total for exemptions and minus either (a) the total of itemized deductions, or (b) the standard deduction, whichever is greater.
Total income For most people, the income from employment, from interest on savings or bonds, and from stock dividends.

Review test

1. A tax imposed on a nonessential or luxury item is called a(n) ______________ tax.
2. A percentage of the estimated market value of property is called the ______________ of the property.
3. A ______________ is 1/1,000 of a dollar.
4. The difference between total income and adjustments to income is called the ______________.
5. The average amount of deductible expenses an individual or family is expected to incur during a year is called the ______________.

In problems 6–9, use only the basic percentage formula to compute sales and excise taxes.

6. The selling price of a baby car seat is $69.99. Find the amount of the sales tax if the tax rate is 6%.
7. Find the total cost of a coffee maker if the selling price is $46.95 and the sales tax rate is 4%.
8. A theater owner decides that the total price of a ticket for a movie (selling price plus sales tax) should be $3.50. What is the selling price if the sales tax rate is 5%?
9. A fishing rod that sells for $72.95 is subject to a 4% sales tax and a 10% excise tax. What is the total cost to the buyer?
10. Find the property tax on a warehouse if the property is assessed at 80% of its market value of $434,000 and the tax rate is 28 mills.
11. Harold Haines's salary was $32,800 last year. During the same year, he had adjustments to income of $2,870, and he made $50 per month in interest from a savings account. What was his adjusted gross income for the year?
12. Edith Miller earned a salary of $28,500 last year. In addition, she received $1,400 in dividends, and she had medical and dental expenses of $822 in excess of the IRS exclusion. Other expenses for the year included mortgage interest charges of $1,040, real estate taxes of $1,677, and charitable contributions of $1,516. Calculate her taxable income if she claims two exemptions and files a return as head of household.

PART 3

Finance

The principles of basic finance from the viewpoint of both the consumer and the businessperson are examined in this part. Topics include simple and compound interest, credit, stocks and bonds, annuities, and amortization.

CHAPTER 9

Simple Interest

Chapter Objectives

I. Learn the meaning of the following terms:

Interest, 299
Time fraction, 303
Exact time, 303
Ordinary time, 303
Exact interest, 306
Ordinary interest, 306
Maturity value, 312
Present value, 313

II. Understand:

The formula for simple interest and its variations, 299–300

The difference between exact time and ordinary time, 303

The difference between ordinary interest and exact interest, 306

The formulas for maturity value and present value, 312–313

III. Apply:

The simple interest formula to solve problems involving loans, 299–301, 307–309

The formulas for maturity value and present value for simple interest loans, 312–314

Section 9.1 Introduction

Money paid for the use of money is called **interest.** Much of the American economy depends on keeping in circulation money that people have but temporarily do not need. The charge for the use of this money is called interest.

Nearly everyone either pays or receives interest at some point during their lifetime. We receive interest from savings accounts or bonds because we, in effect, loan our money for others to use. On the other hand, in the mortgage payments for our house, in the monthly payments for our automobile, or in our charge account at the department store, we are borrowing money, and our payments include charges for interest.

Businesses and governmental agencies frequently need money to finance special projects. So, loans are obtained from banks, life insurance companies, or by the issuance of bonds. In each case, interest is paid to the party supplying the money.

In this chapter, we begin a study of the kinds of interest and the methods used to determine interest for a given loan or investment.

Section 9.2 Simple interest

Simple interest is an annual percentage of the amount of money borrowed or invested. The formula for simple interest is a modification of the basic percentage formula. The equation is

■ (9–1) $$I = Prt$$

where I = interest, P = **principal** (the amount of money borrowed or invested), r = annual rate, and t = the length of time (in years) the principal is borrowed or invested.

Thus, simple interest is a function of three variables—principal, rate, and time. The principal is expressed in dollars, the rate is expressed in percent, and the time is expressed in years. Simple interest is used primarily for short-term loans and investments.

Example 1 A man borrows \$500 for four months at a simple interest rate of 12%. How much interest does he pay?

Solution

$I = ?, P = \$500, r = 12\% = 0.12, t = \frac{4}{12} = \frac{1}{3}$

Using formula 9–1,

$$\begin{aligned} I &= Prt \\ &= \$500 \times 0.12 \times \frac{1}{3} \\ &= \$20 \end{aligned}$$

Note that time is always expressed in years; hence, the time fraction $\frac{4}{12} = \frac{1}{3}$ is used for four months.

Example 2 What is the interest on a \$2,800 loan for six months at $11\frac{1}{4}\%$ simple interest?

Solution

$I = ?, P = \$2{,}800, r = 11\frac{1}{4}\% = 0.1125, t = \frac{6}{12} = 0.5$

Using formula 9–1,

$$I = Prt$$
$$= \$2{,}800 \times 0.1125 \times 0.5$$
$$= \$157.50$$

In formula 9–1, the interest I is the unknown. However, it may be necessary to solve for one of the other variables. From

$$I = Prt$$

we can derive

■ (9–2) $P = \frac{I}{rt}$ (Dividing both sides of formula 9–1 by rt)

■ (9–3) $r = \frac{I}{Pt}$ (Dividing both sides of formula 9–1 by Pt)

■ (9–4) $t = \frac{I}{Pr}$ (Dividing both sides of formula 9–1 by Pr)

Example 3 At a simple interest rate of $9\frac{1}{2}\%$, what principal would earn \$304 interest in six months?

Solution

$I = \$304, P = ?, r = 9\frac{1}{2}\% = 0.095, t = \frac{6}{12} = 0.5$

Using formula 9–2,

$$P = \frac{I}{rt}$$
$$= \frac{\$304}{0.095 \times 0.5}$$
$$= \frac{\$304}{0.0475}$$
$$= \$6{,}400$$

Example 4 Find the simple interest rate necessary for \$3,000 to earn \$270 interest in nine months.

Solution

$I = \$270, P = \$3{,}000, r = ?, t = \frac{9}{12} = 0.75$

Using formula 9–3,

$$r = \frac{I}{Pt}$$

$$= \frac{\$270}{\$3{,}000 \times 0.75}$$

$$= \frac{\$270}{\$2{,}250}$$

$$= 0.12$$

$$= 12\%$$

Example 5 How long will it take for \$1,800 to earn \$156 in interest if the simple interest rate is 13%?

Solution

$I = \$156, P = \$1{,}800, r = 13\% = 0.13, t = ?$

Using formula 9–4,

$$t = \frac{I}{Pr}$$

$$= \frac{\$156}{\$1{,}800 \times 0.13}$$

$$= \frac{156}{234}$$

$$= \frac{2}{3} \text{ years or eight months}$$

Exercises for Section 9.2 In problems 1–12, solve the formula $I = Prt$ for the appropriate variable and compute the value of the indicated quantity.

1. $I = \$150, r = 12\%, t = 2$ months. Find P.
2. $r = 11\%, P = \$2{,}000, I = \$110$. Find t.
3. $P = \$12{,}000, I = \$1{,}280, t = 8$ months. Find r.

4. $P = \$6{,}000$, $r = 14\%$, $t = 5$ months. Find I.
5. $I = \$990$, $r = 16.5\%$, $t = 10$ months. Find P.
6. $r = 9\%$, $P = \$2{,}500.00$, $I = \$56.25$. Find t.
7. $P = \$1{,}600$, $I = \$368$, $t = 2$ years. Find r.
8. $P = \$2{,}000$, $r = 10\frac{1}{4}\%$, $t = 9$ months. Find I.
9. $I = \$500$, $r = 16\%$, $t = 15$ months. Find P.
10. $I = \$551.25$, $P = \$2{,}250.00$, $t = 2$ years. Find r.
11. $I = \$110.25$, $P = \$2{,}800.00$, $r = 15\frac{3}{4}\%$. Find t.
12. $P = \$3{,}500$, $r = 12\frac{1}{4}\%$, $t = 8$ months. Find I.
13. Bob Parker borrowed \$3,000 for four months at a simple interest rate of 12%. How much interest will Bob pay for the loan?
14. Find the interest paid for a loan of \$1,800 for 10 months at 9% simple interest.
15. What is the interest on a \$1,500 loan for six months at $8\frac{3}{4}\%$ simple interest?
16. Myra Williams borrowed \$2,400 for 18 months at a simple interest rate of $14\frac{1}{2}\%$. How much interest will she pay for the loan?
17. Sue Cunningham owns a \$5,000 bond that pays $10\frac{1}{4}\%$ simple interest. How much does she receive quarterly from the bond?
18. Bill Foster invested \$10,000 in a six-month savings certificate offered by his credit union. If the interest rate on the certificate was 11.65%, how much interest did Bill earn?
19. At an interest rate of 9%, how much money would have to be invested to earn \$315 in seven months?
20. Mel Phillips paid \$675 interest on a \$5,000 loan at 18% simple interest. What was the length of the loan?
21. Brenda Jones invested \$15,000.00 in U.S. Treasury bills. At the end of three months, she received \$468.75 in interest. What was the interest rate?
22. To earn \$85 in eight months, how much money would have to be invested at $8\frac{1}{2}\%$ interest?
23. Find the simple interest rate necessary for \$2,500.00 to earn \$543.75 in 18 months.
24. How long will it take \$1,300.00 invested at $9\frac{1}{2}\%$ to earn \$61.75 in interest?

25. Wilma Smith arranged for a loan of \$7,500 for $1\frac{1}{2}$ years at $16\frac{3}{4}\%$ interest. How much interest will she pay?

26. Brett Walker needs to borrow \$4,000 to pay for remodeling his store. If the rate of interest Brett must pay is 14%, and if he is not willing to pay more than \$420 in interest, for how long can he borrow the money?

27. Ned Peters needs to borrow \$3,900 for 16 months. If he cannot pay more than \$700 in interest, and if the least interest rate at which he can borrow the money is $13\frac{3}{4}\%$, can he obtain the loan?

28. The new owner of a small business wishes to borrow some money for operating capital. At an interest rate of $10\frac{1}{2}\%$, how much can she borrow for three months and not pay more than \$100 in interest?

29. June Richardson has arranged to loan \$1,800 to a friend for four months. To receive at least \$100 in interest, what is the smallest interest rate that she can charge?

Section 9.3 Time

Time is measured in years in the simple interest formula; hence, a **time fraction** is used in problems in which the term of the loan is specified in months or days. If the term of the loan is specified in months, then the numerator of the time fraction consists of the term of the loan in months and the denominator consists of the number of months in a year. That is,

■ (9–5) $$t = \frac{\text{Term of the loan in months}}{\text{Number of months in a year}}$$

If the term of a loan is specified in days, a time fraction again is necessary. In this case,

■ (9–6) $$t = \frac{\text{Term of the loan in days}}{\text{Number of days in a year}}$$

When time is measured in days, equation 9–6 is complicated by the use of two calendars: an astronomical calendar and a financial calendar.

The astronomical calendar, called **exact time,** is based on the revolution of the earth around the sun. One orbit requires $365\frac{1}{4}$ days; hence, our year consists of 365 days, with a leap year of 366 days every fourth year.* The year is divided into months of 28 (29), 30, or 31 days, irregularly spaced.

The financial calendar, called **ordinary time** or **banker's year,** eliminates the irregularities of the astronomical calendar by defining a year to consist of 12 months of 30 days per month. A year in ordinary time thus consists of 360 days. Ordinary time is a calendar of convenience since 360 is a multiple of numbers such as 60 and 90. Frequently, the term of a loan is 60 days or 90 days.

*Leap years account for the $\frac{1}{4}$ day accumulation each year, with the extra day added to the month of February (February 29). Leap years occur on years divisible by 4; 1984 and 1988 were leap years. Likewise, 1992, 1996, 2000, and so on are leap years.

In most interest transactions, *if the term of the loan is expressed in days, the numerator of the time fraction will be exact time*. Calculation of exact time may be simplified by the use of appendix B—"The Number of Each Day of the Year"—found at the end of the book. The examples that follow illustrate the use of appendix B in finding exact time. Unless specified, the years are nonleap years.

Example 1 Using exact time, find the number of days from May 14 to September 20 of the same year.*

Solution

Using appendix B and subtracting the first date from the second,

Date		*Day*
September 20	=	263
May 14	=	−134
		129

There are 129 days from May 14 to September 20.

Example 2 Using exact time, find the number of days from January 4, 1992, to April 30, 1992.

Solution

The year 1992 is a leap year; thus,

Date		*Day*	
April 30, 1992	=	121	(120 + 1 day for leap year)
January 4, 1992	=	− 4	
		117	

Example 3 Find the number of days from November 14, 1989, to January 10, 1990, using exact time.

Solution

Because this period includes two different years, the interval must be separated into 1989 time and 1990 time. Then the solutions are added to obtain the total time.

*An interest-bearing document begins to earn interest on the day following its execution and continues to earn interest until the day it is paid. Thus, in counting the days between two dates, the last day is counted, but the first is not.

Date		*Day*
December 31, 1989	=	365
November 14, 1989	=	−318
		47
January 10, 1990	=	+ 10
		57

There are 57 days from November 14, 1989, to January 10, 1990.

Example 4 A loan is executed on June 10 for a term of six months. Find the due date of the loan using exact time.

Solution

Since the term of the loan is stated in months, six months from June 10 is December 10. This is true using either exact time or ordinary time.

One exception to the reasoning of example 4 occurs when the term of a loan ends on a day that does not exist. For instance, a one-month loan executed on March 31 would be due on April 30, since there is no April 31.

Example 5 A loan is executed on June 10 for 180 days. Find the due date of the loan using exact time.

Solution

The term of the loan is in days; hence, from appendix B,

Date	*Day*
June 10 ⟶	161
	+180 days
December 7 ⟵	341

Exercises for Section 9.3 In problems 1–10, use appendix B and exact time to find the number of days from the first date to the second.

1. March 11, 1990, to October 12, 1990
2. June 15, 1990, to December 27, 1990
3. April 24, 1990, to August 15, 1990
4. May 12, 1990, to November 2, 1990
5. February 10, 1992, to July 15, 1992
6. January 19, 1990, to September 12, 1990

7. April 18, 1991, to January 24, 1992
8. June 14, 1991, to February 15, 1992
9. November 14, 1989, to September 13, 1990
10. August 6, 1989, to May 3, 1990

In problems 11–20, use exact time to find the due date of a loan executed on the given date for the given term.

11. May 24, three months
12. September 15, eight months
13. August 17, 60 days
14. March 6, 180 days
15. February 10, 1990, 90 days
16. January 22, 1990, 60 days
17. February 25, 1992, 180 days
18. January 7, 1990, 90 days
19. November 12, 1989, 180 days
20. December 16, 1989, 90 days

Section 9.4 Exact interest and ordinary interest

When the term of a loan is in days, the numerator of the time fraction is usually exact time, but depending on the loan, the denominator may be either exact time or ordinary time:

■ (9–7) $$t = \frac{\text{Exact time}}{365}$$

■ (9–8) $$t = \frac{\text{Exact time}}{360}$$

In time fraction 9–7, both numerator and denominator are in exact time, while in time fraction 9–8, the numerator is in exact time and the denominator is in ordinary time.*

Interest calculations using time fraction 9–7 are called **exact interest.** Exact interest is used by the federal government and by Federal Reserve banks in their transactions with member banks. Interest calculations using time fraction 9–8 are called **ordinary interest, banker's interest,** or **banker's rule.** Ordinary interest is used by many commercial institutions because it generates more interest.

*Actually, there are two additional possibilities, $\frac{\text{Ordinary time}}{365}$ and $\frac{\text{Ordinary time}}{360}$, but these are infrequently used.

Example 1 A loan for \$500 is executed on January 10 at a simple interest rate of 12% and is due on February 20. Calculate the interest using (a) exact interest and (b) ordinary interest.

Solution

From appendix B, the exact time from January 10 to February 20 is 41 days. Thus, with $P = \$500$ and $r = 12\% = 0.12$,

a. $I = Prt$

$= \$500 \times 0.12 \times \frac{41}{365}$

$= \$6.74$ Exact interest

b. $I = Prt$

$= \$500 \times 0.12 \times \frac{41}{360}$

$= \$6.83$ Ordinary interest

In this case, ordinary interest earned \$0.09 more than exact interest.

Example 2 Find the exact interest on \$3,000 at $9\frac{3}{4}\%$ from August 12 to December 5.

Solution

The exact time from August 12 to December 5 is 115 days. Thus, with $I = ?$, $P = \$3{,}000$, $r = 9\frac{3}{4}\% = 0.0975$, and $t = \frac{115}{365}$,

$I = Prt$

$= \$3{,}000 \times 0.0975 \times \frac{115}{365}$

$= \$92.16$

Example 3 A loan of \$1,200 for 90 days earned ordinary interest in the amount of \$33. What was the interest rate?

Solution

$P = \$1{,}200$, $I = \$33$, $r = ?$, $t = \frac{90}{360} = 0.25$

$r = \frac{I}{Pt}$

$= \frac{\$33}{\$1{,}200 \times 0.25}$

$= 0.11$

$= 11\%$

Example 4 How many days would it take to earn \$300 ordinary interest on \$20,000 invested at 15%?

Solution

$I = \$300$, $P = \$20{,}000$, $r = 15\% = 0.15$, $t = ?$

$$t = \frac{I}{Pr}$$

$$= \frac{\$300}{\$20{,}000 \times 0.15}$$

$$= \frac{\$300}{\$3{,}000}$$

$$= 0.10 \text{ years}$$

$$= 0.10 \times 360 \quad \text{(Multiplying by 360 to convert } t \text{ to days)}$$

$$= 36 \text{ days}$$

As shown in section 5.6, it is a common practice for vendors to offer buyers a cash discount for prompt payment. It is usually profitable for a buyer to take advantage of a cash discount, even if it is necessary to borrow money to do so. The next examples illustrate why.

Example 5 An invoice for \$600 contains terms 2/10, n/30. At what interest rate (ordinary interest) could the buyer afford to borrow to take advantage of the cash discount?

Solution

The first step is to calculate the cash discount and the amount to be borrowed:

\$600	Net amount
− 12	Cash discount (\$600 × 0.02)
\$588	Amount to be borrowed

If the buyer is to save money, the interest on the loan must be less than \$12. Since the net amount is due 20 days after the last day of the cash discount, the term of the loan is $\frac{20}{360} = \frac{1}{18}$. Thus, using formula 9–3 with $I = \$12$, $P = \$588$, $r = ?$, and $t = \frac{1}{18}$,

$$r = \frac{I}{Pt}$$

$$= \frac{\$12}{\$588 \times 1/18}$$

$$= 0.3673$$

$$= 36.73\%$$

The buyer could borrow \$588 for 20 days at any interest rate less than 36.73% and save money on the transaction.

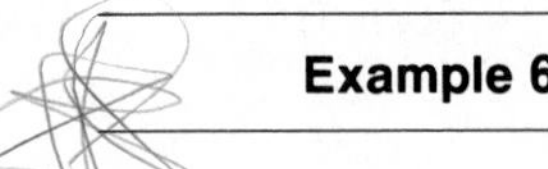

Example 6 An invoice for \$480 contains terms 3/10, n/60. At an interest rate of $10\frac{1}{2}\%$ (ordinary interest), calculate (a) how much would have to be borrowed to take advantage of the cash discount and (b) how much would be saved on the transaction.

Solution

a.

	\$480.00	Net amount
−	14.40	Cash discount (\$480 × 0.03)
	\$465.60	Amount to be borrowed

b. $I = ?$, $P = \$465.60$, $r = 10\frac{1}{2}\% = 0.105$, $t = \frac{50}{360} = \frac{5}{36}$

$$I = Prt$$

$$= \$465.60 \times 0.105 \times \frac{5}{36}$$

$$= \$6.79$$

The interest on the loan is \$6.79. Hence, the amount saved is \$14.40 − \$6.79 = \$7.61

Exercises for Section 9.4

In problems 1–15, find (a) the exact interest and (b) the ordinary interest for the given loans. (Always assume nonleap years.)

1. \$9,500 at 10% for 90 days
2. \$4,500 at 13% for 180 days
3. \$5,200 at $8\frac{1}{4}$% for 60 days
4. \$2,700 at $9\frac{1}{2}$% for 180 days
5. \$5,600 at $8\frac{3}{4}$% for 45 days
6. \$8,200 at $12\frac{3}{4}$% for 65 days
7. \$4,000 at $11\frac{1}{2}$% from May 15 to August 13
8. \$6,200 at $10\frac{1}{4}$% from July 8 to September 6
9. \$3,500 at $9\frac{3}{4}$% from February 4 to August 3
10. \$7,200 at $10\frac{1}{2}$% from January 18 to August 6
11. \$9,800 at $8\frac{3}{4}$% from September 26 to February 3
12. \$5,700 at $8\frac{1}{2}$% from November 12 to July 10
13. \$7,450 at $9\frac{1}{2}$% from October 23 to February 15
14. \$8,230 at $10\frac{3}{4}$% from August 18 to January 20
15. \$14,720 at $9\frac{1}{4}$% from December 5 to February 18

In problems 16–25, find the interest rate for the given loans.

16. \$3,000 earns \$180 ordinary interest in 180 days.
17. \$9,600 earns \$144 ordinary interest in 60 days.
18. \$4,500.00 earns \$99.86 exact interest in 90 days.
19. \$5,700.00 earns \$299.84 exact interest in 120 days.
20. \$2,800 earns \$252 ordinary interest from March 15 to November 10.
21. \$3,800.00 earns \$140.39 ordinary interest from May 6 to September 23.
22. \$6,400.00 earns \$153.42 exact interest from November 11 to February 19.
23. \$7,200.00 earns \$631.73 exact interest from December 4 to July 2.
24. \$5,200.00 earns \$136.50 ordinary interest from October 28 to February 5.
25. \$3,100.00 earns \$151.34 ordinary interest from September 18 to March 27.

In problems 26–31, find the number of days necessary to earn the given amount of interest on the given loan.

26. $600 ordinary interest on $20,000 at 12%

27. $37.50 ordinary interest on $2,500.00 at 9%

28. $136.50 ordinary interest on $4,200.00 at $9\frac{3}{4}$%

29. $706.85 exact interest on $8,600.00 at 10%

30. $270.74 exact interest on $7,200.00 at $15\frac{1}{4}$%

31. $330.82 exact interest on $9,200.00 at $8\frac{3}{4}$%

In problems 32–39, an investment of *P* dollars yields the given amount of interest. Find *P*. (Round to the nearest dollar.)

32. $160 ordinary interest in 180 days at 16%

33. $120 ordinary interest in 60 days at 9%

34. $94.93 exact interest in 90 days at 11%

35. $98.63 exact interest in 120 days at 12%

36. $159.50 ordinary interest at $14\frac{1}{2}$% from May 6 to August 4

37. $142.92 ordinary interest at $8\frac{3}{4}$% from September 5 to January 23

38. $573.25 exact interest at $9\frac{1}{4}$% from July 22 to April 8

39. $483.29 exact interest at $10\frac{1}{2}$% from August 10 to June 6

In problems 40–45, for the given invoice amount and cash discount terms, find the ordinary interest rate at which a buyer could afford to borrow to take advantage of the cash discount.

40. $100; 1/10, n/30

41. $450; 2/15, n/30

42. $680; 3/10, n/30

43. $144.60; 2/15, n/60

44. $375.45; 4/15, n/60

45. $920.33; 5/10, n/30

In problems 46–50, for the given invoice amount, cash discount terms, and ordinary interest rate, find (a) the amount to be borrowed and (b) how much would be saved on the transaction.

46. $200; 2/10, n/30; 9%

47. $500; 3/10, n/30; 12%

48. $1,370; 4/15, n/60; $8\frac{1}{2}$%

49. $782.50; 2/15, n/60; 11%

50. $947.65; 5/15, n/90; $10\frac{3}{4}$%

Section 9.5 Maturity value and present value

When a loan is repaid, the borrower pays the principal plus interest. This sum is called the **amount** or **maturity value.** In symbols,

■ (9–9) $$A = P + I$$

where A = amount or maturity value, P = principal, and I = interest.

In example 1 of section 9.2, the maturity value is

$$\begin{aligned} A &= P + I \\ &= \$500 + \$20 \\ &= \$520 \end{aligned}$$

Thus, the borrower paid \$520 at the end of four months. In example 2 of section 9.2, the maturity value is

$$\begin{aligned} A &= P + I \\ &= \$2{,}800.00 + \$157.50 \\ &= \$2{,}957.50 \end{aligned}$$

The maturity value also can be expressed by a different formula. Since

$$A = P + I$$

and $$I = Prt$$

it follows that $$A = P + Prt \quad \text{(Substitution)}$$

■ (9–10) $$A = P\,(1 + rt) \quad \text{(Distributive property)}$$

If the principal, rate, and time are given, the maturity value can be found directly from formula 9–10.

Example 1

Find the maturity value of \$1,280 invested at a simple interest rate of 9% for three months.

Solution

$A = ?$, $P = \$1{,}280$, $r = 9\% = 0.09$, $t = \frac{3}{12} = 0.25$

Using formula 9–10,

$$\begin{aligned} A &= P\,(1 + rt) \\ &= \$1{,}280\,[1 + (0.09 \times 0.25)] \\ &= \$1{,}280\,(1 + 0.0225) \\ &= \$1{,}280\,(1.0225) \\ &= \$1{,}308.80 \end{aligned}$$

The result can be checked using formulas 9–1 and 9–9:

$$I = Prt$$
$$= \$1{,}280 \times 0.09 \times 0.25$$
$$= \$28.80$$
$$A = P + I$$
$$= \$1{,}280 + \$28.80$$
$$= \$1{,}308.80$$

Example 2 What investment at 12% simple interest would have a maturity value of $500 in 18 months?

Solution

$A = \$500$, $P = ?$, $r = 12\% = 0.12$, $t = \frac{18}{12} = 1.5$

Since P is the unknown, formula 9–10 is first solved for P:

$$A = P\,(1 + rt)$$
$$P\,(1 + rt) = A$$

■ (9–11) $$P = \frac{A}{1 + rt} \quad \text{(Dividing both sides by } 1 + rt\text{)}$$

$$= \frac{\$500}{1 + (0.12 \times 1.5)}$$
$$= \frac{\$500}{1 + 0.18}$$
$$= \frac{\$500}{1.18}$$
$$= \$423.73$$

Formula 9–11 in example 2 is an important variation of formula 9–10. When formula 9–11 is used, P is referred to as the **present value.**

Formulas 9–10 and 9–11 solve opposite kinds of problems. Formula 9–10 answers the question, "What amount A results from the investment of principal P at rate r for time t?" On the other hand, formula 9–11 answers the question, "What principal P invested at rate r for time t will result in amount A?"

Example 3 Find the present value of \$2,000 at 12% for eight months.

Solution

$A = \$2{,}000,\ P = ?,\ r = 12\% = 0.12,\ t = \frac{8}{12} = \frac{2}{3}$

$$P = \frac{A}{1 + rt}$$

$$= \frac{\$2{,}000}{1 + (0.12 \times 2/3)}$$

$$= \frac{\$2{,}000}{1 + 0.08}$$

$$= \frac{\$2{,}000}{1.08}$$

$$= \$1{,}851.85$$

Example 4 In one year, John Sparks plans to modernize his shop by buying new equipment. He estimates that it will require \$6,000 for the new machines. To have the money to purchase the equipment, he wishes to make an investment that will yield \$6,000 one year from now. At $8\frac{1}{2}\%$ simple interest, how much must he invest now to have a total of \$6,000 in one year?

Solution

$A = \$6{,}000,\ P = ?,\ r = 8\frac{1}{2}\% = 0.085,\ t = 1$

$$P = \frac{A}{1 + rt}$$

$$= \frac{\$6{,}000}{1 + (0.085 \times 1)}$$

$$= \frac{\$6{,}000}{1.085}$$

$$= \$5{,}529.95$$

Exercises for Section 9.5

In problems 1–8, use the formula $A = P(1 + rt)$ to compute the maturity value A for the given values of P, r, and t.

1. $P = \$3{,}000,\ r = 10\%,\ t = 1$ year
2. $P = \$4{,}000,\ r = 12\%,\ t = 2$ months
3. $P = \$3{,}600,\ r = 9\frac{1}{2}\%,\ t = 4$ months
4. $P = \$2{,}400,\ r = 16\frac{1}{4}\%,\ t = 15$ months

5. $P = \$1{,}600$, $r = 11\frac{3}{4}\%$, $t = 6$ months

6. $P = \$3{,}250$, $r = 8\frac{1}{4}\%$, $t = 9$ months

7. $P = \$1{,}750$, $r = 9\frac{1}{4}\%$, $t = 8$ months

8. $P = \$2{,}250$, $r = 8\frac{3}{4}\%$, $t = 4$ months

In problems 9–16, use the formula $P = \frac{A}{(1 + rt)}$ to find the present value P for the given values of A, r, and t.

9. $A = \$2{,}460$, $r = 15\%$, $t = 2$ months

10. $A = \$1{,}022.50$, $r = 9\%$, $t = 3$ months

11. $A = \$1{,}563.75$, $r = 8\frac{1}{2}\%$, $t = 6$ months

12. $A = \$2{,}046.25$, $r = 9\frac{1}{4}\%$, $t = 3$ months

13. $A = \$2{,}922.50$, $r = 8\frac{3}{4}\%$, $t = 6$ months

14. $A = \$3{,}326.25$, $r = 14\frac{1}{2}\%$, $t = 9$ months

15. $A = \$4{,}000$, $r = 16\frac{3}{4}\%$, $t = 5$ months

16. $A = \$3{,}000$, $r = 9\frac{3}{4}\%$, $t = 4$ months

17. John Richards borrowed \$2,500 from Leslie Small at 14% interest for three months. How much will John repay Leslie at the end of three months?

18. Dick Welch loaned his neighbor \$2,000 for six months at $8\frac{1}{4}\%$ interest. What amount of money will the neighbor repay Dick at the end of six months?

19. Find the maturity value for a loan of \$3,500 for 14 months at 15% interest.

20. If \$2,800 is borrowed for five years at $8\frac{1}{2}\%$ interest, what is the maturity value of the loan?

21. Joan Parker is planning to spend \$3,000 one year from now for a European tour. How much should she invest now at $8\frac{3}{4}\%$ interest to have the money for her trip?

22. Find the present value of \$1,500 at $10\frac{1}{4}\%$ interest for nine months.

23. What is the present value of \$2,400 at $8\frac{1}{2}\%$ interest for three months?

24. Bob Simmons borrowed \$2,800 for 18 months at $13\frac{3}{4}\%$ interest to pay for new equipment for his auto repair shop. What amount will he repay for the loan?

25. Mary Schmidt was offered \$20,000 for a piece of property or \$21,000 in eight months. If money can be invested at the interest rate of $10\frac{1}{2}\%$, which is the better offer?

26. Arthur Samuels owns some old silver coins. A buyer offered to pay him \$1,800 cash or \$2,000 in 10 months. If money can be invested at the simple interest rate of 15%, which is the better offer?

27. For her antique clock, Sandi King was offered \$1,600 cash or \$1,000 now and \$700 in six months. If money can be invested at the interest rate of $12\frac{1}{2}$%, which is the better offer?

28. Paul Baker estimates that in one year he will need \$4,500 to replace some aging equipment in his grocery store. He has \$3,800 in an investment that will yield the equivalent of $15\frac{1}{2}$% simple interest. Will he be able to purchase the equipment?

29. Max Phillips plans to remodel his store in 15 months. He estimates that the remodeling will cost \$13,800, and he has \$12,000 to invest. Find the least interest rate at which he can invest his money so as to meet his remodeling expenses.

30. At an interest rate of $13\frac{1}{2}$%, how long will it take for an investment of \$4,800 to have a maturity value of \$5,772?

31. June Porter has an opportunity to invest \$2,400 at 15% interest. How long will it take for the maturity value of the investment to reach \$2,820?

32. At what rate of interest will \$3,200 have a maturity value of \$3,554 in nine months?

Glossary

Amount See *maturity value.*
Banker's interest See *ordinary interest.*
Banker's rule See *ordinary interest.*
Banker's year See *ordinary time.*
Exact interest Interest calculations using the time fraction $\frac{\text{Exact time}}{365}$.
Exact time The calendar based on the revolution of the earth around the sun. The year consists of 365 days, with a leap year of 366 days every fourth year. The months have 28 (29), 30, or 31 days, irregularly spaced.
Interest Money paid for the use of money.
Maturity value Also called *amount.* The total amount due (principal plus interest) when a loan is repaid.
Ordinary interest Also called *banker's interest* or *banker's rule.* Interest calculations using the time fraction $\frac{\text{Exact time}}{360}$.
Ordinary time Also called *banker's year.* A financial calendar consisting of 12 months of 30 days per month. A year in ordinary time thus consists of 360 days.
Present value The amount of money (principal) that must be borrowed or invested at a given interest rate for a given length of time to result in a specified maturity value.
Principal The amount of money borrowed or invested.
Simple interest An annual percentage of the amount of money borrowed or invested.
Time fraction A fraction used to express the length of a loan when the loan is specified to be for a number of days or months.

Review test

1. Find the simple interest earned on a $2,000 loan for four months at $10\frac{1}{2}\%$.

2. At a simple interest rate of $11\frac{1}{4}\%$, what principal would earn $90 interest in three months?

3. Find the simple interest rate necessary for $6,500.00 to earn $487.50 interest in eight months.

4. Mary Cunningham invested $2,800.00 at $10\frac{3}{4}\%$ simple interest. How many months will it take for her investment to earn $75.25 in interest?

5. Bill Pell borrowed $2,000 for 45 days at $9\frac{1}{2}\%$ ordinary interest. How much interest did he pay for the loan?

6. How many days would it take $1,825.00 to earn $90.75 exact interest at 11%?

7. An invoice for $800 contains terms 3/10, n/30. At what interest rate (ordinary interest) could the buyer afford to borrow to take advantage of the cash discount?

8. Find the maturity value of a $750 loan at 12% exact interest for 80 days.

9. Six months from now, Julia Bennett plans to remodel her real estate office. She estimates that the remodeling will cost $6,000. How much money must she invest now at $12\frac{1}{2}\%$ simple interest to have $6,000 in six months?

10. Mel Bridges was offered $1,500 cash for his woodworking tools. Another prospective buyer then offered him $1,000 now and $550 in six months. If money can be invested at the interest rate of 14%, which is the better offer?

CHAPTER 10 Simple Discount

Chapter Objectives

I. Learn the meaning of the following terms:

Simple discount, 319

Proceeds, 319

II. Understand:

The difference between simple interest and simple discount, 319–321

The principle of discounting interest-bearing notes, 328–331

The relationship between simple interest and simple discount, 333

III. Learn to:

Solve problems using the simple discount formula, 320–322

Solve problems using variations of the simple discount formula, 324–326

Section 10.1 Introduction

In chapter 9, we discussed simple interest. Another kind of interest is called **simple discount.** For example, suppose John Webster asks a bank to loan him $1,000 for one year. The bank agrees to the loan but presents Webster with $880 and indicates that the $120 difference is a 12% interest charge ($1,000 × 0.12 = $120). Webster accepts the $880, and in one year he will owe the bank $1,000.

The primary difference between this transaction and a simple interest loan is that interest is computed on the maturity value instead of on the principal. This difference between simple interest and simple discount is worth repeating: *Simple interest is a percentage of the principal; simple discount is a percentage of the maturity value.*

Section 10.2 The simple discount formula

Simple discount is another application of the basic percentage equation. The formula is

■ (10–1) $$D = Adt$$

where D = amount of discount, A = maturity value, d = discount percent, and t = term of the loan in years.

In the John Webster loan, the calculations were

$D = ?, A = \$1{,}000, d = 12\% = 0.12, t = 1$

$$\begin{aligned} D &= Adt \\ &= \$1{,}000 \times 0.12 \times 1 \\ &= \$120 \end{aligned}$$

The amount paid to the borrower in a simple discount loan is called the **proceeds** of the loan, rather than the principal. The proceeds of a simple discount transaction are equal to the maturity value minus the discount. That is,

■ (10–2) $$P = A - D$$

where P = proceeds, A = maturity value, and D = amount of discount.

In the Webster transaction,

$$\begin{aligned} P &= A - D \\ &= \$1{,}000 - \$120 \\ &= \$880 \end{aligned}$$

The proceeds may also be thought of as the **present value** of the loan at simple discount.

Example 1 The Farmers State Bank offered to discount a loan of $900 at 14% for six months. Find (a) the discount and (b) the proceeds of the loan.

Solution

a. $D = ?, A = \$900, d = 14\% = 0.14, t = \frac{1}{2} = 0.5$

$$\begin{aligned} D &= Adt \\ &= \$900 \times 0.14 \times 0.5 \\ &= \$63 \end{aligned}$$

b. $P = ?, A = \$900, D = \$63$

$$\begin{aligned} P &= A - D \\ &= \$900 - \$63 \\ &= \$837 \end{aligned}$$

Example 2 For a $680 loan discounted at $11\frac{1}{4}\%$ for two months, find (a) the discount and (b) the present value.

Solution

a. $D = ?, A = \$680, d = 11\frac{1}{4}\% = 0.1125, t = \frac{1}{6}$

$$\begin{aligned} D &= Adt \\ &= \$680 \times 0.1125 \times \frac{1}{6} \\ &= \$12.75 \end{aligned}$$

b. $P = ?, A = \$680.00, D = \$12.75$

$$\begin{aligned} P &= A - D \\ &= \$680.00 - \$12.75 \\ &= \$667.25 \end{aligned}$$

For a given transaction, 12% simple discount is not equivalent to 12% simple interest. To see this, let us return to the John Webster loan and calculate the simple interest rate. $I = \$120$, $P = \$880$, $r = ?$, and $t = 1$; hence,

$$\begin{aligned} r &= \frac{I}{Pt} \\ &= \frac{\$120}{\$880 \times 1} \\ &= 0.13636 \\ &= 13.64\% \text{ (Rounded)} \end{aligned}$$

Thus, a 12% simple discount rate on this loan is equivalent to a simple interest rate of 13.64%. In other words, for a given simple discount percent, it takes a higher simple interest percent to produce the same amount of interest.

Because simple discount earns more interest than the same simple interest percent, simple discount was once popular with banks for short-term loans. But in 1969, Congress enacted legislation requiring lending institutions to disclose the interest charge in terms of a simple interest percent (see section 12.3). As a result, many financial institutions use simple discount only for certain transactions with other banks and in some instances that involve the sale of interest-bearing notes to the public. For example, the Treasury Department uses the terms of simple discount to quote the rates at which short-term Treasury securities (commonly known as T-bills) are sold to the public. Also, simple discount is still used in situations where the federal disclosure act does not apply, such as personal loans between individuals.

Example 3 Linda Parsons purchased a $10,000 three-month Treasury bill discounted at 7.75%. Find (a) the discount and (b) the present value.

Solution

a. $D = ?, A = \$10{,}000, d = 7.75\% = 0.0775, t = \dfrac{1}{4}$

$$\begin{aligned} D &= Adt \\ &= \$10{,}000 \times 0.0775 \times \frac{1}{4} \\ &= \$193.75 \end{aligned}$$

b. $P = ?, A = \$10{,}000, D = \$193.75$

$$\begin{aligned} P &= A - D \\ &= \$10{,}000 - \$193.75 \\ &= \$9{,}806.25 \end{aligned}$$

For short-term simple discount loans, ordinary interest is usually used if the term of the loan is in days.

Example 4 Find the discount on a $1,200 loan at 15% for 45 days.

Solution

$D = ?, A = \$1{,}200, d = 15\% = 0.15, t = \dfrac{45}{360} = \dfrac{1}{8} = 0.125$

$$\begin{aligned} D &= Adt \\ &= \$1{,}200 \times 0.15 \times 0.125 \\ &= \$22.50 \end{aligned}$$

Example 5 A loan of \$575 is executed on November 28 and is due on January 15. What is (a) the discount and (b) the proceeds if the loan is discounted at 9%?

Solution

From appendix B, there are 48 days from November 28 to January 15. Thus, with $A = \$575$, $d = 9\% = 0.09$, and $t = \frac{48}{360} = \frac{2}{15}$,

a. $D = Adt$

$= \$575 \times 0.09 \times \frac{2}{15}$

$= \$6.90$

b. $P = A - D$

$= \$575.00 - \$6.90$

$= \$568.10$

As discussed in chapter 5, some vendors offer anticipation dating to encourage payment of an invoice before the last day of the discount period. If an invoice is paid prior to the expiration of the cash discount period, the buyer can deduct an amount equal to the current bank discount rate for the number of days of early payment. This is illustrated in the next example.

Example 6 An invoice for \$2,500 dated June 1 contains terms 2/10, n/30, anticipation. If the current discount rate is 8% and the invoice is paid on June 5, find the amount to be remitted.

Solution

	\$2,500	List price
−	50	Cash discount (\$2,500 × 0.02)
	\$2,450	

The number of days of early payment is the number of days from June 5 through June 11, or 6 days. Thus,

$D = ?$, $A = \$2,450$, $d = 8\% = 0.08$, $t = \frac{6}{360} = \frac{1}{60}$

$D = Adt$

$= \$2,450 \times 0.08 \times \frac{1}{60}$

$= \$3.27$

Thus, the amount to be remitted is \$2,450.00 − \$3.27 = \$2,446.73

Exercises for Section 10.2

In problems 1–15, find the discount and the proceeds of the given loan.

1. \$5,000 discounted at 10% for three years
2. \$3,000 discounted at 9% for two years
3. \$2,720 discounted at $14\frac{1}{2}$% for one year
4. \$1,420 discounted at $12\frac{1}{4}$% for nine months
5. \$2,250 discounted at $11\frac{3}{4}$% for six months
6. \$450 discounted at $8\frac{1}{2}$% for three months
7. \$2,875 discounted at $10\frac{3}{4}$% for 10 months
8. \$1,150 discounted at $9\frac{1}{2}$% for eight months
9. \$4,275 discounted at $11\frac{1}{2}$% for 18 months
10. \$1,800 discounted at $9\frac{1}{4}$% for six months
11. \$1,900 discounted at 13% for 30 days
12. \$1,400 discounted at $15\frac{3}{4}$% for 60 days
13. \$1,350 discounted at $12\frac{3}{4}$% for 50 days
14. \$760 discounted at $16\frac{1}{2}$% for 200 days
15. \$1,350 discounted at $9\frac{1}{4}$% for 170 days
16. A \$1,200 loan is executed on April 10 and is due July 15. If the loan is discounted at 10%, find the discount and the proceeds.
17. John Blocker negotiates a loan at the bank for \$7,500 for two years, discounted at $12\frac{1}{2}$%. Find the discount and the proceeds of the loan.
18. The Midwest Bank offers to lend Janice Baxter \$3,200 discounted at $11\frac{3}{4}$% for 40 days. Find the discount and the proceeds of the loan.
19. To obtain additional operating capital for his new business, Bob Perkins borrows \$12,000 from his bank, discounted at $15\frac{1}{4}$% for 245 days. Find the discount and the proceeds of the loan.
20. Ray Pittman purchases a \$5,000 three-month Treasury bill discounted at 7.42%. Find (a) the discount and (b) the present value.
21. Find (a) the discount and (b) the present value for a \$10,000 six-month Treasury bill discounted at 6.89%.

22. An invoice for $428.60 dated January 18 contains terms 3/10, n/30, with anticipation. If the current discount rate is 9% and the invoice is paid on January 21, find the amount to be remitted.

23. The terms of an invoice dated October 15 were 2/15, n/30 with anticipation. If the list price was $522.48, the invoice was paid on October 18, and the current discount rate is 8.25%, find the amount to be remitted.

Section 10.3

Other discount formulas

As with simple interest, the formula for simple discount can be solved for any of the other variables:

■ (10–3) $A = \frac{D}{dt}$ (Dividing both sides of formula 10–1 by dt)

■ (10–4) $d = \frac{D}{At}$ (Dividing both sides of formula 10–1 by At)

■ (10–5) $t = \frac{D}{Ad}$ (Dividing both sides of formula 10–1 by Ad)

You should learn to solve formula 10–1 for the appropriate variable rather than attempt to memorize formulas 10–3, 10–4, and 10–5.

Example 1 If a bank discounts a loan at 10% for four months, what is the maturity value if the discount is $40?

Solution

$D = \$40,\ A = ?,\ d = 10\% = \frac{1}{10},\ t = \frac{4}{12} = \frac{1}{3}$

$$A = \frac{D}{dt}$$

$$= \frac{\$40}{\frac{1}{10} \times \frac{1}{3}}$$

$$= \frac{\$40}{\frac{1}{30}}$$

$$= \$1{,}200$$

Example 2 Gilbert Evans received \$350 from Paul Decker and promised to pay him \$400 in nine months. What was the simple discount rate?

Solution

$D = \$400 - \$350 = \$50,\ A = \$400,\ d = ?,\ t = \frac{9}{12} = 0.75$

$$d = \frac{D}{At}$$

$$= \frac{\$50}{\$400 \times 0.75}$$

$$= \frac{\$50}{\$300}$$

$$= 0.1667$$

$$= 16.67\%$$

Example 3 J. D. Godwin received \$192.50 from Clyde McKeever and agreed to repay him \$200.00. If the note Godwin signed was discounted at a simple discount rate of 9%, what was the term of the loan?

Solution

$D = \$200.00 - \$192.50 = \$7.50,\ A = \$200.00,\ d = 9\% = 0.09,\ t = ?$

$$t = \frac{D}{Ad}$$

$$= \frac{\$7.50}{\$200.00 \times 0.09}$$

$$= \frac{\$7.50}{\$18.00} = \frac{7.5}{18} = \frac{15}{36} = \frac{5}{12}$$

$$= 5 \text{ months}$$

The proceeds also can be expressed by a different formula. Since

$$P = A - D$$

and

$$D = Adt$$

it follows that

$$P = A - Adt \qquad \text{(Substitution)}$$

■ (10–6)

$$P = A\,(1 - dt) \qquad \text{(Distributive property)}$$

Example 4 Find the proceeds of a \$670 loan discounted at 12% for five months.

Solution

$P = ?,\ A = \$670,\ d = 12\% = 0.12,\ t = \frac{5}{12}$

$$P = A\,(1 - dt)$$
$$= \$670\left(1 - (0.12 \times \tfrac{5}{12})\right)$$
$$= \$670\,(1 - 0.05)$$
$$= \$670\,(0.95)$$
$$= \$636.50$$

Example 5 The proceeds of a loan are \$1,560. What is the maturity value of the loan if the discount rate is $11\frac{1}{4}\%$ and the term of the loan is 80 days?

Solution

$P = \$1{,}560,\ A = ?,\ d = 11\frac{1}{4}\% = 0.1125,\ t = \frac{80}{360} = \frac{2}{9}$

$$P = A\,(1 - dt)$$

$$A = \frac{P}{1 - dt} \quad \text{(Dividing both sides by } 1 - dt\text{)}$$
$$= \frac{\$1{,}560}{1 - (0.1125 \times 2/9)}$$
$$= \frac{\$1{,}560}{1 - 0.025}$$
$$= \frac{\$1{,}560}{0.975}$$
$$= \$1{,}600$$

Exercises for Section 10.3

In problems 1–12, solve the formula $D = Adt$ for the appropriate variable and compute the value of the indicated quantity.

1. $A = \$1{,}800$, $d = 10\%$, $D = \$540$. Find t.
2. $d = 12\%$, $t = 3$ years, $D = \$216$. Find A.
3. $A = \$1{,}450.00$, $t = 2$ years, $D = \$246.50$. Find d.

4. $A = \$3{,}750$, $d = 9\frac{1}{2}\%$, $t = 4$ years. Find D.

5. $A = \$600$, $t = 6$ months, $D = \$33$. Find d.

6. $A = \$1{,}300.00$, $d = 11\%$, $D = \$35.75$. Find t.

7. $d = 10\frac{1}{2}\%$, $t = 4$ months, $D = \$94.50$. Find A.

8. $A = \$2{,}400.00$, $t = 7$ months, $D = \$157.50$. Find d.

9. $A = \$1{,}440$, $d = 12\frac{1}{2}\%$, $t = 40$ days. Find D.

10. $A = \$2{,}800.00$, $t = 72$ days, $D = \$57.40$. Find d.

11. $d = 11\frac{3}{4}\%$, $t = 180$ days, $D = \$129.25$. Find A.

12. $A = \$900.00$, $t = 64$ days, $D = \$15.60$. Find d.

13. Bill Harris borrowed $4,500 for six months, discounted at 11%. Find the proceeds of the loan.

14. What is the discount on a loan of $1,200 discounted at 12% if the loan is executed on May 24 and is due on November 2?

15. Clementine Williams executed a loan on October 12 for $1,100 discounted at $8\frac{1}{2}\%$. If the loan is due February 16, what are the proceeds?

16. Karen Peters can borrow money from her bank discounted at 10% for two years. If she needs proceeds of $2,600, how much should she borrow?

17. John Butcher needs $6,000 to cover operating expenses for his new store. How much should he borrow if the loan is to be discounted at 12% for six months?

18. The First City Bank approves a loan of $2,000 for two years. If the proceeds are $1,480, what is the discount rate?

19. If the proceeds of a $1,200 loan for six months are $1,149, what is the discount rate?

20. Jennifer Smith needs $7,125 to remodel her store. What is the least amount (maturity value) that she can borrow if the loan is discounted at 15% for 120 days?

21. John Baxter signed a promissory note agreeing to pay the bank $950.00 in 45 days. If the bank charged $15.20 for the loan, what is the discount rate?

22. Paula Forsythe received $1,212.25 from P. J. Thomas and agreed to repay him $1,300.00. If the note Paula signed was discounted at $13\frac{1}{2}\%$, what was the term of the loan?

Section 10.4 Discounting interest-bearing notes

An individual who borrows money is usually required to sign a written agreement that states the conditions of the loan—the term, the rate of interest or discount, and the principal or maturity value of the loan. An example of such an agreement is the **promissory note** shown in figure 10.1. Promissory notes can be written at simple interest, simple discount, or no interest at all. In any event, a note is a promise to pay the maturity value of the loan on the date specified.

Figure 10.1
Promissory note

$ ______ ______ 19__

______ after date ______ promise to pay to

the order of ______

______ Dollars

AT THE OFFICE OF ______ FOR VALUE RECEIVED

WITH INTEREST FROM ______ AT THE RATE OF ______ PER CENT PER ANNUM UNTIL PAID.

NOW, SHOULD IT BECOME NECESSARY TO COLLECT THIS NOTE THROUGH AN ATTORNEY, EITHER OF US, WHETHER MAKER, SECURITY OR ENDORSER ON THIS NOTE, HEREBY AGREES TO PAY ALL COSTS OF SUCH COLLECTION INCLUDING A REASONABLE ATTORNEY'S FEE. THE DRAWERS AND ENDORSERS SEVERALLY WAIVE PRESENTMENT FOR PAYMENT, PROTEST AND NOTICE OF PROTEST AND NON-PAYMENT OF THIS NOTE.

No. ______ ______ (SEAL)

Due ______ ______ (SEAL)

FORM M—FRANKLIN PRINTING CO., TAMPA

A promissory note is both a legal and a negotiable instrument. That is, in addition to a promise to pay, a note may be sold to a third party. In this sense, a promissory note is similar to a personal check; it may be endorsed to a third party for cash, in payment for goods or services, or in retirement of a debt.

Banks are the principal purchasers of promissory notes and do so at a discount. For instance, a businessperson may own a number of promissory notes that must be sold to meet unusual expenses. By discounting the notes at a bank, the businessperson obtains the needed cash, and the bank earns a profit equal to the discount percentage.

When the payee of an interest-bearing note sells the note to a bank, he or she receives the proceeds of the newly discounted note.

Example 1

On March 1, Hal Miller loaned a friend $1,500 at a simple interest rate of $8\frac{1}{2}\%$ with a due date of June 29. On April 10, Hal sold the note to a bank that discounted the note at 10%. How much did Hal receive from the bank?

Solution

From appendix B, there are 120 days from March 1 to June 29 and 80 days from April 10 to June 29. Before the proceeds of the discounted note can be found, we must calculate the maturity value of the simple interest loan using formula 9–10.

$A = ?, P = \$1{,}500, r = 8\frac{1}{2}\% = 0.085, t = \frac{120}{360} = \frac{1}{3}$

$A = P\,(1 + rt)$

$= \$1{,}500 \left(1 + (0.085 \times \frac{1}{3})\right)$

$= \$1{,}542.50$

The proceeds are now calculated using formula 10–6:

$P = ?, A = \$1{,}542.50, d = 10\% = 0.1, t = \frac{80}{360} = \frac{2}{9}$

$P = A\,(1 - dt)$

$= \$1{,}542.50 \left(1 - (0.1 \times \frac{2}{9})\right)$

$= \$1{,}508.22$

The transactions between the two parties can be summarized as follows:

	Hal	*Bank*
Received	$1,508.22	$1,542.50
Expended	− 1,500.00	− 1,508.22
Earned	$ 8.22	$ 34.28

Hal receives $1,508.22 and realizes $8.22 on the loan, despite having to sell the note prior to the maturity date. The bank realizes $34.28 on the transaction.

Example 2 Thirty days before the due date of a $1,200, 90-day loan discounted at 11%, Granite City Bank rediscounted (sold) the note to Franklin Federal Bank at a rate of 9%. How much did Granite City Bank receive from Franklin Federal Bank? How much did Granite City Bank make on the transaction?

Solution

First, the proceeds of the original loan are calculated:

$P = ?, A = \$1{,}200, d = 11\% = 0.11, t = \frac{90}{360} = 0.25$

$P = A\,(1 - dt)$

$= \$1{,}200 \left(1 - (0.11 \times 0.25)\right)$

$= \$1{,}200\,(0.9725)$

$= \$1{,}167$

Next, the proceeds of the rediscounted note are calculated:

$P = ?, A = \$1{,}200, d = 9\% = 0.09, t = \frac{30}{360} = \frac{1}{12}$

$$P = A\,(1 - dt)$$
$$= \$1{,}200\left(1 - (0.09 \times \tfrac{1}{12})\right)$$
$$= \$1{,}200\,(0.9925)$$
$$= \$1{,}191$$

The transactions between the two banks can be summarized as follows:

	Granite City Bank	*Franklin Federal Bank*
Received	$1,191	$1,200
Expended	1,167	1,191
Earned	$ 24	$ 9

Granite City Bank received $1,191 from Franklin Federal Bank and earned $1,191 − $1,167 = $24 on the transaction.

As illustrated in example 2, it is a common practice for financial institutions to charge each other a discount rate lower than that charged to individual borrowers and businesses.

In section 9.4, it was shown that merchants could usually save money by taking advantage of a cash discount in the payment of a bill, even if it meant borrowing at simple interest to do so. An analogous situation occurs when a merchant borrows money at simple discount to take advantage of a cash discount. While an invoice is not an interest-bearing document, it acts as such in that a higher price is paid if the purchaser fails to take advantage of the cash discount. As in the case of borrowing at simple interest, borrowing at simple discount is prudent only if the interest on the loan is less than the cash discount. The maximum possible savings occur when the bill is paid on the last day that the cash discount is offered.

Example 3 The terms of a bill for $1,200 are 2/30, n/60. If the discount rate at a bank is 8%, (a) how much must be borrowed (proceeds) and (b) how much will be saved by taking advantage of the cash discount?

Solution

a. The cash discount is $1,200 × 0.02 = $24; hence,

$1,200	n/60
− 24	Cash discount
$1,176	Amount to be borrowed (proceeds)

b. The net amount is due 30 days after the last day of the cash discount. Thus, we must calculate the maturity value necessary to generate proceeds of \$1,176 in 30 days.

$A = ?, P = \$1,176, d = 8\% = 0.08, t = \frac{30}{360} = \frac{1}{12}$

Solving formula 10–6 for A,

$$A = \frac{P}{1 - dt}$$

$$= \frac{\$1,176}{1 - (0.08 \times 1/12)}$$

$$= \$1,183.89$$

The discount is \$1,183.89 − \$1,176.00 = \$7.89. Thus, the amount saved by borrowing is \$24.00 − \$7.89 = \$16.11.

Example 4 A merchant receives a consignment of goods for \$840 with terms 1/10, n/30. At what discount rate could he afford to borrow money to take advantage of the cash discount?

Solution

The cash discount is \$840 × 0.01 = \$8.40; hence,

\$840.00	n/30
− 8.40	Cash discount
\$831.60	Amount to be borrowed

The net amount is due 20 days after the last day of the cash discount. In borrowing from the bank, the discount percentage must not exceed \$8.40 (the cash discount), or the merchant will lose money. Thus, using formula 10–4, with $D = \$8.40$, $A = \$840.00$, $d = ?$, and $t = \frac{20}{360} = \frac{1}{18}$,

$$d = \frac{D}{At}$$

$$= \frac{\$8.40}{\$840.00 \times 1/18}$$

$$= 0.18$$

$$= 18\%$$

The merchant could afford to borrow money at a discount rate up to 18% and still break even on the transaction.

Exercises for Section 10.4

1. Paul Prentice loaned Bill Butler $3,000 for 90 days at a simple interest rate of 8%. Then, 60 days later, Paul sold the note to a bank that discounted it at 9%. How much did Paul receive from the bank? How much did Paul make on the loan?

2. A $1,400 note bearing 9% simple interest with a term of six months is sold to a bank two months before the due date. If the bank discounts the note at 11%, how much did the payee receive for the note? How much did the payee make on the loan?

3. Two months before the due date, Gateway Bank purchased a one-year, $8,000 note bearing $10\frac{1}{2}$% simple interest. If the bank discounted the note at $12\frac{1}{2}$%, how much did the bank make on the transaction? How much did the original owner of the note make?

4. On April 10, Mary Phillips loaned her sister $2,400 at a simple interest rate of $6\frac{1}{4}$%. The due date of the note was July 19, but on June 29, Mary sold the note to the bank, which discounted it at $8\frac{3}{4}$%. How much did Mary receive for the note? How much did she make on the loan? How much did the bank make on the transaction?

5. Jim Butler loaned his brother-in-law $2,800 on March 2 at a simple interest rate of $7\frac{3}{4}$%. The due date of the note was September 18, but because of an illness in his family, Jim was forced to sell the note to the bank on April 1, and the bank discounted it at $9\frac{1}{4}$%. How much did Jim receive for the note? How much did he lose on the loan? How much did the bank make?

6. Forty-five days before the due date of an $1,800, 180-day loan discounted at 12%, Pacific Bank sold the note to Western Bank at a discount rate of 10%. How much did Pacific Bank receive from Western Bank? How much did Pacific Bank make on the transaction?

7. On June 7, Union Bank loaned $3,700 discounted at $11\frac{1}{4}$%. The due date of the note was November 4, but on September 5, Union Bank sold the note to Central Bank at a discount of $9\frac{3}{4}$%. How much did Union Bank receive for the note? How much did Union Bank make on the transaction?

8. The terms of a bill for $900 are 3/30, n/90. If the discount rate at a bank is 12%, how much must be borrowed (proceeds) to take advantage of the cash discount? How much is saved by taking advantage of the discount?

9. Packard Products receives a consignment of goods for $1,600 with terms of 2/10, n/30. The discount rate at the bank is $8\frac{1}{4}$%. How much should Packard borrow (proceeds) to take advantage of the cash discount? How much will Packard save by borrowing the money?

10. If the terms of a $1,400 bill are 2/20, n/60, find the maximum discount rate at which money could be borrowed to take advantage of the cash discount.

11. Howell Services receives a bill for $2,100 with terms of 2/30, n/120. If the current discount rate for borrowing money is 9%, should the company borrow money to take advantage of the cash discount? Why?

12. Should a company borrow money at a discount rate of 10% to take advantage of the cash discount of an $1,800 bill with terms of 1/10, n/40? Why?

Section 10.5 Simple interest versus simple discount

In section 10.2, it was shown that for a given discount rate, it takes a higher simple interest rate to generate the same amount of interest. In this section, the precise relationship between simple interest and simple discount is given by deriving formulas to convert from one rate to the other. If the formulas

$A = P\,(1 + rt)$ and $P = A\,(1 - dt)$

are solved for the common variable P, then:

$P = \dfrac{A}{1 + rt}$ and $P = A\,(1 - dt)$

Since P is equal to each of these quantities,

(10–7) $$\frac{A}{1 + rt} = A\,(1 - dt)$$

or

(10–8) $$\frac{1}{1 + rt} = 1 - dt$$ (Dividing both sides of formula 10–7 by A)

Solving formula 10–8 for r,

■ (10–9) $$r = \frac{d}{1 - dt}$$

Solving formula 10–8 for d,

■ (10–10) $$d = \frac{r}{1 + rt}$$

Formulas 10–9 and 10–10 give the relationship between simple interest and simple discount. Given one rate, we can solve for the other by using the appropriate formula. Note that only time affects the relationship between the two rates; the maturity value has no effect.

Example 1 What simple interest rate corresponds (a) to a 12% discount rate on a loan for one year and (b) to a $10\frac{1}{2}$% discount rate on a loan for 90 days?

Solution

a. $d = 12\% = 0.12,\ t = 1$

$$\begin{aligned} r &= \frac{d}{1 - dt} \\ &= \frac{0.12}{1 - (0.12 \times 1)} \\ &= 0.1364 \text{ (Rounded)} \\ &= 13.64\% \end{aligned}$$

(Compare with the calculations for the John Webster loan in sections 10.1 and 10.2.)

b. $d = 10\frac{1}{2}\% = 0.105,\ t = \frac{90}{360} = 0.25$

$$\begin{aligned} r &= \frac{d}{1 - dt} \\ &= \frac{0.105}{1 - (0.105 \times 0.25)} \\ &= 0.1078 \text{ (Rounded)} \\ &= 10.78\% \end{aligned}$$

Example 2 Find the discount rate corresponding to a simple interest rate of (a) 9% and (b) $12\frac{1}{4}$% if the term of the loan is six months.

Solution

a. $r = 9\% = 0.09,\ t = \frac{1}{2} = 0.5$

$$\begin{aligned} d &= \frac{r}{1 + rt} \\ &= \frac{0.09}{1 + (0.09 \times 0.5)} \\ &= 0.0861 \text{ (Rounded)} \\ &= 8.61\% \end{aligned}$$

b. $d = 12\frac{1}{4}\% = 0.1225,\ t = \frac{1}{2} = 0.5$

$$d = \frac{r}{1 + rt}$$

$$= \frac{0.1225}{1 + (0.1225 \times 0.5)}$$

$$= 0.1154 \quad \text{(Rounded)}$$

$$= 11.54\%$$

Exercises for Section 10.5

In problems 1–8, find the simple interest rate that corresponds to the given discount rate for the given time.

1. 8%, two years
2. 10%, six months
3. $11\frac{1}{4}\%$, 18 months
4. $11\frac{1}{2}\%$, one year
5. $9\frac{3}{4}\%$, 90 days
6. $8\frac{3}{4}\%$, 40 days
7. $12\frac{1}{4}\%$, 100 days
8. $11\frac{1}{4}\%$, 72 days

In problems 9–17, find the discount rate that corresponds to the given simple interest rate for the given time.

9. 8%, two years
10. 12%, 18 months
11. $9\frac{1}{4}\%$, one year
12. $8\frac{3}{4}\%$, four years
13. $12\frac{1}{4}\%$, three months
14. $14\frac{3}{4}\%$, 40 days
15. $9\frac{3}{4}\%$, 180 days
16. $10\frac{3}{4}\%$, 20 days
17. $11\frac{1}{2}\%$, 60 days
18. Mary Miller needs to borrow some money for 90 days to cover her expenses in opening a new clothing shop. She can obtain the money by borrowing it from a bank at $12\frac{3}{4}\%$ simple interest, or she can borrow it from a friend at $12\frac{1}{2}\%$ discount. Where should she borrow the money?
19. John Parsons is opening a restaurant and wants to borrow some money to buy equipment. He plans to borrow the money for two years. He can get the money from the bank at $9\frac{1}{4}\%$ discount, or he can borrow from a friend at $11\frac{1}{4}\%$ simple interest. Where should he get the money?

20. Jack Bentley can borrow money for two years from the bank at $8\frac{3}{4}\%$ discount, or he can borrow money elsewhere at 10% simple interest. Should he borrow from the bank or obtain the money elsewhere?

21. C. J. Peterson wants to borrow money for four years so that she can remodel her gift shop. Should she obtain the money from the bank at $10\frac{1}{2}\%$ discount or borrow from other sources at 18% simple interest?

Glossary

Present value Also called *proceeds*. The value in current dollars of a future sum found by the formulas $P = A - D$ or $P = A\,(1 - dt)$, where P is the present value, A is the maturity value, D is the amount of the discount, d is the discount percent, and t is the term of the loan or investment in years.

Proceeds See *present value.*

Promissory note A written promise to pay a sum of money at a specified future date.

Simple discount Interest computed on the maturity value of a loan according to the formula $D = Adt$, where D is the amount of simple discount, A is the maturity value, d is the discount percent, and t is the term of the loan in years.

Review test

1. The Lodesville State Bank offered to discount a loan of $2,700 at 10% for three months. Find (a) the discount and (b) the present value.

2. Find the discount and the proceeds on a $1,600 loan at 13% for 45 days.

3. If a bank discounts a loan at 12% for four months, what is the maturity value if the discount is $150?

4. Morton Nickel received $764 from Pat Osten and promised to pay Pat $800 in 180 days. What was the simple discount rate?

5. Find the proceeds of a $950 loan at 8% discount for five months.

6. Find the proceeds of a $1,750 loan at 15% discount for 90 days.

7. What simple interest rate corresponds to a 12% discount rate on a loan for 90 days?

8. What discount rate corresponds to an $11\frac{1}{4}\%$ simple interest rate on a loan for 40 days?

9. The terms of a bill for $900 are 3/10, n/30. If the discount rate is 9%, (a) how much must be borrowed, and (b) how much will be saved by taking advantage of the cash discount?

10. An $840 note for 90 days bearing 9% simple interest is sold to a bank 60 days before the due date. If the bank discounts the note at $10\frac{1}{2}\%$, how much does the seller receive from the bank?

CHAPTER 11

Compound Interest

Chapter Objectives

I. Learn the meaning of the following terms:

Compound amount, 338
Original principal, 338
Nominal rate, 339
Term, 339
Conversion period, 339
Rate per period, 340

II. Understand:

Compound interest, 338
Computing compound interest, 339–341
Present value for compound interest, 348
Daily compounding, 352
Continuous compounding, 354–355
Effective interest rate, 357

III. Use:

The compound interest formula to compute compound interest, 342–343
Compound interest tables to solve compound interest problems, 343–345
Present value tables to compute present value at compound interest, 348–350
Daily interest tables to compute interest compounded daily, 352–354
Continuous compound interest tables to compute interest compounded continuously, 354–355

Section 11.1 Introduction

Compound interest differs from simple interest in that simple interest is computed on a principal that never changes, while compound interest is computed on the principal plus past interest. For this reason, compound interest is frequently described as "interest on interest."

To illustrate the difference between simple interest and compound interest, consider $100 invested for three years at 9% simple interest and 9% interest compounded annually. The calculations are as follows:

	*Simple Interest**		*Compound Interest*	
Year 1	$100.00	Principal	$100.00	Principal
	× 0.09	Rate × time (0.09 × 1)	× 0.09	Rate × time (0.09 × 1)
	$9.00	Interest	$9.00	Interest
Year 2	$100.00	Principal	$109.00	Principal ($100 + $9)
	× 0.09	Rate × time (0.09 × 1)	× 0.09	Rate × time (0.09 × 1)
	$9.00	Interest	$9.81	Interest
Year 3	$100.00	Principal	$118.81	Principal ($109.00 + $9.81)
	× 0.09	Rate × time (0.09 × 1)	× 0.09	Rate × time (0.09 × 1)
	$9.00	Interest	$10.69	Interest

The simple interest is $27.00 for the three years ($9.00 + $9.00 + $9.00), while the compound interest is $29.50 for the same period ($9.00 + $9.81 + $10.69) because interest is computed on interest for the last two years. Thus,

$$A = P + I \qquad\qquad A = P + I$$

$$= \$100 + \$27 \qquad\qquad = \$100.00 + \$29.50$$

$$= \$127 \qquad\qquad = \$129.50$$

In the preceding illustration, compound interest generated more interest than the corresponding rate of simple interest, and this generally is the case. Despite this, however, compound interest is the form of interest paid to investors by banks, savings and loan institutions, and the U.S. government bond program. One reason for this is that compound interest encourages the investor to maintain the interest on deposit; the savings institution thus has funds to invest that it would otherwise be paying out in interest.

There is a close relationship between simple interest and compound interest. As a result, some of the interest terminology must be modified to distinguish between the two. For compound interest, the terms of the formula $A = P + I$ are **compound amount** (also called *future value*), **original principal,** and

*The simple interest calculation using $I = Prt$ is $100 × 0.09 × 3 = $27. However, for this illustration, the interest is calculated annually. (The result is the same.)

compound interest, respectively. The quoted interest rate is the **nominal rate** (rate per annum), and the length of the investment is the **term.** The intervals when interest is added to the principal are called **conversion periods,** or just **periods.** In the previous illustration, the compound amount is \$129.50, the original principal is \$100.00, the compound interest is \$29.50, the nominal rate is 9%, the term is three years, and the conversion period is one year.

The most frequently used conversion periods are monthly, quarterly, semiannually, and annually. The greater the number of conversion periods per year, the greater the compound interest for a given investment.

Section 11.2
Computing compound interest

One method of computing compound interest is the step-by-step calculation shown in section 11.1. At the beginning of each period, the earned interest is added to the principal of the previous period, and interest is calculated using the formula $I = Prt$.

Example 1

Find the compound interest earned on \$100 invested for two years at 10% compounded semiannually.

Solution

$P = \$100$, $r = 0.10$, $t = \frac{1}{2}$

First six months	\$100.00	Original principal
	× 0.05	Rate × time $(0.10 \times \frac{1}{2})$
	\$ 5.00	Interest
Second six months	\$105.00	Principal (\$100 + \$5)
	× 0.05	Rate × time $(0.10 \times \frac{1}{2})$
	\$ 5.25	Interest
Third six months	\$110.25	Principal (\$105.00 + \$5.25)
	× 0.05	Rate × time $(0.10 \times \frac{1}{2})$
	\$ 5.51	Interest
Fourth six months	\$115.76	Principal (\$110.25 + \$5.51)
	× 0.05	Rate × time $(0.10 \times \frac{1}{2})$
	\$ 5.79	Interest

The compound interest is the sum of the interests for each period, or

\$5.00 + \$5.25 + \$5.51 + \$5.79 = \$21.55

Note that in applying the simple interest formula, it was convenient to multiply P by the combination rt. That is, $I = Prt$ is the same as $I = P \times (rt)$.

In compound interest, the combination rt is called the **rate per period** and is equal to the nominal rate divided by the number of periods per year.* If i = rate per period, then

■ (11–1) $$i = \frac{\text{Nominal rate}}{\text{Number of periods per year}}$$

In example 1, 10% per annum compounded semiannually is equal to $\frac{10\%}{2} = 5\%$ per period.

Example 2 Find the rate per period for (a) 12% per annum compounded semiannually, (b) 10% per annum compounded quarterly, and (c) 9% per annum compounded monthly.

Solution

a. The rate per period $i = \frac{12\%}{2} = 6\%$ per six months

b. The rate per period $i = \frac{10\%}{4} = 2\frac{1}{2}\%$ per quarter

c. The rate per period $i = \frac{9\%}{12} = \frac{3}{4}\%$ per month

Example 3 Find the compound amount for $600 invested for one year at 8% per annum compounded quarterly.

Solution

The rate per period i is $\frac{8\%}{4} = 2\%$ per quarter.

First quarter	$600.00	Original principal
	× 0.02	Rate per period
	$ 12.00	Interest
Second quarter	$612.00	Principal ($600 + $12)
	× 0.02	Rate per period
	$ 12.24	Interest
Third quarter	$624.24	Principal ($612.00 + $12.24)
	× 0.02	Rate per period
	$12.4848	Interest
Fourth quarter	$636.72	Principal ($624.24 + $12.48)
	× 0.02	Rate per period
	$12.7344	Interest

*Since $t = \frac{1}{p}$, where t = time and p = number of periods per year, then $r \times t = r \times \frac{1}{p} = \frac{r}{p}$.

Exercises for Section 11.2

In problems 1–10, find the rate per period i for the given nominal rate and conversion period.

1. 11% compounded semiannually
2. 8% compounded quarterly
3. 12% compounded monthly
4. 9% compounded monthly
5. 13% compounded semiannually
6. 14% compounded quarterly
7. 15% compounded monthly
8. 9% compounded semiannually
9. $10\frac{1}{2}$% compounded semiannually
10. $8\frac{1}{2}$% compounded quarterly

In problems 11–20, find the compound interest earned on the given original principal at the given compound interest rate for the indicated term.

11. $2,000 for two years at 8% compounded annually
12. $4,000 for one year at 12% compounded semiannually
13. $3,000 for one year at 14% compounded semiannually
14. $3,000 for two years at 8% compounded semiannually
15. $800 for two years at 10% compounded semiannually
16. $1,200 for one year at 9% compounded quarterly
17. $2,400 for one year at 11% compounded quarterly
18. $500 for one year at 9% compounded monthly
19. $600 for one year at 15% compounded monthly
20. $200 for six months at 13% compounded quarterly

In problems 21–25, find the compound amount for the given original principle invested at the given compound interest rate for the indicated term.

21. $800 for one year at 10% compounded quarterly
22. $900 for two years at 8% compounded semiannually
23. $1,600 for three years at 9% compounded annually
24. $8,000 for five years at 15% compounded annually
25. $2,000 for four years at $11\frac{1}{2}$% compounded semiannually

26. Lynn Bishop placed \$5,000 in a money market account that pays $8\frac{1}{2}\%$ interest compounded quarterly. How much will be in the account after one year?

27. John Foster has \$4,000 to invest for five years. He can either invest it at $11\frac{1}{2}\%$ simple interest or at 10% interest compounded annually. Which interest rate should he choose?

Section 11.3 The compound interest formula

In example 3 of section 11.2, if we multiply the principal \$600 by $(1.02)^4$, where $(1.02)^4 = 1.02 \times 1.02 \times 1.02 \times 1.02$,* the result is:

$$\begin{aligned} \$600 \times (1.02)^4 &= \$600 \times 1.08243216 \\ &= \$649.459296 \\ &= \$649.46 \end{aligned}$$

This is the solution to example 3 of section 11.2.

The decision to multiply \$600.00 by $(1.02)^4$ to obtain \$649.46 was not accidental. It is taken from a formula that can be derived to calculate compound amount.† The formula is:

■ (11–2)
$$A = P(1 + i)^n$$

where A = compound amount, P = principal, i = rate per period, and n = total number of periods. The entire subject of compound interest is contained in formula 11–2.

*In the algebra of exponents, a^n is defined as: $a^n = \underbrace{a \cdot a \cdot a \cdots a}_{n \text{ factors}}$. Thus, $(1.02)^4 = 1.02 \times 1.02 \times 1.02 \times 1.02$.

†Let

I = compound interest
P = original principal
i = rate per period
A_1 = compound amount at the end of the first period

Then

$I = Pi$	
$A_1 = P + I$	
$= P + Pi$	Substitution
$= P(1 + i)$	Distributive property

The compound amount A_2 at the end of the second period is:

$A_2 = A_1 + A_1 i$	
$= A_1(1 + i)$	Distributive property
$= P(1 + i)(1 + i)$	Substitution for A_1
$= P(1 + i)^2$	Where $(1 + i)(1 + i) = (1 + i)^2$

At the end of the third period,

$A_3 = A_2 + A_2 i$	
$= A_2(1 + i)$	Distributive property
$= P(1 + i)^2(1 + i)$	Substitution for A_2
$= P(1 + i)^3$	Where $(1 + i)^2(1 + i) = (1 + i)^3$

Continuing in this fashion, for an investment with a term of n periods, the compound amount A_n is $A_n = P(1 + i)^n$.

Example 1 Find the compound amount and the compound interest for an investment of \$2,000 for three years that pays 10% compounded semiannually.

Solution

$P = \$2{,}000$, $i = \frac{10\%}{2} = 5\% = 0.05$, $n = 3$ years $\times$ 2 periods per year $= 6$ periods

$$A = P(1 + i)^n$$
$$= \$2{,}000\,(1 + 0.05)^6$$
$$= \$2{,}000\,(1.05)^6$$
$$= \$2{,}000\,(1.34009564)$$
$$(1.05 \times 1.05 \times 1.05 \times 1.05 \times 1.05 \times 1.05 = 1.34009564)$$
$$= \$2{,}680.19128$$
$$= \$2{,}680.19$$
$$I = A - P$$
$$= \$2{,}680.19 - \$2{,}000.00$$
$$= \$680.19$$

Section 11.4 Compound interest tables

Applying formula 11–2 in the calculation of compound interest becomes unwieldy when n is a large number, as seen in the last example; finding $(1.05)^6$ is no small task. To simplify these calculations, appendix C provides the value of $(1 + i)^n$ for various combinations of i and n. In example 1 in section 11.3, $i = 5\%$ and $n = 6$. To find $(1.05)^6$, locate the appendix page labeled 5% and column C labeled "Compound Amount." Row 6 of this column is 1.34009564, which is the value of $(1.05)^6$.

Example 1 Find the compound interest on \$4,000 at 11% compounded quarterly for five years.

Solution

$P = \$4{,}000$, $i = \frac{11\%}{4} = 2\frac{3}{4}\% = 0.0275$, $n = 5 \times 4 = 20$

$$A = P(1 + i)^n$$
$$= \$4{,}000\,(1.0275)^{20}$$
$$= \$4{,}000\,(1.72042843) \qquad \text{(Appendix C)}$$
$$= \$6{,}881.71372$$
$$= \$6{,}881.71$$

$$I = A - P$$
$$= \$6{,}881.71 - \$4{,}000.00$$
$$= \$2{,}881.71$$

Appendix C can also be used to find values of i or n.

Example 2 How long will it take for \$2,000.00 to accumulate to \$2,612.10 if the \$2,000.00 is compounded quarterly at 9%?

Solution

$A = \$2{,}612.10,\ i = \dfrac{9\%}{4} = 2\frac{1}{4}\% = 0.0225,\ P = \$2{,}000.00,\ n = ?$

$$A = P(1 + i)^n$$

$$\frac{A}{P} = (1 + i)^n \quad \text{(Dividing both sides by } P\text{)}$$

$$\frac{\$2{,}612.10}{\$2{,}000.00} = (1.0225)^n$$

$$1.30605 = (1.0225)^n$$

In appendix C on the $2\frac{1}{4}\%$ page, 1.30604999 is the entry for $n = 12$; thus, the term is 12 quarters or three years.

Example 3 What interest rate compounded semiannually would be required for \$4,400.00 to accumulate to \$14,111.40 in 10 years?

Solution

$A = \$14{,}111.40,\ P = \$4{,}400.00,\ i = ?,\ n = 10 \times 2 = 20$

$$A = P(1 + i)^n$$

$$\frac{A}{P} = (1 + i)^n \quad \text{(Dividing both sides by } P\text{)}$$

$$\frac{\$14{,}111.40}{\$4{,}400.00} = (1 + i)^{20}$$

$$3.2071363 = (1 + i)^{20}$$

A horizontal scan of the $n = 20$ line of appendix C shows that the entry very close to 3.2071363 is on the page labeled $i = 6\%$. Since interest is compounded semiannually, the nominal rate is $6\% \times 2 = 12\%$.

Example 4 John Talbot invests \$900 in a savings account paying $6\frac{1}{2}\%$ compounded semiannually. After $3\frac{1}{2}$ years, he withdraws \$1,000 from the account and invests in a certificate of deposit paying 11% compounded quarterly, leaving the remainder in the savings account. How much is his total compound amount two years after purchasing the certificate of deposit?

Solution

First $3\frac{1}{2}$ Years

$$P = \$900,\ i = \frac{6\ 1/2\%}{2} = 3\frac{1}{4}\% = 0.0325,\ n = 3\frac{1}{2} \times 2 = 7$$

$$\begin{aligned} A &= P\,(1 + i)^n \\ &= \$900\,(1.0325)^7 \\ &= \$900\,(1.25092255) \qquad \text{(Appendix C)} \\ &= \$1{,}125.83 \end{aligned}$$

Next 2 Years (Certificate of Deposit)

$$P = \$1{,}000,\ i = \frac{11\%}{4} = 2\frac{3}{4}\% = 0.0275,\ n = 2 \times 4 = 8$$

$$\begin{aligned} A &= P\,(1 + i)^n \\ &= \$1{,}000\,(1 + 0.0275)^8 \\ &= \$1{,}000\,(1.24238055) \qquad \text{(Appendix C)} \\ &= \$1{,}242.38 \end{aligned}$$

Next 2 Years (Savings Account)

$$P = \$125.83,\ i = 3\frac{1}{4}\% = 0.0325,\ n = 2 \times 2 = 4$$

$$\begin{aligned} A &= P\,(1 + i)^n \\ &= \$125.83\,(1.0325)^4 \\ &= \$125.83\,(1.13647593) \qquad \text{(Appendix C)} \\ &= \$143.00 \end{aligned}$$

Total compound amount = \$1,242.38 + \$143.00 = \$1,385.38

Exercises for Sections 11.3 and 11.4

In problems 1–6, use the formula $A = P(1 + i)^n$ to find the compound amount and the compound interest on the given original principal at the given compound interest rate for the indicated term.

1. $2,000 for two years at 12% compounded annually
2. $500 for three years at 8% compounded annually
3. $600 for two years at 13% compounded semiannually
4. $700 for two years at 10% compounded semiannually
5. $1,600 for one year at 9% compounded quarterly
6. $500 for one year at 8% compounded quarterly

In problems 7–15, use appendix C to find the compound interest on the given original principal at the given compound interest rate for the indicated term.

7. $800 for three months at 15% compounded monthly
8. $400 for five months at 12% compounded monthly
9. $1,400 for two years at 14% compounded semiannually
10. $2,200 for two years at 12% compounded semiannually
11. $1,000 for five years at 8% compounded quarterly
12. $600 for 10 years at 12% compounded monthly
13. $1,200 for three years at 10% compounded quarterly
14. $800 for eight years at 12% compounded semiannually
15. $2,000 for 20 years at 13% compounded quarterly

In problems 16–20, use appendix C to find how long it would take for the given original principal to accumulate to the given amount at the given compound interest rate.

16. $1,000.00 to $2,011.36 at 15% compounded annually
17. $4,000.00 to $27,488.34 at 11% compounded semiannually
18. $500.00 to $742.97 at 8% compounded quarterly
19. $800.00 to $1,078.28 at 12% compounded monthly
20. $1,400.00 to $1,673.87 at 18% compounded monthly

In problems 21–26, use appendix C to find the compound interest rate that would make the given original principal accumulate to the given amount in the given length of time.

21. $400.00 to $536.04 in three years, interest compounded semiannually
22. $1,500.00 to $2,703.34 in four years, interest compounded quarterly

23. \$3,000.00 to \$3,787.43 in two years, interest compounded semiannually

24. \$1,800.00 to \$1,968.20 in six months, interest compounded monthly

25. \$200.00 to \$297.19 in five years, interest compounded quarterly

26. \$900 to \$969.82 in ten months, interest compounded monthly

27. On the day his son was born, Pedro Dominguez planned for his son's education by placing \$8,000 in an account paying 9% compounded semiannually. Pedro closed the account 18 years later and used the compound amount to send his son to college. How much was the compound amount?

28. In preparation for a tax payment, Janice Jones placed \$1,500 in an account paying 6% compounded monthly. After 10 months, she closed the account. How much money did she receive?

29. A professional baseball player's contract called for \$25,000 to be placed in an account paying 11% compounded quarterly, with the player to receive the compound amount when he retired. If the player retired seven years later, how much did he receive from the account?

30. Following a job transfer, Kerry Grant sold his condominium for \$122,000. While looking for a new home, he put the money into an account that paid 10% compounded quarterly. Eighteen months later he withdrew the compound amount. How much did he withdraw?

31. Carol and Carolyn each have \$3,500 in a savings account. Carol's money is in a bank that pays 8% interest compounded annually. Carolyn's money is invested in a company credit union paying $8\frac{1}{2}$% compounded annually. At the end of two years, how much more will Carolyn have in savings than Carol?

32. Find the length of time it will take for \$10,000 to double if it is invested in an account that pays 12% compounded quarterly.

33. Mary Watkins places \$450 in a savings account paying 9% interest compounded quarterly. After four years, she withdraws \$500 from the account and buys a certificate of deposit that pays 15% interest compounded semiannually, leaving the remainder in the savings account. How much is her total compound amount one year after purchasing the certificate of deposit?

34. Art Landon opens a savings account with \$1,200. The account pays 8% interest compounded semiannually. After $3\frac{1}{2}$ years, he withdraws \$1,000 from the account and buys a certificate of deposit that pays 14% interest compounded quarterly, leaving the remainder in the savings account. How much is his total compound amount $1\frac{1}{2}$ years after purchasing his certificate of deposit?

Section 11.5 Present value

In chapter 9 on simple interest, **present value** was defined as the current value of a future sum of money. This definition also applies to present value at compound interest. Also analogous is the procedure for finding present value; the formula for A is solved for P:

$$A = P(1+i)^n$$

$$\frac{A}{(1+i)^n} = \frac{P(1+i)^n}{(1+i)^n} \qquad \text{Dividing both sides by } (1+i)^n$$

$$\frac{A}{(1+i)^n} = P$$

In the algebra of exponents, $\frac{1}{x^n}$ is defined as x^{-n} for any positive n and nonzero x. Thus,

■ (11–3) $$P = A(1+i)^{-n} \qquad \text{where } \frac{1}{(1+i)^n} = (1+i)^{-n}$$

Present value at compound interest can be calculated by using appendix D, which lists the values of $(1+i)^{-n}$. Similar to finding an entry in the compound interest table, an entry in appendix D is found by locating the appendix page for the rate of interest i and then the nth row of column D "Present Value." This entry is the value of $(1+i)^{-n}$.

Example 1 Find the principal that must be deposited at 14% compounded annually to have an amount of $10,000 in eight years.

Solution

$P = ?$, $A = \$10{,}000$, $i = 14\% = 0.14$, $n = 8$

$$\begin{aligned} P &= A(1+i)^{-n} \\ &= \$10{,}000\,(1.14)^{-8} \\ &= \$10{,}000\,(0.35055905) \qquad \text{(Appendix D)} \\ &= \$3{,}505.59 \end{aligned}$$

Example 2 Find the principal that must be deposited at 8% compounded quarterly to have an amount of $10,000 in five years.

Solution

$P = ?, A = \$10{,}000, i = \frac{8\%}{4} = 2\% = 0.02, n = 5 \times 4 = 20$

$P = A\,(1 + i)^{-n}$

$= \$10{,}000\,(1.02)^{-20}$

$= \$10{,}000\,(0.67297133)$ (Appendix D)

$= \$6{,}729.71$

Check: If a principal of $6,729.71 was invested at 8% compounded quarterly for five years, then by formula 11–2:

$A = P\,(1 + i)^{n}$

$= \$6{,}729.71\,(1.02)^{20}$

$= \$6{,}729.71\,(1.4859474)$ (Appendix C)

$= \$9{,}999.995$

$= \$10{,}000.00$

Example 3 The parents of newborn Terry Morton wanted to establish a savings account that would provide $16,000 for college expenses for Terry at age 18. Their banker calculated the amount to be placed in an account that pays 12% compounded semiannually. How much was put in the savings account?

Solution

$P = ?, A = \$16{,}000, i = \frac{12\%}{2} = 6\% = 0.06, n = 18 \times 2 = 36$

$P = A\,(1 + i)^{-n}$

$= \$16{,}000\,(1.06)^{-36}$

$= \$16{,}000\,(0.12274077)$ (Appendix D)

$= \$1{,}963.85$

The present value of the expected future income from an investment is often used to compare alternate investment proposals.

Example 4 Paul Hawkins is considering two different investment programs. Each program requires the same initial investment, and the projected income of the two programs for each of the first three years is as follows:

Year	Program A	Program B
1	\$2,000	\$1,000
2	1,500	1,200
3	1,000	2,300

If money is worth 9% compounded annually, which is the better investment?

Solution

Since present value is the current value of a future sum of money, the better investment will be the one for which the sum of the present values of the future incomes is largest. The present values of the projected yearly incomes from the two programs are:

Program A

Year	*Income*	*Present Value*	
1	\$2,000	\$2,000 $(1.09)^{-1}$	= \$1,834.86
2	1,500	1,500 $(1.09)^{-2}$	= 1,262.52
3	1,000	1,000 $(1.09)^{-3}$	= 772.18
		Sum	= \$3,869.56

Program B

Year	*Income*	*Present Value*	
1	\$1,000	\$1,000 $(1.09)^{-1}$	= \$ 917.43
2	1,200	1,200 $(1.09)^{-2}$	= 1,010.02
3	2,300	2,300 $(1.09)^{-3}$	= 1,776.02
		Sum	= \$3,703.47

Since the sum of the present values of the yearly incomes from program A exceeds that of program B, program A is the better investment.

Exercises for Section 11.5

In problems 1–10, use appendix D to find the principal that must be invested at the given interest rate to have the given amount after the given period of time.

1. \$4,000 in two years at 12% compounded semiannually
2. \$5,000 in five years at 10% compounded semiannually
3. \$3,000 in three years at 14% compounded annually
4. \$1,600 in one year at 8% compounded quarterly
5. \$1,500 in 10 years at 12% compounded quarterly
6. \$20,000 in 20 years at 12% compounded monthly
7. \$5,000 in four years at 18% compounded monthly
8. \$4,000 in 10 years at 13% compounded semiannually
9. \$1,400 in six years at 11% compounded quarterly
10. \$10,000 in 20 years at 16% compounded quarterly
11. Ten years ago, Jack Philips opened a savings account that paid 6% interest compounded quarterly. He made no deposits or withdrawals after his initial deposit. Today, there is \$3,083.83 in the account. How much did he place in the account initially?
12. John Foster, who is 40 years old, wishes to place enough money in a savings account that pays 10% interest compounded quarterly so that he will have \$20,000 in the account at age 65 to use for retirement. How much should he put in the account?
13. Pam Shuster just inherited \$15,000. She wishes to put enough of her inheritance into a savings account so that five years from now she will still have \$15,000. If the account pays 9% compounded semiannually, how much should she put in the account?
14. Joyce Ruth is planning to tour Europe two years from now, and she estimates that she will need \$3,000 for the trip. How much should she place in a savings account now to have enough money for her trip if the account pays 12% compounded quarterly?
15. John Perry is considering two different investment programs, each requiring the same initial investment. The projected net incomes for each of the first three years are: program A—\$2,500, \$2,500, \$1,500; program B—\$3,000, \$2,500, \$1,000. If money is worth 10% compounded annually, which is the better investment?
16. The Jensens are considering two investment programs, each requiring the same initial investment. Program A is expected to return a net income of \$1,000, \$4,000, \$2,500, and \$500 for each of the first four years. Program B is expected to return \$3,000, \$1,500, \$2,000, and \$1,500. At an interest rate of $9\frac{1}{2}$% compounded annually, which is the better investment?

17. A company is considering the proposals of two advertising firms. Each proposal requires an investment of \$65,000. The first proposal is expected to result in a semiannual increase in net income of \$10,000, \$15,000, and \$20,000 for the first 18 months. The second proposal is expected to return \$10,000, \$12,000, and \$23,000 over the same period. At an interest rate of 10% compounded semiannually, which proposal should the company accept?

Section 11.6 Daily and continuous compounding

Traditionally, savings institutions offered interest at periods that were annual, semiannual, or quarterly. However, in recent years, competition for the savings dollar has resulted in savings plans with shorter conversion periods. The first to be studied is interest compounded daily.

Daily compounding

Interest compounded daily has two advantages. First, the investor earns higher interest, for it has already been demonstrated that the shorter the period, the greater the generated interest. Second, interest is earned for the time it is invested; there is no penalty for withdrawal during an interest period, as there often is on accounts with periods of a quarter or longer.

Daily interest is calculated using formula 11–2, $A = P(1 + i)^n$, the same as for any other interest calculation. Since the conversion period is one day, $i = \frac{r}{365}$, where r = the nominal rate. For ease of calculation, appendix I is a table of values of $(1 + \frac{r}{365})^n$. The headings at the top of the table are values of r; the values of n are given in the left-hand column. An appropriate entry in the table is multiplied by the principal P to obtain the compound amount A.

Example 1 Find the compound amount of \$1,500 invested on July 14 and withdrawn on September 9 if interest is compounded daily at a rate of 10%.

Solution

From appendix B, there are 57 days from July 14 to September 9. Thus,

$A = ?, P = \$1,500, r = 10\% = 0.10, n = 57$

$$A = P\left(1 + \frac{r}{365}\right)^n$$

$$= \$1,500\left(1 + \frac{.10}{365}\right)^{57}$$

$$= \$1,500\ (1.01573684) \qquad \text{(Appendix I)}$$

$$= \$1,523.61$$

Example 2 Leslie Tormes invested \$2,000 on July 24 in a credit union that pays interest at a rate of 9% compounded daily. If the credit union credits the interest to her account quarterly, what was her balance at the end of the quarter?*

Solution

From appendix B, there are 68 days from July 24 to September 30 (the end of the quarter).

$$A = P\left(1 + \frac{r}{365}\right)^n$$

$$= \$2{,}000\left(1 + \frac{.09}{365}\right)^{68}$$

$$= \$2{,}000\ (1.01690638) \qquad \text{(Appendix I)}$$

$$= \$2{,}033.81276$$

$$= \$2{,}033.81$$

The balance as of September 30 is \$2,033.81. The interest earned to this date is

$$\$2{,}033.81 - \$2{,}000.00 = \$33.81$$

Example 3 Continental Federal pays investors interest at a rate of $8\frac{1}{2}$% compounded daily, and deposits made by the tenth of a month earn interest from the first of the month. Jim Click opened an account with a \$500 deposit on April 8 and made an additional deposit of \$700 on May 15. (a) What was the compound amount at the end of the quarter? (b) If Jim receives an interest check quarterly, how much did he receive at the end of the quarter?

Solution

a. The first deposit earns interest from April 1, since it was made during the first 10 days of the month. There are 90 days from April 1 to June 30 (the end of the quarter), and 46 days from May 15 to June 30.

April Deposit

$$A_1 = P\left(1 + \frac{r}{365}\right)^n$$

$$= \$500\left(1 + \frac{.085}{365}\right)^{90}$$

$$= \$500\ (1.02117759)$$

$$= \$510.588795$$

$$= \$510.59$$

May Deposit

$$A_2 = P\left(1 + \frac{r}{365}\right)^n$$

$$= \$700\left(1 + \frac{.085}{365}\right)^{46}$$

$$= \$700\ (1.01076865)$$

$$= \$707.538055$$

$$= \$707.54$$

*Ending dates of the four quarters in a year are March 31, June 30, September 30, and December 31.

The compound amount A is the sum $A_1 + A_2$. Thus,

$$A = A_1 + A_2$$
$$= \$510.59 + \$707.54$$
$$= \$1{,}218.13$$

b. Interest is calculated using:

$$I = A - P$$
$$= \$1{,}218.13 - \$1{,}200.00 \quad (\$1{,}200 = \$500 + \$700)$$
$$= \$18.13$$

Continuous compounding

The most recent innovation in savings plans is the ultimate in compounding: interest compounded continuously. The formula for this form of compounding is

■ (11–4) $$A = Pe^{rt}$$

where A = compound amount, P = principal, r = rate, t = time in years, and e = a mathematical constant approximately equal to 2.7183.

A table of values for e^{rt} is found in appendix J.

Example 4 Find the compound amount of \$1,200 compounded continuously at 10% for six months.

Solution

Using formula 11–4, with $A = ?$, $P = \$1{,}200$, $r = 10\% = 0.10$, $t = \frac{6}{12} = 0.5$,

$$A = Pe^{rt}$$
$$= \$1{,}200e^{(0.10)(0.5)}$$
$$= \$1{,}200e^{(0.05)}$$
$$= \$1{,}200\ (1.0513) \quad \text{(Appendix J)}$$
$$= \$1{,}261.56$$

Example 5 Jim Brown invested \$5,000 in an account that pays interest at $8\frac{1}{2}\%$ compounded continuously. How much was in the account after four years?

Solution

$A = ?,\ P = \$5{,}000,\ r = 0.085,\ t = 4$

$$\begin{aligned} A &= Pe^{rt} \\ &= \$5{,}000e^{(0.085)(4)} \\ &= \$5{,}000e^{(0.34)} \\ &= \$5{,}000\ (1.4049) \qquad \text{(Appendix J)} \\ &= \$7{,}024.50 \end{aligned}$$

How does daily and continuous compounding of interest compare with compounding of interest over longer conversion periods? The entries in table 11.1 give the compound amounts of \$1,000 invested at a rate of 12% compounded quarterly, daily, and continuously. Note that the shorter the conversion period, the greater the amount of compound interest earned.

Table 11.1 Compound Amounts of \$1,000 Invested at 12%

Conversion Period	One Year	Five Years	Ten Years
Quarterly	\$1,125.51	\$1,806.11	\$3,262.04
Daily	1,127.47	1,821.94	3,319.46
Continuously	1,127.50	1,822.10	3,320.10

Exercises for Section 11.6

In problems 1–10, use appendix I to find the compound amount of the given principal invested at the given compound interest rate when interest is compounded daily.

1. \$800 from August 15 to December 7 at 8%
2. \$1,000 from March 7 to September 14 at $9\frac{1}{2}\%$
3. \$750 from April 14 to June 27 at 12%
4. \$1,600 from October 11 to November 2 at $8\frac{1}{2}\%$
5. \$1,500 from May 30 to August 23 at 10%
6. \$900 from June 29 to September 5 at 12%
7. \$1,450 from January 3 to September 13 at 11% (assume nonleap year)

8. $1,575 from July 4 to October 29 at 13%

9. $815 from September 8 to January 27 at 9%

10. $682 from November 15 to January 18 at 11%

In problems 11–16, assume that interest is compounded daily and credited quarterly. Find the amount at the end of the quarter when the given principal is placed in an account that pays the given rate of compound interest.

11. $500 deposited July 15 at 10%

12. $1,500 deposited October 9 at 12%

13. $2,800 deposited November 16 at $8\frac{1}{2}$%

14. $2,200 deposited June 3 at $9\frac{1}{2}$%

15. $600 deposited January 19 at 11% (nonleap year)

16. $1,470 deposited January 5 at 13% (nonleap year)

17. Pete Thomas opened an account at a savings and loan association that pays 8% interest compounded daily, with deposits made by the tenth earning interest from the first. If Pete opened his account on August 7 with $600 and made an additional deposit on September 12 of $400, what was the balance in his account at the end of the quarter?

18. Carolyn James opened a savings account at Fiduciary Federal with $500 on October 9. On November 5, she made an additional deposit of $300. If Fiduciary Federal pays 9% interest compounded daily, with deposits made by the tenth earning interest from the first, what was the balance in her account at the end of the quarter?

In problems 19–26, use appendix J to find the compound amount of the given principal invested at the given compound interest rate when interest is compounded continuously.

19. $2,400 at 14% for two years

20. $1,840 at 11% for three years

21. $920 at 12% for six months

22. $1,600 at 9% for four months

23. $1,450 at 10% for 18 months

24. $2,846 at 13% for five years

25. \$1,420 at $11\frac{1}{2}\%$ for four years

26. \$3,740 at $13\frac{1}{2}\%$ for 10 years

27. Jeanne Phillips wishes to invest \$5,000 for two years. She can invest the money at $9\frac{1}{2}\%$ compounded continuously or 10% compounded semiannually. Which is the better investment?

Section 11.7 Nominal rate versus effective rate

The rate quoted in a compound interest transaction is an annual rate, or nominal rate. When the conversion period is less than one year, the action of interest generating interest results in a rate greater than the nominal rate. For example, if \$100 is invested for one year at 9% compounded quarterly, then

$$\begin{aligned} A &= P(1+i)^n \\ &= \$100\,(1.0225)^4 \\ &= \$100\,(1.09308332) \quad \text{(Appendix C)} \\ &= \$109.31 \end{aligned}$$

The interest earned in one year is \$9.31, which is 9.31% of \$100.00. This is equivalent to \$100.00 invested at 9.31% simple interest, since

$$\begin{aligned} I &= Prt \\ &= \$100 \times 0.0931 \times 1 \\ &= \$9.31 \end{aligned}$$

Compared with the nominal rate of 9%, 9.31% is called the **effective rate** of interest or the **true interest** rate, since it indicates the real earning power of the funds invested.

The effective rate can be read directly from appendix C. For example, consider a principal P invested at 8% compounded semiannually. This means that the rate per period is 4% and that the table entry from appendix C for $n = 2$ is 1.0816.

The table entry of 1.0816 is the compound amount per \$1.00 of principal; that is, \$1.00 invested at 8% compounded semiannually amounts to \$1.0816 in one year. Thus, \$1.00 earns \$0.0816 simple interest in one year. This is equivalent to a simple interest rate of 8.16%, since by the simple interest formula $I = Prt$, the interest I on \$1.00 at 8.16% for one year is $I = \$1 \times 0.0816 \times 1 = \$0.0816$. Thus, the effective rate of interest is 0.0816 or 8.16%.

Example 1 A sum of money is invested at an interest rate of 9% compounded monthly. Find the effective rate of interest.

Solution

$$i = \frac{9\%}{12} = 0.75\% = 0.0075,\ n = 12$$

From appendix C,

$$(1.0075)^{12} = 1.0938069$$

The effective rate is 0.0938069. To the nearest hundredth of a percent, this is 9.38%.

Given the effective rate of interest, the nominal rate can be found.

Example 2 A credit union announces the issuance of savings certificates paying an effective rate of 12.68%. If interest is compounded monthly, what is the nominal rate r?

Solution

An effective rate of 12.68% means that for $n = 12$,

$$(1 + i)^{12} = 1.1268$$

From appendix C, $(1.01)^{12} = 1.12682503$; thus,

$$i = \frac{r}{12} = 0.01$$

$$r = 12 \times 0.01 \quad \text{(Multiplying both sides by 12)}$$

$$r = 0.12$$

$$r = 12\%$$

Exercises for Section 11.7

In problems 1–10, find the effective interest rates (to the nearest hundredth of a percent) for the given rates of compound interest.

1. 10% compounded semiannually
2. 11% compounded quarterly
3. 12% compounded quarterly

4. 9% compounded quarterly
5. 15% compounded monthly
6. 12% compounded semiannually
7. 9% compounded semiannually
8. 13% compounded semiannually
9. 10% compounded quarterly
10. 6% compounded monthly

In problems 11–15, find the nominal interest rates for the given effective rates of interest.

11. 11.30%, interest compounded semiannually
12. 8.16%, interest compounded semiannually
13. 13.65%, interest compounded quarterly
14. 10.38%, interest compounded quarterly
15. 16.08%, interest compounded monthly
16. A savings and loan association issues $1,000 savings certificates with an effective rate of 11.46%. If interest is compounded quarterly, what is the nominal rate?

Glossary

Compound amount Also called *future value.* The total amount accumulated (principal plus interest) from a loan or investment at compound interest.
Compound interest Interest that is periodically computed and added to the previous principal, yielding a new principal for the next interest computation.
Conversion periods The intervals of time when interest is computed and added to the principal.
Effective rate The simple interest rate that generates the same amount of interest in one year as a given compound interest rate.
Nominal rate The rate per annum; the quoted compound interest rate.
Original principal The original amount of money borrowed or invested at compound interest.
Present value The amount of money (original principal) that must be borrowed or invested at a given interest rate for a given length of time to result in a specified compound amount.
Rate per period The nominal rate divided by the number of conversion periods per year.
Term The length of an investment or loan.
True interest rate See *effective rate.*

Review test

1. Find the rate per period for
   a. 10% compounded quarterly
   b. 9% compounded monthly
   c. 13% compounded semiannually
   d. 9% compounded quarterly

2. Using the simple interest formula for each period, find the compound amount for $900 invested for one year in an account that pays 12% interest compounded semiannually. Do not use tables.

3. Using appendix C, find the compound amount and the compound interest for $2,600 invested for three years at 11% compounded quarterly.

4. Gloria Winters will need $25,000 in 18 months for new display cases. Use appendix D to determine how much she should deposit now in an account that pays 12% compounded quarterly to have the money for the cases.

5. How long will it take for $1,000 to accumulate to $1,500 if money is worth 11% compounded quarterly? Use appendix C.

6. On May 14, Henry Stone deposited $800 in an account that pays 9% interest compounded daily. What is the compound amount of the account on June 24? Use appendices B and I.

7. Cynthia Lewis placed $1,500 in an account that pays 8% interest compounded quarterly. Use appendix C to find the effective rate of interest.

8. Harold Cruz is considering two different investment programs. Each program requires the same initial investment, and the projected income of the two programs for each of the first three years is as follows:

Year	Program A	Program B
1	$1,000	$1,200
2	1,400	1,300
3	1,600	1,500

If money is worth 11% compounded semiannually, which is the better investment? Use appendix D.

CHAPTER

12 Consumer Credit

Chapter Objectives

I. Learn the meaning of the following terms:

Finance charge, 366
Down payment, 382
Amount financed, 382
Deferred payment price, 382
Schedule of payments, 382

II. Understand:

The principles of the United States Rule, 363–364
Open-end credit, 366–368
Installment plans, 382
Annual percentage rate, 386–387
The Rule of 78, 392–393

III. Calculate:

The distribution of partial payments, 364
Finance charges for open-end credit accounts, 367–368, 370–371
Finance charges for installment plans, 383
The annual percentage rate for open-end credit and installment plans, 386–389
Annual percentage rate using the constant ratio formula, 390
The amount of the rebate on unearned interest using the Rule of 78, 393–394

Section 12.1 Introduction

Credit has become an American institution. "Buy now—pay later" is an accepted way of life for the consumer, and Americans buy houses, automobiles, appliances, home furnishings, and clothing on credit. In fact, nearly anything may be obtained on credit. The extent to which Americans buy on credit is demonstrated in figure 12.1.

Partly as a result of credit, Americans enjoy the highest standard of living in the world. Credit permits the purchase of items that consumers might not otherwise be able to afford. By apportioning the cost of an item into a series of partial payments over a period of time, consumers are able to purchase items that would be impractical if cash were required.

Convenience is a second reason for the widespread acceptance of consumer credit. The ease of purchasing without needing to carry money has been a significant factor in the increase in credit sales. Americans often pay dearly for this convenience; nevertheless, credit purchases by consumers, business, and government are expected to increase. Indeed, predictions of a "credit economy" and a "cashless-checkless" society are becoming widespread.

This chapter focuses on that segment of consumer credit dealing with charge accounts, credit cards, and installment contracts.

Figure 12.1 Consumer installment credit amounts outstanding

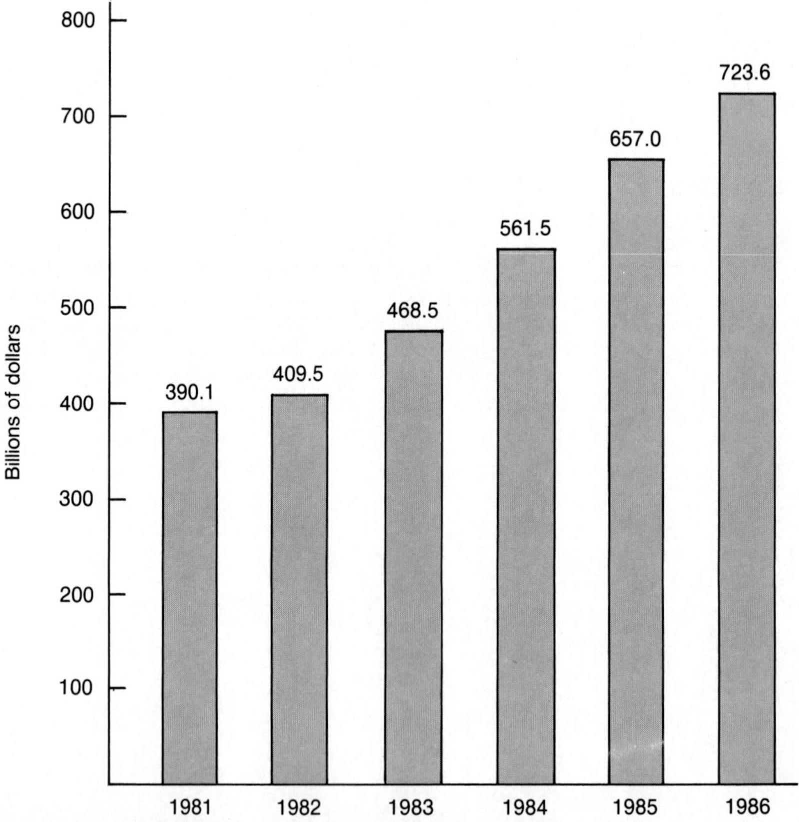

Source: Statistical Abstract

Section 12.2 The United States Rule

There is a key difference between loans at simple interest and those retired by a series of partial payments. In the former, the borrower retains the principal for the entire term of the loan; in the latter, a partial payment normally includes a portion of the principal. As a result, the method of calculating interest can vary.

To illustrate this, consider a loan for $1,000 for one year at 12% simple interest. If this loan is repaid in two installments, how is the interest calculated if $500 is paid at the end of six months? One method is to calculate interest only after the entire principal is repaid. In this case, the interest is $120 ($1,000 × 0.12 × 1), and the second installment is $620. A second method is to calculate interest after the first installment, as shown in the following table:

Principal	Interest	Amount	Payment	New Principal
$1,000	$60.00 ($\$1{,}000 \times 0.12 \times \frac{1}{2}$)	$1,060.00	$500.00	$560.00
560	33.60 ($\$560 \times 0.12 \times \frac{1}{2}$)	593.60	593.60	0.00

Note that by this method the total interest charge is only

$$\$60.00 + \$33.60 = \$93.60$$

The variety of methods for crediting payments to principal and interest has led to numerous lawsuits and finally to a decision by the United States Supreme Court. In this decision, certain principles were established regarding partial payments, and these principles have become known as the **United States Rule.** The essence of the principles is as follows:

1. Distribution of partial payments
   a. If the partial payment exceeds accumulated interest, the difference is deducted from the principal; this new principal is the basis for interest calculations of the next partial payment.
   b. If the partial payment does not exceed the accumulated interest, the interest continues to accrue until the sum of subsequent partial payments equals or exceeds the interest due.

2. Calculation of interest

   a. Interest is calculated on the principal from the first day of the loan to the day of the first partial payment.

   b. For subsequent partial payments, interest is calculated on the remaining principal from the date of the previous payment to the date of the current payment.*

   c. On the maturity date, interest is calculated from the date of the last payment to the maturity date.*

While no time rule is specified by the court, banker's rule ($\frac{\text{Exact days}}{\text{360 days}}$) is used most often, and it is used for all examples and exercises in this chapter.

Example 1 On a \$3,000 loan at 10% interest, payments of \$300, \$50, and \$200 were made at three-month intervals. What is the amount due if the loan is paid off in one year?

Solution

Principal		\$3,000.00
Payment 1	\$300.00	
Less interest (\$3,000 × 0.10 × $\frac{1}{4}$)	75.00	
Applied to principal		225.00
New principal		\$2,775.00
Payment 2	\$ 50.00	
Less interest (\$2,775 × 0.10 × $\frac{1}{4}$)	69.38	
Applied to principal		0.00
New principal		\$2,775.00
Payment 3 (\$200 + \$50)†	\$250.00	
Less interest (\$2,775 × 0.10 × $\frac{1}{2}$)	138.75	
Applied to principal		111.25
New principal		\$2,663.75
Interest (\$2,663.75 × 0.10 × $\frac{1}{4}$)		66.59
Amount due		\$2,730.34

The interest for a term of one year would have been \$3,000 × 0.10 × 1 = \$300. Compared to the charges of \$75.00 + \$138.75 + \$66.59 = \$280.34, a savings of \$19.66 was realized by making partial payments.

*An exception to this is item 1b: If the partial payment does not exceed the accumulated interest, the interest continues to accrue until the sum of subsequent partial payments equals or exceeds the interest due.

†Because the previous payment did not exceed the accrued interest, the previous payment is added to this payment, and interest is calculated for six months. (See item 1b.)

Exercises for Section 12.2

In problems 1–10, find the amount due at the end of one year on the given loan when the indicated partial payments are made at 90-day intervals.

1. $1,000 loan at 12% interest; payments of $200, $200, and $400
2. $2,000 loan at 8% interest; payments of $400, $350, and $700
3. $5,000 loan at 14% interest; payments of $1,000, $2,000, and $400
4. $6,000 loan at 11% interest; payments of $2,000, $1,500, and $2,200
5. $8,000 loan at 9% interest; payments of $4,000, $100, and $2,100
6. $1,500 loan at 13% interest; payments of $400, $35, and $500
7. $800 loan at $10\frac{1}{2}\%$ interest; payments of $20, $500, and $100
8. $2,500 loan at $12\frac{1}{2}\%$ interest; payments of $250, $70, and $600
9. $3,200 loan at $8\frac{1}{2}\%$ interest; payments of $450, $100, and $600
10. $2,700 loan at $9\frac{1}{4}\%$ interest; payments of $40, $300, and $100
11. Joan Reynolds borrowed $6,000 at 10% interest and made payments at two-month intervals of $1,000, $500, $75, $1,200, and $30. How much was due on the loan at the end of the first year?
12. Bob Johnson borrowed $4,000 for two years at 12% interest so that he could remodel his clothing shop. If he made partial payments at three-month intervals of $500, $150, $60, $300, $1,000, $40, and $1,000, how much did he owe at the end of two years?

Section 12.3 The Truth-in-Lending Act

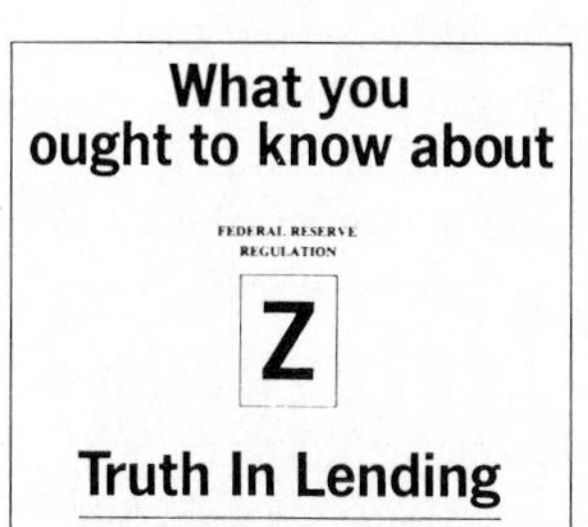

What you ought to know about
FEDERAL RESERVE REGULATION
Z
Truth In Lending
Consumer Credit Cost Disclosure
EFFECTIVE JULY 1, 1969

As the potential uses of credit are many, so are the potential abuses. Following World War II, credit sales rose phenomenally. A number of credit purchases were made by men and women who were not aware of the true cost of credit. Lured by clever advertisements and catch phrases such as "no money down, small monthly payments," these individuals often purchased items solely on their ability to make the monthly payments, not realizing that the total purchase price sometimes included exorbitant fees and high interest rates. Unfortunately, those least able to afford such charges often were the most susceptible to this kind of sales approach, and in some instances, persons and families incurred enormous debts due to repeated and unwise credit purchases.

In 1969, Congress acted to protect the public by passing legislation known as the **Truth-in-Lending Act. Regulation Z** is a Federal Reserve System document that carries out the provisions of this act.

The Truth-in-Lending Act does not regulate interest charges. Its purpose is disclosure—to make consumers aware of the cost of consumer credit and to permit them to make comparisons of credit terms. As defined by the act, consumer credit is credit offered or extended for which a finance charge is or may be imposed or that is repayable in more than four installments. Thus,

Regulation Z applies to banks, savings and loans, credit card issuers, automobile dealers, residential mortgage brokers, and all other individuals or groups that offer or arrange for consumer credit.

Two important concepts embodied in Regulation Z are the finance charge and the annual percentage rate. These are discussed in relation to the two types of credit covered by the regulation.

Section 12.4 The finance charge

In credit purchases covered by Regulation Z, the total price paid by the customer often includes fees other than interest charges. Examples of such fees are credit investigation fees, credit life insurance, or carrying charges. The latter (called carrying charges, time payment differential, or similar names) help defray the additional bookkeeping expenses incurred by the seller in a credit transaction. Regulation Z lumps all such fees, along with interest charges, under the term **finance charge.** Thus, the finance charge is the total of all costs to the buyer for obtaining credit, whether direct or indirect. Regulation Z states that all such costs must be itemized and disclosed to the customer, clearly and conspicuously.

Not all charges are included in the finance charge. Costs that would be paid even if credit was not granted, such as taxes, licenses, and registration fees, may be excluded. However, these, too, must be itemized and disclosed to the buyer.

Section 12.5 Open-end credit

Most consumers are acquainted with **open-end credit,** for this is the credit associated with major credit cards and with the revolving charge accounts of most department stores and retail businesses. In most open-end credit accounts, a monthly finance charge is imposed if the entire balance is not paid by the **payment due date,** usually 25 days after the billing date. The finance charge is a percentage of (1) the unpaid balance or (2) the average daily balance.

In the unpaid balance method, the finance charge is computed on the unpaid balance as of the end of the previous month. The amount of the finance charge varies according to the institution offering the credit and the state in which the account is located, but the charge typically ranges from 1% to 2% of the unpaid balance. In recording payments and finance charges on open-end accounts, the United States Rule is used.

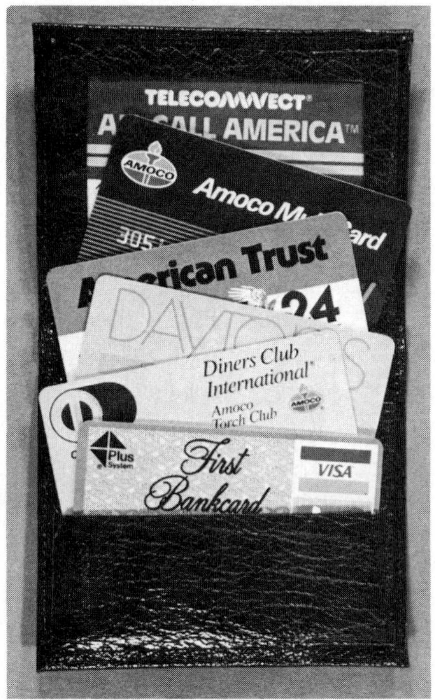

Many consumers rely on several credit cards.

Example 1 The balance on a credit card account with a finance charge of 1.75% per month on the unpaid balance is \$76.40. If monthly payments of \$22.00, \$12.00, \$10.00, and \$15.00 are made, find (a) the remaining balance due and (b) the total paid in finance charges during this period.

Solution

Month	Previous Balance	Current Purchases	Payments	Finance Charge	Credited to Balance	New Balance
1	\$76.40		\$22.00	\$1.34 (\$76.40 × 0.0175)	\$20.66	\$55.74
2	55.74		12.00	0.98 (\$55.74 × 0.0175)	11.02	44.72
3	44.72		10.00	0.78 (\$44.72 × 0.0175)	9.22	35.50
4	35.50		15.00	0.62 (\$35.50 × 0.0175)	14.38	21.12
				\$3.72		

The remaining balance is \$21.12, and a total finance charge of \$3.72 was paid during the period.

Example 2 The outstanding balance on a revolving charge account that carries a finance charge of 1.5% per month on the unpaid balance is $36.20. The following purchases and payments are made on the account:

Month	Purchases	Payments
1	$ 7.48	$15.00
2	22.60	10.00
3	—	20.00

What is the remaining balance following the third payment?

Solution

Month	Previous Balance	Current Purchases	Payments	Finance Charge	Credited to Balance	New Balance
1	$36.20	$ 7.48	$15.00	$0.54	$14.46	$29.22
2	29.22	22.60	10.00	0.44	9.56	42.26
3	42.26		20.00	0.63	19.37	22.89

The finance charge as a percentage of the unpaid balance has all but been replaced by the finance charge as a percentage of the average daily balance because the latter method generates more interest. The **average daily balance** is the sum of the daily balances during the billing cycle divided by the number of days in the cycle. Each **daily balance** is the previous balance plus purchases and cash advances,* less any payments or credits, and excluding any unpaid finance charges made during the billing period.

Like the unpaid balance method, the amount of the finance charge under the average daily balance method varies according to the institution offering the credit and the state in which the account is located, but the charge typically ranges from 1% to 2% of the average daily balance. The finance charge percent may change during the year. Many companies offering open-end credit now link changes in the finance charge percent to changes in some federal index, for example, the average interest rate of Treasury bills. The finance charge percent and the amount of the finance charge appear on the monthly statement following the month in which the finance charge was generated.

*Bank-sponsored credit cards often provide limited cash loans as a part of their credit services.

Example 3 Joanne Miller has a revolving charge account at a department store. Her monthly statement contained the following information:

Previous balance		$45.93
6–20, Payment	$25.00CR	
6–25, Women's wear	26.80	
6–28, Auto department	24.74	
7–2, Craft department	12.00	
7–10, Billing date		

Find: (a) the payment due date and (b) the daily balance for Joanne's account on June 23 and July 5.

Solution

a. The payment due date is 25 days from July 10, which is August 4.
b. The daily balance on June 23 is

$$\$45.93 - \$25.00 = \$20.93$$

The daily balance on July 5 is

$$\$20.93 + \$26.80 + \$24.74 + \$12.00 = \$84.47$$

Example 4 A monthly statement for a credit card account with billing date the 20th of each month contains the following information:

Previous balance		$112.40
10–27, Credit	$46.80CR	
10–31, Charge	22.00	
11–5, Payment	20.00CR	
11–10, Cash advance	50.00	
11–20, Billing date		

Find the average daily balance for the November 20 billing date.

Solution

Since the previous billing date was October 20, the daily balances are as follows:

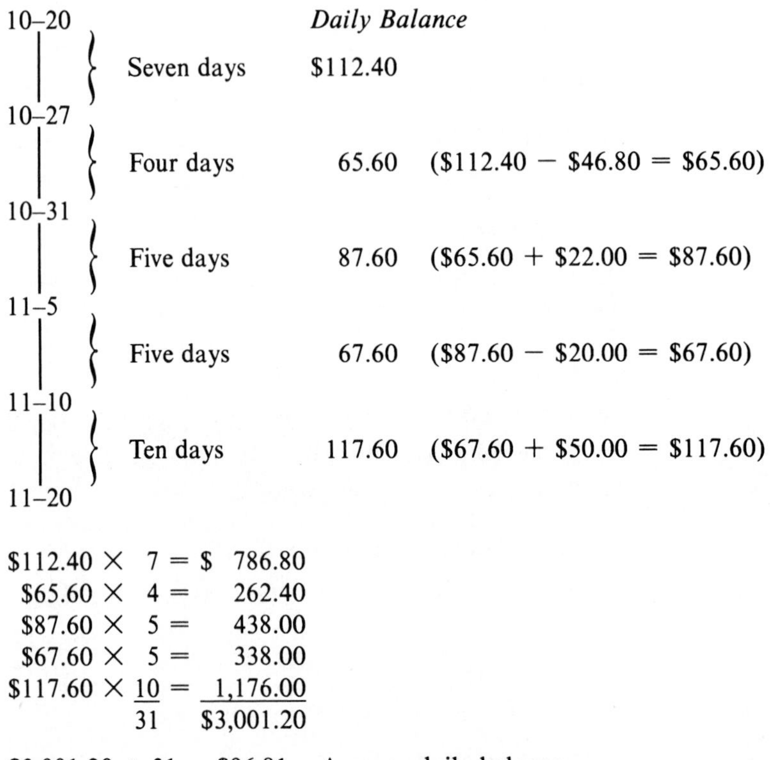

\$112.40 ×	7	=	\$ 786.80
\$65.60 ×	4	=	262.40
\$87.60 ×	5	=	438.00
\$67.60 ×	5	=	338.00
\$117.60 ×	10	=	1,176.00
	31		\$3,001.20

\$3,001.20 ÷ 31 = \$96.81 Average daily balance

Example 5 Rosemary Morley's latest monthly statement from Bank-a-Card (billing date the 18th of each month) contained the following information:

Previous balance		\$355.00
8–5, Payment	\$155.00CR	
8–8, Marshall's Department Store	42.18	
8–10, Fancy French Restaurant	18.60	
8–12, Cash advance—Sunshine National Bank	100.00	
8–18, Billing date		

If the finance charge is 1.5% per month of the average daily balance, find (a) the average daily balance and (b) the finance charge.

Solution

a. There are 18 days from the previous billing date of July 18 to the payment date, 3 days to the department store charge, 2 days to the restaurant charge, 2 days to the cash advance, and then 6 days to the August 18th billing date. Hence,

$355.00 × 18 =	$ 6,390.00	
$200.00 × 3 =	600.00	($355 − $155 = $200)
$242.18 × 2 =	484.36	($200.00 + $ 42.18 = $242.18)
$260.78 × 2 =	521.56	($242.18 + $ 18.60 = $260.78)
$360.78 × 6 =	2,164.68	($260.78 + $100.00 = $360.78)
31	$10,160.60	

$10,160.60 ÷ 31 = $327.76 Average daily balance

b. $327.76 × 0.015 = $4.92 Finance charge

The finance charge as a percentage of the average daily balance places a heavy penalty on the consumer who makes a partial payment late in the billing period. To see this, suppose that in example 5 Rosemary had no transactions other than a partial payment of $350 on August 15. Then the finance charge for the next statement, calculated on both the unpaid balance and the average daily balance, would be as follows:

Unpaid Balance	*Average Daily Balance*
Unpaid balance = $5	$355 × 28 = $9,940
	$ 5 × 3 = 15
	31 $9,955
	$9,955 ÷ 31 = $321.13 Average daily balance
$5 × 0.015 = $0.075	$321.13 × 0.015 = $4.81695
= $0.08 Finance charge	= $4.82 Finance charge

The finance charge calculated on the average daily balance is *60 times* that of the finance charge calculated on the unpaid balance. While this example is admittedly an extreme case, it illustrates that the average daily balance permits a substantial increase in the finance charge without an increase in the interest rate. (It should be noted that some open-end credit plans require a minimum finance charge of $0.50 or more if credit is extended. Even so, the average daily balance in this example yields a finance charge almost 10 times greater than a $0.50 minimum.)

Businesses offering open-end credit accounts are required by Regulation Z to provide new customers with a complete description of the financing, including conditions under which a finance charge can be made, how it is calculated, the periodic rate used, and the minimum periodic payment required. In addition, the seller must send a statement that contains the previous balance, amount and date of each purchase, payments, credits, the finance charge and periodic rate, and the annual percentage rate. Samples of such billing statements are shown in figures 12.2 and 12.3.

Figure 12.2
Sample retailer's billing statement

Example of a retailer's statement, prepared by a manual billing operation, for an account on which the finance charge is determined by a single periodic rate or a minimum charge of 50 cents applicable to balances under a specific amount. It also assumes that the finance charge is computed on the previous balance before deducting payments and/or credits. Separate slips shall accompany each statement, identifying all charges and credits and showing the dates and amounts thereof.

Any Store U.S.A.

MAIN STREET—ANY CITY, U.S.A.

(Customer's name here)

AMT. PAID $________

TO INSURE PROPER CREDIT RETURN THIS PORTION WITH YOUR PAYMENT

PREVIOUS BALANCE	FINANCE CHARGE 50 CENT MINIMUM	PAYMENTS	CREDITS	PURCHASES	NEW BALANCE	MINIMUM PAYMENT

FINANCE CHARGE IS COMPUTED BY A "PERIODIC RATE" OF % PER MONTH (OR A MINIMUM CHARGE OF 50 CENTS FOR BALANCES UNDER $) WHICH IS AN **ANNUAL PERCENTAGE RATE** OF % APPLIED TO THE PREVIOUS BALANCE WITHOUT DEDUCTING CURRENT PAYMENTS AND/OR CREDITS APPEARING ON THIS STATEMENT.

NOTICE

PLEASE SEE ACCOMPANYING STATEMENT(S) FOR IMPORTANT INFORMATION.

PAYMENTS, CREDITS OR CHARGES, RECEIVED AFTER THE DATE SHOWN ABOVE THE ARROW, WHICH IS THE CLOSING DATE OF THIS BILLING CYCLE, WILL APPEAR ON YOUR NEXT STATEMENT. TO AVOID ADDITIONAL FINANCE CHARGES PAY THE "NEW BALANCE" BEFORE THIS DATE NEXT MONTH.

ANY STORE, U.S.A. MAIN STREET, ANY CITY, U.S.A.

This form, when properly completed, will show how a creditor may comply with the disclosure requirements of the provisions of paragraphs (b) and (c) of §226.7 of Regulation Z for the type of credit extended in this example. This form is intended solely for purposes of demonstration and it is not the only format which will permit a creditor to comply with disclosure requirements of Regulation Z.

Figure 12.3
Sample retailer's billing statement

Example of a retailer's descriptive statement, prepared by an automated billing operation, for an account on which the finance charge is determined by a single periodic rate or a minimum charge of 50 cents applicable to balances under a specified amount. It also assumes that the finance charge is computed on the previous balance before deducting payments and/or credits.

(FACE OF FORM)

Any Store U.S.A.
MAIN STREET—ANY CITY, U.S.A.

(Customer's name here)

YOUR ACCOUNT NUMBER IS__________

TO INSURE PROPER CREDIT RETURN THIS PORTION WITH PAYMENT

BILLING DATES		To Your	We Added Your **FINANCE CHARGE**	We Deducted Your		We Added Your
NEXT MO.	THIS MO.	PREVIOUS BALANCE	50¢ MINIMUM	PAYMENTS	CREDITS	PURCHASES

TRANSACTION NO.	DATE	STORE	DEPT. NO.	DEPARTMENT NAME	CHARGES	PAYMENTS & CREDITS

To Avoid Additional Finance Charges, Pay The "New Balance" Before Your Billing Date Next Month.	This Is Your NEW BALANCE	This Is Your MINIMUM PAYMENT	ANNUAL PERCENTAGE RATE
			%

NOTICE: SEE REVERSE SIDE FOR IMPORTANT INFORMATION

(REVERSE SIDE OF FORM)

PAYMENTS, CREDITS OR CHARGES RECEIVED AFTER YOUR BILLING DATE "THIS MONTH" WILL APPEAR ON YOUR NEXT STATEMENT. YOUR **FINANCE CHARGE** IS COMPUTED BY A SINGLE PERIODIC RATE OF % (OR A MINIMUM CHARGE OF 50 CENTS FOR BALANCES UNDER $) WHICH IS AN **ANNUAL PERCENTAGE RATE** OF % APPLIED TO YOUR "PREVIOUS BALANCE" WITHOUT DEDUCTING CURRENT PAYMENTS AND/OR CREDITS APPEARING ON THE FACE OF THIS STATEMENT.

DEPT. NO.	DEPT. NAME	DEPT. NO.	DEPT. NAME	DEPT. NO.	DEPT. NAME
1	MEN'S ACCESSORIES (Shirts, Ties, Socks, etc.)	(In this form of billing, this side of the statement contains a listing of all departments and a brief description of the merchandise sold in each.)			
2	MEN'S CLOTHING (Suits, Sportcoats, Outerwear, etc.)				

ANY STORE, U.S.A., MAIN ST., ANY CITY, U.S.A.

This form, when properly completed, will show how a creditor may comply with the disclosure requirements of the provisions of paragraphs (b) and (c) of §226.7 of Regulation Z for the type of credit extended in this example. This form is intended solely for purposes of demonstration and it is not the only format which will permit a creditor to comply with disclosure requirements of Regulation Z

Exercises for Section 12.5

A description of a credit card account, including the amount of the unpaid balance and the rate of the monthly finance charge, is given in each of problems 1–6. Find the remaining balance due and the total paid in finance charges based on the unpaid balance after the indicated monthly payments are made on the account.

1. Unpaid balance of $212.40; 1.5% per month finance charge; monthly payments of $30.00, $40.00, and $50.00
2. Unpaid balance of $147.32; 1.7% per month finance charge; monthly payments of $10.00, $14.00, and $25.00
3. Unpaid balance of $171.52; 1.75% per month finance charge; monthly payments of $25.00, $40.00, and $70.00
4. Unpaid balance of $314.27; 1.5% per month finance charge; monthly payments of $50.00, $60.00, and $40.00
5. Unpaid balance of $517.63; 1.6% per month finance charge; monthly payments of $105.00, $115.00, $70.00, $80.00, and $115.00
6. Unpaid balance of $605.42; 1.6667% per month finance charge; monthly payments of $115.00, $100.00, $125.00, $80.00, and $110.00

In each of problems 7–12, the outstanding balance, rate of finance charge on the unpaid balance, purchases, and payments are given for a revolving charge account. Find the remaining balance of each account after the indicated payments and purchases are made.

7. Previous balance of $202.02; 1.75% per month finance charge

Month	Purchases	Payments
1	$11.56	$20.00
2	23.41	40.00
3	17.85	50.00

8. Previous balance of $151.42; 1.625% per month finance charge

Month	Purchases	Payments
1	$19.47	$25.00
2	43.15	50.00
3	11.72	50.00

9. Previous balance of $94.27; 1.8% per month finance charge

Month	Purchases	Payments
1	$17.21	$15.00
2	7.62	40.00
3	21.14	30.00

10. Previous balance of $114.21; 1.55% per month finance charge

Month	Purchases	Payments
1	$32.14	$25.00
2	14.21	20.00
3	27.86	25.00

11. Previous balance of $202.11; 1.205% per month finance charge

Month	Purchases	Payments
1	$17.28	$25.00
2	42.81	50.00
3	37.96	25.00
4	5.11	75.00

12. Previous balance of $311.49; 1.75% per month finance charge

Month	Purchases	Payments
1	$58.41	$100.00
2	62.83	75.00
3	19.27	50.00
4	41.52	75.00

In problems 13–18, information from the monthly statement of a credit card account is given. For each of these accounts, the payment due date is 25 days from the billing date. Find (a) the payment due date and (b) the daily balance of each account on each of the specified dates. (Use appendix B to find due dates.)

13. Previous balance $166.40

3–15, Payment	$50.00CR
3–20, Charge	10.12
3–22, Charge	22.45
4–6, Billing date	

(1) March 18, (2) March 26

14. Previous balance $322.17

6–21, Charge	$41.80
6–25, Charge	3.95
6–30, Credit	12.69CR
7–3, Payment	100.00CR
7–10, Charge	16.73
7–19, Billing date	

(1) June 23, (2) July 2, (3) July 8

15. Previous balance $66.63

11–5, Cash advance	$50.00
11–12, Charge	31.09
11–16, Charge	7.95
11–19, Cash advance	25.00
11–30, Billing date	

(1) November 10, (2) November 18, (3) November 24

16. Previous balance $283.57

12–30, Credit	$ 23.60CR
1–4, Charge	16.85
1–10, Credit	33.66CR
1–15, Payment	120.00CR
1–28, Billing date	

(1) January 3, (2) January 8, (3) January 12, (4) January 20

17. Previous balance $49.60

8–14, Payment	$49.60CR
8–17, Charge	66.45
8–18, Charge	22.90
8–20, Cash advance	25.00
8–30, Charge	16.84
9–12, Billing date	

(1) August 16, (2) August 19, (3) August 25, (4) September 3

18. Previous balance $92.25

5–4, Cash advance	$75.00
5–10, Credit	14.88CR
5–15, Payment	20.00CR
5–24, Charge	12.33
6–1, Billing date	

(1) May 9, (2) May 12, (3) May 20, (4) May 25

In problems 19–24, find the average daily balance of the given account as of the given billing date. For each problem, the billing dates fall on the same day of each month.

19. Previous balance $216.90

1–25, Charge	$ 38.00
1–31, Payment	100.00CR

Billing date: February 15

20. Previous balance $62.54

3–22, Credit	$19.30CR
4–1, Charge	18.72
4–3, Payment	25.00CR

Billing date: April 12

21. Previous balance $606.40

9–12, Charge	$ 66.20
9–16, Credit	37.63CR
9–18, Credit	58.00CR
10–1, Payment	200.00CR

Billing date: October 9

22. Previous balance $482.60

7–20, Payment	$200.00CR
7–26, Charge	32.60
8–2, Cash advance	40.00
8–12, Charge	16.65

Billing date: August 15

23. Previous balance $22.90

4–25, Charge	$ 4.67
5–1, Charge	18.30
5–10, Cash advance	100.00
5–12, Charge	16.80
5–15, Payment	25.00CR

Billing date: May 24

24. Previous balance $337.84

6–10, Payment	$150.00CR
6–12, Charge	16.75
6–18, Charge	32.30
6–20, Credit	16.75CR
6–25, Cash advance	75.00

Billing date: July 1

For each of the credit card accounts in problems 25–30, find the average daily balance of each account and compute the finance charge as of the given billing date. For each problem, the billing dates fall on the same day of each month.

25. Previous balance $240.14

4–20, Charge	$ 50.72
4–28, Charge	24.72
5–10, Payment	140.00CR

Billing date: May 15

Finance charge: 1.55% of the average daily balance

26. Previous balance $360.24

3–26, Charge	$ 24.16
4–2, Payment	175.00CR
4–15, Payment	20.00CR

Billing date: April 20

Finance charge: 1.7% of the average daily balance

27. Previous balance $416.18

8–20, Payment	$200.00CR
8–25, Cash advance	50.00
9–4, Charge	16.72
9–8, Charge	72.42

Billing date: September 10

Finance charge: 1.8% of the average daily balance

28. Previous balance $182.78

6–12, Cash advance	$100.00
6–20, Payment	40.00CR
6–28, Charge	17.42
6–30, Payment	50.00CR

Billing date: July 1

Finance charge: 1.5% of the average daily balance

29. Previous balance $316.40

4–20, Payment	$150.00CR
4–22, Credit	27.16CR
4–28, Cash advance	50.00
4–30, Charge	84.15
5–4, Payment	100.00CR

Billing date: May 10

Finance charge: 1.625% of the average daily balance

30. Previous balance $512.16

7–22, Charge	$ 17.29
7–28, Charge	110.12
7–29, Payment	300.00CR
8–7, Credit	17.29CR
8–12, Cash advance	75.00
8–16, Charge	41.16

Billing date: August 20

Finance charge: 1.75% of the average daily balance

In problems 31–34, find the balance of the account as of the last given billing date. For each problem, the billing dates fall on the same day of each month.

31. Previous balance $74.35

4–9, Payment	$ 50.00CR
4–10, Charge	16.20
4–20, Charge	104.35
4–25, Charge	34.50
5–1, Billing date	
5–10, Charge	22.79
5–12, Credit	16.20CR
5–15, Charge	12.00
5–26, Charge	20.40
6–1, Billing date	

Finance charge: 1.8% of the average daily balance

32. Previous balance $82.31

6–5, Charge	$12.16
6–15, Payment	25.00CR
6–17, Charge	33.38
6–20, Charge	41.00
7–1, Billing date	
7–8, Charge	7.83
7–10, Charge	16.40
7–12, Charge	76.70
7–14, Credit	41.00CR
8–1, Billing date	

Finance charge: 1.5% of the average daily balance

33. Previous balance $63.94

9–12, Credit	$ 14.30CR
9–16, Charge	44.80
9–25, Cash advance	75.00
10–10, Billing date	
10–13, Charge	4.70
10–20, Charge	16.35
10–30, Charge	21.25
11–5, Payment	100.00CR
11–10, Billing date	

Finance charge: 1.55% of the average daily balance

34. Previous balance $180.00

3–18, Charge	$ 27.62
3–20, Credit	33.28CR
3–30, Cash advance	100.00
4–3, Payment	200.00CR
4–15, Billing date	
4–18, Cash advance	50.00
4–23, Charge	72.16
4–30, Charge	61.14
5–4, Payment	75.00CR
5–11, Charge	22.17
5–15, Billing date	

Finance charge: 1.6% of the average daily balance

Section 12.6 Installment plans

A second type of consumer credit is credit in return for a series of equal payments at equal intervals over a fixed period of time. This credit, called the **installment plan,** is used in the purchase of "big ticket" items, such as automobiles, furniture, and major appliances. The major features of the installment plan are the down payment, the amount financed, and the amount and schedule of payments.

An accepted principle of the installment plan is that the buyer pay a part of the cash price in the form of a **down payment** or **trade-in.** This creates a sense of ownership for the buyer and provides a safety margin for the vendor. The amount of down payment varies according to the item purchased; for furniture and appliances, 10% of the cash price is a common figure.*

The cash price minus the down payment or trade-in is the **amount financed.**† The sum of the cash price, the finance charge, and any other charges is called the **deferred payment price.**

The **schedule of payments** is determined by dividing the deferred payment price minus the total down payment into a series of equal partial payments. There are two factors to consider: First, the amount of the payment should be relative to the buyer's income and credit status and should correlate with the buyer's pay period. Second, the unpaid balance should be no greater than the resale value of the merchandise.

*The credit rating of the customer may also influence the amount of the down payment.

†The amount financed is also called the unpaid balance of the cash price. Actually, the amount financed may include other items, but these are not discussed in this text.

Example 1 To purchase a new car, Terry Bacon agreed to pay $500 down and a finance charge of 9% per year of the amount financed. If the cash price was $9,882, and if Terry paid off the debt in 48 monthly payments, what was (a) the amount of the finance charge, (b) the deferred payment price, and (c) the monthly payment?

Solution

a. ($9,882 − $500) × 0.09 × 4 yrs. = $3,377.52 Amount of finance charge

b.

	$ 9,882.00	Cash price
+	3,377.52	Finance charge
	$13,259.52	Deferred payment price

c.

	$13,259.52	Deferred payment price
−	500.00	Down payment
	$12,759.52	

$12,759.52 ÷ 48 = $265.82333

Since the division does not result in an even number of cents, the monthly payment would likely be $265.82 for 47 months and $265.98 for the final month.

	$12,493.54	($265.82 × 47)
+	265.98	
	$12,759.52	

Example 2 Sarah Compton purchased a refrigerator with a cash price of $468.95 from a department store. Sarah paid $46.90 down and $26.26 per month for 18 months. Find (a) the amount financed, (b) the deferred payment price, and (c) the finance charge.

Solution

a.

	$468.95	Cash price
−	46.90	Down payment
	$422.05	Amount financed

b.

	$472.68	($26.26 × 18)
+	46.90	Down payment
	$519.58	Deferred payment price

c.

	$519.58	Deferred payment price
−	468.95	Cash price
	$ 50.63	Finance charge

Businesses offering installment plans must provide their customers with a description of the financing. This description must be in printed form (usually a sales contract) and clearly state the terms of the plan, including the items covered in the previous examples, the annual rate, the charge for default or delinquency, and the penalty for prepayment of principal. A sample of the disclosure information required by Regulation Z is shown in figure 12.4.

Figure 12.4
Disclosure information required by Regulation Z

Seller's Name: ______________________ Contract #________

____

RETAIL INSTALLMENT CONTRACT AND SECURITY AGREEMENT

The undersigned (herein called Purchaser, whether one or more) purchases from ______________(seller) and grants to ______________ a security interest in, subject to the terms and conditions hereof, the following described property.

QUANTITY	DESCRIPTION	AMOUNT	
Description of Trade-in:			
	Sales Tax		
	Total		

PURCHASER'S NAME______________________
PURCHASER'S ADDRESS______________________
CITY__________STATE________ZIP________

1. CASH PRICE $________
2. LESS: CASH DOWN PAYMENT $________
3. TRADE-IN ________
4. TOTAL DOWN PAYMENT ________ $________
5. UNPAID BALANCE OF CASH PRICE $________
6. OTHER CHARGES:
   ______________ $________
   ______________ ________
7. AMOUNT FINANCED $________
8. **FINANCE CHARGE** $________
9. TOTAL OF PAYMENTS $________
10. DEFERRED PAYMENT PRICE (1+6+8) $________
11. **ANNUAL PERCENTAGE RATE** ________%

Insurance Agreement

The purchase of insurance coverage is voluntary and not required for credit. (Type of Ins.) insurance coverage is available at a cost of $__________ for the term of credit.

I desire insurance coverage

Signed______________ Date________

I do not desire insurance coverage

Signed______________ Date________

Purchaser hereby agrees to pay to______________ ______________ at their offices shown above the "TOTAL OF PAYMENTS" shown above in ________ monthly installments of $________(final payment to be $________) the first installment being payable ________ 19____, and all subsequent installments on the same day of each consecutive month until paid in full. The finance charge applies from (Date)

Signed______________________

Notice to Buyer: You are entitled to a copy of the contract you sign. You have the right to pay in advance the unpaid balance of this contract and obtain a partial refund of the finance charge based on the "Actuarial Method." [Any other method of computation may be so identified, for example, "Rule of 78's," "Sum of the Digits," etc.]

This form, when properly completed, will show how a creditor may comply with the disclosure requirements of the provisions of paragraphs (b) and (c) of §226.8 of Regulation Z for the type of credit extended in this example. This form is intended solely for purposes of demonstration and it is not the only format which will permit a creditor to comply with disclosure requirements of Regulation Z.

Exercises for Section 12.6

In problems 1–10, the cash price of an item is given along with the percent of the amount financed that is the finance charge. For the given down payment and number of monthly payments, find (a) the amount of the finance charge, (b) the deferred payment price, and (c) the monthly payment.

1. Cash price of \$882.14, finance charge of 10% per year of amount financed, down payment of \$100.00, 18 monthly payments
2. Cash price of \$661.23, finance charge of 12% per year of amount financed, down payment of \$50.00, 12 monthly payments
3. Cash price of \$1,052.18, finance charge of 11% per year of amount financed, down payment of \$150.00, 12 monthly payments
4. Cash price of \$1,623.34, finance charge of 8% per year of amount financed, down payment of \$162.33, 18 monthly payments
5. Cash price of \$1,612.26, finance charge of 9% per year of amount financed, down payment of \$225.00, 18 monthly payments
6. Cash price of \$2,549.34, finance charge of $9\frac{1}{2}\%$ per year of amount financed, down payment of \$401.72, 24 monthly payments
7. Cash price of \$3,271.60, finance charge of $8\frac{1}{2}\%$ per year of amount financed, down payment of \$375.46, 24 monthly payments
8. Cash price of \$4,923.36, finance charge of $10\frac{1}{4}\%$ per year of amount financed, down payment of \$492.34, 30 monthly payments
9. Cash price of \$4,239.45, finance charge of $7\frac{3}{4}\%$ per year of amount financed, down payment of \$518.27, 36 monthly payments
10. Cash price of \$4,332.60, finance charge of $8\frac{3}{4}\%$ per year of amount financed, down payment of \$421.18, 36 monthly payments

In problems 11–20, the cash price of an item is given along with the down payment, the amount paid per month, and the number of months payments are to be made. Find (a) the amount financed, (b) the deferred payment price, and (c) the finance charge.

11. Cash price of \$511.25, down payment of \$75.00, monthly payments of \$21.85 for 24 months
12. Cash price of \$824.11, down payment of \$122.14, monthly payments of \$46.02 for 18 months
13. Cash price of \$421.18, down payment of \$45.26, monthly payments of \$32.80 for 12 months
14. Cash price of \$729.18, down payment of \$72.92, monthly payments of \$43.07 for 18 months

15. Cash price of $1,124.18, down payment of $172.18, monthly payments of $50.84 for 24 months

16. Cash price of $1,021.11, down payment of $212.14, monthly payments of $75.17 for 12 months

17. Cash price of $992.95, down payment of $110.72, monthly payments of $55.91 for 18 months

18. Cash price of $1,795.92, down payment of $333.21, monthly payments of $64.60 for 30 months

19. Cash price of $2,892.11, down payment of $363.81, monthly payments of $89.71 for 36 months

20. Cash price of $2,214.87, down payment of $385.75, monthly payments of $66.05 for 36 months

21. Judy Anderson purchased a living-room suite for $321.18 down and a finance charge of 8% per year of the amount financed. If the cash price was $2,163.33, and if Judy paid off the furniture in 20 monthly payments, find (a) the amount of the finance charge, (b) the deferred payment price, and (c) the monthly payment.

22. Tom Phillips purchased a washing machine for $60.00 down and $42.98 per month for 12 months. If the cash price of the machine was $512.42, find (a) the amount financed, (b) the deferred payment price, and (c) the finance charge.

Section 12.7 The annual percentage rate

A key feature of the truth-in-lending legislation is the requirement that the seller disclose not only the amount of the finance charge but also the annual percent. Because interest is normally expressed as a rate per annum, the requirement that finance charges also be expressed as an annual rate provides the consumer with a truer picture of the cost of consumer credit.

As defined by Regulation Z, the **annual percentage rate** is found by multiplying the unit-period rate by the number of unit-periods in a given year. The regulation further states that the computation must be accurate to the nearest quarter of 1% and that payments are applied first to the finance charge and any remainder to the unpaid balance of the amount financed.

In open-end credit, the unit period is normally one month, and the unit-period rate is the percent per month charge on the unpaid or average daily balance. Thus, a charge of 1% per month is an annual percentage rate (APR) of $1\% \times 12 = 12\%$, $1\frac{1}{2}\%$ per month is an APR of $1\frac{1}{2}\% \times 12 = 18\%$, and $3\frac{1}{2}\%$ per month is an APR of 42%.

For installment plans, the computation is more involved, and APR tables have been prepared by the government to simplify the computation. A portion of these tables is found in appendix K at the end of the book. To calculate the APR using appendix K,

Step 1 Divide the finance charge by the total amount financed and multiply by \$100. (This gives the finance charge per \$100 of the amount to be financed.)

Step 2 Find the number of payments in the first column of appendix K. Follow horizontally across this row to the column with the amount nearest the value obtained in step 1. The top of this column shows the annual percentage rate.

The sample page from appendix K shown on page 388 can be used for the next two examples.

Example 1 An installment contract for a color television set contains the following information: cash price of \$695.00, total down payment of \$150.00, deferred payment price of \$799.25. What is the annual percentage rate if the plan calls for 24 monthly payments?

Solution

\$799.25	Deferred payment price
− 695.00	Cash price
\$104.25	Finance charge

\$695.00	Cash price
− 150.00	Down payment
\$545.00	Amount financed

Step 1: $\frac{\$104.25}{\$545.00} \times \$100.00 = \$19.13$

Step 2: In line 24 of appendix K, the nearest value to \$19.13 is \$19.24. The top of this column shows that the annual percentage rate is 17.5%.

SAMPLE PAGE FROM TABLE FOR COMPUTING ANNUAL PERCENTAGE RATE FOR LEVEL MONTHLY PAYMENT PLANS

NUMBER OF PAYMENTS	ANNUAL PERCENTAGE RATE															
	14.00%	14.25%	14.50%	14.75%	15.00%	15.25%	15.50%	15.75%	16.00%	16.25%	16.50%	16.75%	17.00%	17.25%	17.50%	17.75%
	(FINANCE CHARGE PER $100 OF AMOUNT FINANCED)															
1	1.17	1.19	1.21	1.23	1.25	1.27	1.29	1.31	1.33	1.35	1.37	1.40	1.42	1.44	1.46	1.48
2	1.75	1.78	1.82	1.85	1.88	1.91	1.94	1.97	2.00	2.04	2.07	2.10	2.13	2.16	2.19	2.22
3	2.34	2.38	2.43	2.47	2.51	2.55	2.59	2.64	2.68	2.72	2.76	2.80	2.85	2.89	2.93	2.97
4	2.93	2.99	3.04	3.09	3.14	3.20	3.25	3.30	3.36	3.41	3.46	3.51	3.57	3.62	3.67	3.73
5	3.53	3.59	3.65	3.72	3.78	3.84	3.91	3.97	4.04	4.10	4.16	4.23	4.29	4.35	4.42	4.48
6	4.12	4.20	4.27	4.35	4.42	4.49	4.57	4.64	4.72	4.79	4.87	4.94	5.02	5.09	5.17	5.24
7	4.72	4.81	4.89	4.98	5.06	5.15	5.23	5.32	5.40	5.49	5.58	5.66	5.75	5.83	5.92	6.00
8	5.32	5.42	5.51	5.61	5.71	5.80	5.90	6.00	6.09	6.19	6.29	6.38	6.48	6.58	6.67	6.77
9	5.92	6.03	6.14	6.25	6.35	6.46	6.57	6.68	6.78	6.89	7.00	7.11	7.22	7.32	7.43	7.54
10	6.53	6.65	6.77	6.88	7.00	7.12	7.24	7.36	7.48	7.60	7.72	7.84	7.96	8.08	8.19	8.31
11	7.14	7.27	7.40	7.53	7.66	7.79	7.92	8.05	8.18	8.31	8.44	8.57	8.70	8.83	8.96	9.09
12	7.74	7.89	8.03	8.17	8.31	8.45	8.59	8.74	8.88	9.02	9.16	9.30	9.45	9.59	9.73	9.87
13	8.36	8.51	8.66	8.81	8.97	9.12	9.27	9.43	9.58	9.73	9.89	10.04	10.20	10.35	10.50	10.66
14	8.97	9.13	9.30	9.46	9.63	9.79	9.96	10.12	10.29	10.45	10.62	10.78	10.95	11.11	11.28	11.45
15	9.59	9.76	9.94	10.11	10.29	10.47	10.64	10.82	11.00	11.17	11.35	11.53	11.71	11.88	12.06	12.24
16	10.20	10.39	10.58	10.77	10.95	11.14	11.33	11.52	11.71	11.90	12.09	12.28	12.46	12.65	12.84	13.03
17	10.82	11.02	11.22	11.42	11.62	11.82	12.02	12.22	12.42	12.62	12.83	13.03	13.23	13.43	13.63	13.83
18	11.45	11.66	11.87	12.08	12.29	12.50	12.72	12.93	13.14	13.35	13.57	13.78	13.99	14.21	14.42	14.64
19	12.07	12.30	12.52	12.74	12.97	13.19	13.41	13.64	13.86	14.09	14.31	14.54	14.76	14.99	15.22	15.44
20	12.70	12.93	13.17	13.41	13.64	13.88	14.11	14.35	14.59	14.82	15.06	15.30	15.54	15.77	16.01	16.25
21	13.33	13.58	13.82	14.07	14.32	14.57	14.82	15.06	15.31	15.56	15.81	16.06	16.31	16.56	16.81	17.07
22	13.96	14.22	14.48	14.74	15.00	15.26	15.52	15.78	16.04	16.30	16.57	16.83	17.09	17.36	17.62	17.88
23	14.59	14.87	15.14	15.41	15.68	15.96	16.23	16.50	16.78	17.05	17.32	17.60	17.88	18.15	18.43	18.70
24	15.23	15.51	15.80	16.08	16.37	16.65	16.94	17.22	17.51	17.80	18.09	18.37	18.66	18.95	19.24	19.53
25	15.87	16.17	16.46	16.76	17.06	17.35	17.65	17.95	18.25	18.55	18.85	19.15	19.45	19.75	20.05	20.36
26	16.51	16.82	17.13	17.44	17.75	18.06	18.37	18.68	18.99	19.30	19.62	19.93	20.24	20.56	20.87	21.19
27	17.15	17.47	17.80	18.12	18.44	18.76	19.09	19.41	19.74	20.06	20.39	20.71	21.04	21.37	21.69	22.02
28	17.80	18.13	18.47	18.80	19.14	19.47	19.81	20.15	20.48	20.82	21.16	21.50	21.84	22.18	22.52	22.86
29	18.45	18.79	19.14	19.49	19.83	20.18	20.53	20.88	21.23	21.58	21.94	22.29	22.64	22.99	23.35	23.70
30	19.10	19.45	19.81	20.17	20.54	20.90	21.26	21.62	21.99	22.35	22.72	23.08	23.45	23.81	24.18	24.55
31	19.75	20.12	20.49	20.87	21.24	21.61	21.99	22.37	22.74	23.12	23.50	23.88	24.26	24.64	25.02	25.40
32	20.40	20.79	21.17	21.56	21.95	22.33	22.72	23.11	23.50	23.89	24.28	24.68	25.07	25.46	25.86	26.25
33	21.06	21.46	21.85	22.25	22.65	23.06	23.46	23.86	24.26	24.67	25.07	25.48	25.88	26.29	26.70	27.11
34	21.72	22.13	22.54	22.95	23.37	23.78	24.19	24.61	25.03	25.44	25.86	26.28	26.70	27.12	27.54	27.97
35	22.38	22.80	23.23	23.65	24.08	24.51	24.94	25.36	25.79	26.23	26.66	27.09	27.52	27.96	28.39	28.83
36	23.04	23.48	23.92	24.35	24.80	25.24	25.68	26.12	26.57	27.01	27.46	27.90	28.35	28.80	29.25	29.70
37	23.70	24.16	24.61	25.06	25.51	25.97	26.42	26.88	27.34	27.80	28.26	28.72	29.18	29.64	30.10	30.57
38	24.37	24.84	25.30	25.77	26.24	26.70	27.17	27.64	28.11	28.59	29.06	29.53	30.01	30.49	30.96	31.44
39	25.04	25.52	26.00	26.48	26.96	27.44	27.92	28.41	28.89	29.38	29.87	30.36	30.85	31.34	31.83	32.32
40	25.71	26.20	26.70	27.19	27.69	28.18	28.68	29.18	29.68	30.18	30.68	31.18	31.68	32.19	32.69	33.20
41	26.39	26.89	27.40	27.91	28.41	28.92	29.44	29.95	30.46	30.97	31.49	32.01	32.52	33.04	33.56	34.08
42	27.06	27.58	28.10	28.62	29.15	29.67	30.19	30.72	31.25	31.78	32.31	32.84	33.37	33.90	34.44	34.97
43	27.74	28.27	28.81	29.34	29.88	30.42	30.96	31.50	32.04	32.58	33.13	33.67	34.22	34.76	35.31	35.86
44	28.42	28.97	29.52	30.07	30.62	31.17	31.72	32.28	32.83	33.39	33.95	34.51	35.07	35.63	36.19	36.76
45	29.11	29.67	30.23	30.79	31.36	31.92	32.49	33.06	33.63	34.20	34.77	35.35	35.92	36.50	37.08	37.66
46	29.79	30.36	30.94	31.52	32.10	32.68	33.26	33.84	34.43	35.01	35.60	36.19	36.78	37.37	37.96	38.56
47	30.48	31.07	31.66	32.25	32.84	33.44	34.03	34.63	35.23	35.83	36.43	37.04	37.64	38.25	38.86	39.46
48	31.17	31.77	32.37	32.98	33.59	34.20	34.81	35.42	36.03	36.65	37.27	37.88	38.50	39.13	39.75	40.37
49	31.86	32.48	33.09	33.71	34.34	34.96	35.59	36.21	36.84	37.47	38.10	38.74	39.37	40.01	40.65	41.29
50	32.55	33.18	33.82	34.45	35.09	35.73	36.37	37.01	37.65	38.30	38.94	39.59	40.24	40.89	41.55	42.20
51	33.25	33.89	34.54	35.19	35.84	36.49	37.15	37.81	38.46	39.12	39.79	40.45	41.11	41.78	42.45	43.12
52	33.95	34.61	35.27	35.93	36.60	37.27	37.94	38.61	39.28	39.96	40.63	41.31	41.99	42.67	43.36	44.04
53	34.65	35.32	36.00	36.68	37.36	38.04	38.72	39.41	40.10	40.79	41.48	42.17	42.87	43.57	44.27	44.97
54	35.35	36.04	36.73	37.42	38.12	38.82	39.52	40.22	40.92	41.63	42.33	43.04	43.75	44.47	45.18	45.90
55	36.05	36.76	37.46	38.17	38.88	39.60	40.31	41.03	41.74	42.47	43.19	43.91	44.64	45.37	46.10	46.83
56	36.76	37.48	38.20	38.92	39.65	40.38	41.11	41.84	42.57	43.31	44.05	44.79	45.53	46.27	47.02	47.77
57	37.47	38.20	38.94	39.68	40.42	41.16	41.91	42.65	43.40	44.15	44.91	45.66	46.42	47.18	47.94	48.71
58	38.18	38.93	39.68	40.43	41.19	41.95	42.71	43.47	44.23	45.00	45.77	46.54	47.32	48.09	48.87	49.65
59	38.89	39.66	40.42	41.19	41.96	42.74	43.51	44.29	45.07	45.85	46.64	47.42	48.21	49.01	49.80	50.60
60	39.61	40.39	41.17	41.95	42.74	43.53	44.32	45.11	45.91	46.71	47.51	48.31	49.12	49.92	50.73	51.55

Example 2 Gene Roberts purchased a set of four automobile tires by making six monthly payments of \$33.56. He received \$12.00 credit for his old tires as a trade-in. The cash price was \$51.00 per tire. What annual percentage rate did Gene pay as a result of buying on credit?

Solution

\$201.36	(\$33.56 × 6)
+ 12.00	Trade-in
\$213.36	Deferred payment price

\$213.36	Deferred payment price
− 204.00	Cash price (\$51 × 4)
\$ 9.36	Finance charge

\$204.00	Cash price
− 12.00	Trade-in
\$192.00	Amount financed

$$\frac{\$9.36}{\$192.00} \times \$100.00 = \$4.88$$

In line 6 of appendix K, the nearest value to \$4.88 is \$4.87; hence, the APR is 16.5%.

The annual percentage rate of 16.5% in example 2 means that if interest is computed at 16.5% only on the remaining balance each month, and if the \$33.56 payment is applied to the outstanding balance according to the United States Rule, then the six payments will equal the \$192.00 amount financed plus the \$9.36 finance charge. This is illustrated in the schedule of payments shown in the following table (the final balance of −\$.03 is due to rounding and the approximate annual percentage rate of 16.5%):

(1) Month	(2) Previous Balance	(3) Payment	(4) Interest (Prt = I)		(5) Credited to Balance (3)–(4)	(6) New Balance (2)–(5)
1	\$192.00	\$33.56	$\$192.00 \times .165 \times \frac{1}{12}$	= \$2.64	\$ 30.92	\$161.08
2	161.08	33.56	$161.08 \times .165 \times \frac{1}{12}$	= 2.21	31.35	129.73
3	129.73	33.56	$129.73 \times .165 \times \frac{1}{12}$	= 1.78	31.78	97.95
4	97.95	33.56	$97.95 \times .165 \times \frac{1}{12}$	= 1.35	32.21	65.74
5	65.74	33.56	$65.74 \times .165 \times \frac{1}{12}$	= 0.90	32.66	33.08
6	33.08	33.56	$33.08 \times .165 \times \frac{1}{12}$	= 0.45	33.11	− .03
				\$9.33	\$192.03	

Section 12.8 The constant ratio method

An approximation of the APR can be obtained by using a formula called the **constant ratio method.** The formula is:

■ (12–1)
$$i = \frac{2md}{B(n + 1)}$$

where i = annual interest rate, m = number of possible payments in one year, n = total number of payments, d = finance charge, and B = amount financed. The constant ratio method owes its name to the fact that the ratio of the interest to the total partial payment remains constant for each payment.

The constant ratio method is not sufficiently accurate to be used in place of the APR tables. However, the formula may be used to obtain a reasonable approximation of the APR should the tables not be available.

The constant ratio method computes an interest rate higher than the APR tables, as shown in example 1.

Example 1 Thelma Fricks purchased a vacuum cleaner by paying $15.00 down and $8.24 per month for six months. If the cash price was $59.95, find the annual percentage rate using the constant ratio formula.

Solution

$59.95	Cash price
− 15.00	Down payment
$44.95	Amount financed

$49.44	($8.24 × 6)
− 44.95	Amount financed
$ 4.49	Finance charge

$m = 12$, $n = 6$, $d = \$4.49$, $B = \$44.95$

$$i = \frac{2md}{B(n + 1)}$$

$$= \frac{2 \times 12 \times \$4.49}{\$44.95 \times 7}$$

$$= 0.3424757$$

$$= 34.25\%$$

Note that by the APR tables in appendix K, the annual percentage rate is 33.5%.

Exercises for Sections 12.7 and 12.8

In problems 1–6, find the annual percentage rate for revolving charge accounts with the given monthly interest rate.

1. 1.25%	3. 2.5%	5. 1.8%
2. 2.25%	4. 1.55%	6. 1.75%

In problems 7–15, use appendix K to find the annual percentage rate for the given installment contract.

7. Cash price of $472, down payment of $75, deferred payment price of $525, 18 monthly payments
8. Cash price of $782.40, down payment of $110.00, deferred payment price of $896.62, 24 monthly payments
9. Cash price of $1,287.40, down payment of $225.00, deferred payment price of $1,575.80, 40 monthly payments
10. Cash price of $1,896.52, down payment of $425.50, deferred payment price of $2,245.80, 36 monthly payments
11. Cash price of $2,692.49, down payment of $510.25, deferred payment price of $2,972.75, 26 monthly payments
12. Cash price of $979.42, down payment of $220.15, deferred payment price of $1,142.60, 30 monthly payments
13. Cash price of $1,475.83, down payment of $283.49, deferred payment price of $1,695.43, 28 monthly payments
14. Cash price of $1,064.89, down payment of $106.49, deferred payment price of $1,289.09, 42 monthly payments
15. Cash price of $4,287.50, down payment of $723.89, deferred payment price of $4,893.80, 22 monthly payments

In problems 16–20, use appendix K to find the annual percentage rate when an item with the given cash price is paid for by making the given payments.

16. Cash price of $485.42, 24 monthly payments of $22.79 each
17. Cash price of $859.63, 12 monthly payments of $77.82 each
18. Cash price of $1,152.16, 15 monthly payments of $85.86 each
19. Cash price of $987.24, 30 monthly payments of $38.25 each
20. Cash price of $647.83, 18 monthly payments of $40.96 each

In problems 21–25, use the constant ratio formula to compute the annual percentage rate.

21. Cash price of $743.85, down payment of $50.00, 18 monthly payments of $42.65 each

22. Cash price of $1,142.86, down payment of $225.00, 12 monthly payments of $83.15 each

23. Cash price of $1,857.64, down payment of $410.00, 24 monthly payments of $71.20 each

24. Cash price of $858.19, down payment of $95.00, 20 monthly payments of $43.66 each

25. Cash price of $1,042.80, down payment of $140.00, 18 monthly payments of $55.11 each

26. Bob Johnson purchased a new outboard motor by paying $75.00 down and $54.03 a month for 18 months. If the cash price was $957.75, find the annual percentage rate Bob is paying by (a) using appendix K and (b) using the constant ratio formula.

27. Sylvia Stephens purchased a new sewing machine by paying $50.00 down and $27.66 a month for 24 months. If the cash price was $621.80, find the annual percentage rate Sylvia is paying by (a) using appendix K and (b) using the constant ratio formula.

Section 12.9 The Rule of 78

Installment contracts are designed to pay off the principal and interest charge (finance charge) by a series of partial payments; thus, each payment is part principal and part interest. Should the full amount of the obligation be paid prior to the maturity date, the borrower may be entitled to a rebate on the unearned interest.

The Truth-in-Lending Act requires the lender to disclose the method of calculating such a rebate when the loan is initiated. In the language of the act, the lender must give "a statement of the amount or method of computation of any charge that may be deducted from the amount of any rebate of such unearned finance charge that will be credited to an obligation or refunded to the customer."*

A method commonly used to calculate this rebate is called the **Rule of 78,** or the sum-of-the-balances method. This method assumes that on a 12-month loan, 12 units of principal are outstanding the first month, 11 units are outstanding the second month, 10 units are outstanding the third month, and so on, to the

*If the credit contract does not provide for any rebate of unearned finance charges upon prepayment in full, this must be disclosed.

last or twelfth month, when 1 unit of principal is outstanding. Since the sum of the numbers from 1 to 12 is 78, the total finance charge is divided into 78 units (hence, the name Rule of 78).

Division of the finance charge into 78 units has the following effect on the amount of the rebate: Clearly, there is no rebate if the loan is not paid off until the end of the twelfth month or the maturity date, but if the loan is paid off at the end of the eleventh month, the borrower is entitled to a rebate of $\frac{1}{78}$ of the finance charge. If the loan is paid off at the end of the tenth month, the borrower is entitled to a rebate of $\frac{1}{78} + \frac{2}{78} = \frac{1+2}{78} = \frac{3}{78}$ of the finance charge, and if the loan is paid off at the end of the ninth month, the borrower is entitled to a rebate of $\frac{1+2+3}{78}$ of the finance charge. In general, if a 12-month loan is paid in full at the end of the nth month, then the amount of the rebate R is given by the formula

■ (12–2) $$R = \frac{1 + 2 + \ldots + (12-n)}{78} \times \text{Finance charge}$$

Example 1 Beverly McMillan purchased a set of golf clubs on a 12-month installment contract that included a finance charge of \$40. If she decided to pay off the entire contract at the end of the seventh month, how much would her rebate be under the Rule of 78?

Solution

$n = 7$ and $12 - n = 12 - 7 = 5$

Hence, by formula 12–2,

$$R = \frac{1 + 2 + 3 + 4 + 5}{78} \times \$40$$

$$= \frac{15}{78} \times \$40$$

$$= \$7.69$$

Rebate calculations for contracts other than 12 months duration are the same, except that the number of units is different. For a six-month loan, there are $1 + 2 + 3 + 4 + 5 + 6 = 21$ units; for an 18-month loan, there are 171 units; for a two-year loan, there are 300 units; and so on.

A general formula for the amount of rebate under the sum-of-the-balances method is as follows: If R = amount of rebate, m = total number of months, and n = m minus number of months before prepay, then

■ (12–3) $$R = \frac{n(n + 1)}{m(m + 1)} \times \text{Finance charge}$$

In example 1, $m = 12$, $n = 12 - 7 = 5$, and the finance charge was \$40; thus

$$R = \frac{5(6)}{12(13)} \times \$40$$

$$= \frac{5}{26} \times \$40$$

$$= \$7.69$$

Example 2 To get a new roof put on his house, Danny Swisshelm signed a contract calling for a finance charge of \$234.00 and 24 monthly payments of \$84.75. At the end of the fifteenth month, Danny decided to pay off the entire debt. Under the sum-of-the-balances method, what rebate did Danny receive?

Solution

$m = 24$, $n = 24 - 15 = 9$

$$R = \frac{9(10)}{24(25)} \times \$234$$

$$= \frac{3}{20} \times \$234$$

$$= \$35.10$$

Example 3 K. May McCluskey purchased a vacuum cleaner for a finance charge of \$18 and six payments of \$23 per month. At the end of the fourth month, Mrs. McCluskey decided to pay off the entire amount of the obligation. Find (a) the amount of the rebate and (b) the amount of the final payment.

Solution

a. $m = 6$, $n = 6 - 4 = 2$

$$R = \frac{2(3)}{6(7)} \times \$18$$

$$= \frac{1}{7} \times \$18$$

$$= \$2.57$$

b. If the debt is to be paid off at the end of the fourth month, three payments have been made with three remaining. The remaining payments total $3 \times \$23.00 = \$69.00$. With the rebate, the final payment is $\$69.00 - \$2.57 = \$66.43$.

Exercises for Section 12.9

In problems 1–5, use the Rule of 78 to compute the rebate when a 12-month installment contract with the given finance charge is paid off at the end of the given month.

1. Finance charge of \$60, paid off at the end of the fifth month
2. Finance charge of \$18, paid off at the end of the third month
3. Finance charge of \$24, paid off at the end of the tenth month
4. Finance charge of \$36, paid off at the end of the fourth month
5. Finance charge of \$48, paid off at the end of the eighth month

In problems 6–10, use the sum-of-the-balances method to compute the rebate when an installment contract of the given duration with the given finance charge is paid off at the end of the given month.

6. Two-year contract, \$180 finance charge, paid off at the end of the twelfth month
7. 18-month contract, \$110 finance charge, paid off at the end of the tenth month
8. Six-month contract, \$24 finance charge, paid off at the end of the third month
9. 14-month contract, \$90 finance charge, paid off at the end of the ninth month
10. 20-month contract, \$160 finance charge, paid off at the end of the fourteenth month
11. Bob Jacobs purchased a color television set on a one-year installment contract that included a finance charge of \$68. If Bob paid off the contract at the end of the eighth month, what was his rebate?
12. Jennifer Childress signed a one-year installment contract to purchase some furniture. If the contract included a finance charge of \$74, and if Jennifer paid off the contract at the end of the fifth month, what was her rebate?
13. Craig Ross bought some new equipment for his radiator shop on a 20-month installment contract that included a finance charge of \$236. He was then able to pay off the contract at the end of the sixteenth month. How much was his rebate?
14. Diane Dennis signed an 18-month installment contract to buy some new display items for her clothing shop. If the contract included a finance charge of \$210, and if Diane paid off the contract at the end of the fourteenth month, what was her rebate?

15. Ralph Thomas bought a fishing boat on an installment plan of \$52 a month for one year. At the end of the seventh month, Ralph paid off the contract. If the finance charge was \$64, find the amount of the final payment.

16. Marcia Brennan purchased a refrigerator for a finance charge of \$36 and sixteen monthly payments of \$63 each. At the end of the sixth month, Marcia paid off the contract. What was the amount of the final payment?

Glossary

Amount financed The difference between the cash price and the down payment or trade-in.

Annual percentage rate The cost of credit expressed as an annual percent in accordance with the regulations contained in Regulation Z of the Truth-in-Lending Act.

Average daily balance The sum of the daily balances during a billing cycle divided by the number of days in the cycle.

Constant ratio method A formula for approximating the annual percentage rate. The formula is: $i = \frac{2md}{B(n + 1)}$ where i is the annual interest rate, m is the number of possible payments in one year, n is the total number of payments, d is the finance charge, and B is the amount financed.

Daily balance The previous balance plus purchases and cash advances, less any payments or credits, and excluding any unpaid finance charges made during the billing period.

Deferred payment price The sum of the cash price, the finance charge, and any other charges.

Down payment In an installment contract, a portion of the cash price paid at the time of the sale.

Finance charge The total of all costs to the buyer for obtaining credit, including interest, credit investigation fees, credit life insurance, and carrying charges.

Installment plan A payment plan calling for a series of equal payments over a fixed period of time.

Open-end credit A payment plan in which a finance charge (depending on the balance of the account) is imposed at the end of each billing period and in which the number of payments is not fixed.

Payment due date The date by which full payment must be made on an open-end account to avoid a finance charge.

Regulation Z A Federal Reserve System document implementing the provisions of the Truth-in-Lending Act.

Rule of 78 A method used to calculate the amount of the rebate when the full amount owed under an installment contract is paid prior to the maturity date.

Schedule of payments In an installment plan, a series of equal partial payments found by dividing the deferred payment price minus the total down payment by the total number of payments.

Trade-in An item of merchandise accepted as the down payment on an installment plan.

Truth-in-Lending Act A federal disclosure act requiring sellers to inform buyers of the cost of credit.

United States Rule A method established by a decision of the United States Supreme Court for crediting partial payments toward a debt. The fundamental principle of the rule is that a partial payment is applied first to the interest on the unpaid balance, with any remainder applied to the reduction of the principal.

Review test

In problems 1–5, indicate whether the statement is true or false.

1. A principle of the United States Rule is that if the partial payment does not exceed the accumulated interest, the partial payment is applied only to the principal for that period.
2. The Truth-in-Lending Act was designed to regulate interest charges.
3. In open-end credit, a finance charge is imposed if the entire balance of the account is not paid by the payment due date.
4. The average daily balance is the sum of the daily balances during the billing cycle divided by the number of days in the cycle.
5. The cash price minus the down payment or trade-in is the amount financed.
6. Using the United States Rule, find the amount due at the end of one year on a loan of $600 at 10% if the following payments are made at three-month intervals: $90, $50, $75.
7. Find the new balance after month 2 on the following credit card account if the finance charge is $1\frac{1}{2}$% per month of the unpaid balance:

Month	Previous Balance	Purchases	Payments	Finance Charge	Credited to Balance	New Balance
1	$142.00	$ 0.00	$ 60.00	____	____	____
2	____	200.00	50.00	____	____	____

8. The monthly charge on the following account is 1.8% of the average daily balance. Compute the finance charge. The billing dates fall on the same day of each month.

Previous balance	$160.70
6–20, Charge	$134.50
6–26, Charge	64.48
7–1, Payment	50.00CR
7–10, Billing date	

9. An item of furniture with a cash price of $639.95 is purchased with a payment of $64.00 down, 18 monthly payments, and a finance charge of 11.75% per year of the amount financed. Find (a) the amount of the finance charge, (b) the deferred payment price, and (c) the monthly payment.
10. (a) Compute the rebate on an 18-month installment contract with a finance charge of $75.00 if the contract is paid off at the end of the eighth month. (b) If the contract called for monthly payments of $36.50, find the amount of the final payment.

CHAPTER 13

Annuities

Chapter Objectives

I. Learn the meaning of the following terms:

Annuity, 399
Period of an annuity, 399
Term of an annuity, 399
Annuity certain, 399
Ordinary annuity, 399
Annuity due, 399
Present value of an annuity, 405

II. Understand:

The difference between an ordinary annuity and an annuity due, 399
The accumulated amount of an ordinary annuity, 399–400
The present value of an ordinary annuity, 405–406
The accumulated amount of an annuity due, 409
The present value of an annuity due, 413

III. Calculate:

The accumulated amount of an ordinary annuity, 401–403
The number of payments of an ordinary annuity, 403
The present value of an ordinary annuity, 406–407
The accumulated amount of an annuity due, 410–411
The number of payments of an annuity due, 410
The present value of an annuity due, 413–414

Section 13.1 Introduction

An **annuity** is a series of payments at regular intervals. The payments are normally equal but need not be so. The time interval between payments is called the **period,** and the **term** of an annuity is the time from the beginning of the first period to the end of the last period. Examples of annuities are Social Security payments, mortgage payments on a house, endowments, and installment plan payments.

The type of annuity to be studied in this chapter is the **annuity certain.** The beginning and ending dates of an annuity certain are specified.* There are two basic kinds of annuity certain. If the payment is made at the end of a period, the annuity is called an **ordinary annuity;** if the payment is made at the beginning of a period, the annuity is called an **annuity due.** (See figure 13.1.)

Figure 13.1
Comparison of payment schedules of an ordinary annuity and an annuity due

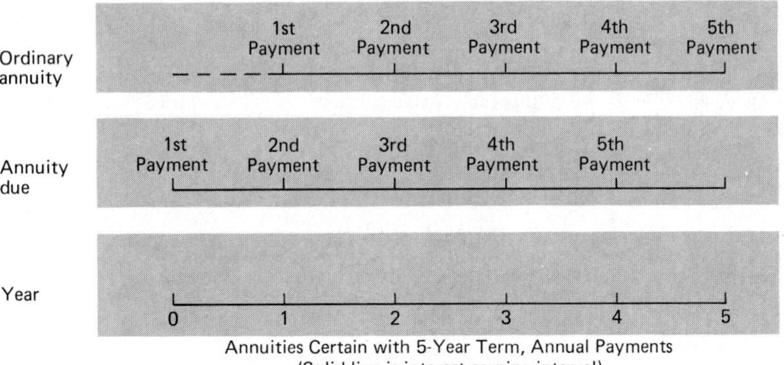

Annuities Certain with 5-Year Term, Annual Payments
(Solid line is interest earning interval)

Section 13.2 Ordinary annuities

To understand an ordinary annuity and its formulas, suppose that on May 1 of each year for five years, $1 is deposited in a savings account paying 10% interest compounded annually. What is the accumulated amount immediately following the last deposit?

The fifth deposit, having just been made, earns no interest; the fourth deposit earns one year's interest; the third deposit earns two years' interest; and so on. By formula 11–2 for compound interest (using appendix C),

Fifth deposit	\$1	= \$1.00000000
Fourth deposit	\$1 $(1.10)^1$	= 1.10000000
Third deposit	\$1 $(1.10)^2$	= 1.21000000
Second deposit	\$1 $(1.10)^3$	= 1.33100000
First deposit	\$1 $(1.10)^4$	= 1.46410000
Accumulated deposit		= \$6.10510000

*If either the beginning or ending date of an annuity is not specified, then the annuity is called a **contingent annuity.** Proceeds of a life insurance policy that are paid in installments are an example of this kind of annuity, in that the beginning payment is contingent on the death of the insured.

The accumulated amount for deposits of \$1 is \$6.10510000. By the same reasoning, it can be shown that had the deposits been \$100 per year, the accumulated amount would be 100 × \$6.10510000 = \$610.510000, and that deposits of \$1,000 per year would result in an accumulated amount of \$1,000 × \$6.10510000 = \$6,105.10000.

This special case leads to a generalization. Consider an ordinary annuity with n payments of \$1 each (n = a counting number) made once a year, and let the annual compound interest rate be i. Then, if the accumulated amount is denoted by $s_{\overline{n}|i}$,

$$s_{\overline{n}|i} = 1 + (1+i) + (1+i)^2 + (1+i)^3 + \cdots + (1+i)^{n-1} \tag{13–1}$$

The right-hand side of this equation can be simplified;* the result is:

■ (13–2)
$$s_{\overline{n}|i} = \frac{(1+i)^n - 1}{i}$$

To demonstrate formula 13–2, consider the previous illustration:

$$\begin{aligned} s_{\overline{5}|0.10} &= \frac{(1.10)^5 - 1}{0.10} \\ &= \frac{1.61051000 - 1}{0.10} \qquad \text{(Appendix C)} \\ &= \frac{.61051000}{0.10} \\ &= 6.1051000 \end{aligned}$$

One final step in the generalization remains. Formula 13–2 is the accumulated amount for payments of \$1. If the payments are P dollars per year, and if the accumulated amount is denoted by S, then

■ (13–3)
$$S = P \cdot s_{\overline{n}|i}$$

Section 13.3 Annuity tables

Annuity computations can be made using a compound interest table such as appendix C. However, the computations are tedious, and for that reason, tables have been prepared for values of $s_{\overline{n}|i}$. Appendix E at the end of the book is such a table. The heading of each page is the value of i; the values of n are in the left-hand column.

*The right-hand side of the equation is in the form of a geometric progression $a + ar + ar^2 + \cdots + ar^{n-1}$, which is equal to $\frac{a(r^n - 1)}{r - 1}$.

Example 1 What is the accumulated amount for annual deposits of \$1,000 in an account paying 8% compounded annually following the twelfth deposit?

Solution

$S = ?, P = \$1{,}000, n = 12, i = 0.08$

$S = P \cdot s_{\overline{n}|i}$

$= \$1{,}000 \cdot s_{\overline{12}|0.08}$

$= \$1{,}000 \times 18.97712646$ (Appendix E)

$= \$18{,}977.12646$

$= \$18{,}977.13$

Exercises for Section 13.3

In problems 1–19, use appendix E and the formula $S = P \cdot s_{\overline{n}|i}$ to find the accumulated amount S when P dollars are invested annually n times in an account paying the given interest rate i compounded annually.

1. $P = \$500, n = 4, i = 12\%$
2. $P = \$800, n = 6, i = 9\%$
3. $P = \$1{,}200, n = 5, i = 8\%$
4. $P = \$1{,}200, n = 8, i = 8\frac{1}{2}\%$
5. $P = \$1{,}600, n = 10, i = 10\%$
6. $P = \$600, n = 15, i = 13\%$
7. $P = \$750, n = 15, i = 9\frac{1}{2}\%$
8. $P = \$400, n = 20, i = 11\%$
9. $P = \$900, n = 40, i = 10\%$
10. $P = \$1{,}300, n = 10, i = 14\%$
11. $P = \$1{,}850, n = 14, i = 15\%$
12. $P = \$1{,}750, n = 22, i = 12\%$
13. $P = \$1{,}250, n = 25, i = 14\%$
14. $P = \$2{,}000, n = 20, i = 8\%$
15. $P = \$3{,}600, n = 18, i = 11\%$
16. $P = \$4{,}750, n = 14, i = 9\%$
17. $P = \$9{,}500, n = 12, i = 8\frac{1}{2}\%$
18. $P = \$6{,}500, n = 25, i = 13\%$
19. $P = \$7{,}000, n = 30, i = 12\%$
20. Carl Jennings decides to start a savings plan by placing \$1,000 a year in a savings account that pays 10% interest compounded annually. How much will Carl have in his savings account after he makes his twentieth deposit?
21. Myra Miller works in a women's clothing store. She wants to open her own shop, so she decides to put \$1,200 a year into a savings account that pays 12% interest compounded annually. How much will she have in her account after she makes her fifth deposit? After she makes her eighth deposit?

22. John Atkins is placing $800 a year in an account that pays 11% interest compounded annually. He intends to use this savings plan to educate his children. How much will John have in the account after he makes his fifteenth deposit?

23. Sarah Stephens is putting $1,600 a year into an account that pays $9\frac{1}{2}\%$ interest compounded annually to save money for a new house. How much will she have in the account after she makes her sixth deposit? After she makes her twelfth deposit?

24. Mechanic Jack Ruse places $2,000 a year in an account paying 13% interest compounded annually to save money to purchase his own auto repair shop. How much will Jack have in the account after he makes his seventh deposit? After he makes his tenth deposit?

25. Janet Richards has decided to put $1,500 a year into an account that pays 10% interest compounded annually so that one day she will be able to open her own business. How much will she have in the account after she makes her fourth deposit? After she makes her seventh deposit?

Section 13.4 Nominal rate

The word *annuity* implies annual payments and a nominal rate, but in practice, the payments and conversion period may be semiannual, quarterly, or monthly.* Analogous to compound interest, formula 13–3 can be used in any annuity calculation as long as the conversion period and the payment period are the same time interval.†

Example 1 Payments of $1,000 are made twice a year and are accumulated at 9% compounded semiannually. What is the accumulated amount following the tenth payment?

Solution

$S = ?, P = \$1{,}000, n = 10, i = \frac{9\%}{2} = 4\frac{1}{2}\% = 0.045$

$$\begin{aligned} S &= P \cdot s_{\overline{n}|i} \\ &= \$1{,}000 \cdot s_{\overline{10}|0.045} \\ &= \$1{,}000 \times 12.28820937 \quad \text{(Appendix E)} \\ &= \$12{,}288.20937 \\ &= \$12{,}288.21 \end{aligned}$$

*__Nominal rate__ and **conversion period** were discussed in section 11.1.

†The conversion period and payment period are not always the same, but such cases are not considered here.

Example 2 To provide for the replacement of machinery, the Krane Company made quarterly deposits of $1,800 in an account that paid 11% interest compounded quarterly. How much was in the fund after the twelfth deposit, and how much interest was earned?

Solution

$S = ?, P = \$1{,}800, n = 12, i = \frac{11\%}{4} = 2\frac{3}{4}\% = 0.0275$

$$
\begin{aligned}
S &= P \cdot s_{\overline{n}|i} \\
&= \$1{,}800 \cdot s_{\overline{12}|0.0275} \\
&= \$1{,}800 \times 13.99213729 \qquad \text{(Appendix E)} \\
&= \$25{,}185.85
\end{aligned}
$$

The total of the deposits is 12 × $1,800 = $21,600; thus, the interest earned is $25,185.85 − $21,600.00 = $3,585.85.

Example 3 How many monthly payments of $150 would it take to accumulate $5,000 if the payments were deposited in an account paying 12% compounded monthly?

Solution

$S = \$5{,}000, P = \$150, n = ?, i = \frac{12\%}{12} = 1\% = 0.01$

$$
\begin{aligned}
S &= P \cdot s_{\overline{n}|i} \\
P \cdot s_{\overline{n}|i} &= S \\
s_{\overline{n}|i} &= \frac{S}{P} \qquad \text{(Dividing both sides by } P\text{)} \\
s_{\overline{n}|0.01} &= \frac{\$5{,}000}{150} \\
&= 33.33333333
\end{aligned}
$$

Appendix E on the page headed 1% shows that the entry nearest to but larger than 33.33333333 is 33.45038766 for $n = 29$. Thus, a minimum of $n = 29$ payments are required. This results in an accumulation of $150 × 33.45038766 = $5,017.56.

Exercises for Section 13.4

In problems 1–10, find the accumulated amount S at the end of the n equal payments of P dollars each into an account that pays the given nominal interest rate.

1. Semiannual payments of $P = \$200$ each, $n = 10$ payments, 8% interest compounded semiannually
2. Semiannual payments of $P = \$350$ each, $n = 15$ payments, 12% interest compounded semiannually
3. Quarterly payments of $P = \$900$ each, $n = 20$ payments, 14% interest compounded quarterly
4. Quarterly payments of $P = \$750$ each, $n = 24$ payments, 10% interest compounded quarterly
5. Monthly payments of $P = \$50$ each, $n = 50$ payments, 12% interest compounded monthly
6. Monthly payments of $P = \$80$ each, $n = 25$ payments, 15% interest compounded monthly
7. Semiannual payments of $P = \$350$ each, $n = 12$ payments, 9% interest compounded semiannually
8. Monthly payments of $P = \$200$ each, $n = 100$ payments, 9% interest compounded monthly
9. Quarterly payments of $P = \$175$ each, $n = 80$ payments, 10% interest compounded quarterly
10. Quarterly payments of $P = \$225$ each, $n = 30$ payments, 11% interest compounded quarterly
11. How many quarterly payments of $500 each would it take to accumulate $20,000 if the payments were deposited in an account paying 8% interest compounded quarterly?
12. Find the number of quarterly payments of $250 each that must be paid into an account earning 13% interest compounded quarterly for there to be $8,000 in the account.
13. If monthly deposits of $71 were put into an account paying 18% compounded monthly, how long would it take to become a millionaire?
14. How many monthly payments of $9,000 would it take to accumulate $400,000 if the payments were deposited in an account paying 9% compounded monthly? How much would actually accumulate?
15. John Peterson has decided to place $200 each month in a credit union savings account that pays 12% compounded monthly so that he can purchase a new car that costs $8,500. How long will it take for the accumulated amount in the account to reach $8,500? How much interest will be earned by the time the account accumulates to $8,500?

16. To offset future expansion expenses, Martin Industries made semiannual deposits of $1,500 each into an account that paid 8% interest compounded semiannually. How much was in the account after the fifteenth deposit? How much interest was earned?

17. Taylor's Transit Company is making quarterly payments of $750 into an account that pays 13% interest compounded quarterly to accumulate $20,000 for the purchase of new equipment. How long will it take for the account to accumulate to $20,000? How much interest will be earned by that time?

18. To provide for future remodeling expenses, the owner of a restaurant made semiannual payments of $500 into an account that paid 11% interest compounded semiannually. How much was in the account after the tenth deposit? How much interest was earned?

19. The Phillips Produce Company is making monthly payments of $600 into an account that pays 9% interest compounded monthly to provide funds for business expansion. How much will be in the account after the twentieth deposit? How much interest will be earned at that time?

20. To provide funds for new research equipment, Conco Labs made semiannual payments of $2,000 each into an account that paid 12% interest compounded semiannually. How long did it take for the account to accumulate to $30,000? How much interest was earned at that time? How much was in the account after the twentieth deposit?

Section 13.5 Present value of an ordinary annuity

The **present value of an annuity** is that current amount that, if invested at a given rate, will result in a specified series of future payments. To understand the formulas for the present value of an ordinary annuity, consider the special case of how much must be deposited now in a bank paying 9% compounded annually to provide for five annual withdrawals of $1, the first withdrawal to be made in one year. See figure 13.1.

The amount to be deposited is the sum of the present values of the separate withdrawals. That is (using appendix D),

First withdrawal	$\$1\ (1.09)^{-1}$ =	$0.91743119
Second withdrawal	$\$1\ (1.09)^{-2}$ =	0.84167999
Third withdrawal	$\$1\ (1.09)^{-3}$ =	0.77218348
Fourth withdrawal	$\$1\ (1.09)^{-4}$ =	0.70842521
Fifth withdrawal	$\$1\ (1.09)^{-5}$ =	0.64993139
Amount deposited now	=	$3.88965126

Thus, a deposit of slightly less than \$3.89 in an account paying 9% compounded annually would provide a fund that would permit \$1 to be withdrawn annually for five years. To withdraw \$100 a year for five years, the deposit would have to be \$100 × 3.88965126 = \$388.965126, and to withdraw \$1,000 a year for five years, a deposit of \$1,000 × 3.88965126 = \$3,889.65126 would be required.

There is a similarity between the preceding discussion and that for the accumulated amount of an ordinary annuity. This similarity extends to the development of a formula for the present value of an annuity. The formula is

■ (13–4) $$A = P \cdot a_{\overline{n}|i}$$

where A = present value of an ordinary annuity, P = amount of each future payment, and $a_{\overline{n}|i}$ = present value of a deposit of \$1 at interest rate per period i for n conversion periods.*

The values of $a_{\overline{n}|i}$ can be found in appendix F. The values in this table are multiplied by P to obtain A.

Example 1 Carl Jefferson sold his business and retired on his sixtieth birthday. He used a part of the money from the sale to purchase an annuity that would pay him \$4,500 a quarter until he began to receive Social Security at age 65. If money is worth 10% compounded quarterly, how much did the annuity cost?

Solution

$A = ?,\ P = \$4{,}500,\ n = 20,\ i = \frac{10\%}{4} = 2\frac{1}{2}\% = 0.025$

$$\begin{aligned} A &= P \cdot a_{\overline{n}|i} \\ &= \$4{,}500 \cdot a_{\overline{20}|0.025} \\ &= \$4{,}500 \times 15.58916229 \qquad \text{(Appendix F)} \\ &= \$70{,}151.23 \end{aligned}$$

Carl received 20 × \$4,500 = \$90,000 in payments; thus, \$90,000.00 − \$70,151.23 = \$19,848.77 was earned in interest.

*For n withdrawals of \$1 each (n a counting number) made annually at compound interest rate i, the present value $a_{\overline{n}|i}$ is

$$a_{\overline{n}|i} = (1+i)^{-1} + (1+i)^{-2} + (1+i)^{-3} + \cdots + (1+i)^{-n} = \frac{1-(1+i)^{-n}}{i}$$

For n withdrawals of P dollars each, the present value is $P \cdot a_{\overline{n}|i}$.

Example 2 For her corner lot, Con Oil offered Margaret Prescott \$40,000 and semiannual payments of \$5,000 for the next five years. If money is worth 12% compounded semiannually, what is the equivalent cash price of the lot?

Solution

$A = ?,\ P = \$5{,}000,\ n = 10,\ i = \dfrac{12\%}{2} = 6\% = 0.06$

$$\begin{aligned} A &= P \cdot a_{\overline{n}|i} \\ &= \$5{,}000 \cdot a_{\overline{10}|0.06} \\ &= \$5{,}000 \times 7.36008705 \qquad \text{(Appendix F)} \\ &= \$36{,}800.44 \end{aligned}$$

Thus, the cash price of the lot is \$40,000.00 + \$36,800.44 = \$76,800.44.

Example 3 If \$75,000 is used to purchase an annuity that pays \$950 a month, and if the interest rate is 9% compounded monthly, approximately how many payments are possible?

Solution

$A = \$75{,}000,\ P = \$950,\ n = ?,\ i = \dfrac{9\%}{12} = \dfrac{3}{4}\% = 0.0075$

$$A = P \cdot a_{\overline{n}|i}$$

$$P \cdot a_{\overline{n}|i} = A$$

$$a_{\overline{n}|i} = \frac{A}{P} \qquad \text{(Dividing both sides by } P\text{)}$$

$$\begin{aligned} a_{\overline{n}|0.0075} &= \frac{\$75{,}000}{\$950} \\ &= 78.94736842 \end{aligned}$$

Appendix F on the page headed $\frac{3}{4}\%$ shows that the value for $a_{\overline{120}|0.0075}$ is 78.94169267. This is the largest entry in the table that is still less than 78.94736842. Thus, $n = 120$ payments are possible.

Exercises for Section 13.5

In problems 1–10, find the present value of an annuity that will provide the given payments for the given length of time when money is worth the given nominal compound interest rate.

1. \$2,000 per year for 10 years, 14% interest compounded annually
2. \$3,500 per year for eight years, 11% interest compounded annually
3. \$800 per quarter for four years, 13% interest compounded quarterly

4. \$1,200 per quarter for two years, 12% interest compounded quarterly
5. \$400 semiannually for six years, 15% interest compounded semiannually
6. \$750 semiannually for 12 years, 10% interest compounded semiannually
7. \$1,500 per month for four years, 9% interest compounded monthly
8. \$1,750 per month for $3\frac{1}{2}$ years, 12% interest compounded monthly
9. \$3,000 per quarter for six years, 11% interest compounded quarterly
10. \$4,750 per quarter for five years, 10% interest compounded quarterly
11. If \$15,000 is used to purchase an annuity that pays \$400 a month, and if the interest rate is 12% compounded monthly, how many full payments will be received from the annuity?
12. How many full payments will be received from an annuity that costs \$10,000 if the payments are \$750 semiannually and money is worth 14% compounded semiannually?
13. Bob Brewster sold some real estate for \$5,000 down and quarterly payments of \$500 for 10 years. If money is worth 8% compounded quarterly, what is the equivalent cash price of the real estate?
14. Sue Johnson purchased an annuity that would pay her son \$400 per month while he was getting his education. How much did the annuity cost if the payments were to continue for four years and money was worth 15% compounded monthly?
15. Jesse Phillips won \$20,000 in a sweepstakes and purchased an annuity with the money that would pay him \$750 quarterly. If money was worth 10% compounded quarterly at the time he purchased the annuity, how many full payments will he receive?
16. Sarah Steadman sold her retail clothing store for \$20,000 in cash and monthly payments of \$500 for four years. If money was worth 12% compounded monthly, what was the equivalent cash selling price of the store?
17. Carol Jackson purchased an annuity that would pay her daughter \$150 a month for 40 months. How much did the annuity cost if money was worth 9% compounded monthly?
18. Ron Jacobson sold one of the branch stores of his business for \$65,000 and used the money to purchase an annuity that would pay him \$5,000 semiannually. If money was worth 12% compounded semiannually at the time he purchased the annuity, how many full payments will he receive?

Section 13.6 Annuities due

The second type of annuity certain is the annuity due. In an annuity due, payments are made at the beginning of the period. Insurance premiums and rent payments are common examples of annuities due.

The accumulated amount and the present value of an annuity due have the same meanings as for an ordinary annuity. Thus, formulas for annuities due can be derived from the formulas and tables of the ordinary annuity.

To determine a formula for the accumulated amount of an annuity due, consider figure 13.1 on page 399 and our first illustration of a $1 annual payment for five years. Note that the annuity due has five interest-earning periods, one more than for the ordinary annuity. This is true in general; that is, if an ordinary annuity has n interest-earning periods, then for the same term an annuity due has $n + 1$ interest-earning periods. Also, the formulas for $s_{\overline{n}|i}$ include the last payment of an ordinary annuity that earns no interest (this is the first term in equation 13–1). The annuity due has no such payment; thus it must be deducted from $s_{\overline{n}|i}$.

Combining this information, the accumulated amount of an annuity due is

■ (13–5) $$\overline{S} = P \cdot (s_{\overline{n+1}|i} - 1)$$

where $\overline{S}$ = accumulated amount of annuity due,* P = payment or deposit, n = number of payments or deposits, and i = rate per period.

*It is customary to designate the accumulated amount and the present value of an annuity due by boldface letters **S** and **A**. For ease of writing, the notations $\overline{S}$ and $\overline{A}$ are used in this text.

Example 1 For 10 years, an annual deposit of $4,000 was made on April 1 in an account paying 15% compounded annually. Find the accumulated amount on April 1 of the eleventh year.

Solution

$\bar{S} = ?,\ P = \$4{,}000,\ n = 10,\ i = 15\% = 0.15$

$$\begin{aligned}\bar{S} &= P\,(s_{\overline{n+1}|i} - 1)\\ &= \$4{,}000\,(s_{\overline{11}|0.15} - 1)\\ &= \$4{,}000\,(24.34927597 - 1) \qquad \text{(Appendix E)}\\ &= \$4{,}000\,(23.34927597)\\ &= \$93{,}397.10\end{aligned}$$

Example 2 How long will it take to accumulate $25,000 if $1,620 is deposited at the beginning of each month in an account that pays interest at 12% compounded monthly?

Solution

$\bar{S} = \$25{,}000,\ P = \$1{,}620,\ n = ?,\ i = \dfrac{12\%}{12} = 1\% = 0.01$

$$\begin{aligned}\bar{S} &= P(s_{\overline{n+1}|i} - 1)\\ P(s_{\overline{n+1}|i} - 1) &= \bar{S}\\ s_{\overline{n+1}|i} - 1 &= \frac{\bar{S}}{P} \qquad \text{(Dividing both sides by } P\text{)}\\ s_{\overline{n+1}|i} &= \frac{\bar{S}}{P} + 1 \qquad \text{(Adding 1 to both sides)}\\ s_{\overline{n+1}|0.01} &= \frac{\$25{,}000}{\$1{,}620} + 1\\ s_{\overline{n+1}|0.01} &= 16.43209877\end{aligned}$$

Appendix E on the page headed 1% shows that the smallest entry greater than 16.43209877 is $s_{\overline{16}|0.01} = 17.25786449$. Since $n + 1 = 16$, $n = 15$. Thus, 15 months will be required.

Example 3 For 20 semiannual deposits of \$1,800 invested at 14% compounded semiannually, find the accumulated amount of (a) an ordinary annuity and (b) an annuity due.

Solution

a. $S = ?, P = \$1{,}800, n = 20, i = \dfrac{14\%}{2} = 7\% = 0.07$

$$\begin{aligned} S &= P \cdot s_{\overline{n}|i} \\ &= \$1{,}800 \cdot s_{\overline{20}|0.07} \\ &= \$1{,}800 \times 40.99549232 \qquad \text{(Appendix E)} \\ &= \$73{,}791.89 \end{aligned}$$

b. $\overline{S} = ?, P = \$1{,}800, n = 20, i = \dfrac{14\%}{2} = 7\% = 0.07$

$$\begin{aligned} \overline{S} &= P\,(s_{\overline{n+1}|i} - 1) \\ &= \$1{,}800\,(s_{\overline{21}|0.07} - 1) \\ &= \$1{,}800\,(44.86517678 - 1) \qquad \text{(Appendix E)} \\ &= \$1{,}800\,(43.86517678) \\ &= \$78{,}957.32 \end{aligned}$$

Note that the accumulated amount for the annuity due is greater than that for the ordinary annuity.

Exercises for Section 13.6

In problems 1–10, find the accumulated amount of the given annuity due when n payments of P dollars each are deposited in an account that pays the given nominal interest rate.

1. \$1,000 per year for five years, 12% interest compounded annually
2. \$1,500 per year for 15 years, 14% interest compounded annually
3. \$700 semiannually for five years, 8% interest compounded semiannually
4. \$400 semiannually for 12 years, 10% interest compounded semiannually
5. \$200 per month for three years, 15% interest compounded monthly
6. \$150 per month for one year, 12% interest compounded monthly
7. \$450 per quarter for four years, 13% interest compounded quarterly
8. \$1,600 per quarter for five years, 11% interest compounded quarterly
9. \$400 per month for four years, 9% interest compounded monthly

10. $775 per quarter for five years, 10% interest compounded quarterly

11. A deposit of $350 is made each month for 24 months into an account that pays 12% interest compounded monthly. Find the accumulated amount in the account at the beginning of the twenty-fifth month.

12. For five years, a deposit of $550 is made at the beginning of each quarter into an account that pays 14% interest compounded quarterly. What is the accumulated amount in the account at the beginning of the first quarter of the sixth year?

13. How long will it take to accumulate $10,000 if $700 is deposited at the beginning of each year into an account that pays interest at 10% compounded annually?

14. If $500 is paid quarterly into an account that pays 12% interest compounded quarterly, how many years will it take to accumulate $15,000 in the account?

15. For 10 quarterly deposits of $600 each invested at 8% compounded quarterly, find the accumulated amount of (a) an ordinary annuity and (b) an annuity due.

16. For 20 monthly deposits of $75 each invested at 12% compounded monthly, find the accumulated amount of (a) an ordinary annuity and (b) an annuity due.

17. To provide funds for an expected increase in operating expenses at her restaurant, Myra Cole decides to deposit $200 each month into an account that pays 9% interest compounded monthly. How much will she have in the account 24 months from now if she makes the first deposit immediately?

18. Bob Schwartz decides to begin a savings plan by depositing $125 each quarter into an account that pays 13% interest compounded quarterly. If he makes his first deposit now, how much will be in the account three years from now?

19. At the beginning of the year, Donna Deer took $2,000 from her savings and placed it in an Individual Retirement Account (IRA) that pays 9.5% compounded annually. If Donna continues this practice for the next 35 years, how much will she have in her IRA account?

20. Each month, Jack and Kay put $187.50 in an IRA account that pays 12% compounded monthly. If they continue to make these deposits until Jack retires in 9 years and 11 months, how much will they have in their IRA account?

Section 13.7 Present value of an annuity due

To determine a formula for the present value of an annuity due, again consider figure 13.1 on page 399. With an annuity due, the present value of the first payment of \$1 is \$1 since there is no interest-earning period. As a result, there are only four periods for calculation of present value, one less than the ordinary annuity. This is true in general; if an ordinary annuity has n periods, the annuity due has $n - 1$ periods when calculating present value. The initial payment is then added to this calculation.

Combining this information, the present value of an annuity due is

$$\overline{A} = P(a_{\overline{n-1}|i} + 1) \qquad (13\text{–}6)$$

where $\overline{A}$ = present value of an annuity due, P = amount of each future payment, n = number of payments, and i = rate per period.

Example 1 Find the present value of an annuity due with semiannual payments of \$3,000 for a term of 10 years if interest is compounded at 14% semiannually.

Solution

$\overline{A} = ?,\ P = \$3{,}000,\ n = 20,\ i = \dfrac{14\%}{2} = 7\% = 0.07$

$$\begin{aligned}\overline{A} &= P(a_{\overline{n-1}|i} + 1)\\ &= \$3{,}000\,(a_{\overline{19}|0.07} + 1)\\ &= \$3{,}000\,(10.33559524 + 1) \qquad \text{(Appendix F)}\\ &= \$3{,}000\,(11.33559524)\\ &= \$34{,}006.79\end{aligned}$$

Example 2 A company retirement fund pays Bob Simmons \$980 at the beginning of each month. If money is worth 9% compounded monthly, what is the present value of the pension for (a) one year and (b) four years?

Solution

a. $\overline{A} = ?,\ P = \$980,\ n = 12,\ i = \dfrac{9\%}{12} = \dfrac{3}{4}\% = 0.0075$

$$\begin{aligned}\overline{A} &= P\,(a_{\overline{n-1}|i} + 1)\\ &= \$980\,(a_{\overline{11}|0.0075} + 1)\\ &= \$980\,(10.52067452 + 1) \qquad \text{(Appendix F)}\\ &= \$980\,(11.52067452)\\ &= \$11{,}290.26\end{aligned}$$

b. $\bar{A} = ?,\ P = \$980,\ n = 48,\ i = \frac{9\%}{12} = \frac{3}{4}\% = 0.0075$

$$\begin{aligned}\bar{A} &= P\,(a_{\overline{n-1}|i} + 1)\\ &= \$980\,(a_{\overline{47}|0.0075} + 1)\\ &= \$980\,(39.48616775 + 1) \qquad \text{(Appendix F)}\\ &= \$980\,(40.48616775)\\ &= \$39{,}676.44\end{aligned}$$

Example 3 What is the present value of (a) an ordinary annuity and (b) an annuity due if $P = \$750$ per month, the term is 30 months, and interest is compounded at 12% monthly?

Solution

a. $A = ?,\ P = \$750,\ n = 30,\ i = \frac{12\%}{12} = 1\% = 0.01$

$$\begin{aligned}A &= P \cdot a_{\overline{n}|i}\\ &= \$750 \cdot a_{\overline{30}|0.01}\\ &= \$750 \times 25.80770822 \qquad \text{(Appendix F)}\\ &= \$19{,}355.78\end{aligned}$$

b. $\bar{A} = ?,\ P = \$750,\ n = 30,\ i = \frac{12\%}{12} = 1\% = 0.01$

$$\begin{aligned}\bar{A} &= P\,(a_{\overline{n-1}|i} + 1)\\ &= \$750\,(a_{\overline{29}|0.01} + 1)\\ &= \$750\,(25.06578530 + 1) \qquad \text{(Appendix F)}\\ &= \$750\,(26.06578530)\\ &= \$19{,}549.34\end{aligned}$$

Note that the present value of the annuity due is greater than that of the ordinary annuity.

Exercises for Section 13.7

In problems 1–10, find the present value for each annuity due using the information provided.

1. \$800 per year for five years, 12% interest compounded annually
2. \$1,400 per year for 10 years, $9\frac{1}{2}\%$ interest compounded annually
3. \$700 per quarter for four years, 15% interest compounded quarterly

4. \$400 per quarter for five years, 13% interest compounded quarterly

5. \$1,200 semiannually for five years, 15% interest compounded semiannually

6. \$2,000 semiannually for eight years, 14% interest compounded semiannually

7. \$200 per month for 48 months, 15% interest compounded monthly

8. \$350 per month for 20 months, 12% interest compounded monthly

9. \$1,250 per quarter for nine years, 10% interest compounded quarterly

10. \$3,400 semiannually for eight years, 9% interest compounded semiannually

11. Find the present value of (a) an ordinary annuity and (b) an annuity due if $P = \$4{,}200$ semiannually, the term is 10 years, and interest is compounded at 11% semiannually.

12. What is the present value of (a) an ordinary annuity and (b) an annuity due if $P = \$250$ monthly, the term is three years, and interest is compounded at 9% monthly.

13. As payment to satisfy an old debt, John Baker agrees to pay his neighbor \$500 quarterly for two years, with the first payment to be made immediately. If money is worth 11% compounded quarterly, what is the equivalent cash value of John's debt to his neighbor?

14. Some teenagers vandalized Lisa Carter's clothing store, and their parents agreed to pay Lisa \$50 per month for two years to cover damages, with the first payment to be made immediately. What is the equivalent cash amount of damage done to the store if money is worth 12% compounded monthly?

15. When Ella Richards graduated from college, her father gave her \$50 and promised to pay her \$50 each month for the next 12 months. If money is worth 9% compounded monthly, what is the equivalent cash value of Ella's gift? (Hint: $n = 13$.)

16. To satisfy a debt to one of its creditors, a company agrees to pay \$3,000 semiannually for six years, with the first payment to be made immediately. If money is worth 13% compounded semiannually, what is the amount of the debt?

17. Atlas Plumbing Supply agreed to pay John Simmons \$2,500 quarterly for five years as compensation for injuries John received on the job. If the first payment was made immediately and if money was worth 12% compounded quarterly, what was the equivalent cash value of the settlement?

18. Bob Jacobs, a truck driver, lost control of his truck and knocked down a wall of a restaurant while making a delivery. To pay for the damages, Bob paid the owner of the restaurant $100 a month for two years, with the first payment made immediately. If money was worth 6% compounded monthly, what was the equivalent cash value of the damage?

Glossary

Annuity Any series of payments at regular intervals of time. The payments are usually equal but need not be so.
Annuity certain An annuity for which the beginning and ending dates are specified.
Annuity due An annuity for which payments are made at the beginning of each period; for example, apartment rent or insurance premiums.
Contingent annuity An annuity for which either the beginning or ending date is not specified.
Conversion period The intervals of time when interest is computed and added to the accumulated amount of an annuity.
Nominal rate The rate per annum; the quoted compound interest rate of an annuity.
Ordinary annuity An annuity for which payments are made at the end of each period; for example, salaries or interest payments.
Period of an annuity The time interval between the payments of an annuity.
Present value of an annuity The current amount of money that, if invested at a given rate, will result in a specified series of future payments.
Term of an annuity The time from the beginning of the first period to the end of the last period of an annuity.

Review test

Use appendices E and F to solve the following problems:

1. What is the accumulated amount of quarterly payments of $400 invested in an ordinary annuity at 11% compounded quarterly following the twelfth payment?
2. James Richards sold some real estate for $25,000 down and semiannual payments of $2,000 for the next 10 years, with the first payment due in six months. If money is worth 9% compounded semiannually, what is the equivalent cash price of the real estate?
3. Which generates the larger accumulated amount: an ordinary annuity of $200 per quarter for two years at 10% compounded quarterly or an annuity due of $65 per month for two years at 12% compounded monthly?
4. How long will it take to accumulate $20,000 if $350 is deposited at the beginning of each month in an account that pays interest at 9% compounded monthly?

5. Find the present value of an annuity due with semiannual payments of $1,500 for a term of six years if money is worth 13% compounded semiannually.

6. Jim Justin purchased 50 shares of stock for his infant daughter and placed the dividends (paid at the end of each quarter) in a savings account paying 9% compounded quarterly. During the first two years, the quarterly dividends were $2.60 per share. Find the amount in the savings account after two years.

7. Sandra Locke used an inheritance of $40,000 to purchase an ordinary annuity that paid $2,500 a quarter. If money was worth 11% compounded quarterly, how many full payments did she receive?

8. Lou Martin is paid on the fifteenth of each month. For 18 months, he placed 15% of his monthly pay of $1,200 in an account paying 9% compounded monthly. How much was in the account on the fifteenth day of the nineteenth month?

9. A business property was purchased for $150,000 down and monthly payments of $10,000 for four years. Find the equivalent cash price if money was worth 9% compounded monthly.

10. Find the difference between the present values of an ordinary annuity and an annuity due if the semiannual payment is $800, the term is 14 years, and money is worth 14% compounded semiannually.

CHAPTER 14

Sinking Funds and Amortization

Chapter Objectives

I. Learn the meaning of the following terms:

Sinking fund, 419

Amortization, 419, 424

II. Understand:

The difference between a sinking fund and the process of amortization, 419, 424

The preparation of a schedule of payments for a sinking fund, 421

The preparation of an amortization schedule, 427

III. Calculate:

The periodic payment of a sinking fund, 419–421

The periodic payment to amortize a debt, 426–427

Section 14.1 Introduction

An annuity established to meet a future obligation is called a **sinking fund.** Businesses establish sinking funds to redeem bonds, to replace worn-out equipment, to expand facilities, or to meet a future debt or anticipated expense. In general, sinking funds retire only the principal of a debt.

If both the principal and accrued interest are gradually retired by partial payments, the process is called **amortization.**

This chapter examines the fundamentals of sinking funds and amortization. While the methods developed are applicable to both kinds of annuities certain, discussion is limited to the ordinary annuity.

Section 14.2 Sinking funds

In a sinking fund, the amount of the obligation, the term, and the current interest rate are known; hence, the problem is to determine the amount of the periodic payment *P*.* This means solving the annuity formula for *P*. The result is†

■ (14–1) $$P = S \times \frac{1}{s_{\overline{n}|i}}$$

Appendix G shows the values for $\frac{1}{s_{\overline{n}|i}}$.

Example 1

The Scorpio Corporation estimates that its plant machinery will be obsolete in another three years. The replacement cost is \$240,000, and the current interest rate is 8% compounded quarterly. How much should the company invest at the end of each quarter to be prepared to purchase new equipment in three years?

Solution

$S = \$240{,}000,\ P = ?,\ n = 12,\ i = \frac{8\%}{4} = 2\% = 0.02$

$$P = S \times \frac{1}{s_{\overline{n}|i}}$$
$$= \$240{,}000 \times \frac{1}{s_{\overline{12}|0.02}}$$
$$= \$240{,}000 \times .07455960 \qquad \text{(Appendix G)}$$
$$= \$17{,}894.304$$
$$= \$17{,}894.30‡$$

*The periodic payment to a sinking fund is often called the *rent*.

†$S = P \times s_{\overline{n}|i}$

$P \times s_{\overline{n}|i} = S$

$P = \frac{S}{s_{\overline{n}|i}}$ (Dividing both sides by $s_{\overline{n}|i}$)

$P = S \times \frac{1}{s_{\overline{n}|i}}$

‡Actually, the fund will accumulate to only \$17,894.30 × 13.41208973 = \$239,999.94 because of rounding. If the firm chose to invest \$17,894.31, the fund would be \$240,000.02.

Example 2 Grey Enterprises plans to replace its fleet of trucks in three years at an estimated cost of $140,000. The company establishes a sinking fund in an account that earns interest at 9% compounded semiannually. What is the amount of the payment at the end of each six months?

Solution

$S = \$140{,}000,\ P = ?,\ n = 6,\ i = \frac{9\%}{2} = 4\frac{1}{2}\% = 0.045$

$$\begin{aligned} P &= S \times \frac{1}{s_{\overline{n}|i}} \\ &= \$140{,}000 \times \frac{1}{s_{\overline{6}|0.045}} \\ &= \$140{,}000 \times 0.14887839 \qquad \text{(Appendix G)} \\ &= \$20{,}842.9746 \\ &= \$20{,}842.97 \end{aligned}$$

Example 3 The Davidson Corporation borrowed $200,000 by issuing bonds redeemable in 10 years. To be able to redeem the bonds at maturity, the company established a sinking fund into which payments were made at the end of each quarter. If the interest rate was 10% compounded quarterly, (a) what was the amount of each payment, and (b) how much total interest was earned?

Solution

$S = \$200{,}000,\ P = ?,\ n = 40,\ i = \frac{10\%}{4} = 2\frac{1}{2}\% = 0.025$

a.

$$\begin{aligned} P &= S \times \frac{1}{s_{\overline{n}|i}} \\ &= \$200{,}000 \times \frac{1}{s_{\overline{40}|0.025}} \\ &= \$200{,}000 \times 0.01483623 \qquad \text{(Appendix G)} \\ &= \$2{,}967.246 \\ &= \$2{,}967.25 \end{aligned}$$

b.

$200,000	Accumulated amount	
− 118,690	Total payments	($2,967.25 × 40)
$ 81,310	Earned interest	

Frequently, it is convenient to have a schedule showing the operation of the sinking fund.

Example 4 To be able to remodel their display rooms 18 months from now, the Regency Company established a sinking fund by making quarterly payments into an account paying 12% compounded quarterly. Prepare a schedule for a remodeling cost of $28,000.

Solution

$$S = \$28{,}000,\ P = ?,\ n = 6,\ i = \frac{12\%}{4} = 3\% = 0.03$$

$$P = S \times \frac{1}{s_{\overline{6}|0.03}}$$

$$= \$28{,}000 \times 0.15459750 \qquad \text{(Appendix G)}$$

$$= \$4{,}328.73$$

	Beginning of Period	**End of Period**		
Period	*Accumulated Amount (1)*	*Earned Interest (2)*	*Periodic Payment (3)*	*Accumulated Amount (1) + (2) + (3)*
1	0	0	$4,328.73	$ 4,328.73
2	$ 4,328.73	$129.86	4,328.73	8,787.32
3	8,787.32	263.62	4,328.73	13,379.67
4	13,379.67	401.39	4,328.73	18,109.79
5	18,109.79	543.29	4,328.73	22,981.81
6	22,981.81	689.45	4,328.73	27,999.99

Since each line in the schedule is a separate interest problem, the interest can be computed using the simple interest formula.* The remaining entries are self-explanatory. The final accumulated amount is 1¢ less than the required amount because of rounding.

Exercises for Section 14.2 In problems 1–6, find the amount of the periodic payment P for the given sinking fund.

1. $S = \$70{,}000$, quarterly payments for five years, 8% interest compounded quarterly
2. $S = \$40{,}000$, semiannual payments for 10 years, 10% interest compounded semiannually
3. $S = \$90{,}000$, quarterly payments for six years, 9% interest compounded quarterly

*Recall that compound interest is simply an accumulation of simple interest calculations (see section 11.2).

4. $S = \$27{,}000$, semiannual payments for eight years, 14% interest compounded semiannually

5. $S = \$16{,}000$, monthly payments for three years, 9% interest compounded monthly

6. $S = \$35{,}000$, semiannual payments for six years, 11% interest compounded semiannually

In problems 7–12, find the amount of the periodic payment P for the given sinking fund, set up a schedule showing the operation of the fund, and compute the total interest earned by the fund.

7. $S = \$22{,}000$, quarterly payments for two years, 8% interest compounded quarterly

8. $S = \$31{,}000$, semiannual payments for three years, 12% interest compounded semiannually

9. $S = \$8{,}000$, monthly payments for six months, 12% interest compounded monthly

10. $S = \$40{,}000$, semiannual payments for four years, 8% interest compounded semiannually

11. $S = \$36{,}000$, quarterly payments for 15 months, 10% interest compounded quarterly

12. $S = \$42{,}000$, semiannual payments for three years, 16% interest compounded semiannually

In problems 13–16, fill in the missing entries in the sinking fund schedules.

13.

	Beginning of Period	**End of Period**		
Period	*Accumulated Amount (1)*	*Earned Interest (2)*	*Periodic Payment (3)*	*Accumulated Amount (1) + (2) + (3)*
1	$ 0.00	$ 0.00	$2,073.72	$2,073.72
2	2,073.72	207.37		
3				
4				
5				
6				

14.

	Beginning of Period	End of Period		
Period	Accumulated Amount (1)	Earned Interest (2)	Periodic Payment (3)	Accumulated Amount (1) + (2) + (3)
1	$ 0.00	$ 0.00		
2	1,332.62	59.97		
3				
4				
5				
6				
7				
8				

15.

	Beginning of Period	End of Period		
Period	Accumulated Amount (1)	Earned Interest (2)	Periodic Payment (3)	Accumulated Amount (1) + (2) + (3)
1	$ 0.00	$ 0.00		
2	6,694.41	167.36		
3				
4				
5				
6				
7				
8				
9				
10				

16.

	Beginning of Period	End of Period		
Period	Accumulated Amount (1)	Earned Interest (2)	Periodic Payment (3)	Accumulated Amount (1) + (2) + (3)
1	$ 0.00	$0.00		
2	647.61	4.86		
3				
4				
5				
6				
7				
8				
9				
10				
11				
12				

17. The Hudson Manufacturing Company plans to replace some of its machinery in two years at an estimated cost of $220,000. The company establishes a sinking fund in an account that earns interest at 10% compounded quarterly. Find the amount of each quarterly payment.

18. Scott Processors issued bonds totaling $725,000 to raise capital for plant modifications. The bonds were redeemable in six years, and the company established a sinking fund, into which payments were made quarterly, to redeem the bonds. If the interest rate was 11% compounded quarterly, find (a) the amount of each payment and (b) the total interest earned.

19. The owner of an appliance store established a sinking fund so that she could remodel her display room in two years. If the account earned interest at 9% compounded monthly, and if the remodeling cost was $9,000, find the amount of the monthly payments into the account.

20. The Harris Company plans to open a branch office in three years at an estimated cost of $430,000. To provide the funds, the company establishes a sinking fund in an account that pays 9% interest compounded semiannually. Find the amount of the semiannual payments into the fund. Prepare a schedule showing the operation of the fund.

Section 14.3 Amortization

In example 3 of section 14.2, a sinking fund was established to redeem bonds that had been issued. But investors buy bonds because the bonds are interest bearing; that is, the bondholder receives not only the original cost of the bond at maturity (principal), but also periodic interest while the bond is in force. Example 3 created a sinking fund to pay off the principal; the interest on the bonds would have had to be paid from another source. If both the principal and accrued interest had been retired by partial payments, the debt would have been *amortized.**

Perhaps the most common example of amortization is mortgage payments on a real estate loan. A portion of each payment is applied to accrued interest, with the remainder applied to the outstanding principal, in accordance with the United States Rule. Table 14.1 compares mortgage payments for a $100,000 loan at different rates of interest.

*In accounting, amortization may have a broader meaning. In this text, however, amortization means the elimination of both the principal and interest of a debt by a series of equal payments at regular intervals.

Table 14.1 Comparing Mortgage Payments

	Monthly Payments on \$100,000 Loan	**Total Mortgage Payments over Life of \$100,000 Loan**
At 6% interest		
30-year term	\$ 599	\$215,640
15-year term	843	151,740
10-year term	1,110	133,200
At 10% interest		
30-year term	\$ 877	\$315,720
15-year term	1,075	193,500
10-year term	1,321	158,520
At 14% interest		
30-year term	\$1,184	\$426,240
15-year term	1,332	239,760
10-year term	1,552	186,240
At 18% interest		
30-year term	\$1,507	\$542,520
15-year term	1,610	289,800
10-year term	1,801	216,120

Other examples of amortization occurred in section 12.6 on installment plans; although the interest calculation is different, the partial payments pay off the entire debt—both principal and finance charge.

Consider a debt A drawing interest at rate i per period. To pay off the entire debt in n periodic payments of amount P, the present value of these future payments must equal A. That is,

(14–2) $$P \times a_{\overline{n}|i} = A$$

Solving formula 14.2 for P:*

■ (14–3) $$P = A \times \frac{1}{a_{\overline{n}|i}}$$

Each payment using formula 14–3 is distributed between principal and interest according to the United States Rule. Values for $\frac{1}{a_{\overline{n}|i}}$ are shown in appendix H.

*$P \times a_{\overline{n}|i} = A$

$$P = \frac{A}{a_{\overline{n}|i}} \quad \text{(Dividing both sides by } a_{\overline{n}|i}\text{)}$$

$$P = A \times \frac{1}{a_{\overline{n}|i}}$$

Example 1 The Growth Corporation acquired a piece of property for \$750,000 by paying \$150,000 down and signing a mortgage for 48 quarterly payments (payments to be made at the end of each quarter). What is the amount of each payment if the nominal rate is 9%?

Solution

$A = \$750{,}000 - \$150{,}000 = \$600{,}000$, $P = ?$, $n = 48$,
$i = 2\frac{1}{4}\% = 0.0225$

$$P = A \times \frac{1}{a_{\overline{n}|i}}$$

$$= \$600{,}000 \times \frac{1}{a_{\overline{48}|0.0225}}$$

$$= \$600{,}000 \times 0.03428233 \qquad \text{(Appendix H)}$$

$$= \$20{,}569.398$$

$$= \$20{,}569.40$$

Example 2 A debt of \$4,850 bears interest at 14% compounded semiannually. What semiannual payment is required to amortize the debt in $2\frac{1}{2}$ years if the payments are made at the end of each six months?

Solution

$A = \$4{,}850$, $P = ?$, $n = 5$, $i = 7\% = 0.07$

$$P = A \times \frac{1}{a_{\overline{n}|i}}$$

$$= \$4{,}850 \times \frac{1}{a_{\overline{5}|0.07}}$$

$$= \$4{,}850 \times 0.24389069 \qquad \text{(Appendix H)}$$

$$= \$1{,}182.8694$$

$$= \$1{,}182.87$$

Example 3 Construct a schedule showing the distribution of payments in example 2 of this section.

Solution

To determine the interest in column 3 of the schedule, again recall that compound interest is a series of simple interest calculations, with the simple interest formula applied to the principal plus interest of the preceding period (column 1).

	Beginning of Period	End of Period			
Period	*Amount of Debt (1)*	*Payment (2)*	*Interest (3)*	*Applied to Principal (4)=(2)−(3)*	*Remaining Debt (5)=(1)−(4)*
1	$4,850.00	$1,182.87	$339.50	$ 843.37	$4,006.63
2	4,006.63	1,182.87	280.46	902.41	3,104.22
3	3,104.22	1,182.87	217.30	965.57	2,138.65
4	2,138.65	1,182.87	149.71	1,033.16	1,105.49
5	1,105.49	1,182.87	77.38	1,105.49	0.00

The schedule showing the distribution of the payments in example 3 is called an *amortization schedule.* Amortization schedules are frequently presented to debtors, particularly in the case of real estate loans.

Exercises for Section 14.3

In problems 1–6, find the periodic payment required to amortize the given debt in the given time.

1. $4,000 debt, bearing interest at 13% compounded annually, annual payments for 10 years
2. $10,000 debt, bearing interest at 8% compounded quarterly, quarterly payments for 12 years
3. $16,000 debt, bearing interest at 10% compounded semiannually, semiannual payments for 20 years
4. $12,500 debt, bearing interest at 12% compounded monthly, monthly payments for $3\frac{1}{2}$ years

5. \$7,500 debt, bearing interest at 9% compounded monthly, monthly payments for three years

6. \$25,000 debt, bearing interest at 14% compounded semiannually, semiannual payments for 10 years

In problems 7–12, find the periodic payment required to amortize the given debt in the given time and construct a schedule showing the distribution of payments.

7. \$5,250 debt, bearing interest at 8% compounded annually, annual payments for four years

8. \$7,420 debt, bearing interest at 13% compounded semiannually, semiannual payments for three years

9. \$3,200 debt, bearing interest at 11% compounded quarterly, quarterly payments for two years

10. \$9,450 debt, bearing interest at 12% compounded monthly, monthly payments for 10 months

11. \$8,700 debt, bearing interest at 9% compounded monthly, monthly payments for one year

12. \$2,400 debt, bearing interest at 12% compounded semiannually, semiannual payments for six years

In problems 13–16, fill in the missing entries in the amortization schedules.

13.

	Beginning of Period	**End of Period**			
Period	*Amount of Debt (1)*	*Payment (2)*	*Interest (3)*	*Applied to Principal (4)=(2)−(3)*	*Remaining Debt (5)=(1)−(4)*
1	\$1,500.00		\$75.00		
2					
3					
4					

14.

Period	Beginning of Period	End of Period			
	Amount of Debt (1)	Payment (2)	Interest (3)	Applied to Principal (4)=(2)−(3)	Remaining Debt (5)=(1)−(4)
1	$5,000.00		$200.00		
2					
3					
4					
5					

15.

Period	Beginning of Period	End of Period			
	Amount of Debt (1)	Payment (2)	Interest (3)	Applied to Principal (4)=(2)−(3)	Remaining Debt (5)=(1)−(4)
1	$11,000.00		$357.50		
2					
3					
4					
5					
6					
7					
8					

16.

Period	Beginning of Period	End of Period			
	Amount of Debt (1)	Payment (2)	Interest (3)	Applied to Principal (4)=(2)−(3)	Remaining Debt (5)=(1)−(4)
1	$32,500.00		$2,437.50		
2					
3					
4					
5					
6					
7					
8					
9					
10					

17. Johnson Properties acquired some acreage for \$340,000 by paying \$100,000 down and signing a mortgage for 24 quarterly payments. If the interest rate is 8% compounded quarterly, what is the amount of each quarterly payment?

18. The Centaur Corporation borrowed \$200,000 to open a new branch office. If the interest rate is 14% compounded semiannually, and if the debt is to be amortized by semiannual payments for 10 years, find the amount of each payment.

19. The Everwear Carpet Outlet borrowed \$175,000 to construct a new warehouse. The company is to amortize the loan in four years by making quarterly payments. If the interest rate is 10% compounded quarterly, find the amount of each payment.

20. For a \$50,000 debt, bearing interest at 10% compounded quarterly, (a) how much total interest is paid if the debt is amortized in eight years? (b) how much more interest is paid if the debt is amortized in ten years?

21. To buy their new house, George and Susan made a down payment and signed a 30-year mortgage for \$78,000. If the interest rate is 9% compounded monthly, find the amount of their monthly mortgage payment.

22. The Haycox Corporation purchased an apartment building for \$180,000 down and a 20-year mortgage for \$788,400. If the interest rate is 12% compounded monthly, find the amount of the corporation's monthly mortgage payment.

23. Four years after borrowing \$60,000, to be amortized at 9% compounded semiannually for 10 years, the Decker Company was forced to refinance the remaining principal at 12% compounded semiannually for 20 years. Find (a) the semiannual payment for the original debt, (b) the semiannual payment for the refinanced debt, and (c) the total additional interest paid as a result of the refinancing.

Glossary

Amortization The retirement of the principal and accrued interest of a debt by a series of partial payments.

Sinking fund An annuity established to meet a future obligation.

Review test

1. A sinking fund is to be established to accumulate $110,000 in four years. How much should be invested quarterly if the interest rate is 11% compounded quarterly?
2. The Fraley Company borrowed $450,000 by issuing bonds that were redeemable in 20 years. To be able to redeem the bonds at maturity, the company established a sinking fund into which payments were made at the end of each six months. If the interest rate was 12% compounded semiannually, find (a) the amount of each payment and (b) the total interest earned.
3. A debt of $16,000 bears interest at 9% compounded quarterly. What quarterly payment is required to amortize the debt in five years if payments are made at the end of each quarter?
4. How much interest is paid if a $6,000 debt, bearing interest at 15% compounded annually, is amortized over four years with payments at the end of each year?
5. Construct an amortization schedule showing the distribution of payments for a $4,700 debt, bearing interest at 10% compounded semiannually, with semiannual payments for three years.
6. Maria Valdez plans to replace a piece of equipment in three years. She anticipates that by that time the equipment will cost 15% more than its present price of $14,400. If money is worth 11% compounded semiannually, how much should she invest at the end of each six months to be able to purchase the equipment in three years?
7. Marion Brothers paid $20,000 down and made payments at the end of each month for three years to amortize the cost of a $200,000 computer. The interest rate was 9% compounded monthly. Find (a) the amount of each payment, (b) the interest paid on the loan, and (c) the total cost of the computer.
8. The McPherson Company purchased some acreage for a down payment of $20,000 and a 10-year mortgage for $227,000. If the interest rate was 15% compounded monthly, find the amount of the company's monthly mortgage payment.

CHAPTER 15 Securities

Chapter Objectives

I. Learn the meaning of the following terms:

Stock dividends, 434
Capital gain, 434
Earnings per share, 443
Price-earnings ratio, 444
Yield, 444
Mortgage bond, 446
Debenture, 446
Nominal yield of a bond, 452
Current yield of a bond, 452
Yield to maturity of a bond, 453

II. Understand:

The concept of common stock, 433
The reasons for purchasing common stock, 434–435
The differences between common stock and preferred stock, 435–436
Trading of stocks, 437–439
The concept of bonds, 446–447
The differences between corporate bonds and corporate stocks, 446
Trading of bonds, 447–449

III. Calculate:

Dividends per share and capital gain of common stock, 434
Buying and selling costs of stocks, 440–441
Earnings per share for common stock, 443
Price-earnings ratio of common stock, 444
Yield of common stock, 444
Buying and selling costs of bonds, 449–450
Current yield of a bond, 452
Yield to maturity of a bond, 453

Section 15.1 Introduction

There are times when a corporation may need funds in excess of those in the company treasury. Plant expansion, acquisition of another company, modernization of facilities, even the birth of the corporation itself may require capital beyond the ability of the company to supply. It may be possible to borrow the money from a lending institution, but there are more advantageous methods of raising capital. Corporations often raise money by selling securities to the public. Two of these securities—corporate stocks and corporate bonds—are the subject of this chapter.

Section 15.2 Common stock

When a company issues **common stock,** it offers for sale to the public part ownership in the company. The word *common* in common stock means that the stockholders own the company in common. A **share** is the unit of issue of stock. Evidence of stock ownership is the **stock certificate,** an engraved or lithographed document on which are entered the owner's name, the number of shares, and the date of issue (see figure 15.1).

If, for example, an individual owns 1,000 shares of a total of 100,000 shares of stock, then that person owns 1% of the corporation. If 100 persons each bought 1,000 shares, then the company would be owned by the 100 persons.

As part owners of the corporation, stockholders have a voice in management. Although the direction of the company is determined by a board of directors, this board is elected by the stockholders, and stockholders have the opportunity to vote on company matters and to suggest changes in corporate policy at the annual meeting of the company.

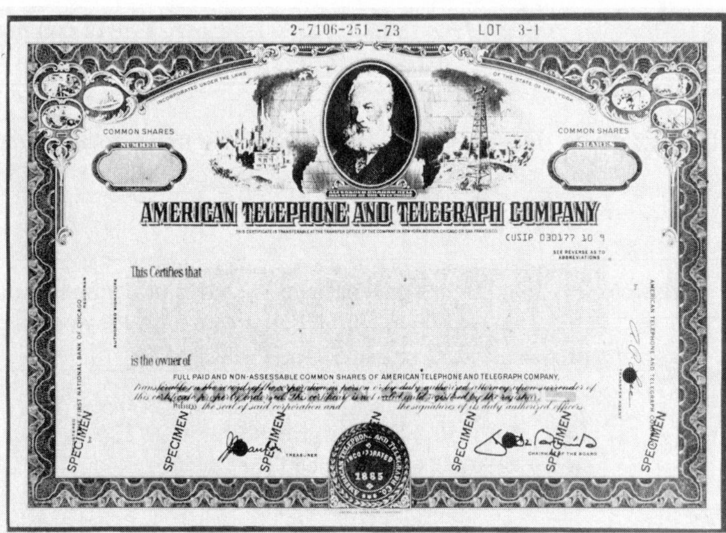

Figure 15.1
Sample stock certificate

Most individuals, however, do not invest in common stock because of part ownership. Instead, they cite the following reasons for buying stock: (1) dividends, (2) capital gain, (3) liquidity and minimum management, and (4) inflation protection.

Dividends

Stock dividends are a percentage of the after-tax profits of a corporation and are usually distributed by the board of directors to the stockholders on a per share basis. Dividends are normally in cash but may be in additional shares of stock or even in property. For example, a dividend of \$0.25 per share to a stockholder who owns 1,000 shares means a payment of $\$0.25 \times 1{,}000 = \$250.00$.

The amount of a dividend often exceeds returns from other forms of investment (for example, bonds or savings accounts), but it should be understood that dividends come from the company's net earnings. A firm that has made no money or that is in financial stress may reduce the amount of the dividend or declare no dividend at all.

The per share dividend is calculated by dividing the total profits to be distributed by the number of outstanding shares.

Example 1

The board of directors of the Craft Corporation voted to distribute 60% of the company's net profits of \$600,000 to the corporation's stockholders. If there are 450,000 outstanding shares of common stock, what was the amount of the declared dividend?

Solution

The amount to be distributed is $\$600{,}000 \times 0.60 = \$360{,}000$.

$\frac{\$360{,}000}{450{,}000} = \$0.80$ Dividend per share of common stock

Capital gain

It is possible for the value of common stock to increase, thus allowing an individual to sell the stock for more than its purchase price. This is called **capital gain.**

Example 2

John Jacobs purchased 500 shares of common stock at \$38.00 a share and later sold them for \$42.50 a share. What was his capital gain?

Solution

\$21,250	Selling price (\$42.50 × 500)
− 19,000	Cost price (\$38 × 500)
\$ 2,250	Capital gain

Liquidity and minimum management Stocks require little attention and may be sold readily for cash. This is not true for all investments, such as real estate.

Inflation protection In general, stock prices increase as prices rise for other commodities, thus protecting the buyer from devaluation of the dollar. Some investments (savings accounts, for example) do not afford this protection.

Section 15.3 Preferred stock

A company may issue another class of stock, called **preferred stock.** Preferred stock differs from common stock in three important ways:

1. Preferred stock dividends are usually fixed and are paid before any dividends are paid to common stockholders.
2. Preferred stock dividends are typically cumulative; that is, should company earnings be insufficient to pay the full dividend per share, the difference is carried over to subsequent dividend distribution payments.
3. In the event of liquidation, preferred stockholders have a claim to the company assets prior to common stockholders.

Example 1 The board of directors of the Orion Corporation voted \$362,000.00 in dividends for the fourth quarter. The company has issued 70,000 shares of preferred stock that pays a quarterly dividend of \$0.60 per share, and there are 640,000 shares of common stock outstanding. Determine the dividend per share of common stock.

Solution

The preferred stock dividends are distributed first. This is already fixed at \$0.60 per share.

\$362,000	Amount to be distributed
− 42,000	Preferred stock dividends (\$0.60 × 70,000)
\$320,000	For distribution to common stockholders

$$\frac{\$320{,}000}{640{,}000} = \$0.50 \text{ per share dividend for common stock}$$

Preferred stock is often described as a hybrid stock because it has characteristics of both common stock and bonds. The chief advantage of preferred stock is its dividend, but there are several disadvantages. Participation in management is restricted, the right to buy additional shares is limited, and the dividend is usually fixed, regardless of the prosperity of the company.

Preferred stocks were issued in large numbers in the latter part of the nineteenth century, when many bankrupt railroads were being reorganized. This type of stock was issued in lieu of common stock to attract investors who wanted a smaller risk than provided by common stock but a greater return than from bonds.

Preferred stock thus occupies an intermediate position between common stock and bonds and must be considered a moderately conservative investment.

Exercises for Sections 15.2 and 15.3

1. The Huron Company is distributing 40% of its net profits of $450,000 to its stockholders. There are 200,000 outstanding shares of common stock in the company. What is the dividend per share of common stock?
2. John Porter owns 200 shares of common stock in the Martin Mining Company. The company has decided to distribute 50% of its first quarter profits of $700,000 to its stockholders. If there are 500,000 outstanding shares of common stock, how much will John receive in dividends?
3. Lucille Porter purchased 100 shares of common stock in the Owens Corporation. The company's board of directors voted to distribute 60% of the company's profits of $225,000 to its stockholders, and there are 300,000 outstanding shares of common stock. How much did Lucille receive?
4. There are 240,000 outstanding shares of common stock in the Otis Manufacturing Company. The company's quarterly profits in 1989 were:

Quarter I:	$210,000
Quarter II:	$160,000
Quarter III:	$140,000
Quarter IV:	$170,000

   If the company distributed 60% of its profits to its 180,000 stockholders, what was the annual dividend per share of common stock in 1989?
5. Myron Industries recorded the following profits in 1989, with the given percentages distributed among the company's stockholders:

Quarter I:	$110,000; 60%
Quarter II:	$180,000; 65%
Quarter III:	$ 90,000; 40%
Quarter IV:	$105,000; 45%

   If there are 213,000 outstanding shares of common stock, what was the annual dividend per share of common stock in 1989?
6. Joan Richards purchased 150 shares of common stock in Continental Industries at $22.25 per share and a year later sold the stock for $26.75 per share. What was her capital gain?

7. At the beginning of the second quarter, Tim O'Connor bought 300 shares of Data Systems common stock at $14.75 per share. The company's board of directors voted to distribute 40% of the company's second-quarter profits of $350,000.00 among its stockholders, and there are 400,000 outstanding shares of common stock. Tim sold his stock at the end of the quarter for $17.25 per share. What was his capital gain? How much did he receive in dividends? What was his total profit on the transaction?

8. The board of directors of the Babson Company voted $150,000.00 in dividends for the third quarter. The company has issued 30,000 shares of preferred stock that pays a quarterly dividend of $0.20 per share, and there are 400,000 shares of common stock outstanding. Determine the dividend per share of common stock.

9. There are 800,000 outstanding shares of common stock in the Lyonkraft Company and 70,000 shares of preferred stock that pay a quarterly dividend of $0.60 per share. For the second quarter, the company will distribute $410,000.00 in dividends. Determine the dividend per share of common stock.

10. Rhonda Myer has 100 shares of preferred and 400 shares of common stock in the Scott Manufacturing Company. For the first quarter, the company will distribute $257,000.00 in dividends. If the preferred stock pays a quarterly dividend of $0.50 a share, and if there are 580,000 shares of common and 50,000 shares of preferred stock outstanding, how much will Rhonda receive in dividends?

Section 15.4 Transactions in stocks

When a corporation first issues stock, it is usually sold at **par value,** the amount printed on the stock certificate. After a share of stock becomes publicly held, the issuing company can no longer control its ownership or its price. As a result, stock is bought and sold like any other commodity.

For major corporations, the principal market for stocks is a stock exchange. In the United States, the largest stock exchanges are the New York Stock Exchange and the American Stock Exchange. At a stock exchange, the price of a stock is determined by the most fundamental of economic concepts—the law of supply and demand. Shares are sold by a two-way auction: Buyers compete with other buyers for the lowest price, and sellers compete with other sellers for the highest price.

The actual trading (buying and selling) of a stock is executed by stock exchange members, called brokers. If an investor wants to buy or sell a share of stock, he or she must place an order with a broker, usually via a local brokerage office. Once the order is placed, the broker bargains for the best possible price, whether the order involves a purchase or a sale.

Figure 15.2
Sample newspaper account of stock transactions

52 Weeks High	Low	Stock	Div.	Yld %	P-E Ratio	Sales 100s	High	low	Close	Net Chg.
31⅝	15¼	Armco	1.20	7.7	10	1692	15¾	15¼	15½	− ¼
39½	21½	Armc	pf2.10	8.8	..	9	24	23⅞	23⅞	+ ⅛
20⅞	14	ArmR	s .80	4.0	5	37	20¼	20⅛	20⅛	− ⅛
18⅜	13¼	ArmWln	1.10	6.9	21	1841	16¼	15⅝	16	+ ⅜
17	13⅞	AroCp	1b	6.5	8	2	15½	15¼	15½	+ ¼
16	7¾	ArowE	.16	1.1	64	66	14⅝	14⅛	14⅝	+ ⅜
24⅞	16⅛	Artra	.20	1.1	65	18	19½	18¾	18¾	− ¾
16⅜	11¾	Arvin	1.12	7.9	12	146	14¼	13⅞	14⅛	+ ⅜
25½	18⅞	Arvin	pf 2	8.9	..	13	22½	22⅛	22½	+ ¼
38	17¼	Asarco	.40	1.6	..	596	25¾	25	25	− ¾
39¾	20½	AshlOil	2.40	8.5	6	261	28¼	27¾	28⅛	+ ⅜
35½	29¼	AshlO	pf4.50	13.	..	5	35	34½	35	+1
41⅜	29¼	AshlO	pf3.96	12.	..	2	34	34	34	.....
39⅜	23⅝	AsdDG	2	5.2	10	642	38½	37⅞	38¼	+ ⅛
64½	42	AsdD	pf4.75	7.4	..	11	64½	64	64	.....
28⅝	14⅝	Athlone	1.60	9.7	6	2	16¾	16½	16½	− ¼
20½	16⅜	AtCyEl	2.28	11.	8	141	20⅜	20	20¼	+ ¼
64	57¾	AtlCE	pf5.87	8.4	..	8	u69¾	69¾	69¾	+5¾
1⅝	⅞	AtlMtro	.04e	4.3	3	143	1	15-16	15-16	.....
50⅜	32¼	AtlRich	2.40	5.6	6	6555	42⅞	41	42⅝	+1¾
32½	27	AtlRc	pf3.75	12.	..	z200	31¾	31½	31½	− ¼
87⅞	77¾	AtlRc	pf2.80	2.8	..	17	102	98	101⅝	+4⅜
20⅜	10⅛	AtlasCp		..	2	66	15½	15⅛	15⅛	− ⅛
29½	20	Augat	.32	1.2	18	87	27⅜	26¾	27	+ ¼
30¼	20⅝	AutoDt	.50	1.8	16	1436	27¼	26⅜	27⅛	+ ⅝
23½	13⅞	AvcoCp	1.20	5.5	8	627	22	21⅜	21⅝	+ ⅛
47	31⅛	Avco	pf 3.20	7.3	..	55	43⅞	43⅞	43⅞	+ ⅜
30	20	Avery	.90	3.2	9	167	28⅞	28⅜	28⅜	− ⅝
52¼	34¾	Avnet	1	2.1	12	627	48	47	47¼	+ ⅛
35⅜	19⅜	Avon	2	8.1	8	1598	25½	24⅝	24¾	− ½
20½	16½	Axia	1.15	6.6	9	x30	17½	17½	17½	+ ⅛
29	12⅜	Aydin	s	..	19	248	u30¾	27⅝	29⅛	.....
		— B—B—B —								
19⅛	11¼	Bairnco	.50	3.0	6	44	16⅞	16½	16¾	+ ⅛
42	18¼	BkrIntl	.92	4.2	5	2766	22¼	21⅛	22	+ ¾
26½	16⅜	Baldor	.32	1.7	11	45	19½	18¾	19	− ⅛
36⅛	18⅜	BaldU	s .88	3.1	6	1841	29⅛	28⅛	28¾	.....
08¾	54¼	BldU	pf 2.06	2.4	..	1	84⅞	84⅞	84⅞	.....
38	27⅛	BallCp	2.08	5.2	6	133	u39⅞	38	39⅝	+1⅞
32⅜	20½	BallyMf	.20	.8	7	3115	25½	24	24½	+ ⅛
29½	21	BaltGE	2.84	10.	7	278	27½	27¼	27½	.....
32	14¾	BanCal	1.20	4.8	16	561	25	23½	25	+1¾
9⅛	5½	BanTx	n .20	3.3	6	167	6	5⅞	6	+ ⅛
30⅜	20	Bandag	.90	3.0	11	19	30	29¾	29¾	− ¼
23½	11	BangP	.80	5.0	..	62	16¼	16	16⅛	+ ⅛
48	24	BanP	pf 2	6.4	..	1	31¼	31¼	31¼	+ ¼
47⅜	32⅞	BkNY	3.20	8.0	4	60	40	39⅜	40	+ ¾
18⅜	12½	BkofVa	1.16	6.3	8	138	u18⅝	18⅛	18½	+ ⅜
24¾	15⅝	BnkAm	1.52	8.7	6	3231	17⅝	16⅞	17½	+ ⅜
28	20½	BkARty	2.40	9.5	10	5	25⅜	25⅜	25⅜	− ⅛
36½	25¼	BankTr	2.05	6.4	4	1493	32⅝	30⅝	32¼	+1⅜
20¾	16⅜	BkTr	pf 2.50	12.	..	14	u20⅞	20¼	20¼	− ¼
34	28½	BkTr	pf 4.22	12.	..	1	u34¼	34¼	34¼	+ ¾
14½	5⅜	Banner	.18	2.9	9	36	6⅜	6⅛	6¼	− ⅜
40¼	21¼	BardCR	.56	1.5	15	336	39⅛	37¾	38¼	− ⅞
20½	11⅛	BarnGp	.60	4.0	..	45	15	14¾	14⅞	+ ⅛
26¾	18¾	Barnet	1.08	4.4	8	365	24½	23⅞	24½	+ ¼
29¼	23	Barnt	pf2.38	8.3	..	82	28¾	28¼	28¾	+ ¼
18⅞	13⅜	BaryWr	.40	2.4	11	77	16⅝	16⅛	16⅝	+ ⅜
6⅛	3⅜	BasRes	.24t	4.9	8	253	5	4⅝	4⅞	− ⅛
53	35¼	Bausch	1.56	4.4	25	321	36⅛	35¼	35¾	+ ¼
43⅞	24¼	BaxTr	s .46	1.1	18	884	41⅞	41¼	41½	.....
11⅝	6⅜	BayFin			42	69	10¾	10¼	10½	+ ¼

52 Weeks High	Low	Stock	Div.	Yld %	P-E Ratio	Sales 100s	High	low	Close	Net Chg.
18½	15¾	CwE	pf 2.37	13.	..	2	18⅛	18⅛	18⅛	− ¼
22½	18¼	CwE	pf 2.87	13.	..	100	22½	22½	22½	+ ¼
61	51	CwE	pf 8.40	14.	..	z90	u62	62	62	+1
16¾	12⅜	ComES	1.88	11.	8	42	16½	16¼	16⅜	+ ⅛
67¾	42⅞	Comsat	2.30	3.6	15	462	65¾	62½	64½	+1¼
29⅞	15½	CoPsyc	s.36	1.2	21	180	29⅛	28⅞	28⅞	.....
15⅛	9¾	Compgr		..	..	32	13¼	13⅛	13¼	+ ⅛
16¼	11⅛	CompSc		..	12	377	15	14¾	14⅞	.....
35⅛	19⅛	Cptvsn		..	18	1259	26⅜	25¼	26⅛	+ ⅝
25	16	ConAgr	.86	4.1	8	138	21⅛	20¾	21	+ ½
33⅜	26¾	ConeMl	2.20	6.8	7	17	32¼	32⅛	32¼	+ ⅛
24¼	18¾	ConnE	n2.80	13.	6	4	22⅜	22⅛	22⅛	+ ⅛
20¼	13⅝	CnnNG	2.20	12.	6	x47	18⅜	17¾	17¾	− ¼
29¼	21¼	Conrac	.80	3.0	14	39	26¼	25⅞	26¼	.....
20¼	13¼	ConEd	s1.68	8.5	5	1028	20	19¾	19⅞	.....
40¾	32⅞	ConE	pf 5	13.	..	1	39	39	39	.....
38⅝	26¼	ConFds	2.12	5.4	7	398	u39¼	38⅛	39¼	+1
90	61⅝	ConF	pf4.50	4.9	..	5	u91	89¼	91	+1
48½	32	CnsFrt	1.60	3.4	5	271	46¾	46⅛	46¾	+ ¼
25¾	20	CnsNG	s1.88	7.7	6	173	24⅜	23⅞	24⅜	+ ½
103½	95 •	CnG	pf10.96	11.	..	z30	103	103	103	− ½
18⅞	15⅞	ConsPw	2.44	13.	6	391	18¾	18½	18⅝	+ ⅛
29½	24⅞	CnPw	pf4.16	14.	..	z520	29	28¾	28¾	+ ¾
32½	26⅛	CnPw	pf4.50	15.	..	z1580	u33	29½	29½	−1
55	44½	CnPw	pf7.72	15.	..	z630	52⅛	51	51	−1½
55¼	45	CnPw	pf7.76	14.	..	z650	54¼	51½	54¼	+1¼
54	40	CnPw	pf7.68	14.	..	z1250	53½	51⅞	53½	.....
28¼	23¾	CnPw	pf 4	14.	..	155	27⅞	27¼	27¾	+ ¼
28¼	23¼	CnPw	pf3.98	14.	..	108	27⅞	26⅞	27⅞	+ ¾
26⅞	22¼	CnPw	pr3.85	15.	..	2	26½	26¼	26½	.....
18	14¾	CnPw	pr2.50	14.	..	10	17½	17⅜	17½	.....
16¼	13¼	CnPw	pr2.23	15.	..	7	15⅜	15¼	15⅜	.....
17⅜	14¼	CnPw	pf2.43	15.	..	6	16⅞	16⅝	16⅝	.....
9⅜	3	ContAir		..	..	353	5⅛	4¾	5	+ ¼
6¾	3⅛	ContCop		..	..	10	4⅛	4	4	− ⅛
8¾	7½	CntC	pf 1.25	16.	..	z80	8	8	8	.....
29	20⅝	CntlCp	2.60	11.	6	518	24¾	24⅜	24½	− ¼
36¼	25⅛	CntlGrp	2.60	8.3	5	300	31¼	30½	31¼	+ ⅜
18	14¼	CntGp	pf 2	12.	..	5	16¾	16¾	16¾	+ ⅛
33¾	28¾	CntGp	pf4.50	14.	..	1	32½	32½	32½	− ½
39¼	15⅛	ContIll	2	12.	5	2101	17⅜	16⅝	17⅜	+ ⅝
19	14⅞	ContTel	1.56	8.9	7	748	17¾	17⅜	17⅝	.....
41⅛	21⅛	CtDat	s .55	1.8	7	1316	30⅞	30	30¼	+ ½
41¼	30¼	CnDt	pf 4.50	13.	..	z20	36	36	36	−1
32	20⅞	Conwod	1.40	4.7	9	47	29¾	29	29½	− ⅜
5¼	2½	CookUn	.07r	2.0	..	46	3½	3⅜	3½	+ ⅛
55¾	19¼	Coopr	1.52	6.4	4	1358	24⅛	23½	23¾	.....
57	26¼	Coopl	pf2.90	9.8	..	53	29½	29⅛	29½	+ ⅜
38	22¼	CoopLb	.80	2.1	12	575	u39	36⅞	38¼	+1⅜
23	12¼	CooprT	.64	2.9	5	97	22⅜	22	22⅛	− ¼
30	12¾	Copwd	s1.16	7.4	6	5	16	15¾	15¾	.....
11½	5¾	Cordura	.60	5.6	9	92	10¾	10½	10⅝	.....
14¾	8¼	CoreIn	.44	4.2	9	44	10½	10¼	10½	.....
60⅛	39¼	CornG	2.32	4.3	14	203	54	53¼	53½	.....
21¾	17½	CorBlk	1.80	8.3	10	52	u22	21¾	21¾	+ ⅛
39¼	25⅜	Cowles	1	2.6	23	61	39	38⅝	39	+ ¼
37¼	23⅞	CoxCm	.28	.9	15	216	32⅞	31⅝	32⅝	+ ⅞
8⅛	5	Craig		..	14	2	6⅝	6⅝	6⅝	− ⅛
36½	17¾	Crane	1.60a	7.4	7	828	22	21¼	21½	− ⅛
39¾	20	CrayRs		..	19	588	27⅝	26¾	27½	+ ½
45⅝	20⅛	Criton		..	9	236	u45¾	45⅝	45⅝	+ ⅛
41⅞	20¾	CrockN	2.40	10.	8	85	23⅝	23	23½	+ ¼
28⅛	16½	CrckN	pf2.18	11.	..	5	19⅜	19	19¼	+ ⅛

Because the trading of stocks is subject to supply and demand, the price of a share fluctuates almost daily. The financial sections of many daily newspapers carry an account of the previous day's activity on an exchange. A portion of such an account is shown in figure 15.2. The meaning of the underlined entry in figure 15.2 is as follows:

$39\frac{3}{4}$	The highest selling price during the past 52 weeks. Stocks are sold in whole dollars and units of eighths of a dollar ($12\frac{1}{2}$ ¢ or $0.125). Thus, the high is $39.75 per share for the past 52 weeks.
$20\frac{1}{2}$	The lowest selling price during the past 52 weeks ($20.50).
AshlOil	Abbreviation for the Ashland Oil and Refining Company.
2.40	The amount of the annual dividend.
8.5	The yield. This is discussed in section 15.6.
6	The price-earnings ratio. This is discussed in section 15.6.
261	The number of reported shares sold for the day, in hundreds.
$28\frac{1}{4}$	The highest selling price of the day ($28.25).
$27\frac{3}{4}$	The lowest selling price of the day ($27.75).
$28\frac{1}{8}$	The last or closing price of the day ($28.125).
$+\frac{3}{8}$	The difference between today's closing price and the closing price of the last session in which the stock was traded. Today's closing price was $28\frac{1}{8}$; the last closing price was $27\frac{3}{4}$.

Note the line in figure 15.2 immediately below the one just discussed. This is a second issue of Ashland Oil, a preferred stock issue. The same information is provided as for common stock.

Section 15.5 Buying and selling costs—stocks

All investors who buy or sell stocks on an exchange pay a commission to the broker who executes the order. The amount of the commission depends on the trading price (the price per share × the number of shares). Commission schedules not only vary from broker to broker but may also be negotiable on large stock purchases.

The basic unit of stock purchase or sale is the **round lot,** which is 100 shares or a multiple thereof.* Orders for other than round lots are called **odd lots.** For odd lots, $\frac{1}{8}$ point ($12\frac{1}{2}$¢) per share is added to the broker's commission. This is called the **odd-lot differential.**

In addition to the broker's commission, the seller of a stock must pay certain fees and taxes. The **Securities and Exchange Commission** (**SEC**), a federal regulatory agency created by Congress in 1934 to help protect investors, levies a fee on the trading price of $.01 per $500.00 in value or fraction thereof. In addition, state or local governments may impose transfer taxes. Transfer taxes are usually computed on a graduated scale according to the trading price of the stock.

*For low-volume stocks, a round lot may consist of only 10 shares.

The costs associated with buying or selling stocks are summarized as follows:

Buyer Pays	*Seller Receives*
Trading price × number of shares purchased	Trading price × number of shares sold
plus	**less**
Basic broker commission (**plus** odd-lot differential for odd-lot orders)	Basic broker commission (**plus** odd-lot differential for odd-lot sales)
	less
	SEC fee
	less
	Transfer taxes (if any)

Example 1 Find the total cost of purchasing 100 shares of stock at $40\frac{1}{2}$ if the broker's commission is $58.45.

Solution

$4,050.00	Trading price ($40.50 × 100)
+ 58.45	Broker's commission
$4,108.45	Total cost

Example 2 What is the total cost of purchasing 40 shares of stock at $35\frac{1}{8}$ if the broker's basic commission amounts to 2.2% of the trading price?

Solution

$1,405.00	Trading price ($35.125 × 40)
+ 30.91	Broker's basic commission ($1,405 × .022)
+ 5.00	Odd-lot differential (.125 × 40)
$1,440.91	Total cost

Example 3 Janis McGuire sold 200 shares of stock at $37\frac{5}{8}$. If the broker's commission amounted to 1.4% of the trading price, what did Janis net from the sale?

Solution

$7,525.00	Trading price ($37.625 × 200)
− 105.35	Broker commission ($7,525 × .014)
− 0.16	SEC fee ($7,525 ÷ $500 = 15.05; 16 × $0.01 = $0.16)
$7,419.49	Net to Janis

Example 4 How much would a seller net from the sale of 80 shares of stock at $16\frac{7}{8}$ if the transfer taxes were $3.35 and the broker's basic commission amounted to 2% of the trading price?

Solution

$1,350.00	Trading price ($16.875 × 80)
− 27.00	Basic commission ($1,350 × .02)
− 10.00	Odd-lot differential (.125 × 80)
− 3.35	Transfer taxes
− 0.03	SEC fee ($1,350 ÷ $500 = 2.7; 3 × $0.01= $0.03)
$1,309.62	Net to seller

Example 5 Lowell Fraley sold 300 shares of stock at $27\frac{1}{4}$. The same day, he purchased 250 shares of a stock at $31\frac{1}{8}$. If the broker's basic commission amounted to 1.4% of the trading price on the sale and 1.36% of the trading price on the purchase, and if transfer taxes on the sale were $12, what was the net result of the transactions?

Solution

Sale

$8,175.00	Trading price ($27.25 × 300)
− 114.45	Broker commission ($8,175 × 0.014)
− 12.00	Transfer tax
− 0.17	SEC fee ($8,175 ÷ $500 = 16.35; 17 × $0.01 = $0.17)
$8,048.38	Net to Lowell from sale

Purchase

$7,781.25	Trading price ($31.125 × 250)
+ 105.83	Basic commission ($7,781.25 × 0.0136)
+ 6.25	Odd-lot differential ($.125 × 50)
$7,893.33	Total cost

$8,048.38	
− 7,893.33	
$ 155.05	Received by Lowell after sale and purchase

Exercises for Sections 15.4 and 15.5

In problems 1–10, determine the total cost of purchasing the indicated number of shares of stock at the given price per share and with the given basic broker commission.

1. 100 shares at \$9.00 per share; \$20.40 commission
2. 100 shares at \$22.50 per share; \$41.25 commission
3. 100 shares at $42\frac{1}{8}$ per share; \$57.91 commission
4. 400 shares at $3\frac{1}{4}$ per share; \$52.90 commission
5. 900 shares at $57\frac{3}{8}$ per share; 0.8% of the trading price
6. 1,300 shares at $40\frac{5}{8}$ per share; 0.9% of the trading price
7. 80 shares at $18\frac{1}{2}$ per share; 2.2% of the trading price
8. 55 shares at $32\frac{7}{8}$ per share; 1.8% of the trading price
9. 140 shares at $15\frac{3}{8}$ per share (100 round lot, 40 odd lot); 2% of the trading price
10. 225 shares at $60\frac{5}{8}$ per share (200 round lot, 25 odd lot); 1.2% of the trading price

In problems 11–20, find the net amount to the seller given (a) the number of shares and the price per share, (b) the basic broker commission, and (c) transfer taxes.

11. (a) 100 shares at \$13.00 per share; (b) \$23.60
12. (a) 100 shares at \$21.50 per share; (b) \$40.00
13. (a) 400 shares at $37\frac{1}{2}$ per share; (b) \$141.25; (c) \$11.25
14. (a) 1500 shares at $43\frac{1}{4}$ per share; (b) \$461.50; (c) \$21.65
15. (a) 600 shares at $14\frac{3}{8}$ per share; (b) \$135.60; (c) \$8.70
16. (a) 500 shares at $22\frac{7}{8}$ per share; (b) \$154.94; (c) \$11.44
17. (a) 70 shares at $7\frac{1}{8}$ per share; (b) \$10.70
18. (a) 65 shares at $12\frac{1}{2}$ per share; (b) \$20.56
19. (a) 150 shares at $10\frac{1}{4}$ per share (100 round lot, 50 odd lot); (b) \$39.99
20. (a) 325 shares at $27\frac{5}{8}$ per share (300 round lot, 25 odd lot); (b) \$102.80

In problems 21–24, find the net result of the transactions given (a) the number of shares and the price per share, (b) the basic broker commission, and (c) transfer taxes.

21. Sold (a) 100 shares at $20\frac{1}{8}$ per share; (b) \$38.16
    Bought (a) 200 shares at $13\frac{1}{2}$ per share; (b) \$46.30

22. Sold (a) 500 shares at $16\frac{1}{4}$ per share; (b) $95.12
Bought (a) 300 shares at 22 per share; (b) $111.40

23. Sold (a) 175 shares at $30\frac{1}{2}$ per share; (b) $50.04; (c) $5.34
Bought (a) 400 shares at $12\frac{7}{8}$ per share; (b) $68.35

24. Sold (a) 160 shares at $9\frac{3}{8}$ per share; (b) $29.50; (c) $2.50
Bought (a) 80 shares at $13\frac{5}{8}$ per share; (b) $36.20

Section 15.6 Valuation indices—stocks

Because of the fluctuation in stock prices, it is possible to make a great amount of money in the stock market; it is also possible to lose a great amount of money.* Consequently, investors have long sought methods to predict market behavior. While some formulas have been successful over a long period of time, no one has yet found a way to "beat the market." The old axiom is still true: "The market can do anything."

Nevertheless, investors use several indicators to evaluate a stock. Among these are (1) earnings per share, (2) the price-earnings ratio, and (3) the yield.

Earnings per share

The **earnings per share** for common stock is found by dividing earnings available for common stock by the number of outstanding shares:

■ (15–1) $$E/S = \frac{\text{Net profit} - \text{Preferred dividends}}{\text{Outstanding shares}}$$

Example 1

In the previous fiscal year, Gartco Corporation had a net profit of $4,600,000, from which preferred stock dividends were $520,000. If there are 1,800,000 outstanding shares, what is the earnings per share?

Solution

$$E/S = \frac{\$4{,}600{,}000 - \$520{,}000}{1{,}800{,}000}$$

$$= \frac{\$4{,}080{,}000}{1{,}800{,}000}$$

$$= \$2.266$$

$$= \$2.27$$

*Two examples of this are Bernard Baruch and Daniel Drew. Baruch once made $700,000 on one stock, Amalgamated Copper. On the other hand, "Uncle Daniel," one of the most ruthless men in Wall Street history and who amassed a fortune of some $13 million, lost it all in the market and died with assets of less than $1,000.

Earnings per share represents the theoretical portion of total earnings owned by a holder of one share of stock. It is not to be confused with dividends, which are actually distributed to stockholders. In examining earnings per share, investors look for an upward trend.

Price-earnings ratio

The **price-earnings ratio** is a number found by dividing the current market price of a share by the earnings per share:

■ (15–2)
$$P/E = \frac{\text{Current market price}}{\text{Earnings per share}}$$

Example 2 Find the price-earnings ratio of a stock selling for $64 with earnings per share of $4.

Solution

$$P/E = \frac{\$64}{\$4} = \frac{16}{1} = 16$$

The price-earnings ratio is 16 to 1.

The price-earnings ratio is the most frequently used indicator of the relationship between stock prices and earnings and represents the amount that investors are currently paying for $1 of the company's earnings. In general, a high price-earnings stock is bought for growth, and a low price-earnings stock is bought for income. Over a period of time, the price-earnings ratio of a given stock tends to fluctuate over a wide range. It is the task of the investor to estimate the "normal" price-earnings ratio.

Yield

Another simple tool for measuring stock valuation is the yield. The **yield** is that percent found by dividing the annual dividend by the current market price:

■ (15–3)
$$\text{Yield} = \frac{\text{Annual dividend}}{\text{Current market price}}$$

Example 3 Find the yield of a stock if it is currently selling at $36\frac{1}{4}$ and paying an annual dividend of $1.60.

Solution

$$\text{Yield} = \frac{\$1.60}{\$36.25}$$

$$= 0.0441379$$

$$= 4.4\%$$

Yield is considered a definite indicator of the reasonableness of a stock price. Slow-growth stocks may be expected to yield as much as 5%, while future-growth stocks may average only 2% to 3%.

Exercises for Section 15.6

In problems 1–4, find the earnings per share for the indicated common stock.

1. Net profit of \$2,390,000; preferred dividends of \$410,000; 900,000 outstanding shares
2. Net profit of \$4,800,000; preferred dividends of \$1,100,000; 1,500,000 outstanding shares
3. Net profit of \$3,676,000; preferred dividends of \$820,000; 1,400,000 outstanding shares
4. Net profit of \$6,255,000; preferred dividends of \$2,150,000; 2,300,000 outstanding shares

In problems 5–8, find the price-earnings ratio of the given stock. (Round to the nearest whole number.)

5. Selling price of stock, \$27.50; earnings per share, \$1.85
6. Selling price of stock, $43\frac{1}{8}$; earnings per share, \$2.25
7. Net profit of company, \$5,620,000; preferred dividends, \$750,000; outstanding shares of common stock, 1,100,000; selling price of stock, $62\frac{3}{8}$
8. Net profit of company, \$4,750,000; preferred dividends, \$1,150,000; outstanding shares of common stock, 875,000; selling price of stock, $52\frac{7}{8}$

In problems 9–13, find the yield of the given stock. (Round to the nearest tenth of a percent.)

9. Annual dividend per share, \$0.60; selling price, \$24.25
10. Annual dividend per share, \$1.20; selling price, \$31.25
11. Annual dividend per share, \$1.55; selling price, $18\frac{1}{8}$
12. Total annual dividends paid, \$2,300,000; outstanding shares of common stock, 1,875,000; selling price, $19\frac{7}{8}$
13. Total annual dividends paid, \$3,111,000; outstanding shares of common stock, 920,000; selling price, $54\frac{3}{8}$
14. Jane Travis is deciding which of three stocks to purchase. Stock A pays dividends of \$1.80 and sells for $28\frac{1}{8}$; stock B pays dividends of \$0.20 and sells for $3\frac{1}{4}$; stock C pays dividends of \$0.90 and sells for $14\frac{1}{8}$. If Jane is interested in income, which stock should she purchase?

Section 15.7 Bonds

Bonds are a second way in which corporations can acquire capital. When a company issues bonds, it is borrowing money from investors. Thus, a bond is like a long-term promissory note. Each **bond** is an agreement to repay the principal (face value or par value) at a specified time and to pay a set annual rate of interest from the day of issue to the day of redemption.*

As an investment, corporate bonds differ from corporate stocks in the following ways:

1. A stockholder is a part owner of the company and has a voice in management; a person who buys bonds simply lends his or her money to the company.
2. A stockholder expects to share in the company's profits; a bondholder expects to receive only a fixed interest payment. However, a stockholder's dividends may fluctuate or may not be paid at all, but a bondholder receives interest payments when due. Failure of the company to pay bond interest constitutes insolvency of the company.
3. In the event of insolvency, bondholders have a prior claim to the company's assets. The claims of bondholders come first, then preferred stockholders, and last, common stockholders.

Obviously, bonds are a more conservative investment than common stock. But, as the risk is smaller, so is the return. The element of financial risk plays a definite role in both the price and profits of corporate securities. The additional investment security of bonds makes them popular with insurance companies, banks, pension funds, and other investors seeking guaranteed incomes. Common stocks are for investors willing to accept financial risk for potential growth and increased profits.

There are several types of corporate bonds, but the most popular is the **mortgage bond,** which pledges the physical property of the corporation as security. This is an example of a secured bond. Unsecured bonds, called **debentures,** are backed only by the general credit of the corporation.

Since the quality of a bond is a measure of its security, it is a practice to rate bonds according to their security features. A triple-A bond, as rated by an investor service company, offers the ultimate safety in principal and income to the investor. Bonds in the B range are medium to fair security risks, while C-rated bonds are considered highly speculative.

Prior to 1964, most bonds were issued as **bearer bonds;** that is, the bonds were payable to the bearer. Bearer bonds do not indicate the owner's name and may be transferred to a new owner by the simple act of delivery. Interest on bearer bonds is collected by presenting to a bank the appropriate dated coupon attached to the bond.

*Although the set interest rate is nominal (annual), it is customary to pay the interest semiannually.

Since 1964, nearly all new corporate bonds are **registered bonds,** meaning that they are issued to specifically named owners. Interest on registered bonds is by check, and the bonds must be returned to a transfer office for reissue when acquired by new owners. Clearly, registered bonds provide more safety than bearer bonds in the event of loss or theft.

Section 15.8 Transactions in bonds

Bonds are sold in denominations ranging from $50 to $10,000, but the most popular denomination is $1,000. Bonds are marketed at a securities exchange or on the over-the-counter market.* Bond transactions at an exchange are reported daily in the financial section of many newspapers. Figure 15.3 shows a sample of such a report. The meaning of the underlined entry is as follows:

AT & T	Abbreviation for American Telephone and Telegraph.
$7\frac{1}{8}$s	The annual interest rate of the bond ($7\frac{1}{8}$%).
03	The maturity date of the bond (2003).
AAA	The bond rating or quality.
10	The bond yield. This is discussed in section 15.10.
294	The volume of sales in thousands of dollars.
70	The closing price in percent of $1,000 face value; that is, the price is $1,000 × 0.70 = $700.
$+\frac{3}{4}$	The change in closing price from the last trading session.

Section 15.9 Buying and selling costs—bonds

As indicated in section 15.8, the market price of a bond is expressed as a percent of its face value, which is customarily $1,000. A price of 95 means that the current market price is 95% of $1,000, or $950. Similarly, a price of 103 means that the current market price is 103% of $1,000, or $1,030. The difference between the market price and the face value is known as a **discount** when the market price is less than the face value and a **premium** when the market price is greater than the face value.

Why should the market price of a bond be other than the face value? There are two reasons: financial risk and interest rates. The ultimate security of any bond is the ability of the company to earn sufficient income to meet its bond obligations. Thus, bond prices in part reflect confidence in the company.

Prevailing interest rates also play a major role in the market price of a bond. Since the interest rate of a bond is fixed, bonds can be marketed competitively against current interest rates only by adjusting the selling price. To illustrate, if

*An over-the-counter market is made up of securities dealers who may or may not be members of an exchange. Stock of companies with insufficient financial qualifications to be listed on an exchange also are traded on over-the-counter markets.

Figure 15.3
Sample newspaper account of bond transactions

Bond	Rating	Yld	$Vol (thds)	Last	Net Chg.
Abbott 7⅝s96	AA	8.7	17	87⅝	+ ⅛
AetnaL 8⅛ 07	AAA	11.	10	74½	+ ¼
AlPw 17⅜s11	BBB	15.	10	115	+ 1¾
AlPw 15¼s10	BBB	14.	83	105⅝	− ⅜
AlPw 12⅝s10	BBB	13.	35	94¼	− ⅛
AlaPw 9¾s04	BBB	13.	65	76½	+ ½
AlaPw 9½s08	BBB	13.	12	76	.....
AlaPw 9¼s07	BBB	13.	97	74¼	+ 1¼
AlaPw 8⅞s03	BBB	12.	55	72¼	− ⅜
AlaPw 8¾s07	BBB	12.	45	72	+ ⅝
AlaPw 8½s01	BBB	12.	10	69¾	+ ¼
AlaPw 8¼s03	BBB	12.	21	67	+ 1
AlaPw 7⅞s02	BBB	12.	20	64½	+ 2½
AlskH 16¼ 99	A	14.	5	113⅛	+ 2
Alexan 5½s96	B	11.	3	52½	+ ½
AllgLS 10¾99	....	14.	10	78⅛	− 1⅛
AlliedCp zr00	A	....	z21900	12½	− ⅛
AlliedCp zr96	A	....	50	22	+ ½
AlliedCp zr92	A	....	2	32¾	.....
AlliedCp zr87	A	....	70	58½	+ ½
All Ch 5.20s91	A	8.3	2	62¾	+ ⅜
AllisChl 16s91	BB	17.	49	92	− ¾
AllisChl 12s90	BB	15.	30	78	+ ½
AMAX 14¼90	BBB	14.	1	100½	.....
AMAX 8½s96	BBB	13.	5	67⅞	+ ¾
AMAX 8s86	....	9.4	12	85½	+ ¼
Amhes 7⅛ 96	BBB	11.	5	66	− 2
AmAirl 11s88	BBB	12.	4	91⅛	+ ⅛
AmAirl 10s89	BBB	13.	26	79¼	+ ⅜
AmAir 4¼s92	BB	9.1	12	46½	− ½
ABrnd 8⅛s85	A	8.6	30	94⅝	.....
ABrnd 5⅞s92	A	8.5	69	69	+ ½
ABrnd 4⅝s90	A	7.5	2	61½	+ 1¼
AForPw 5s30	A	13.	5	40	+ ¼
AMF 10s85	A	10.	3	96	.....
A Med 9½s01	BBB	8.0	13	119	+ 2
A Motor 6s88	CCC	8.0	17	75⅛	+ ⅞
A Sug 5.30s93	BBB	9.2	9	57½	− ½
AT&T 13¼s91	AAA	13.	211	106¼	+ 1
AT&T 10⅜s90	AAA	11.	114	98⅛	+ ½
AT&T 8¾s00	AAA	10.	264	83¾	+ ¼
AT&T 8.80s05	AAA	11.	249	82¾	− ⅛
AT&T 8⅝s07	AAA	11.	131	80⅞	− ⅛
AT&T 7⅛s03	AAA	10.	294	70	+ ¾
AT&T 7s2001	AAA	10.	522	69⅞	+ ⅞
AT&T 4⅜s85	AAA	4.9	35	89½	− ¾
AT&T 3⅞s90	AAA	5.6	15	69	.....
AT&T 3¼s84	AAA	3.6	94	90⅝	− ⅜
AT&T 2⅞s87	AAA	3.6	52	79¾	+ ¼
AT&T 2⅝s86	AAA	3.2	5	82⅛	+ ⅛
Ampex 5½ 94	BBB	7.4	15	74½	− 2½
Ancm 13⅞s02	B	12	50	117	+ 1
Ancmp 9½ 00	B	8.3	58	114	+ 1⅞
AnBsh 11⅞12	A	12.	10	101	.....
Arco PL 8s84	AA	8.2	26	97⅝	+ ⅝
AriPS 12⅛s09	A	12.	10	98	.....
AriPS 7.45s02	A	11.	15	65⅞	− ¼
Armour 5s84	BB	5.3	14	95	.....
Arm C 8.45 84	AA	8.8	2	96	− ¼
Arms Ck 8s96	AA	11.	10	72	− 1
AshOi 8.20s02	BBB	12.	49	67⅜	− ⅜
AssoCp 9¼ 90	A	11.	50	88	+ ⅝
Atchison 4s95	AA	8.0	8	49¾	+ ⅛
AtlRch 8⅝s00	AA	11.	17	82	+ ½
AtRch 11⅜ 10	AA	12.	5	98⅛	+ ⅛
AvcoF 8½s84	A	8.7	72	98	+ 1⅜
AvcoF 8.20 86	A	9.1	11	89¾	− ⅛
AvcoF 7⅞s89	A	9.8	1	80⅝	+ ⅝
AvcoF 7⅞s92	A	11.	5	75¼	+ 5⅜
AvcoM 7½s93	BB	12.	5	63⅝	.....
AvcoM 5½s93	B	8.4	20	65¾	+ ¾
Bald Ul 10s09	BB	14.	2	74	− 1⅞
Bally M 10s06	....	9.2	209	108½	− 1½
Bally Mf 6s98	BB	5.7	42	105	− 1
BaltGs 10⅛83	AA	10.	10	99	+ ¼
BaltGs 9⅜s08	AA	11.	18	82	+ 2
BaltGs 3¼s90	AA	5.4	4	60½	.....
B&O 4½s10a	B	5.5	2	82⅛	− 1⅞
BangP 11¼98	B	14.	5	78½	+ ½
Bk A 13.25s88	AA	13.	5	105	.....
BnkAm 8⅞05	AA	11.	10	80	+ 2
BankAm zr91	AAA	....	125	39⅞	+ ⅝
BankAm zr93	AAA	....	185	32½	+ ⅜
Bnk NY 12s06	....	10.	35	118	− ½
BarnB 12¼06	A	9.8	10	124⅜	− ⅛
BectonD 5s89	A	6.1	66	82	+ ½
Becton 4⅛s88	A	4.5	6	92½	.....
BellC 14½s91	AA	13.	65	108½	+ ⅞
BlTel 11⅞s20	AAA	12.	238	99½	+ ½
BlTPa 9⅝s14	AAA	11.	289	84¼	+ 2¼
BlTPa 9¼s19	AAA	11.	10	81	+ 1
BlTPa 8⅛s17	AAA	11.	10	72¼	+ 1⅜
BlTlPa 8⅝ 06	AAA	11.	20	76⅞	+ 2⅜
BlTPa 7½s13	AAA	11.	2	66¾	.....
BlTlPa 7⅛ 12	AAA	11.	74	65⅛	+ 1¾
BenC 13⅜s91	A	13.	10	102⅜	+ ⅝
Ben C 9.40s85	A	10.	15	93¾	− 1¼
BethS 8.45s05	A	13.	10	63	.....
BethSt 6⅞s99	A	13.	22	55	− ½
BethSt 4½s90	A	7.8	42	57½	+ ⅝
Big3In 8½s06	A	11.	26	80	.....
BlkDk 8.45s85	A	8.9	5	94⅝	− ⅜
Boeing 8⅞s06	AA	9.7	62	91¾	− ¼
BosEd 9¼07	BBB	13.	3	70	+ 7
GenHost 6s90	CC	9.4	10	63½	+ 4⅜
GMAc 14⅝ 89	AA	14.	2	108½	− ½
GMAc 14⅜ 91	AA	13.	25	107¼	− ¾
GMa 13.45s90	AA	14.	75	96⅞	− ¼
GMA 12⅝s85	AA	12.	25	103½	+ ⅜
GMa 11.90s87	AA	12.	280	102½	+ ⅜
GMtA 11¾s00	AA	12.	35	97	.....
GMtA 11⅝s90	AA	12.	35	101	− ¼
GMtA 11¾s89	AA	12.	25	102¼	+ ½
GMtA 10⅞s87	AA	11.	20	100	− ⅛
GMAC 9⅝s89	AA	10.	5	94¾	+ ¾
GMAC 9.40 04	AA	12.	10	81¾	− ⅛
GMAC 9s84	AA	9.2	27	97⅝	− ¼
GMAC 8.70 83	AA	8.8	60	99¼	+ ⅝
GMAC 8⅞s85	AA	9.3	74	95¼	+ ⅜
GMAC 8¾s01	AA	11.	10	78⅜	+ 3⅜
GMAC 8s02	AA	11.	20	72⅜	+ 1½
GMAc 8⅛86A	AA	8.9	20	91	+ ¾
GMAC 8.15 86	AA	9.0	60	90⅝	+ ⅛
GMAC 8⅛s84	AA	8.2	25	99⅜	+ 2⅜
GMAC 8⅝s85	AA	9.1	15	94⅝	+ 1⅞
GMAC 8.20 88	AA	9.3	25	88⅛	.....
GMAC 8⅛s96	AA	11.	10	76⅛	+ ⅛
GMAc 8⅛86B	AA	8.8	15	91⅞	+ ⅛
GMAC 8s0..	AA	11.	55	71	+ ⅛
GMAC 8s93	AA	10.	13	78¾	+ ⅝
GMAC 7.85 98	AA	11.	47	73⅛	+ ⅜
GMAc 7.30s85	AA	7.9	20	93	+ 2¼
GMAC 7¼s95	AA	9.9	25	73⅜	− ⅛
GMAC 7⅛s90	AA	9.1	4	78¼	− ½
GMAC 6¼s88	AA	7.8	64	80¼	+ ¼
GMAC 6s11	AA	11.	5	56½	.....
GMAC 7.35 87	AA	8.4	86	87½	− ⅜
GMAC 4⅞s87	AA	6.2	55	78¾	+ ⅜
GMAC 4⅝s86	AA	5.6	5	83¼	− ⅛
GnMtr 8.05 85	AA	8.5	9	94⅝	+ ⅛
G TelC 8⅞s96	BBB	12.	1	75	+ 7½
Gn Tel 9¾s95	BBB	11.	23	85¼	− 1¾
Gn Tel 9⅜s99	BBB	12.	8	80⅜	+ ¼
Gn Tel 6¼s91	BBB	8.8	2	70⅝	.....
Gen Tel 5s92	BB	5.2	23	97	+ 1
Gen Tel 4s90	BB	4.3	1	92	.....
GaPc 10.70 87	A	15.	50	97⅝	+ ⅝
GaPac 5¼s96	BBB	6.2	81	85	− ½
GaPw 17½ 91	BBB	15.	5	117	+ ⅜
GaPw 16¼ 11	BBB	15.	8	109½	+ ⅝
GaPw 14½ 10	BBB	14.	124	105	+ 1¼
GaPw 11¾ 05	BBB	13.	30	89⅞	+ 1¾
GaPw 11⅝ 00	BBB	13.	20	91	+ 1
Ga Pw 11s09	BBB	13.	33	86⅝	+ ¼
GPwr 10½s09	BBB	13.	45	83	+ 1
Ga Pw 8⅝s04	BBB	12.	2	71	+ ½

a \$1,000 bond paying 6% interest is sold for \$612.25, then the actual return on the investment is $\frac{\$\ 60.00}{\$612.25} = 0.098 = 9.8\%$. Thus, the bond interest plus the difference between the face value and the market price is equivalent to investing at a simple interest rate of 9.8%. In general, as prevailing interest rates increase, bond prices decrease; as prevailing interest rates decrease, bond prices increase.

Another factor in the actual cost of a bond is accrued interest. Because interest is paid only to the owner of a bond, the purchaser pays the seller for all accrued interest since the last interest payment. The interest is computed with the simple-interest formula $I = Prt$, using the financial calendar of a 30-day month and a 360-day year. Most bond interest is paid semiannually.

Both buyer and seller pay a broker's commission, which also adds to the cost of a bond. A typical commission is \$10 per bond or \$25, whichever is greater.* Finally, the seller of a bond is subject to an SEC fee of \$.01 per \$500.00 quotation or fraction thereof.

The costs of buying and selling bonds can be summarized as follows:

Purchase price = Market price + accrued interest + commission

Sale price = Market price + accrued interest − commission − SEC fee

In examples 1–3, the face value of the bonds is \$1,000.

Example 1 Find the cost of buying five Con Oil 9s02 bonds quoted at $89\frac{1}{2}$ if the date of the sale is March 1 and interest is paid on January 1 and July 1.

Solution

The market price per bond is

$$89\tfrac{1}{2}\% \times \$1{,}000 = 0.895 \times \$1{,}000 = \$895 \text{ per bond}$$

January 1 to March 1 is 60 days; thus, $t = \frac{60}{360} = \frac{1}{6}$. The accrued interest per bond is

$$\begin{aligned} I &= Prt \\ &= \$1{,}000 \times 0.09 \times \frac{1}{6} \\ &= \$15 \text{ per bond} \end{aligned}$$

	\$4,475	Market price (\$895 × 5)
+	75	Accrued interest (\$15 × 5)
+	50	Commission (\$10 × 5)
	\$4,600	Cost

*Bond commissions vary, often according to the number of bonds purchased. However, a fixed rate of \$10 per \$1,000 bond or \$25, whichever is greater, is used in the examples and problems of this section.

Example 2 Alice Blake bought 10 Evco $11\frac{1}{2}$s96 bonds quoted at $104\frac{1}{4}$. If the date of the sale was October 1 and interest is paid on January 1 and July 1, what did Alice pay for the bonds?

Solution

The market price per bond is $104\frac{1}{4}\% \times \$1{,}000 = \$1{,}042.50$

July 1 to October 1 is 90 days; thus, $t = \frac{90}{360} = \frac{1}{4} = 0.25$. The accrued interest is

$$
\begin{aligned}
I &= Prt \\
&= \$1{,}000 \times 0.115 \times 0.25 \\
&= \$28.75 \text{ per bond}
\end{aligned}
$$

	\$10,425.00	Market price (\$1,042.50 × 10)
+	287.50	Accrued interest (\$28.75 × 10)
+	100.00	Commission (\$10 × 10)
	\$10,812.50	Cost

Example 3 Richard Whitlock sold two BiCon $8\frac{1}{4}$s98 bonds on November 25. The bonds were quoted at $91\frac{1}{8}$ and paid interest semiannually on March 1 and September 1. How much did Richard net from the sale?

Solution

The market price per bond is $91\frac{1}{8}\% \times \$1{,}000 = \$911.25$.

The time from the last interest payment is two months and 24 days or 84 days.* The accrued interest is

$$
\begin{aligned}
I &= Prt \\
&= \$1{,}000 \times 0.0825 \times \frac{84}{360} \\
&= \$19.25 \text{ per bond}
\end{aligned}
$$

	\$1,822.50	Market price (\$911.25 × 2)
+	38.50	Accrued interest (\$19.25 × 2)
−	25.00	Commission minimum
−	0.04	SEC fee (\$1,822.50 ÷ \$500 = 3.645; 4 × \$0.01 = \$0.04)
	\$1,835.96	Net to Richard

*The *settlement date* is the date that the buyer makes payment and acquires title to the bond. Thus, the interest period is:

September 1 to November 1	= 2 months	= 60 days
November 1 to November 25		= 24 days
Interest period		= 84 days

Exercises for Sections 15.7 through 15.9

In problems 1–8, find the cost of buying the given bonds. (The face value of the bonds is $1,000.)

1. Ten WyCo 7s99 bonds quoted at $62\frac{1}{2}$; date of sale, April 1; interest paid on January 1 and July 1
2. Two Chry 9s96 bonds quoted at $87\frac{1}{4}$; date of sale, October 1; interest paid on January 1 and July 1
3. Eight Grmn $8\frac{1}{4}$s02 bonds quoted at $72\frac{1}{8}$; date of sale, July 1; interest paid on April 1 and October 1
4. Fifteen GMe $7\frac{1}{8}$s14 bonds quoted at $91\frac{1}{4}$; date of sale, July 14; interest paid on January 1 and July 1
5. Nine SCN $6\frac{7}{8}$s98 bonds quoted at $87\frac{1}{2}$; date of sale, April 22; interest paid on February 1 and August 1
6. Four Medco $7\frac{5}{8}$s03 bonds quoted at $64\frac{1}{2}$; date of sale, August 28; interest paid on April 1 and October 1
7. Eight MePw $10\frac{1}{2}$s11 bonds quoted at 103; date of sale, April 1; interest paid on January 1 and July 1
8. Twelve TMA $11\frac{1}{4}$s98 bonds quoted at $105\frac{1}{4}$; date of sale, May 18; interest paid on February 1 and August 1

In problems 9–16, find the net proceeds from the sale of the given bonds. (The face value of the bonds is $1,000.)

9. Three SPac $7\frac{1}{2}$s94 bonds quoted at 78; date of sale, May 1; interest paid on January 1 and July 1
10. Five Arpw $5\frac{1}{4}$s04 bonds quoted at $41\frac{1}{8}$; date of sale, December 1; interest paid on January 1 and July 1
11. Six SunP $6\frac{7}{8}$s02 bonds quoted at $52\frac{3}{8}$; date of sale, February 16; interest paid on February 1 and August 1
12. Nine FnCo $9\frac{1}{4}$s95 bonds quoted at $95\frac{1}{2}$; date of sale, May 27; interest paid on May 1 and November 1
13. Fifteen OCC $8\frac{7}{8}$s93 bonds quoted at $88\frac{1}{4}$; date of sale, June 18; interest paid on March 1 and September 1
14. Twelve BnkC $7\frac{5}{8}$s07 bonds quoted at $74\frac{1}{4}$; date of sale, May 19; interest paid on February 1 and August 1
15. Fifteen MaCr $12\frac{1}{4}$s14 bonds quoted at $108\frac{1}{8}$; date of sale, June 12; interest paid on March 1 and September 1
16. Ten NoGa $11\frac{3}{8}$s09 bonds quoted at $110\frac{1}{2}$; date of sale, February 12; interest paid on February 1 and August 1

17. David Truitt sold four A&O $7\frac{1}{8}$s96 bonds, each with face value of $1,000, on April 14. The bonds were quoted at $82\frac{1}{4}$ and paid semiannual interest on February 1 and August 1. That same day, he used part of the proceeds to purchase three PaC $8\frac{7}{8}$s04 bonds, each with face value of $1,000 and quoted at $92\frac{1}{8}$. If the PaC bonds paid interest on January 1 and July 1, how much did David have left of the proceeds from the sale of the A&O bonds?

18. Janis Boyd sold five StO $8\frac{1}{4}$s07 bonds, each with face value of $1,000, on March 23. The bonds were quoted at $87\frac{1}{8}$ and paid semiannual interest on January 1 and July 1. That same day, she decided to use the proceeds to purchase some MCM $9\frac{1}{8}$s99 bonds, each with face value of $1,000 and quoted at $98\frac{1}{2}$. If the MCM bonds paid interest on March 1 and September 1, how many MCM bonds was she able to buy? How much did she have left of the proceeds from the sale of the StO bonds?

Section 15.10 Valuation indices—bonds

Aside from the yield stated on the bond itself, which is the **nominal yield** (annual interest rate), there are two other valuation indices commonly used by bond investors: current yield and yield to maturity.

Current yield

The **current yield** is that percent found by dividing the annual interest by the current market price:

■ (15–4)
$$\text{Current yield} = \frac{\text{Annual interest}}{\text{Current market price}}$$

As indicated in section 15.9, the current yield is the simple interest rate at which one could invest the market price of the bond and earn the same amount of interest as that generated by the bond. The current yield is the yield quoted in the financial section of a newspaper.

Example 1 Verify the yield for the Gn Tel $6\frac{1}{4}$s91 bonds in figure 15.3. (The face value of the bond is $1,000.)

Solution

Since $6\frac{1}{4} = 6.25\%$, the annual interest is $\$1,000 \times 0.0625 = \$62.50$. From figure 15.3, the trading price is $\$1,000 \times 0.70625 = \$706.25$. Thus,

$$\begin{aligned}\text{Current yield} &= \frac{\$62.50}{\$706.25}\\ &= 0.0884955\\ &= 0.088\\ &= 8.8\%\end{aligned}$$

TAX FREE BONDS

10%
yield to maturity
7.50 current returns

Various New York State agencies are still returning high tax-free returns with as much as 35% capital appreciation (subject to capital gains tax). These bonds offer income exempt from Federal Taxation and New York State and City taxes.

HEINEMAN FRANKLIN, INC.
Investment Bankers
Write or Call (212) 952-0730, (201) 621-6570
One Whitehall Street, New York, N.Y. 10004

Yield to maturity

The most common measure of bond yield is the yield to maturity. The **yield to maturity** is that percent found by dividing the combined annual gain by the average investment. Yields to maturity are normally published in specially prepared bond tables but may be approximated by the following formula:

■ (15–5) $$\text{Yield to maturity} = \frac{\text{Annual interest} + \text{Average capital gain}}{500 + 1/2\ \text{Market price}}$$

where the average capital gain (or loss) is the difference between the face value and the market price divided by the remaining term of the bond.*

Example 2 Find the yield to maturity on a $1,000 bond quoted at 80 if the interest rate is 7% and the remaining term of the bond is 20 years.

Solution

$$\text{Annual interest} = \$1{,}000 \times 0.07 = \$70$$

$$\text{Average capital gain} = \frac{\$1{,}000 - \$800}{20} = \$10$$

$$500 + \frac{1}{2}\ \text{market price} = \$500 + \$400 = \$900$$

$$\begin{aligned}\text{Yield to maturity} &= \frac{\$70 + \$10}{\$900}\\ &= 0.0888888\\ &= 8.9\%\end{aligned}$$

*If there is an average capital loss rather than an average capital gain, then the formula is

$$\text{Yield to maturity} = \frac{\text{Annual interest} - \text{Average capital loss}}{500 + 1/2\ \text{Market price}}$$

Exercises for Section 15.10

In problems 1–8, compute the current yield for the given bonds with face value of $1,000. (Round answers to the nearest tenth of a percent.)

1. GaPw $8\frac{1}{4}$s92 quoted at 93
2. UCar $7\frac{1}{8}$s04 quoted at 82
3. ConP $6\frac{5}{8}$s94 quoted at $71\frac{1}{8}$
4. SMP $7\frac{3}{8}$s99 quoted at $84\frac{3}{8}$
5. DayCo $8\frac{7}{8}$s06 quoted at $97\frac{1}{2}$
6. MWCr $6\frac{1}{8}$s02 quoted at $67\frac{3}{8}$
7. PAA $7\frac{5}{8}$s95 quoted at $85\frac{1}{4}$
8. Bghs $8\frac{3}{8}$s01 quoted at $89\frac{1}{8}$

In problems 9–15, find the yield to maturity for the given bonds with face value of $1,000. (Round answers to the nearest tenth of a percent.)

9. TwCF $7\frac{1}{2}$s quoted at 83; remaining term, 10 years
10. TPL $8\frac{1}{4}$s quoted at 91; remaining term, 20 years
11. PCC $9\frac{1}{8}$s quoted at 94; remaining term, 15 years
12. WstnC $6\frac{7}{8}$s quoted at $71\frac{1}{4}$; remaining term, eight years
13. LTP $7\frac{7}{8}$s quoted at $83\frac{1}{8}$; remaining term, 14 years
14. IntH $8\frac{3}{8}$s quoted at $92\frac{5}{8}$; remaining term, 12 years
15. Frmt $6\frac{3}{8}$s quoted at $68\frac{7}{8}$; remaining term, six years
16. John Boswell is considering purchasing DTT $7\frac{7}{8}$s bonds, each with face value of $1,000 and quoted at $87\frac{5}{8}$. The remaining term of the bonds is 22 years. Compute the current yield and the yield to maturity.
17. Kathy Forbes is trying to decide whether to buy GPL $6\frac{1}{8}$s bonds, each with face value of $1,000 and quoted at $71\frac{1}{8}$, or NLL $8\frac{1}{4}$s bonds, each with face value of $1,000 and quoted at $87\frac{1}{8}$. If the remaining term of the GPL bonds is 12 years and the remaining term of the NLL bonds is eight years, which of the bonds has the greatest yield to maturity?

Glossary

Bearer bond A bond that is issued payable to the bearer. Transfer of ownership is effected by the simple act of delivery.

Bond A written agreement to repay a specified amount of money on a certain date and to pay a specified annual rate of interest during the term of the bond.

Capital gain The selling price of stock minus the purchase price, provided that the selling price is higher.

Common stock Partial ownership of a company without guaranteed dividends; represented by transferable certificates.

Current yield An indicator for evaluating bonds; the percent found by dividing the annual interest by the current market price.

Debenture A bond that is backed only by the general credit of the company.

Discount When a bond is sold at a price less than its face value.
Dividend See *stock dividend.*
Earnings per share An indicator for evaluating common stock; found by dividing the earnings that are available for common stockholders by the number of outstanding shares of common stock.
Mortgage bond A bond that pledges the physical property of the company as security.
Nominal yield The annual interest rate stated on a bond.
Odd lot A number of shares of stock that is not a round lot.
Odd-lot differential An extra commission of $12\frac{1}{2}$¢ per share charged on the purchase or sale of odd-lot orders of stock.
Par value The face amount of a bond, or the amount printed on a stock certificate. When a corporation first issues stock, it is the usual selling price of one share.
Preferred stock Stock with a guaranteed dividend per share that is paid before any dividends are paid to common stockholders.
Premium When a bond is sold at a price greater than its face value.
Price-earnings ratio An indicator for evaluating common stock; the current market price of a share of stock divided by the earnings per share.
Registered bond A bond that is issued to a specifically named owner. Registered bonds must be reissued by a transfer office when acquired by new owners.
Round lot Usually, 100 shares of stock or a multiple thereof; for low-volume stocks, a round lot may be any multiple of 10 shares.
Securities and Exchange Commission (**SEC**) A federal regulatory agency created in 1934 to help protect investors.
Share The unit of issue of stock.
Stock certificate An engraved or lithographed document that serves as evidence of stock ownership.
Stock dividend A portion of the profits of a company distributed to stockholders on a per share basis.
Yield An indicator for evaluating common stock; the percent found by dividing the annual dividend by the current market price.
Yield to maturity An indicator for evaluating bonds; the percent found by dividing the total annual gain by the average investment.

Review test

1. An individual bought 50 shares of a stock at $23\frac{1}{8}$ and later sold them at $30\frac{1}{4}$. The difference in money that the individual received is called ______________.

2. In the event of liquidation, owners of ______________ stock have a claim to assets prior to owners of ______________ stock.

3. The most frequently used indicator of the relationship between stock prices and earnings is the ______________.

4. A ______________ is an example of a secured bond, while a ______________ is an example of an unsecured bond.

5. Two reasons for the market price of a bond to differ from the face value are ______________ and ______________.

6. One hundred shares of a stock or a multiple thereof is called a ______________.

7. A bond offering the ultimate safety in principal and income to an investor would be rated ______________ by an investor service.

8. Mastercraft Industries is distributing 80% of its net profits of $640,000 to its stockholders. If there are 800,000 outstanding shares of common stock, what is the dividend per share?

9. The board of directors of the Amron Company voted $420,000.00 in dividends for the first quarter. The company has issued 80,000 shares of preferred stock that pays a quarterly dividend of $1.20 per share, and there are 720,000 shares of common stock outstanding. Determine the dividend per share of common stock.

10. Gail Barrett purchased 200 shares of stock at $14\frac{3}{8}$ and later sold them at $33\frac{5}{8}$. What was her capital gain?

11. Phil Krueger purchased 60 shares of stock at $27\frac{1}{8}$. If the broker's commission was 2.4% of the trading price, what was the total cost of the stock, including the broker's commission and the odd-lot differential?

12. Last year, Millfield Industries had a net profit of $6,400,000, from which preferred stock dividends were $840,000. If there are 2,400,000 outstanding shares of common stock, what were the earnings per share of common stock?

13. A stock currently sells for $42\frac{1}{2}$ and pays an annual dividend of $2.20. Find the yield. (Round to the nearest tenth of a percent.)

14. Find the current yield on ACC $9\frac{1}{4}$s02 bonds, each with face value of $1,000 and quoted at 89. (Round to the nearest tenth of a percent.)

15. On October 1, Arnold Snell sold six KMrt $8\frac{1}{2}$s98 bonds, each with face value of $1,000 and quoted at $84\frac{1}{4}$. If interest is paid on January 1 and July 1, find the net amount Arnold received from the sale of the bonds.

PART 4

Selected Topics

Insurance is a business necessity, and the chapter on insurance includes detailed coverage of four forms of business insurance: life insurance, group insurance, fire insurance, and automobile insurance. Statistics and graphs have become a vital decision tool for management, and businesses are rapidly converting to metric measurements. Chapters in this part examine these topics.

CHAPTER 16

Insurance

Chapter Objectives

I. Learn the meaning of the following terms:

Peril, 459
Hazard, 459
Insurance, 459
Insurance policy, 459
Insured, 459
Insurer, 459
Face value of a policy, 461
Beneficiary, 461
Mortality table, 463
Net premium, 465
Gross premium, 465
Level premium, 468
Participating and nonparticipating life insurance policies, 470

II. Understand:

The purpose of the parts of a policy, 459
The concepts of term insurance and cash-value insurance, 461
The types of cash-value insurance, 461–463
The calculation of life insurance premiums using a mortality table, 463–466
The concept of level premium, 467–469
The types of nonforfeiture values, 472
The types of settlement options, 473–474
The concept of group insurance, 477–478
Coinsurance and insurer's liability, 481, 484
Types of automobile insurance coverage, 491–492

III. Calculate:

The net premium of a one-year term policy, 465–466
Gross level premiums for various payment periods, 468–470
Nonforfeiture values, 473
Settlement options, 474
Group insurance premiums, 478–479
Fire insurance liability, 484–485
Fire insurance premiums, 486–489
Automobile insurance premiums, 495–496
Automobile insurance claims, 497

Section 16.1 Introduction

The financial loss resulting from illness, death, fire, theft, flood, or countless other hazards can be catastrophic. For protection from such losses, individuals and businesses turn to insurance. Insurance is a means of avoiding possible economic loss.

The fundamental principle of insurance is group sharing of losses. People subject to a particular risk combine their resources and share losses on an equitable basis. This permits each member of the group to be protected against a substantial loss for a relatively small cost. This basic insurance principle is found in the earliest written records. Today, insurance can be purchased for almost any peril, and the insurance industry is one of the largest and most influential businesses in the world.

Because of its unique product, a specialized vocabulary has developed for insurance. The following terminology is common to all types of insurance and must be understood to interpret an insurance contract properly:

Peril An event (fire, accident, illness, etc.) that causes a loss.
Hazard A condition that may create a peril or increase its probability of occurrence.
Insurance A contract whereby a party undertakes to guarantee another party against loss by an accidental event.
Insurance policy The contract wherein the terms and conditions of the insurance are stated.
Insured The person or organization named in an insurance policy to receive the insurance coverage provided by the policy.
Insurer (or **underwriter**) The organization that sells an insurance policy.
Policyholder The owner of an insurance policy.
Premium The cost of an insurance policy.

A typical insurance policy consists of four parts:

1. The **declaration** contains descriptive material indicating who is covered, what is covered, the amount of coverage, and the premium.
2. The **insuring agreement** specifies exactly what perils are covered.
3. The **exclusions** state what the insuring agreement does not cover.
4. The **conditions** are the stipulations that the insured must fulfill to receive the insurance.

Most policies follow the foregoing format with the parts clearly identified. Some deviations from the standard format can be found, but an understanding of these four parts will make them recognizable in any policy.

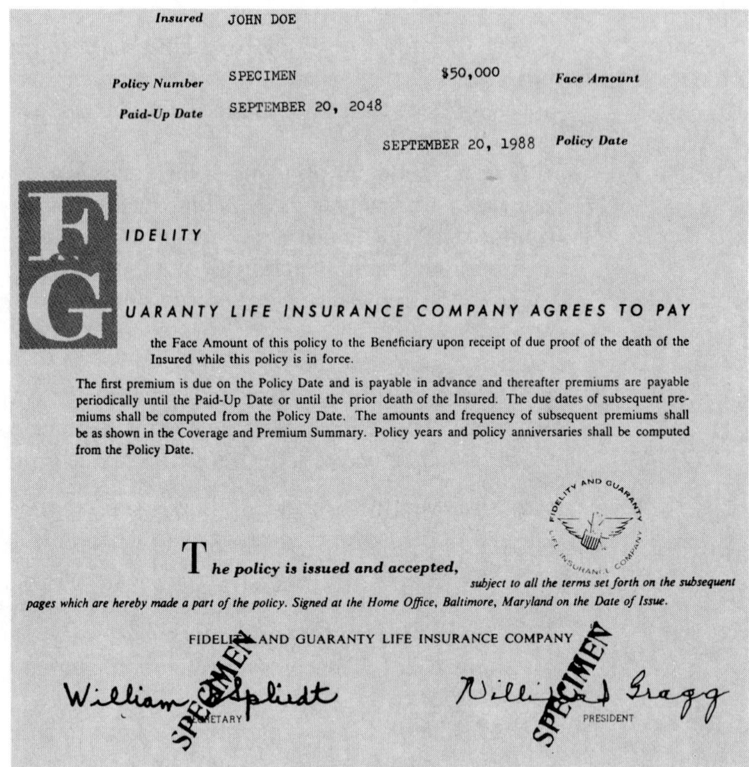
Insured JOHN DOE

Policy Number SPECIMEN $50,000 Face Amount

Paid-Up Date SEPTEMBER 20, 2048

SEPTEMBER 20, 1988 Policy Date

FIDELITY

GUARANTY LIFE INSURANCE COMPANY AGREES TO PAY the Face Amount of this policy to the Beneficiary upon receipt of due proof of the death of the Insured while this policy is in force.

The first premium is due on the Policy Date and is payable in advance and thereafter premiums are payable periodically until the Paid-Up Date or until the prior death of the Insured. The due dates of subsequent premiums shall be computed from the Policy Date. The amounts and frequency of subsequent premiums shall be as shown in the Coverage and Premium Summary. Policy years and policy anniversaries shall be computed from the Policy Date.

The policy is issued and accepted, subject to all the terms set forth on the subsequent pages which are hereby made a part of the policy. Signed at the Home Office, Baltimore, Maryland on the Date of Issue.

FIDELITY AND GUARANTY LIFE INSURANCE COMPANY

SECRETARY PRESIDENT

Figure 16.1 Sample life insurance policy

Every policy should be carefully read to be sure that the coverage desired is so stated, that nothing is excluded from the desired coverage, and that the person or property is described correctly and completely. A sample life insurance policy is shown in figure 16.1.

The kinds and varieties of insurance could easily be the subject of an entire textbook. In this chapter, the discussion is limited to four forms of insurance common to business operations: life insurance, group insurance, fire insurance, and automobile insurance.

Section 16.2 Life insurance

The primary purpose of life insurance is to offset financial need resulting from the death of a person. Upon the death of the insured, the insurance company promises to pay a specified amount of money (the **face value** of the policy) to a person or persons (the **beneficiaries**) named by the policyholder.

There are two categories of life insurance: term insurance and cash-value insurance. Term insurance is pure protection, while cash-value insurance combines protection with a savings account.

Term insurance

Term insurance is protection for a limited period. The period may be as short as the duration of an airplane flight or may extend to age 65 or 70, but common periods for term policies are one, five, or ten years. Term insurance is analogous to rent; it provides protection but develops no equity. The advantage of term insurance is that it provides the maximum life insurance protection for the premium dollars.

Term insurance can be renewable, convertible, or both. Renewable term insurance means that the policyholder has the option of renewing the contract for a limited number of additional periods. Convertibility means that the policyholder can exchange the term policy for a form of cash-value insurance. This conversion is guaranteed regardless of the physical condition of the insured at the time of conversion.

Cash-value insurance

One thing that all individual life insurance policies have in common is that they are constructed on a framework of increasing cost with increasing age. That is, the premium per $1,000 increases each year (see section 16.3).

Because of the unpopularity of an annual price increase, insurance companies have developed the level premium plan. A level premium is the same for each installment, higher than the actual cost of the protection in the lower ages but considerably less than the cost of the protection at the upper ages. The excess premium at the lower ages is invested at compound interest, and the accumulated amount is used to offset the higher protection cost at the upper ages.

The fund thus accumulated is held in trust for the policyholder and represents a savings element called the **cash value.** Cash-value insurance thus combines insurance protection with a guaranteed investment feature.

Cash-value insurance comes in three basic forms—ordinary life, limited payment life, and endowments—and these three forms are discussed here in order of increasing premium cost.

Ordinary life insurance

Also known as whole or straight life insurance, **ordinary life insurance** is characterized by the payment of premiums as long as the insured lives. It is the basic policy of most life insurance companies and usually the most widely sold. In the sense that the policy never has to be renewed or converted, it is often referred to as "permanent" protection.

The extended payment period makes the ordinary life policy the least expensive of the cash-value plans, but most persons do not plan to pay premiums beyond a certain age. At that point, they hope to exercise one of the nonforfeiture options contained in the policy (see section 16.5). Insurance protection ceases with the last payment, but the accumulated cash value may be used to purchase an annuity, to buy other forms of insurance, or in a variety of other ways. This flexibility is one of the advantages of cash-value insurance.

Two recent variations of ordinary life insurance are *universal life insurance* and *variable life insurance.* In universal life policies, premiums are placed in a general fund from which the life insurance company makes investments, and the returns on these investments generate cash value for the policyholder. Thus, it is possible that the rate of cash-value increase will exceed the rate guaranteed by regular ordinary life policies. Variable life insurance is similar to universal life policies, except that policyholders are allowed to specify that premiums be placed in one or more of a variety of separate investment funds, such as stock funds, fixed investment funds, bond funds, and others.

Limited payment life insurance

Limited payment life insurance plans have the same features as ordinary life insurance except that premium payments are limited to a specified period of years. The idea is to pay for a lifetime of coverage during the peak income-earning years. Thus, limited payment policies are sold with payment periods of 10, 15, 20, 25, or 30 years, or to a specified age, such as 65 or 70.

Unless the policyholder exercises one of the settlement options, upon completion of the payments, the insurance remains in force, thus providing permanent or lifetime insurance protection. The higher premiums necessitated by a shorter payment period are offset by greater cash values than for an ordinary policy of the same face value, thus providing a larger fund for use if needed.

Endowment insurance

In contrast to term insurance and the other forms of cash-value insurance that pay the face amount of the policy only in the event of death, **endowment insurance** pays the face amount if the insured is alive as of a specified date, called the maturity date. That is, if the insured dies during the endowment period, the beneficiary receives the face value; if the insured survives the endowment period, the policyholder receives the face value. Typical endowment periods are 10, 15, or 20 years, or may be specified as a particular age—for example, 60 or 65.

Endowment insurance emphasizes the investment feature of cash-value insurance. A traditional use of endowment policies is to provide educational funds for children. However, the "can't miss" feature of this form of insurance makes it the most expensive of the cash-value forms (see section 16.4). Note also that endowment insurance is not permanent insurance; insurance protection ceases upon payment of the face value to the policyholder at the maturity date. Essentially, endowment insurance is a savings plan with insurance to protect the savings program against premature death.

Section 16.3 Life insurance premiums

The instrument used by a life insurance company to price its product is called a mortality table. A **mortality table** indicates the probability of death at each age. Insurance companies have kept careful records of groups of people, recording the number living and dying at each age. These statistics form the basis of a mortality table and are sufficiently accurate to estimate future deaths.

A mortality table widely used by insurance companies is shown in table 16.1. The table indicates the number of deaths and the number of survivors of a hypothetical group of 10,000,000 males from age 0 to age 100 and also gives the number of deaths per 1,000 at each age.

The use of a mortality table can be illustrated in the calculation of the premium of a one-year term policy: Suppose 100,000 males, all age 30, purchased $1,000 of term life insurance for one year. What premium should the insurance company charge for the insurance? According to table 16.1, 213 of this group will die before reaching age 31. Thus, the insurance company would have to pay out a total of $\$1,000 \times 213 = \$213,000$ in claims.* The per insured share of the cost is $\$213,000 \div 100,000 = \$2.13$. In other words, if each of the 100,000 members of the group pays $2.13 to be insured, the $213,000 collected will be exactly the amount needed to pay the beneficiaries of those who died during the year.

Actually, the premium charged would be less than $2.13. Since insurance premiums are paid in advance, the company could invest the money for one year. The present value of $213,000 at a conservative rate of 5% compounded annually is

$$\$213,000 \times 0.95238095 = \$202,857.13 \qquad \text{(Appendix D)}$$

which amounts to

$$\$202,857.14 \div 100,000 = \$2.0285713 = \$2.03$$

per insured member.

*In calculating premiums using table 16.1, insurance actuaries make the following assumptions: (1) premiums are paid in advance, (2) claims are paid at the end of the year, and (3) the death rate is uniform throughout the year.

Table 16.1 Mortality Table

Age	Number Living	Number Dying	Deaths per 1,000	Age	Number Living	Number Dying	Deaths per 1,000
0	10,000,000	70,800	7.08	50	8,762,306	72,902	8.32
1	9,929,200	17,475	1.76	51	8,689,404	79,160	9.11
2	9,911,725	15,066	1.52	52	8,610,244	85,758	9.96
3	9,896,659	14,449	1.46	53	8,524,486	92,832	10.89
4	9,882,210	13,835	1.40	54	8,431,654	100,337	11.90
5	9,868,375	13,322	1.35	55	8,331,317	108,307	13.00
6	9,855,053	12,812	1.30	56	8,223,010	116,849	14.21
7	9,842,241	12,401	1.26	57	8,106,161	125,970	15.54
8	9,829,840	12,091	1.23	58	7,980,191	135,663	17.00
9	9,817,749	11,879	1.21	59	7,844,528	145,830	18.59
10	9,805,870	11,865	1.21	60	7,698,698	156,592	20.34
11	9,794,005	12,047	1.23	61	7,542,106	167,736	22.24
12	9,781,958	12,325	1.26	62	7,374,370	179,271	24.31
13	9,769,633	12,896	1.32	63	7,195,099	191,174	26.57
14	9,756,737	13,562	1.39	64	7,003,925	203,394	29.04
15	9,743,175	14,225	1.46	65	6,800,531	215,917	31.75
16	9,728,950	14,983	1.54	66	6,584,614	228,749	34.74
17	9,713,967	15,737	1.62	67	6,355,865	241,777	38.04
18	9,698,230	16,390	1.69	68	6,114,088	254,835	41.68
19	9,681,840	16,846	1.74	69	5,859,253	267,241	45.61
20	9,664,994	17,300	1.79	70	5,592,012	278,426	49.79
21	9,647,694	17,655	1.83	71	5,313,586	287,731	54.15
22	9,630,039	17,912	1.86	72	5,025,855	294,766	58.65
23	9,612,127	18,167	1.89	73	4,731,089	299,289	63.26
24	9,593,960	18,324	1.91	74	4,431,800	301,894	68.12
25	9,575,636	18,481	1.93	75	4,129,906	303,011	73.37
26	9,557,155	18,732	1.96	76	3,826,895	303,014	79.18
27	9,538,423	18,981	1.99	77	3,523,881	301,997	85.70
28	9,519,442	19,324	2.03	78	3,221,884	299,829	93.06
29	9,500,118	19,760	2.08	79	2,922,055	295,683	101.19
30	9,480,358	20,193	2.13	80	2,626,372	288,848	109.98
31	9,460,165	20,718	2.19	81	2,337,524	278,983	119.35
32	9,439,447	21,239	2.25	82	2,058,541	265,902	129.17
33	9,418,208	21,850	2.32	83	1,792,639	249,858	139.38
34	9,396,358	22,551	2.40	84	1,542,781	231,433	150.01
35	9,373,807	23,528	2.51	85	1,311,348	211,311	161.14
36	9,350,279	24,685	2.64	86	1,100,037	190,108	172.82
37	9,325,594	26,112	2.80	87	909,929	168,455	185.13
38	9,299,482	27,991	3.01	88	741,474	146,997	198.25
39	9,271,491	30,132	3.25	89	594,477	126,303	212.46
40	9,241,359	32,622	3.53	90	468,174	106,809	228.14
41	9,208,737	35,362	3.84	91	361,365	88,813	245.77
42	9,173,375	38,253	4.17	92	272,552	72,480	265.93
43	9,135,122	41,382	4.53	93	200,072	57,881	289.30
44	9,093,740	44,741	4.92	94	142,191	45,026	316.66
45	9,048,999	48,412	5.35	95	97,165	34,128	351.24
46	9,000,587	52,473	5.83	96	63,037	25,250	400.56
47	8,948,114	56,910	6.36	97	37,787	18,456	488.42
48	8,891,204	61,794	6.95	98	19,331	12,916	668.16
49	8,829,410	67,104	7.60	99	6,415	6,415	1,000.00

The calculation of \$2.03 is called the **net premium** because it does not take into consideration the expenses of the company. The premium actually paid is called the **gross premium** and includes the cost of the insurance, the company's overhead expenses, and contingency reserves.

With a net premium of \$2.03 per member, the insurance company records the following:

\$203,000	Premium collected (\$2.03 × 100,000)
+ 10,150	Interest on invested premium (\$203,000 × 0.05)
\$213,150	
− 213,000	Claims paid (\$1,000 × 213)
\$ 150	Surplus (due to rounding of premium)

It is not necessary to insure 100,000 people to determine the premium per individual. This may be found in another way using table 16.1. At age 30, there are 2.13 deaths per 1,000. This is equivalent to $\frac{2.13}{1,000}$ or 0.00213. Multiplying this by the face value of the policy determines the premium; that is, \$1,000 × 0.00213 = \$2.13. At an assumed rate of 5% per annum, the present value of \$2.13 for one year is

$$\$2.13 \times 0.95238095 = \$2.0285713$$
$$= \$2.03 \text{ Net premium}$$

Example 1 Find the net premium for a one-year term policy of \$50,000 sold to a male age 40 if the assumed interest rate is 5% per annum.

Solution

From table 16.1, the death rate is 3.53 per 1,000, or 0.00353. Thus,

$$\$50,000 \times 0.00353 \times 0.95238095 = \$168.10$$

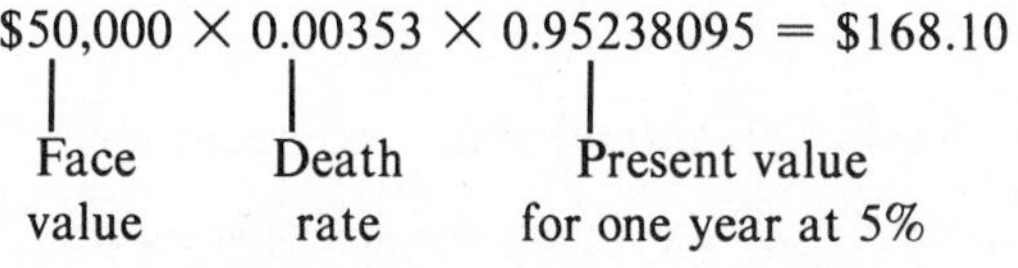

Table 16.1 is based on the experiences of 10,000,000 men. Since women have a longer life expectancy than men, an adjustment must be made if this table is to be used in calculating premiums for females. One approach is to base the premium on an age less than the applicant's actual age. For example, a female age 25 might have her premiums calculated as though she were age 22.

Example 2 Joan Jacobs (age 25) purchased a one-year term policy for $150,000 from the Presidential Insurance Company. Presidential uses a three-year age reduction for females and assumes an interest rate of 5% per annum. Find the net premium.

Solution

From table 16.1, the death rate at age $25 - 3 = 22$ is 1.86 per 1,000 or 0.00186. Thus, the net premium is:

$\$150{,}000 \times 0.00186 \times 0.95238095 = \$265.71$

Exercises for Sections 16.2 and 16.3

In problems 1–10, find the net premium for a one-year term policy with the given face amount and the given interest rate issued to a male of the given age.

1. $150,000; 5%; age 40
2. $80,000; 4%; age 24
3. $120,000; 5%; age 42
4. $70,000; $3\frac{1}{2}$%; age 36
5. $130,000; $4\frac{1}{2}$%; age 52
6. $140,000; 5%; age 49
7. $84,500; $4\frac{1}{2}$%; age 27
8. $47,500; $5\frac{1}{2}$%; age 56
9. $185,000; $4\frac{1}{2}$%; age 37
10. $69,500; $3\frac{1}{2}$%; age 28

In problems 11–16, one-year term policies of the given face amount are issued to females. Find the net premium for the given interest rate and the given age reduction.

11. $57,500; 4%; age 24; three-year age reduction
12. $73,000; 3%; age 42; four-year age reduction
13. $125,000; 5%; age 34; three-year age reduction
14. $88,000; $4\frac{1}{2}$%; age 46; five-year age reduction
15. $120,000; $5\frac{1}{2}$%; age 52; four-year age reduction
16. $45,000; 4%; age 39; three-year age reduction
17. Eloise Clark, age 22, purchased a one-year term policy for $25,000 from a company that uses a two-year age reduction for females. If the interest rate is 4% per annum, what was the net premium for the policy?
18. Find the net premium for a one-year term policy of $80,000 sold to a female, age 37, if the assumed rate of interest is 5% per annum and the company uses a three-year age reduction for females.

19. Bob Forester has been assigned to do extensive traveling for his company during the coming year. He decides to purchase a \$50,000 one-year term policy. If the interest rate is 5% per annum and if Bob is 34 years old, what is the net premium for the policy?

20. Mary Johnson, age 46, purchased a \$30,000 one-year term policy from a company that uses a three-year age reduction for females. At an interest rate of $4\frac{1}{2}\%$ per annum, find the net premium for the policy.

Section 16.4 Level premiums

Premium calculations in section 16.3 were for a one-year term policy. The premiums change each year and escalate rapidly in the later years.* Figure 16.2 graphs the net premium per \$1,000 of a renewable one-year term policy issued at age 30 and assuming an interest rate of 3% per annum.

An annual price increase would make insurance a difficult commodity to sell. Furthermore, during the later years, the cost could well be prohibitive. To overcome this difficulty, insurance companies developed the level premium plan.

Figure 16.2
Line graph of net premium of a renewable one-year term policy

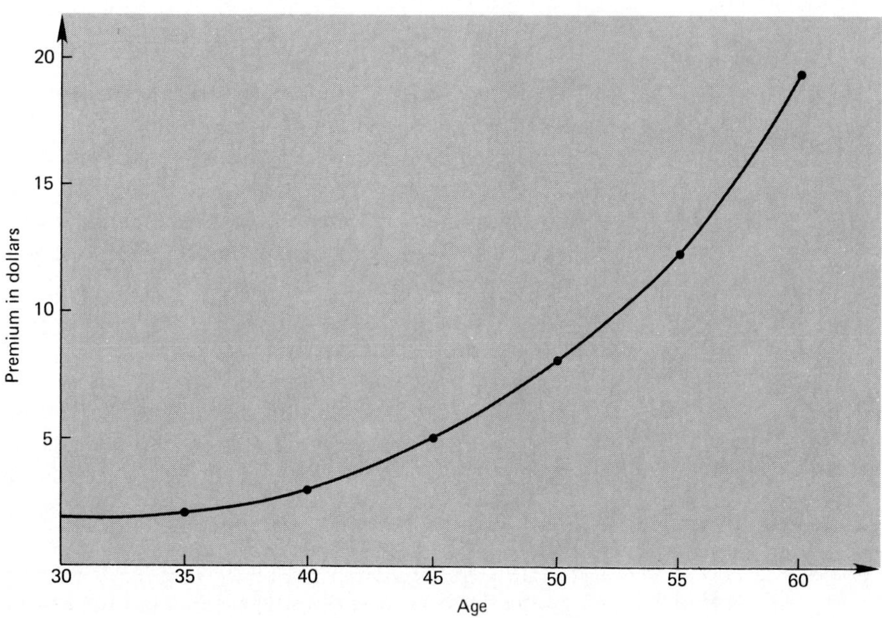

*This is true for all life insurance plans.

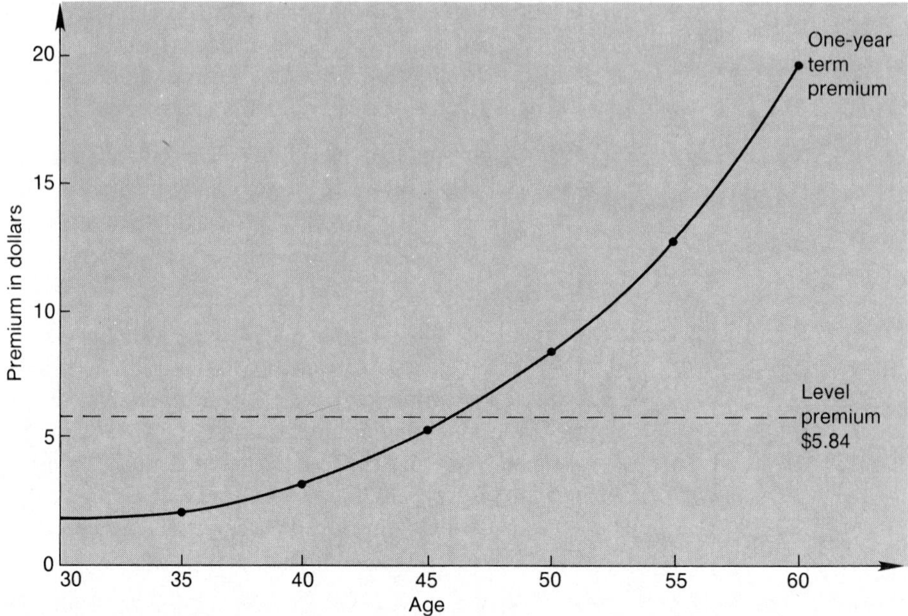

Figure 16.3
Line graph comparison of a yearly renewable term premium and a level premium

A **level premium** is a premium that is the same for each payment. Figure 16.3 illustrates the level premium of a term policy to age 60 compared with the renewable premium of the yearly term policy. Both are issued at age 30, and the rates are based on an interest rate of 3% per annum. Note that the level premium is greater than the renewable premium at the early ages but less at the later ages. The insurance company invests the excess premium from the early ages at compound interest and uses the interest to offset the difference in premium at the higher ages. The excess premium is also used to generate the cash value in cash-value policies.

The methods used to calculate the level premium are beyond the scope of this text, but table 16.2 illustrates the annual gross level premium per $1,000 for four types of policies at selected ages. The total gross premium is found by multiplying the face value of the policy (in thousands) by the appropriate entry in the table.

Example 1 Using table 16.2, what is the annual premium for an ordinary life policy of $45,000 issued to a 50-year-old man?

Solution

$33.60 × 45 = $1,512

Table 16.2 Annual Level Premium Rates per $1,000 Face Value

Age	Ten-Year Renewable Term	Ordinary Life	Twenty-Payment Life	Twenty-Year Endowment
25	$ 9.97	$12.95	$21.50	$43.13
30	11.79	15.31	24.34	43.55
35	14.17	18.40	27.78	44.24
40	17.22	22.36	31.75	45.32
45	21.13	27.44	36.77	46.89
50	25.87	33.60	42.34	49.12
55	31.90	41.44	48.90	52.94
60	40.74	52.31	58.06	59.26

Example 2 Vicky Williams (age 30) purchased a 20-payment life policy from Megapolis Life Insurance Company, which uses a five-year setback in calculating rates for females. If the face value of the policy is $80,000 and Megapolis uses the rates of table 16.2, what is Vicky's annual premium?

Solution

A five-year setback means that Megapolis would use the rate for age 25. Hence,

$21.50 × 80 = $1,720

The level premiums discussed thus far are annual premiums. However, payment periods may also be semiannual, quarterly, or monthly. These rates are a percentage of the annual rate and may be approximated according to table 16.3.*

Table 16.3 Percent of Annual Premium Paid for Different Payment Periods

Payment Period	% of Annual Premium
Semiannual	52
Quarterly	26
Monthly	9

*It is possible to circumvent the increased semiannual and quarterly premiums by the use of multiple policies. For example, in lieu of a single policy of $10,000 with semiannual payments, two $5,000 policies, each with an annual premium, could be purchased at six-month intervals. Not only does this avoid increased premium costs, but it provides greater flexibility for the policyholder and the beneficiary.

Example 3 At age 40, John Higgins purchased a 20-year endowment policy with a face value of $125,000. If the rates are based on tables 16.2 and 16.3, what is the amount of John's monthly premium?

Solution

$\$45.32 \times 125 \times 0.09 = \$509.85$

Although insurance companies are conservative in their estimates of death rates and interest earnings, premiums are based on probabilities, and actual claims could exceed income. One method of guarding against this eventuality is to charge a premium greater than the company expects to need under normal circumstances. The company later refunds a portion of this surplus in the form of dividends. Policies with dividend provisions are called **participating** and are usually marketed by mutual insurance companies.* Generally, dividends begin from one to three years after purchase and increase in size each year. Over a period of time, dividends can substantially reduce the actual insurance cost.

A life insurance policy without the dividend feature is said to be **nonparticipating.** Here the risk of excess claims is borne by the owners of the company, normally the stockholders. As a rule, nonparticipating premiums are considerably less than corresponding participating policies, but there are no provisions for dividends.

Exercises for Section 16.4

In problems 1–10, use table 16.2 to find the annual premium for the given policy if the insured is a male of the given age.

1. $180,000 10-year renewable term; age 40
2. $100,000 20-year endowment; age 30
3. $60,000 20-payment life; age 35
4. $120,000 ordinary life; age 55
5. $125,000 20-payment life; age 25
6. $80,000 10-year renewable term; age 60
7. $85,000 ordinary life; age 45
8. $50,000 20-year endowment; age 60
9. $135,000 ordinary life; age 35
10. $250,000 10-year renewable term; age 40

*A mutual life insurance company is owned by the policyholders who share in the company's surplus earnings in the form of dividends. Nonparticipating policies are usually sold by a stock life insurance company, which is a corporation owned by the stockholders. Surplus earnings of a stock company are distributed to the stockholders as dividends.

In problems 11–16, find the annual premium for the given policy if the insured is a female and the company uses a five-year age reduction.

11. $125,000 20-payment life; age 40
12. $50,000 ordinary life; age 30
13. $75,000 10-year renewable term; age 55
14. $60,000 20-year endowment; age 45
15. $145,000 20-payment life; age 35
16. $80,000 10-year renewable term; age 50

In problems 17–22, use tables 16.2 and 16.3 to find the net premium for the given periodic payment on the given policy if the insured is a male.

17. $60,000 ordinary life; age 35; monthly payment
18. $120,000 10-year renewable term; age 50; quarterly payment
19. $50,000 20-year endowment; age 40; semiannual payment
20. $75,000 20-payment life; age 25; monthly payment
21. $50,000 10-year renewable term; age 60; semiannual payment
22. $200,000 ordinary life; age 45; quarterly payment

In problems 23–28, use tables 16.2 and 16.3 to find the net premium for the given periodic payment on the given policy if the insured is a female. (Use a five-year age reduction.)

23. $85,000 20-year endowment; age 40; monthly payment
24. $145,000 20-payment life; age 35; quarterly payment
25. $200,000 10-year renewable term; age 45; semiannual payment
26. $125,000 20-payment life; age 35; monthly payment
27. $75,000 ordinary life; age 30; quarterly payment
28. $130,000 20-year endowment; age 35; semiannual payment
29. Mary Johnson, age 35, purchased a 20-payment life policy of $80,000. The company uses a five-year age reduction for females. How much is the semiannual premium?
30. Preston French bought a $50,000 ordinary life policy upon the birth of his first child. If he was 25 years old at the time, what was his quarterly premium?

31. Victoria Peters decides to buy a 20-year endowment of $65,000. She is 45 years old, and the company uses a five-year age reduction for females. How much is her monthly premium?

32. When Elvin Harrison was married, he purchased a $100,000 10-year renewable term policy. If he was 30 years old at the time, how much was his quarterly premium?

Section 16.5 Nonforfeiture values

A cash-value insurance policy contains three **nonforfeiture values,** or surrender options, in the event of nonpayment of premiums:

1. *Cash value* The policyholder may receive the cash value of the policy in cash. This terminates the contract, and the company has no other obligation under the policy. Normally, cash values begin to accrue after one or two years.

2. *Reduced paid-up insurance* Under this option, the cash value is used to purchase protection without further premiums. The face amount of the new policy depends on the amount of cash value and the attained age of the insured, but will be less than the original policy. If the original policy was a life policy, the protection is for life; if the original policy was an endowment, the protection continues to the maturity date, at which time the policyholder receives the reduced face value as a cash settlement.

3. *Extended term insurance* With this option, the insurance protection is continued at the face amount by using the cash value to purchase a paid-up term policy. The length of the term depends on the attained age of the insured and the amount of the cash value. This option automatically goes into effect if the policyholder does not elect an option within a specified number of days after failure to make a premium payment.

Table 16.4 illustrates minimum paid-up nonforfeiture values per $1,000 face value for a policy issued at age 35.

Table 16.4 Minimum Paid-Up Nonforfeiture Values per $1,000 Face Value for a Policy Issued at Age 35

	Ordinary Life				**Twenty-Payment Life**				**Twenty-Year Endowment**				
End of Year	*Cash Value*	*Extended Term Years*	*Extended Term Days*	*Reduced Paid-Up*	*Cash Value*	*Extended Term Years*	*Extended Term Days*	*Reduced Paid-Up*	*Cash Value*	*Extended Term Years*	*Extended Term Days*	*Pure Endow-ment*	*Reduced Paid-Up*
3	$ 17.00	4	38	$ 37.97	$ 45.93	9	190	$102.57	$ 84.12	14	313	—	$125.76
5	51.31	9	47	109.84	103.95	15	125	222.53	172.42	15	—	$119.14	246.02
10	140.96	14	91	272.40	259.55	21	291	501.56	412.23	10	—	462.39	523.45
15	235.14	15	183	412.25	431.88	24	352	757.17	684.38	5	—	755.79	772.52
20	331.58	15	72	530.91	624.55	Fully	paid	up	1,000.00	at	maturity		
25	427.84	14	60	630.46	—	—	—	—	—	—	—	—	—
30	520.74	12	310	712.57	—	—	—	—	—	—	—	—	—

Example 1 Twenty-five years after purchase, Herb Goldberg (age 60) elected to surrender his $40,000 ordinary life policy. To what is Herb entitled under the nonforfeiture options of his policy? (Refer to table 16.4.)

Solution

a. *Cash value option* The per $1,000 cash value at the end of 25 years is $427.84. Hence, Herb could elect to receive $\$427.84 \times 40 = \$17,113.60$ in cash.

b. *Reduced paid-up insurance option* Under this option, Herb could elect to receive a paid-up policy with a face value of $\$630.46 \times 40 = \$25,218.40$.

c. *Extended term insurance option* Under this option, Herb could elect to continue his $40,000 coverage for a period of 14 years and 60 days beyond the surrender date.

Section 16.6 Settlement options

It is the prerogative of the policyholder (or in some cases, the beneficiary) to designate the manner in which the proceeds are distributed, and insurance companies offer a variety of options called **settlement options.*** Typically, the options fall into the following four categories:

1. *Cash* The beneficiary may receive the proceeds in cash, generally referred to as a lump-sum payment. Technically, this is not an option because the policy usually provides for this payment unless another option is selected.

2. *Interest option* Under this option, the proceeds remain with the company, and only interest earned on the proceeds is paid to the beneficiary, with provisions for later lump-sum payment or gradual withdrawal.

3. *Installment option* This option liquidates the principal and interest of the proceeds according to one of two plans:

    a. *Fixed period* The payments are spread over a given period of time, with the longer the period, the smaller the installment.
    b. *Fixed amount* Each payment is for a specified amount, with the larger the amount, the shorter the time until the fund is exhausted.

*Because of dividends or policy loans, the actual amount paid by the insurance company may be more or less than the face value of the policy. Hence, the term "proceeds" is used to designate the payment to the beneficiary.

4. *Life income annuity* The proceeds are converted to a life annuity form of income. Several plans are available and may include a *period certain* that provides for a guaranteed number of payments to the beneficiary or to a second beneficiary in the event the primary beneficiary dies before the guaranteed time elapses.

Tables of settlement values often appear in the policy. Table 16.5 illustrates such tables for selected ages.

Table 16.5 Monthly Payment per $1,000 of Proceeds

Option C		**Option D**					
Fixed Period Payments					*Life Income with Payments Certain*		
					Number of Installments		
Years	*Payment*	*Male*	*Female*	*Life Income*	*100*	*120*	*240*
1	$84.32	20	25	$2.95	$2.93	$2.92	$2.86
2	42.71	25	30	3.09	3.07	3.06	2.99
3	28.84	30	35	3.26	3.23	3.22	3.15
4	21.91	35	40	3.49	3.46	3.45	3.35
5	17.75	40	45	3.77	3.73	3.72	3.59
6	14.98	45	50	4.12	4.04	4.02	3.85
7	13.00	50	55	4.58	4.50	4.47	4.19
8	11.52	55	60	5.16	5.02	4.97	4.52
9	10.37	60	65	5.90	5.68	5.50	4.86
10	9.45	65	70	6.88	6.40	6.23	5.13

Example 1 Nell Butterfield (age 50) is the beneficiary of a $20,000 ordinary life policy. She selects the life income option with 100 payments certain. Find the monthly payment using table 16.5.

Solution

For a female age 50, the payment per $1,000 is $4.04. Hence,

$4.04 × 20 = $80.80

Section 16.7 Business uses of life insurance

While the primary use of life insurance is to protect the dependents of the insured against financial loss, businesses also need protection against the loss of a valuable worker. For example, consider a drug company with a chemist who is developing a drug anticipated to be highly successful and profitable to the company. The unexpected loss of this individual may curtail production, affect credit, reduce dividends, or damage the company in other ways. To offset the estimated financial loss, the company may purchase a life insurance policy for this key employee. The company is the beneficiary of the policy and pays the premiums. This form of insurance is called "key man insurance" and is designed to provide cash for the company during the readjustment period following the death of a key employee.

A second use of life insurance in business is for business continuation. For example, in a partnership form of business organization, the general rule of law calls for the dissolution and liquidation upon death of a general partner, with the surviving partners responsible for paying the estate of the deceased his or her share of the business. Because forced liquidation is costly, many partnerships enter into an agreement that binds the surviving partners to purchase at a predetermined price the interest of the first partner to die. One method of purchase is with a life insurance policy. Each partner is insured for his or her share, the policy being owned by the other partners. In the event of death, the proceeds of the policy are used to purchase the deceased partner's share of the business. All parties benefit by this arrangement, and it eliminates the need for liquidation.

Exercises for Sections 16.5 through 16.7

In problems 1–11, use table 16.4 to find the cash value received when the given policy is surrendered after the given number of years.

1. $60,000 ordinary life; 15 years
2. $40,000 20-year endowment; 10 years
3. $50,000 20-payment life; five years
4. $55,000 20-year endowment; five years
5. $45,000 ordinary life; 30 years
6. $65,000 20-payment life; 15 years
7. A $75,000 ordinary life policy is surrendered after 15 years for reduced paid-up insurance. What is the face amount and the term of the new policy?
8. If an $80,000 20-year endowment policy is surrendered after five years for extended term insurance, what is the length of the term of the new policy? What is the face amount of the new term insurance policy?

9. Russ Overmeyer surrendered his $50,000 20-payment life policy after 10 years for reduced paid-up insurance. Find the face amount and the term of the new policy.

10. Find the length of the term when a $35,000 ordinary life policy is surrendered for extended term insurance after 25 years. What is the face amount of the new term insurance policy?

11. A 20-year endowment policy is surrendered after three years for reduced paid-up insurance. If the face amount of the endowment policy was $65,000, what is the face amount and the term of the new policy?

In problems 12–23, use table 16.5 to find the amount of the monthly payment to the beneficiary of a policy with the given proceeds when the given settlement option is selected.

12. Proceeds: $30,000; payee: male, age 40; settlement option: life income

13. Proceeds: $65,000; payee: female, age 60; settlement option: fixed period payments for five years

14. Proceeds: $85,000; payee: male, age 20; settlement option: life income, payments certain, 120 installments

15. Proceeds: $50,000; payee: female, age 45; settlement option: life income

16. Proceeds: $40,000; payee: female, age 35; settlement option: life income, payments certain, 240 installments

17. Proceeds: $80,000; payee: male, age 55; settlement option: life income, payments certain, 100 installments

18. Proceeds: $75,000; payee: male, age 40; settlement option: life income

19. Proceeds: $100,000; payee: male, age 25; settlement option: fixed period payments for 10 years

20. Proceeds: $45,000; payee: female, age 50; settlement option: fixed period payments for six years

21. Pasco Phillips, age 35, is the beneficiary of a $125,000 ordinary life policy, payable as life income. Find the monthly payments that he will receive.

22. Jean Tatum is to receive the proceeds of $40,000 from her father's life insurance in fixed period payments for eight years. If Jean is 45 when her father dies, what are her monthly payments?

23. Find the monthly payments to the beneficiary (male, age 50) of a life insurance policy with proceeds of $130,000 if the proceeds are payable as life income with payments certain in 120 installments.

Section 16.8 Group insurance

Group insurance provides insurance protection to the employees of an organization. Under a group plan, a master contract issued to a company may provide both life insurance and nonoccupational disability insurance to participating employees. Many plans also provide coverage for dependents of employees.

Compared with individual insurance, a group insurance plan contains a number of unique features. Among these are

1. Medical examinations usually are not required for employees actively at work.
2. Benefits are automatically determined by wage bracket, position, or some other employee classification.
3. The cost is shared by the employer. Most plans call for the employer to pay a portion of the total premium. This lowers the cost to the employee and encourages participation in the plan. A minimum percent of employee participation (usually 75%) is required to originate the contract and keep it in force.
4. The actual cost of the insurance is based on the experience of the organization rather than on the experience of the insurance company.

Group contracts may provide a variety of coverages, including:

1. *Term life insurance* The basic plan is yearly renewable term insurance with the same features as individual policies.
2. *In-hospital expense* This coverage pays a specified amount for hospital daily room and board and for miscellaneous hospital charges.
3. *Surgical expense* This benefit pays a surgeon for fees resulting from a surgical procedure. The amount paid is usually specified by a surgical schedule. The maximum benefit on such a schedule may range from $200 to $900.
4. *Major medical expense* This coverage pays a percent (usually 80%) of all covered expenses in excess of a deductible.* Designed to cover the catastrophic illness, maximum benefits under this coverage may be written for $100,000, $200,000, or higher. In a typical plan, benefits under this coverage become payable only after exhaustion of other health benefits and satisfaction of the deductible.

*A deductible is a portion of covered expenses paid by the insured.

Other coverages available under a group plan include:

1. Accidental death and dismemberment
2. Weekly indemnity
3. Long-term disability
4. In-hospital medical care
5. Diagnostic expense
6. Dental care

Section 16.9 Group insurance premiums

Net premiums for group term life insurance are found by multiplying the rate per $1,000 at each age by the number of thousands of insured at that age, adding the results, and dividing by the total amount of insurance to obtain an average rate per $1,000. This rate is charged every employee, regardless of age.* The premium is the product of the rate and the number of thousands of insurance. Premiums are paid monthly.

Example 1 Rainbow Industries has the following group life insurance coverage for its employees:

Officers	$40,000
Supervisors	$25,000
All other employees	$12,000

What is the monthly premium for an individual in each classification if the total premium is $656 and the total insurance is $800,000?

Solution

The rate per $1,000 is $\frac{\$656}{800} = \$0.82$. Thus,

Officers	$\$0.82 \times 40 = \$32.80$
Supervisors	$\$0.82 \times 25 = \$20.50$
All other employees	$\$0.82 \times 12 = \$9.84$

The premium for other group benefits is the sum of the rates for each benefit. The rates vary according to the amount of coverage and the characteristics of the group. The actual premium paid by the employee depends on (1) the contribution of the employer and (2) whether or not dependents are also covered.

*In a company with a normal flow of new, young employees replacing retiring or deceased employees, the average age remains relatively constant, resulting in an almost level premium for the group each year.

Table 16.6 Sample Monthly Premiums for a Variety of Coverages

Coverage		Monthly Premiums Employee	Dependents
A.	Life insurance	$ 0.52/$1,000	—
B.	Accidental death and dismemberment	0.12/$1,000	—
C.	Weekly indemnity	4.84	—
D.	Hospitalization	12.68	$24.56
E.	Surgical expense	4.04	10.36
F.	In-hospital medical care	0.80	1.44
G.	Major medical	3.72	5.80

Example 2 Harry Wurts works for a company that carries coverages A ($5,000), B ($5,000), D, E, and G in table 16.6. Harry insures his family, and the company contributes 75% of the employee (only) premium. How much is Harry's monthly premium?

Solution

The total monthly premiums are

Coverage	*Employee*	*Dependents*
A	$ 2.60	—
B	0.60	—
D	12.68	$24.56
E	4.04	10.36
G	3.72	5.80
Total	$23.64	$40.72

Harry pays 25% of the employee premium, or $23.64 × 0.25 = $5.91, plus the dependent premium for a total of $5.91 + $40.72 = $46.63.

Exercises for Sections 16.8 and 16.9

1. A company provides $10,000 worth of group term life insurance for each of its employees. Find the monthly premium for each employee if the total monthly premium is $315 and the total insurance is $300,000.

2. If $15,000 worth of group term life insurance is provided to each employee of a company, and if the total monthly premium is $292 and the total insurance is $400,000, what is the monthly premium for each employee?

3. Find the monthly group life insurance premium for each employee of a company that provides all employees with $10,000 worth of group term life insurance if the total monthly premium is $385 and the total insurance is $500,000.

4. The executives of Rockford Enterprises are eligible for $25,000 worth of group term life insurance. All other employees are eligible for $10,000 worth of insurance. Find the monthly premium for each executive and for each of the other employees if the total premium is $195 and the total insurance is $250,000.

5. The Minton Company has the following group life insurance coverage for its employees:

Executives	$20,000
Supervisors	$15,000
Other employees	$10,000

What is the monthly premium for an individual in each classification if the total premium is $528 and the total insurance is $800,000?

6. Find the monthly premium for an employee in each classification at the Buford Corporation if the total premium is $996, the total insurance is $1,200,000, and the company provides the following coverages:

Officers	$40,000
Supervisors	$20,000
Other employees	$15,000

In problems 7–12, use table 16.6 to compute the monthly premium for an employee with the given insurance coverage.

7. Coverage: A ($10,000), B ($10,000), D, and E; no dependents; company contributes 65% of the premium

8. Coverage: A ($10,000), B ($10,000), C, D, and E; dependents insured; company contributes 70% of the employee (only) premium

9. Coverage: A ($8,000), B ($8,000), D, E, F, and G; no dependents; company contributes 85% of the premium

10. Coverage: A ($7,500), B ($7,500), C, D, E, and F; dependents insured; company contributes 70% of the employee (only) premium

11. Coverage: A ($14,000), B ($14,000), D, E, and F; dependents insured; company contributes 100% of the employee (only) premium

12. Coverage: A ($9,000), B ($9,000), C, D, E, F, and G; dependents insured; company contributes 100% of the employee (only) premium

Section 16.10
Fire insurance

Both individuals and businesses need to protect their property from loss. Insurance of this type is called property and liability insurance. This section reviews one of the basic coverages of property and liability insurance—fire insurance.

Fire insurance indemnifies the insured for direct losses arising from uncontrolled fire, lightning, and damage to property suffered while the insured is moving the property to safety. Most fire insurance policies conform to a standard fire contract. This contract came into existence because of confusion caused when every company wrote its own policy. Every word and phrase of the standard policy has been interpreted by the courts. The standard policy indicates who is insured; where, when, what property is covered, and what is not covered; the amount of coverage; the premium; and the conditions under which coverage is suspended.

Three factors affect the actual amount paid by the insurance company in the event of a loss: (1) the face value of the policy, (2) the actual damage to the property, and (3) coinsurance. While fire insurance policies have a fixed face value that establishes the maximum liability of the company, most fires seldom cause total destruction, and the insurance company is responsible only for the value of the actual loss, or the cost to repair or replace. Figure 16.4 shows an example of a "Sworn Statement in Proof of Loss" form, which must be filled out by the insured following a fire.

The probability of a fire causing only a partial loss has led many businesses to insure their property for only a fraction of its total value. However, an insurance company cannot afford to pay a loss in full if the premiums are based on the partial value of the property. This situation has led to the practice of coinsurance.

As used in this context, **coinsurance** means that the insurance company and the insured share the risk. The most common ratio is 80%/20%; that is, the insured agrees to carry insurance equal to at least 80 percent of the value of the property. Thus, for a property worth $100,000, the insured would carry a policy of $80,000; in the event of a total loss, the company would pay $80,000, while the insured would absorb $20,000 of the loss.

In a fire insurance policy with a coinsurance clause, the insurer's liability (the amount paid by the insurance company) is the least of the following amounts:

1. The face value of the policy
2. The actual loss
3. The amount determined by

$$\frac{\text{Amount of insurance carried}}{\text{Property value} \times \text{Coinsurance }\%} \times \text{Loss}$$

Figure 16.4
Sworn statement in proof of loss form

AMERICAN STATES INSURANCE

SWORN STATEMENT IN PROOF OF LOSS

POLICY PREFIX & NUMBER

PLEASE CHECK COMPANY ✓

- [ ] American States
- [ ] American Economy
- [ ] American States of Texas
- [ ] ______________________

AMOUNT OF POLICY

$______________

AGENCY NAME, LOCATION

POLICY PERIOD (FROM, TO)

By the above numbered policy of insurance you insured

....

against loss by..upon the property described under Schedule "A," according to the terms and conditions of the said policy and all forms, endorsements, transfers and assignments attached thereto.

1. Time and Origin: A loss occurred about the hour of..............................o'clock.......................M. on the............... day of.., 19......... The cause and origin of said loss were:

....

....

2. Occupancy: The building described, or containing the property described, was occupied at the time of the loss as follows, and for no other purpose whatever:

....

3. Title and Interest: At the time of the loss and when this policy was acquired, the interest of your insured in the property described therein was sole and unconditional ownership, and no other person or persons had any interest therein or incumbrance thereon. (State any exceptions in detail)..

....

....

4. Changes: Since the said policy was acquired there has been no assignment thereof, or change of ownership, use, occupancy, possession, location or exposure of the property described, or of your insured's interest therein. (State in detail any exceptions)..

....

5. Total Insurance: The total amount of insurance upon the property described by this policy was, at the time of the loss, $.., as more particularly specified on the reverse side under Schedule "C", besides which there was no policy or other contract of insurance, written or oral, valid or invalid.

6. The Cash Value of said property at the time of the loss was . . . . $..............................

7. The Whole Loss and Damage as stated under Schedule "B" was . . . . $..............................

8. The Amount Claimed under the above numbered policy is . . . . $..............................

Subrogation: The Insured hereby subrogates the said Company to all rights and causes of action the said Insured has against any person, persons or corporation whomsoever for damage arising out of or incident to said loss or damage to said property.

The said loss did not originate by any Act, design or procurement on the part of your insured, or this affiant; nothing has been done by or with the privity or consent of your insured or this affiant, to violate the conditions of the policy, or render it void; no articles are mentioned herein or in annexed schedules but such as were in the building damaged or destroyed, and belonging to, and in possession of the said insured at the time of said loss; no property saved has in any manner been concealed, and no attempt to deceive the said company, as to the extent of said loss, has in any manner been made. Any other information that may be required will be furnished and considered a part of this proof.

The furnishing of this blank or the preparation of proofs by a representative of the above insurance company is not a waiver of any of its rights.

The undersigned claimant hereby declares he is a native born or naturalized citizen of the United States of America and that he has no connection whatsoever with any foreign government or agency unless otherwise stated hereon.............

....

The undersigned claimant further declares that he is not, by virtue of orders or regulations of the United States Government, prohibited, as a national of a foreign country or otherwise, from accepting payment of within claim, unless otherwise stated hereon..

....

State of.. ....

County of ....*Insured*

Subscribed and sworn to before me this..........................*day of*...19..........

Form 3-119 (1-69) ....*Notary Public*

Figure 16.4
(continued)

SCHEDULE "A"—POLICY FORM

Policy Form No.......................................Dated.......................................
Item 1. $..............................on...
Item 2. $..............................on...
Item 3. $..............................on...
Item 4. $..............................on...
Item 5. $..............................on...
Coinsurance, Average, or Distribution Clause, if any..
Loss, if any, payable to...

SCHEDULE "B"
STATEMENT OF CASH VALUE AND LOSS AND DAMAGE

Item No. Shown on Policy		Cash Value		Loss and Damage	
Totals:					

SCHEDULE "C"—APPORTIONMENT

Policy No.	Expires	Name of Company	Item No......				Item No......			
			Insures		Pays		Insures		Pays	
Totals:										

By..*Adjuster*

....

IMPORTANT

IF IT IS DESIRED THAT THE LOSS CHECK BE MADE PAYABLE TO ANY THIRD PARTY, REPAIRMAN, CONTRACTOR, ETC., THE FOLLOWING MUST BE COMPLETED AND SIGNED BY THE INSURED:

CERTIFICATE OF SATISFACTION:

THIS IS TO CERTIFY That the loss and damage referred to on the reverse side has been repaired and/or replaced to the entire satisfaction of the undersigned by.. and authorization is hereby given to the Insurance Company to whom this proof of loss is directed, to pay the above named the full amount of loss, and in consideration thereof, the undersigned hereby forever discharges said Insurance Company from any further liability for loss or damage occurring on the date or dates mentioned.

....
Insured

The coinsurance clause places a penalty on the insured who carries a face value less than the coinsurance percent, as shown in the following examples. To encourage insureds to carry insurance equal to the coinsurance percent, companies offer a rate reduction for this amount of insurance.

Example 1 Property worth \$400,000 is insured for \$240,000. If the policy contains an 80% coinsurance clause and a fire causes \$120,000 damage, what is the liability of the insurance company?

Solution

1. The face value is \$240,000.
2. The actual loss is \$120,000.
3. $\frac{\$240{,}000}{\$400{,}000 \times 0.80} \times \$120{,}000 = \frac{\$240{,}000}{\$320{,}000} \times \$120{,}000$

$= \$90{,}000$

The least amount is \$90,000; hence, this is the insurer's liability.

Had the insured carried the full amount of insurance required by the coinsurance clause (\$320,000), the company would have paid the full amount of the loss since

$$\frac{\$320{,}000}{\$400{,}000 \times 0.80} \times \$120{,}000 = 1 \times \$120{,}000 = \$120{,}000$$

Example 2 Property worth \$200,000 is insured for \$150,000. If the fire insurance policy contains an 80% coinsurance clause, what is the insurer's liability on a fire that causes \$170,000 damage?

Solution

1. The face value is \$150,000.
2. The actual loss is \$170,000.
3. $\frac{\$150{,}000}{\$200{,}000 \times 0.80} \times \$170{,}000 = \frac{\$150{,}000}{\$160{,}000} \times \$170{,}000$

$= \$159{,}375$

The insurer's liability is the least of the three amounts, or the face value of \$150,000.

Fire insurance on a building may be spread over several companies. This can occur when additional insurance is purchased over a period of time, when new additions are built, or when the value of the building is too great for a single company to accept the risk. The next example illustrates payment of a claim by multiple carriers.

Example 3 A building worth \$400,000 incurred fire damage of \$150,000. The fire insurance coverage of \$300,000 contained an 80% coinsurance clause and was divided among Company A (\$150,000), Company B (\$90,000), and Company C (\$60,000). Find the amount paid by each company in settlement of the claim.

Solution

1. The face value is \$300,000.
2. The actual loss is \$150,000.
3. $\frac{\$300{,}000}{\$400{,}000 \times 0.80} \times \$150{,}000 = \$112{,}500$

The least of these amounts is \$112,500, which was split among the three companies according to the ratio of the amount of coverage to the total face value. Thus,

Paid by	*Amount*	
A	\$56,250	$\left(\$112{,}500 \times \frac{\$150{,}000}{\$300{,}000}\right)$
B	33,750	$\left(\$112{,}500 \times \frac{\$90{,}000}{\$300{,}000}\right)$
C	22,500	$\left(\$112{,}500 \times \frac{\$60{,}000}{\$300{,}000}\right)$
Total	\$112,500	

Section 16.11 Fire insurance premiums

A number of factors affect the premium charged for fire insurance. Among these are

1. Construction (brick, frame, etc.)
2. Occupancy (flammability of contents)
3. Protection facilities (fire-fighting equipment, water supply, etc.)
4. Exposure (congestion of area, hazardous property nearby, etc.)
5. Geographical location (losses vary by state)

Fire insurance premiums are quoted as a rate per \$100 of insurance coverage, and the calculation is an application of the basic percentage formula $P = BR$, where P = premium, B = face value of the policy in hundreds of dollars, and R = rate per \$100. Premium calculations are rounded to the nearest dollar in the last step.

In table 16.7 fire insurance rates are shown for four building construction categories in five areas.

Table 16.7 Annual Rates for Each \$100 of Insurance

	Building Category							
	A		*B*		*C*		*D*	
Area	*Building*	*Contents*	*Building*	*Contents*	*Building*	*Contents*	*Building*	*Contents*
1	\$0.23	\$0.24	\$0.31	\$0.33	\$0.35	\$0.38	\$0.40	\$0.44
2	0.26	0.29	0.35	0.39	0.39	0.44	0.43	0.49
3	0.30	0.34	0.40	0.45	0.44	0.49	0.48	0.55
4	0.36	0.41	0.51	0.56	0.55	0.61	0.59	0.66
5	0.44	0.50	0.60	0.67	0.70	0.77	0.82	0.90

Example 1 Use table 16.7 to find the total fire insurance premium for the specified coverages for the given area and category:

(a) Building, \$200,000; contents, \$85,000; area 1; category B
(b) Building, \$315,000; contents, \$64,000; area 4; category C

Solution

(a) Building: $P = ?,\ B = 200{,}000/100 = 2{,}000,\ R = \$0.31$

$$\begin{aligned} P &= BR \\ &= 2{,}000 \times \$0.31 \\ &= \$620 \end{aligned}$$

Contents: $P = ?,\ B = 85{,}000/100 = 850,\ R = \$0.33$

$$\begin{aligned} P &= BR \\ &= 850 \times \$0.33 \\ &= \$280.50 \end{aligned}$$

\$620 + \$280.50 = \$900.50. Rounded to the nearest dollar, the total premium is \$901.

(b) Building: $P = ?, B = 315{,}000/100 = 3{,}150, R = \$0.55$

$$P = BR$$
$$= 3{,}100 \times \$0.55$$
$$= \$1{,}732.50$$

Contents: $P = ?, B = 64{,}000/100 = 640, R = \$0.61$

$$P = BR$$
$$= 640 \times \$0.61$$
$$= \$390.40$$

$1,732.50 + $390.40 = $2,122.90. Rounded to the nearest dollar, the total premium is $2,123.

While premiums are quoted for one year, policies may be in force for less than one year.* In this event, the premium charged is a percentage of the annual premium, according to a short-term rate table. Table 16.8 is an abbreviated version of such a table.

Table 16.8 Short-Term Rate Table

Time in Force	% of Annual Rate	Time in Force	% of Annual Rate
5 days	7	5 months	60
10 days	10	6 months	70
15 days	13	7 months	75
20 days	16	8 months	80
25 days	18	9 months	85
1 month	20	10 months	90
2 months	30	11 months	95
3 months	40	12 months	100
4 months	50		

The premium is less if the insurance company cancels the policy. For the examples and problems in this text, a figure of 10% less than the premium calculated from table 16.8 is used.

*Policies in force for less than one year may be because of (1) temporary protection need, (2) cancellation by the insured, or (3) cancellation by the insurance company.

Example 2 The need for additional space caused Alan Labeda to sell his property and move his electronics store to a new location. He canceled a fire insurance policy (coverage: building, \$78,000; contents, \$50,000; area 1; category B) five months after paying the annual premium. What refund did Alan receive?

Solution

First, the annual premium is calculated. Using table 16.7,

Building: $P = ?$, $B = 78{,}000/100 = 780$, $R = \$0.31$

$$P = BR$$
$$= 780 \times \$0.31$$
$$= \$241.80$$

Contents: $P = ?$, $B = 50{,}000/100 = 500$, $R = \$0.33$

$$P = BR$$
$$= 500 \times \$0.33$$
$$= \$165$$

$\$241.80 + \$165 = \$406.80$. Rounded to the nearest dollar, the total annual premium is \$407.

From table 16.8, the premium is 60% of the annual premium. Alan receives the difference. That is,

\$407.00	Annual premium
− 244.20	Short-term premium (\$407 × 0.60)
\$162.80	Refund to Alan

Example 3 After a fire of suspicious origin, the Heartford Insurance Company canceled a seven-month-old policy with an annual premium of $680. What refund did the policyholder receive?

Solution

From table 16.8,

$$\begin{aligned} P &= BR \\ &= \$680 \times 0.75 \\ &= \$510 \end{aligned}$$

Since the insurance company canceled the policy, the premium is 10% less than $510; that is, 90% of $510. Thus,

$680	Annual premium
− 459	Short-term premium ($510 × 0.90)
$221	Refund

Exercises for Sections 16.10 and 16.11

In problems 1–8, find the insurer's liability for a fire that causes the given amount of damage.

1. Property value: $120,000; amount of insurance: $78,000; coinsurance clause: 80%; fire causes $40,000 damage
2. Property value: $320,000; amount of insurance: $224,000; coinsurance clause: 80%; fire causes $190,000 damage
3. Property value: $150,000; amount of insurance: $110,000; coinsurance clause: 80%; fire causes $50,000 damage
4. Property value: $400,000; amount of insurance: $200,000; coinsurance clause: 80%; fire causes $300,000 damage
5. Property value: $180,000; amount of insurance: $130,000; coinsurance clause: 80%; fire causes $180,000 damage
6. Property value: $260,000; amount of insurance: $200,000; coinsurance clause: 80%; fire causes $220,000 damage
7. Property value: $375,000; amount of insurance: $270,000 carried by A ($180,000) and B ($90,000); coinsurance clause: 80%; fire causes $230,000 damage

8. Property value: $625,000; amount of insurance: $400,000 carried by A ($200,000), B ($100,000), and C ($100,000); coinsurance clause: 80%; fire causes $300,000 damage

9. Use table 16.7 to find the annual premium for a fire insurance policy that will insure a category D building located in area 3 for $250,000 and the contents for $120,000.

10. Sam Donaldson opened a sporting goods store and purchased $110,000 worth of fire insurance for the building and $65,000 for the contents. If the building is rated category A and is located in area 2, how much was the annual premium for the policy?

11. When Jennifer Smith opened her clothing store, she insured the building for $130,000 and the contents for $80,000. What was her annual insurance premium if the building is located in area 2 and is rated category C?

In problems 12–21, use tables 16.7 and 16.8 to find the premium for a fire insurance policy for the given coverage when the policy is in force for the given period of time.

12. Coverage: building, $230,000; contents, $165,000; category B; area 5; time in force: four months; policy canceled by insured.

13. Coverage: building, $115,000; contents, $40,000; category C; area 3; time in force: 10 months; policy canceled by insurance company.

14. Coverage: building, $320,000; contents, $100,000; category D; area 1; time in force: two months; policy canceled by insurance company.

15. Coverage: building, $180,000; contents, $30,000; category A; area 2; time in force: 20 days; policy canceled by insured.

16. Coverage: building, $80,000; contents, $20,000; category D; area 5; time in force: seven months; policy canceled by insurance company.

17. Coverage: building, $145,000; contents, $60,000; category B; area 3; time in force: five days; policy canceled by insured.

18. Coverage: building, $220,000; contents, $50,000; category C; area 1; time in force: eight months; policy canceled by insurance company.

19. John Dirkson insured his building for $120,000 and the contents for $70,000, but after six months he went out of business and canceled his policy. If the building was rated category B and located in area 4, how much did John pay for his insurance coverage for the six months that he was in business?

20. Find the premium for a fire insurance policy to insure a category A building for $130,000 and the contents for $90,000 if the building is located in area 2, the policy is in force for eight months, and the policy is canceled by the insured.

21. Laura Nesbitt insured her building (category B, area 5) for $110,000 and the contents for $50,000. Eleven months later, the company canceled her policy because she failed to correct fire hazards in her business. How much did Laura have to pay for the 11 months of coverage?

Section 16.12

Automobile insurance

In the United States, the automobile has evolved from an expensive luxury to an expensive necessity. Transportation experts predict that the automobile will continue to be the primary means of public transportation for the remainder of the century. At the same time, increased costs and spiraling energy prices have pushed the cost of driving toward 50¢ per mile.

One factor in the increased expense of owning and operating an automobile has been the spectacular increase in automobile accident costs. For example, in one decade, the average bodily injury claim increased 107%, from $1,604 to $3,316, and the average property damage claim rose 109%, from $294 to an estimated $615.

The likelihood of being involved in an accident is also increasing. According to statistics published by the New York State Insurance Department, during the first year, there is a 1 in 4 chance that the typical driver will be involved in at least one motor vehicle accident. During five years, the chances are better than 3 out of 4. During twenty years, the chances are 99 out of 100.

Faced with the mounting cost of accidents and the probability of involvement, most drivers protect themselves with **automobile insurance.** Indeed, in most states it is compulsory that a driver carry some form of automobile insurance.

Automobile insurance policies are tailored to individual needs. Hence, insurance companies offer a variety of coverages and protection amounts. Among the standard coverages are

1. **Bodily injury liability** This coverage applies when the policyholder's car causes injury or death to persons in other cars or to passengers in his or her car. When claims are brought against the policyholder, the insurance company provides legal defense and pays for bodily injury damages up to the limit of the policy should the policyholder be found legally liable. Bodily injury liability is compulsory in many states, with minimum coverage of 5/10, meaning that the insurance company will pay up to $5,000 for the injuries sustained by one person and up to $10,000 for all injuries resulting from one accident. Many policyholders elect to carry coverage amounts much higher than the minimum.

2. **Property damage liability** This coverage applies when the policyholder's car damages property belonging to others. Usually, the property is another automobile, but it can be other items, such as buildings, lampposts, fire hydrants, and trees. When claims are brought against the policyholder, the insurance company provides legal defense and pays property damage up to the limit of the policy should the policyholder be found legally liable. The minimum coverage is usually $5,000, which means that the insurance company will pay up to this amount for each accident. Many drivers carry more than the minimum amount.

3. **Medical expenses** Under this coverage, the insurance company pays medical, surgical, X-ray, dental, and funeral expenses up to the limit of the policy. The coverage applies to the policyholder and his or her immediate family, whether in their own car, another car, or struck by a car while walking. It also applies to passengers in the policyholder's automobile. Payment is made regardless of who is at fault.

4. **Comprehensive damage** This coverage pays for any damage to the policyholder's car caused by falling objects, fire, theft, missiles, explosion, riot or civil commotion, or collision with a bird or animal. The coverage does not include damage resulting from collision with another automobile or object. Comprehensive insurance can be purchased with a deductible. For example, with a $50 deductible, the policyholder pays for the first $50 of loss per accident, while the insurance company pays any remainder. The higher the deductible, the lower the premium for the insurance.

5. **Collision damage** This coverage applies when the policyholder's car is damaged from collision with a vehicle or an object or as the result of turning over. Damages are paid by the insurance company regardless of who is at fault. Most collision insurance is sold with a $50 or $100 deductible.

6. **Uninsured motorist protection** This coverage reimburses the policyholder for injuries caused by an uninsured motorist or a hit-and-run driver. Coverage is normally limited to bodily injury claims, but some policies may include property damage. Protection is extended to the policyholder, relatives or passengers in the insured automobile, and any other person who would have legal right to collect for bodily injuries suffered through the negligence of an uninsured driver. In some states, uninsured motorist coverage is compulsory.

Section 16.13 Automobile insurance premiums

Insurance premiums are a function of risk. In automobile insurance, the primary factors affecting risk are

1. *Territory in which the vehicle is operated* The probability of an accident is greater in cities than in rural areas.
2. *Usage and miles driven* The more miles driven, the greater the probability of an accident. Also, vehicles used for business are more likely to be involved in an accident than those driven for personal use.
3. *Make, model, and age of the vehicle* The newer and more expensive the automobile, the greater the cost of repair or replacement.
4. *Age, sex, and marital status of the driver* Statistics indicate that unmarried males under age 25 have more accidents than any other age group.

Factors 1 through 3 are used to establish base rates for the standard insurance coverages, as shown in tables 16.9 through 16.11. The total annual base rate is then multiplied by the age, sex, and marital status factor contained in table 16.12 to obtain the net annual premium.

Table 16.9 Liability and Medical Expense Premiums

Coverage	Territory 1	Territory 2	Territory 3	Territory 4
Bodily Injury				
10/20	$33	$44	$55	$62
15/30	35	46	59	66
25/50	39	50	66	70
50/100	49	60	75	80
100/200	55	66	80	86
200/300	64	75	90	94
Property Damage				
$ 5,000	$32	$35	$38	$42
10,000	34	37	40	44
25,000	36	39	43	48
50,000	38	41	46	52
100,000	40	43	49	56
Medical Expense				
$ 1,000	$ 3	$ 5	$ 8	$10
2,500	6	10	16	20
5,000	8	14	20	25

Table 16.10 Comprehensive and Collision Premiums

		Territory 1				Territory 2				Territory 3				Territory 4			
		Comprehen.		*Collision*		*Comprehen.*		*Collision*		*Comprehen.*		*Collision*		*Comprehen.*		*Collision*	
Model Class	*Age*	*Full Cov.*	*$50 Ded.*	*$50 Ded.*	*$100 Ded.*	*Full Cov.*	*$50 Ded.*	*$50 Ded.*	*$100 Ded.*	*Full Cov.*	*$50 Ded.*	*$50 Ded.*	*$100 Ded.*	*Full Cov.*	*$50 Ded.*	*$50 Ded.*	*$100 Ded.*
A–C	1	$10	$ 6	$ 60	$50	$12	$ 8	$ 62	$52	$15	$11	$64	$54	$19	$15	$ 68	$57
	2–3	9	5	51	43	11	7	53	45	14	10	55	47	18	14	63	50
	4–5	8	4	42	35	10	6	44	37	13	9	46	39	17	13	54	41
	6	6	3	35	28	8	5	37	30	11	8	39	32	15	12	47	34
D	1	13	7	67	56	15	9	69	58	18	12	71	60	22	16	74	63
	2–3	11	6	57	47	13	8	59	49	16	11	61	51	20	15	64	54
	4–5	10	5	47	39	12	7	49	41	15	10	51	43	19	14	54	45
	6	7	4	37	31	9	6	39	33	12	9	41	35	16	13	44	37
E	1	15	9	73	61	17	11	75	63	20	14	77	65	24	18	80	67
	2–3	13	7	63	52	15	9	65	54	18	12	67	56	22	16	77	58
	4–5	12	6	51	43	14	8	53	45	17	11	55	47	21	15	65	50
	6	9	5	41	34	11	7	43	36	14	10	45	38	18	14	55	40
F	1	21	12	87	72	23	14	89	74	26	17	91	76	30	21	94	79
	2–3	18	11	74	62	20	13	76	64	23	16	78	66	27	20	82	68
	4–5	16	9	61	51	18	11	63	53	21	14	65	55	25	18	69	58
	6	12	7	48	40	14	9	50	42	17	12	52	44	21	16	56	46
G	1	26	15	100	84	28	17	102	86	31	20	104	89	35	24	107	91
	2–3	22	12	85	71	24	14	87	73	27	17	89	75	33	21	92	78
	4–5	20	11	70	59	22	13	72	61	25	16	74	64	32	20	77	66
	6	14	8	55	46	16	10	57	48	19	13	59	50	26	17	62	53

Table 16.11 Uninsured Motorist Premiums

Limits	**Premium**	**Limits**	**Premium**
$ 10,000	$ 6	$100,000	$21
15,000	10	200,000	23
25,000	12	300,000	25
50,000	16		

Table 16.12 Rating Factors

	Age	Driver Training	Pleasure	Work (Less Than 15 Miles)	Work (15 Miles or More)	Business Use
No youthful operator	Female 30-64	—	1.30	1.55	1.75	1.75
	Male or female 65 or over	—	1.30	1.55	1.75	1.75
	All others	—	1.40	1.65	1.85	1.85
Unmarried female	18–20	Yes	1.60	1.85	1.85	1.85
		No	1.65	1.90	1.90	1.90
	21–24	—	1.40	1.65	1.85	1.85
	25–29	—	1.40	1.65	1.85	1.85
Married male	18–20	Yes	1.95	2.20	2.20	2.20
		No	2.05	2.30	2.30	2.30
	21–24	—	1.55	1.80	1.85	1.85
	25–29	—	1.40	1.65	1.85	1.85
Unmarried male—not owner, not principal operator	18–20	Yes	2.30	2.55	2.55	2.55
		No	2.60	2.85	2.85	2.85
	21–24	—	1.90	2.15	2.15	2.15
	25–29	—	1.40	1.65	1.85	1.85
Unmarried male—owner or principal operator	18–20	Yes	2.95	3.20	3.20	3.20
		No	3.25	3.50	3.50	3.50
	21–24	—	2.40	2.65	2.65	2.65
	25–29	—	2.05	2.30	2.30	2.30

Example 1 Find the annual premium of an automobile policy for the following driver and coverages:

Driver

Male, age 30
Territory 3
Car: D class, two years old
Miles to and from work: 22

Coverages

Bodily injury liability: 25/50
Property damage liability: 25
Comprehensive: $50 deductible
Collision: $50 deductible

Solution

Base premiums		
Bodily injury liability	$ 66.00	(Table 16.9)
Property damage liability	43.00	(Table 16.9)
Comprehensive	11.00	(Table 16.10)
Collision	61.00	(Table 16.10)
Total	$181.00	
Rating factor	× 1.85	(Table 16.12)
Annual premium	$334.85	

Example 2 Upon graduation from college at age 22, Helen Adkins decided to open a florist shop. Since she would have to use her four-year-old, class F station wagon for delivery, she changed her automobile insurance to insure it as a business vehicle. Helen is unmarried and lives in a territory 2 area. She purchased the following coverage: bodily injury and property damage liability, 50/100/50; medical expense, $5,000; comprehensive and collision, $50 deductible each; and uninsured motorist, $10,000. Find Helen's annual premium.

Solution

Base premiums	
Bodily injury liability (50/100)	$ 60.00
Property damage liability (50)	41.00
Medical expense ($5,000)	14.00
Comprehensive ($50 deductible, class F)	11.00
Collision ($50 deductible, class F)	63.00
Uninsured motorist ($10,000)	6.00
Total	$195.00
Rating factor	× 1.85
Annual premium	$360.75

Example 3 Jeff Bachman, age 25 and married, uses his car for business as a customer service representative and is reimbursed for mileage by his company. Jeff lives in a territory 1 area and drives a new class A car that he insures for bodily injury liability, 100/200; property damage liability, 100; comprehensive, full coverage; and collision, $50 deductible. Calculate Jeff's annual premium.

Solution

Base premiums	
Bodily injury liability (100/200)	$ 55.00
Property damage liability (100)	40.00
Comprehensive (full coverage)	10.00
Collision ($50 deductible)	60.00
Total	$165.00
Rating factor	× 1.85
Annual premium	$305.25

Example 4 While driving to work on a foggy highway, Janice's car rear-ended a slower moving car, causing $3,800 damage to her car and $1,100 to the other car. The other driver suffered whiplash and other injuries and was awarded $15,000 in a resultant lawsuit. Janice's medical expenses were $750. Janice carried the following automobile insurance: bodily injury and property damage liability, 25/50/10; comprehensive and collision, each with a $50 deductible. (a) How much did Janice's insurance company pay in settlement of the claim? (b) How much did Janice pay beyond her insurance coverage?

Solution

	(a) *Paid by Insurance company*	*(b)* *Paid by Janice*
Collision Damage		
Policyholder car	$3,750	$50
Other vehicle	1,100	
Bodily injury liability	15,000	
Medical Expense		750
Total	$19,850	$800

Exercises for Sections 16.12 and 16.13

In problems 1–10, find the annual premium of an automobile policy for the given driver and indicated coverages.

1\.

Driver	*Coverages*
Male, age 37	Bodily injury liability: 15/30
Territory 2	Property damage liability: 10
Car: F class, five years old	Medical expense: $2,500
Miles to and from work: 10	Collision: $50 deductible

2\.

Driver	*Coverages*
Female, age 42	Bodily injury liability: 100/200
Territory 4	Property damage liability: 100
Car: C class, three years old	Comprehensive: full
Miles to and from work: 18	Collision: $100 deductible

3\.

Driver	*Coverages*
Male, age 22, married	Bodily injury liability: 10/20
Territory 3	Property damage liability: 5
Car: A class, new	Medical expense: $1,000
Miles to and from work: 35	Uninsured motorist: $15,000
	Comprehensive: $50 deductible
	Collision: $50 deductible

4. *Driver*

Male, age 23, unmarried, owner
Territory 4
Car: G class, five years old
Miles to and from work: 8

Coverages

Bodily injury liability: 25/50
Property damage liability: 25
Medical expense: $5,000
Comprehensive: $50 deductible
Collision: $100 deductible

5. *Driver*

Female, age 24, unmarried
Territory 1
Car: E class, six years old
Business use

Coverages

Bodily injury liability: 15/30
Property damage liability: 10
Medical expense: $2,500
Collision: $100 deductible
Uninsured motorist: $25,000

6. *Driver*

Female, age 26, married
Territory 4
Car: B class, two years old
Business use

Coverages

Bodily injury liability: 10/20
Property damage liability: 5
Collision: $100 deductible
Comprehensive: $50 deductible
Uninsured motorist: $15,000

7. *Driver*

Male, age 18, unmarried, not owner, not principal operator, no driver training
Territory 2
Car: G class, three years old
Pleasure use

Coverages

Bodily injury liability: 25/50
Property damage liability: 10
Medical expense: $1,000
Collision: $50 deductible
Comprehensive: full
Uninsured motorist: $25,000

8. *Driver*

Male, age 67
Territory 1
Car: F class, new
Pleasure use

Coverages

Bodily injury liability: 200/300
Property damage liability: 100
Medical expense: $5,000
Collision: $50 deductible
Comprehensive: full
Uninsured motorist: $300,000

9. *Driver*

Male, age 20, unmarried, owner, completed driver training
Territory 3
Car: C class, six years old
Miles to and from work: 5

Coverages

Bodily injury liability: 15/30
Property damage liability: 10
Medical expense: $5,000
Collision: $100 deductible
Uninsured motorist: $15,000

10.

Driver	*Coverages*
Female, age 19, unmarried, completed driver training Territory 2 Car: B class, two years old Miles to and from work: 22	Bodily injury liability: 50/100 Property damage liability: 50 Medical expense: $2,500 Comprehensive: $50 deductible Collision: $100 deductible Uninsured motorist: $50,000

11. Greg Foster sells real estate and uses his own car for business purposes. He lives in a territory 3 area and drives a class F car that is one year old. Greg is married, 28 years old, and has the following insurance coverage: bodily injury and property damage liability, 25/50/10; medical expense, $2,500; comprehensive, full coverage; collision, $50 deductible; and uninsured motorist, $50,000. How much is Greg's annual premium?

12. Barbara DeVane is a sales representative for a pharmaceutical company. She uses her own car to call on wholesalers and is reimbursed by the company according to her business mileage. She lives in a territory 4 area and drives a three-year-old, class B car that she insures for the following coverage: bodily injury and property damage liability, 100/200/50; comprehensive, $50 deductible; collision, $100 deductible; and uninsured motorist, $25,000. If Barbara is married and 32 years old, how much is her annual premium?

13. Bob Simmons works as a used book salesman to earn enough money so that he can return to college. Bob is 20 years old, unmarried, owns his own car, and took a driver training course in high school. He uses his car in his sales job and lives in a territory 1 area. Find the amount of the annual insurance premium on his two-year-old, class D car for 15/30 bodily injury liability coverage, $50 deductible collision coverage, $5,000 medical expense coverage, and $25,000 uninsured motorist coverage.

14. Tony Mendoza purchased a new class B sports car that he drives only for pleasure, since he also owns a pickup truck that he drives to his construction business. Tony is not married, lives in a territory 2 area, and is 29 years old. He insured his new sports car for the following coverage: bodily injury liability, 50/100; property damage liability, $10,000; medical expense, $2,500; comprehensive, full coverage; collision, $50 deductible; and uninsured motorist, $100,000. How much is Tony's annual premium?

15. In example 4, when Janice's policy came up for renewal, Janice lived in territory 1, was a 19-year-old unmarried female without driver training who drove her two-year-old, class D car 20 miles to work. As a result of the accident, the insurance company calculated her normal annual premium, then doubled the amount. What was her new premium?

16. Charlene Smith swerved to avoid hitting a child who darted into the street, lost control when the car jumped the curb, and crashed into a brick wall, causing $350 damage to the wall and $780 damage to her car. The cuts and bruises Charlene sustained resulted in a medical bill of $83. Charlene carried the following automobile insurance: bodily injury and property damage liability, 50/100/50; comprehensive and collision, each with a $100 deductible. (a) How much did Charlene's insurance company pay in settling the claim? (b) How much out-of-pocket expense did Charlene incur?

17. Hal Stoopid ran a red light and hit another automobile broadside, causing $3,475 damage to the other automobile and $4,200 damage to his own car. A friend in Hal's car and the driver of the other car were seriously injured. When an investigation revealed that Hal's blood alcohol content was above the legal limit, the driver of the other car and his friend's parents sued and were awarded $100,000 and $80,000 respectively. Hal carried the following automobile insurance: bodily injury and property damage liability, 15/30/10; comprehensive and collision, each with a $100 deductible. (a) Find the amount Hal's insurance company paid in settlement of the claim. (b) Hal's parents negotiated a loan to pay the difference between the total claim and the amount paid by Hal's insurance company. What was the amount of the loan?

18. Larry Leadfoot failed to negotiate a turn and crashed into a tree causing $5,600 damage to his car. Neither Larry nor his girlfriend were wearing seat belts, and they suffered serious injuries resulting in medical expenses of $6,000 and $11,500 respectively. A suit by the girlfriend's father resulted in an award of $25,000. Larry had the following automobile insurance: bodily injury and property damage liability, 10/20/10; comprehensive and collision, each with a $50 deductible; medical expense, $2,500. In settling the claim, (a) How much did the insurance company pay, and (b) how much did Larry have to pay beyond his insurance coverage?

19. Daisy unsuccessfully tried to pass a truck on a two-lane highway and crashed her small foreign car head-on into a full-size sedan. Daisy's car was totaled and damage to the sedan was $6,975. The only survivor of the accident was the driver of the sedan who was hospitalized and incurred medical bills totaling $6,500. Daisy's insurance had recently been canceled, while the other driver carried the following coverage: bodily injury and property damage liability, 100/200/100; comprehensive and collision, full; uninsured motorist, $50,000. Find the amount paid to the surviving driver in settlement of the claim.

Glossary

Automobile insurance Insurance protection for injuries to persons or damages to property caused by a motor vehicle.
Beneficiary The person named to receive the proceeds or benefits of an insurance policy.
Bodily injury liability In automobile insurance, coverage when the policyholder's car causes injury or death to persons in other cars or to passengers in the policyholder's car.
Cash value A fund that accumulates within a life insurance policy (except for term insurance) that may be borrowed against or paid in cash to the policyholder if the policy is canceled.
Coinsurance The sharing of a risk by the insurance company and the insured; a feature found in major medical group insurance and in fire insurance.
Collision damage In automobile insurance, coverage when the policyholder's car is damaged from collision with a vehicle or object.
Comprehensive damage In automobile insurance, coverage for damage to the policyholder's car by fire, theft, explosion, falling objects, and so on.
Conditions A description of what an individual must do to receive an insurance policy.
Declaration In an insurance policy, descriptive material indicating who is covered, what is covered, the amount of coverage, and the premium.
Endowment insurance Insurance that pays the beneficiary upon death of the insured or pays the insured if the insured is alive on the maturity date of the policy.
Exclusions A description of what the insuring agreement does not cover in an insurance policy.
Face value A specified amount of money to be paid to the beneficiary upon the death of the insured or, in the case of endowment insurance, to the insured if the insured is alive on the maturity date.
Gross premium The premium paid by the policyholder. It includes the cost of the insurance plus the cost of the insurance company's overhead.
Group insurance Insurance for the employees of a company under a master plan issued to the company. Both life insurance and nonoccupational health coverage are commonly offered under group plans.
Hazard A condition that may create a peril or increase its probability of occurrence.
Insurance A contract whereby a party undertakes to guarantee another party against loss by an accidental event.
Insurance policy The contract wherein the terms and conditions of the insurance are stated.
Insured The person or organization named in an insurance policy to receive the insurance coverage provided by the policy.
Insurer Also called *underwriter.* The organization that sells an insurance policy.
Insuring agreement A description of the perils that are covered by an insurance policy.
Level premium A premium that is the same for each payment.
Limited payment life insurance A life insurance plan in which the premiums are limited to a specified number of years.
Medical expenses In automobile insurance, coverage for medical, surgical, X-ray, dental, and funeral expenses for the policyholder, family of the policyholder, or passengers in the policyholder's car.
Mortality table A table indicating the probability of death at each age; used by insurance companies as a basis for life insurance rates.
Net premium A life insurance premium based only on a mortality table, without taking into consideration the expenses of the company.
Nonforfeiture values Options by which the policyholder may utilize the cash value in the event premium payments are discontinued. These options include cash, reduced paid-up insurance, or extended term insurance.
Nonparticipating policy An insurance policy with rates lower than the participating rate but with no provision for dividends.
Ordinary life insurance A life insurance policy characterized by the payment of premiums as long as the insured lives.

Participating policy An insurance policy offered by a mutual insurance company or a stock insurance company in which an overcharge is made on the premium with the idea of returning a dividend to the policyholder.
Peril An event that causes a loss, such as fire, accident, illness, and so on.
Policyholder The owner of an insurance policy.
Premium The cost of an insurance policy.
Property damage liability In automobile insurance, coverage when the policyholder's car damages property belonging to others.
Settlement options Options by which the policyholder (or in some cases the beneficiary) can designate the manner in which the proceeds are to be distributed. Options include cash, interest payments, installments of principal and interest, or a life income annuity.
Term life insurance Insurance that provides protection for a limited period of time and develops no nonforfeiture values.
Uninsured motorist protection In automobile insurance, reimbursement to the policyholder for damage caused by an uninsured motorist or a hit-and-run driver.

Review test

1. A condition that may create a peril or increase its probability of occurrence is called a ________________.
2. In a typical insurance policy, the ________________ sets forth exactly what perils are covered.
3. Life insurance characterized by the payment of premiums as long as the insured lives is called ________________.
4. Life insurance policies marketed by mutual insurance companies that have a dividend provision are called ________________.
5. A nonforfeiture option whereby the cash value is used to purchase life insurance protection without further premiums is called ________________.
6. Automobile insurance that applies when the policyholder's car damages property belonging to others is called ____________.
7. The two categories of life insurance are ________________ and ________________.
8. Find the premium for a one-year term policy of $25,000 sold to a 38-year-old male if the assumed interest rate is 4% per annum.
9. Using tables 16.2 and 16.3, find the monthly premium for a 50-year-old female who purchases a 20-payment life policy with a face value of $60,000, if the insurance company uses a five-year setback.
10. Property worth $200,000 is insured for $150,000. If the fire insurance policy contains an 80% coinsurance clause and a fire causes $100,000 damage, what is the liability of the insurance company?
11. A married, 25-year-old male who lives in territory 1 insures his new class A car for the following coverages: comprehensive, full coverage; collision, $50 deductible; bodily injury liability, 50/100; property damage liability, $25,000; medical expense, $5,000. If the car is driven 20 miles to work, what is the annual premium?

CHAPTER 17

Statistics and Graphs

Chapter Objectives

I. Learn the meaning of the following terms:

Array, 504
Frequency distribution, 504–505
Relative and cumulative frequency distributions, 505–506
Line graph, 506
Bar graph, 507
Circle graph, 507
Pictogram, 508
The Greek letter sigma (Σ), 521
Measures of location, 522
Arithmetic mean, 522
Median, 524
Mode, 525
Bimodal, 525
Modal class, 531
Measures of variation, 535
Standard deviation, 535
Normal distribution, 538
Index number, 540

II. Understand:

How to summarize data into
1. An array, 504
2. A frequency distribution, 504–505
3. A relative frequency distribution, 505
4. A cumulative frequency distribution, 505–506

Graph distortions, 508–511
The advantages and disadvantages of the mean, median, and mode, 523–525
Normal distributions, 538

III. Calculate:

The mean, median, and mode of
1. Ungrouped data, 523–525
2. Grouped data, 528–531

The standard deviation, 536
The price relative, 541
The simple aggregate index, 542
The Laspeyres index, 543

Section 17.1 Introduction

The word *statistics* has more than one meaning. In its most common usage, statistics refers to a collection of numerical data. Statistics may also refer to the analysis and interpretation of such data. In the singular, the word statistic may denote a particular item of data or a measure calculated from data.

Each of these connotations has an application in business. A characterization of the contemporary business enterprise is the accumulation of numerous reports, graphs, and other forms of numerical data from both internal and external sources. The proper utilization of this data is crucial to successful business practices. In this chapter, several of the basic methods used to summarize and categorize numerical data are introduced.

Section 17.2 Data organization and graphs

Arrays

Before statistical analysis can take place, the data to be analyzed must be arranged in a usable form. One such arrangement, called an **array,** involves ordering data from high to low or from low to high. For example, the number of sales at register 9 of the R. D. Davis Company for a two-week period is recorded in table 17.1.

Table 17.1 Sales at Register 9

Week	Monday	Tuesday	Wednesday	Thursday	Friday	Saturday
1	10	12	15	9	22	32
2	7	15	16	17	20	29

An array of the data in table 17.1 would be:

7, 9, 10, 12, 15, 15, 16, 17, 20, 22, 29, 32

An array serves to detail the overall pattern, but its usefulness is limited to sets with a small number of values. The ordering of data with a large number of values is tedious unless data-processing equipment is available.

Frequency distributions

A second method of summarizing or describing a set of data involves arranging the values in a frequency distribution. In a **frequency distribution,** the values are grouped into **classes;** then a tally is made of the number or frequency of the values in each class. This tally is called the **class frequency.**

Table 17.2 shows a frequency distribution of the data in table 17.1.

Table 17.2 Frequency Distribution of Table 17.1 Data

Class	Tally	Frequency
5–9	//	2
10–14	//	2
15–19	////	4
20–24	//	2
25–29	/	1
30–34	/	1

Frequency distributions are described as **numerical** when the data are grouped according to numerical size (such as in table 17.2) and as **categorical** when sorted according to a qualitative description.* The number of classes in a frequency distribution is arbitrary but should range from 6 to 15. It is also desirable to make class intervals of equal length whenever possible.†

Another method of presenting data is the **relative frequency distribution,** in which relative class frequencies are found by dividing class frequencies by the total number in the sample. Table 17.3 is a relative frequency distribution of the data in table 17.1.

Table 17.3 Relative Frequency Distribution of Table 17.1 Data

Class	Frequency	Relative Frequency	Percent
5–9	2	0.1667	16.67
10–14	2	0.1667	16.67
15–19	4	0.3333	33.33
20–24	2	0.1667	16.67
25–29	1	0.0833	8.33
30–34	1	0.0833	8.33
	12	1.0000	

A **cumulative frequency distribution** is one in which the entry for each line in the table is the class frequency plus the sum of the frequencies of all preceding lines. A cumulative frequency distribution of the data in table 17.1 is shown in table 17.4.

*One example of a categorical distribution would be arranging the data according to categories of sales, such as records, tapes, phonographs, televisions, and so on.

†The length of a class interval is the difference between successive lower class limits. For example, the length of the class interval 5–9 is $10 - 5 = 5$.

Table 17.4 Cumulative Frequency Distribution of Table 17.1 Data

Class	Cumulative Frequency
Less than 10	2
Less than 15	4
Less than 20	8
Less than 25	10
Less than 30	11
Less than 35	12

Graphs In business, **graphs** are often used to present statistical information. Graphs can be more useful than charts or aggregates of figures in presenting data, and graphs are particularly useful in spotting trends. Graphs frequently used in business are line graphs, bar graphs, pictograms, and circle graphs.

Line graphs are the most widely used kind of graph. Figure 17.1 is a line graph of the data for week one in table 17.1, where the horizontal (x-axis) represents time and the vertical (y-axis) represents frequency. The dots indicate the frequency for the given day and the graph is formed by connecting the dots with line segments.

Figure 17.1
Line graph of data for week one in table 17.1

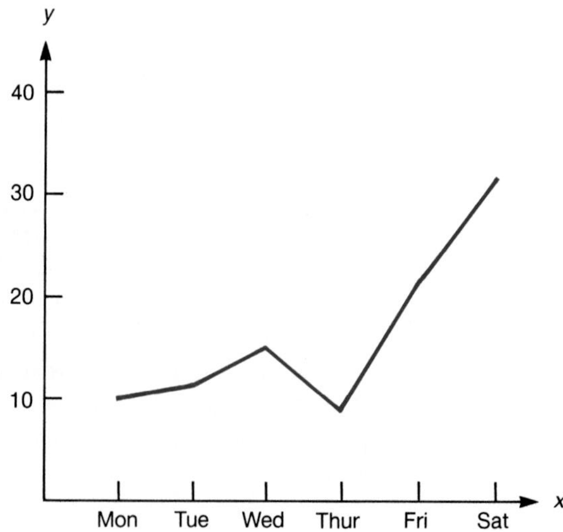

A second type of graph is the bar graph. **Bar graphs** are similar to line graphs in that they are also drawn in reference to an x- and y-axis, but instead of points, bar graphs use bars projecting from an axis. Figure 17.2 is a bar graph of the data in table 17.2. Note that the height of the bars in the figure corresponds to points on a line graph.

Figure 17.2
Bar graph of table 17.2

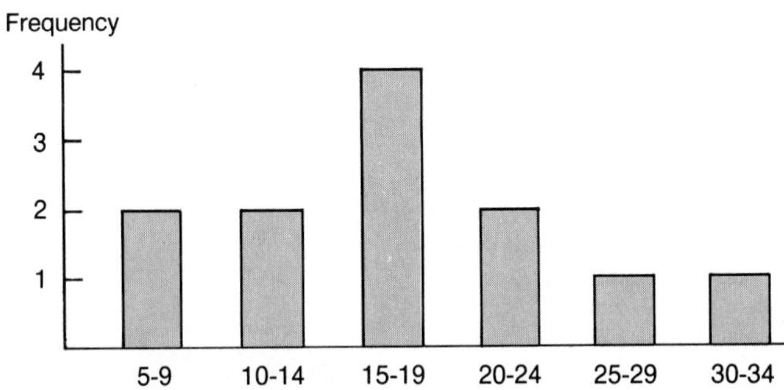

Circle graphs, also known as pie charts, use a circle as a base for the graph. Figure 17.3 is a circle graph of table 17.3.

Figure 17.3
Circle graph of table 17.3

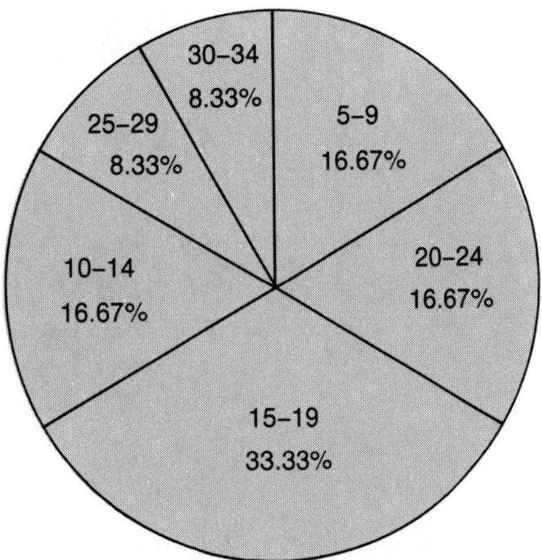

To construct a circle graph, each item of data must be converted to degrees. For example, in table 17.3, class 15–19 had a frequency of 4, or 33.33% of the total. Since

$$360° \times 0.3333 = 120°$$

this class is represented by that part of the circle with a central angle of 120°.

A **pictogram** is a modified form of a bar graph in which pictures are used to represent quantity. Figure 17.4 is a pictogram of the employment record of the Whitman Company taken from the following data.

Total Employment

Year	Men	Women
1981	50	20
1985	65	40
1989	70	55

Pictograms are almost always displayed horizontally; thus, years are scaled on the vertical axis.

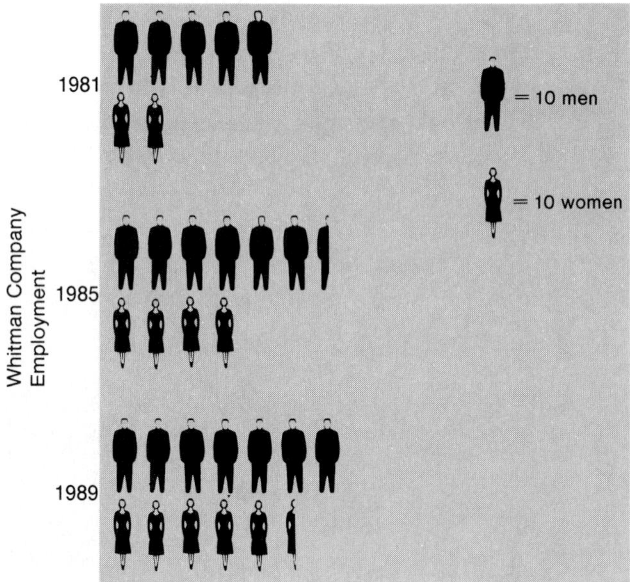

Figure 17.4
Pictogram of Whitman Company employment

Graph distortions Care must be exercised in the construction of a graph, since it is possible to present a graph that is accurate, yet misleading. To see this, let us see how a graph of the earnings per share of the Armstrong Company (figure 17.5) was reshaped by (1) the board of directors of the company and (2) a dissident stockholder seeking control of the company.

Figure 17.5
Earnings per share of the Armstrong Company

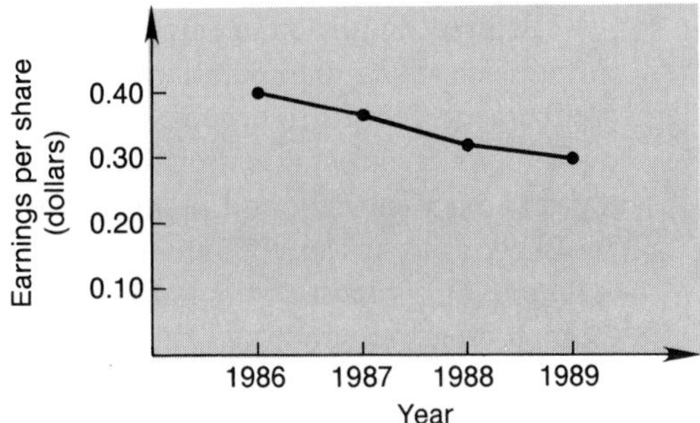

The board of directors naturally wants to minimize the declining earnings of the company. Therefore, in their annual report to stockholders, they present figure 17.6(a) as a graph of the company earnings. By stretching the scale of the x-axis and shortening that of the y-axis, the decline in earnings appears minimal.

Figure 17.6
Distortions of the earnings per share of the Armstrong Company

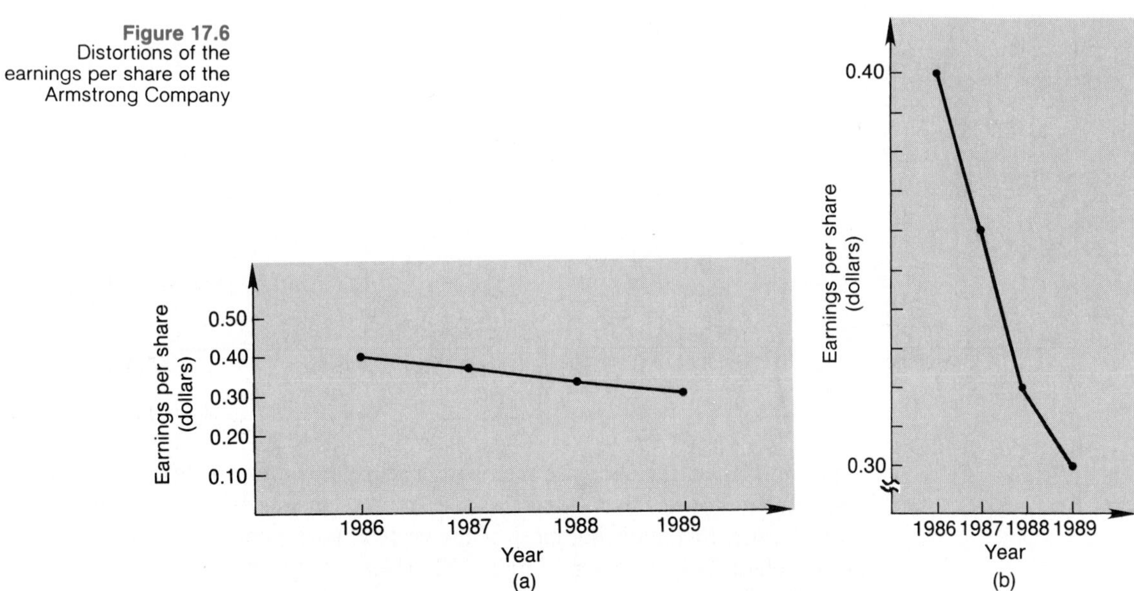

On the other hand, in an open letter to stockholders, Mr. Dissident Stockholder charges the company with mismanagement and calls for an immediate change in the company leadership. He supports his charge with the graph of the company's earnings record shown in figure 17.6(b).

By stretching the scale on the y-axis, shortening the scale of the x-axis, and eliminating most of the vertical portion of the graph, Mr. D. S. has presented an earnings record that appears calamitous. In both cases, the graphs were accurately drawn but created opposite impressions.

The preceding is an example of how graphs can be manipulated to create an impression. Such manipulations may be accidental, but all too often they are deliberate attempts to deceive. In pointing out these distortions, our purpose is to help you avoid unintentional errors in graph construction and to encourage a critical examination of all published graphs.

Bar graphs are susceptible to the same distortions as line graphs. For example, in a report to the home office on reduction of energy consumption, a branch manager submitted the graph shown in figure 17.7(a).

Figure 17.7
Kilowatt hours consumed by Oregon branch

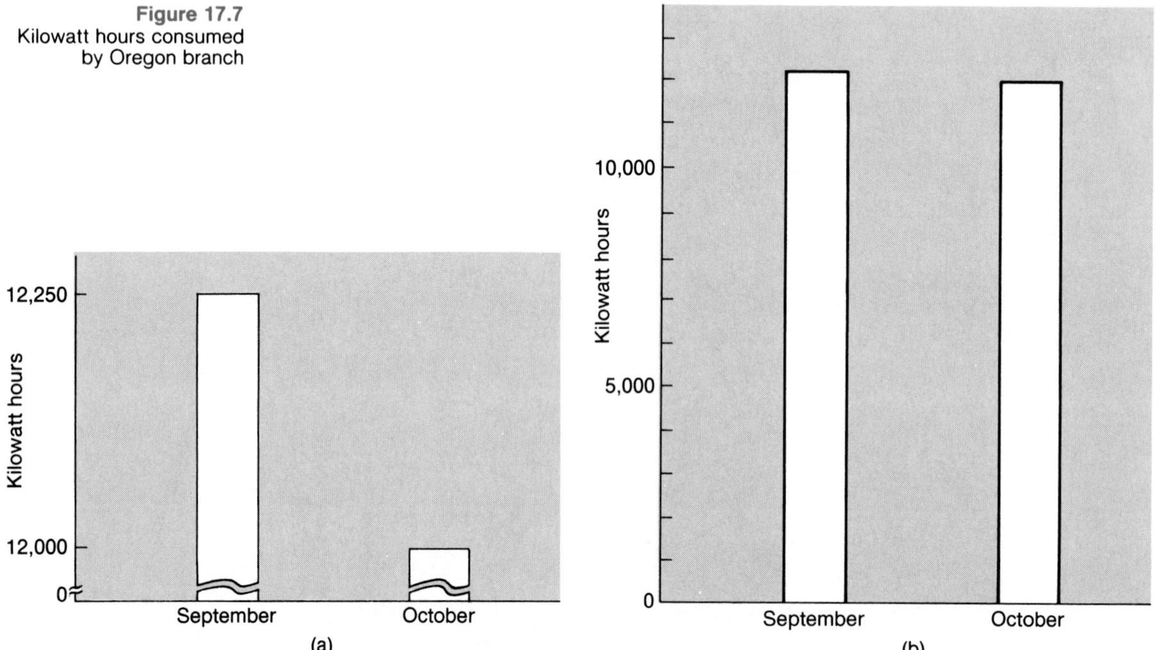

At first glance, the decrease seems impressive; however, the actual reduction is only about 2%. In this instance, a false impression was created by using a detailed scale, then omitting most of the vertical portion of the graph. The correct relationship is shown in figure 17.7(b).

Figure 17.8(a) shows a distortion of a pictogram. In this case, a twofold increase in company assets has been depicted by a figure whose radius is twice that of the 1988 figure. Although the radius is only twice as large, the *area* of the 1989 figure is *four times* that of the 1988 figure!

The correct method of graphing the increase is shown in figure 17.8(b).

Figure 17.8
Assets of a company

Exercises for Section 17.2

Use the following data to solve problems 1–12:

A	5	21	14	33	19	27	9	15
B	7	13	24	15	32	37	41	11
C	43	12	8	26	31	23	39	18
D	9	18	27	25	29	19	8	23

1. Arrange the data in line A in an array.
2. Arrange the data in line D in an array.
3. Arrange the data in lines A and C in an array.
4. Arrange the data in lines B and D in an array.
5. Arrange the data in lines B and C in an array.
6. Complete the following table using the data in lines A and C:

Class	Frequency
0–9	
10–19	
20–29	
30–39	
40–49	

7. Complete the following table using the data in lines B and D:

Class	Frequency
0–9	
10–19	
20–29	
30–39	
40–49	

8. Complete the following table using the data in lines B and C:

Class	Frequency
0–9	
10–19	
20–29	
30–39	
40–49	

9. Complete the following table using the data in lines A and D:

Class	Frequency	Relative Frequency	Percent
0–9			
10–19			
20–29			
30–39			
40–49			

10. Complete the following table using the data in lines A and B:

Class	Frequency	Relative Frequency	Percent
0–9			
10–19			
20–29			
30–39			
40–49			

11. Complete the following table using the data in lines A and D:

Class	Frequency	Cumulative Frequency
0–9		
10–19		
20–29		
30–39		
40–49		

12. Complete the following table using the data in lines B and D:

Class	Frequency	Cumulative Frequency
0–9		
10–19		
20–29		
30–39		
40–49		

13. The number of sales reported by each of ten salespersons at a used car outlet last week are given in the following table:

Salesperson	Number of Sales	Salesperson	Number of Sales
J. H.	15	R. S.	16
A. B.	7	B. A.	12
D. T.	11	C. D.	9
P. Z.	4	E. T.	8
D. D.	13	E. S.	5

Construct a frequency distribution of this data using class intervals of five.

14. The following numbers represent the number of years that the ten employees at the Simpson Company have yet to work before being eligible for retirement: 5, 11, 14, 2, 21, 8, 14, 9, 18, 12. Construct a frequency distribution of this data using class intervals of four.

15. Construct a relative frequency distribution of the data in problem 13.

16. Construct a relative frequency distribution of the data in problem 14.

17. The biweekly net earnings of 12 employees at the Concord Company are $390, $420, $405, $470, $510, $475, $460, $492, $505, $435, $425, and $395. Construct a cumulative frequency distribution of this data using class intervals of $20 and starting with $380.

18. The following numbers represent the final exam scores of students in a biology class:

62	59	91	80	87	56
72	68	78	87	76	75
42	98	72	75	70	55
52	83	72	71	99	89
69	73	74	59	63	91

Construct a cumulative frequency distribution of this data using class intervals of 10 and starting with 40.

19. The Golden State Corporation reported profits of $1.25 per share in 1986, $1.75 in 1987, $2.00 in 1988, and $1.50 in 1989. Construct a line graph of the company's profits for the four years.

20. The annual maintenance costs of the Omega Manufacturing Company for a five-year period are as follows: 1985, $50,000; 1986, $70,000; 1987, $85,000; 1988, $90,000; 1989, $95,000. Prepare a line graph to illustrate this data.

21. Superior Products manufactures blade housings for lawn mowers. The following table gives the production cost per unit based on the number of units produced per month:

Number of units produced	600	800	1,000	1,200
Production cost per unit	$8.00	$7.00	$6.50	$6.25

Construct a line graph for this data. Use the graph to estimate the production cost per unit if 700 units are produced per month.

22. The following table gives the gross sales and production costs of the Braxton Company for the first six months of 19__:

	Jan.	**Feb.**	**March**	**April**	**May**	**June**
Gross sales	$27,000	$31,000	$26,000	$27,500	$33,000	$33,500
Production costs	$18,000	$20,000	$17,000	$17,500	$21,500	$22,000

On the same set of axes, draw a line graph of the gross sales and a line graph of the production costs.

23. Culver Enterprises presented the following bar graph to summarize the number of male and female employees in its work force at the beginning of each of the years shown:

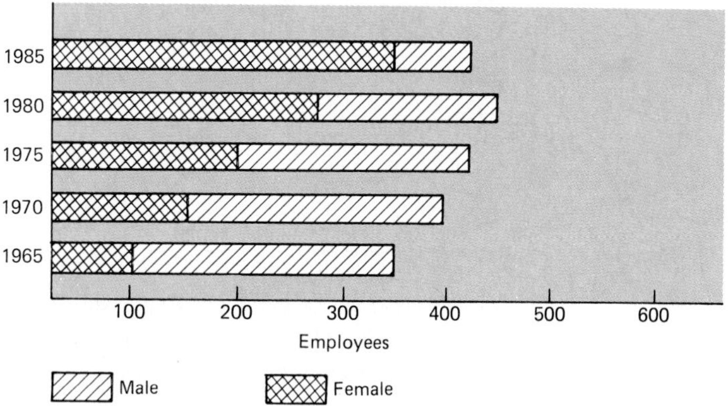

How many female employees were at Culver at the beginning of 1980? What was the total work force at the beginning of 1970? How many male employees were there at the beginning of 1985?

24. Construct a vertical bar graph that shows the number of units produced each month at the Concord Manufacturing Company: January, 4,500; February, 4,800; March, 5,200; April, 5,800; May, 4,200; June, 3,800.

25. Using the data given in the following table, construct a horizontal bar graph of the sales of the five branch stores of the Friendly Wholesale Farm Supply Company:

Branch	**Sales**
Riverview	$230,000
Eastport	320,000
Gulf	280,000
Brooksville	360,000
Sumter	220,000

26. The employment records of the Bradston Company yield the following data on the number of male and female employees at the company at the beginning of the years indicated:

Year	Male	Female
1960	800	50
1965	850	250
1970	900	400
1975	1,150	700
1980	1,250	950
1985	1,300	1,150

On the same set of axes, construct side-by-side vertical bar graphs showing the number of male employees and the number of female employees for each of the six years.

27. The first-quarter sales of Adamson's Men's Store were distributed as follows: suits, 32%; sport coats, 25%; slacks, 18%; shirts, 16%; shoes, 6%; miscellaneous, 3%. Construct a circle graph of the first-quarter sales.

28. The Eagle Manufacturing Company reported the following use of the company's sales dollar: production, 40¢; operating expenses, 25¢; research, 15¢; taxes, 15¢; miscellaneous, 5¢. Construct a circle graph that represents the use of the sales dollar.

29. The sales last year at Sander's Sporting Goods Store were distributed as follows: sports equipment, 64%; clothing, 28%; books, 6%; miscellaneous, 2%. Prepare a circle graph of the store's sales.

30. John and Pat Weber prepared the following monthly budget for their family: food, $320; housing, $230; clothing, $160; savings, $100; recreation and miscellaneous, $120. Find the percent of each expenditure and construct a circle graph of the budget.

31. Huffman Industries manufactures farm equipment. The company produced 40,000 tractors in 1987, 45,000 in 1988, and 55,000 in 1989.

    Let the symbol  represent 10,000 tractors, and prepare a pictogram showing the company's production for the three years.

32. Employment records at the Hammond Company reveal that the company employed 20 women and 40 men in 1975, 40 women and 45 men in 1980, and 55 women and 50 men in 1985. Prepare a pictogram for this data.

    Use the symbol  to represent 10 men and the symbol  to represent 10 women.

33. The net income of the Kenyon Company for the years 1985–1989 is as follows: 1985, $60,000; 1986, $70,000; 1987, $90,000; 1988, $80,000; 1989, $110,000. Construct a pictogram that shows the net income for each year. Use the symbol to represent $20,000.

34. Sterling Auto Sales sold 2,500 cars in 1970, 3,750 cars in 1975, 4,000 cars in 1980, and 3,500 cars in 1985. Using the symbol to represent 500 cars, construct a pictogram of the company's sales for the four years.

35. Kelsey Industries reported profits of $0.60 per share in 1986, $0.70 per share in 1987, $0.50 per share in 1988, and $0.40 per share in 1989. Which of the following line graphs most accurately represents this data? What is wrong with the other two graphs?

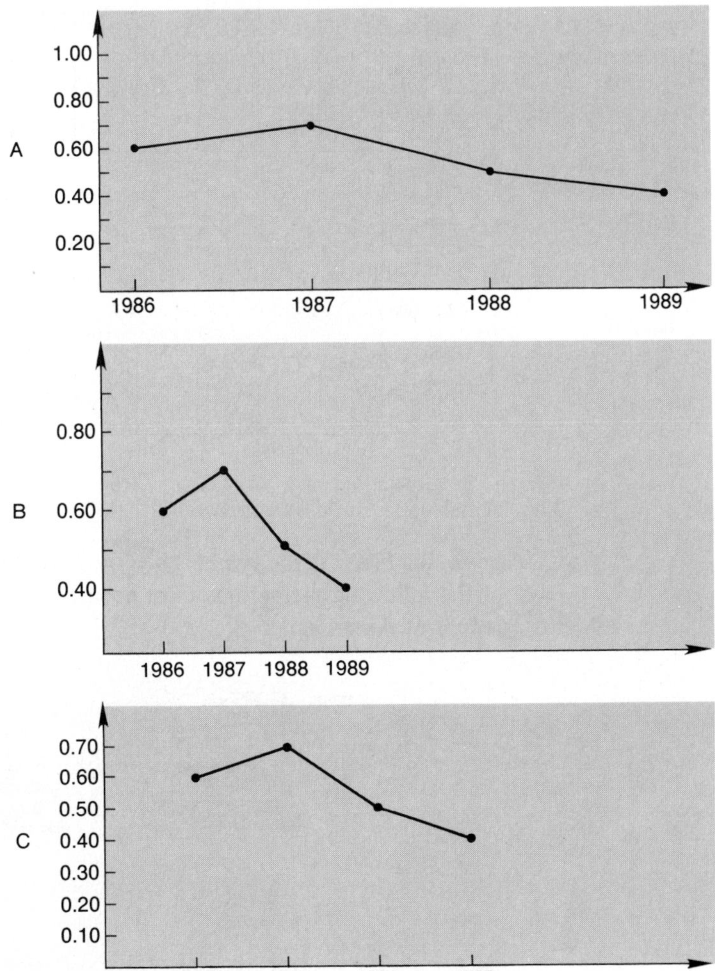

36. Robertson's Electrical Supply recorded sales of \$19,000 in January, \$21,500 in February, \$17,000 in March, and \$15,000 in April. Which of the following bar graphs most accurately represents this information? What is wrong with the other two graphs?

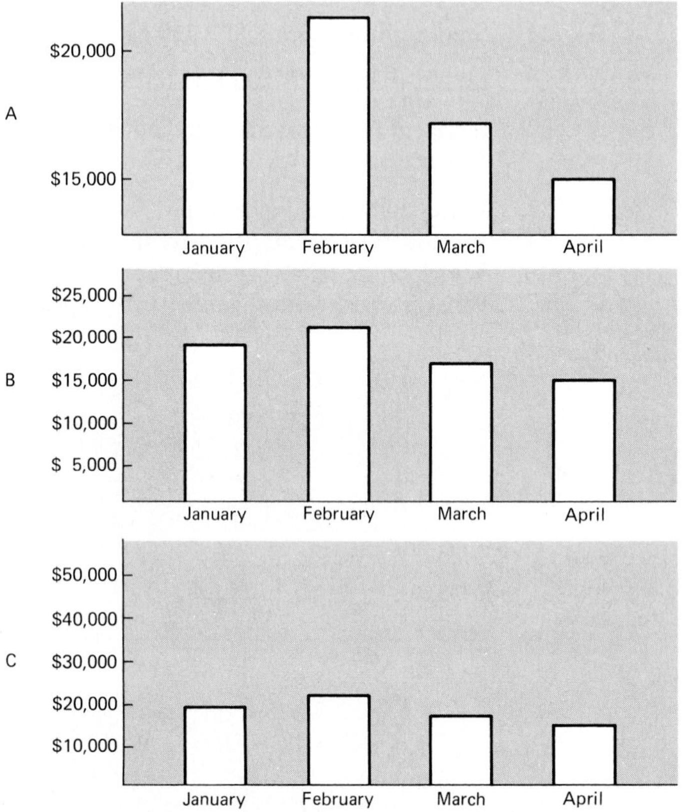

37. Americana Builders constructed 1,000 new homes in 1983 and 4,000 new homes in 1988. If the symbol represents 1,000 homes, which of the following pictograms most accurately reflects the construction record at Americana?

38. Employment records at the Bradshaw Company show that in 1979 15% of the employees were members of minority groups; in 1984, the figure rose to 20%; and in 1989, to 30%. Which of the following line graphs most accurately represents this data? What is wrong with the other two graphs?

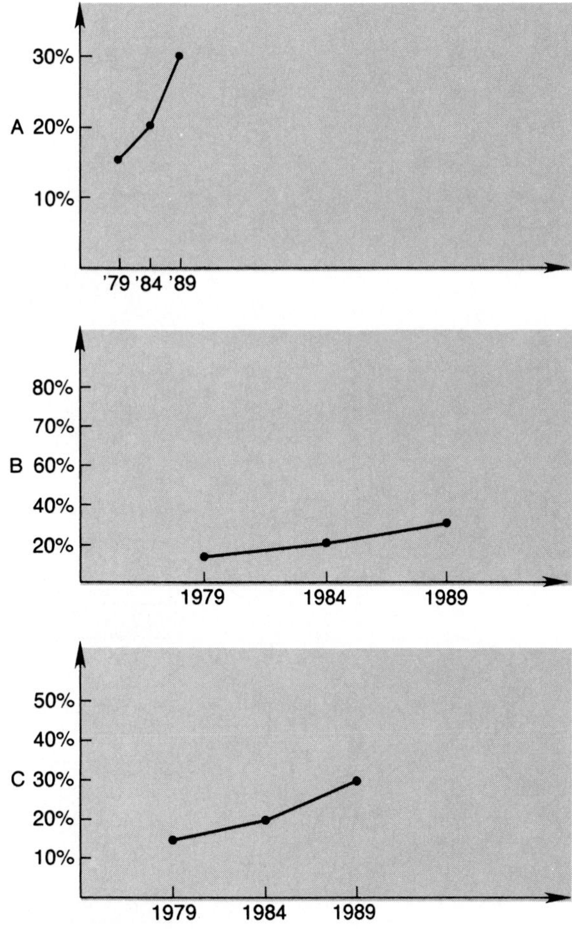

39. The sales record at the Clayton Candy Company for the first quarter of this year is as follows: January, $12,000; February, $16,000; March, $8,000; and April, $10,000. Which of the following bar graphs most accurately represents this information? What is wrong with the other two graphs?

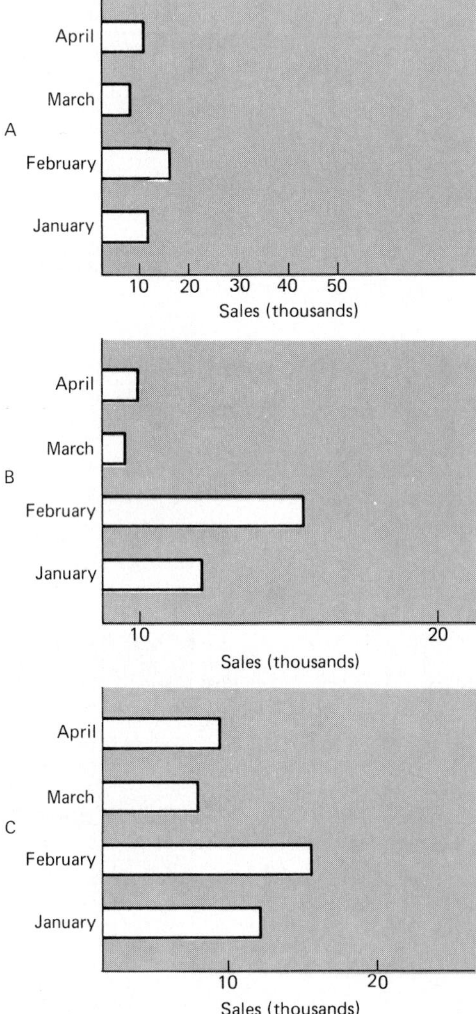

40. Braxton Builders reported net income of \$20,000 in 1988 and \$40,000 in 1989. If the symbol [\$] represents \$10,000, which of the following pictograms most accurately represents the net income of the company for the two years?

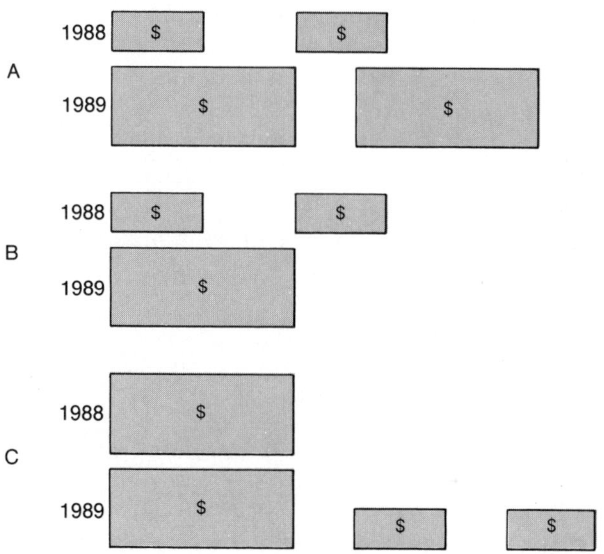

Section 17.3 Measures of location

Statisticians use a number of techniques to describe quantitative data. Numerical and graphical displays were covered in section 17.2. The sections that follow cover arithmetic methods. Before describing these arithmetic techniques, it is necessary to introduce a mathematical notation used in these measures.

The Greek letter **sigma** (Σ) is a notation used for "sum" or "add." For example, if the values in a distribution are x_1, x_2, x_3, x_4, and x_5, the sum of these values can be denoted by $\sum_{i=1}^{5} x_i$. That is,

$$\sum_{i=1}^{5} x_i = x_1 + x_2 + x_3 + x_4 + x_5 \tag{17–1}$$

The notation $\Sigma\, x_i$ means sum (add) all of the x_i's. The notation below and above the sigma symbol indicates the range of the x_i's, in this case from one to five.

The notation $\sum_{i=1}^{7} y_i$ means the sum of y_1 through y_7; that is,

$$\sum_{i=1}^{7} y_i = y_1 + y_2 + y_3 + y_4 + y_5 + y_6 + y_7 \tag{17–2}$$

Example 1 Find: $\sum_{i=1}^{4} x_i$ if $x_1 = 2, x_2 = 4, x_3 = 9, x_4 = 16$

Solution

$$\begin{aligned}\sum_{i=1}^{4} x_i &= x_1 + x_2 + x_3 + x_4 \\ &= 2 + 4 + 9 + 16 \\ &= 31\end{aligned}$$

Example 2 Find: $\sum_{i=1}^{3} (x_i + y_i)$ if $x_1 = 4, x_2 = 9, x_3 = 14, y_1 = 8, y_2 = 22, y_3 = 7$

Solution

$$\begin{aligned}\sum_{i=1}^{3} (x_i + y_i) &= (x_1 + y_1) + (x_2 + y_2) + (x_3 + y_3) \\ &= (4 + 8) + (9 + 22) + (14 + 7) \\ &= 12 + 31 + 21 \\ &= 64\end{aligned}$$

Measures of location (or **measures of central tendency**) are numbers indicative of the "center" or "average" of a set of data. The measures of location discussed in this section are (1) the arithmetic mean, (2) the median, and (3) the mode. There are advantages and disadvantages to each measure; hence, more than one may be utilized for a given set of data.

The arithmetic mean

The arithmetic mean is the most popular measure of location and is that value usually associated with the word "average." Average weight, batting average, and average sales are examples of the arithmetic mean. The **arithmetic mean** or **mean** is the sum of the values of a set of data divided by the total number of values. That is, for a set containing n values, the arithmetic mean (denoted by $\bar{x}$) is given by the formula

■ (17–3) $$\bar{x} = \frac{\sum_{i=1}^{n} x_i}{n}$$

Example 1 Find the mean of the data in the following array:

7, 9, 10, 12, 15, 15, 16, 17, 20, 22, 29, 32

Solution

$x_1 = 7, x_2 = 9, x_3 = 10, \ldots, x_{12} = 32$; hence,

$$\bar{x} = \frac{\sum_{i=1}^{12} x_i}{12} = \frac{204}{12} = 17$$

Example 2 Sixteen pieceworkers of the Hudgins Company produced the following number of pieces in one day's work: 22, 24, 20, 22, 26, 26, 23, 30, 28, 22, 20, 24, 28, 27, 26, 24. What was the mean number of pieces produced by the 16 workers?

Solution

$$\bar{x} = \frac{\sum_{i=1}^{16} x_i}{16} = \frac{392}{16} = 24.5$$

As a measure of central tendency, the mean has several advantages. The mean always exists, it is unique in the sense that a set of data has only one mean, and it takes into account each item of the data. A disadvantage of the mean is that it is affected by extreme values; that is, an unusually high or low value shifts the mean toward this value. The mean of the data 2, 3, 4, 5, 6 is $\frac{20}{5} = 4$, but the mean of the data 2, 3, 4, 5, 16 is $\frac{30}{5} = 6$. The mean of the second set of data was shifted toward the extreme value.

The median In an array of n values, the **median** is (1) the middle value of the array if n is odd and (2) the mean of the two middle values if n is even.

Example 3 Find the median of (a) 2, 4, 6, 8, 10, and (b) 2, 4, 6, 8, 10, 12.

Solution

a. $n = 5$; thus, the median is the middle value 6

b. $n = 6$; thus, the median is the mean of the two middle values; that is,

$$\frac{6 + 8}{2} = 7$$

Example 4 Find the median of the data in the following array:

7, 9, 10, 12, 15, 15, 16, 17, 20, 22, 29, 32

Solution

$n = 12$; hence, the median is the mean of the sixth and seventh values:

$$\frac{15 + 16}{2} = \frac{31}{2} = 15.5$$

Example 5 During an eleven-day period, the closing stock prices of the Hanson Corporation were

$21\frac{1}{4}, 21\frac{3}{8}, 21\frac{1}{4}, 21\frac{1}{2}, 21\frac{5}{8}, 21\frac{1}{2}, 21\frac{3}{4}, 22, 22\frac{1}{4}, 21\frac{7}{8}, 21\frac{5}{8}$

What was the median closing price of the stock during this period?

Solution

First, arrange the prices in an array

$21\frac{1}{4}, 21\frac{1}{4}, 21\frac{3}{8}, 21\frac{1}{2}, 21\frac{1}{2}, 21\frac{5}{8}, 21\frac{5}{8}, 21\frac{3}{4}, 21\frac{7}{8}, 22, 22\frac{1}{4}$

The sixth or middle value is $21\frac{5}{8}$. This is the median closing price of the stock.

Like the mean, the median is unique and always exists. The median requires a minimum of calculation; unlike the mean, it is not affected by extreme values. On the other hand, to find the median, the values must be arranged in an array, a tedious task for large values of n. A more significant disadvantage is that in statistical problems of estimation and tests of hypotheses, the median is less useful than the mean.

The mode A third measure of location is the mode. The **mode** is that value, class, or category that has the highest frequency.

Example 6 Find the mode of the data in the following array:

7, 9, 10, 12, 15, 15, 16, 17, 20, 22, 29, 32

Solution

The value with the highest frequency is 15, which occurs twice.

The chief advantage of the mode is that it requires no calculation. On the other hand, the mode may not exist (for example, the set of data 4, 5, 6, 7 has no mode), or if it does exist, it may not be unique. The array 2, 4, 4, 6, 6, 8 has two modes—4 and 6—and is said to be **bimodal.**

The principal value of the mode lies with categorical data. Suppose a poll indicated the following preferences for package size:

Size A = 157
Size B = 84
Size C = 120
Size D = 95

The frequency of 157 clearly indicates that size A is the mode.

Exercises for Section 17.3

1. Compute $\sum_{i=1}^{3} x_i$, when $x_1 = 4$, $x_2 = 3$, and $x_3 = 7$.

2. If $y_1 = 10$, $y_2 = 9$, $y_3 = 4$, and $y_4 = 6$, find $\sum_{i=1}^{4} y_i$.

3. Find $\sum_{i=1}^{3} (y_i - 2)$, when $y_1 = 6$, $y_2 = 8$, and $y_3 = 12$.

4. Find $\sum_{i=1}^{4} (2x_i)$, when $x_1 = 3$, $x_2 = 1$, $x_3 = 5$, and $x_4 = 8$.

5. If $x_1 = 6$, $x_2 = 10$, $x_3 = 8$, and $x_4 = 4$, what is the value of $\sum_{i=1}^{4} (3x_i - 1)$?

6. If $x_1 = 10$, $x_2 = 12$, $x_3 = 20$, $y_1 = 4$, $y_2 = 6$, and $y_3 = 11$, find $\sum_{i=1}^{3} (x_i + y_i)$.

7. In problem 6, find $\sum_{i=1}^{3} (x_i \cdot y_i)$.

8. In problem 6, find $\sum_{i=1}^{3} (4x_i - y_i)$.

9. Find $\sum_{i=1}^{4} (2x_i + 4) + \sum_{i=1}^{3} (4y_i - 1)$, when $x_1 = 2$, $x_2 = 7$, $x_3 = 11$, $x_4 = 6$, $y_1 = 2$, $y_2 = 4$, and $y_3 = 8$.

10. Find $\sum_{i=1}^{3} (6x_i - 1) - \sum_{i=1}^{4} (3y_i + 2)$, when $x_1 = 2$, $x_2 = 3$, $x_3 = 1$, $y_1 = 1$, $y_2 = 1$, $y_3 = 3$, and $y_4 = 2$.

Use the following data to solve problems 11–22:

A	7	11	5	19	6	12	12	21	14	12	14
B	18	4	7	2	16	23	15	15	9	14	
C	6	11	15	14	13	7	13	24	18	17	16
D	15	9	12	18	7	10	14	15	11	13	

11. Find the mean of the data in line A.

12. Find the mean of the data in line B.

13. Find the mean of the data in line C.

14. What is the median of line A?

15. What is the median of line B?

16. What is the median of line C?

17. Find the mode of line A.

18. Find the mode of line B.

19. Find the mode of line C.

20. Find the mean, median, and mode of line D.

21. Find the mean, median, and mode of lines A and B.

22. Find the mean, median, and mode of lines C and D.

23. A sales representative for the Burns Corporation reported the following daily sales for the past week: Monday, $7,200; Tuesday, $9,200; Wednesday, $10,400; Thursday, $12,100; and Friday, $8,400. Find her mean daily sales for the week.

24. Twelve pieceworkers at Parker Industries produced the following number of pieces in one day's work: 42, 51, 46, 44, 38, 40, 49, 53, 46, 47, 44, 48. What was the mean number of pieces produced by the workers?

25. The prices of nine stocks on the New York Stock Exchange are $14, $47, $60, $22, $12, $38, $67, $54, and $58. Find the median price of the stock.

26. The six employees of the Central Variety Store earn weekly salaries of $260, $265, $280, $240, $244, and $310. Find the median salary.

27. Earl Bowers decided to purchase a new television set and priced the set in seven different stores. The prices he found were $465, $420, $455, $435, $455, $440, and $470. Find (a) the mean price and (b) the mode of the prices.

28. The annual salaries of the employees at the Dunfield Company are given in the following table. Find (a) the mean annual salary, (b) the median of the salaries, and (c) the mode of the annual salaries.

Annual Salary	Frequency
$24,200	2
25,500	4
25,800	8
25,900	3
26,400	1
27,200	3

Section 17.4 Frequency distributions and measures of location

When a set of data contains a large number of values, measures of location are more efficiently calculated using a frequency distribution.

The arithmetic mean

The mean of a distribution with k classes is found by using the formula

■ (17–4)
$$\bar{x} = \frac{\sum_{i=1}^{k} f_i x_i}{\sum_{i=1}^{k} f_i}$$

where f_i = class frequency and x_i = midpoint of class interval.*

*The class midpoint is the mean of the boundaries of the class interval.

Example 1 Find the mean of the data in table 17.2.

Solution

There are six classes; hence, $k = 6$.

Class	Frequency (f_i)	Class Midpoint (x_i)	$f_i x_i$
5–9	2	7	14
10–14	2	12	24
15–19	4	17	68
20–24	2	22	44
25–29	1	27	27
30–34	1	32	32
	12		209

$$\bar{x} = \frac{\sum_{i=1}^{6} f_i x_i}{\sum_{i=1}^{6} f_i}$$

$$= \frac{209}{12}$$

$$= 17.416$$

$$= 17.42$$

The difference between 17.42 and the actual mean of 17 results from using the midpoint of the class intervals in place of the actual values. If the sample contains a large number of values, this error is quite small.

Example 2 Gasoline sales at a Sure Oil station were recorded as follows:

Amount	Number of Sales
Less than $10.00	16
$10.00–$19.99	26
20.00– 29.99	52
30.00– 39.99	12
40.00– 49.99	4

Find the mean sale at the station.

Solution

Class	Frequency (f_i)	Class Midpoint (x_i)	$f_i x_i$
$ 0.00–$ 9.99	16	$ 4.995	$ 79.92
10.00– 19.99	26	14.995	389.87
20.00– 29.99	52	24.995	1,299.74
30.00– 39.99	12	34.995	419.94
40.00– 49.99	4	44.995	179.98
	110		$2,369.45

$$\bar{x} = \frac{\sum_{i=1}^{5} f_i x_i}{\sum_{i=1}^{5} f_i}$$

$$= \frac{\$2{,}369.45}{110}$$

$$= \$21.54$$

The median In a set of data that contains n values, the median is a number that is at least as large as $\frac{n}{2}$ of the values and no larger than $\frac{n}{2}$ of the values. For the frequency distribution shown in table 17.2, $\frac{n}{2} = \frac{12}{2} = 6$, which means that the median must occur in the class 15–19. Assuming that the values are equally distributed in that interval, the following formula can be used to find the median:

■ (17–5) $$m = b + \frac{cd}{f_m}$$

where m = median, b = lower boundary of the class containing the median, c = length of the class interval, f_m = frequency of the class containing the median, and d = the difference between $\frac{n}{2}$ and the cumulative frequency up to b.

Example 3 Using formula 17–5, find the median of the data in table 17.2.

Solution

$\frac{n}{2} = 6, b = 15, c = 5, f_m = 4, d = 6 - 4 = 2$

$$m = b + \frac{cd}{f_m}$$
$$= 15 + \frac{10}{4}$$
$$= 15 + 2.5$$
$$= 17.5$$

The discrepancy between 17.5 and the median of 15.5 calculated in example 4 of section 17.3 results from assuming that the values in the class are uniformly distributed over the interval.* For data with a large number of values, uniform distribution is more likely to occur, and the calculated value approximates the median with little error.

Example 4 The following table records the reliability of an electronic component:

Hours	Frequency
700– 799	86
800– 899	82
900– 999	64
1,000–1,099	32
1,100–1,199	10

What is the median number of hours the component may be expected to perform?

Solution

$\frac{n}{2} = \frac{274}{2} = 137$; hence, the median class is 800–899.

$b = 800, c = 100, f_m = 82, d = 137 - 86 = 51$

*In class 15–19, the values were distributed as follows:

//	/	/		
15	16	17	18	19

$$m = b + \frac{cd}{f_m}$$

$$= 800 + \frac{100 \times 51}{82}$$

$$= 800 + 62.20$$

$$= 862.20 \text{ hours}$$

The mode The mode of a frequency distribution cannot be identified; hence, it is customary to report only the modal class. The **modal class** of a frequency distribution is the class with the highest frequency.

Example 5 Find the modal class of the data in table 17.2.

Solution

The class with the greatest frequency is the class 15–19; hence, it is the modal class.

If a single value of the mode is necessary, the midpoint of the modal class may be used. In this event, the mode of the data in table 17.2 is:

$$\frac{15 + 19}{2} = 17$$

Example 6 A survey indicated the following number of flavors of ice cream carried by area supermarkets and drugstores:

Number of Flavors	Frequency
1–5	2
6–10	11
11–15	9
16–20	1

Find (a) the modal class and (b) a single modal value.

Solution

a. The modal class is 6–10.

b. The modal value is $\frac{6 + 10}{2} = 8$.

Exercises for Section 17.4

In problems 1–5, fill in the missing entries in the given frequency distribution and use the formula $\bar{x} = (\sum_{i=1}^{k} f_i x_i)/(\sum_{i=1}^{k} f_i)$ to find the mean of the data in the distribution.

1.

Class	Frequency (f_i)	Class Midpoint (x_i)	$f_i x_i$
5–9	1	____	____
10–14	3	____	____
15–19	4	____	____
20–24	4	____	____
25–29	2	____	____

2.

Class	Frequency (f_i)	Class Midpoint (x_i)	$f_i x_i$
0–4	2	____	____
5–9	6	____	____
10–14	8	____	____
15–19	8	____	____
20–24	10	____	____
25–29	7	____	____
30–34	6	____	____
35–39	3	____	____

3.

Class	Frequency (f_i)	Class Midpoint (x_i)	$f_i x_i$
0–9	2	____	____
10–19	3	____	____
20–29	2	____	____
30–39	4	____	____
40–49	1	____	____

4.

Class	Frequency (f_i)	Class Midpoint (x_i)	$f_i x_i$
0–8	1	____	____
9–17	2	____	____
18–26	3	____	____
27–35	2	____	____
36–44	4	____	____
45–53	1	____	____
54–62	1	____	____

5.

Class	Frequency (f_i)	Class Midpoint (x_i)	f_ix_i
0–10	2	______	___
11–21	4	______	___
22–32	6	______	___
33–43	5	______	___
44–54	7	______	___
55–65	3	______	___
66–76	1	______	___

6. Use the formula $m = b + \frac{cd}{f_m}$ to find the median of the data given in problem 1.

7. Repeat problem 6 for the data given in problem 2.

8. Repeat problem 6 for the data given in problem 3.

9. Repeat problem 6 for the data given in problem 4.

10. Find the modal class of the frequency distribution in problem 1. What is the modal value?

11. Find the modal class and the modal value for the frequency distribution in problem 2.

12. Find the modal class and the modal value for the frequency distribution in problem 5.

13. A survey of the number of brands of cereal carried by area supermarkets yielded the following data:

Number of Brands	Frequency
1–5	4
6–10	11
11–15	14
16–20	3

Find (a) the mean, (b) the median, and (c) the modal class.

14. The Eltec Company manufactures light bulbs. The number of hours of useful life of one of the company's products is indicated by the following data:

Hours	Frequency
160–179	12
180–199	102
200–219	120
220–239	110
240–259	60
260–279	4

Find (a) the mean, (b) the median, and (c) the modal class.

15. Sales at a local convenience store were recorded as follows:

Amount	Number of Sales
Less than $2.00	42
$ 2.00–$ 3.99	126
4.00– 5.99	130
6.00– 7.99	72
8.00– 9.99	84
10.00– 11.99	20

Find (a) the mean, (b) the median, and (c) the modal class.

16. A survey of the employees at a manufacturing plant yielded the following frequency distribution of the weekly amount spent for food:

Amount Spent	Frequency
$ 50–$ 59	38
60– 69	62
70– 79	74
80– 89	46
90– 99	23
100– 109	18
110– 119	5

Find (a) the mean, (b) the median, and (c) the modal class.

Section 17.5 Measures of variation and the normal distribution

Equally important to measures of location that describe the "center" of a set of data are **measures of variation** that describe the amount of scatter or variation among the values.

The range

One measure of variation is the **range,** the difference between the largest and smallest data values. The range is not always reliable in describing the dispersion of data values. To illustrate, consider the following data arrays:

A 1,10,11,13,14,23
B 1,2,3,21,22,23

Each set has the same mean, median, and range (12,12, and 22, respectively), but most of the values of A are grouped around the mean, while the values of B are near the end values.

The most important statistical measure used to describe data variation is the standard deviation.

The standard deviation

The **standard deviation** is defined by the formula*

■ (17–6)
$$s = \sqrt{\frac{\sum_{i=1}^{n} (x_i - \bar{x})^2}{(n-1)}}$$

but is more easily calculated by the formula

■ (17–7)
$$s = \sqrt{\frac{n \cdot \sum_{i=1}^{n} x_i^2 - (\sum_{i=1}^{n} x_i)^2}{n(n-1)}}$$

where s = standard deviation, n = total number of values, and x_i = data values.

The standard deviation describes the amount of scatter in a set of data in that the larger the value of s the greater the amount of scatter.

* $\sqrt{}$ denotes the square root. The square root of a nonnegative number a is that nonnegative number b such that $b \times b = a$. For example, $\sqrt{36} = 6$ because $6 \times 6 = 36$.

Example 1 Using table 17.5 to find the necessary square roots, find the standard deviation of each of the data arrays A and B on page 535.

Solution

Using formula 17–7,

A		B	
x_i	x_i^2	x_i	x_i^2
1	1	1	1
10	100	2	4
11	121	3	9
13	169	21	441
14	196	22	484
23	529	23	529
$\sum_1^6 x_i = 72$	$\sum_1^6 x_i^2 = 1{,}116$	$\sum_1^6 x_i = 72$	$\sum_1^6 x_i^2 = 1468$

A:

$$s = \sqrt{\frac{6(1{,}116) - 72^2}{6(5)}}$$

$$s = \sqrt{50.4}$$

$$s \approx \sqrt{50}$$

$$s = 7.07$$

B:

$$s = \sqrt{\frac{6(1468) - 72^2}{6(5)}}$$

$$s = \sqrt{120.8}$$

$$s \approx \sqrt{121}$$

$$s = 11.00$$

The larger standard deviation of B indicates a wider dispersion of data values than for A.

For a frequency distribution with k classes, a formula for the standard deviation s is

■ (17–8)
$$s = \sqrt{\frac{\sum_{i=1}^{k} (x_i - \bar{x})^2 \cdot f_i}{n - 1}}$$

where the variables have the same meaning as in formula 17–4.

Measures of central tendency and measures of variation are used to make large collections of data more understandable. With a measure of central tendency, the statistician seeks to produce one number that is representative of all values, while with a measure of variation, one number is sought that describes the "spread" of the values.

Table 17.5 Square Roots

n	$\sqrt{n}$	n	$\sqrt{n}$	n	$\sqrt{n}$	n	$\sqrt{n}$
1	1	51	7.14	101	10.05	151	12.29
2	1.41	52	7.21	102	10.10	152	12.33
3	1.73	53	7.28	103	10.15	153	12.37
4	2.00	54	7.35	104	10.20	154	12.41
5	2.24	55	7.42	105	10.25	155	12.45
6	2.45	56	7.48	106	10.30	156	12.49
7	2.65	57	7.55	107	10.34	157	12.53
8	2.83	58	7.62	108	10.39	158	12.57
9	3.00	59	7.68	109	10.44	159	12.61
10	3.16	60	7.75	110	10.49	160	12.65
11	3.32	61	7.81	111	10.54	161	12.69
12	3.46	62	7.87	112	10.58	162	12.73
13	3.61	63	7.94	113	10.63	163	12.77
14	3.74	64	8.00	114	10.68	164	12.81
15	3.87	65	8.06	115	10.72	165	12.85
16	4.00	66	8.12	116	10.77	166	12.88
17	4.12	67	8.19	117	10.82	167	12.92
18	4.24	68	8.25	118	10.86	168	12.96
19	4.36	69	8.31	119	10.91	169	13.00
20	4.47	70	8.37	120	10.95	170	13.04
21	4.58	71	8.43	121	11.00	171	13.08
22	4.69	72	8.49	122	11.05	172	13.11
23	4.80	73	8.54	123	11.09	173	13.15
24	4.90	74	8.60	124	11.14	174	13.19
25	5.00	75	8.66	125	11.18	175	13.23
26	5.10	76	8.72	126	11.22	176	13.27
27	5.20	77	8.77	127	11.27	177	13.30
28	5.29	78	8.83	128	11.31	178	13.34
29	5.39	79	8.89	129	11.36	179	13.38
30	5.48	80	8.94	130	11.40	180	13.42
31	5.57	81	9.00	131	11.45	181	13.45
32	5.66	82	9.06	132	11.49	182	13.49
33	5.74	83	9.11	133	11.53	183	13.53
34	5.83	84	9.17	134	11.58	184	13.56
35	5.92	85	9.22	135	11.62	185	13.60
36	6.00	86	9.27	136	11.66	186	13.64
37	6.08	87	9.33	137	11.70	187	13.67
38	6.16	88	9.38	138	11.75	188	13.71
39	6.24	89	9.43	139	11.79	189	13.75
40	6.32	90	9.49	140	11.83	190	13.78
41	6.40	91	9.54	141	11.87	191	13.82
42	6.48	92	9.59	142	11.92	192	13.86
43	6.56	93	9.64	143	11.96	193	13.89
44	6.63	94	9.70	144	12.00	194	13.93
45	6.71	95	9.75	145	12.04	195	13.96
46	6.78	96	9.80	146	12.08	196	14.00
47	6.86	97	9.85	147	12.12	197	14.04
48	6.93	98	9.90	148	12.17	198	14.07
49	7.00	99	9.95	149	12.21	199	14.11
50	7.07	100	10.00	150	12.25	200	14.14

Normal distribution

For many sets of data, if the sample is large, the graph of the frequency distribution tends to resemble the bell-shaped curve shown in figure 17.9. This graph is called a **normal curve,** and distributions of data that are approximated by a normal curve are called **normal distributions.***

Normal distributions are common and occur in a variety of circumstances. For example, I.Q. scores, the heights of adult males or females, baseball batting averages, the size of peas, and the density of the stars are all normally distributed. That is, if a frequency distribution is obtained for a large number of measurements of one of these variables, the corresponding graph tends to look like a normal curve.

The normal curve has several interesting properties. The mean, median, and mode are identical and occur at the point where the curve reaches its maximum height. In addition, approximately 68% of all values differ from the mean by less than one standard deviation, approximately 95% of the data differ from the mean by less than two standard deviations, and approximately 99% of the data differ from the mean by less than three standard deviations. See figure 17.10.

Example 2

A time study made on 250 workers indicated that the mean time for performing a certain task was 36 minutes with a standard deviation of 8 minutes. Assuming that the times were normally distributed, approximately how many workers completed the task in 28 to 44 minutes?

Solution

The time frame of 28 to 44 minutes is one standard deviation to the left and to the right of the mean. Hence, approximately $250 \times 0.68 = 170$ workers completed the task in 28 to 44 minutes.

Figure 17.9
A normal curve

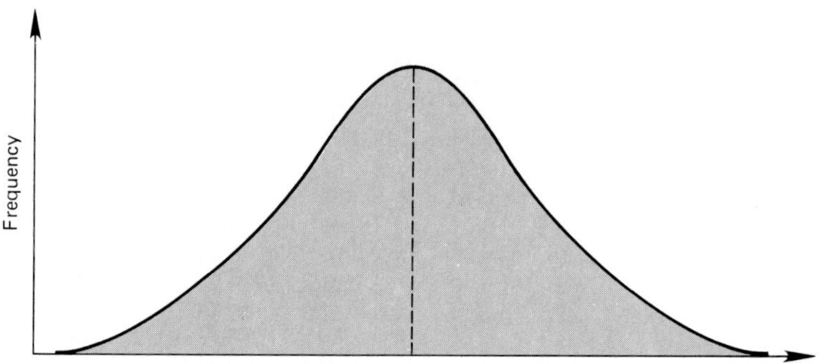

*The data values in a distribution are either *discrete* or *continuous*. A count always yields discrete data, while measurements will usually yield continuous data. The normal curve is the graph of a distribution of continuous data, but the graphs of distributions of discrete data may resemble the normal curve.

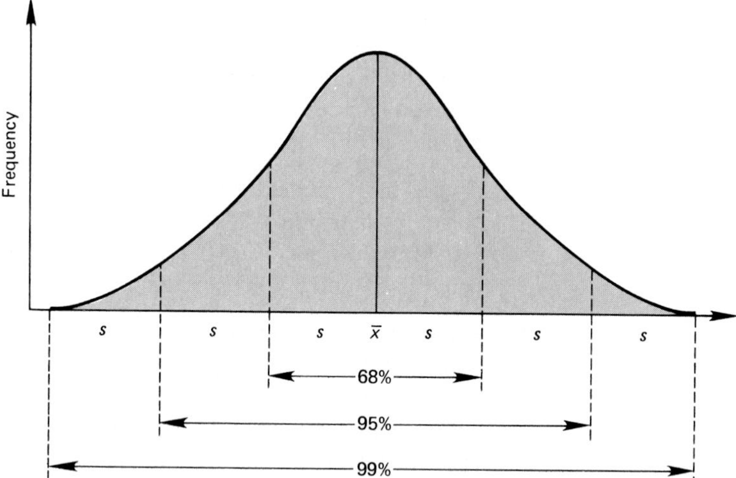

Figure 17.10
Standard deviations on a normal curve

Exercises for Section 17.5

In problems 1–5, use formula 17–7 and table 17.5 to compute the standard deviation of the given data.

1. 11, 4, 23, 16, 4, 15
2. 6, 2, 12, 8, 4, 8
3. 5, 11, 15, 14, 13, 6, 12, 11
4. 10, 15, 11, 20, 25, 14, 16, 21
5. 4, 6, 2, 8, 5, 12, 9, 7, 8, 6, 10, 8
6. The weekly salaries of the employees at the Curtis Company are given in the following table:

Weekly Salary	Frequency
$220	3
230	9
250	6
260	2

   Compute the standard deviation for this data.

7. The number of sales reported by each of eight salespeople at a furniture store last week were 12, 8, 10, 11, 15, 6, 10, and 8. Compute the standard deviation for this data.

8. The number of years of service of the 10 employees of the Quality Clothing Store are 23, 5, 10, 16, 4, 8, 14, 8, 17, and 8. Compute the standard deviation for this data. What percent of the employees have served a number of years that is within one standard deviation of the mean?

9. A class of 40 students was given an examination. The scores were normally distributed. If the mean score on the exam was 75 and the standard deviation was 10, approximately how many students scored between 65 and 85 on the exam? How many scored between 55 and 95?

10. An analysis of the weekly salaries paid to the assembly-line workers at a manufacturing plant revealed a mean weekly salary of \$173 with a standard deviation of \$12. If the plant employs 72 assembly-line workers and if their salaries are normally distributed, approximately how many workers earn between \$161 and \$185 per week? How many earn between \$149 and \$197 per week?

11. Sunshine Breakfast Cereal is sold in boxes marked with a net weight of 12 ounces. The true net weight is normally distributed, with a mean of 12 ounces and a standard deviation of 0.1 ounce. If a grocer receives a shipment of 200 boxes of the cereal, how many boxes will have an actual net weight between 12.2 and 12.3 ounces? How many will have a net weight between 11.8 and 11.9 ounces?

12. Suppose the waist size of adult men is normally distributed, with a mean of 35 inches and a standard deviation of 1 inch. A clothing manufacturer is introducing a new line of dress slacks for men, and 5,000 pairs of the slacks will be test-marketed. How many of the 5,000 pairs manufactured should be between a size 33 waist and a size 37 waist?

Section 17.6 Index numbers

An **index number** is a statistical measure designed to show changes with respect to some characteristic, such as time, geographic location, income, profession, and so on. Although mainly used in business and economics, index numbers also have applications in such fields as psychology, sociology, public health, and government.

The price relative One of the simplest of the index numbers is the **price relative,** the ratio of a given year's price to a base year's price multiplied by 100:

■ (17–9) $$\text{Price relative} = \frac{p_n}{p_o} \cdot 100$$

where p_n = new price or the given year price and p_o = old price or the base year price.

Example 1 The average residential electric bill for 1,000 kilowatt hours in 1975 was \$18.31; in 1985, it was \$48.76. Compute the price relative (to the nearest whole number) using 1975 as the base year.

Solution

Using formula 17–9, with p_n = \$48.76 and p_o = \$18.31,

$$\begin{aligned}\text{Price relative} &= \frac{p_n}{p_o} \cdot 100\\ &= \frac{\$48.76}{\$18.31} \cdot 100\\ &= 266\end{aligned}$$

The price relative in example 1 compares 1985 electricity prices with 1975 electricity prices in the following sense: For every \$100 spent on electricity in 1975, it took \$266 in 1985 to purchase the same number of kilowatt hours.

The simple aggregate index The price relative compares prices of a single item; other indexes seek to compare prices of a related group of items. For example, the **simple aggregate index** is found by dividing the sum of the prices for a given year by the sum of the prices for the base year and then multiplying the result by 100:

■ (17–10) $$\text{Simple aggregate index} = \frac{\Sigma p_n}{\Sigma p_o} \cdot 100$$

where Σp_n = sum of the given year prices and Σp_o= sum of the base year prices.

Example 2 For selected meats, the price per pound in 1976 and 1986 was as follows:

	1976 Price	1986 Price
Sirloin steak	$1.76	$3.05
Pork chops	1.61	2.25
Chicken	0.58	0.72
Bacon	1.22	1.89
Frankfurters	1.09	1.75

Compute the simple aggregate index (to the nearest whole number) using the year 1976 as the base year.

Solution

Using formula 17–10, with Σp_n = sum of the 1986 prices and Σp_o = sum of the 1976 prices,

$$\text{Simple aggregate index} = \frac{\Sigma p_n}{\Sigma p_o} \cdot 100$$

$$= \frac{\$3.05 + \$2.25 + \$0.72 + \$1.89 + \$1.75}{\$1.76 + \$1.61 + \$0.58 + \$1.22 + \$1.09} \cdot 100$$

$$= \frac{\$9.66}{\$6.26} \cdot 100$$

$$= 154$$

If the prices in example 2 are representative of all meats, then the index number 154 indicates that the combined 1986 meat prices are 154% of those of 1976, or that it would take $154 in 1986 to buy the same quantity of meat that $100 would purchase in 1976.

A major weakness of the simple aggregate index is that prices are not related to quantities. For instance, in example 2, sirloin steak and frankfurters were treated equally, although sales of frankfurters undoubtedly far exceeded sales of sirloin steaks.

The Laspeyres index

An index designed to consider both quantity and price is the **Laspeyres index,** named after the statistician who first suggested its use. The formula is

■ (17–11) $$I = \frac{\Sigma p_n q_o}{\Sigma p_o q_o} \cdot 100$$

where $\Sigma p_n q_o$ = sum of the products of the given year prices and the corresponding base year quantities and $\Sigma p_o q_o$ = sum of the products of the base year prices and the corresponding base year quantities.

Example 3 Softwood prices (per 1,000 board feet) and production (in billions of board feet) are shown in the following table:

	Price		Production
	1985	*1990*	*1985*
Douglas fir	$165.90	$432.20	7.33
Southern pine	57.00	155.40	6.97
Ponderosa pine	71.20	206.10	3.54

Using 1985 as the base year, compute (to the nearest whole number) the Laspeyres index.

Solution

$$\begin{aligned} \mathrm{I} &= \frac{\Sigma p_n q_o}{\Sigma p_o q_o} \cdot 100 \\ &= \frac{\$432.20(7.33) + \$155.40(6.97) + \$206.10(3.54)}{\$165.90(7.33) + \$\ 57.00(6.97) + \$\ 71.20(3.54)} \cdot 100 \\ &= \frac{\$4{,}980.76}{\$1{,}865.39} \cdot 100 \\ &= 267 \end{aligned}$$

The Laspeyres index is an example of a *weighted index* in which the prices are adjusted by the corresponding amount produced. Many of the indexes used today are weighted indexes, particularly those published by the federal government.

The consumer price index

Perhaps the most widely known of the weighted indexes is the **Consumer Price Index (CPI).** Calculated monthly by the U.S. Department of Labor, the CPI is a measure of the average change in the prices paid by urban consumers for a fixed market basket of consumer goods and services. The CPI compares what the market basket of goods and services costs this month with what the same market basket cost a month, a year, or several years ago.

The CPI market basket is developed from detailed expenditure information provided by a sampling of families and individuals on what they actually buy. All expenditure items have been classified into about 250 categories, arranged into seven major groups as shown in table 17.6.

Table 17.6 Consumer Price Index 1988 (1982–84 = 100)

1988	All Items	Food	Apparel	Transportation	Shelter	Medical Care	Entertainment
Jan.	115.7	115.7	110.4	107.1	116.2	134.4	118.1
May	117.5	117.0	116.3	108.1	117.7	137.5	119.7
Sept.	119.8	120.2	117.8	109.7	119.9	140.4	121.3

For the Consumer Price Index, 1982–84 is the base period. Thus, in September of 1988, it cost $120.20 for the same amount of food that $100.00 would buy in the period 1982–84. The Consumer Price Index is an important index in that many government and private cost-of-living increases are linked to the CPI, such as social security payments and cost-of-living increases in collective bargaining contracts.

Other government indexes of importance to businesses include the following:

Gross National Product (GNP) Issued quarterly by the U.S. Department of Commerce, this index measures the market value of the nation's total output of goods and services. Historically, economic policymakers have aimed for growth in the GNP of about 3% after discounting increases due to inflation, because they consider this to be the nation's growth potential. A decline in the GNP for two consecutive quarters is usually considered to denote a recession.

Composite Index of Leading Indicators Prepared monthly by the U.S. Department of Commerce, this index is a composite of 12 other indexes that are weighted to show their importance to the overall economy. This index is designed to foreshadow economic trends in the months ahead. Strong gains in the index are considered signs of healthy economic growth, while several consecutive months of decline are regarded as signaling the onset of a recession.

U.S. Export and Import Merchandise Trade Prepared by the U.S. Bureau of the Census from customs data, this index measures the nation's trade performance in imports and exports.

Exercises for Section 17.6

1. The average monthly residential heating cost in a midwestern city was $24.70 in 1980 and $72.90 in 1990. Compute the price relative, using 1980 as the base year. (Round to the nearest whole number.)

2. The annual company cost of employee benefits at the Preston Company was $984.82 per employee in 1983 and $1,420.36 in 1988. Using 1983 as the base year, find the price relative for employee benefits. (Round to the nearest whole number.)

3. The cost of fuel at Rosen Industries rose from $0.48 per gallon in 1975 to $1.08 per gallon in 1985. To the nearest whole number, find the price relative using 1975 as the base year.

4. Use table 17.6 to determine how much an individual spent in January, 1988 for medical care that cost $100 in 1982–84. How much did groceries costing $20 in 1982–84 cost in May, 1988?

5. Use table 17.6 to determine how much it cost in September, 1988 to purchase clothing that cost $100 in 1982–84. How much did housing worth $78,500 in 1982–84 cost in January, 1988?

6. Use table 17.6 to find the percent increase in the cost of medical care from January to May. What is the percent increase in transportation costs from January to September? (Round to the nearest tenth of a percent.)

7. Production costs (per unit produced) at Carter Enterprises are shown in the following table:

	Cost	
	1984	*1989*
Labor	$400.20	$ 615.10
Materials	931.16	1,540.20
Maintenance	54.08	82.80

Using 1984 as the base year, compute (to the nearest whole number) the simple aggregate index of the production costs.

8. The retail prices of the air-conditioning units produced at Brentwood Refrigeration are shown in the following table:

	Retail Prices		**Number of Units Produced (Hundreds)**
	1980	*1985*	*1980*
Model 12	$302.10	$ 532.18	87.3
Model 12-D	570.90	908.42	101.4
Model 12-XL	924.14	1,514.86	62.3

Compute (to the nearest whole number) the simple aggregate index of the retail prices, using 1980 as the base year.

9. The production costs per unit of the computers produced at Elway Electronics are shown in the following table:

	Production Costs 1980	Production Costs 1986	Number of Units Produced (Hundreds) 1980
Model E-400	$ 348.20	$ 520.10	76.4
Model E-800	764.80	914.40	112.8
Model E-1200	1,480.10	1,920.30	48.2

Find the simple aggregate index (to the nearest whole number) of the production costs, using 1980 as the base year.

10. Using the 1980 production figures as weights for retail prices, compute (to the nearest whole number) the Laspeyres index for the data given in problem 8.

11. Compute (to the nearest whole number) the Laspeyres index for the data given in problem 9. Use the 1980 production figures as weights for production costs.

Glossary

Arithmetic mean Also called the *mean*. The sum of the values of a set of data divided by the number of pieces of data.

Array An arrangement of numerical data in order from low to high or from high to low.

Bar graph A graph that compares several related pieces of data using horizontal or vertical bars.

Bimodal A set of data for which two pieces of data occur most frequently, thereby resulting in two modes.

Categorical frequency distribution A frequency distribution of data sorted according to a qualitative description.

Circle graph A graph used to illustrate the distribution of goods or money by using portions of a circle.

Classes The groups into which data are placed in a frequency distribution.

Class frequency The number of pieces of data in a class of a frequency distribution.

Composite Index of Leading Indicators An index issued monthly by the U.S. Department of Commerce that is a composite of 12 other indexes and is designed to foreshadow economic trends in the months ahead.

Consumer Price Index (CPI) An index issued monthly by the U.S. Labor Department that measures retail price changes for specific items of food, clothing, shelter, fuels, and services.

Cumulative frequency distribution A frequency distribution in which the entry for each line of the table is the class frequency plus the sum of the preceding class frequencies.

Frequency distribution A tabulation of data obtained by grouping the data into classes and tallying the number or frequency of pieces of data in each class.

Graph A representation of statistical or numerical data by visual means.

Gross National Product (GNP) An index issued quarterly by the U.S. Department of Commerce that measures the market value of the nation's total output of goods and services.

Index number A statistical measure designed to show changes with respect to some characteristic, usually time.
Laspeyres index The ratio of the sum of the products of the given year prices and the corresponding base year quantities to the sum of the products of the base year prices and the corresponding base year quantities, multiplied by 100.
Line graph A graph that uses a broken line to illustrate how one quantity changes with respect to another.
Mean See *arithmetic mean.*
Measures of central tendency See *measures of location.*
Measures of location Numbers used to indicate the "center" or "average" of a collection of data. The mean, median, and mode are measures of location.
Measures of variation Measures that describe the amount of "scatter" or variation in a collection of data.
Median For an array of n pieces of data, the middle value if n is odd and the mean of the two middle values if n is even.
Modal class In a frequency distribution, the class with the highest frequency.
Mode The piece of data that occurs most frequently in a set of data.
Normal curve The graph of a normal distribution.
Normal distribution A frequency distribution for which the graph is a bell-shaped curve and approximately 68% of the data differ from the mean by less than one standard deviation, 95% of the data differ from the mean by less than two standard deviations, and 99% of the data differ from the mean by less than three standard deviations.
Numerical frequency distribution A frequency distribution of data grouped according to numerical size.
Pictogram A modified form of a bar graph in which pictures are used to represent quantity.
Price relative The ratio of a given year's price to a base year's price, multiplied by 100.
Range The difference between the largest and smallest data values.
Relative frequency distribution A frequency distribution in which relative class frequencies are indicated for each class. Each relative class frequency is the class frequency divided by the total number of pieces of data.
Sigma (Σ) A notation used to indicate a sum.
Simple aggregate index The ratio of the sum of the prices for a given year to the sum of the prices for a base year, multiplied by 100.
Standard deviation A number used to indicate the amount of scatter or variation among the values in a set of data.
U.S. Export and Import Merchandise Trade An index prepared by the U.S. Bureau of the Census that measures the nation's trade performance in imports and exports.

Review test

Use the following data for problems 1–4:

12	8	0	3	3	10
10	16	7	14	8	4
2	8	13	8	11	7

1. Arrange the data in an array and find the median.
2. Find the mean of the data.
3. Find the mode of the data.
4. Complete the following cumulative frequency distribution of the data:

Class	Cumulative Frequency
0–3	
4–7	
8–11	
12–15	
16–19	

For problems 5–7, use the information given in the following frequency distribution:

Class	Frequency
0–4	2
5–9	5
10–14	12
15–19	10
20–24	8
25–29	3

5. Find the mean of the data in the distribution.
6. Find the median of the data in the distribution.
7. Find the modal class of the data.
8. Compute the standard deviation of the data in the following array: 1, 2, 3, 5, 9. Use table 17.5 to find the necessary square root.
9. Two students each took five exams in an English class. One student scored higher than the other on all but one exam, yet their mean scores for the five exams were the same. Give an example of such exam scores.
10. The breaking strength of a new synthetic fiber is normally distributed, with a mean of 150 pounds and a standard deviation of 3 pounds. If 500 samples of the fiber are tested, approximately how many of the samples will have a breaking strength of between 144 and 156 pounds?
11. The cost of solvent at Burgess Products rose from $0.46 per gallon in 1984 to $0.74 per gallon in 1988. To the nearest whole number, find the price relative using 1984 as the base year.
12. Production costs (per unit produced) at Elpen Enterprises are shown in the following table:

	Cost	
	1985	*1990*
Labor	$204.14	$ 480.20
Materials	612.80	1,042.80
Maintenance	72.14	104.46

Using 1985 as the base year, compute (to the nearest whole number) the simple aggregate index of the production costs.

13. Prices and quantities sold of three brands of shock absorbers are shown in the following table:

	Prices		Quantities	
	1981	*1986*	*1981*	*1986*
A	$ 3	$ 6	240	212
B	5	10	165	104
C	11	15	110	98

Compute (to the nearest whole number) the Laspeyres index, using 1981 as the base year.

14. The profits per share of Elco stock were $0.80 in 1985, $0.40 in 1986, $0.20 in 1987, $1.00 in 1988, and $1.20 in 1989. Construct a line graph to illustrate this data.

15. Glenridge Poultry Products reported the following sales for the years 1985–1989:

Year	Chickens	Turkeys
1985	$180,000	$ 70,000
1986	210,000	100,000
1987	250,000	120,000
1988	260,000	150,000
1989	280,000	180,000

On the same set of axes, construct side-by-side horizontal bar graphs of chicken sales and turkey sales for each of the five years.

16. Allied Parcel Service delivered 80,000 parcels in 1986, 100,000 parcels in 1987, 140,000 parcels in 1988, and 160,000 parcels in 1989. Using the symbol ▭ to represent 40,000 parcels, construct a pictogram showing the number of parcels delivered in each of the four years.

17. Prentice Pharmaceuticals reported that in 1988, 50¢ of each sales dollar was used for research, 25¢ was used for operating expenses, 15¢ was used for taxes, and 10¢ was used for miscellaneous expenses. Construct a circle graph that represents the use of the company's sales dollar in 1988.

CHAPTER 18 The Metric System

Chapter Objectives

I. Learn the meaning of the following terms:

Meter, 552
Square meter, 555
Are, 555
Liter, 558
Gram, 559
Metric ton, 559

II. Understand:

Prefixes used in the metric system, 553
Metric units of length, 553–554
Metric units of area, 555
Metric units of capacity, 558
Metric units of weight, 559
Fahrenheit and Celsius temperature scales, 566

III. Perform:

Conversions between metric units, 554–556, 558–561
Conversions between metric units and English units, 564–565
Conversions between Fahrenheit and Celsius temperature scales, 566–567

Section 18.1 Introduction

The system of weights and measures used in the United States has its heritage in the English system of weights and measures, which in turn can be traced to ancient Roman and Egyptian customs. These ancient standards were imprecise and largely based on anatomical dimensions. For example, in Egypt, a basic unit of length was the cubit, the distance from the elbow to the tip of the middle finger. The Egyptians divided the cubit into seven palms and each palm into four digits, a word also meaning finger. Thus, every person carried his or her own measuring system, but because these lengths vary among individuals, everyone had a different "ruler."

In the latter part of the eighteenth century, a commission of French scientists developed a system that has become the international standard of weights and measures. Called the metric system, it has been adopted by almost every civilized country except the United States (see figures 18.1 and 18.2).*

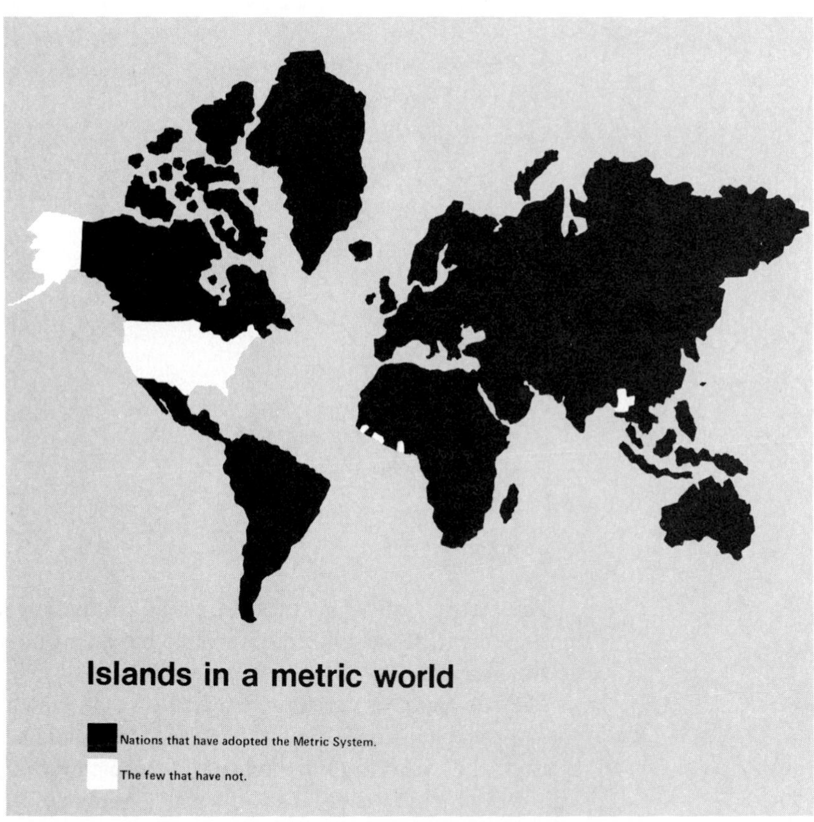

Figure 18.1
Islands in a metric world

*American scientists already express scientific measurements in metric units, but the general public continues to use the system of feet, miles, pounds, gallons, and so on. Plans to convert the entire country to the metric system currently are being discussed.

Figure 18.2 Australian stamps used to promote metric conversion

The metric system has two distinct advantages over other forms of measurement: It has a fixed, invariable base, and its numerical system is decimal based.

The basic unit of measurement is the **meter,** which was defined to be $\frac{1}{10{,}000{,}000}$ of the distance from the equator to either the North or South Pole.* As a result, the meter is approximately 39.37 inches or approximately 1.093 yards. This unit of length is also used to establish units of area, capacity, and weight, as will be seen in the sections that follow.

Decimal multiples and fractions of the basic unit are designated by Greek and Latin prefixes. The value and meaning of these designations are shown in table 18.1.

*A more recent definition of the meter is 1,650,763.73 wavelengths of the orange-red light of krypton 86.

Table 18.1 Prefixes Used in the Metric System

Prefix (Abbreviation)	Meaning	Numerical Value
Giga (G)	One billion	1,000,000,000
Mega (M)	One million	1,000,000
Kilo (k)	One thousand	1,000
Hecto (h)	One hundred	100
Deka (dk)	Ten	10
Deci (d)	One tenth	$\frac{1}{10} = 0.1$
Centi (c)	One hundredth	$\frac{1}{100} = 0.01$
Milli (m)	One thousandth	$\frac{1}{1{,}000} = 0.001$
Micro (u)	One millionth	$\frac{1}{1{,}000{,}000} = 0.000001$
Nano (n)	One billionth	$\frac{1}{1{,}000{,}000{,}000} = 0.000000001$

Thus, a dekameter is 10 meters, a kilometer is 1,000 meters, a centimeter is $\frac{1}{100}$ of a meter, and a millimeter is $\frac{1}{1{,}000}$ of a meter. The decimal base makes calculations with the metric system much simpler than with the U.S. system. For example, any denomination can be changed to a higher one by moving the decimal point to the left and changed to a lower one by moving the decimal point to the right. Thus,

1.725 dekameters = 17.25 meters = 172.5 decimeters

Section 18.2 Metric units of length and area

The meter is the basic unit of the metric system. The **kilometer** is used to measure long distances, while for small lengths the **centimeter** and the **millimeter** are the most common forms. Multiples and submultiples of the meter are shown in table 18.2.

Table 18.2 Multiples and Submultiples of the Meter

1 kilometer (km)	= 1,000 meters	1 meter	= 0.001 kilometer
1 hectometer (hm)	= 100 meters	1 meter	= 0.01 hectometer
1 dekameter (dkm)	= 10 meters	1 meter	= 0.1 dekameter
1 meter (m)	= Basic unit of length	1 meter	= Basic unit of length
1 decimeter (dm)	= 0.1 meter	1 meter	= 10 decimeters
1 centimeter (cm)	= 0.01 meter	1 meter	= 100 centimeters
1 millimeter (mm)	= 0.001 meter	1 meter	= 1,000 millimeters

Figure 18.3
The metric system

kilo (k)	hecto (h)	deka (dk)	unit	deci (d)	centi (c)	milli (m)
1,000	100	10	1	0.1	0.01	0.001

Because the metric system is decimal based, each metric prefix corresponds to a decimal position as indicated in figure 18.3. As a result, converting from one metric measure of length to another is just a matter of relocating the decimal point. To relocate the decimal point, the following steps can be used:

1. Arrange the metric measures according to their decimal position as described in figure 18.3.
2. Count the number of positions from the given measure to the desired measure.
3. Move the decimal point of the given measure the same number of spaces and in the same direction as step 2, adding zeros as necessary.

Example 1 Find the number of meters in 37 kilometers.

Solution

Step 1 kilometer hectometer dekameter meter
Step 2 given → desired
(right 3 spaces)

Step 3 37 0 0 0.

Thus, 37 kilometers = 37,000 meters

Example 2 A football field is approximately 91.44 meters long. Express this length in dekameters.

Solution

Step 1 dekameters meters
Step 2 desired ← given
(left 1 space)

Step 3 9. 1 4 4

Thus, 91.44 meters = 9.144 dekameters

Example 3 The proposed site for a new packing plant has a frontage along a main highway of 3.2 hectometers. How many decimeters is this?

Solution

Step 1 hectometers dekameters meters decimeters
Step 2 given → desired (right 3 spaces)

Step 3 3.2 0 0.

Thus, 3.2 hm = 3,200 dm

Example 4 The Payne Corporation manufactures stainless steel rods that retail for $4.75 per meter. Find the total cost of 20 rods, each of which is 82 centimeters long.

Solution

Step 1 m dm cm
Step 2 desired ← given (left 2 spaces)

Step 3 0.8 2

Thus, 82 cm = 0.82 m

0.82 × $4.75 = $3.90 per rod
20 × $3.90 = $78.00 total cost

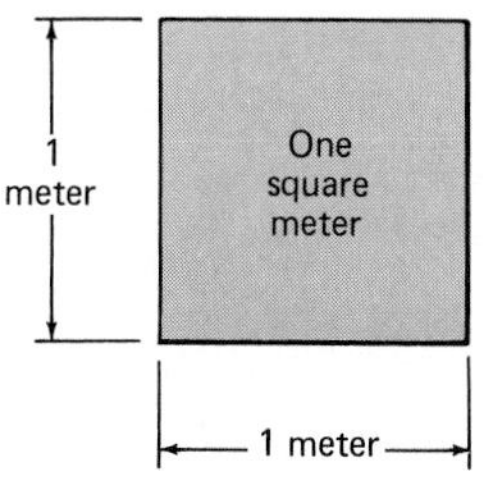

Figure 18.4
A square meter, the basic unit of area in the metric system

The basic unit of area in the metric system is the **square meter,** which is the area of a square with sides 1 meter in length (see figure 18.4). For most land measurements, the **are** (100 square meters), the **hectare** (100 ares), and the square kilometer are used. For small areas, the square meter and the square centimeter are common. Abbreviations for these units are

Square meter	m^2
Are	a
Hectare	ha
Square kilometer	km^2
Square centimeter	cm^2

Example 5 Feed-Tex purchased 21.4 hectares of farmland. If the cost was $80 per are, find the total cost of the land.

Solution

1 ha = 100 a

21.4 ha = 21.4 × 100 a = 2,140 a

2,140 × $80 = $171,200

Example 6 An executive desk is 180 centimeters long and 75 centimeters wide. What is the area of the desk in square meters?

Solution

1 cm = 0.01 m

180 cm = 180 × 0.01 m = 1.8 m

75 cm = 75 × 0.01 m = 0.75 m

Area = 1.8 m × 0.75 m = 1.35 m^2

Exercises for Section 18.2

In problems 1–14, convert the given length or area to the metric units specified.

1. a. 28 kilometers to meters
   b. 72 meters to dekameters
2. a. 109 hectometers to meters
   b. 62 meters to decimeters
3. a. 721 dekameters to meters
   b. 7.05 meters to centimeters
4. a. 14.78 kilometers to meters
   b. 0.781 meters to millimeters
5. a. 157 dekameters to decimeters
   b. 32,214 millimeters to centimeters
6. a. 47,100 millimeters to centimeters
   b. 2.17 hectometers to centimeters

7. a. 0.0024 square meters to square centimeters
   b. 14 square kilometers to ares

8. a. 11,400 square centimeters to square meters
   b. 2,500 ares to hectares

9. 621 dm = ________ dkm = ________ hm

10. 87.2 km = ________ dm = ________ cm

11. 32,240 mm = ________ dkm = ________ dm

12. 0.723 km = ________ hm = ________ dm

13. 0.19 km^2 = ________ m^2 = ________ a

14. 481.7 a = ________ ha = ________ km^2

15. A proposed new office building for the downtown business district is to be 74.2 meters high. Express this height in (a) dekameters and (b) hectometers.

16. Jake Scott ordered a new sign for his hardware store. The sign was rectangular in shape, 2.61 meters long, and 0.48 meters high. Express the dimensions of the sign in (a) decimeters and (b) centimeters.

17. A new pencil is about 2 decimeters long. The width of the pencil is about 7 millimeters, and the thickness of its lead is about 2 millimeters. Express these measurements in (a) centimeters and (b) meters.

18. The scale on a map is 1 centimeter = 80 kilometers. If the distance between two cities on the map is 5.5 centimeters, how long will it take to drive from one city to another at an average speed of 88 kilometers per hour?

19. An art supply store is selling picture-framing material for $5.40 per meter. Find the total cost of six pieces of the material, each of which is 75 centimeters long.

20. Century Developers recently purchased 1.3 square kilometers of property for $92 per are. What was the total purchase price for the property?

21. Joan Barrett is installing new glass shelves in one of the display cases in her shop. Each shelf is 275 centimeters long and 48 centimeters wide, and four shelves will be required. If the glass costs $125.50 per square meter, how much will all four shelves cost?

Section 18.3 Metric units of capacity and weight

The basic unit of capacity in the metric system is the liter. A **liter** is slightly larger than a quart and is the capacity of a cubic container measuring 10 centimeters on each side (see figure 18.5).

Multiples and submultiples of the liter are shown in table 18.3.

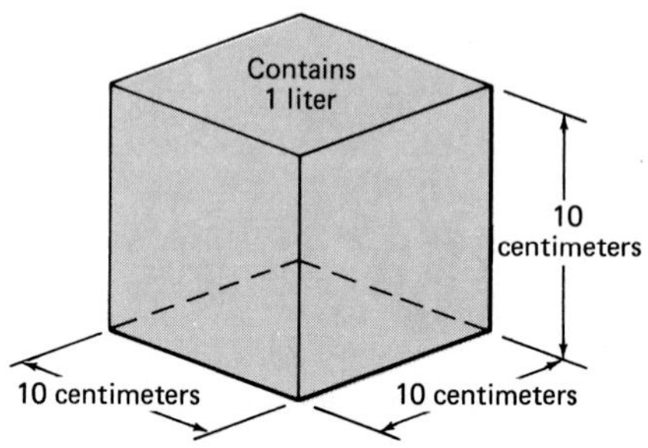

Figure 18.5 A liter, the basic unit of capacity in the metric system

Table 18.3 Multiples and Submultiples of the Liter

1 kiloliter (kl)	= 1,000 liters	1 liter	= 0.001 kiloliter
1 hectoliter (hl)	= 100 liters	1 liter	= 0.01 hectoliter
1 dekaliter (dkl)	= 10 liters	1 liter	= 0.1 dekaliter
1 liter (l)	= Basic unit of capacity	1 liter	= Basic unit of capacity
1 deciliter (dl)	= 0.1 liter	1 liter	= 10 deciliters
1 centiliter (cl)	= 0.01 liter	1 liter	= 100 centiliters
1 milliliter (ml)	= 0.001 liter	1 liter	= 1,000 milliliters

The techniques for converting from one metric unit of capacity to another are similar to the conversion procedures for metric units of length.

Example 1 Find the number of liters in 468 centiliters.

Solution

Step 1 liter deciliter centiliter
Step 2 desired ← (left 2 spaces) given
Step 3 4.68

Hence, 468 centiliters = 4.68 liters

Example 2 A storage tank has a capacity of 550 kiloliters. How many dekaliters will the tank hold?

Solution

Step 1 kl hl dkl
Step 2 given → desired (right 2 spaces)
Step 3 550 0 0.

Thus, 550 kl = 55,000 dkl

Example 3 A synthetic polymer is sold in 100 milliliter bottles. How many liters are there in a case of 24 bottles?

Solution

The case contains a total of 24 × 100 = 2,400 ml

Step 1 liter dl cl ml
Step 2 desired ← given (left 3 spaces)
Step 3 2. 4 0 0

Thus, there are 2.4 liters in a case of 24 bottles.

The unit of weight in the metric system is the gram. A **gram** is the weight of 1 cubic centimeter of distilled water at its greatest density, which is at 39.2°F (4°C) at sea level. Because a gram weighs only 0.353 ounces, the **kilogram** (1,000 grams) is the standard for most small weights. For heavy items, the **metric ton** (1,000 kilograms) is used. Multiples and submultiples of the gram are shown in table 18.4.

Table 18.4 Multiples and Submultiples of the Gram

1 kilogram (kg)	= 1,000 grams	1 gram	= 0.001 kilogram
1 hectogram (hg)	= 100 grams	1 gram	= 0.01 hectogram
1 dekagram (dkg)	= 10 grams	1 gram	= 0.1 dekagram
1 gram (g)	= Basic unit of weight	1 gram	= Basic unit of weight
1 decigram (dg)	= 0.1 gram	1 gram	= 10 decigrams
1 centigram (cg)	= 0.01 gram	1 gram	= 100 centigrams
1 milligram (mg)	= 0.001 gram	1 gram	= 1,000 milligrams

The techniques for converting from one metric unit of weight to another are similar to the conversion procedures for length and capacity.

Example 4 Find the number of kilograms in 1,686 grams.

Solution

Step 1 kilograms hectograms dekagrams grams
Step 2 desired ← (left 3 spaces) given
Step 3 1.6 8 6

Thus, 1,686 grams = 1.686 kilograms

Example 5 Find the number of milligrams in 0.042 hectograms.

Solution

Step 1 hg dkg g dg cg mg
Step 2 given (right 5 spaces) → desired
Step 3 0 4 2 0 0.

Thus, 0.042 hectograms = 4,200 milligrams

Example 6 A tobacco company advertises a low tar brand of cigarette containing an average of 10 milligrams of tar per cigarette. How many decigrams of tar are contained in a carton (200 cigarettes) of this brand?

Solution

At an average of 10 mg per cigarette, a carton contains 200 × 10 = 2,000 milligrams of tar.

Step 1 dg cg mg
Step 2 desired ← (left 2 spaces) given
Step 3 20. 0 0

Thus, a carton contains 20 decigrams of tar.

Example 7 A diesel locomotive weighs 150 metric tons. What is its weight in kilograms?

Solution

A metric ton (t) is 1,000 kilograms. Hence,

1 t = 1,000 kg
150 t = 150 × 1,000 = 150,000 kilograms

Exercises for Section 18.3

In problems 1–14, convert the given capacity or weight to the metric units specified.

1. a. 47 hectoliters to liters
   b. 27,420 liters to kiloliters
2. a. 52 kiloliters to liters
   b. 37 liters to deciliters
3. a. 2,710 milliliters to liters
   b. 5.21 liters to centiliters
4. a. 251.8 deciliters to liters
   b. 420.8 liters to dekaliters
5. a. 67 dekagrams to grams
   b. 38,240 grams to hectograms
6. a. 3.14 kilograms to grams
   b. 87 grams to centigrams
7. a. 78.3 hectograms to grams
   b. 41.23 grams to decigrams
8. a. 18.7 metric tons to kilograms
   b. 9.83 grams to milligrams
9. 420 dl = ________ dkl = ________ ml
10. 27.84 kl = ________ dkl = ________ dl
11. 270,000 ml = ________ hl = ________ cl
12. 2.16 kg = ________ hg = ________ dg
13. 714,000 mg = ________ dg = ________ dkg

14. 0.00214 t = ________ kg = ________ hg

15. Beth Walters is planning a party for 15 people. She estimates that each person will drink 600 milliliters of soft drink. How many 1-liter bottles of soft drink should she purchase for the party?

16. A liquid baby formula is sold in 450-milliliter jars, and 48 jars are packed in a case. How many deciliters of formula does a case contain?

17. Betty Patterson takes 25 milliliters of medicine each day. When she filled the prescription, the bottle contained 5.25 deciliters. For how many days will the bottle of medicine last?

18. A 6-hectoliter aquarium is being filled at the rate of 0.5 dekaliters per minute. How long will it take to fill the aquarium?

19. A storage tank for fuel oil is leaking at the rate of 300 centiliters per hour. If the tank contains 0.6 kiloliters of oil, how long will it take for all the oil to leak out?

20. Jake Anderson purchased a new car that gets 14 kilometers per liter. How far can Jake go on (a) 4 dekaliters of gasoline and (b) 520 centiliters of gasoline?

21. The Patterson's new baby girl weighed 3.4 kilograms at birth. What was the baby's weight in (a) dekagrams and (b) decigrams?

22. The Nut House sells mixed nuts for $6.10 per kilogram. Find the cost of (a) 8 hectograms and (b) 400 dekagrams.

23. If a 4.5 kilogram bag of dog food is priced at $3.78, how much does it cost per day to feed a dog 250 grams of the dog food daily?

24. A foreign country purchased 1,200,000 metric tons of fertilizer for $240,000,000. Find the price of the fertilizer per kilogram.

25. The Mid-County Power Company uses 588 metric tons of coal each week at its main generating plant. The plant operates seven days a week, 24 hours a day. How many kilograms of coal per hour does the plant use?

26. A breakfast cereal is packaged in two sizes of boxes. The 250-gram box sells for $1.05, and the 350-gram box sells for $1.54. Find the unit price per gram of the cereal for each of the two sizes of boxes. Which size box is the better buy?

Section 18.4 Metric units versus English units

Until such time as the United States converts entirely to the metric system, it will be necessary to maintain a conversion table (see table 18.5) showing the relationship between metric and English units.

Table 18.5 Metric-English Conversion Factors

Metric to English		**English to Metric**	
Length			
Meter (m)	= 1.093 yards	Yard	= 0.9144 meter
	= 3.281 feet	Foot	= 0.3048 meter
	= 39.370 inches	Inch	= 0.0254 meter
Kilometer (km)	= 0.621 mile	Mile	= 1.609 kilometers
Area			
Square meter (m^2)	= 1.196 square yards	Square yard	= 0.836 square meter
	= 10.764 square feet	Square foot	= 0.092 square meter
Square centimeter (cm^2)	= 0.155 square inch	Square inch	= 6.45 square centimeters
Square kilometer (km^2)	= 0.386 square mile	Square mile	= 2.590 square kilometers
Hectare (ha)	= 2.471 acres	Acre	= 0.405 hectare
Capacity			
Liter (l)	= 1.056 U.S. liquid quarts	U.S. liquid quart	= 0.946 liter
	= 0.908 dry quart	Dry quart	= 1.111 liters
	= 0.264 U.S. gallon	U.S. gallon	= 3.785 liters
Hectoliter (hl)	= 2.837 U.S. bushels	U.S. bushel	= 0.352 hectoliter
Weight			
Gram (g)	= 15.432 grains	Grain	= 0.0648 gram
	= 0.0352 avoirdupois ounce	Avoirdupois ounce	= 28.35 grams
Kilogram (kg)	= 2.2046 pounds avoirdupois	Pound	= 0.4536 kilogram
Metric ton (t)	= 2,204.62 pounds avoirdupois	Short ton	= 0.9072 metric ton
	= 1.1023 short tons		

Example 1 Karl's Auto Parts specializes in foreign car parts. A voltage regulator 10.1 centimeters in length is to be mailed to a customer. How long a box (in inches) is required if $\frac{1}{2}$ inch of packing is used on each end?

Solution

1 cm = .01 m = 0.3937 inches (Table 18.5)

10.1 cm = 10.1 × 0.3937 inches

= 3.98 inches

Packing = 1.00 inch

Total length = 4.98 inches

Karl will no doubt use a 5-inch box to mail the part.

Example 2 The Sikes Company purchased 150 hectares of land in Spain for construction of a branch factory. If the total price was $70,000, what was the cost per acre?

Solution

1 ha = 2.471 acres

150 ha = 150 × 2.471 acres

= 370.65 acres

$$\frac{\$70{,}000}{370.65} = \$188.86 \text{ per acre}$$

Example 3 The Moroni Import Company received a shipment of 50 hectoliters of olive oil. What was the shipment in gallons?

Solution

1 hl = 100 liters

50 hl = 50 × 100 liters

= 5,000 liters

1 liter = 0.264 gallons (Table 18.5)

5,000 liters = 5,000 × 0.264 gallons

= 1,320 gallons

Metric recipe

Queen cakes

100 g butter or margarine
100 g castor sugar
150 g self-raising flour
pinch of salt
2 eggs
25 mℓ milk
100 g currants

Cream the fat and sugar together until light and fluffy.

Sieve or mix the flour and salt.

Add the eggs, one at a time, to the creamed mixture with a spoonful of flour, stir then beat.

Beat in the milk with a little more flour.

Stir in the currants with the remaining flour.

Divide the mixture evenly between about 20 baking cases, smooth level.

Bake for 15–20 minutes at 190 °C (375 °F) gas mark 5.

Metric recipe leaflets are on sale from UKFEHE, 36 Ravenscroft Avenue, London NW11 8AU.

Recipe supplied by the United Kingdom Home Economics Federation.

Example 4 A poor grain harvest forced the Soviet government to purchase 3,000,000 metric tons of wheat on the open market. What is the U.S. equivalent in tons?

Solution

1 t = 1.1023 tons (Table 18.5)

$$3{,}000{,}000 \text{ t} = 3{,}000{,}000 \times 1.1023 \text{ tons}$$
$$= 3{,}306{,}900 \text{ tons}$$

A part of the planned conversion to the metric system is a change in temperature measurement. The present system in the United States of measuring temperature by degrees Fahrenheit will be replaced by the degrees Celsius measurement system.

The difference between the two systems involves the freezing and boiling points of water. In the Fahrenheit system, water freezes at 32° and boils at 212°, a difference of 180°. In the Celsius system, water freezes at 0° and boils at 100°. Thus, while the degree Celsius is not defined in terms of the meter, as are the other metric units, it is decimal based.

To convert between degrees Fahrenheit (°F) and degrees Celsius (°C), the following formulas are used:

■ (18–1) $$C = \frac{5}{9}(F-32)$$ To convert from Fahrenheit to Celsius

■ (18–2) $$F = \frac{9}{5}C + 32$$ To convert from Celsius to Fahrenheit

Example 5 The normal body temperature of a human being is 98.6°F. Express this temperature in degrees Celsius.

Solution

Using formula 18–1,

$$C = \frac{5}{9}(F-32)$$

$$= \frac{5}{9}(98.6-32)$$

$$= \frac{5}{9}(66.6)$$

$$= 37°C$$

Example 6 Superheated steam used to drive steam turbines can reach 1,050°F. To the nearest tenth of a degree, what is this temperature in degrees Celsius?

Solution

Using formula 18–1,

$$C = \frac{5}{9}(F-32)$$

$$= \frac{5}{9}(1{,}050-32)$$

$$= \frac{5}{9}(1{,}018)$$

$$= 565.6°C$$

Example 7 During the summer, a European city recorded a high temperature of 28°C. To the nearest tenth of a degree, what is this temperature in degrees Fahrenheit?

Solution

Using formula 18–2,

$$F = \frac{9}{5}C + 32$$

$$= \frac{9}{5}(28) + 32$$

$$= 82.4°F$$

Example 8 As a protection against spoilage during shipping, some meat products were packed in dry ice, which has a temperature of −78.5°C. To the nearest tenth of a degree, what is the temperature of dry ice in degrees Fahrenheit?

Solution

Using formula 18–2,

$$F = \frac{9}{5}C + 32$$

$$= \frac{9}{5}(-78.5) + 32$$

$$= -109.3°F$$

Exercises for Section 18.4

In problems 1–28, fill in the blanks. Round your answers to the second decimal place.

1. 10 meters = ________ feet
2. 1,500 meters = ________ miles
3. 45 millimeters = ________ inches
4. 60 kilometers = ________ miles
5. 4,500 meters = ________ yards
6. 48 inches = ________ centimeters
7. 100 yards = ________ meters
8. 12 miles = ________ kilometers
9. 6 feet = ________ meters
10. 350 feet = ________ dekameters
11. 12 square meters = ________ square yards
12. 66 square centimeters = ________ square inches
13. 4 square kilometers = ________ square miles
14. 7 square meters = ________ square feet
15. 44 hectares = ________ acres
16. 12 square yards = ________ square meters
17. 144 square inches = ________ square centimeters
18. $4\frac{1}{2}$ square miles = ________ square kilometers
19. 30 square feet = ________ square meters
20. 75 acres = ________ hectares
21. 6 liters = ________ liquid quarts
22. $2\frac{1}{2}$ liters = ________ pints
23. 16 liters = ________ gallons
24. 110 hectoliters = ________ bushels
25. 36 gallons = ________ liters
26. 14 liquid quarts = ________ liters
27. 62 bushels = ________ hectoliters
28. 24 liquid quarts = ________ liters

In problems 29–40, round answers to the nearest tenth of a degree.

29. 68°F = ________ °C

30. 140°F = ________ °C

31. −49°F = ________ °C

32. −22°F = ________ °C

33. 20°F = ________ °C

34. 6°F = ________ °C

35. 35°C = ________ °F

36. 70°C = ________ °F

37. −10°C = ________ °F

38. −25°C = ________ °F

39. 8°C = ________ °F

40. 138°C = ________ °F

In problems 41–49, round answers to the second decimal place.

41. The Ferris Company sold 200 gallons of molasses to a European firm for $4.40 per gallon. What was the price per liter?

42. Visitors to a country in the Middle East are advised that the speed limit is 90 kilometers per hour. What is the speed limit in miles per hour?

43. A British plant consumes 12 metric tons of coal every eight hours. How many pounds of coal per hour is this?

44. The Wheeling Tool and Die Company received an order for some brass fittings from a foreign firm. One of the specifications called for a hole of 32 millimeters in diameter. What is the size of the hole in inches?

45. A buyer for the Romulus Corporation can buy an item at $0.26 per pound or $0.55 per kilogram. Which is the best price?

46. The Monroe Packing Company sold a total of 120 metric tons of citrus products to a Japanese import company in one year. Find the number of pounds of citrus products sold.

47. The engine of a foreign car is rated at 1,500 cubic centimeters. How many cubic inches is this? (Note: 1 cubic inch = 16.387 cubic centimeters.)

48. A recipe for a cake called for an oven setting of 175°C. What is this temperature in degrees Fahrenheit?

49. As part of a special military training program, a group of technicians was subjected to temperatures as high as 392°F. How many degrees Celsius is this?

Glossary

Are 100 square meters.
Centimeter 1/100 meter.
Gram The weight of 1 cubic centimeter of distilled water at its greatest density.
Hectare 100 ares.
Kilogram 1,000 grams.
Kilometer 1,000 meters.
Liter The capacity of a cubic container measuring 10 centimeters on each side.
Meter The basic unit of measurement in the metric system. It was originally defined as $\frac{1}{10,000,000}$ of the distance from the equator to a pole. The current definition of a meter is 1,650,763.73 wavelengths of the orange-red light of krypton 86.
Metric ton 1,000 kilograms.
Millimeter 1/1,000 meter.
Square meter The basic unit of area in the metric system. The area of a square with sides 1 meter in length.

Review test

In problems 1–10, convert the given measure to the metric units specified.

1. 36 meters to hectometers
2. 16 kiloliters to liters
3. 6.73 grams to decigrams
4. 223 deciliters to dekaliters
5. 7.12 hectometers to centimeters
6. 16 square kilometers to ares
7. 267,490 kilograms to metric tons
8. 720,000 ml = ________ hl = ________ cl
9. 48.72 kl = ________ dkl = ________ dl
10. 4,102 dg = ________ dkg = ________ cg
11. A can of refrigeration oil is priced at $4 per liter. What is the cost of 250 milliliters?
12. John Good purchased a 2.25-kilogram bag of fertilizer. If a plant requires three applications of fertilizer during the growing season at 150 grams per application, how many plants can John fertilize for the entire growing season?
13. Cold water for the air-conditioning system of a manufacturing plant is maintained at 50°F. What is this temperature in degrees Celsius?
14. A lens has a focal length of 250 millimeters. Express this length in inches. (Note: 1 meter = 39.37 inches.)

Appendixes

Appendix A Calculators

Introduction

Hand-held calculators are a remarkable product of modern microelectronics technology. Compact and versatile, these machines have steadily increased in sophistication as they have decreased in price. Today, almost everyone can afford the cost of a calculator.

Because calculators have become an integral part of contemporary business, prospective business students should become adept at performing calculations on these miniature computers. The purpose of this section is to describe the functions common to most hand-held calculators and to demonstrate how calculators can be used to solve a variety of basic arithmetic problems.

Basic operations

The logic found in most general purpose calculators is "algebraic logic." Calculations in this logic are performed in the order in which they are entered. This is illustrated as follows (the reader should practice these calculations as described):

Problem	*Calculator Entries*	*Register Displays*
24 + 26 =	[2] [4] [+] [2] [6] [=]	24 26 50
(24 + 26) − 10 =	[2] [4] [+] [2] [6] [−] [1] [0] [=]	24 26 50 10 40
(24 + 26) × 10 =	[2] [4] [+] [2] [6] [×] [1] [0] [=]	24 26 50 10 500
(24 + 26) ÷ 10 =	[2] [4] [+] [2] [6] [÷] [1] [0] [=]	24 26 50 10 5
(7 × 22) − 11 =	[7] [×] [2] [2] [−] [1] [1] [=]	7 22 154 11
7 × (22 − 11) =	[2] [2] [−] [1] [1] [×] [7] [=]	22 11 11 7 77
(20 + 15) ÷ 5 =	[2] [0] [+] [1] [5] [÷] [5] [=]	20 15 35 5 7
20 + (15 ÷ 5) =	[1] [5] [÷] [5] [+] [2] [0] [=]	15 5 3 20 23

Operations with decimals and percents

Most calculators have a "floating" decimal point mode that automatically locates the decimal point. To enter decimal numbers, the decimal point key [·] is used.

Problem	Calculator Entries	Register Displays
1.265 + 3.721 =	[1] [·] [2] [6] [5] [+]	1.265 3.721 4.986
	[3] [·] [7] [2] [1] [=]	
166 − 33.749 =	[1] [6] [6] [−]	166 33.749
	[3] [3] [·] [7] [4] [9] [=]	132.251
1.48 × 9.43 =	[1] [·] [4] [8] [×]	1.48 9.43 13.9564
	[9] [·] [4] [3] [=]	
27.893 ÷ 14 =	[2] [7] [·] [8] [9] [3]	27.893 14
	[÷] [1] [4] [=]	1.9923571

For convenience in locating the decimal point when multiplying or dividing a number by a percent, calculators are frequently equipped with a percent key [%].

Problem	Calculator Entries	Register Displays
$200 × 11% =	[2] [0] [0] [×] [1] [1] [%]	200 11 22
$\frac{30.63}{44\%} =$	[3] [0] [·] [6] [3]	30.63 44
	[÷] [4] [4] [%]	69.613636

Note that the percent key performs the function of the equals key in addition to correctly placing the decimal point in the answer.

Memory calculations

Many hand-held calculators permit an item of data to be stored in a "memory," a feature that can be a considerable convenience when performing arithmetic operations. In a typical arrangement, four keys are used with a memory. The [M+] key stores the register number in the memory or adds the register number to any number already in the memory. For example,

Memory Number	Calculator Entry	Register Display	New Memory Number
0	[1] [2] [0] [M+]	120	120
80	[1] [2] [0] [M+]	120	200 (80 + 120)

The [M−] key subtracts the register number from any number in the memory.

Memory Number	*Calculator Entry*	*Register Display*	*New Memory Number*
200	[4] [0] [M−]	40	160 (200 − 40)

The [MR] key recalls any number in the memory and displays it in the register, while the [MC] key clears the memory to the number zero. For instance,

Memory Number	*Calculator Entry*	*Register Display*	*New Memory Number*
200	[MR]	200	200
200	[MC]	0	0

The use of the memory keys is illustrated in the following examples (the initial memory number is 0 in each example):

Problem	*Calculator Entries*	*Register Displays*
27 ÷ (6 + 3) =	[6] [M+] [3] [M+]	6 3 27 9 3
	[2] [7] [÷] [MR] [=]	
(8 + 12) ÷	[4] [×] [3] [−] [2] [=] [M+]	4 3 12 2 10
[(4 × 3) − 2] =	[8] [+] [1] [2] [÷] [MR] [=]	8 12 20 10 2
620 − (478 × 40%) =	[4] [7] [8] [×] [4] [0] [%]	478 40 191.2
	[M+] [6] [2] [0] [−] [MR] [=]	620 191.2 428.8
(500 × 6%) +	[5] [0] [0] [×] [6] [%] [M+]	500 6 30
(300 × 7.25%) +	[3] [0] [0] [×] [7] [.] [2] [5]	300 7.25 21.75
(475 × 8%)	[%] [M+] [4] [7] [5] [×]	475 8 38 89.75
	[8] [%] [M+] [MR]	
$36.95	[3] [6] [.] [9] [5] [−] [2] [1]	36.95 21.85
− 21.85	[.] [8] [5] [=] [M+] [×]	15.1 40 6.04
=	[4] [0] [%] [M−] [MR]	9.06
− ____ (40% of line above)		
=		

Fractions Before discussing operations with fractions, recall that every fraction has a decimal representation found by dividing the numerator by the denominator (see chap. 4). The decimal representation of a fraction will be a decimal that is either terminating or infinitely repeating. For example, the following fractions have terminating decimal representations:

$$\frac{1}{2} = 0.5$$

$$\frac{5}{4} = 1.25$$

$$\frac{375}{1000} = 0.375$$

On the other hand, some fractions that have infinitely repeating decimal representations are:

$\frac{1}{3} = 0.33333\ldots$ (the 3s repeat infinitely)

$\frac{4}{9} = 0.4444\ldots$ (the 4s repeat infinitely)

$\frac{1}{6} = 0.1666\ldots$ (the 6s repeat infinitely)

$\frac{5}{11} = 0.454545\ldots$ (the pair of digits 45 repeats infinitely)

On a typical hand-held calculator, the register will display a decimal number up to seven decimal places. Hence, a fraction with an infinitely repeating decimal representation can be approximated at best only to the seventh decimal place. Approximating an infinite decimal introduces a certain amount of error into the calculation. The rougher the approximation, the greater is the error. This is particularly true in multiplication and division problems. To see this, consider the following calculations involving the fraction $\frac{4}{9} = 0.444\ldots$ that were performed on a calculator with a register display up to the seventh decimal place.

Product	*Answer*	*Error*
$710{,}550 \times \frac{4}{9}$	315,800	0
$710{,}550 \times 0.4444444$	315,799.96	0.04
$710{,}550 \times 0.444444$	315,799.68	0.32
$710{,}550 \times 0.44444$	315,796.84	3.16
$710{,}550 \times 0.4444$	315,768.42	31.58
$710{,}550 \times 0.444$	315,484.20	315.8
$710{,}550 \times 0.44$	312,642	3,158
$710{,}550 \times 0.4$	284,220	31,580

In this text, multiplication and division involving fractions with infinitely repeating decimal expansions will be performed using the fraction instead of a decimal approximation. The final answer will then be rounded to the desired accuracy. If the fraction has a terminating decimal representation, the decimal representation will ordinarily be used.

Problem	*Calculator Entries*	*Register Displays*
$710{,}550 \times \frac{4}{9} =$	[7] [1] [0] [5] [5] [0] [×]	710550 4 2842200
	[4] [÷] [9] [=]	9 315800
$134.20 \times \frac{3}{4} =$	[1] [3] [4] [.] [2] [0]	134.20 0.75
	[×] [.] [7] [5] [=]	100.65
$237{,}000 \times \frac{2}{3} =$	[2] [3] [7] [0] [0] [0] [×]	237000 2 474000 3
	[2] [÷] [3] [=]	158000
$726 \div \frac{7}{11} =$	[7] [2] [6] [×] [1] [1]	726 11 7986
$\left(\text{or } 726 \times \frac{11}{7}\right)$	[÷] [7] [=]	7 1140.8571
$\frac{120}{588 \times 5/18} =$	[5] [8] [8] [×] [5]	588 5 2940 18
	[÷] [1] [8] [=] [M+]	163.3333 120
	[1] [2] [0] [÷] [MR] [=]	163.33333 0.7346938
$\frac{\$1{,}560}{1 - (0.1125 \times 2/9)} =$	[1] [M+] [.] [1] [1] [2] [5]	1 0.1125 2 0.225
	[×] [2] [÷] [9] [=]	9 0.025 1560 0.975
	[M−] [1] [5] [6] [0] [÷]	1600
	[MR] [=]	

Percents can also be expressed either as a fraction or a decimal (see chap. 4). For example,

Percent	*Fraction*	*Decimal Representation*
25%	$\frac{1}{4}$	0.25
60%	$\frac{60}{100}$ or $\frac{6}{10}$	0.60
$16\frac{2}{3}\%$	$\frac{1}{6}$	0.16666 . . .
$33\frac{1}{3}\%$	$\frac{1}{3}$	0.3333 . . .
$41\frac{2}{3}\%$	$\frac{5}{12}$	0.416666 . . .

Again, in this text multiplication and division involving percents with infinitely repeating decimal representations will be performed using the fraction instead of the decimal approximation. For percents with terminating decimal representations, the decimal representation will ordinarily be used.

Problem	*Calculator Entries*	*Register Displays*
$\$2,800 \times 11\frac{1}{4}\% =$	[2] [8] [0] [0] [×] [.] [1] [1] [2] [5] [=]	2800 0.1125 315
$\frac{144}{36\%} =$	[1] [4] [4] [÷] [3] [6] [%]	144 36 400
$500 \times 30\% \times 10\% =$	[5] [0] [0] [×] [3] [0] [%] [×] [1] [0] [%]	500 30 150 10 15
$\$162.70 \times 33\frac{1}{3}\% =$	[1] [6] [2] [.] r 7 0 [÷] [3] [=]	162.70 3 54.233333
$\frac{\$2,000}{1 + (12\% \times 2/3)} =$	[.] [1] [2] [×] [2] [÷] [3] [+] [1] [=] [M+] [2] [0] [0] [0] [÷] [MR] [=]	0.12 2 0.24 3 0.08 1 1.08 2000 1.08 1851.8518
$\frac{\$1,225}{1 - (16\frac{2}{3}\% \times 3/4)} =$	[1] [M+] [.] [7] [5] [÷] [6] [=] [M−] [1] [2] [2] [5] [÷] [MR] [=]	1 0.75 6 0.125 1225 0.875 1400

Exercises Use a calculator to work each of the following problems.

1. (1,373 + 1,099) − 755 =
2. (16,472 − 11,384) × 107 =
3. (547 × 213) − 97,461 =
4. 3,472 + (2,520 ÷ 56) =
5. (517 + 112) ÷ 17 =
6. 17,849 + (324 × 277) =
7. 23 × (1,943 ÷ 29) =
8. 67,892 × (10,021 − 9,924) =
9. (247.87 + 113.97) − 14.29 =
10. (165.92 − 54.71) × 2.39 =

11.
```
       143.82
        73.81
       496.14
       501.27
     +  23.79
Total
     − 114.72
     =
```

12.
```
     1,572.14
       276.18
        14.92
       978.50
    +1,421.83
Total
     ×     14
     =
```

13.
```
       878.22
     5,476.18
     7,985.14
     2,430.02
    +7,218.98
Total
     ×     43
     =
```

14.
```
        11.75
       102.09
        14.17
       123.91
     +  98.27
Total
     −  27.83
     =
```

15. 1,872.73 + (5.7 ÷ 1.25) =
16. 117.83 + (269.85 ÷ 15.42) =
17. (1,375.34 × 279.5) − 216,421.78 =
18. (273.92 + 318.22) ÷ (49.25 − 28.40) =
19. (473.25 × 37.4) − (603.10 ÷ 40.75) =

20. $(2.133 \div 39.5) + [(47.7 \div 3) + 6.71] =$

21. $(5{,}428.172 - 18.09) \div [(2.81 \times 7.1) - 1.002] =$

22. $(328.017 \times 5.11) - (17.21208 \div 2.32) =$

23. $(2{,}148.83 + 4{,}879.14) - (8{,}972.04 \times 20\%) =$

24. $(10{,}781.14 - 1{,}419.27) + (4{,}275.80 \times 40\%) =$

25.
$1{,}400 \times 14\% =$
$2{,}750 \times 17\% =$
$1{,}220 \times 13\% =$ ______
Total =

26.
$1{,}872 \times 21\% =$
$3{,}248 \times 19\% =$
$5{,}710 \times 4\% =$ ______
Total =

27.
$1{,}643.10 \times 20\% =$
$1{,}878.40 \times 15\% =$
$2{,}232.50 \times 8\% =$ ______
Total =
Less (30% of total) = ______
=

28.
$6{,}472.83 \times 15\% =$
$2{,}391.17 \times 12\% =$
$3{,}472.08 \times 31\% =$
$984.28 \times 17\% =$ ______
Total =
Less (24% of total) = ______
=

29. $(2{,}314.85 - 426.21) \times \frac{2}{9} =$

30. $(40{,}625.17 + 431.82) \times \frac{7}{11} =$

31. $(17{,}249.15) - (321.06 \times \frac{5}{6}) =$

32. $(8{,}472.15) \div (752.91 \times \frac{1}{3}) =$

33. $\dfrac{1{,}462.14}{1 + (0.09 \times 3/4)} =$

34. $\dfrac{2{,}702.12}{1 + (0.07 \times 2/5)} =$

35. $\dfrac{1{,}428.90}{1 + (0.1284 \times 1/6)} =$

36. $\dfrac{5{,}672.83}{1 + (0.0801 \times 2/3)} =$

37. $\dfrac{3{,}412.80}{1 - (14\% \times 1/3)} =$

38. $\dfrac{2{,}742.91}{1 - (11\% \times 5/6)} =$

39. $\dfrac{4{,}279.83}{1 + (33\frac{1}{3}\% \times 3/5)} =$

40. $\dfrac{1{,}872.19}{1 - (41\frac{2}{3}\% \times 3/4)} =$

Appendix B The number of each day of the year

Day of Month	Jan.	Feb.	Mar.	April	May	June	July	Aug.	Sept.	Oct.	Nov.	Dec.	Day of Month
1	1	32	60	91	121	152	182	213	244	274	305	335	*1*
2	2	33	61	92	122	153	183	214	245	275	306	336	*2*
3	3	34	62	93	123	154	184	215	246	276	307	337	*3*
4	4	35	63	94	124	155	185	216	247	277	308	338	*4*
5	5	36	64	95	125	156	186	217	248	278	309	339	*5*
6	6	37	65	96	126	157	187	218	249	279	310	340	*6*
7	7	38	66	97	127	158	188	219	250	280	311	341	*7*
8	8	39	67	98	128	159	189	220	251	281	312	342	*8*
9	9	40	68	99	129	160	190	221	252	282	313	343	*9*
10	10	41	69	100	130	161	191	222	253	283	314	344	*10*
11	11	42	70	101	131	162	192	223	254	284	315	345	*11*
12	12	43	71	102	132	163	193	224	255	285	316	346	*12*
13	13	44	72	103	133	164	194	225	256	286	317	347	*13*
14	14	45	73	104	134	165	195	226	257	287	318	348	*14*
15	15	46	74	105	135	166	196	227	258	288	319	349	*15*
16	16	47	75	106	136	167	197	228	259	289	320	350	*16*
17	17	48	76	107	137	168	198	229	260	290	321	351	*17*
18	18	49	77	108	138	169	199	230	261	291	322	352	*18*
19	19	50	78	109	139	170	200	231	262	292	323	353	*19*
20	20	51	79	110	140	171	201	232	263	293	324	354	*20*
21	21	52	80	111	141	172	202	233	264	294	325	355	*21*
22	22	53	81	112	142	173	203	234	265	295	326	356	*22*
23	23	54	82	113	143	174	204	235	266	296	327	357	*23*
24	24	55	83	114	144	175	205	236	267	297	328	358	*24*
25	25	56	84	115	145	176	206	237	268	298	329	359	*25*
26	26	57	85	116	146	177	207	238	269	299	330	360	*26*
27	27	58	86	117	147	178	208	239	270	300	331	361	*27*
28	28	59	87	118	148	179	209	240	271	301	332	362	*28*
29	29		88	119	149	180	210	241	272	302	333	363	*29*
30	30		89	120	150	181	211	242	273	303	334	364	*30*
31	31		90		151		212	243		304		365	*31*

Note. In leap years, after February 28, add 1 to the tabulated number.

Appendixes C–H Compound amount, present value, amount of annuity, present value of annuity, sinking fund, and amortization

Rate ¼%	C Compound Amount	D Present Value	E Amount of Annuity	F Present Value of Annuity	G Sinking Fund	H Amortization	
n	$(1+i)^n$	$(1+i)^{-n}$	$s_{\overline{n}\rvert i}$	$a_{\overline{n}\rvert i}$	$1/s_{\overline{n}\rvert i}$	$1/a_{\overline{n}\rvert i}$	n
1	1.00250000	0.99750623	1.00000000	0.99750623	1.00000000	1.00250000	1
2	1.00500625	0.99501869	2.00250000	1.99252492	0.49937578	0.50187578	2
3	1.00751877	0.99253734	3.00750625	2.98506227	0.33250139	0.33500139	3
4	1.01003756	0.99006219	4.01502502	3.97512446	0.24906445	0.25156445	4
5	1.01256266	0.98759321	5.02506258	4.96271766	0.19900250	0.20150250	5
6	1.01509406	0.98513038	6.03762523	5.94784804	0.16562803	0.16812803	6
7	1.01763180	0.98267370	7.05271930	6.93052174	0.14178928	0.14428928	7
8	1.02017588	0.98022314	8.07035110	7.91074487	0.12391035	0.12641035	8
9	1.02272632	0.97777869	9.09052697	8.88852357	0.11000462	0.11250462	9
10	1.02528313	0.97534034	10.11325329	9.86386391	0.09888015	0.10138015	10
11	1.02784634	0.97290807	11.13853642	10.83677198	0.08977840	0.09227840	11
12	1.03041596	0.97048187	12.16638277	11.80725384	0.08219370	0.08469370	12
13	1.03299200	0.96806171	13.19679872	12.77531555	0.07577595	0.07827595	13
14	1.03557448	0.96564759	14.22979072	13.74096314	0.07027510	0.07277510	14
15	1.03816341	0.96323949	15.26536520	14.70420264	0.06550777	0.06800777	15
16	1.04075882	0.96083740	16.30352861	15.66504004	0.06133642	0.06383642	16
17	1.04336072	0.95844130	17.34428743	16.62348133	0.05765587	0.06015587	17
18	1.04596912	0.95605117	18.38764815	17.57953250	0.05438433	0.05688433	18
19	1.04858404	0.95366700	19.43361727	18.53319950	0.05145722	0.05395722	19
20	1.05120550	0.95128878	20.48220131	19.48448828	0.04882288	0.05132288	20
21	1.05383352	0.94891649	21.53340682	20.43340477	0.04643947	0.04893947	21
22	1.05646810	0.94655011	22.58724033	21.37995488	0.04427278	0.04677278	22
23	1.05910927	0.94418964	23.64370843	22.32414452	0.04229455	0.04479455	23
24	1.06175704	0.94183505	24.70281770	23.26597957	0.04048121	0.04298121	24
25	1.06441144	0.93948634	25.76457475	24.20546591	0.03881298	0.04131298	25
26	1.06707247	0.93714348	26.82898619	25.14260939	0.03727312	0.03977312	26
27	1.06974015	0.93480646	27.89605865	26.07741585	0.03584736	0.03834736	27
28	1.07241450	0.93247527	28.96579880	27.00989112	0.03452347	0.03702347	28
29	1.07509553	0.93014990	30.03821330	27.94004102	0.03329093	0.03579093	29
30	1.07778327	0.92783032	31.11330883	28.86787134	0.03214059	0.03464059	30
31	1.08047773	0.92551653	32.19109210	29.79338787	0.03106449	0.03356449	31
32	1.08317892	0.92320851	33.27156983	30.71659638	0.03005569	0.03255569	32
33	1.08588687	0.92090624	34.35474876	31.63750262	0.02910806	0.03160806	33
34	1.08860159	0.91860972	35.44063563	32.55611234	0.02821620	0.03071620	34
35	1.09132309	0.91631892	36.52923722	33.47243126	0.02737533	0.02987533	35
36	1.09405140	0.91403384	37.62056031	34.38646510	0.02658121	0.02908121	36
37	1.09678653	0.91175445	38.71461171	35.29821955	0.02583004	0.02833004	37
38	1.09952850	0.90948075	39.81139824	36.20770030	0.02511843	0.02761843	38
39	1.10227732	0.90721272	40.91092673	37.11491302	0.02444335	0.02694335	39
40	1.10503301	0.90495034	42.01320405	38.01986336	0.02380204	0.02630204	40
41	1.10779559	0.90269361	43.11823706	38.92255697	0.02319204	0.02569204	41
42	1.11056508	0.90044250	44.22603265	39.82299947	0.02261112	0.02511112	42
43	1.11334149	0.89819701	45.33659774	40.72119648	0.02205724	0.02455724	43
44	1.11612485	0.89595712	46.44993923	41.61715359	0.02152855	0.02402855	44
45	1.11891516	0.89372281	47.56606408	42.51087640	0.02102339	0.02352339	45
46	1.12171245	0.89149407	48.68497924	43.40237047	0.02054022	0.02304022	46
47	1.12451673	0.88927090	49.80669169	44.29164137	0.02007762	0.02257762	47
48	1.12732802	0.88705326	50.93120842	45.17869463	0.01963433	0.02213433	48
49	1.13014634	0.88484116	52.05853644	46.06353580	0.01920915	0.02170915	49
50	1.13297171	0.88263457	53.18868278	46.94617037	0.01880099	0.02130099	50
80	1.22109795	0.81893512	88.43918139	72.42595169	0.01130721	0.01380721	80
100	1.28362489	0.77904379	113.44995550	88.38248346	0.00881446	0.01131446	100
120	1.34935355	0.74109562	139.74141888	103.56175308	0.00715607	0.00965607	120
240	1.82075500	0.54922271	328.30199813	180.31091441	0.00304598	0.00554598	240
360	2.45684221	0.40702655	582.73688460	237.18938150	0.00171604	0.00421604	360

Rate ⅓%	C Compound Amount	D Present Value	E Amount of Annuity	F Present Value of Annuity	G Sinking Fund	H Amortization	
n	$(1+i)^n$	$(1+i)^{-n}$	$s_{\overline{n}\rvert i}$	$a_{\overline{n}\rvert i}$	$1/s_{\overline{n}\rvert i}$	$1/a_{\overline{n}\rvert i}$	n
1	1.00333333	0.99667774	1.00000000	0.99667774	1.00000000	1.00333333	1
2	1.00667778	0.99336652	2.00333333	1.99004426	0.49916805	0.50250139	2
3	1.01003337	0.99006630	3.01001111	2.98011056	0.33222469	0.33555802	3
4	1.01340015	0.98677704	4.02004448	3.96688760	0.24875347	0.25208680	4
5	1.01677815	0.98349871	5.03344463	4.95038631	0.19867110	0.20200444	5
6	1.02016741	0.98023127	6.05022278	5.93061759	0.16528317	0.16861650	6
7	1.02356797	0.97697469	7.07039019	6.90759228	0.14143491	0.14476824	7
8	1.02697986	0.97372893	8.09395816	7.88132121	0.12354895	0.12688228	8
9	1.03040313	0.97049395	9.12093802	8.85181516	0.10963785	0.11297118	9
10	1.03383780	0.96726972	10.15134114	9.81908487	0.09850915	0.10184248	10
11	1.03728393	0.96405620	11.18517895	10.78314107	0.08940402	0.09273736	11
12	1.04074154	0.96085335	12.22246288	11.74399442	0.08181657	0.08514990	12
13	1.04421068	0.95766115	13.26320442	12.70165557	0.07539656	0.07872989	13
14	1.04769138	0.95447955	14.30741510	13.65613512	0.06989383	0.07322716	14
15	1.05118369	0.95130852	15.35510648	14.60744364	0.06512491	0.06845825	15
16	1.05468763	0.94814803	16.40629017	15.55559167	0.06095223	0.06428557	16
17	1.05820326	0.94499803	17.46097781	16.50058970	0.05727056	0.06060389	17
18	1.06173060	0.94185851	18.51918107	17.44244821	0.05399807	0.05733140	18
19	1.06526971	0.93872941	19.58091167	18.38117762	0.05107015	0.05440348	19
20	1.06882060	0.93561071	20.64618137	19.31678832	0.04843511	0.05176844	20
21	1.07238334	0.93250236	21.71500198	20.24929069	0.04605111	0.04938445	21
22	1.07595795	0.92940435	22.78738532	21.17869504	0.04388393	0.04721726	22
23	1.07954448	0.92631663	23.86334327	22.10501167	0.04190528	0.04523861	23
24	1.08314296	0.92323916	24.94288775	23.02825083	0.04009159	0.04342492	24
25	1.08675344	0.92017192	26.02603071	23.94842275	0.03842307	0.04175640	25
26	1.09037595	0.91711487	27.11278414	24.86553763	0.03688297	0.04021630	26
27	1.09401053	0.91406798	28.20316009	25.77960561	0.03545702	0.03879035	27
28	1.09765724	0.91103121	29.29717062	26.69063682	0.03413299	0.03746632	28
29	1.10131609	0.90800453	30.39482786	27.59864135	0.03290033	0.03623367	29
30	1.10498715	0.90498790	31.49614395	28.50362925	0.03174992	0.03508325	30
31	1.10867044	0.90198130	32.60113110	29.40561055	0.03067378	0.03400712	31
32	1.11236601	0.89898468	33.70980154	30.30459523	0.02966496	0.03299830	32
33	1.11607389	0.89599802	34.82216754	31.20059325	0.02871734	0.03205067	33
34	1.11979414	0.89302128	35.93824143	32.09361454	0.02782551	0.03115885	34
35	1.12352679	0.89005444	37.05803557	32.98366898	0.02698470	0.03031803	35
36	1.12727187	0.88709745	38.18156236	33.87076642	0.02619065	0.02952399	36
37	1.13102945	0.88415028	39.30883423	34.75491670	0.02543957	0.02877291	37
38	1.13479955	0.88121290	40.43986368	35.63612960	0.02472808	0.02806141	38
39	1.13858221	0.87828528	41.57466322	36.51441488	0.02405311	0.02738644	39
40	1.14237748	0.87536739	42.71324543	37.38978228	0.02341194	0.02674527	40
41	1.14618541	0.87245920	43.85562292	38.26224147	0.02280209	0.02613543	41
42	1.15000603	0.86956066	45.00180833	39.13180213	0.02222133	0.02555466	42
43	1.15383938	0.86667175	46.15181436	39.99847389	0.02166762	0.02500095	43
44	1.15768551	0.86379245	47.30565374	40.86226633	0.02113912	0.02447246	44
45	1.16154446	0.86092270	48.46333925	41.72318903	0.02063415	0.02396749	45
46	1.16541628	0.85806249	49.62488371	42.58125153	0.02015118	0.02348451	46
47	1.16930100	0.85521179	50.79029999	43.43646332	0.01968880	0.02302213	47
48	1.17319867	0.85237055	51.95960099	44.28883387	0.01924572	0.02257905	48
49	1.17710933	0.84953876	53.13279966	45.13837263	0.01882077	0.02215410	49
50	1.18103303	0.84671637	54.30990899	45.98508900	0.01841285	0.02174618	50
80	1.30502632	0.76626807	91.50789532	70.11957849	0.01092802	0.01426135	80
100	1.39483902	0.71692861	118.45170537	84.92141663	0.00844226	0.01177559	100
120	1.49083268	0.67076608	147.24980472	98.77017486	0.00679118	0.01012451	120
240	2.22258209	0.44992714	366.77462607	165.02185825	0.00272647	0.00605980	240
360	3.31349801	0.30179587	694.04940433	209.46124046	0.00144082	0.00477415	360

Rate ½%	C Compound Amount	D Present Value	E Amount of Annuity	F Present Value of Annuity	G Sinking Fund	H Amortization	
n	$(1+i)^n$	$(1+i)^{-n}$	$S_{\overline{n}\rvert i}$	$A_{\overline{n}\rvert i}$	$1/S_{\overline{n}\rvert i}$	$1/A_{\overline{n}\rvert i}$	n
1	1.00500000	0.99502488	1.00000000	0.99502488	1.00000000	1.00500000	1
2	1.01002500	0.99007450	2.00500000	1.98509938	0.49875312	0.50375312	2
3	1.01507513	0.98514876	3.01502500	2.97024814	0.33167221	0.33667221	3
4	1.02015050	0.98024752	4.03010013	3.95049566	0.24813279	0.25313279	4
5	1.02525125	0.97537067	5.05025063	4.92586633	0.19800997	0.20300997	5
6	1.03037751	0.97051808	6.07550188	5.89638441	0.16459546	0.16959546	6
7	1.03552940	0.96568963	7.10587939	6.86207404	0.14072854	0.14572854	7
8	1.04070704	0.96088520	8.14140879	7.82295924	0.12282886	0.12782886	8
9	1.04591058	0.95610468	9.18211583	8.77906392	0.10890736	0.11390736	9
10	1.05114013	0.95134794	10.22802641	9.73041186	0.09777057	0.10277057	10
11	1.05639583	0.94661487	11.27916654	10.67702673	0.08865903	0.09365903	11
12	1.06167781	0.94190534	12.33556237	11.61893207	0.08106643	0.08606643	12
13	1.06698620	0.93721924	13.39724018	12.55615131	0.07464224	0.07964224	13
14	1.07232113	0.93255646	14.46422639	13.48870777	0.06913609	0.07413609	14
15	1.07768274	0.92791688	15.53654752	14.41662465	0.06436436	0.06936436	15
16	1.08307115	0.92330037	16.61423026	15.33992502	0.06018937	0.06518937	16
17	1.08848651	0.91870684	17.69730141	16.25863186	0.05650579	0.06150579	17
18	1.09392894	0.91413616	18.78578791	17.17276802	0.05323173	0.05823173	18
19	1.09939858	0.90958822	19.87971685	18.08235624	0.05030253	0.05530253	19
20	1.10489558	0.90506290	20.97911544	18.98741915	0.04766645	0.05266645	20
21	1.11042006	0.90056010	22.08401101	19.88797925	0.04528163	0.05028163	21
22	1.11597216	0.89607971	23.19443107	20.78405896	0.04311380	0.04811380	22
23	1.12155202	0.89162160	24.31040322	21.67568055	0.04113465	0.04613465	23
24	1.12715978	0.88718567	25.43195524	22.56286622	0.03932061	0.04432061	24
25	1.13279558	0.88277181	26.55911502	23.44563803	0.03765186	0.04265186	25
26	1.13845955	0.87837991	27.69191059	24.32401794	0.03611163	0.04111163	26
27	1.14415185	0.87400986	28.83037015	25.19802780	0.03468565	0.03968565	27
28	1.14987261	0.86966155	29.97452200	26.06768936	0.03336167	0.03836167	28
29	1.15562197	0.86533488	31.12439461	26.93302423	0.03212914	0.03712914	29
30	1.16140008	0.86102973	32.28001658	27.79405397	0.03097892	0.03597892	30
31	1.16720708	0.85674600	33.44141666	28.65079997	0.02990304	0.03490304	31
32	1.17304312	0.85248358	34.60862375	29.50328355	0.02889453	0.03389453	32
33	1.17890833	0.84824237	35.78166686	30.35152592	0.02794727	0.03294727	33
34	1.18480288	0.84402226	36.96057520	31.19554818	0.02705586	0.03205586	34
35	1.19072689	0.83982314	38.14537807	32.03537132	0.02621550	0.03121550	35
36	1.19668052	0.83564492	39.33610496	32.87101624	0.02542194	0.03042194	36
37	1.20266393	0.83148748	40.53278549	33.70250372	0.02467139	0.02967139	37
38	1.20867725	0.82735073	41.73544942	34.52985445	0.02396045	0.02896045	38
39	1.21472063	0.82323455	42.94412666	35.35308900	0.02328607	0.02828607	39
40	1.22079424	0.81913886	44.15884730	36.17222786	0.02264552	0.02764552	40
41	1.22689821	0.81506354	45.37964153	36.98729141	0.02203631	0.02703631	41
42	1.23303270	0.81100850	46.60653974	37.79829991	0.02145622	0.02645622	42
43	1.23919786	0.80697363	47.83957244	38.60527354	0.02090320	0.02590320	43
44	1.24539385	0.80295884	49.07877030	39.40823238	0.02037541	0.02537541	44
45	1.25162082	0.79896402	50.32416415	40.20719640	0.01987117	0.02487117	45
46	1.25787892	0.79498907	51.57578497	41.00218547	0.01938894	0.02438894	46
47	1.26416832	0.79103390	52.83366390	41.79321937	0.01892733	0.02392733	47
48	1.27048916	0.78709841	54.09783222	42.58031778	0.01848503	0.02348503	48
49	1.27684161	0.78318250	55.36832138	43.36350028	0.01806087	0.02306087	49
50	1.28322581	0.77928607	56.64516299	44.14278635	0.01765376	0.02265376	50
80	1.49033857	0.67098847	98.06771357	65.80230538	0.01019704	0.01519704	80
100	1.64666849	0.60728678	129.33369842	78.54264477	0.00773194	0.01273194	100
120	1.81939673	0.54963273	163.87934681	90.07345333	0.00610205	0.01110205	120
240	3.31020448	0.30209614	462.04089516	139.58077168	0.00216431	0.00716431	240
360	6.02257521	0.16604193	1004.51504245	166.79161439	0.00099551	0.00599551	360

Rate ¾%	C Compound Amount	D Present Value	E Amount of Annuity	F Present Value of Annuity	G Sinking Fund	H Amortization	
n	$(1+i)^n$	$(1+i)^{-n}$	$S_{\overline{n}\rceil i}$	$A_{\overline{n}\rceil i}$	$1/S_{\overline{n}\rceil i}$	$1/A_{\overline{n}\rceil i}$	n
1	1.00750000	0.99255583	1.00000000	0.99255583	1.00000000	1.00750000	1
2	1.01505625	0.98516708	2.00750000	1.97772291	0.49813200	0.50563200	2
3	1.02266917	0.97783333	3.02255625	2.95555624	0.33084579	0.33834579	3
4	1.03033919	0.97055417	4.04522542	3.92611041	0.24720501	0.25470501	4
5	1.03806673	0.96332920	5.07556461	4.88943961	0.19702242	0.20452242	5
6	1.04585224	0.95615802	6.11363135	5.84559763	0.16356891	0.17106891	6
7	1.05369613	0.94904022	7.15948358	6.79463785	0.13967488	0.14717488	7
8	1.06159885	0.94197540	8.21317971	7.73661325	0.12175552	0.12925552	8
9	1.06956084	0.93496318	9.27477856	8.67157642	0.10781929	0.11531929	9
10	1.07758255	0.92800315	10.34433940	9.59957958	0.09667123	0.10417123	10
11	1.08566441	0.92109494	11.42192194	10.52067452	0.08755094	0.09505094	11
12	1.09380690	0.91423815	12.50758636	11.43491267	0.07995148	0.08745148	12
13	1.10201045	0.90743241	13.60139325	12.34234508	0.07352188	0.08102188	13
14	1.11027553	0.90067733	14.70340370	13.24302242	0.06801146	0.07551146	14
15	1.11860259	0.89397254	15.81367923	14.13699495	0.06323639	0.07073639	15
16	1.12699211	0.88731766	16.93228183	15.02431261	0.05905879	0.06655879	16
17	1.13544455	0.88071231	18.05927394	15.90502492	0.05537321	0.06287321	17
18	1.14396039	0.87415614	19.19471849	16.77918107	0.05209766	0.05959766	18
19	1.15254009	0.86764878	20.33867888	17.64682984	0.04916740	0.05666740	19
20	1.16118414	0.86118985	21.49121897	18.50801969	0.04653063	0.05403063	20
21	1.16989302	0.85477901	22.65240312	19.36279870	0.04414543	0.05164543	21
22	1.17866722	0.84841589	23.82229614	20.21121459	0.04197748	0.04947748	22
23	1.18750723	0.84210014	25.00096336	21.05331473	0.03999846	0.04749846	23
24	1.19641353	0.83583140	26.18847059	21.88914614	0.03818474	0.04568474	24
25	1.20538663	0.82960933	27.38488412	22.71875547	0.03651650	0.04401650	25
26	1.21442703	0.82343358	28.59027075	23.54218905	0.03497693	0.04247693	26
27	1.22353523	0.81730380	29.80469778	24.35949286	0.03355176	0.04105176	27
28	1.23271175	0.81121966	31.02823301	25.17071251	0.03222871	0.03972871	28
29	1.24195709	0.80518080	32.26094476	25.97589331	0.03099723	0.03849723	29
30	1.25127176	0.79918690	33.50290184	26.77508021	0.02984816	0.03734816	30
31	1.26065630	0.79323762	34.75417361	27.56831783	0.02877352	0.03627352	31
32	1.27011122	0.78733262	36.01482991	28.35565045	0.02776634	0.03526634	32
33	1.27963706	0.78147158	37.28494113	29.13712203	0.02682048	0.03432048	33
34	1.28923434	0.77565418	38.56457819	29.91277621	0.02593053	0.03343053	34
35	1.29890359	0.76988008	39.85381253	30.68265629	0.02509170	0.03259170	35
36	1.30864537	0.76414896	41.15271612	31.44680525	0.02429973	0.03179973	36
37	1.31846021	0.75846051	42.46136149	32.20526576	0.02355082	0.03105082	37
38	1.32834866	0.75281440	43.77982170	32.95808016	0.02284157	0.03034157	38
39	1.33831128	0.74721032	45.10817037	33.70529048	0.02216893	0.02966893	39
40	1.34834861	0.74164796	46.44648164	34.44693844	0.02153016	0.02903016	40
41	1.35846123	0.73612701	47.79483026	35.18306545	0.02092276	0.02842276	41
42	1.36864969	0.73064716	49.15329148	35.91371260	0.02034452	0.02784452	42
43	1.37891456	0.72520809	50.52194117	36.63892070	0.01979338	0.02729338	43
44	1.38925642	0.71980952	51.90085573	37.35873022	0.01926751	0.02676751	44
45	1.39967584	0.71445114	53.29011215	38.07318136	0.01876521	0.02626521	45
46	1.41017341	0.70913264	54.68978799	38.78231401	0.01828495	0.02578495	46
47	1.42074971	0.70385374	56.09996140	39.48616775	0.01782532	0.02532532	47
48	1.43140533	0.69861414	57.52071111	40.18478189	0.01738504	0.02488504	48
49	1.44214087	0.69341353	58.95211644	40.87819542	0.01696292	0.02446292	49
50	1.45295693	0.68825165	60.39425732	41.56644707	0.01655787	0.02405787	50
80	1.81804398	0.55004170	109.07253072	59.99444012	0.00916821	0.01666821	80
100	2.11108384	0.47369033	148.14451201	70.17462272	0.00675017	0.01425017	100
120	2.45135708	0.40793730	193.51427708	78.94169267	0.00516758	0.01266758	120
240	6.00915152	0.16641284	667.88686993	111.14495403	0.00149726	0.00899726	240
360	14.73057612	0.06788601	1830.74348307	124.28186568	0.00054623	0.00804623	360

Rate 1%	C Compound Amount	D Present Value	E Amount of Annuity	F Present Value of Annuity	G Sinking Fund	H Amortization	
n	$(1 + i)^n$	$(1 + i)^{-n}$	$s_{\overline{n}\|i}$	$a_{\overline{n}\|i}$	$1/s_{\overline{n}\|i}$	$1/a_{\overline{n}\|i}$	n
1	1.01000000	0.99009901	1.00000000	0.99009901	1.00000000	1.01000000	1
2	1.02010000	0.98029605	2.01000000	1.97039506	0.49751244	0.50751244	2
3	1.03030100	0.97059015	3.03010000	2.94098521	0.33002211	0.34002211	3
4	1.04060401	0.96098034	4.06040100	3.90196555	0.24628109	0.25628109	4
5	1.05101005	0.95146569	5.10100501	4.85343124	0.19603980	0.20603980	5
6	1.06152015	0.94204524	6.15201506	5.79547647	0.16254837	0.17254837	6
7	1.07213535	0.93271805	7.21353521	6.72819453	0.13862828	0.14862828	7
8	1.08285671	0.92348322	8.28567056	7.65167775	0.12069029	0.13069029	8
9	1.09368527	0.91433982	9.36852727	8.56601758	0.10674036	0.11674036	9
10	1.10462213	0.90528695	10.46221254	9.47130453	0.09558208	0.10558208	10
11	1.11566835	0.89632372	11.56683467	10.36762825	0.08645408	0.09645408	11
12	1.12682503	0.88744923	12.68250301	11.25507747	0.07884879	0.08884879	12
13	1.13809328	0.87866260	13.80932804	12.13374007	0.07241482	0.08241482	13
14	1.14947421	0.86996297	14.94742132	13.00370304	0.06690117	0.07690117	14
15	1.16096896	0.86134947	16.09689554	13.86505252	0.06212378	0.07212378	15
16	1.17257864	0.85282126	17.25786449	14.71787378	0.05794460	0.06794460	16
17	1.18430443	0.84437749	18.43044314	15.56225127	0.05425806	0.06425806	17
18	1.19614748	0.83601731	19.61474757	16.39826858	0.05098205	0.06098205	18
19	1.20810895	0.82773992	20.81089504	17.22600850	0.04805175	0.05805175	19
20	1.22019004	0.81954447	22.01900399	18.04555297	0.04541531	0.05541531	20
21	1.23239194	0.81143017	23.23919403	18.85698313	0.04303075	0.05303075	21
22	1.24471586	0.80339621	24.47158598	19.66037934	0.04086372	0.05086372	22
23	1.25716302	0.79544179	25.71630183	20.45582113	0.03888584	0.04888584	23
24	1.26973465	0.78756613	26.97346485	21.24338726	0.03707347	0.04707347	24
25	1.28243200	0.77976844	28.24319950	22.02315570	0.03540675	0.04540675	25
26	1.29525631	0.77204796	29.52563150	22.79520366	0.03386888	0.04386888	26
27	1.30820888	0.76440392	30.82088781	23.55960759	0.03244553	0.04244553	27
28	1.32129097	0.75683557	32.12909669	24.31644316	0.03112444	0.04112444	28
29	1.33450388	0.74934215	33.45038766	25.06578530	0.02989502	0.03989502	29
30	1.34784892	0.74192292	34.78489153	25.80770822	0.02874811	0.03874811	30
31	1.36132740	0.73457715	36.13274045	26.54228537	0.02767573	0.03767573	31
32	1.37494068	0.72730411	37.49406785	27.26958947	0.02667089	0.03667089	32
33	1.38869009	0.72010307	38.86900853	27.98969255	0.02572744	0.03572744	33
34	1.40257699	0.71297334	40.25769862	28.70266589	0.02483997	0.03483997	34
35	1.41660276	0.70591420	41.66027560	29.40858009	0.02400368	0.03400368	35
36	1.43076878	0.69892495	43.07687836	30.10750504	0.02321431	0.03321431	36
37	1.44507647	0.69200490	44.50764714	30.79950994	0.02246805	0.03246805	37
38	1.45952724	0.68515337	45.95272361	31.48466330	0.02176150	0.03176150	38
39	1.47412251	0.67836967	47.41225085	32.16303298	0.02109160	0.03109160	39
40	1.48886373	0.67165314	48.88637336	32.83468611	0.02045560	0.03045560	40
41	1.50375237	0.66500311	50.37523709	33.49968922	0.01985102	0.02985102	41
42	1.51878989	0.65841892	51.87898946	34.15810814	0.01927563	0.02927563	42
43	1.53397779	0.65189992	53.39777936	34.81000806	0.01872737	0.02872737	43
44	1.54931757	0.64544546	54.93175715	35.45545352	0.01820441	0.02820441	44
45	1.56481075	0.63905492	56.48107472	36.09450844	0.01770505	0.02770505	45
46	1.58045885	0.63272764	58.04588547	36.72723608	0.01722775	0.02722775	46
47	1.59626344	0.62646301	59.62634432	37.35369909	0.01677111	0.02677111	47
48	1.61222608	0.62026041	61.22260777	37.97395949	0.01633384	0.02633384	48
49	1.62834834	0.61411921	62.83483385	38.58807871	0.01591474	0.02591474	49
50	1.64463182	0.60803882	64.46318218	39.19611753	0.01551273	0.02551273	50
80	2.21671522	0.45111794	121.67152172	54.88820611	0.00821885	0.01821885	80
100	2.70481383	0.36971121	170.48138294	63.02887877	0.00586574	0.01586574	100
120	3.30038689	0.30299478	230.03868946	69.70052203	0.00434709	0.01434709	120
240	10.89255365	0.09180584	989.25536539	90.81941635	0.00101086	0.01101086	240
360	35.94964133	0.02781669	3494.96413277	97.21833108	0.00028613	0.01028613	360

Rate 1¼%	C Compound Amount	D Present Value	E Amount of Annuity	F Present Value of Annuity	G Sinking Fund	H Amortization	
n	$(1+i)^n$	$(1+i)^{-n}$	$S_{\overline{n}\rvert i}$	$A_{\overline{n}\rvert i}$	$1/S_{\overline{n}\rvert i}$	$1/A_{\overline{n}\rvert i}$	n
1	1.01250000	0.98765432	1.00000000	0.98765432	1.00000000	1.01250000	1
2	1.02515625	0.97546106	2.01250000	1.96311538	0.49689441	0.50939441	2
3	1.03797070	0.96341833	3.03765625	2.92653371	0.32920117	0.34170117	3
4	1.05094534	0.95152428	4.07562695	3.87805798	0.24536102	0.25786102	4
5	1.06408215	0.93977706	5.12657229	4.81783504	0.19506211	0.20756211	5
6	1.07738318	0.92817488	6.19065444	5.74600992	0.16153381	0.17403381	6
7	1.09085047	0.91671593	7.26803762	6.66272585	0.13758872	0.15008872	7
8	1.10448610	0.90539845	8.35888809	7.56812429	0.11963314	0.13213314	8
9	1.11829218	0.89422069	9.46337420	8.46234498	0.10567055	0.11817055	9
10	1.13227083	0.88318093	10.58166637	9.34552591	0.09450307	0.10700307	10
11	1.14642422	0.87227746	11.71393720	10.21780337	0.08536839	0.09786839	11
12	1.16075452	0.86150860	12.86036142	11.07931197	0.07775831	0.09025831	12
13	1.17526395	0.85087269	14.02111594	11.93018466	0.07132100	0.08382100	13
14	1.18995475	0.84036809	15.19637988	12.77055275	0.06580515	0.07830515	14
15	1.20482918	0.82999318	16.38633463	13.60054592	0.06102646	0.07352646	15
16	1.21988955	0.81974635	17.59116382	14.42029227	0.05684672	0.06934672	16
17	1.23513817	0.80962602	18.81105336	15.22991829	0.05316023	0.06566023	17
18	1.25057739	0.79963064	20.04619153	16.02954893	0.04988479	0.06238479	18
19	1.26620961	0.78975866	21.29676893	16.81930759	0.04695548	0.05945548	19
20	1.28203723	0.78000855	22.56297854	17.59931613	0.04432039	0.05682039	20
21	1.29806270	0.77037881	23.84501577	18.36969495	0.04193749	0.05443749	21
22	1.31428848	0.76086796	25.14307847	19.13056291	0.03977238	0.05227238	22
23	1.33071709	0.75147453	26.45736695	19.88203744	0.03779666	0.05029666	23
24	1.34735105	0.74219707	27.78808403	20.62423451	0.03598665	0.04848665	24
25	1.36419294	0.73303414	29.13543508	21.35726865	0.03432247	0.04682247	25
26	1.38124535	0.72398434	30.49962802	22.08125299	0.03278729	0.04528729	26
27	1.39851092	0.71504626	31.88087337	22.79629925	0.03136677	0.04386677	27
28	1.41599230	0.70621853	33.27938429	23.50251778	0.03004863	0.04254863	28
29	1.43369221	0.69749978	34.69537659	24.20001756	0.02882228	0.04132228	29
30	1.45161336	0.68888867	36.12906880	24.88890623	0.02767854	0.04017854	30
31	1.46975853	0.68038387	37.58068216	25.56929010	0.02660942	0.03910942	31
32	1.48813051	0.67198407	39.05044069	26.24127418	0.02560791	0.03810791	32
33	1.50673214	0.66368797	40.53857120	26.90496215	0.02466786	0.03716786	33
34	1.52556629	0.65549429	42.04530334	27.56045644	0.02378387	0.03628387	34
35	1.54463587	0.64740177	43.57086963	28.20785822	0.02295111	0.03545111	35
36	1.56394382	0.63940916	45.11550550	28.84726737	0.02216533	0.03466533	36
37	1.58349312	0.63151522	46.67944932	29.47878259	0.02142270	0.03392270	37
38	1.60328678	0.62371873	48.26294243	30.10250133	0.02071983	0.03321983	38
39	1.62332787	0.61601850	49.86622921	30.71851983	0.02005365	0.03255365	39
40	1.64361946	0.60841334	51.48955708	31.32693316	0.01942141	0.03192141	40
41	1.66416471	0.60090206	53.13317654	31.92783522	0.01882063	0.03132063	41
42	1.68496677	0.59348352	54.79734125	32.52131874	0.01824906	0.03074906	42
43	1.70602885	0.58615656	56.48230801	33.10747530	0.01770466	0.03020466	43
44	1.72735421	0.57892006	58.18833687	33.68639536	0.01718557	0.02968557	44
45	1.74894614	0.57177290	59.91569108	34.25816825	0.01669012	0.02919012	45
46	1.77080797	0.56471397	61.66463721	34.82288222	0.01621675	0.02871675	46
47	1.79294306	0.55774219	63.43544518	35.38062442	0.01576406	0.02826406	47
48	1.81535485	0.55085649	65.22838824	35.93148091	0.01533075	0.02783075	48
49	1.83804679	0.54405579	67.04374310	36.47553670	0.01491563	0.02741563	49
50	1.86102237	0.53733905	68.88178989	37.01287575	0.01451763	0.02701763	50
80	2.70148494	0.37016679	136.11879526	50.38665706	0.00734652	0.01984652	80
100	3.46340427	0.28873326	197.07234200	56.90133936	0.00507428	0.01757428	100
120	4.44021323	0.22521441	275.21705832	61.98284725	0.00363350	0.01613350	120
240	19.71549352	0.05072153	1497.23948148	75.94227758	0.00066790	0.01316790	240
360	87.54099514	0.01142322	6923.27961085	79.08614244	0.00014444	0.01264444	360

Rate 1½%	C Compound Amount	D Present Value	E Amount of Annuity	F Present Value of Annuity	G Sinking Fund	H Amortization	
n	$(1+i)^n$	$(1+i)^{-n}$	$S_{\overline{n}\rceil i}$	$A_{\overline{n}\rceil i}$	$1/S_{\overline{n}\rceil i}$	$1/A_{\overline{n}\rceil i}$	n
1	1.01500000	0.98522167	1.00000000	0.98522167	1.00000000	1.01500000	1
2	1.03022500	0.97066175	2.01500000	1.95588342	0.49627792	0.51127792	2
3	1.04567837	0.95631699	3.04522500	2.91220042	0.32838296	0.34338296	3
4	1.06136355	0.94218423	4.09090338	3.85438465	0.24444479	0.25944479	4
5	1.07728400	0.92826033	5.15226693	4.78264497	0.19408932	0.20908932	5
6	1.09344326	0.91454219	6.22955093	5.69718717	0.16052521	0.17552521	6
7	1.10984491	0.90102679	7.32299419	6.59821396	0.13655616	0.15155616	7
8	1.12649259	0.88771112	8.43283911	7.48592508	0.11858402	0.13358402	8
9	1.14338998	0.87459224	9.55933169	8.36051732	0.10460982	0.11960982	9
10	1.16054083	0.86166723	10.70272167	9.22218455	0.09343418	0.10843418	10
11	1.17794894	0.84893323	11.86326249	10.07111779	0.08429384	0.09929384	11
12	1.19561817	0.83638742	13.04121143	10.90750521	0.07667999	0.09167999	12
13	1.21355244	0.82402702	14.23682960	11.73153222	0.07024036	0.08524036	13
14	1.23175573	0.81184928	15.45038205	12.54338150	0.06472332	0.07972332	14
15	1.25023207	0.79985150	16.68213778	13.34323301	0.05994436	0.07494436	15
16	1.26898555	0.78803104	17.93236984	14.13126405	0.05576508	0.07076508	16
17	1.28802033	0.77638526	19.20135539	14.90764931	0.05207966	0.06707966	17
18	1.30734064	0.76491159	20.48937572	15.67256089	0.04880578	0.06380578	18
19	1.32695075	0.75360747	21.79671636	16.42616837	0.04587847	0.06087847	19
20	1.34685501	0.74247042	23.12366710	17.16863879	0.04324574	0.05824574	20
21	1.36705783	0.73149795	24.47052211	17.90013673	0.04086550	0.05586550	21
22	1.38756370	0.72068763	25.83757994	18.62082437	0.03870332	0.05370332	22
23	1.40837715	0.71003708	27.22514364	19.33086145	0.03673075	0.05173075	23
24	1.42950281	0.69954392	28.63352080	20.03040537	0.03492410	0.04992410	24
25	1.45094535	0.68920583	30.06302361	20.71961120	0.03326345	0.04826345	25
26	1.47270953	0.67902052	31.51396896	21.39863172	0.03173196	0.04673196	26
27	1.49480018	0.66898574	32.98667850	22.06761746	0.03031527	0.04531527	27
28	1.51722218	0.65909925	34.48147867	22.72671671	0.02900108	0.04400108	28
29	1.53998051	0.64935887	35.99870085	23.37607558	0.02777878	0.04277878	29
30	1.56308022	0.63976243	37.53868137	24.01583801	0.02663919	0.04163919	30
31	1.58652642	0.63030781	39.10176159	24.64614582	0.02557430	0.04057430	31
32	1.61032432	0.62099292	40.68828801	25.26713874	0.02457710	0.03957710	32
33	1.63447918	0.61181568	42.29861233	25.87895442	0.02364144	0.03864144	33
34	1.65899637	0.60277407	43.93309152	26.48172849	0.02276189	0.03776189	34
35	1.68388132	0.59386608	45.59208789	27.07559458	0.02193363	0.03693363	35
36	1.70913954	0.58508974	47.27596921	27.66068431	0.02115240	0.03615240	36
37	1.73477663	0.57644309	48.98510874	28.23712740	0.02041437	0.03541437	37
38	1.76079828	0.56792423	50.71988538	28.80505163	0.01971613	0.03471613	38
39	1.78721025	0.55953126	52.48068366	29.36458288	0.01905463	0.03405463	39
40	1.81401841	0.55126232	54.26789391	29.91584520	0.01842710	0.03342710	40
41	1.84122868	0.54311559	56.08191232	30.45896079	0.01783106	0.03283106	41
42	1.86884712	0.53508925	57.92314100	30.99405004	0.01726426	0.03226426	42
43	1.89687982	0.52718153	59.79198812	31.52123157	0.01672465	0.03172465	43
44	1.92533302	0.51939067	61.68886794	32.04062223	0.01621038	0.03121038	44
45	1.95421301	0.51171494	63.61420096	32.55233718	0.01571976	0.03071976	45
46	1.98352621	0.50415265	65.56841398	33.05648983	0.01525125	0.03025125	46
47	2.01327910	0.49670212	67.55194018	33.55319195	0.01480342	0.02980342	47
48	2.04347829	0.48936170	69.56521929	34.04255365	0.01437500	0.02937500	48
49	2.07413046	0.48212975	71.60869758	34.52468339	0.01396478	0.02896478	49
50	2.10524242	0.47500468	73.68282804	34.99968807	0.01357168	0.02857168	50
80	3.29066279	0.30389015	152.71085247	46.40732349	0.00654832	0.02154832	80
100	4.43204565	0.22562944	228.80304330	51.62470367	0.00437057	0.01937057	100
120	5.96932287	0.16752319	331.28819149	55.49845411	0.00301852	0.01801852	120
240	35.63281555	0.02806402	2308.85437027	64.79573209	0.00043312	0.01543312	240
360	212.70378089	0.00470137	14113.58539279	66.35324174	0.00007085	0.01507085	360

Rate 1¾%	C Compound Amount	D Present Value	E Amount of Annuity	F Present Value of Annuity	G Sinking Fund	H Amortization	
n	$(1+i)^n$	$(1+i)^{-n}$	$S_{\overline{n}\rceil i}$	$A_{\overline{n}\rceil i}$	$1/S_{\overline{n}\rceil i}$	$1/A_{\overline{n}\rceil i}$	n
1	1.01750000	0.98280098	1.00000000	0.98280098	1.00000000	1.01750000	1
2	1.03530625	0.96589777	2.01750000	1.94869875	0.49566295	0.51316295	2
3	1.05342411	0.94928528	3.05280625	2.89798403	0.32756746	0.34506746	3
4	1.07185903	0.93295851	4.10623036	3.83094254	0.24353237	0.26103237	4
5	1.09061656	0.91691254	5.17808939	4.74785508	0.19312142	0.21062142	5
6	1.10970235	0.90114254	6.26870596	5.64899762	0.15952256	0.17702256	6
7	1.12912215	0.88564378	7.37840831	6.53464139	0.13553059	0.15303059	7
8	1.14888178	0.87041157	8.50753045	7.40505297	0.11754292	0.13504292	8
9	1.16898721	0.85544135	9.65641224	8.26049432	0.10355813	0.12105813	9
10	1.18944449	0.84072860	10.82539945	9.10122291	0.09237534	0.10987534	10
11	1.21025977	0.82626889	12.01484394	9.92749181	0.08323038	0.10073038	11
12	1.23143931	0.81205788	13.22510371	10.73954969	0.07561377	0.09311377	12
13	1.25298950	0.79809128	14.45654303	11.53764097	0.06917283	0.08667283	13
14	1.27491682	0.78436490	15.70953253	12.32200587	0.06365562	0.08115562	14
15	1.29722786	0.77087459	16.98444935	13.09288046	0.05887739	0.07637739	15
16	1.31992935	0.75761631	18.28167721	13.85049677	0.05469958	0.07219958	16
17	1.34302811	0.74458605	19.60160656	14.59508282	0.05101623	0.06851623	17
18	1.36653111	0.73177990	20.94463468	15.32686272	0.04774492	0.06524492	18
19	1.39044540	0.71919401	22.31116578	16.04605673	0.04482061	0.06232061	19
20	1.41477820	0.70682458	23.70161119	16.75288130	0.04219122	0.05969122	20
21	1.43953681	0.69466789	25.11638938	17.44754919	0.03981464	0.05731464	21
22	1.46472871	0.68272028	26.55592620	18.13026948	0.03765638	0.05515638	22
23	1.49036146	0.67097817	28.02065490	18.80124764	0.03568796	0.05318796	23
24	1.51644279	0.65943800	29.51101637	19.46068565	0.03388565	0.05138565	24
25	1.54298054	0.64809632	31.02745915	20.10878196	0.03222952	0.04972952	25
26	1.56998269	0.63694970	32.57043969	20.74573166	0.03070269	0.04820269	26
27	1.59745739	0.62599479	34.14042238	21.37172644	0.02929079	0.04679079	27
28	1.62541290	0.61522829	35.73787977	21.98695474	0.02798151	0.04548151	28
29	1.65385762	0.60464697	37.36329267	22.59160171	0.02676424	0.04426424	29
30	1.68280013	0.59424764	39.01715029	23.18584934	0.02562975	0.04312975	30
31	1.71224913	0.58402716	40.69995042	23.76987650	0.02457005	0.04207005	31
32	1.74221349	0.57398247	42.41219955	24.34385897	0.02357812	0.04107812	32
33	1.77270223	0.56411053	44.15441305	24.90796951	0.02264779	0.04014779	33
34	1.80372452	0.55440839	45.92711527	25.46237789	0.02177363	0.03927363	34
35	1.83528970	0.54487311	47.73083979	26.00725100	0.02095082	0.03845082	35
36	1.86740727	0.53550183	49.56612949	26.54275283	0.02017507	0.03767507	36
37	1.90008689	0.52629172	51.43353675	27.06904455	0.01944257	0.03694257	37
38	1.93333841	0.51724002	53.33362365	27.58628457	0.01874990	0.03624990	38
39	1.96717184	0.50834400	55.26696206	28.09462857	0.01809399	0.03559399	39
40	2.00159734	0.49960098	57.23413390	28.59422955	0.01747209	0.03497209	40
41	2.03662530	0.49100834	59.23573124	29.08523789	0.01688170	0.03438170	41
42	2.07226624	0.48256348	61.27235654	29.56780136	0.01632057	0.03382057	42
43	2.10853090	0.47426386	63.34462278	30.04206522	0.01578666	0.03328666	43
44	2.14543019	0.46610699	65.45315367	30.50817221	0.01527810	0.03277810	44
45	2.18297522	0.45809040	67.59858386	30.96626261	0.01479321	0.03229321	45
46	2.22117728	0.45021170	69.78155908	31.41647431	0.01433043	0.03183043	46
47	2.26004789	0.44246850	72.00273637	31.85894281	0.01388836	0.03138836	47
48	2.29959872	0.43485848	74.26278425	32.29380129	0.01346569	0.03096569	48
49	2.33984170	0.42737934	76.56238298	32.72118063	0.01306124	0.03056124	49
50	2.38078893	0.42002883	78.90222468	33.14120946	0.01267391	0.03017391	50
80	4.00639192	0.24960114	171.79382424	42.87993474	0.00582093	0.02332093	80
100	5.66815594	0.17642422	266.75176789	47.06147304	0.00374880	0.02124880	100
120	8.01918343	0.12470098	401.09619608	50.01708709	0.00249317	0.01999317	120
240	64.30730291	0.01555033	3617.56016603	56.25426666	0.00027643	0.01777643	240
360	515.69205797	0.00193914	29410.97474135	57.03204904	0.00003400	0.01753400	360

Rate 2%	C Compound Amount	D Present Value	E Amount of Annuity	F Present Value of Annuity	G Sinking Fund	H Amortization	
n	$(1+i)^n$	$(1+i)^{-n}$	$S_{\overline{n}\rceil i}$	$A_{\overline{n}\rceil i}$	$1/S_{\overline{n}\rceil i}$	$1/A_{\overline{n}\rceil i}$	n
1	1.02000000	0.98039216	1.00000000	0.98039216	1.00000000	1.02000000	1
2	1.04040000	0.96116878	2.02000000	1.94156094	0.49504950	0.51504950	2
3	1.06120800	0.94232233	3.06040000	2.88388327	0.32675467	0.34675467	3
4	1.08243216	0.92384543	4.12160800	3.80772870	0.24262375	0.26262375	4
5	1.10408080	0.90573081	5.20404016	4.71345951	0.19215839	0.21215839	5
6	1.12616242	0.88797138	6.30812096	5.60143089	0.15852581	0.17852581	6
7	1.14868567	0.87056018	7.43428338	6.47199107	0.13451196	0.15451196	7
8	1.17165938	0.85349037	8.58296905	7.32548144	0.11650980	0.13650980	8
9	1.19509257	0.83675527	9.75462843	8.16223671	0.10251544	0.12251544	9
10	1.21899442	0.82034830	10.94972100	8.98258501	0.09132653	0.11132653	10
11	1.24337431	0.80426304	12.16871542	9.78684805	0.08217794	0.10217794	11
12	1.26824179	0.78849318	13.41208973	10.57534122	0.07455960	0.09455960	12
13	1.29360663	0.77303253	14.68033152	11.34837375	0.06811835	0.08811835	13
14	1.31947876	0.75787502	15.97393815	12.10624877	0.06260197	0.08260197	14
15	1.34586834	0.74301473	17.29341692	12.84926350	0.05782547	0.07782547	15
16	1.37278571	0.72844581	18.63928525	13.57770931	0.05365013	0.07365013	16
17	1.40024142	0.71416256	20.01207096	14.29187188	0.04996984	0.06996984	17
18	1.42824625	0.70015937	21.41231238	14.99203125	0.04670210	0.06670210	18
19	1.45681117	0.68643076	22.84055863	15.67846201	0.04378177	0.06378177	19
20	1.48594740	0.67297133	24.29736980	16.35143334	0.04115672	0.06115672	20
21	1.51566634	0.65977582	25.78331719	17.01120916	0.03878477	0.05878477	21
22	1.54597967	0.64683904	27.29898354	17.65804820	0.03663140	0.05663140	22
23	1.57689926	0.63415592	28.84496321	18.29220412	0.03466810	0.05466810	23
24	1.60843725	0.62172149	30.42186247	18.91392560	0.03287110	0.05287110	24
25	1.64060599	0.60953087	32.03029972	19.52345647	0.03122044	0.05122044	25
26	1.67341811	0.59757928	33.67090572	20.12103576	0.02969923	0.04969923	26
27	1.70688648	0.58586204	35.34432383	20.70689780	0.02829309	0.04829309	27
28	1.74102421	0.57437455	37.05121031	21.28127236	0.02698967	0.04698967	28
29	1.77584469	0.56311231	38.79223451	21.84438466	0.02577836	0.04577836	29
30	1.81136158	0.55207089	40.56807921	22.39645555	0.02464992	0.04464992	30
31	1.84758882	0.54124597	42.37944079	22.93770152	0.02359635	0.04359635	31
32	1.88454059	0.53063330	44.22702961	23.46833482	0.02261061	0.04261061	32
33	1.92223140	0.52022873	46.11157020	23.98856355	0.02168653	0.04168653	33
34	1.96067603	0.51002817	48.03380160	24.49859172	0.02081867	0.04081867	34
35	1.99988955	0.50002761	49.99447763	24.99861933	0.02000221	0.04000221	35
36	2.03988734	0.49022315	51.99436719	25.48884248	0.01923285	0.03923285	36
37	2.08068509	0.48061093	54.03425453	25.96945341	0.01850678	0.03850678	37
38	2.12229879	0.47118719	56.11493962	26.44064060	0.01782057	0.03782057	38
39	2.16474477	0.46194822	58.23723841	26.90258883	0.01717114	0.03717114	39
40	2.20803966	0.45289042	60.40198318	27.35547924	0.01655575	0.03655575	40
41	2.25220046	0.44401021	62.61002284	27.79948945	0.01597188	0.03597188	41
42	2.29724447	0.43530413	64.86222330	28.23479358	0.01541729	0.03541729	42
43	2.34318936	0.42676875	67.15946777	28.66156233	0.01488993	0.03488993	43
44	2.39005314	0.41840074	69.50265712	29.07996307	0.01438794	0.03438794	44
45	2.43785421	0.41019680	71.89271027	29.49015987	0.01390962	0.03390962	45
46	2.48661129	0.40215373	74.33056447	29.89231360	0.01345342	0.03345342	46
47	2.53634352	0.39426836	76.81717576	30.28658196	0.01301792	0.03301792	47
48	2.58707039	0.38653761	79.35351927	30.67311957	0.01260184	0.03260184	48
49	2.63881179	0.37895844	81.94058966	31.05207801	0.01220396	0.03220396	49
50	2.69158803	0.37152788	84.57940145	31.42360589	0.01182321	0.03182321	50
80	4.87543916	0.20510973	193.77195780	39.74451359	0.00516071	0.02516071	80
100	7.24464612	0.13803297	312.23230591	43.09835164	0.00320274	0.02320274	100
120	10.76516303	0.09289223	488.25815171	45.35538850	0.00204810	0.02204810	120
240	115.88873515	0.00862897	5744.43675765	49.56855168	0.00017408	0.02017408	240
360	1247.56112775	0.00080156	62328.05638744	49.95992180	0.00001604	0.02001604	360

Rate 2¼%	C Compound Amount	D Present Value	E Amount of Annuity	F Present Value of Annuity	G Sinking Fund	H Amortization	
n	$(1+i)^n$	$(1+i)^{-n}$	$s_{\overline{n}\rvert i}$	$a_{\overline{n}\rvert i}$	$1/s_{\overline{n}\rvert i}$	$1/a_{\overline{n}\rvert i}$	n
1	1.02250000	0.97799511	1.00000000	0.97799511	1.00000000	1.02250000	1
2	1.04550625	0.95647444	2.02250000	1.93446955	0.49443758	0.51693758	2
3	1.06903014	0.93542732	3.06800625	2.86989687	0.32594458	0.34844458	3
4	1.09308332	0.91484335	4.13703639	3.78474021	0.24171893	0.26421893	4
5	1.11767769	0.89471232	5.23011971	4.67945253	0.19120021	0.21370021	5
6	1.14282544	0.87502427	6.34779740	5.55447680	0.15753496	0.18003496	6
7	1.16853901	0.85576946	7.49062284	6.41024626	0.13350025	0.15600025	7
8	1.19483114	0.83693835	8.65916186	7.24718461	0.11548462	0.13798462	8
9	1.22171484	0.81852161	9.85399300	8.06570622	0.10148170	0.12398170	9
10	1.24920343	0.80051013	11.07570784	8.86621635	0.09028768	0.11278768	10
11	1.27731050	0.78289499	12.32491127	9.64911134	0.08113649	0.10363649	11
12	1.30604999	0.76566748	13.60222177	10.41477882	0.07351740	0.09601740	12
13	1.33543611	0.74881905	14.90827176	11.16359787	0.06707686	0.08957686	13
14	1.36548343	0.73234137	16.24370788	11.89593924	0.06156230	0.08406230	14
15	1.39620680	0.71622628	17.60919130	12.61216551	0.05678852	0.07928852	15
16	1.42762146	0.70046580	19.00539811	13.31263131	0.05261663	0.07511663	16
17	1.45974294	0.68505212	20.43301957	13.99768343	0.04894039	0.07144039	17
18	1.49258716	0.66997763	21.89276251	14.66766106	0.04567720	0.06817720	18
19	1.52617037	0.65523484	23.38534966	15.32289590	0.04276182	0.06526182	19
20	1.56050920	0.64081647	24.91152003	15.96371237	0.04014207	0.06264207	20
21	1.59562066	0.62671538	26.47202923	16.59042775	0.03777572	0.06027572	21
22	1.63152212	0.61292457	28.06764989	17.20335232	0.03562821	0.05812821	22
23	1.66823137	0.59943724	29.69917201	17.80278955	0.03367097	0.05617097	23
24	1.70576658	0.58624668	31.36740338	18.38903624	0.03188023	0.05438023	24
25	1.74414632	0.57334639	33.07316996	18.96238263	0.03023599	0.05273599	25
26	1.78338962	0.56072997	34.81731628	19.52311260	0.02872134	0.05122134	26
27	1.82351588	0.54839117	36.60070590	20.07150376	0.02732188	0.04982188	27
28	1.86454499	0.53632388	38.42422178	20.60782764	0.02602525	0.04852525	28
29	1.90649725	0.52452213	40.28876677	21.13234977	0.02482081	0.04732081	29
30	1.94939344	0.51298008	42.19526402	21.64532985	0.02369934	0.04619934	30
31	1.99325479	0.50169201	44.14465746	22.14702186	0.02265280	0.04515280	31
32	2.03810303	0.49065233	46.13791226	22.63767419	0.02167415	0.04417415	32
33	2.08396034	0.47985558	48.17601528	23.11752977	0.02075722	0.04325722	33
34	2.13084945	0.46929641	50.25997563	23.58682618	0.01989655	0.04239655	34
35	2.17879356	0.45896960	52.39082508	24.04579577	0.01908731	0.04158731	35
36	2.22781642	0.44887002	54.56961864	24.49466579	0.01832522	0.04082522	36
37	2.27794229	0.43899268	56.79743506	24.93365848	0.01760643	0.04010643	37
38	2.32919599	0.42933270	59.07537735	25.36299118	0.01692753	0.03942753	38
39	2.38160290	0.41988528	61.40457334	25.78287646	0.01628543	0.03878543	39
40	2.43518897	0.41064575	63.78617624	26.19352221	0.01567738	0.03817738	40
41	2.48998072	0.40160954	66.22136521	26.59513174	0.01510087	0.03760087	41
42	2.54600528	0.39277216	68.71134592	26.98790390	0.01455364	0.03705364	42
43	2.60329040	0.38412925	71.25735121	27.37203316	0.01403364	0.03653364	43
44	2.66186444	0.37567653	73.86064161	27.74770969	0.01353901	0.03603901	44
45	2.72175639	0.36740981	76.52250605	28.11511950	0.01306805	0.03556805	45
46	2.78299590	0.35932500	79.24426243	28.47444450	0.01261921	0.03511921	46
47	2.84561331	0.35141809	82.02725834	28.82586259	0.01219107	0.03469107	47
48	2.90963961	0.34368518	84.87287165	29.16954777	0.01178233	0.03428233	48
49	2.97510650	0.33612242	87.78251126	29.50567019	0.01139179	0.03389179	49
50	3.04204640	0.32872608	90.75761776	29.83439627	0.01101836	0.03351836	50
80	5.93014530	0.16862993	219.11756877	36.94978079	0.00456376	0.02706376	80
100	9.25404630	0.10806084	366.84650213	39.64174052	0.00272594	0.02522594	100
120	14.44102439	0.06924717	597.37886184	41.36679266	0.00167398	0.02417398	120
240	208.54318547	0.00479517	9224.14157653	44.23132578	0.00010841	0.02260841	240

Rate 2½%	C Compound Amount	D Present Value	E Amount of Annuity	F Present Value of Annuity	G Sinking Fund	H Amortization	
n	$(1+i)^n$	$(1+i)^{-n}$	$S_{\overline{n}\rceil i}$	$A_{\overline{n}\rceil i}$	$1/S_{\overline{n}\rceil i}$	$1/A_{\overline{n}\rceil i}$	n
1	1.02500000	0.97560976	1.00000000	0.97560976	1.00000000	1.02500000	1
2	1.05062500	0.95181440	2.02500000	1.92742415	0.49382716	0.51882716	2
3	1.07689062	0.92859941	3.07562500	2.85602356	0.32513717	0.35013717	3
4	1.10381289	0.90595064	4.15251563	3.76197421	0.24081788	0.26581788	4
5	1.13140821	0.88385429	5.25632852	4.64582850	0.19024686	0.21524686	5
6	1.15969342	0.86229687	6.38773673	5.50812536	0.15654997	0.18154997	6
7	1.18868575	0.84126524	7.54743015	6.34939060	0.13249543	0.15749543	7
8	1.21840290	0.82074657	8.73611590	7.17013717	0.11446735	0.13946735	8
9	1.24886297	0.80072836	9.95451880	7.97086553	0.10045689	0.12545689	9
10	1.28008454	0.78119840	11.20338177	8.75206393	0.08925876	0.11425876	10
11	1.31208666	0.76214478	12.48346631	9.51420871	0.08010596	0.10510596	11
12	1.34488882	0.74355589	13.79555297	10.25776460	0.07248713	0.09748713	12
13	1.37851104	0.72542038	15.14044179	10.98318497	0.06604827	0.09104827	13
14	1.41297382	0.70772720	16.51895284	11.69091217	0.06053652	0.08553652	14
15	1.448[illegible]9817	0.69046556	17.93192666	12.38137773	0.05576646	0.08076646	15
16	1.48450562	0.67362493	19.38022483	13.05500266	0.05159899	0.07659899	16
17	1.52161826	0.65719506	20.86473045	13.71219772	0.04792777	0.07292777	17
18	1.55965872	0.64116591	22.38634871	14.35336363	0.04467008	0.06967008	18
19	1.59865019	0.62552772	23.94600743	14.97889134	0.04176062	0.06676062	19
20	1.63861644	0.61027094	25.54465761	15.58916229	0.03914713	0.06414713	20
21	1.67958185	0.59538629	27.18327405	16.18454857	0.03678733	0.06178733	21
22	1.72157140	0.58086467	28.86285590	16.76541324	0.03464661	0.05964661	22
23	1.76461068	0.56669724	30.58442730	17.33211048	0.03269638	0.05769638	23
24	1.80872595	0.55287535	32.34903798	17.88498583	0.03091282	0.05591282	24
25	1.85394410	0.53939059	34.15776393	18.42437642	0.02927592	0.05427592	25
26	1.90029270	0.526[illegible]472	36.01170803	18.95061114	0.02776875	0.05276875	26
27	1.94780002	0.513[illegible]973	37.91200073	19.46401087	0.02637687	0.05137687	27
28	1.99649502	0.50087778	39.85980075	19.96488866	0.02508793	0.05008793	28
29	2.04640739	0.48866125	41.85629577	20.45354991	0.02389127	0.04889127	29
30	2.09756758	0.47674269	43.90270316	20.93029259	0.02277764	0.04777764	30
31	2.15000677	0.46511481	46.00027074	21.39540741	0.02173900	0.04673900	31
32	2.20375694	0.45377055	48.15027751	21.84917796	0.02076831	0.04576831	32
33	2.25885086	0.44270298	50.35403445	22.29188094	0.01985938	0.04485938	33
34	2.31532213	0.43190534	52.61288531	22.72378628	0.01900675	0.04400675	34
35	2.37320519	0.42137107	54.92820744	23.14515734	0.01820558	0.04320558	35
36	2.43253532	0.41109372	57.30141263	23.55625107	0.01745158	0.04245158	36
37	2.49334870	0.40106705	59.73394794	23.95731812	0.01674090	0.04174090	37
38	2.55568242	0.39128492	62.22729664	24.34860304	0.01607012	0.04107012	38
39	2.61957448	0.38174139	64.78297906	24.73034443	0.01543615	0.04043615	39
40	2.68506384	0.37243062	67.40255354	25.10277505	0.01483623	0.03983623	40
41	2.75219043	0.36334695	70.08761737	25.46612200	0.01426786	0.03926786	41
42	2.82099520	0.35448483	72.83980781	25.82060683	0.01372876	0.03872876	42
43	2.89152008	0.34583886	75.66080300	26.16644569	0.01321688	0.03821688	43
44	2.96380808	0.33740376	78.55232308	26.50384945	0.01273037	0.03773037	44
45	3.03790328	0.32917440	81.51613116	26.83302386	0.01226751	0.03726751	45
46	3.11385086	0.32114576	84.55403443	27.15416962	0.01182676	0.03682676	46
47	3.19169713	0.31331294	87.66788530	27.46748255	0.01140669	0.03640669	47
48	3.27148956	0.30567116	90.85958243	27.77315371	0.01100599	0.03600599	48
49	3.35327680	0.29821576	94.13107199	28.07136947	0.01062348	0.03562348	49
50	3.43710872	0.29094221	97.48434879	28.36231168	0.01025806	0.03525806	50
80	7.20956782	0.13870457	248.38271265	34.45181722	0.00402605	0.02902605	80
100	11.81371635	0.08464737	432.54865404	36.61410526	0.00231188	0.02731188	100
120	19.35814983	0.05165783	734.32599335	37.93368683	0.00136179	0.02636179	120
240	374.73796499	0.00266853	14949.51859948	39.89325875	0.00006689	0.02506689	240

Rate 2¾%	C Compound Amount	D Present Value	E Amount of Annuity	F Present Value of Annuity	G Sinking Fund	H Amortization	
n	$(1+i)^n$	$(1+i)^{-n}$	$s_{\overline{n}\mid i}$	$a_{\overline{n}\mid i}$	$1/s_{\overline{n}\mid i}$	$1/a_{\overline{n}\mid i}$	n
1	1.02750000	0.97323601	1.00000000	0.97323601	1.00000000	1.02750000	1
2	1.05575625	0.94718833	2.02750000	1.92042434	0.49321825	0.52071825	2
3	1.08478955	0.92183779	3.08325625	2.84226213	0.32433243	0.35183243	3
4	1.11462126	0.89716573	4.16804580	3.73942787	0.23992059	0.26742059	4
5	1.14527334	0.87315400	5.28266706	4.61258186	0.18929832	0.21679832	5
6	1.17676836	0.84978491	6.42794040	5.46236678	0.15557083	0.18307083	6
7	1.20912949	0.82704128	7.60470876	6.28940806	0.13149747	0.15899747	7
8	1.24238055	0.80490635	8.81383825	7.09431441	0.11345795	0.14095795	8
9	1.27654602	0.78336385	10.05621880	7.87767826	0.09944095	0.12694095	9
10	1.31165103	0.76239791	11.33276482	8.64007616	0.08823972	0.11573972	10
11	1.34772144	0.74199310	12.64441585	9.38206926	0.07908629	0.10658629	11
12	1.38478378	0.72213440	13.99213729	10.10420366	0.07146871	0.09896871	12
13	1.42286533	0.70280720	15.37692107	10.80701086	0.06503252	0.09253252	13
14	1.46199413	0.68399728	16.79978639	11.49100814	0.05952457	0.08702457	14
15	1.50219896	0.66569078	18.26178052	12.15669892	0.05475917	0.08225917	15
16	1.54350944	0.64787424	19.76397948	12.80457315	0.05059710	0.07809710	16
17	1.58595595	0.63053454	21.30748892	13.43510769	0.04693186	0.07443186	17
18	1.62956973	0.61365892	22.89344487	14.04876661	0.04368063	0.07118063	18
19	1.67438290	0.59723496	24.52301460	14.64600157	0.04077802	0.06827802	19
20	1.72042843	0.58125057	26.19739750	15.22725213	0.03817173	0.06567173	20
21	1.76774021	0.56569398	27.91782593	15.79294612	0.03581941	0.06331941	21
22	1.81635307	0.55055375	29.68556615	16.34349987	0.03368640	0.06118640	22
23	1.86630278	0.53581874	31.50191921	16.87931861	0.03174410	0.05924410	23
24	1.91762610	0.52147809	33.36822199	17.40079670	0.02996863	0.05746863	24
25	1.97036082	0.50752126	35.28584810	17.90831795	0.02833997	0.05583997	25
26	2.02454575	0.49393796	37.25620892	18.40225592	0.02684116	0.05434116	26
27	2.08022075	0.48071821	39.28075467	18.88297413	0.02545776	0.05295776	27
28	2.13742682	0.46785227	41.36097542	19.35082640	0.02417738	0.05167738	28
29	2.19620606	0.45533068	43.49840224	19.80615708	0.02298935	0.05048935	29
30	2.25660173	0.44314421	45.69460831	20.24930130	0.02188442	0.04938442	30
31	2.31865828	0.43128391	47.95121003	20.68058520	0.02085453	0.04835453	31
32	2.38242138	0.41974103	50.26986831	21.10032623	0.01989263	0.04739263	32
33	2.44793797	0.40850708	52.65228969	21.50883332	0.01899253	0.04649253	33
34	2.51525626	0.39757380	55.10022765	21.90640712	0.01814875	0.04564875	34
35	2.58442581	0.38693314	57.61548391	22.29334026	0.01735645	0.04485645	35
36	2.65549752	0.37657727	60.19990972	22.66991753	0.01661132	0.04411132	36
37	2.72852370	0.36649856	62.85540724	23.03641609	0.01590953	0.04340953	37
38	2.80355810	0.35668959	65.58393094	23.39310568	0.01524764	0.04274764	38
39	2.88065595	0.34714316	68.38748904	23.74024884	0.01462256	0.04212256	39
40	2.95987399	0.33785222	71.26814499	24.07810106	0.01403151	0.04153151	40
41	3.04127052	0.32880995	74.22801898	24.40691101	0.01347200	0.04097200	41
42	3.12490546	0.32000968	77.26928950	24.72692069	0.01294175	0.04044175	42
43	3.21084036	0.31144495	80.39419496	25.03836563	0.01243871	0.03993871	43
44	3.29913847	0.30310944	83.60503532	25.34147507	0.01196100	0.03946100	44
45	3.38986478	0.29499702	86.90417379	25.63647209	0.01150693	0.03900693	45
46	3.48308606	0.28710172	90.29403857	25.92357381	0.01107493	0.03857493	46
47	3.57887093	0.27941773	93.77712463	26.20299154	0.01066358	0.03816358	47
48	3.67728988	0.27193940	97.35599556	26.47493094	0.01027158	0.03777158	48
49	3.77841535	0.26466122	101.03328544	26.73959215	0.00989773	0.03739773	49
50	3.88232177	0.25757783	104.81170079	26.99716998	0.00954092	0.03704092	50
80	8.76085402	0.11414412	282.21287345	32.21294098	0.00354342	0.03104342	80
100	15.07242234	0.06634634	511.72444867	33.95104232	0.00195418	0.02945418	100
120	25.93102392	0.03856385	906.58268797	34.96131471	0.00110304	0.02860304	120
240	672.41800150	0.00148717	24415.20005439	36.30955745	0.00004096	0.02754096	240

Rate 3%	C Compound Amount	D Present Value	E Amount of Annuity	F Present Value of Annuity	G Sinking Fund	H Amortization	
n	$(1+i)^n$	$(1+i)^{-n}$	$s_{\overline{n}\rvert i}$	$a_{\overline{n}\rvert i}$	$1/s_{\overline{n}\rvert i}$	$1/a_{\overline{n}\rvert i}$	n
1	1.03000000	0.97087379	1.00000000	0.97087379	1.00000000	1.03000000	1
2	1.06090000	0.94259591	2.03000000	1.91346970	0.49261084	0.52261084	2
3	1.09272700	0.91514166	3.09090000	2.82861135	0.32353036	0.35353036	3
4	1.12550881	0.88848705	4.18362700	3.71709840	0.23902705	0.26902705	4
5	1.15927407	0.86260878	5.30913581	4.57970719	0.18835457	0.21835457	5
6	1.19405230	0.83748426	6.46840988	5.41719144	0.15459750	0.18459750	6
7	1.22987387	0.81309151	7.66246218	6.23028296	0.13050635	0.16050635	7
8	1.26677008	0.78940923	8.89233605	7.01969219	0.11245639	0.14245639	8
9	1.30477318	0.76641673	10.15910613	7.78610892	0.09843386	0.12843386	9
10	1.34391638	0.74409391	11.46387931	8.53020284	0.08723051	0.11723051	10
11	1.38423387	0.72242128	12.80779569	9.25262411	0.07807745	0.10807745	11
12	1.42576089	0.70137988	14.19202956	9.95400399	0.07046209	0.10046209	12
13	1.46853371	0.68095134	15.61779045	10.63495533	0.06402954	0.09402954	13
14	1.51258972	0.66111781	17.08632416	11.29607314	0.05852634	0.08852634	14
15	1.55796742	0.64186195	18.59891389	11.93793509	0.05376658	0.08376658	15
16	1.60470644	0.62316694	20.15688130	12.56110203	0.04961085	0.07961085	16
17	1.65284763	0.60501645	21.76158774	13.16611847	0.04595253	0.07595253	17
18	1.70243306	0.58739461	23.41443537	13.75351308	0.04270870	0.07270870	18
19	1.75350605	0.57028603	25.11686844	14.32379911	0.03981388	0.06981388	19
20	1.80611123	0.55367575	26.87037449	14.87747486	0.03721571	0.06721571	20
21	1.86029457	0.53754928	28.67648572	15.41502414	0.03487178	0.06487178	21
22	1.91610341	0.52189250	30.53678030	15.93691664	0.03274739	0.06274739	22
23	1.97358651	0.50669175	32.45288370	16.44360839	0.03081390	0.06081390	23
24	2.03279411	0.49193374	34.42647022	16.93554212	0.02904742	0.05904742	24
25	2.09377793	0.47760557	36.45926432	17.41314769	0.02742787	0.05742787	25
26	2.15659127	0.46369473	38.55304225	17.87684242	0.02593829	0.05593829	26
27	2.22128901	0.45018906	40.70963352	18.32703147	0.02456421	0.05456421	27
28	2.28792768	0.43707675	42.93092252	18.76410823	0.02329323	0.05329323	28
29	2.35656551	0.42434636	45.21885020	19.18845459	0.02211467	0.05211467	29
30	2.42726247	0.41198676	47.57541571	19.60044135	0.02101926	0.05101926	30
31	2.50008035	0.39998715	50.00267818	20.00042849	0.01999893	0.04999893	31
32	2.57508276	0.38833703	52.50275852	20.38876553	0.01904662	0.04904662	32
33	2.65233524	0.37702625	55.07784128	20.76579178	0.01815612	0.04815612	33
34	2.73190530	0.36604490	57.73017652	21.13183668	0.01732196	0.04732196	34
35	2.81386245	0.35538340	60.46208181	21.48722007	0.01653929	0.04653929	35
36	2.89827833	0.34503243	63.27594427	21.83225250	0.01580379	0.04580379	36
37	2.98522668	0.33498294	66.17422259	22.16723544	0.01511162	0.04511162	37
38	3.07478348	0.32522615	69.15944927	22.49246159	0.01445934	0.04445934	38
39	3.16702698	0.31575355	72.23423275	22.80821513	0.01384385	0.04384385	39
40	3.26203779	0.30655684	75.40125973	23.11477197	0.01326238	0.04326238	40
41	3.35989893	0.29762800	78.66329753	23.41239997	0.01271241	0.04271241	41
42	3.46069589	0.28895922	82.02319645	23.70135920	0.01219167	0.04219167	42
43	3.56451677	0.28054294	85.48389234	23.98190213	0.01169811	0.04169811	43
44	3.67145227	0.27237178	89.04840911	24.25427392	0.01122985	0.04122985	44
45	3.78159584	0.26443862	92.71986139	24.51871254	0.01078518	0.04078518	45
46	3.89504372	0.25673653	96.50145723	24.77544907	0.01036254	0.04036254	46
47	4.01189503	0.24925876	100.39650095	25.02470783	0.00996051	0.03996051	47
48	4.13225188	0.24199880	104.40839598	25.26670664	0.00957777	0.03957777	48
49	4.25621944	0.23495029	108.54064785	25.50165693	0.00921314	0.03921314	49
50	4.38390602	0.22810708	112.79686729	25.72976401	0.00886549	0.03886549	50
80	10.64089056	0.09397710	321.36301855	30.20076345	0.00311175	0.03311175	80
100	19.21863198	0.05203284	607.28773270	31.59890534	0.00164667	0.03164667	100
120	34.71098714	0.02880932	1123.69957119	32.37302261	0.00088992	0.03088992	120
240	1204.85262793	0.00082998	40128.42093093	33.30566743	0.00002492	0.03002492	240

Rate 3¼%	C Compound Amount	D Present Value	E Amount of Annuity	F Present Value of Annuity	G Sinking Fund	H Amortization	
n	$(1+i)^n$	$(1+i)^{-n}$	$s_{\overline{n}\rceil i}$	$a_{\overline{n}\rceil i}$	$1/s_{\overline{n}\rceil i}$	$1/a_{\overline{n}\rceil i}$	n
1	1.03250000	0.96852300	1.00000000	0.96852300	1.00000000	1.03250000	1
2	1.06605625	0.93803681	2.03250000	1.90655981	0.49200492	0.52450492	2
3	1.10070308	0.90851022	3.09855625	2.81507003	0.32273095	0.35523095	3
4	1.13647593	0.87991305	4.19925933	3.69498308	0.23813723	0.27063723	4
5	1.17341140	0.85221603	5.33573526	4.54719911	0.18741560	0.21991560	5
6	1.21154727	0.82539083	6.50914665	5.37258994	0.15362997	0.18612997	6
7	1.25092255	0.79941000	7.72069392	6.17199994	0.12952204	0.16202204	7
8	1.29157754	0.77424698	8.97161647	6.94624692	0.11146263	0.14396263	8
9	1.33355381	0.74987601	10.26319401	7.69612292	0.09743555	0.12993555	9
10	1.37689430	0.72627216	11.59674781	8.42239508	0.08623107	0.11873107	10
11	1.42164337	0.70341129	12.97364212	9.12580637	0.07707936	0.10957936	11
12	1.46784678	0.68127002	14.39528548	9.80707639	0.06946719	0.10196719	12
13	1.51555180	0.65982568	15.86313226	10.46690207	0.06303925	0.09553925	13
14	1.56480723	0.63905635	17.37868406	11.10595842	0.05754176	0.09004176	14
15	1.61566347	0.61894078	18.94349129	11.72489920	0.05278858	0.08528858	15
16	1.66817253	0.59945838	20.55915476	12.32435758	0.04864013	0.08114013	16
17	1.72238814	0.58058923	22.22732729	12.90494681	0.04498966	0.07748966	17
18	1.77836575	0.56231402	23.94971543	13.46726083	0.04175415	0.07425415	18
19	1.83616264	0.54461407	25.72808118	14.01187490	0.03886804	0.07136804	19
20	1.89583792	0.52747125	27.56424382	14.53934615	0.03627888	0.06877888	20
21	1.95745266	0.51086804	29.46008174	15.05021419	0.03394424	0.06644424	21
22	2.02106987	0.49478745	31.41753440	15.54500163	0.03182936	0.06432936	22
23	2.08675464	0.47921302	33.43860426	16.02421466	0.02990555	0.06240555	23
24	2.15457416	0.46412884	35.52535890	16.48834349	0.02814891	0.06064891	24
25	2.22459782	0.44951945	37.67993307	16.93786295	0.02653933	0.05903933	25
26	2.29689725	0.43536993	39.90453089	17.37323288	0.02505981	0.05755981	26
27	2.37154641	0.42166579	42.20142815	17.79489867	0.02369588	0.05619588	27
28	2.44862167	0.40839302	44.57297456	18.20329169	0.02243512	0.05493512	28
29	2.52820188	0.39553803	47.02159623	18.59882973	0.02126682	0.05376682	29
30	2.61036844	0.38308768	49.54979811	18.98191741	0.02018172	0.05268172	30
31	2.69520541	0.37102923	52.16016655	19.35294664	0.01917172	0.05167172	31
32	2.78279959	0.35935035	54.85537196	19.71229699	0.01822976	0.05072976	32
33	2.87324058	0.34803908	57.63817155	20.06033607	0.01734961	0.04984961	33
34	2.96662089	0.33708385	60.51141213	20.39741992	0.01652581	0.04902581	34
35	3.06303607	0.32647346	63.47803302	20.72389339	0.01575348	0.04825348	35
36	3.16258475	0.31619706	66.54106909	21.04009045	0.01502831	0.04752831	36
37	3.26536875	0.30624413	69.70365384	21.34633457	0.01434645	0.04684645	37
38	3.37149323	0.29660448	72.96902259	21.64293905	0.01370445	0.04620445	38
39	3.48106676	0.28726826	76.34051582	21.93020732	0.01309920	0.04559920	39
40	3.59420143	0.27822592	79.82158259	22.20843324	0.01252794	0.04502794	40
41	3.71101298	0.26946820	83.41578402	22.47790144	0.01198814	0.04448814	41
42	3.83162090	0.26098615	87.12679700	22.73888759	0.01147753	0.04397753	42
43	3.95614858	0.25277109	90.95841791	22.99165869	0.01099403	0.04349403	43
44	4.08472341	0.24481462	94.91456649	23.23647330	0.01053579	0.04303579	44
45	4.21747692	0.23710859	98.99928990	23.47358189	0.01010108	0.04260108	45
46	4.35454492	0.22964512	103.21676682	23.70322701	0.00968835	0.04218835	46
47	4.49606763	0.22241658	107.57131174	23.92564360	0.00929616	0.04179616	47
48	4.64218983	0.21541558	112.06737937	24.14105917	0.00892320	0.04142320	48
49	4.79306100	0.20863494	116.70956920	24.34969412	0.00856828	0.04106828	49
50	4.94883548	0.20206774	121.50263020	24.55176185	0.00823027	0.04073027	50
80	12.91828395	0.07740966	366.71642920	28.38739500	0.00272690	0.03522690	80
100	24.49097262	0.04083137	722.79915765	29.51288088	0.00138351	0.03388351	100
120	46.43091470	0.02153737	1397.87429832	30.10654232	0.00071537	0.03321537	120
240	2155.82983946	0.00046386	66302.45659888	30.75495820	0.00001508	0.03251508	240

Rate 3½%	C Compound Amount	D Present Value	E Amount of Annuity	F Present Value of Annuity	G Sinking Fund	H Amortization	
n	$(1 + i)^n$	$(1 + i)^{-n}$	$S_{\overline{n}\rceil i}$	$A_{\overline{n}\rceil i}$	$1/S_{\overline{n}\rceil i}$	$1/A_{\overline{n}\rceil i}$	n
1	1.03500000	0.96618357	1.00000000	0.96618357	1.00000000	1.03500000	1
2	1.07122500	0.93351070	2.03500000	1.89969428	0.49140049	0.52640049	2
3	1.10871788	0.90194271	3.10622500	2.80163698	0.32193418	0.35693418	3
4	1.14752300	0.87144223	4.21494287	3.67307921	0.23725114	0.27225114	4
5	1.18768631	0.84197317	5.36246588	4.51505238	0.18648137	0.22148137	5
6	1.22925533	0.81350064	6.55015218	5.32855302	0.15266821	0.18766821	6
7	1.27227926	0.78599096	7.77940751	6.11454398	0.12854449	0.16354449	7
8	1.31680904	0.75941156	9.05168677	6.87395554	0.11047665	0.14547665	8
9	1.36289735	0.73373097	10.36849581	7.60768651	0.09644601	0.13144601	9
10	1.41059876	0.70891881	11.73139316	8.31660532	0.08524137	0.12024137	10
11	1.45996972	0.68494571	13.14199192	9.00155104	0.07609197	0.11109197	11
12	1.51106866	0.66178330	14.60196164	9.66333433	0.06848395	0.10348395	12
13	1.56395606	0.63940415	16.11303030	10.30273849	0.06206157	0.09706157	13
14	1.61869452	0.61778179	17.67698636	10.92052028	0.05657073	0.09157073	14
15	1.67534883	0.59689062	19.29568088	11.51741090	0.05182507	0.08682507	15
16	1.73398604	0.57670591	20.97102971	12.09411681	0.04768483	0.08268483	16
17	1.79467555	0.55720378	22.70501575	12.65132059	0.04404313	0.07904313	17
18	1.85748920	0.53836114	24.49969130	13.18968173	0.04081684	0.07581684	18
19	1.92250132	0.52015569	26.35718050	13.70983742	0.03794033	0.07294033	19
20	1.98978886	0.50256588	28.27968181	14.21240330	0.03536108	0.07036108	20
21	2.05943147	0.48557090	30.26947068	14.69797420	0.03303659	0.06803659	21
22	2.13151158	0.46915063	32.32890215	15.16712484	0.03093207	0.06593207	22
23	2.20611448	0.45328563	34.46041373	15.62041047	0.02901880	0.06401880	23
24	2.28332849	0.43795713	36.66652821	16.05836760	0.02727283	0.06227283	24
25	2.36324498	0.42314699	38.94985669	16.48151459	0.02567404	0.06067404	25
26	2.44595856	0.40883767	41.31310168	16.89035226	0.02420540	0.05920540	26
27	2.53156711	0.39501224	43.75906024	17.28536451	0.02285241	0.05785241	27
28	2.62017196	0.38165434	46.29062734	17.66701885	0.02160265	0.05660265	28
29	2.71187798	0.36874815	48.91079930	18.03576700	0.02044538	0.05544538	29
30	2.80679370	0.35627841	51.62267728	18.39204541	0.01937133	0.05437133	30
31	2.90503148	0.34423035	54.42947098	18.73627576	0.01837240	0.05337240	31
32	3.00670759	0.33258971	57.33450247	19.06886547	0.01744150	0.05244150	32
33	3.11194235	0.32134271	60.34121005	19.39020818	0.01657242	0.05157242	33
34	3.22086033	0.31047605	63.45315240	19.70068423	0.01575966	0.05075966	34
35	3.33359045	0.29997686	66.67401274	20.00066110	0.01499835	0.04999835	35
36	3.45026611	0.28983272	70.00760318	20.29049381	0.01428416	0.04928416	36
37	3.57102543	0.28003161	73.45786930	20.57052542	0.01361325	0.04861325	37
38	3.69601132	0.27056194	77.02889472	20.84108736	0.01298214	0.04798214	38
39	3.82537171	0.26141250	80.72490604	21.10249987	0.01238775	0.04738775	39
40	3.95925972	0.25257247	84.55027775	21.35507234	0.01182728	0.04682728	40
41	4.09783381	0.24403137	88.50953747	21.59910371	0.01129822	0.04629822	41
42	4.24125799	0.23577910	92.60737128	21.83488281	0.01079828	0.04579828	42
43	4.38970202	0.22780590	96.84862928	22.06268870	0.01032539	0.04532539	43
44	4.54334160	0.22010231	101.23833130	22.28279102	0.00987768	0.04487768	44
45	4.70235855	0.21265924	105.78167290	22.49545026	0.00945343	0.04445343	45
46	4.86694110	0.20546787	110.48403145	22.70091813	0.00905108	0.04405108	46
47	5.03728404	0.19851968	115.35097255	22.89943780	0.00866919	0.04366919	47
48	5.21358898	0.19180645	120.38825659	23.09124425	0.00830646	0.04330646	48
49	5.39606459	0.18532024	125.60184557	23.27656450	0.00796167	0.04296167	49
50	5.58492686	0.17905337	130.99791016	23.45561787	0.00763371	0.04263371	50
80	15.67573754	0.06379285	419.30678685	26.74877567	0.00238489	0.03738489	80
100	31.19140798	0.03206011	862.61165666	27.65542540	0.00115927	0.03615927	100
120	62.06431624	0.01611232	1744.69474973	28.11107663	0.00057317	0.03557317	120

Rate 3¾%	C Compound Amount	D Present Value	E Amount of Annuity	F Present Value of Annuity	G Sinking Fund	H Amortization	
n	$(1+i)^n$	$(1+i)^{-n}$	$S_{\overline{n}\mid i}$	$A_{\overline{n}\mid i}$	$1/S_{\overline{n}\mid i}$	$1/A_{\overline{n}\mid i}$	n
1	1.03750000	0.96385542	1.00000000	0.96385542	1.00000000	1.03750000	1
2	1.07640625	0.92901727	2.03750000	1.89287270	0.49079755	0.52829755	2
3	1.11677148	0.89543834	3.11390625	2.78831103	0.32114005	0.35864005	3
4	1.15865042	0.86307310	4.23067773	3.65138413	0.23636875	0.27386875	4
5	1.20209981	0.83187768	5.38932815	4.48326181	0.18555189	0.22305189	5
6	1.24717855	0.80180981	6.59142796	5.28507162	0.15171219	0.18921219	6
7	1.29394774	0.77282874	7.83860650	6.05790036	0.12757370	0.16507370	7
8	1.34247078	0.74489517	9.13255425	6.80279553	0.10949839	0.14699839	8
9	1.39281344	0.71797125	10.47502503	7.52076677	0.09546517	0.13296517	9
10	1.44504394	0.69202048	11.86783847	8.21278725	0.08426134	0.12176134	10
11	1.49923309	0.66700769	13.31288241	8.87979494	0.07511521	0.11261521	11
12	1.55545433	0.64289898	14.81211550	9.52269392	0.06751230	0.10501230	12
13	1.61378387	0.61966167	16.36756983	10.14235558	0.06109642	0.09859642	13
14	1.67430076	0.59726426	17.98135370	10.73961984	0.05561317	0.09311317	14
15	1.73708704	0.57567639	19.65565447	11.31529623	0.05087595	0.08837595	15
16	1.80222781	0.55486881	21.39274151	11.87016504	0.04674483	0.08424483	16
17	1.86981135	0.53481331	23.19496932	12.40497835	0.04311280	0.08061280	17
18	1.93992927	0.51548271	25.06478067	12.92046106	0.03989662	0.07739662	18
19	2.01267662	0.49685080	27.00470994	13.41731187	0.03703058	0.07453058	19
20	2.08815200	0.47889234	29.01738656	13.89620421	0.03446210	0.07196210	20
21	2.16645770	0.46158298	31.10553856	14.35778719	0.03214862	0.06964862	21
22	2.24769986	0.44489926	33.27199626	14.80268645	0.03005531	0.06755531	22
23	2.33198860	0.42881856	35.51969612	15.23150501	0.02815339	0.06565339	23
24	2.41943818	0.41331910	37.85168472	15.64482411	0.02641890	0.06391890	24
25	2.51016711	0.39837985	40.27112290	16.04320396	0.02483169	0.06233169	25
26	2.60429838	0.38398058	42.78129001	16.42718454	0.02337470	0.06087470	26
27	2.70195956	0.37010176	45.38558838	16.79728630	0.02203343	0.05953343	27
28	2.80328305	0.35672459	48.08754794	17.15401089	0.02079540	0.05829540	28
29	2.90840616	0.34383093	50.89083099	17.49784183	0.01964991	0.05714991	29
30	3.01747139	0.33140331	53.79923715	17.82924513	0.01858762	0.05608762	30
31	3.13062657	0.31942487	56.81670855	18.14867001	0.01760046	0.05510046	31
32	3.24802507	0.30787940	59.94733512	18.45654941	0.01668131	0.05418131	32
33	3.36982601	0.29675123	63.19536019	18.75330063	0.01582395	0.05332395	33
34	3.49619448	0.28602528	66.56518619	19.03932591	0.01502287	0.05252287	34
35	3.62730178	0.27568702	70.06138067	19.31501293	0.01427320	0.05177320	35
36	3.76332559	0.26572242	73.68868245	19.58073535	0.01357060	0.05107060	36
37	3.90445030	0.25611800	77.45200804	19.83685335	0.01291122	0.05041122	37
38	4.05086719	0.24686072	81.35645834	20.08371407	0.01229159	0.04979159	38
39	4.20277471	0.23793805	85.40732553	20.32165212	0.01170860	0.04920860	39
40	4.36037876	0.22933788	89.61010024	20.55098999	0.01115946	0.04865946	40
41	4.52389296	0.22104855	93.97047900	20.77203855	0.01064164	0.04814164	41
42	4.69353895	0.21305885	98.49437196	20.98509739	0.01015286	0.04765286	42
43	4.86954666	0.20535793	103.18791091	21.19045532	0.00969106	0.04719106	43
44	5.05215466	0.19793535	108.05745757	21.38839067	0.00925434	0.04675434	44
45	5.24161046	0.19078106	113.10961223	21.57917173	0.00884098	0.04634098	45
46	5.43817085	0.18388536	118.35122269	21.76305709	0.00844943	0.04594943	46
47	5.64210226	0.17723890	123.78939354	21.94029599	0.00807824	0.04557824	47
48	5.85368109	0.17083268	129.43149579	22.11112866	0.00772609	0.04522609	48
49	6.07319413	0.16465800	135.28517689	22.27578666	0.00739179	0.04489179	49
50	6.30093891	0.15870651	141.35837102	22.43449317	0.00707422	0.04457422	50
80	19.01290292	0.05259586	480.34407791	25.26411037	0.00208184	0.03958184	80
100	39.70183119	0.02518776	1032.04883168	25.99499320	0.00096895	0.03846895	100
120	82.90345805	0.01206222	2184.09221454	26.34500739	0.00045786	0.03795786	120

Rate 4%	C Compound Amount	D Present Value	E Amount of Annuity	F Present Value of Annuity	G Sinking Fund	H Amortization	
n	$(1 + i)^n$	$(1 + i)^{-n}$	$S_{\overline{n}\rceil i}$	$A_{\overline{n}\rceil i}$	$1/S_{\overline{n}\rceil i}$	$1/A_{\overline{n}\rceil i}$	n
1	1.04000000	0.96153846	1.00000000	0.96153846	1.00000000	1.04000000	1
2	1.08160000	0.92455621	2.04000000	1.88609467	0.49019608	0.53019608	2
3	1.12486400	0.88899636	3.12160000	2.77509103	0.32034854	0.36034854	3
4	1.16985856	0.85480419	4.24646400	3.62989522	0.23549005	0.27549005	4
5	1.21665290	0.82192711	5.41632256	4.45182233	0.18462711	0.22462711	5
6	1.26531902	0.79031453	6.63297546	5.24213686	0.15076190	0.19076190	6
7	1.31593178	0.75991781	7.89829448	6.00205467	0.12660961	0.16660961	7
8	1.36856905	0.73069021	9.21422626	6.73274487	0.10852783	0.14852783	8
9	1.42331181	0.70258674	10.58279531	7.43533161	0.09449299	0.13449299	9
10	1.48024428	0.67556417	12.00610712	8.11089578	0.08329094	0.12329094	10
11	1.53945406	0.64958093	13.48635141	8.76047671	0.07414904	0.11414904	11
12	1.60103222	0.62459705	15.02580546	9.38507376	0.06655217	0.10655217	12
13	1.66507351	0.60057409	16.62683768	9.98564785	0.06014373	0.10014373	13
14	1.73167645	0.57747508	18.29191119	10.56312293	0.05466897	0.09466897	14
15	1.80094351	0.55526450	20.02358764	11.11838743	0.04994110	0.08994110	15
16	1.87298125	0.53390818	21.82453114	11.65229561	0.04582000	0.08582000	16
17	1.94790050	0.51337325	23.69751239	12.16566885	0.04219852	0.08219852	17
18	2.02581652	0.49362812	25.64541288	12.65929697	0.03899333	0.07899333	18
19	2.10684918	0.47464242	27.67122940	13.13393940	0.03613862	0.07613862	19
20	2.19112314	0.45638695	29.77807858	13.59032634	0.03358175	0.07358175	20
21	2.27876807	0.43883360	31.96920172	14.02915995	0.03128011	0.07128011	21
22	2.36991879	0.42195539	34.24796979	14.45111533	0.02919881	0.06919881	22
23	2.46471554	0.40572633	36.61788858	14.85684167	0.02730906	0.06730906	23
24	2.56330416	0.39012147	39.08260412	15.24696314	0.02558683	0.06558683	24
25	2.66583633	0.37511680	41.64590829	15.62207994	0.02401196	0.06401196	25
26	2.77246978	0.36068923	44.31174462	15.98276918	0.02256738	0.06256738	26
27	2.88336858	0.34681657	47.08421440	16.32958575	0.02123854	0.06123854	27
28	2.99870332	0.33347747	49.96758298	16.66306322	0.02001298	0.06001298	28
29	3.11865145	0.32065141	52.96628630	16.98371463	0.01887993	0.05887993	29
30	3.24339751	0.30831867	56.08493775	17.29203330	0.01783010	0.05783010	30
31	3.37313341	0.29646026	59.32833526	17.58849356	0.01685535	0.05685535	31
32	3.50805875	0.28505794	62.70146867	17.87355150	0.01594859	0.05594859	32
33	3.64838110	0.27409417	66.20952742	18.14764567	0.01510357	0.05510357	33
34	3.79431634	0.26355209	69.85790851	18.41119776	0.01431477	0.05431477	34
35	3.94608899	0.25341547	73.65222486	18.66461323	0.01357732	0.05357732	35
36	4.10393255	0.24366872	77.59831385	18.90828195	0.01288688	0.05288688	36
37	4.26808986	0.23429685	81.70224640	19.14257880	0.01223957	0.05223957	37
38	4.43881345	0.22528543	85.97033626	19.36786423	0.01163192	0.05163192	38
39	4.61636599	0.21662061	90.40914971	19.58448484	0.01106083	0.05106083	39
40	4.80102063	0.20828904	95.02551570	19.79277388	0.01052349	0.05052349	40
41	4.99306145	0.20027793	99.82653633	19.99305181	0.01001738	0.05001738	41
42	5.19278391	0.19257493	104.81959778	20.18562674	0.00954020	0.04954020	42
43	5.40049527	0.18516820	110.01238169	20.37079494	0.00908989	0.04908989	43
44	5.61651508	0.17804635	115.41287696	20.54884129	0.00866454	0.04866454	44
45	5.84117568	0.17119841	121.02939204	20.72003970	0.00826246	0.04826246	45
46	6.07482271	0.16461386	126.87056772	20.88465356	0.00788205	0.04788205	46
47	6.31781562	0.15828256	132.94539043	21.04293612	0.00752189	0.04752189	47
48	6.57052824	0.15219476	139.26320604	21.19513088	0.00718065	0.04718065	48
49	6.83334937	0.14634112	145.83373429	21.34147200	0.00685712	0.04685712	49
50	7.10668335	0.14071262	152.66708366	21.48218462	0.00655020	0.04655020	50
80	23.04979907	0.04338433	551.24497675	23.91539185	0.00181408	0.04181408	80
100	50.50494818	0.01980004	1237.62370461	24.50499900	0.00080800	0.04080800	100
120	110.66256080	0.00903648	2741.56402011	24.77408800	0.00036476	0.04036476	120

Rate 4½%	C Compound Amount	D Present Value	E Amount of Annuity	F Present Value of Annuity	G Sinking Fund	H Amortization	
n	$(1 + i)^n$	$(1 + i)^{-n}$	$S_{\overline{n}\mid i}$	$A_{\overline{n}\mid i}$	$1/S_{\overline{n}\mid i}$	$1/A_{\overline{n}\mid i}$	n
1	1.04500000	0.95693780	1.00000000	0.95693780	1.00000000	1.04500000	1
2	1.09202500	0.91572995	2.04500000	1.87266775	0.48899756	0.53399756	2
3	1.14116612	0.87629660	3.13702500	2.74896435	0.31877336	0.36377336	3
4	1.19251860	0.83856134	4.27819112	3.58752570	0.23374365	0.27874365	4
5	1.24618194	0.80245105	5.47070973	4.38997674	0.18279164	0.22779164	5
6	1.30226012	0.76789574	6.71689166	5.15787248	0.14887839	0.19387839	6
7	1.36086183	0.73482846	8.01915179	5.89270094	0.12470147	0.16970147	7
8	1.42210061	0.70318513	9.38001362	6.59588607	0.10660965	0.15160965	8
9	1.48609514	0.67290443	10.80211423	7.26879050	0.09257447	0.13757447	9
10	1.55296942	0.64392768	12.28820937	7.91271818	0.08137882	0.12637882	10
11	1.62285305	0.61619874	13.84117879	8.52891692	0.07224818	0.11724818	11
12	1.69588143	0.58966386	15.46403184	9.11858078	0.06466619	0.10966619	12
13	1.77219610	0.56427164	17.15991327	9.68285242	0.05827535	0.10327535	13
14	1.85194492	0.53997286	18.93210937	10.22282528	0.05282032	0.09782032	14
15	1.93528244	0.51672044	20.78405429	10.73954573	0.04811381	0.09311381	15
16	2.02237015	0.49446932	22.71933673	11.23401505	0.04401537	0.08901537	16
17	2.11337681	0.47317639	24.74170689	11.70719143	0.04041758	0.08541758	17
18	2.20847877	0.45280037	26.85508370	12.15999180	0.03723690	0.08223690	18
19	2.30786031	0.43330179	29.06356246	12.59329359	0.03440734	0.07940734	19
20	2.41171402	0.41464286	31.37142277	13.00793645	0.03187614	0.07687614	20
21	2.52024116	0.39678743	33.78313680	13.40472388	0.02960057	0.07460057	21
22	2.63365201	0.37970089	36.30337795	13.78442476	0.02754565	0.07254565	22
23	2.75216635	0.36335013	38.93702996	14.14777489	0.02568249	0.07068249	23
24	2.87601383	0.34770347	41.68919631	14.49547837	0.02398703	0.06898703	24
25	3.00543446	0.33273060	44.56521015	14.82820896	0.02243903	0.06743903	25
26	3.14067901	0.31840248	47.57064460	15.14661145	0.02102137	0.06602137	26
27	3.28200956	0.30469137	50.71132361	15.45130282	0.01971946	0.06471946	27
28	3.42969999	0.29157069	53.99333317	15.74287351	0.01852081	0.06352081	28
29	3.58403649	0.27901502	57.42303316	16.02188853	0.01741461	0.06241461	29
30	3.74531813	0.26700002	61.00706966	16.28888854	0.01639154	0.06139154	30
31	3.91385745	0.25550241	64.75238779	16.54439095	0.01544345	0.06044345	31
32	4.08998104	0.24449991	68.66624524	16.78889086	0.01456320	0.05956320	32
33	4.27403018	0.23397121	72.75622628	17.02286207	0.01374453	0.05874453	33
34	4.46636154	0.22389589	77.03025646	17.24675796	0.01298191	0.05798191	34
35	4.66734781	0.21425444	81.49661800	17.46101240	0.01227045	0.05727045	35
36	4.87737846	0.20502817	86.16396581	17.66604058	0.01160578	0.05660578	36
37	5.09686049	0.19619921	91.04134427	17.86223979	0.01098402	0.05598402	37
38	5.32621921	0.18775044	96.13820476	18.04999023	0.01040169	0.05540169	38
39	5.56589908	0.17966549	101.46442398	18.22965572	0.00985567	0.05485567	39
40	5.81636454	0.17192870	107.03032306	18.40158442	0.00934315	0.05434315	40
41	6.07810094	0.16452507	112.84668760	18.56610949	0.00886158	0.05386158	41
42	6.35161548	0.15744026	118.92478854	18.72354975	0.00840868	0.05340868	42
43	6.63743818	0.15066054	125.27640402	18.87421029	0.00798235	0.05298235	43
44	6.93612290	0.14417276	131.91384220	19.01838305	0.00758071	0.05258071	44
45	7.24824843	0.13796437	138.84996510	19.15634742	0.00720202	0.05220202	45
46	7.57441961	0.13202332	146.09821353	19.28837074	0.00684471	0.05184471	46
47	7.91526849	0.12633810	153.67263314	19.41470884	0.00650734	0.05150734	47
48	8.27145557	0.12089771	161.58790163	19.53560654	0.00618858	0.05118858	48
49	8.64367107	0.11569158	169.85935720	19.65129813	0.00588722	0.05088722	49
50	9.03263627	0.11070965	178.50302828	19.76200778	0.00560215	0.05060215	50
80	33.83009643	0.02955948	729.55769854	21.56534493	0.00137069	0.04637069	80
100	81.58851803	0.01225663	1790.85595627	21.94985274	0.00055839	0.04555839	100
120	196.76817320	0.00508212	4350.40384897	22.10928616	0.00022986	0.04522986	120

Rate 5%	C Compound Amount	D Present Value	E Amount of Annuity	F Present Value of Annuity	G Sinking Fund	H Amortization	
n	$(1+i)^n$	$(1+i)^{-n}$	$s_{\overline{n}\rvert i}$	$a_{\overline{n}\rvert i}$	$1/s_{\overline{n}\rvert i}$	$1/a_{\overline{n}\rvert i}$	n
1	1.05000000	0.95238095	1.00000000	0.95238095	1.00000000	1.05000000	1
2	1.10250000	0.90702948	2.05000000	1.85941043	0.48780488	0.53780488	2
3	1.15762500	0.86383760	3.15250000	2.72324803	0.31720856	0.36720856	3
4	1.21550625	0.82270247	4.31012500	3.54595050	0.23201183	0.28201183	4
5	1.27628156	0.78352617	5.52563125	4.32947667	0.18097480	0.23097480	5
6	1.34009564	0.74621540	6.80191281	5.07569207	0.14701747	0.19701747	6
7	1.40710042	0.71068133	8.14200845	5.78637340	0.12281982	0.17281982	7
8	1.47745544	0.67683936	9.54910888	6.46321276	0.10472181	0.15472181	8
9	1.55132822	0.64460892	11.02656432	7.10782168	0.09069008	0.14069008	9
10	1.62889463	0.61391325	12.57789254	7.72173493	0.07950457	0.12950457	10
11	1.71033936	0.58467929	14.20678716	8.30641422	0.07038889	0.12038889	11
12	1.79585633	0.55683742	15.91712652	8.86325164	0.06282541	0.11282541	12
13	1.88564914	0.53032135	17.71298285	9.39357299	0.05645577	0.10645577	13
14	1.97993160	0.50506795	19.59863199	9.89864094	0.05102397	0.10102397	14
15	2.07892818	0.48101710	21.57856359	10.37965804	0.04634229	0.09634229	15
16	2.18287459	0.45811152	23.65749177	10.83776956	0.04226991	0.09226991	16
17	2.29201832	0.43629669	25.84036636	11.27406625	0.03869914	0.08869914	17
18	2.40661923	0.41552065	28.13238467	11.68958690	0.03554622	0.08554622	18
19	2.52695020	0.39573396	30.53900391	12.08532086	0.03274501	0.08274501	19
20	2.65329771	0.37688948	33.06595410	12.46221034	0.03024259	0.08024259	20
21	2.78596259	0.35894236	35.71925181	12.82115271	0.02799611	0.07799611	21
22	2.92526072	0.34184987	38.50521440	13.16300258	0.02597051	0.07597051	22
23	3.07152376	0.32557131	41.43047512	13.48857388	0.02413682	0.07413682	23
24	3.22509994	0.31006791	44.50199887	13.79864179	0.02247090	0.07247090	24
25	3.38635494	0.29530277	47.72709882	14.09394457	0.02095246	0.07095246	25
26	3.55567269	0.28124073	51.11345376	14.37518530	0.01956432	0.06956432	26
27	3.73345632	0.26784832	54.66912645	14.64303362	0.01829186	0.06829186	27
28	3.92012914	0.25509364	58.40258277	14.89812726	0.01712253	0.06712253	28
29	4.11613560	0.24294632	62.32271191	15.14107358	0.01604551	0.06604551	29
30	4.32194238	0.23137745	66.43884750	15.37245103	0.01505144	0.06505144	30
31	4.53803949	0.22035947	70.76078988	15.59281050	0.01413212	0.06413212	31
32	4.76494147	0.20986617	75.29882937	15.80267667	0.01328042	0.06328042	32
33	5.00318854	0.19987254	80.06377084	16.00254921	0.01249004	0.06249004	33
34	5.25334797	0.19035480	85.06695938	16.19290401	0.01175545	0.06175545	34
35	5.51601537	0.18129029	90.32030735	16.37419429	0.01107171	0.06107171	35
36	5.79181614	0.17265741	95.83632272	16.54685171	0.01043446	0.06043446	36
37	6.08140694	0.16443563	101.62813886	16.71128734	0.00983979	0.05983979	37
38	6.38547729	0.15660536	107.70954580	16.86789271	0.00928423	0.05928423	38
39	6.70475115	0.14914797	114.09502309	17.01704067	0.00876462	0.05876462	39
40	7.03998871	0.14204568	120.79977424	17.15908635	0.00827816	0.05827816	40
41	7.39198815	0.13528160	127.83976295	17.29436796	0.00782229	0.05782229	41
42	7.76158756	0.12883962	135.23175110	17.42320758	0.00739471	0.05739471	42
43	8.14966693	0.12270440	142.99333866	17.54591198	0.00699333	0.05699333	43
44	8.55715028	0.11686133	151.14300559	17.66277331	0.00661625	0.05661625	44
45	8.98500779	0.11129651	159.70015587	17.77406982	0.00626173	0.05626173	45
46	9.43425818	0.10599668	168.68516366	17.88006650	0.00592820	0.05592820	46
47	9.90597109	0.10094921	178.11942185	17.98101571	0.00561421	0.05561421	47
48	10.40126965	0.09614211	188.02539294	18.07715782	0.00531843	0.05531843	48
49	10.92133313	0.09156391	198.42666259	18.16872173	0.00503965	0.05503965	49
50	11.46739979	0.08720373	209.34799572	18.25592546	0.00477674	0.05477674	50
80	49.56144107	0.02017698	971.22882134	19.59646048	0.00102962	0.05102962	80
100	131.50125785	0.00760449	2610.02515693	19.84791020	0.00038314	0.05038314	100
120	348.91198567	0.00286605	6958.23971334	19.94267895	0.00014371	0.05014371	120

Rate 5½%	C Compound Amount	D Present Value	E Amount of Annuity	F Present Value of Annuity	G Sinking Fund	H Amortization	
n	$(1+i)^n$	$(1+i)^{-n}$	$s_{\overline{n}\mid i}$	$a_{\overline{n}\mid i}$	$1/s_{\overline{n}\mid i}$	$1/a_{\overline{n}\mid i}$	n
1	1.05500000	0.94786730	1.00000000	0.94786730	1.00000000	1.05500000	1
2	1.11302500	0.89845242	2.05500000	1.84631971	0.48661800	0.54161800	2
3	1.17424137	0.85161366	3.16802500	2.69793338	0.31565407	0.37065407	3
4	1.23882465	0.80721674	4.34226638	3.50515012	0.23029449	0.28529449	4
5	1.30696001	0.76513435	5.58109103	4.27028448	0.17917644	0.23417644	5
6	1.37884281	0.72524583	6.88805103	4.99553031	0.14517895	0.20017895	6
7	1.45467916	0.68743681	8.26689384	5.68296712	0.12096442	0.17596442	7
8	1.53468651	0.65159887	9.72157300	6.33456599	0.10286401	0.15786401	8
9	1.61909427	0.61762926	11.25625951	6.95219525	0.08883946	0.14383946	9
10	1.70814446	0.58543058	12.87535379	7.53762583	0.07766777	0.13266777	10
11	1.80209240	0.55491050	14.58349825	8.09253633	0.06857065	0.12357065	11
12	1.90120749	0.52598152	16.38559065	8.61851785	0.06102923	0.11602923	12
13	2.00577390	0.49856068	18.28679814	9.11707853	0.05468426	0.10968426	13
14	2.11609146	0.47256937	20.29257203	9.58964790	0.04927912	0.10427912	14
15	2.23247649	0.44793305	22.40866350	10.03758094	0.04462560	0.09962560	15
16	2.35526270	0.42458109	24.64113999	10.46216203	0.04058254	0.09558254	16
17	2.48480215	0.40244653	26.99640269	10.86460856	0.03704197	0.09204197	17
18	2.62146627	0.38146590	29.48120483	11.24607447	0.03391992	0.08891992	18
19	2.76564691	0.36157906	32.10267110	11.60765352	0.03115006	0.08615006	19
20	2.91775749	0.34272896	34.86831801	11.95038248	0.02867933	0.08367933	20
21	3.07823415	0.32486158	37.78607550	12.27524406	0.02646478	0.08146478	21
22	3.24753703	0.30792567	40.86430965	12.58316973	0.02447123	0.07947123	22
23	3.42615157	0.29187267	44.11184669	12.87504239	0.02266965	0.07766965	23
24	3.61458990	0.27665656	47.53799825	13.15169895	0.02103580	0.07603580	24
25	3.81339235	0.26223370	51.15258816	13.41393266	0.01954935	0.07454935	25
26	4.02312893	0.24856275	54.96598051	13.66249541	0.01819307	0.07319307	26
27	4.24440102	0.23560450	58.98910943	13.89809991	0.01695228	0.07195228	27
28	4.47784307	0.22332181	63.23351045	14.12142172	0.01581440	0.07081440	28
29	4.72412444	0.21167944	67.71135353	14.33310116	0.01476857	0.06976857	29
30	4.98395129	0.20064402	72.43547797	14.53374517	0.01380539	0.06880539	30
31	5.25806861	0.19018390	77.41942926	14.72392907	0.01291665	0.06791665	31
32	5.54726238	0.18026910	82.67749787	14.90419817	0.01209519	0.06709519	32
33	5.85236181	0.17087119	88.22476025	15.07506936	0.01133469	0.06633469	33
34	6.17424171	0.16196321	94.07712207	15.23703257	0.01062958	0.06562958	34
35	6.51382501	0.15351963	100.25136378	15.39055220	0.00997493	0.06497493	35
36	6.87208538	0.14551624	106.76518879	15.53606843	0.00936635	0.06436635	36
37	7.25005008	0.13793008	113.63727417	15.67399851	0.00879993	0.06379993	37
38	7.64880283	0.13073941	120.88732425	15.80473793	0.00827217	0.06327217	38
39	8.06948699	0.12392362	128.53612708	15.92866154	0.00777991	0.06277991	39
40	8.51330877	0.11746314	136.60561407	16.04612469	0.00732034	0.06232034	40
41	8.98154076	0.11133947	145.11892285	16.15746416	0.00689090	0.06189090	41
42	9.47552550	0.10553504	154.10046360	16.26299920	0.00648927	0.06148927	42
43	9.99667940	0.10003322	163.57598910	16.36303242	0.00611337	0.06111337	43
44	10.54649677	0.09481822	173.57266850	16.45785063	0.00576128	0.06076128	44
45	11.12655409	0.08987509	184.11916527	16.54772572	0.00543127	0.06043127	45
46	11.73851456	0.08518965	195.24571936	16.63291537	0.00512175	0.06012175	46
47	12.38413287	0.08074849	206.98423392	16.71366386	0.00483129	0.05983129	47
48	13.06526017	0.07653885	219.36836679	16.79020271	0.00455854	0.05955854	48
49	13.78384948	0.07254867	232.43362696	16.86275139	0.00430230	0.05930230	49
50	14.54196120	0.06876652	246.21747645	16.93151790	0.00406145	0.05906145	50
80	72.47642628	0.01379759	1299.57138693	17.93095291	0.00076948	0.05576948	80
100	211.46863567	0.00472883	3826.70246680	18.09583939	0.00026132	0.05526132	100
120	617.01419577	0.00162071	11200.25810482	18.15235076	0.00008928	0.05508928	120

Rate 6%	C Compound Amount	D Present Value	E Amount of Annuity	F Present Value of Annuity	G Sinking Fund	H Amortization	
n	$(1+i)^n$	$(1+i)^{-n}$	$S_{\overline{n}\rceil i}$	$A_{\overline{n}\rceil i}$	$1/S_{\overline{n}\rceil i}$	$1/A_{\overline{n}\rceil i}$	n
1	1.06000000	0.94339623	1.00000000	0.94339623	1.00000000	1.06000000	1
2	1.12360000	0.88999644	2.06000000	1.83339267	0.48543689	0.54543689	2
3	1.19101600	0.83961928	3.18360000	2.67301195	0.31410981	0.37410981	3
4	1.26247696	0.79209366	4.37461600	3.46510561	0.22859149	0.28859149	4
5	1.33822558	0.74725817	5.63709296	4.21236379	0.17739640	0.23739640	5
6	1.41851911	0.70496054	6.97531854	4.91732433	0.14336263	0.20336263	6
7	1.50363026	0.66505711	8.39383765	5.58238144	0.11913502	0.17913502	7
8	1.59384807	0.62741237	9.89746791	6.20979381	0.10103594	0.16103594	8
9	1.68947896	0.59189846	11.49131598	6.80169227	0.08702224	0.14702224	9
10	1.79084770	0.55839478	13.18079494	7.36008705	0.07586796	0.13586796	10
11	1.89829856	0.52678753	14.97164264	7.88687458	0.06679294	0.12679294	11
12	2.01219647	0.49696936	16.86994120	8.38384394	0.05927703	0.11927703	12
13	2.13292826	0.46883902	18.88213767	8.85268296	0.05296011	0.11296011	13
14	2.26090396	0.44230096	21.01506593	9.29498393	0.04758491	0.10758491	14
15	2.39655819	0.41726506	23.27596988	9.71224899	0.04296276	0.10296276	15
16	2.54035168	0.39364628	25.67252808	10.10589527	0.03895214	0.09895214	16
17	2.69277279	0.37136442	28.21287976	10.47725969	0.03544480	0.09544480	17
18	2.85433915	0.35034379	30.90565255	10.82760348	0.03235654	0.09235654	18
19	3.02559950	0.33051301	33.75999170	11.15811649	0.02962086	0.08962086	19
20	3.20713547	0.31180473	36.78559120	11.46992122	0.02718456	0.08718456	20
21	3.39956360	0.29415540	39.99272668	11.76407662	0.02500455	0.08500455	21
22	3.60353742	0.27750510	43.39229028	12.04158172	0.02304557	0.08304557	22
23	3.81974966	0.26179726	46.99582769	12.30337898	0.02127848	0.08127848	23
24	4.04893464	0.24697855	50.81557735	12.55035753	0.01967900	0.07967900	24
25	4.29187072	0.23299863	54.86451200	12.78335616	0.01822672	0.07822672	25
26	4.54938296	0.21981003	59.15638272	13.00316619	0.01690435	0.07690435	26
27	4.82234594	0.20736795	63.70576568	13.21053414	0.01569717	0.07569717	27
28	5.11168670	0.19563014	68.52811162	13.40616428	0.01459255	0.07459255	28
29	5.41838790	0.18455674	73.63979832	13.59072102	0.01357961	0.07357961	29
30	5.74349117	0.17411013	79.05818622	13.76483115	0.01264891	0.07264891	30
31	6.08810064	0.16425484	84.80167739	13.92908599	0.01179222	0.07179222	31
32	6.45338668	0.15495740	90.88977803	14.08404339	0.01100234	0.07100234	32
33	6.84058988	0.14618622	97.34316471	14.23022961	0.01027293	0.07027293	33
34	7.25102528	0.13791153	104.18375460	14.36814114	0.00959843	0.06959843	34
35	7.68608679	0.13010522	111.43477987	14.49824636	0.00897386	0.06897386	35
36	8.14725200	0.12274077	119.12086666	14.62098713	0.00839483	0.06839483	36
37	8.63608712	0.11579318	127.26811866	14.73678031	0.00785743	0.06785743	37
38	9.15425235	0.10923885	135.90420578	14.84601916	0.00735812	0.06735812	38
39	9.70350749	0.10305552	145.05845813	14.94907468	0.00689377	0.06689377	39
40	10.28571794	0.09722219	154.76196562	15.04629687	0.00646154	0.06646154	40
41	10.90286101	0.09171905	165.04768356	15.13801592	0.00605886	0.06605886	41
42	11.55703267	0.08652740	175.95054457	15.22454332	0.00568342	0.06568342	42
43	12.25045463	0.08162962	187.50757724	15.30617294	0.00533312	0.06533312	43
44	12.98548191	0.07700908	199.75803188	15.38318202	0.00500606	0.06500606	44
45	13.76461083	0.07265007	212.74351379	15.45583209	0.00470050	0.06470050	45
46	14.59048748	0.06853781	226.50812462	15.52436990	0.00441485	0.06441485	46
47	15.46591673	0.06465831	241.09861210	15.58902821	0.00414768	0.06414768	47
48	16.39387173	0.06099840	256.56452882	15.65002661	0.00389765	0.06389765	48
49	17.37750403	0.05754566	272.95840055	15.70757227	0.00366356	0.06366356	49
50	18.42015427	0.05428836	290.33590458	15.76186064	0.00344429	0.06344429	50
80	105.79599348	0.00945215	1746.59989137	16.50913077	0.00057254	0.06057254	80
100	339.30208351	0.00294723	5638.36805857	16.61754623	0.00017736	0.06017736	100
120	1088.18774784	0.00091896	18119.79579725	16.65135068	0.00005519	0.06005519	120

Rate 6½%	C Compound Amount	D Present Value	E Amount of Annuity	F Present Value of Annuity	G Sinking Fund	H Amortization	
n	$(1+i)^n$	$(1+i)^{-n}$	$s_{\overline{n}\rvert i}$	$a_{\overline{n}\rvert i}$	$1/s_{\overline{n}\rvert i}$	$1/a_{\overline{n}\rvert i}$	n
1	1.06500000	0.93896714	1.00000000	0.93896714	1.00000000	1.06500000	1
2	1.13422500	0.88165928	2.06500000	1.82062642	0.48426150	0.54926150	2
3	1.20794963	0.82784909	3.19922500	2.64847551	0.31257570	0.37757570	3
4	1.28646635	0.77732309	4.40717463	3.42579860	0.22690274	0.29190274	4
5	1.37008666	0.72988084	5.69364098	4.15567944	0.17563454	0.24063454	5
6	1.45914230	0.68533412	7.06372764	4.84101356	0.14156831	0.20656831	6
7	1.55398655	0.64350621	8.52286994	5.48451977	0.11733137	0.18233137	7
8	1.65499567	0.60423119	10.07685648	6.08875096	0.09923730	0.16423730	8
9	1.76257039	0.56735323	11.73185215	6.65610419	0.08523803	0.15023803	9
10	1.87713747	0.53272604	13.49442254	7.18883022	0.07410469	0.13910469	10
11	1.99915140	0.50021224	15.37156001	7.68904246	0.06505521	0.13005521	11
12	2.12909624	0.46968285	17.37071141	8.15872532	0.05756817	0.12256817	12
13	2.26748750	0.44101676	19.49980765	8.59974208	0.05128256	0.11628256	13
14	2.41487418	0.41410025	21.76729515	9.01384233	0.04594048	0.11094048	14
15	2.57184101	0.38882652	24.18216933	9.40266885	0.04135278	0.10635278	15
16	2.73901067	0.36509533	26.75401034	9.76776418	0.03737757	0.10237757	16
17	2.91704637	0.34281251	29.49302101	10.11057670	0.03390633	0.09890633	17
18	3.10665438	0.32188969	32.41006738	10.43246638	0.03085461	0.09585461	18
19	3.30858691	0.30224384	35.51672176	10.73471022	0.02815575	0.09315575	19
20	3.52364506	0.28379703	38.82530867	11.01850725	0.02575640	0.09075640	20
21	3.75268199	0.26647608	42.34895373	11.28498333	0.02361333	0.08861333	21
22	3.99660632	0.25021228	46.10163573	11.53519562	0.02169120	0.08669120	22
23	4.25638573	0.23494111	50.09824205	11.77013673	0.01996078	0.08496078	23
24	4.53305081	0.22060198	54.35462778	11.99073871	0.01839770	0.08339770	24
25	4.82769911	0.20713801	58.88767859	12.19787673	0.01698148	0.08198148	25
26	5.14149955	0.19449579	63.71537769	12.39237251	0.01569480	0.08069480	26
27	5.47569702	0.18262515	68.85687725	12.57499766	0.01452288	0.07952288	27
28	5.83161733	0.17147902	74.33257427	12.74647668	0.01345305	0.07845305	28
29	6.21067245	0.16101316	80.16419159	12.90748984	0.01247440	0.07747440	29
30	6.61436616	0.15118607	86.37486405	13.05867591	0.01157744	0.07657744	30
31	7.04429996	0.14195875	92.98923021	13.20063465	0.01075393	0.07575393	31
32	7.50217946	0.13329460	100.03353017	13.33392925	0.00999665	0.07499665	32
33	7.98982113	0.12515925	107.53570963	13.45908850	0.00929924	0.07429924	33
34	8.50915950	0.11752042	115.52553076	13.57660892	0.00865610	0.07365610	34
35	9.06225487	0.11034781	124.03469026	13.68695673	0.00806226	0.07306226	35
36	9.65130143	0.10361297	133.09694513	13.79056970	0.00751332	0.07251332	36
37	10.27863603	0.09728917	142.74824656	13.88785887	0.00700534	0.07200534	37
38	10.94674737	0.09135134	153.02688259	13.97921021	0.00653480	0.07153480	38
39	11.65828595	0.08577590	163.97362996	14.06498611	0.00609854	0.07109854	39
40	12.41607453	0.08054075	175.63191590	14.14552687	0.00569373	0.07069373	40
41	13.22311938	0.07562512	188.04799044	14.22115199	0.00531779	0.07031779	41
42	14.08262214	0.07100950	201.27110981	14.29216149	0.00496842	0.06996842	42
43	14.99799258	0.06667559	215.35373195	14.35883708	0.00464352	0.06964352	43
44	15.97286209	0.06260619	230.35172453	14.42144327	0.00434119	0.06934119	44
45	17.01109813	0.05878515	246.32458662	14.48022842	0.00405968	0.06905968	45
46	18.11681951	0.05519733	263.33568475	14.53542575	0.00379743	0.06879743	46
47	19.29441278	0.05182848	281.45250426	14.58725422	0.00355300	0.06855300	47
48	20.54854961	0.04866524	300.74691704	14.63591946	0.00332505	0.06832505	48
49	21.88420533	0.04569506	321.29546665	14.68161451	0.00311240	0.06811240	49
50	23.30667868	0.04290616	343.17967198	14.72452067	0.00291393	0.06791393	50
80	154.15890683	0.00648681	2356.29087423	15.28481826	0.00042440	0.06542440	80
100	543.20127103	0.00184094	8341.55801588	15.35629326	0.00011988	0.06511988	100
120	1914.04847717	0.00052245	29431.51503337	15.37657765	0.00003398	0.06503398	120

Rate 7%	C Compound Amount	D Present Value	E Amount of Annuity	F Present Value of Annuity	G Sinking Fund	H Amortization	
n	$(1+i)^n$	$(1+i)^{-n}$	$S_{\overline{n}\rceil i}$	$A_{\overline{n}\rceil i}$	$1/S_{\overline{n}\rceil i}$	$1/A_{\overline{n}\rceil i}$	n
1	1.07000000	0.93457944	1.00000000	0.93457944	1.00000000	1.07000000	1
2	1.14490000	0.87343873	2.07000000	1.80801817	0.48309179	0.55309179	2
3	1.22504300	0.81629788	3.21490000	2.62431604	0.31105167	0.38105167	3
4	1.31079601	0.76289521	4.43994300	3.38721126	0.22522812	0.29522812	4
5	1.40255173	0.71298618	5.75073901	4.10019744	0.17389069	0.24389069	5
6	1.50073035	0.66634222	7.15329074	4.76653966	0.13979580	0.20979580	6
7	1.60578148	0.62274974	8.65402109	5.38928940	0.11555322	0.18555322	7
8	1.71818618	0.58200910	10.25980257	5.97129851	0.09746776	0.16746776	8
9	1.83845921	0.54393374	11.97798875	6.51523225	0.08348647	0.15348647	9
10	1.96715136	0.50834929	13.81644796	7.02358154	0.07237750	0.14237750	10
11	2.10485195	0.47509280	15.78359932	7.49867434	0.06335690	0.13335690	11
12	2.25219159	0.44401196	17.88845127	7.94268630	0.05590199	0.12590199	12
13	2.40984500	0.41496445	20.14064286	8.35765074	0.04965085	0.11965085	13
14	2.57853415	0.38781724	22.55048786	8.74546799	0.04434494	0.11434494	14
15	2.75903154	0.36244602	25.12902201	9.10791401	0.03979462	0.10979462	15
16	2.95216375	0.33873460	27.88805355	9.44664860	0.03585765	0.10585765	16
17	3.15881521	0.31657439	30.84021730	9.76322299	0.03242519	0.10242519	17
18	3.37993228	0.29586392	33.99903251	10.05908691	0.02941260	0.09941260	18
19	3.61652754	0.27650833	37.37896479	10.33559524	0.02675301	0.09675301	19
20	3.86968446	0.25841900	40.99549232	10.59401425	0.02439293	0.09439293	20
21	4.14056237	0.24151309	44.86517678	10.83552733	0.02228900	0.09228900	21
22	4.43040174	0.22571317	49.00573916	11.06124050	0.02040577	0.09040577	22
23	4.74052986	0.21094688	53.43614090	11.27218738	0.01871393	0.08871393	23
24	5.07236695	0.19714662	58.17667076	11.46933400	0.01718902	0.08718902	24
25	5.42743264	0.18424918	63.24903772	11.65358318	0.01581052	0.08581052	25
26	5.80735292	0.17219549	68.67647036	11.82577867	0.01456103	0.08456103	26
27	6.21386763	0.16093037	74.48382328	11.98670904	0.01342573	0.08342573	27
28	6.64883836	0.15040221	80.69769091	12.13711125	0.01239193	0.08239193	28
29	7.11425705	0.14056282	87.34652927	12.27767407	0.01144865	0.08144865	29
30	7.61225504	0.13136712	94.46078632	12.40904118	0.01058640	0.08058640	30
31	8.14511290	0.12277301	102.07304137	12.53181419	0.00979691	0.07979691	31
32	8.71527080	0.11474113	110.21815426	12.64655532	0.00907292	0.07907292	32
33	9.32533975	0.10723470	118.93342506	12.75379002	0.00840807	0.07840807	33
34	9.97811354	0.10021934	128.25876481	12.85400936	0.00779674	0.07779674	34
35	10.67658148	0.09366294	138.23687835	12.94767230	0.00723396	0.07723396	35
36	11.42394219	0.08753546	148.91345984	13.03520776	0.00671531	0.07671531	36
37	12.22361814	0.08180884	160.33740202	13.11701660	0.00623685	0.07623685	37
38	13.07927141	0.07645686	172.56102017	13.19347345	0.00579505	0.07579505	38
39	13.99482041	0.07145501	185.64029158	13.26492846	0.00538676	0.07538676	39
40	14.97445784	0.06678038	199.63511199	13.33170884	0.00500914	0.07500914	40
41	16.02266989	0.06241157	214.60956983	13.39412041	0.00465962	0.07465962	41
42	17.14425678	0.05832857	230.63223972	13.45244898	0.00433591	0.07433591	42
43	18.34435475	0.05451268	247.77649650	13.50696167	0.00403590	0.07403590	43
44	19.62845959	0.05094643	266.12085125	13.55790810	0.00375769	0.07375769	44
45	21.00245176	0.04761349	285.74931084	13.60552159	0.00349957	0.07349957	45
46	22.47262338	0.04449859	306.75176260	13.65002018	0.00325996	0.07325996	46
47	24.04570702	0.04158747	329.22438598	13.69160764	0.00303744	0.07303744	47
48	25.72890651	0.03886679	353.27009300	13.73047443	0.00283070	0.07283070	48
49	27.52992997	0.03632410	378.99899951	13.76679853	0.00263853	0.07263853	49
50	29.45702506	0.03394776	406.52892947	13.80074629	0.00245985	0.07245985	50
80	224.23438758	0.00445962	3189.06267969	14.22200544	0.00031357	0.07031357	80
100	867.71632557	0.00115245	12381.66179381	14.26925071	0.00008076	0.07008076	100
120	3357.78838289	0.00029782	47954.11975557	14.28145978	0.00002085	0.07002085	120

Rate 7½%	C Compound Amount	D Present Value	E Amount of Annuity	F Present Value of Annuity	G Sinking Fund	H Amortization	
n	$(1+i)^n$	$(1+i)^{-n}$	$S_{\overline{n}\vert i}$	$A_{\overline{n}\vert i}$	$1/S_{\overline{n}\vert i}$	$1/A_{\overline{n}\vert i}$	n
1	1.07500000	0.93023256	1.00000000	0.93023256	1.00000000	1.07500000	1
2	1.15562500	0.86533261	2.07500000	1.79556517	0.48192771	0.55692771	2
3	1.24229688	0.80496057	3.23062500	2.60052574	0.30953763	0.38453763	3
4	1.33546914	0.74880053	4.47292188	3.34932627	0.22356751	0.29856751	4
5	1.43562933	0.69655863	5.80839102	4.04588490	0.17216472	0.24716472	5
6	1.54330153	0.64796152	7.24402034	4.69384642	0.13804489	0.21304489	6
7	1.65904914	0.60275490	8.78732187	5.29660132	0.11380032	0.18880032	7
8	1.78347783	0.56070223	10.44637101	5.85730355	0.09572702	0.17072702	8
9	1.91723866	0.52158347	12.22984883	6.37888703	0.08176716	0.15676716	9
10	2.06103156	0.48519393	14.14708750	6.86408096	0.07068593	0.14568593	10
11	2.21560893	0.45134319	16.20811906	7.31542415	0.06169747	0.13669747	11
12	2.38177960	0.41985413	18.42372799	7.73527827	0.05427783	0.12927783	12
13	2.56041307	0.39056198	20.80550759	8.12584026	0.04806420	0.12306420	13
14	2.75244405	0.36331347	23.36592066	8.48915373	0.04279737	0.11779737	14
15	2.95887735	0.33796602	26.11836470	8.82711975	0.03828724	0.11328724	15
16	3.18079315	0.31438699	29.07724206	9.14150674	0.03439116	0.10939116	16
17	3.41935264	0.29245302	32.25803521	9.43395976	0.03100003	0.10600003	17
18	3.67580409	0.27204932	35.67738785	9.70600908	0.02802896	0.10302896	18
19	3.95148940	0.25306913	39.35319194	9.95907821	0.02541090	0.10041090	19
20	4.24785110	0.23541315	43.30468134	10.19449136	0.02309219	0.09809219	20
21	4.56643993	0.21898897	47.55253244	10.41348033	0.02102937	0.09602937	21
22	4.90892293	0.20371067	52.11897237	10.61719101	0.01918687	0.09418687	22
23	5.27709215	0.18949830	57.02789530	10.80668931	0.01753528	0.09253528	23
24	5.67287406	0.17627749	62.30498744	10.98296680	0.01605008	0.09105008	24
25	6.09833961	0.16397906	67.97786150	11.14694586	0.01471067	0.08971067	25
26	6.55571508	0.15253866	74.07620112	11.29948452	0.01349961	0.08849961	26
27	7.04739371	0.14189643	80.63191620	11.44138095	0.01240204	0.08740204	27
28	7.57594824	0.13199668	87.67930991	11.57337763	0.01140520	0.08640520	28
29	8.14414436	0.12278761	95.25525816	11.69616524	0.01049811	0.08549811	29
30	8.75495519	0.11422103	103.39940252	11.81038627	0.00967124	0.08467124	30
31	9.41157683	0.10625212	112.15435771	11.91663839	0.00891628	0.08391628	31
32	10.11744509	0.09883918	121.56593454	12.01547757	0.00822599	0.08322599	32
33	10.87625347	0.09194343	131.68337963	12.10742099	0.00759397	0.08259397	33
34	11.69197248	0.08552877	142.55963310	12.19294976	0.00701461	0.08201461	34
35	12.56887042	0.07956164	154.25160558	12.27251141	0.00648291	0.08148291	35
36	13.51153570	0.07401083	166.82047600	12.34652224	0.00599447	0.08099447	36
37	14.52490088	0.06884729	180.33201170	12.41536952	0.00554533	0.08054533	37
38	15.61426844	0.06404399	194.85691258	12.47941351	0.00513197	0.08013197	38
39	16.78533858	0.05957580	210.47118102	12.53898931	0.00475124	0.07975124	39
40	18.04423897	0.05541935	227.25651960	12.59440866	0.00440031	0.07940031	40
41	19.39755689	0.05155288	245.30075857	12.64596155	0.00407663	0.07907663	41
42	20.85237366	0.04795617	264.69831546	12.69391772	0.00377789	0.07877789	42
43	22.41630168	0.04461039	285.55068912	12.73852811	0.00350201	0.07850201	43
44	24.09752431	0.04149804	307.96699080	12.78002615	0.00324710	0.07824710	44
45	25.90483863	0.03860283	332.06451511	12.81862898	0.00301146	0.07801146	45
46	27.84770153	0.03590961	357.96935375	12.85453858	0.00279354	0.07779354	46
47	29.93627915	0.03340428	385.81705528	12.88794287	0.00259190	0.07759190	47
48	32.18150008	0.03107375	415.75333442	12.91901662	0.00240527	0.07740527	48
49	34.59511259	0.02890582	447.93483451	12.94792244	0.00223247	0.07723247	49
50	37.18974603	0.02688913	482.52994709	12.97481157	0.00207241	0.07707241	50
80	325.59456000	0.00307130	4327.92746666	13.29238261	0.00023106	0.07523106	80
100	1383.07720993	0.00072303	18427.69613233	13.32369299	0.00005427	0.07505427	100
120	5875.10604790	0.00017021	78321.41397195	13.33106387	0.00001277	0.07501277	120

Rate 8%	C Compound Amount	D Present Value	E Amount of Annuity	F Present Value of Annuity	G Sinking Fund	H Amortization	
n	$(1+i)^n$	$(1+i)^{-n}$	$s_{\overline{n}\rvert i}$	$a_{\overline{n}\rvert i}$	$1/s_{\overline{n}\rvert i}$	$1/a_{\overline{n}\rvert i}$	n
1	1.08000000	0.92592593	1.00000000	0.92592593	1.00000000	1.08000000	1
2	1.16640000	0.85733882	2.08000000	1.78326475	0.48076923	0.56076923	2
3	1.25971200	0.79383224	3.24640000	2.57709699	0.30803351	0.38803351	3
4	1.36048896	0.73502985	4.50611200	3.31212684	0.22192080	0.30192080	4
5	1.46932808	0.68058320	5.86660096	3.99271004	0.17045645	0.25045645	5
6	1.58687432	0.63016963	7.33592904	4.62287966	0.13631539	0.21631539	6
7	1.71382427	0.58349040	8.92280336	5.20637006	0.11207240	0.19207240	7
8	1.85093021	0.54026888	10.63662763	5.74663894	0.09401476	0.17401476	8
9	1.99900463	0.50024897	12.48755784	6.24688791	0.08007971	0.16007971	9
10	2.15892500	0.46319349	14.48656247	6.71008140	0.06902949	0.14902949	10
11	2.33163900	0.42888286	16.64548746	7.13896426	0.06007634	0.14007634	11
12	2.51817012	0.39711376	18.97712646	7.53607802	0.05269502	0.13269502	12
13	2.71962373	0.36769792	21.49529658	7.90377594	0.04652181	0.12652181	13
14	2.93719362	0.34046104	24.21492030	8.24423698	0.04129685	0.12129685	14
15	3.17216911	0.31524170	27.15211393	8.55947869	0.03682954	0.11682954	15
16	3.42594264	0.29189047	30.32428304	8.85136916	0.03297687	0.11297687	16
17	3.70001805	0.27026895	33.75022569	9.12163811	0.02962943	0.10962943	17
18	3.99601950	0.25024903	37.45024374	9.37188714	0.02670210	0.10670210	18
19	4.31570106	0.23171206	41.44626324	9.60359920	0.02412763	0.10412763	19
20	4.66095714	0.21454821	45.76196430	9.81814741	0.02185221	0.10185221	20
21	5.03383372	0.19865575	50.42292144	10.01680316	0.01983225	0.09983225	21
22	5.43654041	0.18394051	55.45675516	10.20074366	0.01803207	0.09803207	22
23	5.87146365	0.17031528	60.89329557	10.37105895	0.01642217	0.09642217	23
24	6.34118074	0.15769934	66.76475922	10.52875828	0.01497796	0.09497796	24
25	6.84847520	0.14601790	73.10593995	10.67477619	0.01367878	0.09367878	25
26	7.39635321	0.13520176	79.95441515	10.80997795	0.01250713	0.09250713	26
27	7.98806147	0.12518682	87.35076836	10.93516477	0.01144810	0.09144810	27
28	8.62710639	0.11591372	95.33882983	11.05107849	0.01048891	0.09048891	28
29	9.31727490	0.10732752	103.96593622	11.15840601	0.00961854	0.08961854	29
30	10.06265689	0.09937733	113.28321111	11.25778334	0.00882743	0.08882743	30
31	10.86766944	0.09201605	123.34586800	11.34979939	0.00810728	0.08810728	31
32	11.73708300	0.08520005	134.21353744	11.43499944	0.00745081	0.08745081	32
33	12.67604964	0.07888893	145.95062044	11.51388837	0.00685163	0.08685163	33
34	13.69013361	0.07304531	158.62667007	11.58693367	0.00630411	0.08630411	34
35	14.78534429	0.06763454	172.31680368	11.65456822	0.00580326	0.08580326	35
36	15.96817184	0.06262458	187.10214797	11.71719279	0.00534467	0.08534467	36
37	17.24562558	0.05798572	203.07031981	11.77517851	0.00492440	0.08492440	37
38	18.62527563	0.05369048	220.31594540	11.82886899	0.00453894	0.08453894	38
39	20.11529768	0.04971341	238.94122103	11.87858240	0.00418513	0.08418513	39
40	21.72452150	0.04603093	259.05651871	11.92461333	0.00386016	0.08386016	40
41	23.46248322	0.04262123	280.78104021	11.96723457	0.00356149	0.08356149	41
42	25.33948187	0.03946411	304.24352342	12.00669867	0.00328684	0.08328684	42
43	27.36664042	0.03654084	329.58300530	12.04323951	0.00303414	0.08303414	43
44	29.55597166	0.03383411	356.94964572	12.07707362	0.00280152	0.08280152	44
45	31.92044939	0.03132788	386.50561738	12.10840150	0.00258728	0.08258728	45
46	34.47408534	0.02900730	418.42606677	12.13740880	0.00238991	0.08238991	46
47	37.23201217	0.02685861	452.90015211	12.16426741	0.00220799	0.08220799	47
48	40.21057314	0.02486908	490.13216428	12.18913649	0.00204027	0.08204027	48
49	43.42741899	0.02302693	530.34273742	12.21216341	0.00188557	0.08188557	49
50	46.90161251	0.02132123	573.77015642	12.23348464	0.00174286	0.08174286	50
80	471.95483426	0.00211885	5886.93542831	12.47351441	0.00016987	0.08016987	80
100	2199.76125634	0.00045459	27484.51570427	12.49431757	0.00003638	0.08003638	100

Rate 8½%	C Compound Amount	D Present Value	E Amount of Annuity	F Present Value of Annuity	G Sinking Fund	H Amortization	
n	$(1 + i)^n$	$(1 + i)^{-n}$	$s_{\overline{n}\rvert i}$	$a_{\overline{n}\rvert i}$	$1/s_{\overline{n}\rvert i}$	$1/a_{\overline{n}\rvert i}$	n
1	1.08500000	0.92165899	1.00000000	0.92165899	1.00000000	1.08500000	1
2	1.17722500	0.84945529	2.08500000	1.77111427	0.47961631	0.56461631	2
3	1.27728913	0.78290810	3.26222500	2.55402237	0.30653925	0.39153925	3
4	1.38585870	0.72157428	4.53951413	3.27559666	0.22028789	0.30528789	4
5	1.50365669	0.66504542	5.92537283	3.94064208	0.16876575	0.25376575	5
6	1.63146751	0.61294509	7.42902952	4.55358717	0.13460708	0.21960708	6
7	1.77014225	0.56492635	9.06049702	5.11851352	0.11036922	0.19536922	7
8	1.92060434	0.52066945	10.83063927	5.63918297	0.09233065	0.17733065	8
9	2.08385571	0.47987968	12.75124361	6.11906264	0.07842372	0.16342372	9
10	2.26098344	0.44228542	14.83509932	6.56134806	0.06740771	0.15240771	10
11	2.45316703	0.40763633	17.09608276	6.96898439	0.05849293	0.14349293	11
12	2.66168623	0.37570168	19.54924979	7.34468607	0.05115286	0.13615286	12
13	2.88792956	0.34626883	22.21093603	7.69095490	0.04502287	0.13002287	13
14	3.13340357	0.31914178	25.09886559	8.01009668	0.03984244	0.12484244	14
15	3.39974288	0.29413989	28.23226916	8.30423658	0.03542046	0.12042046	15
16	3.68872102	0.27109667	31.63201204	8.57533325	0.03161354	0.11661354	16
17	4.00226231	0.24985869	35.32073306	8.82519194	0.02831198	0.11331198	17
18	4.34245461	0.23028450	39.32299538	9.05547644	0.02543041	0.11043041	18
19	4.71156325	0.21224378	43.66544998	9.26772022	0.02290140	0.10790140	19
20	5.11204612	0.19561639	48.37701323	9.46333661	0.02067097	0.10567097	20
21	5.54657005	0.18029160	53.48905936	9.64362821	0.01869541	0.10369541	21
22	6.01802850	0.16616738	59.03562940	9.80979559	0.01693892	0.10193892	22
23	6.52956092	0.15314965	65.05365790	9.96294524	0.01537193	0.10037193	23
24	7.08457360	0.14115176	71.58321882	10.10409700	0.01396975	0.09896975	24
25	7.68676236	0.13009378	78.66779242	10.23419078	0.01271168	0.09771168	25
26	8.34013716	0.11990210	86.35455478	10.35409288	0.01158017	0.09658017	26
27	9.04904881	0.11050885	94.69469193	10.46460174	0.01056025	0.09556025	27
28	9.81821796	0.10185148	103.74374075	10.56645321	0.00963914	0.09463914	28
29	10.65276649	0.09387233	113.56195871	10.66032554	0.00880577	0.09380577	29
30	11.55825164	0.08651828	124.21472520	10.74684382	0.00805058	0.09305058	30
31	12.54070303	0.07974035	135.77297684	10.82658416	0.00736524	0.09236524	31
32	13.60666279	0.07349341	148.31367987	10.90007757	0.00674247	0.09174247	32
33	14.76322913	0.06773586	161.92034266	10.96781343	0.00617588	0.09117588	33
34	16.01810360	0.06242936	176.68357179	11.03024279	0.00565984	0.09065984	34
35	17.37964241	0.05753858	192.70167539	11.08778137	0.00518937	0.09018937	35
36	18.85691201	0.05303095	210.08131780	11.14081233	0.00476006	0.08976006	36
37	20.45974953	0.04887645	228.93822981	11.18968878	0.00436799	0.08936799	37
38	22.19882824	0.04504742	249.39797935	11.23473620	0.00400966	0.08900966	38
39	24.08572865	0.04151836	271.59680759	11.27625457	0.00368193	0.08868193	39
40	26.13301558	0.03826577	295.68253624	11.31452034	0.00338201	0.08838201	40
41	28.35432190	0.03526799	321.81555182	11.34978833	0.00310737	0.08810737	41
42	30.76443927	0.03250506	350.16987372	11.38229339	0.00285576	0.08785576	42
43	33.37941660	0.02995858	380.93431299	11.41225197	0.00262512	0.08762512	43
44	36.21666702	0.02761160	414.31372959	11.43986357	0.00241363	0.08741363	44
45	39.29508371	0.02544848	450.53039661	11.46531205	0.00221961	0.08721961	45
46	42.63516583	0.02345482	489.82548032	11.48876686	0.00204154	0.08704154	46
47	46.25915492	0.02161734	532.46064615	11.51038420	0.00187807	0.08687807	47
48	50.19118309	0.01992382	578.71980107	11.53030802	0.00172795	0.08672795	48
49	54.45743365	0.01836297	628.91098416	11.54867099	0.00159005	0.08659005	49
50	59.08631551	0.01692439	683.36841782	11.56559538	0.00146334	0.08646334	50
80	682.93450332	0.00146427	8022.75886259	11.74747919	0.00012465	0.08512465	80
100	3491.19268107	0.00028644	41061.09036551	11.76133606	0.00002435	0.08502435	100

Rate 9%	C Compound Amount	D Present Value	E Amount of Annuity	F Present Value of Annuity	G Sinking Fund	H Amortization	
n	$(1+i)^n$	$(1+i)^{-n}$	$S_{\overline{n}\rceil i}$	$A_{\overline{n}\rceil i}$	$1/S_{\overline{n}\rceil i}$	$1/A_{\overline{n}\rceil i}$	n
1	1.09000000	0.91743119	1.00000000	0.91743119	1.00000000	1.09000000	1
2	1.18810000	0.84167999	2.09000000	1.75911119	0.47846890	0.56846890	2
3	1.29502900	0.77218348	3.27810000	2.53129467	0.30505476	0.39505476	3
4	1.41158161	0.70842521	4.57312900	3.23971988	0.21866866	0.30866866	4
5	1.53862395	0.64993139	5.98471061	3.88965126	0.16709246	0.25709246	5
6	1.67710011	0.59626733	7.52333456	4.48591859	0.13291978	0.22291978	6
7	1.82803912	0.54703424	9.20043468	5.03295284	0.10869052	0.19869052	7
8	1.99256264	0.50186628	11.02847380	5.53481911	0.09067438	0.18067438	8
9	2.17189328	0.46042778	13.02103644	5.99524689	0.07679880	0.16679880	9
10	2.36736367	0.42241081	15.19292972	6.41765770	0.06582009	0.15582009	10
11	2.58042641	0.38753285	17.56029339	6.80519055	0.05694666	0.14694666	11
12	2.81266478	0.35553473	20.14071980	7.16072528	0.04965066	0.13965066	12
13	3.06580461	0.32617865	22.95338458	7.48690392	0.04356656	0.13356656	13
14	3.34172703	0.29924647	26.01918919	7.78615039	0.03843317	0.12843317	14
15	3.64248246	0.27453804	29.36091622	8.06068843	0.03405888	0.12405888	15
16	3.97030588	0.25186976	33.00339868	8.31255819	0.03029991	0.12029991	16
17	4.32763341	0.23107318	36.97370456	8.54363137	0.02704625	0.11704625	17
18	4.71712042	0.21199374	41.30133797	8.75562511	0.02421229	0.11421229	18
19	5.14166125	0.19448967	46.01845839	8.95011478	0.02173041	0.11173041	19
20	5.60441077	0.17843089	51.16011964	9.12854567	0.01954648	0.10954648	20
21	6.10880774	0.16369806	56.76453041	9.29224373	0.01761663	0.10761663	21
22	6.65860043	0.15018171	62.87333815	9.44242544	0.01590499	0.10590499	22
23	7.25787447	0.13778139	69.53193858	9.58020683	0.01438188	0.10438188	23
24	7.91108317	0.12640494	76.78981305	9.70661177	0.01302256	0.10302256	24
25	8.62308066	0.11596784	84.70089623	9.82257960	0.01180625	0.10180625	25
26	9.39915792	0.10639251	93.32397689	9.92897211	0.01071536	0.10071536	26
27	10.24508213	0.09760781	102.72313481	10.02657992	0.00973491	0.09973491	27
28	11.16713952	0.08954845	112.96821694	10.11612837	0.00885205	0.09885205	28
29	12.17218208	0.08215454	124.13535646	10.19828291	0.00805572	0.09805572	29
30	13.26767847	0.07537114	136.30753855	10.27365404	0.00733635	0.09733635	30
31	14.46176953	0.06914783	149.57521702	10.34280187	0.00668560	0.09668560	31
32	15.76332879	0.06343838	164.03698655	10.40624025	0.00609619	0.09609619	32
33	17.18202838	0.05820035	179.80031534	10.46444060	0.00556173	0.09556173	33
34	18.72841093	0.05339481	196.98234372	10.51783541	0.00507660	0.09507660	34
35	20.41396792	0.04898607	215.71075465	10.56682148	0.00463584	0.09463584	35
36	22.25122503	0.04494135	236.12472257	10.61176282	0.00423505	0.09423505	36
37	24.25383528	0.04123059	258.37594760	10.65299342	0.00387033	0.09387033	37
38	26.43668046	0.03782623	282.62978288	10.69081965	0.00353820	0.09353820	38
39	28.81598170	0.03470296	309.06646334	10.72552261	0.00323555	0.09323555	39
40	31.40942005	0.03183758	337.88244504	10.75736020	0.00295961	0.09295961	40
41	34.23626786	0.02920879	369.29186510	10.78656899	0.00270789	0.09270789	41
42	37.31753197	0.02679706	403.52813296	10.81336604	0.00247814	0.09247814	42
43	40.67610984	0.02458446	440.84566492	10.83795050	0.00226837	0.09226837	43
44	44.33695973	0.02255455	481.52177477	10.86050504	0.00207675	0.09207675	44
45	48.32728610	0.02069224	525.85873450	10.88119729	0.00190165	0.09190165	45
46	52.67674185	0.01898371	574.18602060	10.90018100	0.00174160	0.09174160	46
47	57.41764862	0.01741625	626.86276245	10.91759725	0.00159525	0.09159525	47
48	62.58523700	0.01597821	684.28041107	10.93357546	0.00146139	0.09146139	48
49	68.21790833	0.01465891	746.86564807	10.94823436	0.00133893	0.09133893	49
50	74.35752008	0.01344854	815.08355640	10.96168290	0.00122687	0.09122687	50
80	986.55166813	0.00101363	10950.57409031	11.09984854	0.00009132	0.09009132	80
100	5529.04079183	0.00018086	61422.67546473	11.10910152	0.00001628	0.09001628	100

Rate 9½%	C Compound Amount	D Present Value	E Amount of Annuity	F Present Value of Annuity	G Sinking Fund	H Amortization	
n	$(1+i)^n$	$(1+i)^{-n}$	$S_{\overline{n}\|i}$	$A_{\overline{n}\|i}$	$1/S_{\overline{n}\|i}$	$1/A_{\overline{n}\|i}$	n
1	1.09500000	0.91324201	1.00000000	0.91324201	1.00000000	1.09500000	1
2	1.19902500	0.83401097	2.09500000	1.74725298	0.47732697	0.57232697	2
3	1.31293237	0.76165385	3.29402500	2.50890683	0.30357997	0.39857997	3
4	1.43766095	0.69557429	4.60695737	3.20448112	0.21706300	0.31206300	4
5	1.57423874	0.63522767	6.04461833	3.83970879	0.16543642	0.26043642	5
6	1.72379142	0.58011659	7.61885707	4.41982538	0.13125328	0.22625328	6
7	1.88755161	0.52978684	9.34264849	4.94961222	0.10703603	0.20203603	7
8	2.06686901	0.48382360	11.23020009	5.43343581	0.08904561	0.18404561	8
9	2.26322156	0.44184803	13.29706910	5.87528385	0.07520454	0.17020454	9
10	2.47822761	0.40351419	15.56029067	6.27879803	0.06426615	0.15926615	10
11	2.71365924	0.36850611	18.03851828	6.64730414	0.05543693	0.15043693	11
12	2.97145686	0.33653526	20.75217752	6.98383940	0.04818771	0.14318771	12
13	3.25374527	0.30733813	23.72363438	7.29117753	0.04215206	0.13715206	13
14	3.56285107	0.28067410	26.97737965	7.57185163	0.03706809	0.13206809	14
15	3.90132192	0.25632337	30.54023072	7.82817500	0.03274370	0.12774370	15
16	4.27194750	0.23408527	34.44155263	8.06226028	0.02903470	0.12403470	16
17	4.67778251	0.21377651	38.71350013	8.27603678	0.02583078	0.12083078	17
18	5.12217185	0.19522969	43.39128265	8.47126647	0.02304610	0.11804610	18
19	5.60877818	0.17829195	48.51345450	8.64955842	0.02061284	0.11561284	19
20	6.14161210	0.16282370	54.12223267	8.81238212	0.01847670	0.11347670	20
21	6.72506525	0.14869744	60.26384478	8.96107956	0.01659370	0.11159370	21
22	7.36394645	0.13579675	66.98891003	9.09687631	0.01492784	0.10992784	22
23	8.06352137	0.12401530	74.35285649	9.22089161	0.01344938	0.10844938	23
24	8.82955590	0.11325598	82.41637785	9.33414759	0.01213351	0.10713351	24
25	9.66836371	0.10343012	91.24593375	9.43757770	0.01095939	0.10595939	25
26	10.58685826	0.09445673	100.91429745	9.53203443	0.00990940	0.10490940	26
27	11.59260979	0.08626185	111.50115571	9.61829629	0.00896852	0.10396852	27
28	12.69390772	0.07877795	123.09376551	9.69707423	0.00812389	0.10312389	28
29	13.89982896	0.07194333	135.78767323	9.76901756	0.00736444	0.10236444	29
30	15.22031271	0.06570167	149.68750218	9.83471924	0.00668058	0.10168058	30
31	16.66624241	0.06000153	164.90781489	9.89472076	0.00606399	0.10106399	31
32	18.24953544	0.05479592	181.57405731	9.94951668	0.00550739	0.10050739	32
33	19.98324131	0.05004193	199.82359275	9.99955861	0.00500441	0.10000441	33
34	21.88164924	0.04570039	219.80683406	10.04525901	0.00454945	0.09954945	34
35	23.96040591	0.04173552	241.68848330	10.08699453	0.00413756	0.09913756	35
36	26.23664448	0.03811463	265.64888921	10.12510916	0.00376437	0.09876437	36
37	28.72912570	0.03480788	291.88553369	10.15991704	0.00342600	0.09842600	37
38	31.45839264	0.03178802	320.61465939	10.19170506	0.00311901	0.09811901	38
39	34.44693994	0.02903015	352.07305203	10.22073521	0.00284032	0.09784032	39
40	37.71939924	0.02651156	386.51999197	10.24724677	0.00258719	0.09758719	40
41	41.30274216	0.02421147	424.23939121	10.27145824	0.00235716	0.09735716	41
42	45.22650267	0.02211093	465.54213337	10.29356917	0.00214803	0.09714803	42
43	49.52302042	0.02019263	510.76863604	10.31376180	0.00195783	0.09695783	43
44	54.22770736	0.01844076	560.29165647	10.33220255	0.00178478	0.09678478	44
45	59.37933956	0.01684087	614.51936383	10.34904343	0.00162729	0.09662729	45
46	65.02037682	0.01537979	673.89870340	10.36442322	0.00148390	0.09648390	46
47	71.19731262	0.01404547	738.91908022	10.37846870	0.00135333	0.09635333	47
48	77.96105732	0.01282692	810.11639284	10.39129561	0.00123439	0.09623439	48
49	85.36735777	0.01171408	888.07745016	10.40300969	0.00112603	0.09612603	49
50	93.47725675	0.01069779	973.44480793	10.41370748	0.00102728	0.09602728	50
80	1422.75307883	0.00070286	14965.82188238	10.51891724	0.00006682	0.09506682	80
100	8737.99753007	0.00011444	91968.39505341	10.52511113	0.00001087	0.09501087	100

Rate 10%	C Compound Amount	D Present Value	E Amount of Annuity	F Present Value of Annuity	G Sinking Fund	H Amortization	
n	$(1 + i)^n$	$(1 + i)^{-n}$	$s_{\overline{n}\mid i}$	$a_{\overline{n}\mid i}$	$1/s_{\overline{n}\mid i}$	$1/a_{\overline{n}\mid i}$	n
1	1.10000000	0.90909091	1.00000000	0.90909091	1.00000000	1.10000000	1
2	1.21000000	0.82644628	2.10000000	1.73553719	0.47619048	0.57619048	2
3	1.33100000	0.75131480	3.31000000	2.48685199	0.30211480	0.40211480	3
4	1.46410000	0.68301346	4.64100000	3.16986545	0.21547080	0.31547080	4
5	1.61051000	0.62092132	6.10510000	3.79078677	0.16379748	0.26379748	5
6	1.77156100	0.56447393	7.71561000	4.35526070	0.12960738	0.22960738	6
7	1.94871710	0.51315812	9.48717100	4.86841882	0.10540550	0.20540550	7
8	2.14358881	0.46650738	11.43588810	5.33492620	0.08744402	0.18744402	8
9	2.35794769	0.42409762	13.57947691	5.75902382	0.07364054	0.17364054	9
10	2.59374246	0.38554329	15.93742460	6.14456711	0.06274539	0.16274539	10
11	2.85311671	0.35049390	18.53116706	6.49506101	0.05396314	0.15396314	11
12	3.13842838	0.31863082	21.38428377	6.81369182	0.04676332	0.14676332	12
13	3.45227121	0.28966438	24.52271214	7.10335620	0.04077852	0.14077852	13
14	3.79749834	0.26333125	27.97498336	7.36668746	0.03574622	0.13574622	14
15	4.17724817	0.23939205	31.77248169	7.60607951	0.03147378	0.13147378	15
16	4.59497299	0.21762914	35.94972986	7.82370864	0.02781662	0.12781662	16
17	5.05447028	0.19784467	40.54470285	8.02155331	0.02466413	0.12466413	17
18	5.55991731	0.17985879	45.59917313	8.20141210	0.02193022	0.12193022	18
19	6.11590904	0.16350799	51.15909045	8.36492009	0.01954687	0.11954687	19
20	6.72749995	0.14864363	57.27499949	8.51356372	0.01745962	0.11745962	20
21	7.40024994	0.13513057	64.00249944	8.64869429	0.01562439	0.11562439	21
22	8.14027494	0.12284597	71.40274939	8.77154026	0.01400506	0.11400506	22
23	8.95430243	0.11167816	79.54302433	8.88321842	0.01257181	0.11257181	23
24	9.84973268	0.10152560	88.49732676	8.98474402	0.01129978	0.11129978	24
25	10.83470594	0.09229600	98.34705943	9.07704002	0.01016807	0.11016807	25
26	11.91817654	0.08390545	109.18176538	9.16094547	0.00915904	0.10915904	26
27	13.10999419	0.07627768	121.09994191	9.23722316	0.00825764	0.10825764	27
28	14.42099361	0.06934335	134.20993611	9.30656651	0.00745101	0.10745101	28
29	15.86309297	0.06303941	148.63092972	9.36960591	0.00672807	0.10672807	29
30	17.44940227	0.05730855	164.49402269	9.42691447	0.00607925	0.10607925	30
31	19.19434250	0.05209868	181.94342496	9.47901315	0.00549621	0.10549621	31
32	21.11377675	0.04736244	201.13776745	9.52637559	0.00497172	0.10497172	32
33	23.22515442	0.04305676	222.25154420	9.56943236	0.00449941	0.10449941	33
34	25.54766986	0.03914251	245.47669862	9.60857487	0.00407371	0.10407371	34
35	28.10243685	0.03558410	271.02436848	9.64415897	0.00368971	0.10368971	35
36	30.91268053	0.03234918	299.12680533	9.67650816	0.00334306	0.10334306	36
37	34.00394859	0.02940835	330.03948586	9.70591651	0.00302994	0.10302994	37
38	37.40434344	0.02673486	364.04343445	9.73265137	0.00274692	0.10274692	38
39	41.14477779	0.02430442	401.44777789	9.75695579	0.00249098	0.10249098	39
40	45.25925557	0.02209493	442.59255568	9.77905072	0.00225941	0.10225941	40
41	49.78518112	0.02008630	487.85181125	9.79913702	0.00204980	0.10204980	41
42	54.76369924	0.01826027	537.63699237	9.81739729	0.00185999	0.10185999	42
43	60.24006916	0.01660025	592.40069161	9.83399753	0.00168805	0.10168805	43
44	66.26407608	0.01509113	652.64076077	9.84908867	0.00153224	0.10153224	44
45	72.89048369	0.01371921	718.90483685	9.86280788	0.00139100	0.10139100	45
46	80.17953205	0.01247201	791.79532054	9.87527989	0.00126295	0.10126295	46
47	88.19748526	0.01133819	871.97485259	9.88661808	0.00114682	0.10114682	47
48	97.01723378	0.01030745	960.17233785	9.89692553	0.00104148	0.10104148	48
49	106.71895716	0.00937041	1057.18957163	9.90629594	0.00094590	0.10094590	49
50	117.39085288	0.00851855	1163.90852880	9.91481449	0.00085917	0.10085917	50
80	2048.40021459	0.00048819	20474.00214585	9.99511814	0.00004884	0.10004884	80

Rate 11%	C Compound Amount	D Present Value	E Amount of Annuity	F Present Value of Annuity	G Sinking Fund	H Amortization	
n	$(1+i)^n$	$(1+i)^{-n}$	$s_{\overline{n}\vert i}$	$a_{\overline{n}\vert i}$	$1/s_{\overline{n}\vert i}$	$1/a_{\overline{n}\vert i}$	n
1	1.11000000	0.90090090	1.00000000	0.90090090	1.00000000	1.11000000	1
2	1.23210000	0.81162243	2.11000000	1.71252333	0.47393365	0.58393365	2
3	1.36763100	0.73119138	3.34210000	2.44371472	0.29921307	0.40921307	3
4	1.51807041	0.65873097	4.70973100	3.10244569	0.21232635	0.32232635	4
5	1.68505816	0.59345133	6.22780141	3.69589702	0.16057031	0.27057031	5
6	1.87041455	0.53464084	7.91285957	4.23053785	0.12637656	0.23637656	6
7	2.07616015	0.48165841	9.78327412	4.71219626	0.10221527	0.21221527	7
8	2.30453777	0.43392650	11.85943427	5.14612276	0.08432105	0.19432105	8
9	2.55803692	0.39092477	14.16397204	5.53704753	0.07060166	0.18060166	9
10	2.83942099	0.35218448	16.72200896	5.88923201	0.05980143	0.16980143	10
11	3.15175729	0.31728331	19.56142995	6.20651533	0.05112101	0.16112101	11
12	3.49845060	0.28584082	22.71318724	6.49235615	0.04402729	0.15402729	12
13	3.88328016	0.25751426	26.21163784	6.74987040	0.03815099	0.14815099	13
14	4.31044098	0.23199482	30.09491800	6.98186523	0.03322820	0.14322820	14
15	4.78458949	0.20900435	34.40535898	7.19086958	0.02906524	0.13906524	15
16	5.31089433	0.18829220	39.18994847	7.37916178	0.02551675	0.13551675	16
17	5.89509271	0.16963262	44.50084281	7.54879440	0.02247148	0.13247148	17
18	6.54355291	0.15282218	50.39593551	7.70161657	0.01984287	0.12984287	18
19	7.26334373	0.13767764	56.93948842	7.83929421	0.01756250	0.12756250	19
20	8.06231154	0.12403391	64.20283215	7.96332812	0.01557564	0.12557564	20
21	8.94916581	0.11174226	72.26514368	8.07507038	0.01383793	0.12383793	21
22	9.93357404	0.10066870	81.21430949	8.17573908	0.01231310	0.12231310	22
23	11.02626719	0.09069252	91.14788353	8.26643160	0.01097118	0.12097118	23
24	12.23915658	0.08170498	102.17415072	8.34813658	0.00978721	0.11978721	24
25	13.58546380	0.07360809	114.41330730	8.42174466	0.00874024	0.11874024	25
26	15.07986482	0.06631359	127.99877110	8.48805826	0.00781258	0.11781258	26
27	16.73864995	0.05974197	143.07863592	8.54780023	0.00698916	0.11698916	27
28	18.57990145	0.05382160	159.81728587	8.60162183	0.00625715	0.11625715	28
29	20.62369061	0.04848793	178.39718732	8.65010976	0.00560547	0.11560547	29
30	22.89229657	0.04368282	199.02087793	8.69379257	0.00502460	0.11502460	30
31	25.41044919	0.03935389	221.91317450	8.73314646	0.00450627	0.11450627	31
32	28.20559861	0.03545395	247.32362369	8.76860042	0.00404329	0.11404329	32
33	31.30821445	0.03194050	275.52922230	8.80054092	0.00362938	0.11362938	33
34	34.75211804	0.02877522	306.83743675	8.82931614	0.00325905	0.11325905	34
35	38.57485103	0.02592363	341.58955480	8.85523977	0.00292749	0.11292749	35
36	42.81808464	0.02335462	380.16440582	8.87859438	0.00263044	0.11263044	36
37	47.52807395	0.02104020	422.98249046	8.89963458	0.00236416	0.11236416	37
38	52.75616209	0.01895513	470.51056441	8.91858971	0.00212535	0.11212535	38
39	58.55933991	0.01707670	523.26672650	8.93566641	0.00191107	0.11191107	39
40	65.00086731	0.01538441	581.82606641	8.95105082	0.00171873	0.11171873	40
41	72.15096271	0.01385983	646.82693372	8.96491065	0.00154601	0.11154601	41
42	80.08756861	0.01248633	718.97789643	8.97739698	0.00139086	0.11139086	42
43	88.89720115	0.01124895	799.06546504	8.98864593	0.00125146	0.11125146	43
44	98.67589328	0.01013419	887.96266619	8.99878011	0.00112617	0.11112617	44
45	109.53024154	0.00912990	986.63855947	9.00791001	0.00101354	0.11101354	45
46	121.57856811	0.00822513	1096.16880101	9.01613515	0.00091227	0.11091227	46
47	134.95221060	0.00741003	1217.74736912	9.02354518	0.00082119	0.11082119	47
48	149.79695377	0.00667570	1352.69957973	9.03022088	0.00073926	0.11073926	48
49	166.27461868	0.00601415	1502.49653350	9.03623503	0.00066556	0.11066556	49
50	184.56482674	0.00541815	1668.77115218	9.04165318	0.00059924	0.11059924	50
80	4225.11275048	0.00023668	38401.02500437	9.08875745	0.00002604	0.11002604	80

Rate 12%	C Compound Amount	D Present Value	E Amount of Annuity	F Present Value of Annuity	G Sinking Fund	H Amortization	
n	$(1+i)^n$	$(1+i)^{-n}$	$S_{\overline{n}\rvert i}$	$A_{\overline{n}\rvert i}$	$1/S_{\overline{n}\rvert i}$	$1/A_{\overline{n}\rvert i}$	n
1	1.12000000	0.89285714	1.00000000	0.89285714	1.00000000	1.12000000	1
2	1.25440000	0.79719388	2.12000000	1.69005102	0.47169811	0.59169811	2
3	1.40492800	0.71178025	3.37440000	2.40183127	0.29634898	0.41634898	3
4	1.57351936	0.63551808	4.77932800	3.03734935	0.20923444	0.32923444	4
5	1.76234168	0.56742686	6.35284736	3.60477620	0.15740973	0.27740973	5
6	1.97382269	0.50663112	8.11518904	4.11140732	0.12322572	0.24322572	6
7	2.21068141	0.45234922	10.08901173	4.56375654	0.09911774	0.21911774	7
8	2.47596318	0.40388323	12.29969314	4.96763977	0.08130284	0.20130284	8
9	2.77307876	0.36061002	14.77565631	5.32824979	0.06767889	0.18767889	9
10	3.10584821	0.32197324	17.54873507	5.65022303	0.05698416	0.17698416	10
11	3.47854999	0.28747610	20.65458328	5.93769913	0.04841540	0.16841540	11
12	3.89597599	0.25667509	24.13313327	6.19437423	0.04143681	0.16143681	12
13	4.36349311	0.22917419	28.02910926	6.42354842	0.03567720	0.15567720	13
14	4.88711229	0.20461981	32.39260238	6.62816823	0.03087125	0.15087125	14
15	5.47356576	0.18269626	37.27971466	6.81086449	0.02682424	0.14682424	15
16	6.13039365	0.16312166	42.75328042	6.97398615	0.02339002	0.14339002	16
17	6.86604089	0.14564434	48.88367407	7.11963049	0.02045673	0.14045673	17
18	7.68996580	0.13003959	55.74971496	7.24967008	0.01793731	0.13793731	18
19	8.61276169	0.11610678	63.43968075	7.36577686	0.01576300	0.13576300	19
20	9.64629309	0.10366677	72.05244244	7.46944362	0.01387878	0.13387878	20
21	10.80384826	0.09255961	81.69873554	7.56200324	0.01224009	0.13224009	21
22	12.10031006	0.08264251	92.50258380	7.64464575	0.01081051	0.13081051	22
23	13.55234726	0.07378796	104.60289386	7.71843370	0.00955996	0.12955996	23
24	15.17862893	0.06588210	118.15524112	7.78431581	0.00846344	0.12846344	24
25	17.00006441	0.05882331	133.33387006	7.84313911	0.00749997	0.12749997	25
26	19.04007214	0.05252081	150.33393446	7.89565992	0.00665186	0.12665186	26
27	21.32488079	0.04689358	169.37400660	7.94255350	0.00590409	0.12590409	27
28	23.88386649	0.04186927	190.69888739	7.98442277	0.00524387	0.12524387	28
29	26.74993047	0.03738327	214.58275388	8.02180604	0.00466021	0.12466021	29
30	29.95992212	0.03337792	241.33268434	8.05518397	0.00414366	0.12414366	30
31	33.55511278	0.02980172	271.29260646	8.08498569	0.00368606	0.12368606	31
32	37.58172631	0.02660868	304.84771924	8.11159436	0.00328033	0.12328033	32
33	42.09153347	0.02375775	342.42944555	8.13535211	0.00292031	0.12292031	33
34	47.14251748	0.02121227	384.52097901	8.15656438	0.00260064	0.12260064	34
35	52.79961958	0.01893953	431.66349649	8.17550391	0.00231662	0.12231662	35
36	59.13557393	0.01691029	484.46311607	8.19241421	0.00206414	0.12206414	36
37	66.23184280	0.01509848	543.59869000	8.20751269	0.00183959	0.12183959	37
38	74.17966394	0.01348078	609.83053280	8.22099347	0.00163980	0.12163980	38
39	83.08122361	0.01203641	684.01019674	8.23302988	0.00146197	0.12146197	39
40	93.05097044	0.01074680	767.09142034	8.24377668	0.00130363	0.12130363	40
41	104.21708689	0.00959536	860.14239079	8.25337204	0.00116260	0.12116260	41
42	116.72313732	0.00856728	964.35947768	8.26193932	0.00103696	0.12103696	42
43	130.72991380	0.00764936	1081.08261500	8.26958868	0.00092500	0.12092500	43
44	146.41750346	0.00682978	1211.81252880	8.27641846	0.00082521	0.12082521	44
45	163.98760387	0.00609802	1358.23003226	8.28251648	0.00073625	0.12073625	45
46	183.66611634	0.00544466	1522.21763613	8.28796115	0.00065694	0.12065694	46
47	205.70605030	0.00486131	1705.88375247	8.29282245	0.00058621	0.12058621	47
48	230.39077633	0.00434045	1911.58980276	8.29716290	0.00052312	0.12052312	48
49	258.03766949	0.00387540	2141.98057909	8.30103831	0.00046686	0.12046686	49
50	289.00218983	0.00346018	2400.01824858	8.30449849	0.00041666	0.12041666	50
80	8658.48310008	0.00011549	72145.69250066	8.33237089	0.00001386	0.12001386	80

Rate 13%	C Compound Amount	D Present Value	E Amount of Annuity	F Present Value of Annuity	G Sinking Fund	H Amortization	
n	$(1+i)^n$	$(1+i)^{-n}$	$S_{\overline{n}\rceil i}$	$A_{\overline{n}\rceil i}$	$1/S_{\overline{n}\rceil i}$	$1/A_{\overline{n}\rceil i}$	n
1	1.13000000	0.88495575	1.00000000	0.88495575	1.00000000	1.13000000	1
2	1.27690000	0.78314668	2.13000000	1.66810244	0.46948357	0.59948357	2
3	1.44289700	0.69305016	3.40690000	2.36115260	0.29352197	0.42352197	3
4	1.63047361	0.61331873	4.84979700	2.97447133	0.20619420	0.33619420	4
5	1.84243518	0.54275994	6.48027061	3.51723126	0.15431454	0.28431454	5
6	2.08195175	0.48031853	8.32270579	3.99754979	0.12015323	0.25015323	6
7	2.35260548	0.42506064	10.40465754	4.42261043	0.09611080	0.22611080	7
8	2.65844419	0.37615986	12.75726302	4.79877029	0.07838672	0.20838672	8
9	3.00404194	0.33288483	15.41570722	5.13165513	0.06486890	0.19486890	9
10	3.39456739	0.29458835	18.41974915	5.42624348	0.05428956	0.18428956	10
11	3.83586115	0.26069765	21.81431654	5.68694113	0.04584145	0.17584145	11
12	4.33452310	0.23070589	25.65017769	5.91764702	0.03898608	0.16898608	12
13	4.89801110	0.20416450	29.98470079	6.12181152	0.03335034	0.16335034	13
14	5.53475255	0.18067655	34.88271190	6.30248807	0.02866750	0.15866750	14
15	6.25427038	0.15989075	40.41746444	6.46237882	0.02474178	0.15474178	15
16	7.06732553	0.14149624	46.67173482	6.60387506	0.02142624	0.15142624	16
17	7.98607785	0.12521791	53.73906035	6.72909298	0.01860844	0.14860844	17
18	9.02426797	0.11081231	61.72513819	6.83990529	0.01620085	0.14620085	18
19	10.19742280	0.09806399	70.74940616	6.93796928	0.01413439	0.14413439	19
20	11.52308776	0.08678229	80.94682896	7.02475158	0.01235379	0.14235379	20
21	13.02108917	0.07679849	92.46991672	7.10155007	0.01081433	0.14081433	21
22	14.71383077	0.06796327	105.49100590	7.16951334	0.00947948	0.13947948	22
23	16.62662877	0.06014448	120.20483667	7.22965782	0.00831913	0.13831913	23
24	18.78809051	0.05322521	136.83146543	7.28288303	0.00730826	0.13730826	24
25	21.23054227	0.04710195	155.61955594	7.32998498	0.00642593	0.13642593	25
26	23.99051277	0.04168314	176.85009821	7.37166812	0.00565451	0.13565451	26
27	27.10927943	0.03688774	200.84061098	7.40855586	0.00497907	0.13497907	27
28	30.63348575	0.03264402	227.94989040	7.44119988	0.00438693	0.13438693	28
29	34.61583890	0.02888851	258.58337616	7.47008839	0.00386722	0.13386722	29
30	39.11589796	0.02556505	293.19921506	7.49565344	0.00341065	0.13341065	30
31	44.20096469	0.02262394	332.31511301	7.51827738	0.00300919	0.13300919	31
32	49.94709010	0.02002119	376.51607771	7.53829857	0.00265593	0.13265593	32
33	56.44021181	0.01771786	426.46316781	7.55601643	0.00234487	0.13234487	33
34	63.77743935	0.01567953	482.90337962	7.57169596	0.00207081	0.13207081	34
35	72.06850647	0.01387569	546.68081897	7.58557164	0.00182922	0.13182922	35
36	81.43741231	0.01227937	618.74932544	7.59785101	0.00161616	0.13161616	36
37	92.02427591	0.01086670	700.18673775	7.60871771	0.00142819	0.13142819	37
38	103.98743178	0.00961655	792.21101365	7.61833426	0.00126229	0.13126229	38
39	117.50579791	0.00851022	896.19844543	7.62684447	0.00111582	0.13111582	39
40	132.78155163	0.00753117	1013.70424333	7.63437564	0.00098648	0.13098648	40
41	150.04315335	0.00666475	1146.48579497	7.64104039	0.00087223	0.13087223	41
42	169.54876328	0.00589801	1296.52894831	7.64693840	0.00077129	0.13077129	42
43	191.59010251	0.00521948	1466.07771159	7.65215787	0.00068209	0.13068209	43
44	216.49681583	0.00461901	1657.66781410	7.65677688	0.00060326	0.13060326	44
45	244.64140189	0.00408762	1874.16462994	7.66086450	0.00053357	0.13053357	45
46	276.44478414	0.00361736	2118.80603183	7.66448185	0.00047196	0.13047196	46
47	312.38260608	0.00320120	2395.25081596	7.66768306	0.00041749	0.13041749	47
48	352.99234487	0.00283292	2707.63342204	7.67051598	0.00036933	0.13036933	48
49	398.88134970	0.00250701	3060.62576691	7.67302299	0.00032673	0.13032673	49
50	450.73592516	0.00221859	3459.50711660	7.67524158	0.00028906	0.13028906	50

Rate 14%	C Compound Amount	D Present Value	E Amount of Annuity	F Present Value of Annuity	G Sinking Fund	H Amortization	
n	$(1+i)^n$	$(1+i)^{-n}$	$S_{\overline{n}\rvert i}$	$A_{\overline{n}\rvert i}$	$1/S_{\overline{n}\rvert i}$	$1/A_{\overline{n}\rvert i}$	n
1	1.14000000	0.87719298	1.00000000	0.87719298	1.00000000	1.14000000	1
2	1.29960000	0.76946753	2.14000000	1.64666051	0.46728972	0.60728972	2
3	1.48154400	0.67497152	3.43960000	2.32163203	0.29073148	0.43073148	3
4	1.68896016	0.59208028	4.92114400	2.91371230	0.20320478	0.34320478	4
5	1.92541458	0.51936866	6.61010416	3.43308097	0.15128355	0.29128355	5
6	2.19497262	0.45558655	8.53551874	3.88866752	0.11715750	0.25715750	6
7	2.50226879	0.39963732	10.73049137	4.28830484	0.09319238	0.23319238	7
8	2.85258642	0.35055905	13.23276016	4.63886389	0.07557002	0.21557002	8
9	3.25194852	0.30750794	16.08534658	4.94637184	0.06216838	0.20216838	9
10	3.70722131	0.26974381	19.33729510	5.21611565	0.05171354	0.19171354	10
11	4.22623230	0.23661738	23.04451641	5.45273302	0.04339427	0.18339427	11
12	4.81790482	0.20755910	27.27074871	5.66029213	0.03666933	0.17666933	12
13	5.49241149	0.18206939	32.08865353	5.84236151	0.03116366	0.17116366	13
14	6.26134910	0.15970999	37.58106503	6.00207150	0.02660914	0.16660914	14
15	7.13793798	0.14009648	43.84241413	6.14216799	0.02280896	0.16280896	15
16	8.13724930	0.12289165	50.98035211	6.26505964	0.01961540	0.15961540	16
17	9.27646420	0.10779969	59.11760141	6.37285933	0.01691544	0.15691544	17
18	10.57516918	0.09456113	68.39406560	6.46742046	0.01462115	0.15462115	18
19	12.05569287	0.08294836	78.96923479	6.55036883	0.01266316	0.15266316	19
20	13.74348987	0.07276172	91.02492766	6.62313055	0.01098600	0.15098600	20
21	15.66757845	0.06382607	104.76841753	6.68695662	0.00954486	0.14954486	21
22	17.86103944	0.05598778	120.43599598	6.74294441	0.00830317	0.14830317	22
23	20.36158496	0.04911209	138.29703542	6.79205650	0.00723081	0.14723081	23
24	23.21220685	0.04308078	158.65862038	6.83513728	0.00630284	0.14630284	24
25	26.46191581	0.03779016	181.87082723	6.87292744	0.00549841	0.14549841	25
26	30.16658403	0.03314926	208.33274304	6.90607670	0.00480001	0.14480001	26
27	34.38990579	0.02907830	238.49932707	6.93515500	0.00419288	0.14419288	27
28	39.20449260	0.02550728	272.88923286	6.96066228	0.00366449	0.14366449	28
29	44.69312156	0.02237481	312.09372546	6.98303709	0.00320417	0.14320417	29
30	50.95015858	0.01962702	356.78684702	7.00266411	0.00280279	0.14280279	30
31	58.08318078	0.01721669	407.73700561	7.01988080	0.00245256	0.14245256	31
32	66.21482609	0.01510236	465.82018639	7.03498316	0.00214675	0.14214675	32
33	75.48490175	0.01324768	532.03501249	7.04823084	0.00187958	0.14187958	33
34	86.05278799	0.01162077	607.51991423	7.05985161	0.00164604	0.14164604	34
35	98.10017831	0.01019366	693.57270223	7.07004528	0.00144181	0.14144181	35
36	111.83420328	0.00894181	791.67288054	7.07898708	0.00126315	0.14126315	36
37	127.49099173	0.00784369	903.50708382	7.08683078	0.00110680	0.14110680	37
38	145.33973058	0.00688043	1030.99807555	7.09371121	0.00096993	0.14096993	38
39	165.68729286	0.00603547	1176.33780613	7.09974667	0.00085010	0.14085010	39
40	188.88351386	0.00529427	1342.02509898	7.10504094	0.00074514	0.14074514	40
41	215.32720580	0.00464410	1530.90861284	7.10968504	0.00065321	0.14065321	41
42	245.47301461	0.00407377	1746.23581864	7.11375880	0.00057266	0.14057266	42
43	279.83923665	0.00357348	1991.70883325	7.11733228	0.00050208	0.14050208	43
44	319.01672979	0.00313463	2271.54806990	7.12046692	0.00044023	0.14044023	44
45	363.67907196	0.00274968	2590.56479969	7.12321659	0.00038602	0.14038602	45
46	414.59414203	0.00241200	2954.24387165	7.12562859	0.00033850	0.14033850	46
47	472.63732191	0.00211579	3368.83801368	7.12774438	0.00029684	0.14029684	47
48	538.80654698	0.00185595	3841.47533559	7.12960033	0.00026032	0.14026032	48
49	614.23946356	0.00162803	4380.28188258	7.13122836	0.00022830	0.14022830	49
50	700.23298846	0.00142810	4994.52134614	7.13265646	0.00020022	0.14020022	50

Rate 15%	C Compound Amount	D Present Value	E Amount of Annuity	F Present Value of Annuity	G Sinking Fund	H Amortization	
n	$(1+i)^n$	$(1+i)^{-n}$	$s_{\overline{n}\rvert i}$	$a_{\overline{n}\rvert i}$	$1/s_{\overline{n}\rvert i}$	$1/a_{\overline{n}\rvert i}$	n
1	1.15000000	0.86956522	1.00000000	0.86956522	1.00000000	1.15000000	1
2	1.32250000	0.75614367	2.15000000	1.62570888	0.46511628	0.61511628	2
3	1.52087500	0.65751623	3.47250000	2.28322512	0.28797696	0.43797696	3
4	1.74900625	0.57175325	4.99337500	2.85497836	0.20026535	0.35026535	4
5	2.01135719	0.49717674	6.74238125	3.35215510	0.14831555	0.29831555	5
6	2.31306077	0.43232760	8.75373844	3.78448269	0.11423691	0.26423691	6
7	2.66001988	0.37593704	11.06679920	4.16041973	0.09036036	0.24036036	7
8	3.05902286	0.32690177	13.72681908	4.48732151	0.07285009	0.22285009	8
9	3.51787629	0.28426241	16.78584195	4.77158392	0.05957402	0.20957402	9
10	4.04555774	0.24718471	20.30371824	5.01876863	0.04925206	0.19925206	10
11	4.65239140	0.21494322	24.34927597	5.23371185	0.04106898	0.19106898	11
12	5.35025011	0.18690715	29.00166737	5.42061900	0.03448078	0.18448078	12
13	6.15278762	0.16252796	34.35191748	5.58314696	0.02911046	0.17911046	13
14	7.07570576	0.14132866	40.50470510	5.72447561	0.02468849	0.17468849	14
15	8.13706163	0.12289449	47.58041086	5.84737010	0.02101705	0.17101705	15
16	9.35762087	0.10686477	55.71747249	5.95423487	0.01794769	0.16794769	16
17	10.76126400	0.09292589	65.07509336	6.04716076	0.01536686	0.16536686	17
18	12.37545361	0.08080512	75.83635737	6.12796587	0.01318629	0.16318629	18
19	14.23177165	0.07026532	88.21181097	6.19823119	0.01133635	0.16133635	19
20	16.36653739	0.06110028	102.44358262	6.25933147	0.00976147	0.15976147	20
21	18.82151800	0.05313068	118.81012001	6.31246215	0.00841679	0.15841679	21
22	21.64474570	0.04620059	137.63163801	6.35866274	0.00726577	0.15726577	22
23	24.89145756	0.04017443	159.27638372	6.39883717	0.00627839	0.15627839	23
24	28.62517619	0.03493428	184.16784127	6.43377145	0.00542983	0.15542983	24
25	32.91895262	0.03037764	212.79301747	6.46414909	0.00469940	0.15469940	25
26	37.85679551	0.02641534	245.71197009	6.49056442	0.00406981	0.15406981	26
27	43.53531484	0.02296986	283.56876560	6.51353428	0.00352648	0.15352648	27
28	50.06561207	0.01997379	327.10408044	6.53350807	0.00305713	0.15305713	28
29	57.57545388	0.01736851	377.16969250	6.55087658	0.00265133	0.15265133	29
30	66.21177196	0.01510305	434.74514638	6.56597964	0.00230020	0.15230020	30
31	76.14353775	0.01313309	500.95691834	6.57911273	0.00199618	0.15199618	31
32	87.56506841	0.01142008	577.10045609	6.59053281	0.00173280	0.15173280	32
33	100.69982867	0.00993050	664.66552450	6.60046331	0.00150452	0.15150452	33
34	115.80480298	0.00863522	765.36535317	6.60909853	0.00130657	0.15130657	34
35	133.17552342	0.00750889	881.17015615	6.61660742	0.00113485	0.15113485	35
36	153.15185194	0.00652947	1014.34567957	6.62313689	0.00098586	0.15098586	36
37	176.12462973	0.00567780	1167.49753151	6.62881468	0.00085653	0.15085653	37
38	202.54332419	0.00493722	1343.62216123	6.63375190	0.00074426	0.15074426	38
39	232.92482281	0.00429323	1546.16548542	6.63804513	0.00064676	0.15064676	39
40	267.86354623	0.00373324	1779.09030823	6.64177837	0.00056209	0.15056209	40
41	308.04307817	0.00324630	2046.95385447	6.64502467	0.00048853	0.15048853	41
42	354.24953990	0.00282287	2354.99693264	6.64784754	0.00042463	0.15042463	42
43	407.38697088	0.00245467	2709.24647253	6.65030221	0.00036911	0.15036911	43
44	468.49501651	0.00213449	3116.63344341	6.65243670	0.00032086	0.15032086	44
45	538.76926899	0.00185608	3585.12845992	6.65429279	0.00027893	0.15027893	45
46	619.58465934	0.00161398	4123.89772891	6.65590677	0.00024249	0.15024249	46
47	712.52235824	0.00140346	4743.48238825	6.65731024	0.00021082	0.15021082	47
48	819.40071197	0.00122040	5456.00474648	6.65853064	0.00018328	0.15018328	48
49	942.31081877	0.00106122	6275.40545846	6.65959186	0.00015935	0.15015935	49
50	1083.65744158	0.00092280	7217.71627723	6.66051466	0.00013855	0.15013855	50

Rate 16%	C Compound Amount	D Present Value	E Amount of Annuity	F Present Value of Annuity	G Sinking Fund	H Amortization	
n	$(1+i)^n$	$(1+i)^{-n}$	$S_{\overline{n}\rvert i}$	$A_{\overline{n}\rvert i}$	$1/S_{\overline{n}\rvert i}$	$1/A_{\overline{n}\rvert i}$	n
1	1.16000000	0.86206897	1.00000000	0.86206897	1.00000000	1.16000000	1
2	1.34560000	0.74316290	2.16000000	1.60523187	0.46296296	0.62296296	2
3	1.56089600	0.64065767	3.50560000	2.24588954	0.28525787	0.44525787	3
4	1.81063936	0.55229110	5.06649600	2.79818064	0.19737507	0.35737507	4
5	2.10034166	0.47611302	6.87713536	3.27429365	0.14540938	0.30540938	5
6	2.43639632	0.41044225	8.97747702	3.68473591	0.11138987	0.27138987	6
7	2.82621973	0.35382953	11.41387334	4.03856544	0.08761268	0.24761268	7
8	3.27841489	0.30502546	14.24009307	4.34359090	0.07022426	0.23022426	8
9	3.80296127	0.26295298	17.51850797	4.60654388	0.05708249	0.21708249	9
10	4.41143508	0.22668360	21.32146924	4.83322748	0.04690108	0.20690108	10
11	5.11726469	0.19541690	25.73290432	5.02864438	0.03886075	0.19886075	11
12	5.93602704	0.16846284	30.85016901	5.19710722	0.03241473	0.19241473	12
13	6.88579137	0.14522659	36.78619605	5.34233381	0.02718411	0.18718411	13
14	7.98751799	0.12519534	43.67198742	5.46752915	0.02289797	0.18289797	14
15	9.26552087	0.10792701	51.65950541	5.57545616	0.01935752	0.17935752	15
16	10.74800420	0.09304053	60.92502627	5.66849669	0.01641362	0.17641362	16
17	12.46768488	0.08020735	71.67303048	5.74870404	0.01395225	0.17395225	17
18	14.46251446	0.06914427	84.14071536	5.81784831	0.01188485	0.17188485	18
19	16.77651677	0.05960713	98.60322981	5.87745544	0.01014166	0.17014166	19
20	19.46075945	0.05138546	115.37974658	5.92884090	0.00866703	0.16866703	20
21	22.57448097	0.04429781	134.84050604	5.97313871	0.00741617	0.16741617	21
22	26.18639792	0.03818776	157.41498700	6.01132647	0.00635264	0.16635264	22
23	30.37622159	0.03292049	183.60138492	6.04424696	0.00544658	0.16544658	23
24	35.23641704	0.02837973	213.97760651	6.07262669	0.00467339	0.16467339	24
25	40.87424377	0.02446528	249.21402355	6.09709197	0.00401262	0.16401262	25
26	47.41412277	0.02109076	290.08826732	6.11818273	0.00344723	0.16344723	26
27	55.00038241	0.01818169	337.50239009	6.13636443	0.00296294	0.16296294	27
28	63.80044360	0.01567387	392.50277250	6.15203830	0.00254775	0.16254775	28
29	74.00851458	0.01351196	456.30321610	6.16555026	0.00219153	0.16219153	29
30	85.84987691	0.01164824	530.31173068	6.17719850	0.00188568	0.16188568	30
31	99.58585721	0.01004159	616.16160759	6.18724008	0.00162295	0.16162295	31
32	115.51959437	0.00865654	715.74746480	6.19589662	0.00139714	0.16139714	32
33	134.00272947	0.00746253	831.26705917	6.20335916	0.00120298	0.16120298	33
34	155.44316618	0.00643322	965.26978864	6.20979238	0.00103598	0.16103598	34
35	180.31407277	0.00554588	1120.71295482	6.21533826	0.00089229	0.16089229	35
36	209.16432441	0.00478093	1301.02702759	6.22011919	0.00076862	0.16076862	36
37	242.63061632	0.00412149	1510.19135201	6.22424068	0.00066217	0.16066217	37
38	281.45151493	0.00355301	1752.82196833	6.22779369	0.00057051	0.16057051	38
39	326.48375732	0.00306294	2034.27348326	6.23085663	0.00049158	0.16049158	39
40	378.72115849	0.00264047	2360.75724058	6.23349709	0.00042359	0.16042359	40
41	439.31654385	0.00227626	2739.47839907	6.23577336	0.00036503	0.16036503	41
42	509.60719087	0.00196230	3178.79494293	6.23773565	0.00031458	0.16031458	42
43	591.14434141	0.00169163	3688.40213380	6.23942729	0.00027112	0.16027112	43
44	685.72743603	0.00145831	4279.54647520	6.24088559	0.00023367	0.16023367	44
45	795.44382580	0.00125716	4965.27391123	6.24214275	0.00020140	0.16020140	45
46	922.71483793	0.00108376	5760.71773703	6.24322651	0.00017359	0.16017359	46
47	1070.34921199	0.00093427	6683.43257496	6.24416078	0.00014962	0.16014962	47
48	1241.60508591	0.00080541	7753.78178695	6.24496619	0.00012897	0.16012897	48
49	1440.26189966	0.00069432	8995.38687286	6.24566051	0.00011117	0.16011117	49
50	1670.70380360	0.00059855	10435.64877252	6.24625906	0.00009583	0.16009583	50

Rate 17%	C Compound Amount	D Present Value	E Amount of Annuity	F Present Value of Annuity	G Sinking Fund	H Amortization	
n	$(1+i)^n$	$(1+i)^{-n}$	$s_{\overline{n}\vert i}$	$a_{\overline{n}\vert i}$	$1/s_{\overline{n}\vert i}$	$1/a_{\overline{n}\vert i}$	n
1	1.17000000	0.85470085	1.00000000	0.85470085	1.00000000	1.17000000	1
2	1.36890000	0.73051355	2.17000000	1.58521441	0.46082949	0.63082949	2
3	1.60161300	0.62437056	3.53890000	2.20958496	0.28257368	0.45257368	3
4	1.87388721	0.53365005	5.14051300	2.74323501	0.19453311	0.36453311	4
5	2.19244804	0.45611115	7.01440021	3.19934616	0.14256386	0.31256386	5
6	2.56516420	0.38983859	9.20684825	3.58918475	0.10861480	0.27861480	6
7	3.00124212	0.33319538	11.77201245	3.92238013	0.08494724	0.25494724	7
8	3.51145328	0.28478237	14.77325456	4.20716251	0.06768989	0.23768989	8
9	4.10840033	0.24340374	18.28470784	4.45056624	0.05469051	0.22469051	9
10	4.80682839	0.20803738	22.39310817	4.65860363	0.04465660	0.21465660	10
11	5.62398922	0.17780973	27.19993656	4.83641336	0.03676479	0.20676479	11
12	6.58006738	0.15197413	32.82392578	4.98838748	0.03046558	0.20046558	12
13	7.69867884	0.12989242	39.40399316	5.11827990	0.02537814	0.19537814	13
14	9.00745424	0.11101916	47.10267200	5.22929906	0.02123022	0.19123022	14
15	10.53872146	0.09488817	56.11012623	5.32418723	0.01782209	0.18782209	15
16	12.33030411	0.08110100	66.64884769	5.40528823	0.01500401	0.18500401	16
17	14.42645581	0.06931709	78.97915180	5.47460533	0.01266157	0.18266157	17
18	16.87895329	0.05924538	93.40560761	5.53385071	0.01070600	0.18070600	18
19	19.74837535	0.05063708	110.28456090	5.58448778	0.00906745	0.17906745	19
20	23.10559916	0.04327955	130.03293626	5.62776734	0.00769036	0.17769036	20
21	27.03355102	0.03699107	153.13853542	5.66475841	0.00653004	0.17653004	21
22	31.62925470	0.03161630	180.17208644	5.69637471	0.00555025	0.17555025	22
23	37.00622799	0.02702248	211.80134114	5.72339719	0.00472141	0.17472141	23
24	43.29728675	0.02309614	248.80756913	5.74649332	0.00401917	0.17401917	24
25	50.65782550	0.01974029	292.10485588	5.76623361	0.00342343	0.17342343	25
26	59.26965584	0.01687204	342.76268138	5.78310565	0.00291747	0.17291747	26
27	69.34549733	0.01442055	402.03233722	5.79752619	0.00248736	0.17248736	27
28	81.13423187	0.01232525	471.37783454	5.80985145	0.00212144	0.17212144	28
29	94.92705129	0.01053440	552.51206642	5.82038585	0.00180992	0.17180992	29
30	111.06465001	0.00900376	647.43911771	5.82938962	0.00154455	0.17154455	30
31	129.94564051	0.00769553	758.50376772	5.83708514	0.00131839	0.17131839	31
32	152.03639940	0.00657737	888.44940823	5.84366252	0.00112556	0.17112556	32
33	177.88258730	0.00562169	1040.48580763	5.84928420	0.00096109	0.17096109	33
34	208.12262714	0.00480486	1218.36839493	5.85408906	0.00082077	0.17082077	34
35	243.50347375	0.00410672	1426.49102206	5.85819578	0.00070102	0.17070102	35
36	284.89906429	0.00351002	1669.99449581	5.86170579	0.00059880	0.17059880	36
37	333.33190522	0.00300001	1954.89356010	5.86470581	0.00051154	0.17051154	37
38	389.99832910	0.00256411	2288.22546532	5.86726992	0.00043702	0.17043702	38
39	456.29804505	0.00219155	2678.22379443	5.86946147	0.00037338	0.17037338	39
40	533.86871271	0.00187312	3134.52183948	5.87133459	0.00031903	0.17031903	40
41	624.62639387	0.00160096	3668.39055219	5.87293555	0.00027260	0.17027260	41
42	730.81288083	0.00136834	4293.01694606	5.87430389	0.00023294	0.17023294	42
43	855.05107057	0.00116952	5023.82982689	5.87547341	0.00019905	0.17019905	43
44	1000.40975257	0.00099959	5878.88089746	5.87647300	0.00017010	0.17017010	44
45	1170.47941051	0.00085435	6879.29065003	5.87732735	0.00014536	0.17014536	45
46	1369.46091029	0.00073021	8049.77006054	5.87805756	0.00012423	0.17012423	46
47	1602.26926504	0.00062411	9419.23097083	5.87868168	0.00010617	0.17010617	47
48	1874.65504010	0.00053343	11021.50023587	5.87921511	0.00009073	0.17009073	48
49	2193.34639691	0.00045592	12896.15527597	5.87967103	0.00007754	0.17007754	49
50	2566.21528439	0.00038968	15089.50167288	5.88006071	0.00006627	0.17006627	50

Rate 18%	C Compound Amount	D Present Value	E Amount of Annuity	F Present Value of Annuity	G Sinking Fund	H Amortization	
n	$(1+i)^n$	$(1+i)^{-n}$	$S_{\overline{n}\rvert i}$	$A_{\overline{n}\rvert i}$	$1/S_{\overline{n}\rvert i}$	$1/A_{\overline{n}\rvert i}$	n
1	1.18000000	0.84745763	1.00000000	0.84745763	1.00000000	1.18000000	1
2	1.39240000	0.71818443	2.18000000	1.56564206	0.45871560	0.63871560	2
3	1.64303200	0.60863087	3.57240000	2.17427293	0.27992386	0.45992386	3
4	1.93877776	0.51578888	5.21543200	2.69006180	0.19173867	0.37173867	4
5	2.28775776	0.43710922	7.15420976	3.12717102	0.13977784	0.31977784	5
6	2.69955415	0.37043154	9.44196752	3.49760256	0.10591013	0.28591013	6
7	3.18547390	0.31392503	12.14152167	3.81152759	0.08236200	0.26236200	7
8	3.75885920	0.26603816	15.32699557	4.07756576	0.06524436	0.24524436	8
9	4.43545386	0.22545607	19.08585477	4.30302183	0.05239482	0.23239482	9
10	5.23383555	0.19106447	23.52130863	4.49408629	0.04251464	0.22251464	10
11	6.17592595	0.16191904	28.75514419	4.65600533	0.03477639	0.21477639	11
12	7.28759263	0.13721953	34.93107014	4.79322486	0.02862781	0.20862781	12
13	8.59935930	0.11628773	42.21866276	4.90951259	0.02368621	0.20368621	13
14	10.14724397	0.09854893	50.81802206	5.00806152	0.01967806	0.19967806	14
15	11.97374789	0.08351604	60.96526603	5.09157756	0.01640278	0.19640278	15
16	14.12902251	0.07077630	72.93901392	5.16235386	0.01371008	0.19371008	16
17	16.67224656	0.05997992	87.06803642	5.22233378	0.01148527	0.19148527	17
18	19.67325094	0.05083044	103.74028298	5.27316422	0.00963946	0.18963946	18
19	23.21443611	0.04307664	123.41353392	5.31624087	0.00810284	0.18810284	19
20	27.39303460	0.03650563	146.62797002	5.35274650	0.00681998	0.18681998	20
21	32.32378083	0.03093698	174.02100463	5.38368347	0.00574643	0.18574643	21
22	38.14206138	0.02621778	206.34478546	5.40990125	0.00484626	0.18484626	22
23	45.00763243	0.02221845	244.48684684	5.43211970	0.00409020	0.18409020	23
24	53.10900627	0.01882920	289.49447928	5.45094890	0.00345430	0.18345430	24
25	62.66862740	0.01595695	342.60348554	5.46690585	0.00291883	0.18291883	25
26	73.94898033	0.01352284	405.27211294	5.48042868	0.00246748	0.18246748	26
27	87.25979679	0.01146003	479.22109327	5.49188872	0.00208672	0.18208672	27
28	102.96656021	0.00971189	566.48089006	5.50160061	0.00176528	0.18176528	28
29	121.50054105	0.00823042	669.44745027	5.50983102	0.00149377	0.18149377	29
30	143.37063844	0.00697493	790.94799132	5.51680595	0.00126431	0.18126431	30
31	169.17735336	0.00591096	934.31862976	5.52271691	0.00107030	0.18107030	31
32	199.62927696	0.00500929	1103.49598312	5.52772619	0.00090621	0.18090621	32
33	235.56254681	0.00424516	1303.12526008	5.53197135	0.00076739	0.18076739	33
34	277.96380524	0.00359759	1538.68780689	5.53556894	0.00064990	0.18064990	34
35	327.99729018	0.00304881	1816.65161213	5.53861775	0.00055046	0.18055046	35
36	387.03680242	0.00258373	2144.64890232	5.54120148	0.00046628	0.18046628	36
37	456.70342685	0.00218960	2531.68570473	5.54339108	0.00039499	0.18039499	37
38	538.91004369	0.00185560	2988.38913158	5.54524668	0.00033463	0.18033463	38
39	635.91385155	0.00157254	3527.29917527	5.54681922	0.00028350	0.18028350	39
40	750.37834483	0.00133266	4163.21302682	5.54815188	0.00024020	0.18024020	40
41	885.44644690	0.00112937	4913.59137165	5.54928126	0.00020352	0.18020352	41
42	1044.82680734	0.00095710	5799.03781854	5.55023835	0.00017244	0.18017244	42
43	1232.89563266	0.00081110	6843.86462588	5.55104945	0.00014612	0.18014612	43
44	1454.81684654	0.00068737	8076.76025854	5.55173682	0.00012381	0.18012381	44
45	1716.68387891	0.00058252	9531.57710507	5.55231934	0.00010491	0.18010491	45
46	2025.68697712	0.00049366	11248.26098399	5.55281300	0.00008890	0.18008890	46
47	2390.31063300	0.00041836	13273.94796110	5.55323136	0.00007534	0.18007534	47
48	2820.56654694	0.00035454	15664.25859410	5.55358590	0.00006384	0.18006384	48
49	3328.26852539	0.00030046	18484.82514104	5.55388635	0.00005410	0.18005410	49
50	3927.35685996	0.00025462	21813.09366643	5.55414098	0.00004584	0.18004584	50

Rate 19%	C Compound Amount	D Present Value	E Amount of Annuity	F Present Value of Annuity	G Sinking Fund	H Amortization	
n	$(1+i)^n$	$(1+i)^{-n}$	$S_{\overline{n}\|i}$	$A_{\overline{n}\|i}$	$1/S_{\overline{n}\|i}$	$1/A_{\overline{n}\|i}$	n
1	1.19000000	0.84033613	1.00000000	0.84033613	1.00000000	1.19000000	1
2	1.41610000	0.70616482	2.19000000	1.54650095	0.45662100	0.64662100	2
3	1.68515900	0.59341581	3.60610000	2.13991677	0.27730789	0.46730789	3
4	2.00533921	0.49866875	5.29125900	2.63858552	0.18899094	0.37899094	4
5	2.38635366	0.41904937	7.29659821	3.05763489	0.13705017	0.32705017	5
6	2.83976086	0.35214233	9.68295187	3.40977722	0.10327429	0.29327429	6
7	3.37931542	0.29591792	12.52271273	3.70569514	0.07985490	0.26985490	7
8	4.02138535	0.24867052	15.90202814	3.95436567	0.06288506	0.25288506	8
9	4.78544856	0.20896683	19.92341349	4.16333249	0.05019220	0.24019220	9
10	5.69468379	0.17560238	24.70886205	4.33893487	0.04047131	0.23047131	10
11	6.77667371	0.14756502	30.40354584	4.48649989	0.03289090	0.22289090	11
12	8.06424172	0.12400422	37.18021955	4.61050411	0.02689602	0.21689602	12
13	9.59644764	0.10420523	45.24446127	4.71470933	0.02210215	0.21210215	13
14	11.41977269	0.08756742	54.84090891	4.80227675	0.01823456	0.20823456	14
15	13.58952950	0.07358606	66.26068160	4.87586282	0.01509191	0.20509191	15
16	16.17154011	0.06183703	79.85021111	4.93769985	0.01252345	0.20252345	16
17	19.24413273	0.05196389	96.02175122	4.98966374	0.01041431	0.20041431	17
18	22.90051795	0.04366713	115.26588395	5.03333087	0.00867559	0.19867559	18
19	27.25161636	0.03669507	138.16640190	5.07002594	0.00723765	0.19723765	19
20	32.42942347	0.03083619	165.41801826	5.10086214	0.00604529	0.19604529	20
21	38.59101393	0.02591277	197.84744173	5.12677490	0.00505440	0.19505440	21
22	45.92330658	0.02177544	236.43845566	5.14855034	0.00422943	0.19422943	22
23	54.64873482	0.01829869	282.36176223	5.16684902	0.00354156	0.19354156	23
24	65.03199444	0.01537705	337.01049706	5.18222607	0.00296727	0.19296727	24
25	77.38807338	0.01292189	402.04249150	5.19514796	0.00248730	0.19248730	25
26	92.09180733	0.01085873	479.43056488	5.20600669	0.00208581	0.19208581	26
27	109.58925072	0.00912498	571.52237221	5.21513167	0.00174971	0.19174971	27
28	130.41120836	0.00766805	681.11162293	5.22279972	0.00146819	0.19146819	28
29	155.18933794	0.00644374	811.52283129	5.22924347	0.00123225	0.19123225	29
30	184.67531215	0.00541491	966.71216923	5.23465837	0.00103443	0.19103443	30
31	219.76362146	0.00455034	1151.38748139	5.23920872	0.00086852	0.19086852	31
32	261.51870954	0.00382382	1371.15110285	5.24303254	0.00072931	0.19072931	32
33	311.20726435	0.00321329	1632.66981239	5.24624583	0.00061249	0.19061249	33
34	370.33664458	0.00270025	1943.87707675	5.24894607	0.00051444	0.19051444	34
35	440.70060705	0.00226911	2314.21372133	5.25121519	0.00043211	0.19043211	35
36	524.43372239	0.00190682	2754.91432838	5.25312201	0.00036299	0.19036299	36
37	624.07612965	0.00160237	3279.34805077	5.25472438	0.00030494	0.19030494	37
38	742.65059428	0.00134653	3903.42418042	5.25607090	0.00025619	0.19025619	38
39	883.75420719	0.00113154	4646.07477470	5.25720244	0.00021524	0.19021524	39
40	1051.66750656	0.00095087	5529.82898189	5.25815331	0.00018084	0.19018084	40
41	1251.48433281	0.00079905	6581.49648845	5.25895236	0.00015194	0.19015194	41
42	1489.26635604	0.00067147	7832.98082126	5.25962383	0.00012767	0.19012767	42
43	1772.22696369	0.00056426	9322.24717730	5.26018810	0.00010727	0.19010727	43
44	2108.95008679	0.00047417	11094.47414099	5.26066227	0.00009013	0.19009013	44
45	2509.65060328	0.00039846	13203.42422777	5.26106073	0.00007574	0.19007574	45
46	2986.48421790	0.00033484	15713.07483105	5.26139557	0.00006364	0.19006364	46
47	3553.91621930	0.00028138	18699.55904895	5.26167695	0.00005348	0.19005348	47
48	4229.16030097	0.00023645	22253.47526825	5.26191340	0.00004494	0.19004494	48
49	5032.70075815	0.00019870	26482.63556922	5.26211210	0.00003776	0.19003776	49
50	5988.91390220	0.00016698	31515.33632737	5.26227908	0.00003173	0.19003173	50

Rate 20%	C Compound Amount	D Present Value	E Amount of Annuity	F Present Value of Annuity	G Sinking Fund	H Amortization	
n	$(1+i)^n$	$(1+i)^{-n}$	$S_{\overline{n}\rvert i}$	$A_{\overline{n}\rvert i}$	$1/S_{\overline{n}\rvert i}$	$1/A_{\overline{n}\rvert i}$	n
1	1.20000000	0.83333333	1.00000000	0.83333333	1.00000000	1.20000000	1
2	1.44000000	0.69444444	2.20000000	1.52777778	0.45454545	0.65454545	2
3	1.72800000	0.57870370	3.64000000	2.10648148	0.27472527	0.47472527	3
4	2.07360000	0.48225309	5.36800000	2.58873457	0.18628912	0.38628912	4
5	2.48832000	0.40187757	7.44160000	2.99061214	0.13437970	0.33437970	5
6	2.98598400	0.33489798	9.92992000	3.32551012	0.10070575	0.30070575	6
7	3.58318080	0.27908165	12.91590400	3.60459176	0.07742393	0.27742393	7
8	4.29981696	0.23256804	16.49908480	3.83715980	0.06060942	0.26060942	8
9	5.15978035	0.19380670	20.79890176	4.03096650	0.04807946	0.24807946	9
10	6.19173642	0.16150558	25.95868211	4.19247209	0.03852276	0.23852276	10
11	7.43008371	0.13458799	32.15041853	4.32706007	0.03110379	0.23110379	11
12	8.91610045	0.11215665	39.58050224	4.43921673	0.02526496	0.22526496	12
13	10.69932054	0.09346388	48.49660269	4.53268061	0.02062000	0.22062000	13
14	12.83918465	0.07788657	59.19592323	4.61056717	0.01689306	0.21689306	14
15	15.40702157	0.06490547	72.03510787	4.67547264	0.01388212	0.21388212	15
16	18.48842589	0.05408789	87.44212945	4.72956054	0.01143614	0.21143614	16
17	22.18611107	0.04507324	105.93055534	4.77463378	0.00944015	0.20944015	17
18	26.62333328	0.03756104	128.11666640	4.81219482	0.00780539	0.20780539	18
19	31.94799994	0.03130086	154.73999969	4.84349568	0.00646245	0.20646245	19
20	38.33759992	0.02608405	186.68799962	4.86957973	0.00535653	0.20535653	20
21	46.00511991	0.02173671	225.02559955	4.89131644	0.00444394	0.20444394	21
22	55.20614389	0.01811393	271.03071946	4.90943037	0.00368962	0.20368962	22
23	66.24737267	0.01509494	326.23686335	4.92452531	0.00306526	0.20306526	23
24	79.49684720	0.01257912	392.48423602	4.93710442	0.00254787	0.20254787	24
25	95.39621664	0.01048260	471.98108322	4.94758702	0.00211873	0.20211873	25
26	114.47545997	0.00873550	567.37729986	4.95632252	0.00176250	0.20176250	26
27	137.37055197	0.00727958	681.85275984	4.96360210	0.00146659	0.20146659	27
28	164.84466236	0.00606632	819.22331180	4.96966841	0.00122067	0.20122067	28
29	197.81359483	0.00505526	984.06797417	4.97472368	0.00101619	0.20101619	29
30	237.37631380	0.00421272	1181.88156900	4.97893640	0.00084611	0.20084611	30
31	284.85157656	0.00351060	1419.25788280	4.98244700	0.00070459	0.20070459	31
32	341.82189187	0.00292550	1704.10945936	4.98537250	0.00058682	0.20058682	32
33	410.18627025	0.00243792	2045.93135123	4.98781042	0.00048877	0.20048877	33
34	492.22352430	0.00203160	2456.11762148	4.98984201	0.00040715	0.20040715	34
35	590.66822915	0.00169300	2948.34114577	4.99153501	0.00033917	0.20033917	35
36	708.80187499	0.00141083	3539.00937493	4.99294584	0.00028256	0.20028256	36
37	850.56224998	0.00117569	4247.81124991	4.99412154	0.00023542	0.20023542	37
38	1020.67469998	0.00097974	5098.37349989	4.99510128	0.00019614	0.20019614	38
39	1224.80963997	0.00081645	6119.04819987	4.99591773	0.00016342	0.20016342	39
40	1469.77156797	0.00068038	7343.85783985	4.99659811	0.00013617	0.20013617	40
41	1763.72588156	0.00056698	8813.62940781	4.99716509	0.00011346	0.20011346	41
42	2116.47105788	0.00047248	10577.35528938	4.99763758	0.00009454	0.20009454	42
43	2539.76526945	0.00039374	12693.82634725	4.99803131	0.00007878	0.20007878	43
44	3047.71832334	0.00032811	15233.59161670	4.99835943	0.00006564	0.20006564	44
45	3657.26198801	0.00027343	18281.30994004	4.99863286	0.00005470	0.20005470	45
46	4388.71438561	0.00022786	21938.57192805	4.99886071	0.00004558	0.20004558	46
47	5266.45726273	0.00018988	26327.28631366	4.99905060	0.00003798	0.20003798	47
48	6319.74871528	0.00015823	31593.74357640	4.99920883	0.00003165	0.20003165	48
49	7583.69845834	0.00013186	37913.49229168	4.99934069	0.00002638	0.20002638	49
50	9100.43815000	0.00010988	45497.19075001	4.99945058	0.00002198	0.20002198	50

Appendix I Compound daily interest factors for a 365-day year

Day	*6.00%*	*6.25%*	*6.50%*	*6.75%*	*7.00%*	*7.25%*	*7.50%*	*7.75%*
1	1.00016438	1.00017123	1.00017808	1.00018493	1.00019178	1.00019863	1.00020548	1.00021233
2	1.00032879	1.00034250	1.00035620	1.00036990	1.00038360	1.00039730	1.00041100	1.00042470
3	1.00049323	1.00051379	1.00053434	1.00055490	1.00057545	1.00059601	1.00061657	1.00063712
4	1.00065770	1.00068511	1.00071252	1.00073993	1.00076734	1.00079476	1.00082217	1.00084959
5	1.00082219	1.00085646	1.00089073	1.00092500	1.00095927	1.00099355	1.00102782	1.00106209
6	1.00098671	1.00102784	1.00106897	1.00111010	1.00115124	1.00119237	1.00123351	1.00127465
7	1.00115125	1.00119925	1.00124724	1.00129524	1.00134324	1.00139124	1.00143924	1.00148725
8	1.00131583	1.00137068	1.00142555	1.00148041	1.00153528	1.00159015	1.00164502	1.00169989
9	1.00148043	1.00154215	1.00160388	1.00166562	1.00172735	1.00178909	1.00185084	1.00191258
10	1.00164505	1.00171365	1.00178225	1.00185085	1.00191946	1.00198808	1.00205670	1.00212532
11	1.00180971	1.00188518	1.00196065	1.00203613	1.00211161	1.00218710	1.00226260	1.00233810
12	1.00197439	1.00205673	1.00213908	1.00222144	1.00230380	1.00238617	1.00246854	1.00255092
13	1.00213910	1.00222832	1.00231754	1.00240678	1.00249602	1.00258527	1.00267453	1.00276379
14	1.00230383	1.00239993	1.00249604	1.00259216	1.00268828	1.00278441	1.00288056	1.00297671
15	1.00246859	1.00257157	1.00267457	1.00277757	1.00288058	1.00298360	1.00308663	1.00318967
16	1.00263338	1.00274325	1.00285312	1.00296301	1.00307291	1.00318282	1.00329274	1.00340268
17	1.00279820	1.00291495	1.00303171	1.00314849	1.00326528	1.00338208	1.00349890	1.00361573
18	1.00296304	1.00308668	1.00321034	1.00333400	1.00345769	1.00358139	1.00370510	1.00382882
19	1.00312791	1.00325844	1.00338899	1.00351955	1.00365013	1.00378073	1.00391134	1.00404196
20	1.00329281	1.00343023	1.00356768	1.00370514	1.00384261	1.00398011	1.00411762	1.00425515
21	1.00345774	1.00360205	1.00374639	1.00389075	1.00403513	1.00417953	1.00432395	1.00446838
22	1.00362269	1.00377390	1.00392514	1.00407640	1.00422769	1.00437899	1.00453031	1.00468166
23	1.00378767	1.00394578	1.00410392	1.00426209	1.00442028	1.00457849	1.00473672	1.00489498
24	1.00395267	1.00411769	1.00428274	1.00444781	1.00461291	1.00477803	1.00494318	1.00510835
25	1.00411771	1.00428963	1.00446158	1.00463356	1.00480557	1.00497761	1.00514967	1.00532177
26	1.00428277	1.00446160	1.00464046	1.00481935	1.00499827	1.00517723	1.00535621	1.00553522
27	1.00444785	1.00463359	1.00481937	1.00500517	1.00519101	1.00537688	1.00556279	1.00574873
28	1.00461297	1.00480562	1.00499831	1.00519103	1.00538379	1.00557658	1.00576941	1.00596228
29	1.00477811	1.00497768	1.00517728	1.00537692	1.00557660	1.00577632	1.00597608	1.00617587
30	1.00494328	1.00514976	1.00535628	1.00556285	1.00576945	1.00597610	1.00618279	1.00638951
31	1.00510848	1.00532188	1.00553532	1.00574881	1.00596234	1.00617592	1.00638953	1.00660320
32	1.00527370	1.00549402	1.00571439	1.00593480	1.00615526	1.00637577	1.00659633	1.00681693
33	1.00543895	1.00566619	1.00589349	1.00612083	1.00634823	1.00657567	1.00680316	1.00703071
34	1.00560423	1.00583840	1.00607262	1.00630689	1.00654122	1.00677561	1.00701004	1.00724453
35	1.00576953	1.00601063	1.00625178	1.00649299	1.00673426	1.00697558	1.00721696	1.00745839
36	1.00593486	1.00618289	1.00643098	1.00667913	1.00692733	1.00717560	1.00742392	1.00767231
37	1.00610022	1.00635518	1.00661021	1.00686529	1.00712044	1.00737565	1.00763093	1.00788626
38	1.00626561	1.00652750	1.00678947	1.00705149	1.00731359	1.00757575	1.00783797	1.00810027
39	1.00643102	1.00669985	1.00696876	1.00723773	1.00750677	1.00777588	1.00804506	1.00831432
40	1.00659646	1.00687223	1.00714808	1.00742400	1.00769999	1.00797606	1.00825220	1.00852841
41	1.00676193	1.00704464	1.00732743	1.00761030	1.00789325	1.00817627	1.00845937	1.00874255
42	1.00692743	1.00721708	1.00750682	1.00779664	1.00808654	1.00837653	1.00866659	1.00895673
43	1.00709295	1.00738955	1.00768624	1.00798302	1.00827987	1.00857682	1.00887385	1.00917097
44	1.00725850	1.00756205	1.00786569	1.00816942	1.00847324	1.00877715	1.00908115	1.00938524
45	1.00742407	1.00773458	1.00804517	1.00835587	1.00866665	1.00897753	1.00928850	1.00959956
46	1.00758968	1.00790714	1.00822469	1.00854234	1.00886009	1.00917794	1.00949589	1.00981393
47	1.00775531	1.00807972	1.00840424	1.00872885	1.00905357	1.00937839	1.00970332	1.01002834
48	1.00792097	1.00825234	1.00858382	1.00891540	1.00924709	1.00957889	1.00991079	1.01024280
49	1.00808665	1.00842498	1.00876343	1.00910198	1.00944064	1.00977942	1.01011831	1.01045730
50	1.00825237	1.00859766	1.00894307	1.00928859	1.00963423	1.00997999	1.01032586	1.01067185

Day	6.00%	6.25%	6.50%	6.75%	7.00%	7.25%	7.50%	7.75%
51	1.00841811	1.00877037	1.00912274	1.00947524	1.00982786	1.01018060	1.01053347	1.01088645
52	1.00858387	1.00894310	1.00930245	1.00966193	1.01002153	1.01038126	1.01074111	1.01110109
53	1.00874967	1.00911586	1.00948219	1.00984865	1.01021523	1.01058195	1.01094880	1.01131577
54	1.00891549	1.00928866	1.00966196	1.01003540	1.01040897	1.01078268	1.01115653	1.01153051
55	1.00908134	1.00946148	1.00984176	1.01022219	1.01060275	1.01098345	1.01136430	1.01174528
56	1.00924722	1.00963433	1.01002160	1.01040901	1.01079656	1.01118426	1.01157211	1.01196011
57	1.00941312	1.00980722	1.01020146	1.01059586	1.01099041	1.01138512	1.01177997	1.01217497
58	1.00957905	1.00998013	1.01038136	1.01078275	1.01118430	1.01158601	1.01198787	1.01238989
59	1.00974501	1.01015307	1.01056129	1.01096968	1.01137823	1.01178694	1.01219581	1.01260485
60	1.00991099	1.01032604	1.01074126	1.01115664	1.01157219	1.01198791	1.01240380	1.01281985
61	1.01007701	1.01049904	1.01092125	1.01134364	1.01176619	1.01218892	1.01261183	1.01303490
62	1.01024305	1.01067207	1.01110128	1.01153066	1.01196023	1.01238997	1.01281990	1.01325000
63	1.01040911	1.01084513	1.01128134	1.01171773	1.01215430	1.01259106	1.01302801	1.01346514
64	1.01057521	1.01101822	1.01146143	1.01190483	1.01234842	1.01279220	1.01323617	1.01368033
65	1.01074133	1.01119134	1.01164155	1.01209196	1.01254256	1.01299337	1.01344437	1.01389556
66	1.01090748	1.01136449	1.01182171	1.01227913	1.01273675	1.01319458	1.01365261	1.01411084
67	1.01107366	1.01153767	1.01200190	1.01246633	1.01293097	1.01339583	1.01386089	1.01432617
68	1.01123986	1.01171088	1.01218212	1.01265357	1.01312523	1.01359712	1.01406922	1.01454154
69	1.01140609	1.01188412	1.01236237	1.01284084	1.01331953	1.01379845	1.01427759	1.01475695
70	1.01157235	1.01205739	1.01254265	1.01302814	1.01351387	1.01399982	1.01448600	1.01497242
71	1.01173864	1.01223068	1.01272297	1.01321549	1.01370824	1.01420123	1.01469446	1.01518792
72	1.01190495	1.01240401	1.01290331	1.01340286	1.01390265	1.01440268	1.01490296	1.01540348
73	1.01207129	1.01257737	1.01308369	1.01359027	1.01409710	1.01460417	1.01511150	1.01561908
74	1.01223766	1.01275075	1.01326411	1.01377772	1.01429158	1.01480570	1.01532008	1.01583472
75	1.01240405	1.01292417	1.01344455	1.01396520	1.01448610	1.01500728	1.01552871	1.01605041
76	1.01257048	1.01309762	1.01362503	1.01415271	1.01468066	1.01520889	1.01573738	1.01626615
77	1.01273693	1.01327109	1.01380554	1.01434026	1.01487526	1.01541054	1.01594610	1.01648193
78	1.01290340	1.01344460	1.01398608	1.01452784	1.01506989	1.01561223	1.01615485	1.01669776
79	1.01306991	1.01361813	1.01416665	1.01471546	1.01526456	1.01581396	1.01636365	1.01691363
80	1.01323644	1.01379170	1.01434725	1.01490311	1.01545927	1.01601573	1.01657249	1.01712955
81	1.01340300	1.01396529	1.01452789	1.01509080	1.01565402	1.01621754	1.01678138	1.01734552
82	1.01356959	1.01413892	1.01470856	1.01527852	1.01584880	1.01641939	1.01699030	1.01756153
83	1.01373620	1.01431257	1.01488926	1.01546628	1.01604362	1.01662129	1.01719928	1.01777759
84	1.01390284	1.01448625	1.01507000	1.01565407	1.01623848	1.01682322	1.01740829	1.01799369
85	1.01406951	1.01465997	1.01525076	1.01584190	1.01643337	1.01702519	1.01761735	1.01820984
86	1.01423621	1.01483371	1.01543156	1.01602976	1.01662831	1.01722720	1.01782644	1.01842604
87	1.01440293	1.01500748	1.01561239	1.01621765	1.01682328	1.01742925	1.01803559	1.01864228
88	1.01456968	1.01518129	1.01579325	1.01640559	1.01701828	1.01763134	1.01824477	1.01885857
89	1.01473646	1.01535512	1.01597415	1.01659355	1.01721333	1.01783348	1.01845400	1.01907490
90	1.01490327	1.01552898	1.01615507	1.01678155	1.01740841	1.01803565	1.01866327	1.01929128
91	1.01507010	1.01570287	1.01633603	1.01696959	1.01760353	1.01823786	1.01887259	1.01950770
92	1.01523696	1.01587679	1.01651703	1.01715766	1.01779869	1.01844011	1.01908194	1.01972417
93	1.01540385	1.01605075	1.01669805	1.01734576	1.01799388	1.01864241	1.01929134	1.01994069
94	1.01557077	1.01622473	1.01687910	1.01753390	1.01818911	1.01884474	1.01950079	1.02015725
95	1.01573771	1.01639874	1.01706019	1.01772207	1.01838438	1.01904711	1.01971027	1.02037386
96	1.01590468	1.01657278	1.01724131	1.01791028	1.01857969	1.01924953	1.01991980	1.02059052
97	1.01607168	1.01674685	1.01742247	1.01809853	1.01877503	1.01945198	1.02012938	1.02080722
98	1.01623870	1.01692095	1.01760365	1.01828680	1.01897041	1.01965447	1.02033899	1.02102396
99	1.01640576	1.01709508	1.01778487	1.01847512	1.01916583	1.01985701	1.02054865	1.02124076
100	1.01657284	1.01726924	1.01796612	1.01866347	1.01936129	1.02005958	1.02075835	1.02145760

Day	6.00%	6.25%	6.50%	6.75%	7.00%	7.25%	7.50%	7.75%
101	1.01673994	1.01744343	1.01814740	1.01885185	1.01955678	1.02026220	1.02096810	1.02167448
102	1.01690708	1.01761765	1.01832871	1.01904027	1.01975231	1.02046485	1.02117789	1.02189141
103	1.01707424	1.01779190	1.01851006	1.01922872	1.01994788	1.02066755	1.02138772	1.02210839
104	1.01724143	1.01796618	1.01869144	1.01941721	1.02014349	1.02087028	1.02159759	1.02232541
105	1.01740865	1.01814049	1.01887285	1.01960573	1.02033913	1.02107306	1.02180751	1.02254248
106	1.01757589	1.01831483	1.01905429	1.01979429	1.02053481	1.02127587	1.02201747	1.02275959
107	1.01774317	1.01848920	1.01923577	1.01998288	1.02073053	1.02147873	1.02222747	1.02297676
108	1.01791047	1.01866359	1.01941727	1.02017151	1.02092629	1.02168163	1.02243752	1.02319396
109	1.01807780	1.01883802	1.01959881	1.02036017	1.02112208	1.02188456	1.02264761	1.02341122
110	1.01824515	1.01901248	1.01978039	1.02054886	1.02131792	1.02208754	1.02285774	1.02362852
111	1.01841253	1.01918697	1.01996199	1.02073760	1.02151378	1.02229056	1.02306792	1.02384586
112	1.01857994	1.01936149	1.02014363	1.02092636	1.02170969	1.02249362	1.02327814	1.02406325
113	1.01874738	1.01953604	1.02032530	1.02111516	1.02190564	1.02269671	1.02348840	1.02428069
114	1.01891485	1.01971062	1.02050700	1.02130400	1.02210162	1.02289985	1.02369871	1.02449818
115	1.01908234	1.01988522	1.02068873	1.02149287	1.02229764	1.02310303	1.02390905	1.02471571
116	1.01924986	1.02005986	1.02087050	1.02168178	1.02249369	1.02330625	1.02411945	1.02493328
117	1.01941741	1.02023453	1.02105230	1.02187072	1.02268979	1.02350951	1.02432988	1.02515091
118	1.01958498	1.02040923	1.02123413	1.02205969	1.02288592	1.02371281	1.02454036	1.02536858
119	1.01975259	1.02058395	1.02141599	1.02224871	1.02308209	1.02391615	1.02475088	1.02558629
120	1.01992022	1.02075871	1.02159789	1.02243775	1.02327830	1.02411953	1.02496145	1.02580405
121	1.02008788	1.02093350	1.02177982	1.02262683	1.02347454	1.02432295	1.02517206	1.02602186
122	1.02025556	1.02110832	1.02196178	1.02281595	1.02367083	1.02452641	1.02538271	1.02623971
123	1.02042327	1.02128316	1.02214377	1.02300510	1.02386715	1.02472991	1.02559340	1.02645761
124	1.02059102	1.02145804	1.02232580	1.02319429	1.02406351	1.02493346	1.02580414	1.02667556
125	1.02075878	1.02163295	1.02250786	1.02338351	1.02425990	1.02513704	1.02601492	1.02689355
126	1.02092658	1.02180789	1.02268995	1.02357276	1.02445633	1.02534066	1.02622575	1.02711159
127	1.02109440	1.02198285	1.02287207	1.02376205	1.02465281	1.02554433	1.02643662	1.02732968
128	1.02126225	1.02215785	1.02305422	1.02395138	1.02484931	1.02574803	1.02664753	1.02754781
129	1.02143013	1.02233288	1.02323641	1.02414074	1.02504586	1.02595177	1.02685848	1.02776599
130	1.02159804	1.02250793	1.02341863	1.02433014	1.02524244	1.02615556	1.02706948	1.02798421
131	1.02176597	1.02268302	1.02360088	1.02451957	1.02543907	1.02635939	1.02728052	1.02820248
132	1.02193393	1.02285814	1.02378317	1.02470903	1.02563573	1.02656325	1.02749161	1.02842080
133	1.02210192	1.02303328	1.02396549	1.02489853	1.02583242	1.02676716	1.02770274	1.02863916
134	1.02226994	1.02320846	1.02414784	1.02508807	1.02602916	1.02697110	1.02791391	1.02885757
135	1.02243798	1.02338367	1.02433022	1.02527764	1.02622593	1.02717509	1.02812512	1.02907603
136	1.02260606	1.02355891	1.02451263	1.02546725	1.02642274	1.02737912	1.02833638	1.02929453
137	1.02277416	1.02373417	1.02469508	1.02565689	1.02661959	1.02758319	1.02854768	1.02951308
138	1.02294228	1.02390947	1.02487756	1.02584656	1.02681648	1.02778730	1.02875903	1.02973167
139	1.02311044	1.02408480	1.02506007	1.02603628	1.02701340	1.02799145	1.02897042	1.02995032
140	1.02327862	1.02426015	1.02524262	1.02622602	1.02721036	1.02819564	1.02918185	1.03016900
141	1.02344683	1.02443554	1.02542520	1.02641580	1.02740736	1.02839987	1.02939333	1.03038774
142	1.02361507	1.02461096	1.02560781	1.02660562	1.02760440	1.02860414	1.02960485	1.03060652
143	1.02378333	1.02478640	1.02579045	1.02679547	1.02780147	1.02880845	1.02981641	1.03082535
144	1.02395163	1.02496188	1.02597312	1.02698536	1.02799858	1.02901280	1.03002801	1.03104422
145	1.02411995	1.02513739	1.02615583	1.02717528	1.02819573	1.02921720	1.03023966	1.03126314
146	1.02428830	1.02531293	1.02633857	1.02736524	1.02839292	1.02942163	1.03045136	1.03148211
147	1.02445667	1.02548849	1.02652134	1.02755523	1.02859015	1.02962610	1.03066309	1.03170112
148	1.02462508	1.02566409	1.02670415	1.02774526	1.02878741	1.02983062	1.03087487	1.03192018
149	1.02479351	1.02583972	1.02688699	1.02793532	1.02898471	1.03003517	1.03108670	1.03213929
150	1.02496197	1.02601538	1.02706986	1.02812542	1.02918205	1.03023977	1.03129856	1.03235844

Day	6.00%	6.25%	6.50%	6.75%	7.00%	7.25%	7.50%	7.75%
151	1.02513045	1.02619106	1.02725276	1.02831555	1.02937943	1.03044441	1.03151048	1.03257764
152	1.02529897	1.02636678	1.02743570	1.02850572	1.02957685	1.03064908	1.03172243	1.03279689
153	1.02546751	1.02654253	1.02761866	1.02869592	1.02977430	1.03085380	1.03193443	1.03301618
154	1.02563608	1.02671831	1.02780166	1.02888616	1.02997179	1.03105856	1.03214647	1.03323552
155	1.02580468	1.02689411	1.02798470	1.02907643	1.03016932	1.03126336	1.03235855	1.03345490
156	1.02597330	1.02706995	1.02816776	1.02926674	1.03036689	1.03146820	1.03257068	1.03367434
157	1.02614196	1.02724582	1.02835086	1.02945709	1.03056449	1.03167308	1.03278285	1.03389381
158	1.02631064	1.02742172	1.02853399	1.02964746	1.03076213	1.03187800	1.03299507	1.03411334
159	1.02647935	1.02759765	1.02871716	1.02983788	1.03095981	1.03208296	1.03320733	1.03433291
160	1.02664808	1.02777361	1.02890035	1.03002833	1.03115753	1.03228797	1.03341963	1.03455253
161	1.02681685	1.02794959	1.02908358	1.03021881	1.03135529	1.03249301	1.03363198	1.03477220
162	1.02698564	1.02812561	1.02926684	1.03040933	1.03155308	1.03269809	1.03384437	1.03499191
163	1.02715446	1.02830166	1.02945014	1.03059989	1.03175091	1.03290322	1.03405680	1.03521167
164	1.02732331	1.02847774	1.02963346	1.03079048	1.03194878	1.03310838	1.03426928	1.03543147
165	1.02749218	1.02865385	1.02981682	1.03098110	1.03214669	1.03331359	1.03448180	1.03565132
166	1.02766108	1.02882999	1.03000022	1.03117176	1.03234464	1.03351884	1.03469437	1.03587122
167	1.02783001	1.02900616	1.03018364	1.03136246	1.03254262	1.03372413	1.03490697	1.03609117
168	1.02799897	1.02918236	1.03036710	1.03155319	1.03274064	1.03392945	1.03511963	1.03631116
169	1.02816796	1.02935859	1.03055059	1.03174396	1.03293870	1.03413482	1.03533232	1.03653120
170	1.02833697	1.02953485	1.03073411	1.03193476	1.03313680	1.03434023	1.03554506	1.03675128
171	1.02850601	1.02971114	1.03091767	1.03212560	1.03333494	1.03454569	1.03575784	1.03697141
172	1.02867508	1.02988746	1.03110125	1.03231647	1.03353311	1.03475118	1.03597067	1.03719159
173	1.02884418	1.03006381	1.03128487	1.03250738	1.03373132	1.03495671	1.03618354	1.03741182
174	1.02901331	1.03024019	1.03146853	1.03269832	1.03392957	1.03516228	1.03639646	1.03763209
175	1.02918246	1.03041660	1.03165221	1.03288930	1.03412786	1.03536790	1.03660941	1.03785241
176	1.02935164	1.03059304	1.03183593	1.03308031	1.03432619	1.03557355	1.03682242	1.03807278
177	1.02952085	1.03076951	1.03201968	1.03327136	1.03452455	1.03577925	1.03703546	1.03829319
178	1.02969009	1.03094602	1.03220347	1.03346245	1.03472295	1.03598499	1.03724855	1.03851365
179	1.02985935	1.03112255	1.03238729	1.03365357	1.03492139	1.03619076	1.03746168	1.03873416
180	1.03002864	1.03129911	1.03257114	1.03384472	1.03511987	1.03639658	1.03767486	1.03895471
181	1.03019796	1.03147570	1.03275502	1.03403591	1.03531839	1.03660244	1.03788808	1.03917531
182	1.03036731	1.03165232	1.03293893	1.03422714	1.03551694	1.03680834	1.03810135	1.03939596
183	1.03053668	1.03182898	1.03312288	1.03441840	1.03571553	1.03701429	1.03831466	1.03961665
184	1.03070609	1.03200566	1.03330686	1.03460970	1.03591416	1.03722027	1.03852801	1.03983739
185	1.03087552	1.03218237	1.03349088	1.03480103	1.03611283	1.03742629	1.03874140	1.04005818
186	1.03104498	1.03235912	1.03367492	1.03499240	1.03631154	1.03763235	1.03895484	1.04027901
187	1.03121446	1.03253589	1.03385900	1.03518380	1.03651028	1.03783846	1.03916833	1.04049989
188	1.03138398	1.03271269	1.03404311	1.03537524	1.03670907	1.03804461	1.03938186	1.04072082
189	1.03155352	1.03288953	1.03422726	1.03556671	1.03690789	1.03825079	1.03959543	1.04094180
190	1.03172309	1.03306639	1.03441144	1.03575822	1.03710675	1.03845702	1.03980904	1.04116282
191	1.03189269	1.03324329	1.03459565	1.03594976	1.03730564	1.03866329	1.04002270	1.04138389
192	1.03206232	1.03342021	1.03477989	1.03614134	1.03750458	1.03886960	1.04023641	1.04160500
193	1.03223197	1.03359717	1.03496416	1.03633296	1.03770355	1.03907595	1.04045015	1.04182616
194	1.03240165	1.03377416	1.03514847	1.03652461	1.03790256	1.03928234	1.04066394	1.04204737
195	1.03257136	1.03395117	1.03533281	1.03671629	1.03810161	1.03948877	1.04087778	1.04226863
196	1.03274110	1.03412822	1.03551719	1.03690802	1.03830070	1.03969525	1.04109166	1.04248993
197	1.03291087	1.03430529	1.03570160	1.03709977	1.03849983	1.03990176	1.04130558	1.04271128
198	1.03308066	1.03448240	1.03588604	1.03729157	1.03869899	1.04010832	1.04151955	1.04293268
199	1.03325048	1.03465954	1.03607051	1.03748339	1.03889819	1.04031492	1.04173356	1.04315413
200	1.03342033	1.03483671	1.03625501	1.03767526	1.03909744	1.04052155	1.04194761	1.04337562

Day	*6.00%*	*6.25%*	*6.50%*	*6.75%*	*7.00%*	*7.25%*	*7.50%*	*7.75%*
201	1.03359021	1.03501390	1.03643955	1.03786716	1.03929671	1.04072823	1.04216171	1.04359716
202	1.03376011	1.03519113	1.03662412	1.03805909	1.03949603	1.04093495	1.04237586	1.04381874
203	1.03393005	1.03536839	1.03680873	1.03825106	1.03969539	1.04114171	1.04259004	1.04404038
204	1.03410001	1.03554568	1.03699337	1.03844306	1.03989478	1.04134852	1.04280427	1.04426206
205	1.03427000	1.03572300	1.03717804	1.03863511	1.04009421	1.04155536	1.04301855	1.04448378
206	1.03444001	1.03590035	1.03736274	1.03882718	1.04029368	1.04176224	1.04323287	1.04470556
207	1.03461006	1.03607773	1.03754747	1.03901929	1.04049319	1.04196917	1.04344723	1.04492738
208	1.03478013	1.03625514	1.03773224	1.03921144	1.04069274	1.04217614	1.04366164	1.04514925
209	1.03495023	1.03643258	1.03791705	1.03940362	1.04089232	1.04238314	1.04387609	1.04537116
210	1.03512036	1.03661005	1.03810188	1.03959584	1.04109195	1.04259019	1.04409058	1.04559312
211	1.03529052	1.03678755	1.03828675	1.03978810	1.04129161	1.04279728	1.04430512	1.04581513
212	1.03546070	1.03696509	1.03847165	1.03998039	1.04149131	1.04300441	1.04451971	1.04603719
213	1.03563091	1.03714265	1.03865658	1.04017271	1.04169105	1.04321158	1.04473433	1.04625929
214	1.03580116	1.03732024	1.03884155	1.04036507	1.04189082	1.04341880	1.04494900	1.04648144
215	1.03597142	1.03749787	1.03902655	1.04055747	1.04209064	1.04362605	1.04516372	1.04670364
216	1.03614172	1.03767552	1.03921158	1.04074990	1.04229049	1.04383335	1.04537848	1.04692589
217	1.03631205	1.03785320	1.03939664	1.04094237	1.04249038	1.04404068	1.04559328	1.04714818
218	1.03648240	1.03803092	1.03958174	1.04113487	1.04269031	1.04424806	1.04580813	1.04737052
219	1.03665278	1.03820866	1.03976687	1.04132741	1.04289028	1.04445548	1.04602302	1.04759291
220	1.03682319	1.03838644	1.03995204	1.04151998	1.04309028	1.04466294	1.04623796	1.04781534
221	1.03699362	1.03856424	1.04013723	1.04171259	1.04329033	1.04487044	1.04645294	1.04803782
222	1.03716409	1.03874208	1.04032246	1.04190524	1.04349041	1.04507799	1.04666796	1.04826035
223	1.03733458	1.03891995	1.04050773	1.04209792	1.04369053	1.04528557	1.04688303	1.04848293
224	1.03750510	1.03909785	1.04069302	1.04229064	1.04389069	1.04549320	1.04709815	1.04870555
225	1.03767565	1.03927577	1.04087835	1.04248339	1.04409089	1.04570086	1.04731330	1.04892822
226	1.03784623	1.03945373	1.04106371	1.04267618	1.04429113	1.04590857	1.04752850	1.04915094
227	1.03801683	1.03963172	1.04124911	1.04286900	1.04449140	1.04611632	1.04774375	1.04937370
228	1.03818747	1.03980974	1.04143454	1.04306186	1.04469172	1.04632411	1.04795904	1.04959651
229	1.03835813	1.03998779	1.04162000	1.04325476	1.04489207	1.04653194	1.04817437	1.04981937
230	1.03852882	1.04016587	1.04180549	1.04344769	1.04509246	1.04673981	1.04838975	1.05004228
231	1.03869953	1.04034398	1.04199102	1.04364065	1.04529289	1.04694773	1.04860517	1.05026523
232	1.03887028	1.04052212	1.04217658	1.04383365	1.04549335	1.04715568	1.04882064	1.05048824
233	1.03904105	1.04070029	1.04236217	1.04402669	1.04569386	1.04736368	1.04903615	1.05071129
234	1.03921185	1.04087849	1.04254780	1.04421977	1.04589440	1.04757172	1.04925171	1.05093438
235	1.03938268	1.04105673	1.04273346	1.04441287	1.04609499	1.04777980	1.04946731	1.05115752
236	1.03955354	1.04123499	1.04291915	1.04460602	1.04629561	1.04798792	1.04968295	1.05138072
237	1.03972442	1.04141328	1.04310487	1.04479920	1.04649627	1.04819608	1.04989864	1.05160395
238	1.03989534	1.04159161	1.04329063	1.04499242	1.04669697	1.04840428	1.05011437	1.05182724
239	1.04006628	1.04176996	1.04347642	1.04518567	1.04689770	1.04861253	1.05033015	1.05205057
240	1.04023725	1.04194835	1.04366225	1.04537896	1.04709848	1.04882081	1.05054597	1.05227395
241	1.04040825	1.04212676	1.04384811	1.04557228	1.04729929	1.04902914	1.05076184	1.05249738
242	1.04057927	1.04230521	1.04403400	1.04576564	1.04750014	1.04923751	1.05097775	1.05272086
243	1.04075033	1.04248369	1.04421992	1.04595903	1.04770103	1.04944592	1.05119370	1.05294438
244	1.04092141	1.04266219	1.04440588	1.04615246	1.04790196	1.04965437	1.05140970	1.05316795
245	1.04109252	1.04284073	1.04459187	1.04634593	1.04810293	1.04986286	1.05162574	1.05339157
246	1.04126366	1.04301930	1.04477789	1.04653943	1.04830393	1.05007140	1.05184183	1.05361523
247	1.04143483	1.04319790	1.04496395	1.04673297	1.04850498	1.05027997	1.05205796	1.05383895
248	1.04160602	1.04337653	1.04515004	1.04692655	1.04870606	1.05048859	1.05227414	1.05406271
249	1.04177724	1.04355519	1.04533616	1.04712015	1.04890718	1.05069725	1.05249036	1.05428651
250	1.04194849	1.04373388	1.04552231	1.04731380	1.04910834	1.05090595	1.05270662	1.05451037

Day	6.00%	6.25%	6.50%	6.75%	7.00%	7.25%	7.50%	7.75%
251	1.04211977	1.04391260	1.04570850	1.04750748	1.04930954	1.05111469	1.05292293	1.05473427
252	1.04229108	1.04409135	1.04589473	1.04770120	1.04951078	1.05132347	1.05313929	1.05495822
253	1.04246242	1.04427014	1.04608098	1.04789495	1.04971206	1.05153230	1.05335569	1.05518222
254	1.04263378	1.04444895	1.04626727	1.04808874	1.04991337	1.05174117	1.05357213	1.05540627
255	1.04280517	1.04462779	1.04645359	1.04828257	1.05011472	1.05195007	1.05378862	1.05563036
256	1.04297659	1.04480667	1.04663995	1.04847643	1.05031612	1.05215902	1.05400515	1.05585450
257	1.04314804	1.04498557	1.04682633	1.04867032	1.05051755	1.05236801	1.05422172	1.05607869
258	1.04331952	1.04516451	1.04701275	1.04886425	1.05071902	1.05257704	1.05443835	1.05630292
259	1.04349102	1.04534348	1.04719921	1.04905822	1.05092052	1.05278612	1.05465501	1.05652721
260	1.04366255	1.04552247	1.04738570	1.04925223	1.05112207	1.05299523	1.05487172	1.05675154
261	1.04383411	1.04570150	1.04757222	1.04944627	1.05132366	1.05320439	1.05508847	1.05697592
262	1.04400570	1.04588056	1.04775877	1.04964034	1.05152528	1.05341359	1.05530527	1.05720034
263	1.04417732	1.04605965	1.04794536	1.04983445	1.05172694	1.05362283	1.05552212	1.05742482
264	1.04434897	1.04623877	1.04813198	1.05002860	1.05192864	1.05383211	1.05573901	1.05764934
265	1.04452064	1.04641792	1.04831863	1.05022278	1.05213038	1.05404143	1.05595594	1.05787391
266	1.04469234	1.04659710	1.04850532	1.05041700	1.05233216	1.05425080	1.05617292	1.05809853
267	1.04486407	1.04677631	1.04869204	1.05061126	1.05253398	1.05446020	1.05638994	1.05832319
268	1.04503583	1.04695556	1.04887879	1.05080555	1.05273583	1.05466965	1.05660700	1.05854790
269	1.04520762	1.04713483	1.04906558	1.05099988	1.05293773	1.05487914	1.05682411	1.05877266
270	1.04537943	1.04731413	1.04925240	1.05119424	1.05313966	1.05508867	1.05704127	1.05899747
271	1.04555128	1.04749347	1.04943925	1.05138864	1.05334163	1.05529824	1.05725847	1.05922233
272	1.04572315	1.04767283	1.04962614	1.05158307	1.05354364	1.05550786	1.05747572	1.05944723
273	1.04589505	1.04785223	1.04981306	1.05177754	1.05374569	1.05571751	1.05769301	1.05967218
274	1.04606698	1.04803166	1.05000001	1.05197205	1.05394778	1.05592721	1.05791034	1.05989718
275	1.04623893	1.04821111	1.05018700	1.05216659	1.05414991	1.05613695	1.05812772	1.06012223
276	1.04641092	1.04839060	1.05037402	1.05236117	1.05435207	1.05634673	1.05834514	1.06034732
277	1.04658293	1.04857012	1.05056107	1.05255579	1.05455428	1.05655655	1.05856261	1.06057246
278	1.04675497	1.04874967	1.05074816	1.05275044	1.05475652	1.05676641	1.05878012	1.06079765
279	1.04692704	1.04892925	1.05093528	1.05294512	1.05495880	1.05697632	1.05899768	1.06102289
280	1.04709914	1.04910886	1.05112243	1.05313985	1.05516113	1.05718627	1.05921528	1.06124818
281	1.04727126	1.04928850	1.05130962	1.05333461	1.05536348	1.05739626	1.05943293	1.06147351
282	1.04744342	1.04946818	1.05149683	1.05352940	1.05556588	1.05760629	1.05965062	1.06169889
283	1.04761560	1.04964788	1.05168409	1.05372423	1.05576832	1.05781636	1.05986836	1.06192432
284	1.04778781	1.04982761	1.05187137	1.05391910	1.05597080	1.05802647	1.06008614	1.06214980
285	1.04796005	1.05000738	1.05205869	1.05411400	1.05617331	1.05823663	1.06030396	1.06237532
286	1.04813232	1.05018717	1.05224605	1.05430894	1.05637587	1.05844683	1.06052184	1.06260090
287	1.04830461	1.05036700	1.05243343	1.05450392	1.05657846	1.05865707	1.06073975	1.06282652
288	1.04847694	1.05054686	1.05262085	1.05469893	1.05678109	1.05886735	1.06095771	1.06305219
289	1.04864929	1.05072675	1.05280831	1.05489397	1.05698376	1.05907767	1.06117572	1.06327790
290	1.04882167	1.05090667	1.05299579	1.05508906	1.05718647	1.05928804	1.06139377	1.06350367
291	1.04899408	1.05108661	1.05318331	1.05528418	1.05738922	1.05949844	1.06161186	1.06372948
292	1.04916652	1.05126660	1.05337086	1.05547933	1.05759200	1.05970889	1.06183000	1.06395534
293	1.04933898	1.05144661	1.05355845	1.05567452	1.05779483	1.05991938	1.06204818	1.06418125
294	1.04951148	1.05162665	1.05374607	1.05586975	1.05799769	1.06012991	1.06226641	1.06440720
295	1.04968400	1.05180672	1.05393372	1.05606501	1.05820060	1.06034049	1.06248469	1.06463321
296	1.04985655	1.05198683	1.05412141	1.05626031	1.05840354	1.06055110	1.06270301	1.06485926
297	1.05002913	1.05216696	1.05430913	1.05645565	1.05860652	1.06076176	1.06292137	1.06508536
298	1.05020174	1.05234713	1.05449689	1.05665102	1.05880954	1.06097246	1.06313978	1.06531151
299	1.05037437	1.05252732	1.05468467	1.05684643	1.05901260	1.06118320	1.06335823	1.06553771
300	1.05054704	1.05270755	1.05487249	1.05704187	1.05921570	1.06139398	1.06357673	1.06576395

Day	6.00%	6.25%	6.50%	6.75%	7.00%	7.25%	7.50%	7.75%
301	1.05071973	1.05288781	1.05506035	1.05723735	1.05941884	1.06160481	1.06379527	1.06599024
302	1.05089245	1.05306810	1.05524823	1.05743287	1.05962201	1.06181567	1.06401386	1.06621658
303	1.05106520	1.05324842	1.05543616	1.05762842	1.05982523	1.06202658	1.06423249	1.06644297
304	1.05123798	1.05342877	1.05562411	1.05782401	1.06002848	1.06223753	1.06445117	1.06666941
305	1.05141078	1.05360915	1.05581210	1.05801964	1.06023178	1.06244853	1.06466989	1.06689589
306	1.05158362	1.05378956	1.05600012	1.05821530	1.06043511	1.06265956	1.06488866	1.06712242
307	1.05175648	1.05397001	1.05618817	1.05841099	1.06063848	1.06287064	1.06510747	1.06734901
308	1.05192937	1.05415048	1.05637626	1.05860673	1.06084189	1.06308175	1.06532633	1.06757563
309	1.05210229	1.05433098	1.05656438	1.05880250	1.06104534	1.06329291	1.06554524	1.06780231
310	1.05227524	1.05451152	1.05675254	1.05899830	1.06124883	1.06350412	1.06576418	1.06802904
311	1.05244822	1.05469209	1.05694073	1.05919415	1.06145235	1.06371536	1.06598318	1.06825581
312	1.05262122	1.05487269	1.05712895	1.05939002	1.06165592	1.06392665	1.06620221	1.06848263
313	1.05279426	1.05505331	1.05731721	1.05958594	1.06185953	1.06413797	1.06642130	1.06870950
314	1.05296732	1.05523397	1.05750550	1.05978189	1.06206317	1.06434934	1.06664042	1.06893642
315	1.05314041	1.05541467	1.05769382	1.05997788	1.06226685	1.06456076	1.06685960	1.06916338
316	1.05331353	1.05559539	1.05788217	1.06017390	1.06247058	1.06477221	1.06707881	1.06939040
317	1.05348667	1.05577614	1.05807056	1.06036996	1.06267434	1.06498371	1.06729808	1.06961746
318	1.05365985	1.05595692	1.05825899	1.06056606	1.06287814	1.06519524	1.06751738	1.06984457
319	1.05383305	1.05613774	1.05844745	1.06076219	1.06308198	1.06540682	1.06773674	1.07007173
320	1.05400629	1.05631858	1.05863594	1.06095836	1.06328586	1.06561845	1.06795614	1.07029894
321	1.05417955	1.05649946	1.05882446	1.06115456	1.06348977	1.06583011	1.06817558	1.07052619
322	1.05435284	1.05668037	1.05901302	1.06135080	1.06369373	1.06604181	1.06839507	1.07075350
323	1.05452616	1.05686131	1.05920161	1.06154708	1.06389773	1.06625356	1.06861460	1.07098085
324	1.05469950	1.05704228	1.05939023	1.06174339	1.06410176	1.06646535	1.06883418	1.07120825
325	1.05487288	1.05722328	1.05957889	1.06193974	1.06430584	1.06667719	1.06905380	1.07143570
326	1.05504628	1.05740431	1.05976758	1.06213613	1.06450995	1.06688906	1.06927347	1.07166319
327	1.05521971	1.05758537	1.05995631	1.06233255	1.06471410	1.06710098	1.06949318	1.07189074
328	1.05539318	1.05776646	1.06014507	1.06252901	1.06491829	1.06731293	1.06971294	1.07211833
329	1.05556666	1.05794759	1.06033386	1.06272550	1.06512252	1.06752493	1.06993275	1.07234597
330	1.05574018	1.05812874	1.06052269	1.06292204	1.06532680	1.06773698	1.07015260	1.07257366
331	1.05591373	1.05830993	1.06071155	1.06311860	1.06553110	1.06794906	1.07037249	1.07280140
332	1.05608730	1.05849115	1.06090044	1.06331521	1.06573545	1.06816119	1.07059243	1.07302919
333	1.05626091	1.05867239	1.06108937	1.06351185	1.06593984	1.06837336	1.07081241	1.07325702
334	1.05643454	1.05885367	1.06127833	1.06370853	1.06614427	1.06858557	1.07103244	1.07348491
335	1.05660820	1.05903498	1.06146733	1.06390524	1.06634873	1.06879782	1.07125252	1.07371284

Day	6.00%	6.25%	6.50%	6.75%	7.00%	7.25%	7.50%	7.75%
336	1.05678189	1.05921633	1.06165636	1.06410199	1.06655324	1.06901012	1.07147264	1.07394082
337	1.05695561	1.05939770	1.06184542	1.06429877	1.06675778	1.06922246	1.07169281	1.07416885
338	1.05712935	1.05957910	1.06203451	1.06449560	1.06696237	1.06943484	1.07191302	1.07439692
339	1.05730313	1.05976054	1.06222364	1.06469246	1.06716699	1.06964726	1.07213327	1.07462505
340	1.05747693	1.05994200	1.06241281	1.06488935	1.06737165	1.06985972	1.07235357	1.07485322
341	1.05765076	1.06012350	1.06260200	1.06508628	1.06757635	1.07007223	1.07257392	1.07508144
342	1.05782462	1.06030503	1.06279123	1.06528325	1.06778109	1.07028478	1.07279431	1.07530972
343	1.05799851	1.06048659	1.06298050	1.06548025	1.06798587	1.07049737	1.07301475	1.07553803
344	1.05817243	1.06066818	1.06316980	1.06567730	1.06819069	1.07071000	1.07323523	1.07576640
345	1.05834638	1.06084980	1.06335913	1.06587437	1.06839555	1.07092268	1.07345576	1.07599482
346	1.05852035	1.06103145	1.06354849	1.06607149	1.06860045	1.07113539	1.07367633	1.07622328
347	1.05869435	1.06121313	1.06373789	1.06626864	1.06880539	1.07134815	1.07389695	1.07645180
348	1.05886839	1.06139485	1.06392732	1.06646582	1.06901036	1.07156095	1.07411761	1.07668036
349	1.05904245	1.06157659	1.06411679	1.06666305	1.06921538	1.07177380	1.07433832	1.07690897
350	1.05921654	1.06175837	1.06430629	1.06686031	1.06942043	1.07198669	1.07455908	1.07713763
351	1.05939065	1.06194018	1.06449582	1.06705760	1.06962553	1.07219961	1.07477988	1.07736633
352	1.05956480	1.06212202	1.06468539	1.06725493	1.06983066	1.07241259	1.07500072	1.07759509
353	1.05973897	1.06230389	1.06487499	1.06745230	1.07003583	1.07262560	1.07522161	1.07782389
354	1.05991318	1.06248579	1.06506463	1.06764971	1.07024105	1.07283865	1.07544255	1.07805275
355	1.06008741	1.06266772	1.06525430	1.06784715	1.07044630	1.07305175	1.07566353	1.07828165
356	1.06026167	1.06284969	1.06544400	1.06804463	1.07065159	1.07326489	1.07588456	1.07851060
357	1.06043596	1.06303168	1.06563374	1.06824214	1.07085692	1.07347808	1.07610563	1.07873960
358	1.06061028	1.06321371	1.06582351	1.06843970	1.07106229	1.07369130	1.07632675	1.07896865
359	1.06078463	1.06339576	1.06601331	1.06863728	1.07126770	1.07390457	1.07654791	1.07919774
360	1.06095900	1.06357785	1.06620315	1.06883491	1.07147315	1.07411788	1.07676912	1.07942689
361	1.06113341	1.06375997	1.06639302	1.06903257	1.07167864	1.07433123	1.07699037	1.07965608
362	1.06130784	1.06394212	1.06658293	1.06923027	1.07188416	1.07454463	1.07721167	1.07988532
363	1.06148230	1.06412430	1.06677287	1.06942800	1.07208973	1.07475806	1.07743302	1.08011461
364	1.06165679	1.06430652	1.06696284	1.06962577	1.07229534	1.07497154	1.07765441	1.08034395
365	1.06183131	1.06448876	1.06715285	1.06982358	1.07250098	1.07518506	1.07787584	1.08057334

Day	8.00%	8.25%	8.50%	8.75%	9.00%	9.25%	9.50%	9.75%
1	1.00021918	1.00022603	1.00023288	1.00023973	1.00024658	1.00025342	1.00026027	1.00026712
2	1.00043840	1.00045211	1.00046581	1.00047951	1.00049321	1.00050691	1.00052062	1.00053432
3	1.00065768	1.00067824	1.00069879	1.00071935	1.00073991	1.00076047	1.00078103	1.00080158
4	1.00087700	1.00090442	1.00093183	1.00095925	1.00098667	1.00101408	1.00104150	1.00106892
5	1.00109637	1.00113065	1.00116493	1.00119920	1.00123348	1.00126777	1.00130205	1.00133633
6	1.00131579	1.00135693	1.00139807	1.00143922	1.00148036	1.00152151	1.00156266	1.00160381
7	1.00153526	1.00158327	1.00163128	1.00167929	1.00172730	1.00177532	1.00182334	1.00187136
8	1.00175477	1.00180965	1.00186453	1.00191942	1.00197431	1.00202920	1.00208409	1.00213899
9	1.00197433	1.00203609	1.00209784	1.00215960	1.00222137	1.00228314	1.00234491	1.00240668
10	1.00219394	1.00226257	1.00233121	1.00239985	1.00246849	1.00253714	1.00260579	1.00267445
11	1.00241360	1.00248911	1.00256463	1.00264015	1.00271568	1.00279121	1.00286674	1.00294228
12	1.00263331	1.00271570	1.00279810	1.00288051	1.00296292	1.00304534	1.00312776	1.00321019
13	1.00285307	1.00294234	1.00303163	1.00312092	1.00321023	1.00329953	1.00338885	1.00347817
14	1.00307287	1.00316904	1.00326521	1.00336140	1.00345759	1.00355380	1.00365001	1.00374623
15	1.00329272	1.00339578	1.00349885	1.00360193	1.00370502	1.00380812	1.00391123	1.00401435
16	1.00351262	1.00362258	1.00373254	1.00384252	1.00395251	1.00406251	1.00417252	1.00428255
17	1.00373257	1.00384942	1.00396629	1.00408317	1.00420006	1.00431696	1.00443388	1.00455081
18	1.00395256	1.00407632	1.00420009	1.00432387	1.00444767	1.00457148	1.00469531	1.00481915
19	1.00417261	1.00430327	1.00443394	1.00456463	1.00469534	1.00482607	1.00495681	1.00508756
20	1.00439270	1.00453027	1.00466785	1.00480546	1.00494308	1.00508071	1.00521837	1.00535604
21	1.00461284	1.00475732	1.00490182	1.00504633	1.00519087	1.00533543	1.00548000	1.00562460
22	1.00483303	1.00498442	1.00513583	1.00528727	1.00543873	1.00559020	1.00574170	1.00589322
23	1.00505327	1.00521158	1.00536991	1.00552826	1.00568664	1.00584504	1.00600347	1.00616192
24	1.00527355	1.00543878	1.00560403	1.00576931	1.00593462	1.00609995	1.00626531	1.00643069
25	1.00549389	1.00566604	1.00583822	1.00601042	1.00618266	1.00635492	1.00652721	1.00669953
26	1.00571427	1.00589335	1.00607245	1.00625159	1.00643076	1.00660996	1.00678919	1.00696845
27	1.00593470	1.00612071	1.00630674	1.00649281	1.00667892	1.00686506	1.00705123	1.00723743
28	1.00615518	1.00634812	1.00654109	1.00673410	1.00692714	1.00712022	1.00731334	1.00750649
29	1.00637571	1.00657558	1.00677549	1.00697544	1.00717542	1.00737545	1.00757551	1.00777561
30	1.00659628	1.00680309	1.00700994	1.00721684	1.00742377	1.00763074	1.00783776	1.00804482
31	1.00681691	1.00703066	1.00724445	1.00745829	1.00767217	1.00788610	1.00810007	1.00831409
32	1.00703758	1.00725827	1.00747902	1.00769981	1.00792064	1.00814152	1.00836245	1.00858343
33	1.00725830	1.00748594	1.00771363	1.00794138	1.00816917	1.00839701	1.00862491	1.00885285
34	1.00747907	1.00771366	1.00794831	1.00818301	1.00841776	1.00865257	1.00888742	1.00912234
35	1.00769988	1.00794143	1.00818304	1.00842469	1.00866641	1.00890818	1.00915001	1.00939190
36	1.00792075	1.00816925	1.00841782	1.00866644	1.00891512	1.00916387	1.00941267	1.00966153
37	1.00814166	1.00839713	1.00865265	1.00890824	1.00916390	1.00941961	1.00967539	1.00993123
38	1.00836263	1.00862505	1.00888755	1.00915011	1.00941273	1.00967542	1.00993818	1.01020101
39	1.00858364	1.00885303	1.00912249	1.00939203	1.00966163	1.00993130	1.01020104	1.01047086
40	1.00880470	1.00908106	1.00935749	1.00963400	1.00991059	1.01018724	1.01046397	1.01074078
41	1.00902581	1.00930914	1.00959255	1.00987604	1.01015960	1.01044325	1.01072697	1.01101077
42	1.00924696	1.00953727	1.00982766	1.01011813	1.01040868	1.01069932	1.01099004	1.01128083
43	1.00946817	1.00976545	1.01006283	1.01036028	1.01065783	1.01095546	1.01125317	1.01155097
44	1.00968942	1.00999369	1.01029805	1.01060249	1.01090703	1.01121166	1.01151637	1.01182118
45	1.00991072	1.01022197	1.01053332	1.01084476	1.01115629	1.01146792	1.01177964	1.01209146
46	1.01013207	1.01045031	1.01076865	1.01108709	1.01140562	1.01172425	1.01204298	1.01236181
47	1.01035347	1.01067870	1.01100403	1.01132947	1.01165501	1.01198065	1.01230639	1.01263224
48	1.01057492	1.01090714	1.01123947	1.01157191	1.01190446	1.01223711	1.01256987	1.01290274
49	1.01079641	1.01113564	1.01147497	1.01181441	1.01215397	1.01249364	1.01283342	1.01317331
50	1.01101796	1.01136418	1.01171052	1.01205697	1.01240354	1.01275023	1.01309703	1.01344395

Day	8.00%	8.25%	8.50%	8.75%	9.00%	9.25%	9.50%	9.75%
51	1.01123955	1.01159278	1.01194612	1.01229959	1.01265317	1.01300688	1.01336071	1.01371466
52	1.01146119	1.01182142	1.01218178	1.01254226	1.01290287	1.01326360	1.01362446	1.01398545
53	1.01168288	1.01205012	1.01241749	1.01278499	1.01315263	1.01352039	1.01388828	1.01425631
54	1.01190462	1.01227887	1.01265326	1.01302779	1.01340245	1.01377724	1.01415217	1.01452724
55	1.01212641	1.01250768	1.01288909	1.01327063	1.01365233	1.01403416	1.01441613	1.01479824
56	1.01234825	1.01273653	1.01312496	1.01351354	1.01390227	1.01429114	1.01468016	1.01506932
57	1.01257013	1.01296544	1.01336090	1.01375651	1.01415227	1.01454818	1.01494425	1.01534047
58	1.01279206	1.01319440	1.01359688	1.01399953	1.01440234	1.01480530	1.01520841	1.01561169
59	1.01301404	1.01342340	1.01383293	1.01424261	1.01465246	1.01506247	1.01547265	1.01588298
60	1.01323608	1.01365247	1.01406903	1.01448575	1.01490265	1.01531971	1.01573695	1.01615435
61	1.01345815	1.01388158	1.01430518	1.01472895	1.01515290	1.01557702	1.01600132	1.01642579
62	1.01368028	1.01411074	1.01454139	1.01497221	1.01540321	1.01583439	1.01626576	1.01669730
63	1.01390246	1.01433996	1.01477765	1.01521552	1.01565358	1.01609183	1.01653026	1.01696888
64	1.01412468	1.01456923	1.01501397	1.01545890	1.01590402	1.01634933	1.01679484	1.01724054
65	1.01434696	1.01479855	1.01525034	1.01570233	1.01615452	1.01660690	1.01705949	1.01751227
66	1.01456928	1.01502792	1.01548677	1.01594582	1.01640508	1.01686454	1.01732420	1.01778407
67	1.01479165	1.01525735	1.01572325	1.01618937	1.01665570	1.01712223	1.01758898	1.01805594
68	1.01501407	1.01548682	1.01595979	1.01643298	1.01690638	1.01738000	1.01785383	1.01832789
69	1.01523654	1.01571635	1.01619638	1.01667664	1.01715712	1.01763783	1.01811876	1.01859991
70	1.01545906	1.01594593	1.01643303	1.01692037	1.01740793	1.01789572	1.01838375	1.01887200
71	1.01568162	1.01617556	1.01666974	1.01716415	1.01765880	1.01815368	1.01864880	1.01914416
72	1.01590424	1.01640525	1.01690650	1.01740799	1.01790973	1.01841171	1.01891393	1.01941640
73	1.01612690	1.01663498	1.01714331	1.01765189	1.01816072	1.01866980	1.01917913	1.01968871
74	1.01634962	1.01686477	1.01738018	1.01789585	1.01841177	1.01892795	1.01944439	1.01996109
75	1.01657238	1.01709461	1.01761710	1.01813986	1.01866289	1.01918617	1.01970973	1.02023355
76	1.01679519	1.01732450	1.01785408	1.01838394	1.01891406	1.01944446	1.01997513	1.02050608
77	1.01701805	1.01755444	1.01809112	1.01862807	1.01916530	1.01970281	1.02024061	1.02077868
78	1.01724096	1.01778444	1.01832821	1.01887226	1.01941660	1.01996123	1.02050615	1.02105135
79	1.01746391	1.01801448	1.01856535	1.01911651	1.01966797	1.02021972	1.02077176	1.02132410
80	1.01768692	1.01824458	1.01880255	1.01936082	1.01991939	1.02047826	1.02103744	1.02159692
81	1.01790997	1.01847473	1.01903981	1.01960519	1.02017088	1.02073688	1.02130319	1.02186981
82	1.01813308	1.01870494	1.01927712	1.01984961	1.02042243	1.02099556	1.02156901	1.02214278
83	1.01835623	1.01893519	1.01951448	1.02009410	1.02067404	1.02125430	1.02183490	1.02241581
84	1.01857943	1.01916550	1.01975190	1.02033864	1.02092571	1.02151311	1.02210085	1.02268892
85	1.01880268	1.01939586	1.01998938	1.02058324	1.02117745	1.02177199	1.02236688	1.02296211
86	1.01902598	1.01962627	1.02022691	1.02082790	1.02142924	1.02203093	1.02263297	1.02323537
87	1.01924933	1.01985673	1.02046450	1.02107262	1.02168110	1.02228994	1.02289914	1.02350870
88	1.01947273	1.02008725	1.02070214	1.02131740	1.02193302	1.02254901	1.02316537	1.02378210
89	1.01969617	1.02031782	1.02093984	1.02156224	1.02218501	1.02280815	1.02343168	1.02405557
90	1.01991967	1.02054844	1.02117759	1.02180713	1.02243705	1.02306736	1.02369805	1.02432912
91	1.02014321	1.02077911	1.02141540	1.02205208	1.02268916	1.02332663	1.02396449	1.02460275
92	1.02036680	1.02100983	1.02165326	1.02229710	1.02294133	1.02358597	1.02423100	1.02487644
93	1.02059045	1.02124061	1.02189118	1.02254217	1.02319356	1.02384537	1.02449758	1.02515021
94	1.02081414	1.02147144	1.02212916	1.02278730	1.02344586	1.02410483	1.02476423	1.02542405
95	1.02103788	1.02170232	1.02236719	1.02303249	1.02369821	1.02436437	1.02503095	1.02569797
96	1.02126167	1.02193325	1.02260527	1.02327773	1.02395063	1.02462397	1.02529774	1.02597195
97	1.02148550	1.02216424	1.02284342	1.02352304	1.02420311	1.02488363	1.02556460	1.02624601
98	1.02170939	1.02239527	1.02308161	1.02376841	1.02445566	1.02514336	1.02583153	1.02652015
99	1.02193333	1.02262636	1.02331986	1.02401383	1.02470826	1.02540316	1.02609852	1.02679436
100	1.02215731	1.02285750	1.02355817	1.02425931	1.02496093	1.02566302	1.02636559	1.02706864

Day	8.00%	8.25%	8.50%	8.75%	9.00%	9.25%	9.50%	9.75%
101	1.02238135	1.02308870	1.02379653	1.02450485	1.02521366	1.02592295	1.02663273	1.02734299
102	1.02260543	1.02331994	1.02403495	1.02475045	1.02546645	1.02618294	1.02689993	1.02761742
103	1.02282956	1.02355124	1.02427343	1.02499611	1.02571931	1.02644300	1.02716721	1.02789192
104	1.02305375	1.02378259	1.02451196	1.02524183	1.02597222	1.02670313	1.02743455	1.02816649
105	1.02327798	1.02401400	1.02475054	1.02548761	1.02622520	1.02696332	1.02770197	1.02844114
106	1.02350226	1.02424545	1.02498918	1.02573345	1.02647825	1.02722358	1.02796945	1.02871586
107	1.02372659	1.02447696	1.02522788	1.02597934	1.02673135	1.02748390	1.02823701	1.02899065
108	1.02395096	1.02470852	1.02546663	1.02622529	1.02698452	1.02774429	1.02850463	1.02926552
109	1.02417539	1.02494013	1.02570544	1.02647131	1.02723774	1.02800475	1.02877232	1.02954046
110	1.02439987	1.02517180	1.02594430	1.02671738	1.02749104	1.02826527	1.02904008	1.02981548
111	1.02462439	1.02540351	1.02618322	1.02696351	1.02774439	1.02852586	1.02930792	1.03009056
112	1.02484897	1.02563528	1.02642219	1.02720970	1.02799781	1.02878651	1.02957582	1.03036572
113	1.02507359	1.02586710	1.02666122	1.02745595	1.02825129	1.02904723	1.02984379	1.03064096
114	1.02529827	1.02609898	1.02690031	1.02770226	1.02850483	1.02930802	1.03011183	1.03091627
115	1.02552299	1.02633090	1.02713945	1.02794862	1.02875843	1.02956887	1.03037994	1.03119165
116	1.02574776	1.02656288	1.02737864	1.02819505	1.02901210	1.02982979	1.03064812	1.03146710
117	1.02597258	1.02679491	1.02761790	1.02844153	1.02926583	1.03009077	1.03091638	1.03174263
118	1.02619745	1.02702700	1.02785721	1.02868808	1.02951962	1.03035182	1.03118470	1.03201824
119	1.02642237	1.02725913	1.02809657	1.02893468	1.02977347	1.03061294	1.03145309	1.03229391
120	1.02664734	1.02749132	1.02833599	1.02918134	1.03002739	1.03087412	1.03172155	1.03256966
121	1.02687236	1.02772356	1.02857546	1.02942807	1.03028137	1.03113537	1.03199008	1.03284549
122	1.02709743	1.02795586	1.02881500	1.02967485	1.03053541	1.03139669	1.03225868	1.03312138
123	1.02732255	1.02818820	1.02905458	1.02992169	1.03078951	1.03165807	1.03252735	1.03339735
124	1.02754771	1.02842060	1.02929423	1.03016859	1.03104368	1.03191952	1.03279609	1.03367340
125	1.02777293	1.02865305	1.02953392	1.03041554	1.03129791	1.03218103	1.03306490	1.03394952
126	1.02799820	1.02888556	1.02977368	1.03066256	1.03155220	1.03244261	1.03333378	1.03422571
127	1.02822351	1.02911811	1.03001349	1.03090964	1.03180656	1.03270426	1.03360273	1.03450197
128	1.02844887	1.02935072	1.03025336	1.03115677	1.03206098	1.03296597	1.03387175	1.03477831
129	1.02867429	1.02958338	1.03049328	1.03140397	1.03231546	1.03322775	1.03414084	1.03505473
130	1.02889975	1.02981610	1.03073326	1.03165122	1.03257000	1.03348959	1.03441000	1.03533121
131	1.02912526	1.03004886	1.03097329	1.03189854	1.03282461	1.03375151	1.03467923	1.03560777
132	1.02935082	1.03028168	1.03121338	1.03214591	1.03307928	1.03401348	1.03494853	1.03588441
133	1.02957644	1.03051456	1.03145352	1.03239334	1.03333401	1.03427553	1.03521790	1.03616112
134	1.02980210	1.03074748	1.03169373	1.03264083	1.03358880	1.03453764	1.03548734	1.03643790
135	1.03002781	1.03098046	1.03193398	1.03288838	1.03384366	1.03479982	1.03575685	1.03671476
136	1.03025357	1.03121349	1.03217430	1.03313599	1.03409858	1.03506206	1.03602643	1.03699169
137	1.03047937	1.03144657	1.03241467	1.03338366	1.03435357	1.03532437	1.03629608	1.03726869
138	1.03070523	1.03167971	1.03265509	1.03363139	1.03460861	1.03558675	1.03656580	1.03754577
139	1.03093114	1.03191289	1.03289557	1.03387918	1.03486372	1.03584919	1.03683559	1.03782292
140	1.03115710	1.03214613	1.03313611	1.03412703	1.03511889	1.03611170	1.03710545	1.03810015
141	1.03138311	1.03237943	1.03337670	1.03437494	1.03537413	1.03637428	1.03737538	1.03837745
142	1.03160916	1.03261277	1.03361735	1.03462290	1.03562942	1.03663692	1.03764539	1.03865483
143	1.03183527	1.03284617	1.03385806	1.03487093	1.03588479	1.03689963	1.03791546	1.03893228
144	1.03206142	1.03307962	1.03409882	1.03511901	1.03614021	1.03716240	1.03818560	1.03920980
145	1.03228763	1.03331313	1.03433964	1.03536716	1.03639570	1.03742525	1.03845581	1.03948740
146	1.03251388	1.03354668	1.03458051	1.03561536	1.03665125	1.03768816	1.03872610	1.03976507
147	1.03274019	1.03378029	1.03482144	1.03586363	1.03690686	1.03795113	1.03899645	1.04004281
148	1.03296654	1.03401396	1.03506243	1.03611195	1.03716253	1.03821417	1.03926687	1.04032063
149	1.03319295	1.03424767	1.03530347	1.03636033	1.03741827	1.03847728	1.03953737	1.04059853
150	1.03341940	1.03448144	1.03554457	1.03660878	1.03767407	1.03874046	1.03980793	1.04087649

Day	8.00%	8.25%	8.50%	8.75%	9.00%	9.25%	9.50%	9.75%
151	1.03364590	1.03471526	1.03578572	1.03685728	1.03792994	1.03900370	1.04007857	1.04115454
152	1.03387245	1.03494914	1.03602693	1.03710584	1.03818587	1.03926701	1.04034927	1.04143265
153	1.03409906	1.03518306	1.03626820	1.03735446	1.03844186	1.03953039	1.04062005	1.04171084
154	1.03432571	1.03541704	1.03650952	1.03760314	1.03869791	1.03979383	1.04089089	1.04198911
155	1.03455241	1.03565108	1.03675090	1.03785188	1.03895403	1.04005734	1.04116181	1.04226745
156	1.03477916	1.03588516	1.03699233	1.03810068	1.03921021	1.04032091	1.04143280	1.04254586
157	1.03500596	1.03611930	1.03723383	1.03834954	1.03946645	1.04058456	1.04170386	1.04282435
158	1.03523281	1.03635349	1.03747537	1.03859846	1.03972276	1.04084827	1.04197498	1.04310291
159	1.03545971	1.03658773	1.03771698	1.03884744	1.03997913	1.04111204	1.04224618	1.04338155
160	1.03568666	1.03682203	1.03795864	1.03909648	1.04023556	1.04137589	1.04251745	1.04366026
161	1.03591366	1.03705638	1.03820035	1.03934558	1.04049206	1.04163980	1.04278879	1.04393905
162	1.03614071	1.03729079	1.03844213	1.03959474	1.04074862	1.04190377	1.04306020	1.04421791
163	1.03636781	1.03752524	1.03868396	1.03984395	1.04100524	1.04216782	1.04333169	1.04449684
164	1.03659496	1.03775975	1.03892584	1.04009323	1.04126193	1.04243193	1.04360324	1.04477585
165	1.03682216	1.03799431	1.03916778	1.04034257	1.04151868	1.04269611	1.04387486	1.04505494
166	1.03704941	1.03822893	1.03940978	1.04059197	1.04177549	1.04296035	1.04414655	1.04533410
167	1.03727671	1.03846360	1.03965183	1.04084142	1.04203237	1.04322466	1.04441832	1.04561333
168	1.03750406	1.03869832	1.03989395	1.04109094	1.04228931	1.04348904	1.04469015	1.04589264
169	1.03773145	1.03893309	1.04013611	1.04134052	1.04254631	1.04375349	1.04496206	1.04617202
170	1.03795890	1.03916792	1.04037834	1.04159015	1.04280338	1.04401800	1.04523403	1.04645148
171	1.03818640	1.03940280	1.04062062	1.04183985	1.04306051	1.04428258	1.04550608	1.04673101
172	1.03841395	1.03963773	1.04086295	1.04208961	1.04331770	1.04454723	1.04577820	1.04701061
173	1.03864155	1.03987272	1.04110534	1.04233942	1.04357495	1.04481194	1.04605039	1.04729029
174	1.03886919	1.04010776	1.04134779	1.04258930	1.04383227	1.04507672	1.04632265	1.04757005
175	1.03909689	1.04034285	1.04159030	1.04283923	1.04408966	1.04534157	1.04659498	1.04784988
176	1.03932464	1.04057800	1.04183286	1.04308923	1.04434710	1.04560649	1.04686738	1.04812978
177	1.03955243	1.04081320	1.04207548	1.04333929	1.04460461	1.04587147	1.04713985	1.04840976
178	1.03978028	1.04104845	1.04231816	1.04358940	1.04486219	1.04613652	1.04741240	1.04868982
179	1.04000818	1.04128375	1.04256089	1.04383958	1.04511983	1.04640164	1.04768501	1.04896995
180	1.04023613	1.04151911	1.04280367	1.04408981	1.04537753	1.04666682	1.04795770	1.04925015
181	1.04046412	1.04175453	1.04304652	1.04434011	1.04563529	1.04693207	1.04823045	1.04953043
182	1.04069217	1.04198999	1.04328942	1.04459046	1.04589312	1.04719739	1.04850328	1.04981079
183	1.04092027	1.04222551	1.04353238	1.04484088	1.04615101	1.04746278	1.04877618	1.05009122
184	1.04114841	1.04246108	1.04377539	1.04509135	1.04640897	1.04772823	1.04904915	1.05037172
185	1.04137661	1.04269670	1.04401846	1.04534189	1.04666698	1.04799375	1.04932219	1.05065230
186	1.04160486	1.04293238	1.04426159	1.04559249	1.04692507	1.04825934	1.04959530	1.05093295
187	1.04183315	1.04316811	1.04450478	1.04584314	1.04718321	1.04852499	1.04986848	1.05121368
188	1.04206150	1.04340390	1.04474802	1.04609386	1.04744142	1.04879071	1.05014173	1.05149448
189	1.04228990	1.04363974	1.04499131	1.04634463	1.04769969	1.04905650	1.05041506	1.05177536
190	1.04251834	1.04387563	1.04523467	1.04659547	1.04795803	1.04932236	1.05068845	1.05205632
191	1.04274684	1.04411157	1.04547808	1.04684636	1.04821643	1.04958828	1.05096192	1.05233734
192	1.04297539	1.04434757	1.04572155	1.04709732	1.04847490	1.04985427	1.05123546	1.05261845
193	1.04320399	1.04458362	1.04596507	1.04734834	1.04873342	1.05012033	1.05150907	1.05289963
194	1.04343263	1.04481973	1.04620865	1.04759941	1.04899202	1.05038646	1.05178275	1.05318088
195	1.04366133	1.04505588	1.04645229	1.04785055	1.04925067	1.05065265	1.05205650	1.05346221
196	1.04389008	1.04529209	1.04669598	1.04810175	1.04950939	1.05091892	1.05233032	1.05374361
197	1.04411888	1.04552836	1.04693973	1.04835301	1.04976817	1.05118524	1.05260422	1.05402509
198	1.04434773	1.04576468	1.04718354	1.04860432	1.05002702	1.05145164	1.05287818	1.05430665
199	1.04457662	1.04600105	1.04742741	1.04885570	1.05028593	1.05171810	1.05315222	1.05458828
200	1.04480557	1.04623747	1.04767133	1.04910714	1.05054491	1.05198464	1.05342633	1.05486998

Day	8.00%	8.25%	8.50%	8.75%	9.00%	9.25%	9.50%	9.75%
201	1.04503457	1.04647395	1.04791531	1.04935864	1.05080395	1.05225123	1.05370051	1.05515176
202	1.04526362	1.04671048	1.04815934	1.04961020	1.05106305	1.05251790	1.05397476	1.05543362
203	1.04549272	1.04694707	1.04840343	1.04986181	1.05132221	1.05278463	1.05424908	1.05571555
204	1.04572187	1.04718371	1.04864758	1.05011349	1.05158144	1.05305144	1.05452347	1.05599756
205	1.04595107	1.04742040	1.04889179	1.05036523	1.05184074	1.05331831	1.05479794	1.05627964
206	1.04618032	1.04765715	1.04913605	1.05061703	1.05210010	1.05358524	1.05507247	1.05656180
207	1.04640962	1.04789395	1.04938037	1.05086889	1.05235952	1.05385225	1.05534708	1.05684403
208	1.04663897	1.04813080	1.04962475	1.05112081	1.05261900	1.05411932	1.05562176	1.05712634
209	1.04686837	1.04836770	1.04986918	1.05137279	1.05287855	1.05438646	1.05589651	1.05740872
210	1.04709782	1.04860466	1.05011367	1.05162484	1.05313817	1.05465367	1.05617133	1.05769118
211	1.04732732	1.04884168	1.05035822	1.05187694	1.05339785	1.05492094	1.05644623	1.05797371
212	1.04755687	1.04907874	1.05060282	1.05212910	1.05365759	1.05518828	1.05672119	1.05825632
213	1.04778647	1.04931586	1.05084748	1.05238132	1.05391739	1.05545569	1.05699623	1.05853901
214	1.04801612	1.04955304	1.05109220	1.05263361	1.05417726	1.05572317	1.05727134	1.05882177
215	1.04824582	1.04979027	1.05133697	1.05288595	1.05443720	1.05599072	1.05754652	1.05910460
216	1.04847558	1.05002755	1.05158181	1.05313835	1.05469720	1.05625833	1.05782177	1.05938751
217	1.04870538	1.05026488	1.05182670	1.05339082	1.05495726	1.05652602	1.05809710	1.05967050
218	1.04893523	1.05050227	1.05207164	1.05364334	1.05521738	1.05679377	1.05837249	1.05995356
219	1.04916514	1.05073971	1.05231664	1.05389593	1.05547758	1.05706158	1.05864796	1.06023670
220	1.04939509	1.05097721	1.05256170	1.05414858	1.05573783	1.05732947	1.05892350	1.06051991
221	1.04962509	1.05121476	1.05280682	1.05440128	1.05599815	1.05759742	1.05919911	1.06080320
222	1.04985515	1.05145236	1.05305200	1.05465405	1.05625853	1.05786544	1.05947479	1.06108657
223	1.05008525	1.05169002	1.05329723	1.05490688	1.05651898	1.05813353	1.05975054	1.06137001
224	1.05031541	1.05192773	1.05354251	1.05515977	1.05677949	1.05840169	1.06002637	1.06165353
225	1.05054562	1.05216550	1.05378786	1.05541272	1.05704007	1.05866991	1.06030226	1.06193712
226	1.05077587	1.05240331	1.05403326	1.05566573	1.05730071	1.05893821	1.06057823	1.06222079
227	1.05100618	1.05264119	1.05427872	1.05591880	1.05756141	1.05920657	1.06085427	1.06250453
228	1.05123654	1.05287911	1.05452424	1.05617193	1.05782218	1.05947500	1.06113039	1.06278835
229	1.05146695	1.05311709	1.05476981	1.05642512	1.05808301	1.05974349	1.06140657	1.06307225
230	1.05169740	1.05335512	1.05501545	1.05667837	1.05834391	1.06001206	1.06168283	1.06335622
231	1.05192791	1.05359321	1.05526113	1.05693169	1.05860487	1.06028069	1.06195916	1.06364027
232	1.05215847	1.05383135	1.05550688	1.05718506	1.05886590	1.06054939	1.06223556	1.06392439
233	1.05238908	1.05406955	1.05575268	1.05743849	1.05912699	1.06081816	1.06251203	1.06420859
234	1.05261974	1.05430780	1.05599854	1.05769199	1.05938814	1.06108700	1.06278857	1.06449286
235	1.05285045	1.05454610	1.05624446	1.05794555	1.05964936	1.06135591	1.06306519	1.06477721
236	1.05308122	1.05478445	1.05649043	1.05819916	1.05991064	1.06162488	1.06334188	1.06506164
237	1.05331203	1.05502286	1.05673647	1.05845284	1.06017199	1.06189392	1.06361864	1.06534614
238	1.05354289	1.05526133	1.05698256	1.05870658	1.06043340	1.06216303	1.06389547	1.06563072
239	1.05377380	1.05549985	1.05722870	1.05896038	1.06069488	1.06243221	1.06417237	1.06591538
240	1.05400477	1.05573842	1.05747491	1.05921424	1.06095642	1.06270146	1.06444935	1.06620011
241	1.05423578	1.05597704	1.05772117	1.05946816	1.06121803	1.06297077	1.06472640	1.06648491
242	1.05446685	1.05621572	1.05796749	1.05972214	1.06147970	1.06324015	1.06500352	1.06676980
243	1.05469797	1.05645446	1.05821386	1.05997619	1.06174143	1.06350961	1.06528071	1.06705476
244	1.05492913	1.05669324	1.05846030	1.06023029	1.06200323	1.06377913	1.06555798	1.06733979
245	1.05516035	1.05693209	1.05870679	1.06048445	1.06226510	1.06404871	1.06583531	1.06762490
246	1.05539162	1.05717098	1.05895334	1.06073868	1.06252702	1.06431837	1.06611272	1.06791009
247	1.05562294	1.05740993	1.05919994	1.06099297	1.06278902	1.06458809	1.06639020	1.06819535
248	1.05585431	1.05764894	1.05944660	1.06124731	1.06305107	1.06485789	1.06666776	1.06848069
249	1.05608573	1.05788799	1.05969332	1.06150172	1.06331320	1.06512775	1.06694538	1.06876611
250	1.05631720	1.05812710	1.05994010	1.06175619	1.06357538	1.06539768	1.06722308	1.06905160

Day	8.00%	8.25%	8.50%	8.75%	9.00%	9.25%	9.50%	9.75%
251	1.05654872	1.05836627	1.06018694	1.06201072	1.06383763	1.06566768	1.06750085	1.06933717
252	1.05678029	1.05860549	1.06043383	1.06226531	1.06409995	1.06593774	1.06777870	1.06962281
253	1.05701191	1.05884476	1.06068078	1.06251997	1.06436233	1.06620788	1.06805661	1.06990854
254	1.05724359	1.05908409	1.06092779	1.06277468	1.06462478	1.06647808	1.06833460	1.07019433
255	1.05747531	1.05932347	1.06117485	1.06302946	1.06488729	1.06674835	1.06861266	1.07048021
256	1.05770709	1.05956291	1.06142198	1.06328429	1.06514986	1.06701869	1.06889079	1.07076616
257	1.05793891	1.05980240	1.06166916	1.06353919	1.06541250	1.06728910	1.06916899	1.07105218
258	1.05817079	1.06004194	1.06191640	1.06379415	1.06567521	1.06755958	1.06944727	1.07133829
259	1.05840272	1.06028154	1.06216369	1.06404917	1.06593798	1.06783012	1.06972562	1.07162447
260	1.05863470	1.06052120	1.06241104	1.06430425	1.06620081	1.06810074	1.07000404	1.07191072
261	1.05886673	1.06076090	1.06265845	1.06455939	1.06646371	1.06837142	1.07028254	1.07219705
262	1.05909881	1.06100066	1.06290592	1.06481459	1.06672667	1.06864217	1.07056110	1.07248346
263	1.05933094	1.06124048	1.06315345	1.06506985	1.06698970	1.06891299	1.07083974	1.07276995
264	1.05956312	1.06148035	1.06340103	1.06532518	1.06725279	1.06918388	1.07111845	1.07305651
265	1.05979535	1.06172027	1.06364867	1.06558057	1.06751595	1.06945484	1.07139724	1.07334315
266	1.06002764	1.06196025	1.06389637	1.06583601	1.06777918	1.06972587	1.07167609	1.07362986
267	1.06025997	1.06220028	1.06414413	1.06609152	1.06804246	1.06999696	1.07195502	1.07391666
268	1.06049236	1.06244037	1.06439194	1.06634709	1.06830582	1.07026813	1.07223403	1.07420352
269	1.06072479	1.06268051	1.06463982	1.06660272	1.06856923	1.07053936	1.07251310	1.07449047
270	1.06095728	1.06292070	1.06488775	1.06685841	1.06883272	1.07081066	1.07279225	1.07477749
271	1.06118982	1.06316095	1.06513573	1.06711417	1.06909626	1.07108203	1.07307147	1.07506459
272	1.06142241	1.06340126	1.06538378	1.06736998	1.06935988	1.07135347	1.07335076	1.07535176
273	1.06165505	1.06364161	1.06563188	1.06762586	1.06962356	1.07162497	1.07363013	1.07563901
274	1.06188774	1.06388203	1.06588004	1.06788180	1.06988730	1.07189655	1.07390956	1.07592634
275	1.06212048	1.06412249	1.06612826	1.06813780	1.07015111	1.07216820	1.07418907	1.07621375
276	1.06235328	1.06436301	1.06637654	1.06839386	1.07041498	1.07243991	1.07446866	1.07650123
277	1.06258612	1.06460359	1.06662487	1.06864998	1.07067892	1.07271169	1.07474831	1.07678879
278	1.06281902	1.06484422	1.06687326	1.06890616	1.07094292	1.07298354	1.07502804	1.07707642
279	1.06305196	1.06508490	1.06712171	1.06916241	1.07120699	1.07325546	1.07530784	1.07736414
280	1.06328496	1.06532564	1.06737022	1.06941871	1.07147112	1.07352745	1.07558772	1.07765192
281	1.06351801	1.06556643	1.06761879	1.06967508	1.07173532	1.07379951	1.07586767	1.07793979
282	1.06375111	1.06580728	1.06786741	1.06993151	1.07199958	1.07407164	1.07614769	1.07822773
283	1.06398426	1.06604818	1.06811609	1.07018800	1.07226391	1.07434384	1.07642778	1.07851575
284	1.06421746	1.06628914	1.06836483	1.07044455	1.07252831	1.07461610	1.07670795	1.07880385
285	1.06445072	1.06653015	1.06861363	1.07070116	1.07279276	1.07488844	1.07698819	1.07909202
286	1.06468402	1.06677121	1.06886248	1.07095784	1.07305729	1.07516084	1.07726850	1.07938027
287	1.06491738	1.06701233	1.06911140	1.07121458	1.07332188	1.07543331	1.07754888	1.07966860
288	1.06515078	1.06725351	1.06936037	1.07147137	1.07358653	1.07570585	1.07782934	1.07995701
289	1.06538424	1.06749474	1.06960940	1.07172823	1.07385125	1.07597846	1.07810987	1.08024549
290	1.06561775	1.06773602	1.06985848	1.07198515	1.07411604	1.07625114	1.07839048	1.08053405
291	1.06585131	1.06797736	1.07010763	1.07224214	1.07438089	1.07652389	1.07867115	1.08082268
292	1.06608492	1.06821875	1.07035683	1.07249918	1.07464580	1.07679671	1.07895190	1.08111139
293	1.06631858	1.06846020	1.07060609	1.07275629	1.07491079	1.07706959	1.07923273	1.08140018
294	1.06655230	1.06870170	1.07085541	1.07301346	1.07517583	1.07734255	1.07951362	1.08168905
295	1.06678606	1.06894325	1.07110479	1.07327068	1.07544094	1.07761558	1.07979459	1.08197800
296	1.06701988	1.06918486	1.07135423	1.07352798	1.07570612	1.07788867	1.08007563	1.08226702
297	1.06725375	1.06942653	1.07160372	1.07378533	1.07597136	1.07816183	1.08035675	1.08255612
298	1.06748766	1.06966825	1.07185327	1.07404274	1.07623667	1.07843507	1.08063794	1.08284529
299	1.06772163	1.06991002	1.07210288	1.07430022	1.07650205	1.07870837	1.08091920	1.08313455
300	1.06795566	1.07015185	1.07235255	1.07455776	1.07676748	1.07898174	1.08120053	1.08342388

Day	8.00%	8.25%	8.50%	8.75%	9.00%	9.25%	9.50%	9.75%
301	1.06818973	1.07039373	1.07260227	1.07481536	1.07703299	1.07925518	1.08148194	1.08371328
302	1.06842385	1.07063567	1.07285206	1.07507302	1.07729856	1.07952869	1.08176342	1.08400277
303	1.06865803	1.07087767	1.07310190	1.07533074	1.07756419	1.07980227	1.08204498	1.08429233
304	1.06889225	1.07111971	1.07335180	1.07558852	1.07782989	1.08007592	1.08232661	1.08458197
305	1.06912653	1.07136182	1.07360176	1.07584637	1.07809566	1.08034964	1.08260831	1.08487169
306	1.06936086	1.07160397	1.07385178	1.07610428	1.07836149	1.08062342	1.08289008	1.08516148
307	1.06959524	1.07184619	1.07410185	1.07636225	1.07862739	1.08089728	1.08317193	1.08545135
308	1.06982967	1.07208845	1.07435199	1.07662028	1.07889335	1.08117121	1.08345385	1.08574130
309	1.07006416	1.07233077	1.07460218	1.07687838	1.07915938	1.08144520	1.08373585	1.08603133
310	1.07029869	1.07257315	1.07485243	1.07713653	1.07942548	1.08171927	1.08401792	1.08632143
311	1.07053328	1.07281558	1.07510273	1.07739475	1.07969163	1.08199340	1.08430006	1.08661162
312	1.07076791	1.07305807	1.07535310	1.07765303	1.07995786	1.08226760	1.08458227	1.08690188
313	1.07100260	1.07330061	1.07560353	1.07791137	1.08022415	1.08254188	1.08486456	1.08719221
314	1.07123734	1.07354320	1.07585401	1.07816977	1.08049051	1.08281622	1.08514692	1.08748263
315	1.07147213	1.07378585	1.07610455	1.07842824	1.08075693	1.08309063	1.08542936	1.08777312
316	1.07170698	1.07402856	1.07635515	1.07868677	1.08102342	1.08336511	1.08571187	1.08806369
317	1.07194187	1.07427132	1.07660581	1.07894536	1.08128997	1.08363967	1.08599445	1.08835434
318	1.07217682	1.07451413	1.07685652	1.07920401	1.08155659	1.08391429	1.08627711	1.08864506
319	1.07241182	1.07475700	1.07710730	1.07946272	1.08182328	1.08418898	1.08655984	1.08893586
320	1.07264687	1.07499993	1.07735813	1.07972150	1.08209003	1.08446374	1.08684264	1.08922674
321	1.07288197	1.07524291	1.07760902	1.07998033	1.08235684	1.08473857	1.08712552	1.08951770
322	1.07311712	1.07548594	1.07785997	1.08023923	1.08262373	1.08501347	1.08740847	1.08980874
323	1.07335232	1.07572903	1.07811098	1.08049819	1.08289067	1.08528844	1.08769149	1.09009985
324	1.07358758	1.07597217	1.07836205	1.08075722	1.08315769	1.08556348	1.08797459	1.09039104
325	1.07382288	1.07621537	1.07861317	1.08101630	1.08342477	1.08583858	1.08825776	1.09068231
326	1.07405824	1.07645863	1.07886436	1.08127545	1.08369191	1.08611376	1.08854101	1.09097366
327	1.07429365	1.07670194	1.07911560	1.08153466	1.08395913	1.08638901	1.08882432	1.09126508
328	1.07452911	1.07694530	1.07936690	1.08179393	1.08422640	1.08666433	1.08910772	1.09155658
329	1.07476463	1.07718872	1.07961826	1.08205327	1.08449375	1.08693972	1.08939118	1.09184816
330	1.07500019	1.07743219	1.07986968	1.08231266	1.08476116	1.08721517	1.08967472	1.09213982
331	1.07523581	1.07767572	1.08012116	1.08257212	1.08502863	1.08749070	1.08995834	1.09243156
332	1.07547148	1.07791931	1.08037269	1.08283164	1.08529617	1.08776630	1.09024202	1.09272337
333	1.07570720	1.07816295	1.08062428	1.08309122	1.08556378	1.08804196	1.09052579	1.09301526
334	1.07594297	1.07840664	1.08087594	1.08335087	1.08583145	1.08831770	1.09080962	1.09330723
335	1.07617879	1.07865039	1.08112765	1.08361058	1.08609919	1.08859351	1.09109353	1.09359928

Day	8.00%	8.25%	8.50%	8.75%	9.00%	9.25%	9.50%	9.75%
336	1.07641467	1.07889419	1.08137942	1.08387035	1.08636700	1.08886938	1.09137751	1.09389141
337	1.07665059	1.07913805	1.08163125	1.08413018	1.08663487	1.08914533	1.09166157	1.09418361
338	1.07688657	1.07938197	1.08188313	1.08439007	1.08690281	1.08942135	1.09194570	1.09447589
339	1.07712260	1.07962594	1.08213508	1.08465003	1.08717081	1.08969743	1.09222991	1.09476825
340	1.07735868	1.07986996	1.08238708	1.08491005	1.08743888	1.08997359	1.09251419	1.09506069
341	1.07759482	1.08011404	1.08263914	1.08517013	1.08770702	1.09024981	1.09279854	1.09535321
342	1.07783100	1.08035818	1.08289127	1.08543027	1.08797522	1.09052611	1.09308297	1.09564580
343	1.07806724	1.08060237	1.08314345	1.08569048	1.08824349	1.09080248	1.09336747	1.09593847
344	1.07830353	1.08084662	1.08339568	1.08595075	1.08851182	1.09107891	1.09365204	1.09623122
345	1.07853987	1.08109092	1.08364798	1.08621108	1.08878022	1.09135542	1.09393669	1.09652405
346	1.07877626	1.08133527	1.08390034	1.08647147	1.08904869	1.09163200	1.09422142	1.09681696
347	1.07901270	1.08157968	1.08415275	1.08673193	1.08931722	1.09190864	1.09450621	1.09710994
348	1.07924920	1.08182415	1.08440523	1.08699244	1.08958582	1.09218536	1.09479108	1.09740301
349	1.07948575	1.08206867	1.08465776	1.08725302	1.08985448	1.09246215	1.09507603	1.09769615
350	1.07972235	1.08231325	1.08491035	1.08751367	1.09012321	1.09273900	1.09536105	1.09798937
351	1.07995900	1.08255788	1.08516300	1.08777437	1.09039201	1.09301593	1.09564614	1.09828267
352	1.08019570	1.08280257	1.08541571	1.08803514	1.09066087	1.09329293	1.09593131	1.09857605
353	1.08043246	1.08304731	1.08566848	1.08829597	1.09092980	1.09356999	1.09621655	1.09886950
354	1.08066926	1.08329211	1.08592131	1.08855686	1.09119880	1.09384713	1.09650187	1.09916303
355	1.08090612	1.08353696	1.08617419	1.08881782	1.09146786	1.09412434	1.09678726	1.09945665
356	1.08114303	1.08378187	1.08642714	1.08907884	1.09173699	1.09440162	1.09707273	1.09975034
357	1.08138000	1.08402684	1.08668014	1.08933992	1.09200619	1.09467897	1.09735827	1.10004411
358	1.08161701	1.08427186	1.08693320	1.08960106	1.09227545	1.09495638	1.09764388	1.10033795
359	1.08185408	1.08451693	1.08718632	1.08986227	1.09254478	1.09523387	1.09792957	1.10063188
360	1.08209120	1.08476206	1.08743950	1.09012354	1.09281417	1.09551143	1.09821533	1.10092588
361	1.08232837	1.08500725	1.08769274	1.09038487	1.09308363	1.09578906	1.09850117	1.10121997
362	1.08256559	1.08525249	1.08794604	1.09064626	1.09335316	1.09606676	1.09878708	1.10151413
363	1.08280286	1.08549779	1.08819940	1.09090772	1.09362276	1.09634453	1.09907306	1.10180837
364	1.08304019	1.08574314	1.08845282	1.09116923	1.09389242	1.09662237	1.09935912	1.10210269
365	1.08327757	1.08598855	1.08870629	1.09143082	1.09416214	1.09690028	1.09964526	1.10239708

Day	10.00%	10.25%	10.50%	10.75%	11.00%	11.25%	11.50%	11.75%
1	1.00027397	1.00028082	1.00028767	1.00029452	1.00030137	1.00030822	1.00031507	1.00032192
2	1.00054802	1.00056172	1.00057543	1.00058913	1.00060283	1.00061653	1.00063024	1.00064394
3	1.00082214	1.00084270	1.00086326	1.00088382	1.00090438	1.00092494	1.00094550	1.00096606
4	1.00109634	1.00112376	1.00115118	1.00117860	1.00120602	1.00123345	1.00126087	1.00128829
5	1.00137061	1.00140490	1.00143918	1.00147347	1.00150776	1.00154205	1.00157634	1.00161063
6	1.00164496	1.00168611	1.00172727	1.00176842	1.00180958	1.00185074	1.00189190	1.00193306
7	1.00191939	1.00196741	1.00201544	1.00206347	1.00211150	1.00215953	1.00220757	1.00225560
8	1.00219388	1.00224878	1.00230369	1.00235859	1.00241350	1.00246841	1.00252333	1.00257825
9	1.00246846	1.00253024	1.00259202	1.00265381	1.00271560	1.00277739	1.00283919	1.00290099
10	1.00274311	1.00281177	1.00288044	1.00294911	1.00301779	1.00308647	1.00315516	1.00322385
11	1.00301783	1.00309338	1.00316894	1.00324450	1.00332007	1.00339564	1.00347122	1.00354680
12	1.00329263	1.00337507	1.00345752	1.00353998	1.00362244	1.00370491	1.00378738	1.00386986
13	1.00356750	1.00365684	1.00374619	1.00383554	1.00392490	1.00401427	1.00410364	1.00419302
14	1.00384245	1.00393869	1.00403494	1.00413119	1.00422745	1.00432372	1.00442000	1.00451629
15	1.00411748	1.00422062	1.00432377	1.00442693	1.00453010	1.00463328	1.00473646	1.00483966
16	1.00439258	1.00450263	1.00461268	1.00472275	1.00483283	1.00494292	1.00505303	1.00516314
17	1.00466776	1.00478471	1.00490168	1.00501866	1.00513566	1.00525267	1.00536969	1.00548672
18	1.00494301	1.00506688	1.00519076	1.00531466	1.00543858	1.00556250	1.00568645	1.00581040
19	1.00521833	1.00534912	1.00547993	1.00561075	1.00574158	1.00587244	1.00600331	1.00613419
20	1.00549374	1.00563145	1.00576918	1.00590692	1.00604468	1.00618247	1.00632027	1.00645808
21	1.00576921	1.00591385	1.00605851	1.00620318	1.00634788	1.00649259	1.00663733	1.00678208
22	1.00604477	1.00619633	1.00634792	1.00649953	1.00665116	1.00680281	1.00695449	1.00710618
23	1.00632040	1.00647890	1.00663742	1.00679596	1.00695453	1.00711313	1.00727175	1.00743039
24	1.00659610	1.00676154	1.00692700	1.00709249	1.00725800	1.00742354	1.00758911	1.00775470
25	1.00687188	1.00704426	1.00721666	1.00738910	1.00756156	1.00773405	1.00790656	1.00807911
26	1.00714774	1.00732706	1.00750641	1.00768579	1.00786521	1.00804465	1.00822412	1.00840363
27	1.00742367	1.00760994	1.00779624	1.00798258	1.00816895	1.00835535	1.00854178	1.00872825
28	1.00769967	1.00789290	1.00808615	1.00827945	1.00847278	1.00866614	1.00885954	1.00905298
29	1.00797576	1.00817593	1.00837615	1.00857641	1.00877670	1.00897703	1.00917740	1.00937781
30	1.00825191	1.00845905	1.00866623	1.00887345	1.00908072	1.00928802	1.00949536	1.00970275
31	1.00852815	1.00874225	1.00895640	1.00917059	1.00938482	1.00959910	1.00981342	1.01002779
32	1.00880446	1.00902553	1.00924664	1.00946781	1.00968902	1.00991028	1.01013158	1.01035294
33	1.00908084	1.00930888	1.00953698	1.00976512	1.00999331	1.01022155	1.01044984	1.01067819
34	1.00935730	1.00959232	1.00982739	1.01006251	1.01029769	1.01053292	1.01076821	1.01100354
35	1.00963384	1.00987583	1.01011789	1.01036000	1.01060216	1.01084439	1.01108667	1.01132900
36	1.00991045	1.01015943	1.01040847	1.01065757	1.01090673	1.01115595	1.01140523	1.01165457
37	1.01018714	1.01044310	1.01069914	1.01095523	1.01121139	1.01146761	1.01172389	1.01198024
38	1.01046390	1.01072686	1.01098988	1.01125298	1.01151614	1.01177936	1.01204265	1.01230601
39	1.01074074	1.01101069	1.01128072	1.01155081	1.01182098	1.01209121	1.01236152	1.01263189
40	1.01101766	1.01129461	1.01157163	1.01184873	1.01212591	1.01240316	1.01268048	1.01295787
41	1.01129465	1.01157860	1.01186263	1.01214674	1.01243093	1.01271520	1.01299954	1.01328396
42	1.01157171	1.01186267	1.01215372	1.01244484	1.01273605	1.01302734	1.01331871	1.01361016
43	1.01184886	1.01214683	1.01244488	1.01274303	1.01304126	1.01333957	1.01363797	1.01393646
44	1.01212608	1.01243106	1.01273614	1.01304130	1.01334656	1.01365190	1.01395734	1.01426286
45	1.01240337	1.01271537	1.01302747	1.01333966	1.01365195	1.01396433	1.01427680	1.01458937
46	1.01268074	1.01299977	1.01331889	1.01363811	1.01395743	1.01427685	1.01459637	1.01491598
47	1.01295819	1.01328424	1.01361039	1.01393665	1.01426301	1.01458947	1.01491604	1.01524270
48	1.01323571	1.01356879	1.01390198	1.01423527	1.01456868	1.01490219	1.01523580	1.01556953
49	1.01351331	1.01385342	1.01419365	1.01453399	1.01487444	1.01521500	1.01555567	1.01589646
50	1.01379098	1.01413814	1.01448540	1.01483279	1.01518029	1.01552791	1.01587564	1.01622349

Day	10.00%	10.25%	10.50%	10.75%	11.00%	11.25%	11.50%	11.75%
51	1.01406873	1.01442293	1.01477724	1.01513168	1.01548624	1.01584091	1.01619571	1.01655063
52	1.01434656	1.01470780	1.01506916	1.01543066	1.01579227	1.01615402	1.01651588	1.01687788
53	1.01462447	1.01499275	1.01536117	1.01572972	1.01609840	1.01646721	1.01683616	1.01720523
54	1.01490244	1.01527778	1.01565326	1.01602887	1.01640462	1.01678051	1.01715653	1.01753269
55	1.01518050	1.01556290	1.01594544	1.01632811	1.01671094	1.01709390	1.01747700	1.01786025
56	1.01545863	1.01584809	1.01623769	1.01662744	1.01701734	1.01740739	1.01779758	1.01818792
57	1.01573684	1.01613336	1.01653004	1.01692686	1.01732384	1.01772097	1.01811825	1.01851569
58	1.01601512	1.01641871	1.01682246	1.01722637	1.01763043	1.01803465	1.01843903	1.01884357
59	1.01629348	1.01670415	1.01711497	1.01752596	1.01793711	1.01834843	1.01875991	1.01917155
60	1.01657192	1.01698966	1.01740757	1.01782564	1.01824389	1.01866230	1.01908089	1.01949964
61	1.01685043	1.01727525	1.01770025	1.01812541	1.01855076	1.01897628	1.01940197	1.01982784
62	1.01712902	1.01756093	1.01799301	1.01842527	1.01885772	1.01929034	1.01972315	1.02015614
63	1.01740769	1.01784668	1.01828586	1.01872522	1.01916477	1.01960451	1.02004443	1.02048454
64	1.01768643	1.01813251	1.01857879	1.01902526	1.01947192	1.01991877	1.02036582	1.02081306
65	1.01796525	1.01841843	1.01887180	1.01932538	1.01977916	1.02023313	1.02068730	1.02114167
66	1.01824414	1.01870442	1.01916490	1.01962559	1.02008649	1.02054758	1.02100889	1.02147040
67	1.01852311	1.01899050	1.01945809	1.01992589	1.02039391	1.02086214	1.02133058	1.02179923
68	1.01880216	1.01927665	1.01975136	1.02022628	1.02070143	1.02117679	1.02165237	1.02212816
69	1.01908128	1.01956289	1.02004471	1.02052676	1.02100903	1.02149153	1.02197426	1.02245720
70	1.01936048	1.01984920	1.02033815	1.02082733	1.02131674	1.02180638	1.02229625	1.02278635
71	1.01963976	1.02013560	1.02063167	1.02112798	1.02162453	1.02212132	1.02261834	1.02311560
72	1.01991912	1.02042207	1.02092528	1.02142872	1.02193242	1.02243635	1.02294054	1.02344496
73	1.02019855	1.02070863	1.02121897	1.02172956	1.02224040	1.02275149	1.02326283	1.02377443
74	1.02047805	1.02099527	1.02151274	1.02203048	1.02254847	1.02306672	1.02358523	1.02410400
75	1.02075763	1.02128199	1.02180660	1.02233148	1.02285663	1.02338205	1.02390773	1.02443368
76	1.02103729	1.02156878	1.02210055	1.02263258	1.02316489	1.02369747	1.02423033	1.02476346
77	1.02131703	1.02185566	1.02239458	1.02293377	1.02347324	1.02401300	1.02455303	1.02509335
78	1.02159684	1.02214262	1.02268869	1.02323504	1.02378169	1.02432862	1.02487584	1.02542335
79	1.02187673	1.02242966	1.02298289	1.02353641	1.02409022	1.02464434	1.02519874	1.02575345
80	1.02215670	1.02271678	1.02327717	1.02383786	1.02439885	1.02496015	1.02552175	1.02608366
81	1.02243674	1.02300398	1.02357154	1.02413940	1.02470758	1.02527606	1.02584486	1.02641397
82	1.02271686	1.02329127	1.02386599	1.02444103	1.02501639	1.02559207	1.02616807	1.02674439
83	1.02299706	1.02357863	1.02416053	1.02474275	1.02532530	1.02590818	1.02649139	1.02707492
84	1.02327733	1.02386607	1.02445515	1.02504456	1.02563430	1.02622438	1.02681480	1.02740555
85	1.02355768	1.02415360	1.02474985	1.02534645	1.02594340	1.02654069	1.02713832	1.02773629
86	1.02383811	1.02444120	1.02504464	1.02564844	1.02625259	1.02685709	1.02746194	1.02806714
87	1.02411861	1.02472889	1.02533952	1.02595051	1.02656187	1.02717358	1.02778566	1.02839809
88	1.02439919	1.02501665	1.02563448	1.02625268	1.02687124	1.02749018	1.02810948	1.02872915
89	1.02467985	1.02530450	1.02592953	1.02655493	1.02718071	1.02780687	1.02843341	1.02906032
90	1.02496058	1.02559243	1.02622466	1.02685727	1.02749027	1.02812366	1.02875743	1.02939159
91	1.02524139	1.02588044	1.02651987	1.02715970	1.02779993	1.02844055	1.02908156	1.02972297
92	1.02552228	1.02616853	1.02681517	1.02746222	1.02810968	1.02875753	1.02940579	1.03005446
93	1.02580325	1.02645670	1.02711056	1.02776483	1.02841952	1.02907461	1.02973013	1.03038605
94	1.02608429	1.02674495	1.02740603	1.02806753	1.02872945	1.02939180	1.03005456	1.03071775
95	1.02636541	1.02703328	1.02770158	1.02837032	1.02903948	1.02970907	1.03037910	1.03104956
96	1.02664660	1.02732169	1.02799722	1.02867319	1.02934960	1.03002645	1.03070374	1.03138147
97	1.02692788	1.02761019	1.02829295	1.02897616	1.02965982	1.03034392	1.03102848	1.03171349
98	1.02720923	1.02789876	1.02858876	1.02927921	1.02997012	1.03066150	1.03135333	1.03204562
99	1.02749065	1.02818742	1.02888465	1.02958236	1.03028053	1.03097917	1.03167827	1.03237785
100	1.02777216	1.02847616	1.02918064	1.02988559	1.03059102	1.03129693	1.03200332	1.03271019

Day	10.00%	10.25%	10.50%	10.75%	11.00%	11.25%	11.50%	11.75%
101	1.02805374	1.02876498	1.02947670	1.03018891	1.03090161	1.03161480	1.03232847	1.03304264
102	1.02833540	1.02905388	1.02977285	1.03049232	1.03121229	1.03193276	1.03265373	1.03337519
103	1.02861713	1.02934286	1.03006909	1.03079582	1.03152307	1.03225082	1.03297908	1.03370785
104	1.02889895	1.02963192	1.03036541	1.03109942	1.03183394	1.03256898	1.03330454	1.03404062
105	1.02918084	1.02992106	1.03066182	1.03140310	1.03214490	1.03288724	1.03363011	1.03437350
106	1.02946281	1.03021029	1.03095831	1.03170686	1.03245596	1.03320560	1.03395577	1.03470648
107	1.02974485	1.03049959	1.03125488	1.03201072	1.03276711	1.03352405	1.03428154	1.03503957
108	1.03002697	1.03078898	1.03155155	1.03231467	1.03307836	1.03384260	1.03460741	1.03537277
109	1.03030917	1.03107845	1.03184829	1.03261871	1.03338970	1.03416125	1.03493338	1.03570608
110	1.03059145	1.03136800	1.03214513	1.03292284	1.03370113	1.03448000	1.03525945	1.03603949
111	1.03087380	1.03165763	1.03244205	1.03322705	1.03401265	1.03479885	1.03558563	1.03637301
112	1.03115623	1.03194734	1.03273905	1.03353136	1.03432427	1.03511779	1.03591191	1.03670663
113	1.03143874	1.03223713	1.03303614	1.03383576	1.03463599	1.03543683	1.03623829	1.03704037
114	1.03172133	1.03252701	1.03333331	1.03414024	1.03494780	1.03575598	1.03656478	1.03737421
115	1.03200399	1.03281696	1.03363057	1.03444482	1.03525970	1.03607522	1.03689137	1.03770816
116	1.03228673	1.03310700	1.03392792	1.03474948	1.03557170	1.03639455	1.03721806	1.03804222
117	1.03256955	1.03339712	1.03422535	1.03505424	1.03588379	1.03671399	1.03754486	1.03837638
118	1.03285244	1.03368732	1.03452287	1.03535908	1.03619597	1.03703353	1.03787175	1.03871065
119	1.03313542	1.03397760	1.03482047	1.03566402	1.03650825	1.03735316	1.03819875	1.03904503
120	1.03341847	1.03426797	1.03511816	1.03596904	1.03682062	1.03767289	1.03852586	1.03937952
121	1.03370160	1.03455841	1.03541593	1.03627416	1.03713309	1.03799272	1.03885306	1.03971411
122	1.03398480	1.03484894	1.03571379	1.03657936	1.03744565	1.03831265	1.03918037	1.04004882
123	1.03426809	1.03513955	1.03601174	1.03688465	1.03775830	1.03863268	1.03950779	1.04038363
124	1.03455145	1.03543024	1.03630977	1.03719004	1.03807105	1.03895281	1.03983530	1.04071854
125	1.03483489	1.03572101	1.03660788	1.03749551	1.03838389	1.03927303	1.04016292	1.04105357
126	1.03511840	1.03601186	1.03690609	1.03780108	1.03869683	1.03959335	1.04049065	1.04138870
127	1.03540200	1.03630280	1.03720437	1.03810673	1.03900986	1.03991378	1.04081847	1.04172395
128	1.03568567	1.03659381	1.03750275	1.03841247	1.03932299	1.04023430	1.04114640	1.04205930
129	1.03596942	1.03688491	1.03780121	1.03871831	1.03963621	1.04055492	1.04147443	1.04239475
130	1.03625325	1.03717609	1.03809975	1.03902423	1.03994953	1.04087564	1.04180257	1.04273032
131	1.03653715	1.03746735	1.03839838	1.03933024	1.04026294	1.04119646	1.04213081	1.04306599
132	1.03682113	1.03775870	1.03869710	1.03963635	1.04057644	1.04151737	1.04245915	1.04340177
133	1.03710519	1.03805012	1.03899591	1.03994254	1.04089004	1.04183839	1.04278760	1.04373766
134	1.03738933	1.03834163	1.03929479	1.04024883	1.04120373	1.04215950	1.04311615	1.04407366
135	1.03767355	1.03863322	1.03959377	1.04055520	1.04151752	1.04248072	1.04344480	1.04440977
136	1.03795784	1.03892489	1.03989283	1.04086167	1.04183140	1.04280203	1.04377356	1.04474598
137	1.03824221	1.03921664	1.04019198	1.04116822	1.04214538	1.04312344	1.04410242	1.04508230
138	1.03852666	1.03950848	1.04049121	1.04147487	1.04245945	1.04344495	1.04443138	1.04541873
139	1.03881119	1.03980039	1.04079053	1.04178160	1.04277361	1.04376656	1.04476045	1.04575527
140	1.03909580	1.04009239	1.04108994	1.04208843	1.04308787	1.04408827	1.04508962	1.04609192
141	1.03938048	1.04038447	1.04138943	1.04239535	1.04340223	1.04441008	1.04541889	1.04642868
142	1.03966524	1.04067664	1.04168901	1.04270235	1.04371668	1.04473198	1.04574827	1.04676554
143	1.03995008	1.04096888	1.04198867	1.04300945	1.04403122	1.04505399	1.04607775	1.04710251
144	1.04023500	1.04126121	1.04228842	1.04331664	1.04434586	1.04537610	1.04640734	1.04743959
145	1.04052000	1.04155362	1.04258826	1.04362392	1.04466060	1.04569830	1.04673703	1.04777678
146	1.04080507	1.04184611	1.04288818	1.04393128	1.04497543	1.04602061	1.04706682	1.04811408
147	1.04109022	1.04213868	1.04318819	1.04423874	1.04529035	1.04634301	1.04739672	1.04845149
148	1.04137545	1.04243134	1.04348828	1.04454629	1.04560537	1.04666551	1.04772672	1.04878900
149	1.04166076	1.04272407	1.04378846	1.04485393	1.04592048	1.04698811	1.04805683	1.04912663
150	1.04194615	1.04301689	1.04408873	1.04516166	1.04623569	1.04731082	1.04838704	1.04946436

Day	*10.00%*	*10.25%*	*10.50%*	*10.75%*	*11.00%*	*11.25%*	*11.50%*	*11.75%*
151	1.04223161	1.04330980	1.04438909	1.04546949	1.04655100	1.04763362	1.04871735	1.04980220
152	1.04251716	1.04360278	1.04468953	1.04577740	1.04686640	1.04795652	1.04904777	1.05014015
153	1.04280278	1.04389585	1.04499005	1.04608540	1.04718189	1.04827952	1.04937829	1.05047821
154	1.04308848	1.04418900	1.04529067	1.04639350	1.04749748	1.04860262	1.04970892	1.05081638
155	1.04337425	1.04448223	1.04559137	1.04670168	1.04781316	1.04892582	1.05003965	1.05115465
156	1.04366011	1.04477554	1.04589215	1.04700995	1.04812894	1.04924912	1.05037048	1.05149304
157	1.04394604	1.04506894	1.04619303	1.04731832	1.04844482	1.04957252	1.05070142	1.05183153
158	1.04423206	1.04536241	1.04649399	1.04762678	1.04876079	1.04989601	1.05103246	1.05217014
159	1.04451815	1.04565597	1.04679503	1.04793533	1.04907685	1.05021961	1.05136361	1.05250885
160	1.04480432	1.04594962	1.04709617	1.04824396	1.04939301	1.05054331	1.05169486	1.05284767
161	1.04509057	1.04624334	1.04739739	1.04855269	1.04970927	1.05086711	1.05202622	1.05318660
162	1.04537689	1.04653715	1.04769869	1.04886151	1.05002562	1.05119101	1.05235768	1.05352564
163	1.04566330	1.04683104	1.04800008	1.04917042	1.05034206	1.05151500	1.05268924	1.05386479
164	1.04594978	1.04712502	1.04830156	1.04947943	1.05065860	1.05183910	1.05302091	1.05420405
165	1.04623634	1.04741907	1.04860313	1.04978852	1.05097524	1.05216330	1.05335269	1.05454341
166	1.04652298	1.04771321	1.04890478	1.05009770	1.05129197	1.05248759	1.05368456	1.05488289
167	1.04680970	1.04800743	1.04920652	1.05040698	1.05160880	1.05281199	1.05401655	1.05522247
168	1.04709650	1.04830173	1.04950835	1.05071635	1.05192572	1.05313649	1.05434863	1.05556217
169	1.04738337	1.04859612	1.04981026	1.05102580	1.05224274	1.05346108	1.05468083	1.05590197
170	1.04767033	1.04889059	1.05011226	1.05133535	1.05255986	1.05378578	1.05501312	1.05624189
171	1.04795736	1.04918514	1.05041435	1.05164499	1.05287707	1.05411058	1.05534552	1.05658191
172	1.04824447	1.04947977	1.05071652	1.05195472	1.05319437	1.05443548	1.05567803	1.05692204
173	1.04853166	1.04977449	1.05101879	1.05226455	1.05351177	1.05476047	1.05601064	1.05726228
174	1.04881893	1.05006929	1.05132113	1.05257446	1.05382927	1.05508557	1.05634336	1.05760264
175	1.04910628	1.05036417	1.05162357	1.05288446	1.05414686	1.05541077	1.05667618	1.05794310
176	1.04939370	1.05065914	1.05192609	1.05319456	1.05446455	1.05573607	1.05700910	1.05828367
177	1.04968121	1.05095419	1.05222870	1.05350475	1.05478234	1.05606146	1.05734213	1.05862435
178	1.04996879	1.05124932	1.05253139	1.05381503	1.05510021	1.05638696	1.05767527	1.05896514
179	1.05025646	1.05154453	1.05283418	1.05412540	1.05541819	1.05671256	1.05800851	1.05930604
180	1.05054420	1.05183983	1.05313705	1.05443586	1.05573626	1.05703826	1.05834185	1.05964705
181	1.05083202	1.05213521	1.05344000	1.05474641	1.05605443	1.05736406	1.05867530	1.05998817
182	1.05111992	1.05243067	1.05374305	1.05505706	1.05637269	1.05768996	1.05900886	1.06032940
183	1.05140789	1.05272622	1.05404618	1.05536779	1.05669105	1.05801596	1.05934252	1.06067073
184	1.05169595	1.05302184	1.05434940	1.05567862	1.05700951	1.05834206	1.05967629	1.06101218
185	1.05198409	1.05331756	1.05465271	1.05598954	1.05732806	1.05866826	1.06001016	1.06135374
186	1.05227230	1.05361335	1.05495610	1.05630055	1.05764670	1.05899456	1.06034413	1.06169541
187	1.05256060	1.05390923	1.05525958	1.05661165	1.05796545	1.05932097	1.06067821	1.06203719
188	1.05284897	1.05420519	1.05556315	1.05692284	1.05828428	1.05964747	1.06101240	1.06237908
189	1.05313742	1.05450123	1.05586680	1.05723413	1.05860322	1.05997407	1.06134669	1.06272108
190	1.05342595	1.05479736	1.05617054	1.05754551	1.05892225	1.06030078	1.06168109	1.06306319
191	1.05371456	1.05509357	1.05647437	1.05785698	1.05924138	1.06062758	1.06201559	1.06340540
192	1.05400325	1.05538986	1.05677829	1.05816854	1.05956060	1.06095449	1.06235020	1.06374773
193	1.05429202	1.05568624	1.05708230	1.05848019	1.05987992	1.06128149	1.06268491	1.06409017
194	1.05458087	1.05598270	1.05738639	1.05879193	1.06019934	1.06160860	1.06301973	1.06443272
195	1.05486979	1.05627924	1.05769057	1.05910377	1.06051885	1.06193581	1.06335465	1.06477538
196	1.05515880	1.05657587	1.05799484	1.05941570	1.06083846	1.06226312	1.06368968	1.06511815
197	1.05544788	1.05687258	1.05829919	1.05972772	1.06115816	1.06259053	1.06402482	1.06546103
198	1.05573705	1.05716937	1.05860363	1.06003983	1.06147796	1.06291804	1.06436006	1.06580402
199	1.05602629	1.05746625	1.05890816	1.06035203	1.06179786	1.06324565	1.06469540	1.06614713
200	1.05631561	1.05776321	1.05921278	1.06066433	1.06211785	1.06357336	1.06503086	1.06649034

Day	10.00%	10.25%	10.50%	10.75%	11.00%	11.25%	11.50%	11.75%
201	1.05660501	1.05806025	1.05951748	1.06097671	1.06243794	1.06390118	1.06536641	1.06683366
202	1.05689449	1.05835738	1.05982228	1.06128919	1.06275813	1.06422909	1.06570208	1.06717709
203	1.05718405	1.05865459	1.06012716	1.06160177	1.06307841	1.06455711	1.06603785	1.06752064
204	1.05747369	1.05895188	1.06043213	1.06191443	1.06339879	1.06488522	1.06637372	1.06786429
205	1.05776341	1.05924926	1.06073718	1.06222718	1.06371927	1.06521344	1.06670970	1.06820805
206	1.05805321	1.05954672	1.06104233	1.06254003	1.06403984	1.06554176	1.06704579	1.06855193
207	1.05834309	1.05984426	1.06134756	1.06285297	1.06436051	1.06587018	1.06738198	1.06889591
208	1.05863304	1.06014189	1.06165288	1.06316600	1.06468128	1.06619870	1.06771828	1.06924001
209	1.05892308	1.06043960	1.06195828	1.06347913	1.06500214	1.06652733	1.06805468	1.06958422
210	1.05921320	1.06073740	1.06226378	1.06379234	1.06532310	1.06685605	1.06839119	1.06992854
211	1.05950339	1.06103527	1.06256936	1.06410565	1.06564416	1.06718488	1.06872781	1.07027297
212	1.05979367	1.06133324	1.06287503	1.06441905	1.06596531	1.06751380	1.06906453	1.07061751
213	1.06008402	1.06163128	1.06318079	1.06473255	1.06628656	1.06784283	1.06940136	1.07096216
214	1.06037446	1.06192941	1.06348664	1.06504613	1.06660791	1.06817196	1.06973830	1.07130692
215	1.06066497	1.06222762	1.06379257	1.06535981	1.06692935	1.06850119	1.07007534	1.07165179
216	1.06095556	1.06252592	1.06409859	1.06567358	1.06725089	1.06883052	1.07041248	1.07199678
217	1.06124623	1.06282430	1.06440470	1.06598744	1.06757253	1.06915996	1.07074974	1.07234187
218	1.06153699	1.06312277	1.06471090	1.06630140	1.06789426	1.06948949	1.07108710	1.07268708
219	1.06182782	1.06342131	1.06501719	1.06661545	1.06821609	1.06981913	1.07142456	1.07303239
220	1.06211873	1.06371995	1.06532356	1.06692959	1.06853802	1.07014887	1.07176214	1.07337782
221	1.06240972	1.06401866	1.06563003	1.06724382	1.06886005	1.07047871	1.07209981	1.07372336
222	1.06270079	1.06431746	1.06593658	1.06755815	1.06918217	1.07080865	1.07243760	1.07406901
223	1.06299194	1.06461635	1.06624322	1.06787256	1.06950439	1.07113870	1.07277549	1.07441477
224	1.06328318	1.06491531	1.06654994	1.06818707	1.06982671	1.07146884	1.07311349	1.07476065
225	1.06357449	1.06521436	1.06685676	1.06850168	1.07014912	1.07179909	1.07345159	1.07510663
226	1.06386588	1.06551350	1.06716366	1.06881637	1.07047163	1.07212944	1.07378980	1.07545273
227	1.06415735	1.06581272	1.06747066	1.06913116	1.07079424	1.07245989	1.07412812	1.07579893
228	1.06444890	1.06611202	1.06777774	1.06944604	1.07111694	1.07279044	1.07446654	1.07614525
229	1.06474053	1.06641141	1.06808491	1.06976102	1.07143974	1.07312110	1.07480507	1.07649168
230	1.06503224	1.06671088	1.06839216	1.07007608	1.07176264	1.07345185	1.07514371	1.07683823
231	1.06532403	1.06701044	1.06869951	1.07039124	1.07208564	1.07378271	1.07548246	1.07718488
232	1.06561589	1.06731008	1.06900694	1.07070649	1.07240874	1.07411367	1.07582131	1.07753164
233	1.06590784	1.06760980	1.06931447	1.07102184	1.07273193	1.07444473	1.07616026	1.07787852
234	1.06619987	1.06790961	1.06962208	1.07133728	1.07305522	1.07477590	1.07649933	1.07822551
235	1.06649198	1.06820950	1.06992978	1.07165281	1.07337860	1.07510716	1.07683850	1.07857261
236	1.06678417	1.06850948	1.07023756	1.07196843	1.07370209	1.07543853	1.07717778	1.07891982
237	1.06707644	1.06880954	1.07054544	1.07228415	1.07402567	1.07577000	1.07751716	1.07926714
238	1.06736879	1.06910969	1.07085341	1.07259996	1.07434935	1.07610158	1.07785665	1.07961458
239	1.06766122	1.06940991	1.07116146	1.07291586	1.07467312	1.07643325	1.07819625	1.07996213
240	1.06795373	1.06971023	1.07146960	1.07323186	1.07499700	1.07676503	1.07853596	1.08030979
241	1.06824632	1.07001063	1.07177783	1.07354795	1.07532097	1.07709691	1.07887577	1.08065756
242	1.06853899	1.07031111	1.07208615	1.07386413	1.07564504	1.07742889	1.07921569	1.08100544
243	1.06883174	1.07061168	1.07239456	1.07418040	1.07596921	1.07776098	1.07955572	1.08135343
244	1.06912457	1.07091233	1.07270306	1.07449677	1.07629347	1.07809316	1.07989585	1.08170154
245	1.06941748	1.07121306	1.07301164	1.07481323	1.07661783	1.07842545	1.08023609	1.08204976
246	1.06971048	1.07151388	1.07332032	1.07512979	1.07694229	1.07875784	1.08057644	1.08239809
247	1.07000355	1.07181479	1.07362908	1.07544643	1.07726685	1.07909034	1.08091690	1.08274653
248	1.07029670	1.07211578	1.07393793	1.07576318	1.07759151	1.07942293	1.08125746	1.08309509
249	1.07058993	1.07241685	1.07424687	1.07608001	1.07791626	1.07975563	1.08159813	1.08344376
250	1.07088324	1.07271801	1.07455590	1.07639694	1.07824111	1.08008843	1.08193891	1.08379254

Day	10.00%	10.25%	10.50%	10.75%	11.00%	11.25%	11.50%	11.75%
251	1.07117664	1.07301925	1.07486502	1.07671396	1.07856606	1.08042134	1.08227979	1.08414143
252	1.07147011	1.07332058	1.07517423	1.07703107	1.07889111	1.08075434	1.08262078	1.08449043
253	1.07176366	1.07362199	1.07548353	1.07734828	1.07921625	1.08108745	1.08296188	1.08483955
254	1.07205730	1.07392349	1.07579291	1.07766558	1.07954150	1.08142066	1.08330309	1.08518878
255	1.07235101	1.07422507	1.07610239	1.07798298	1.07986684	1.08175398	1.08364440	1.08553812
256	1.07264480	1.07452673	1.07641195	1.07830046	1.08019228	1.08208740	1.08398583	1.08588758
257	1.07293868	1.07482848	1.07672160	1.07861805	1.08051781	1.08242092	1.08432736	1.08623714
258	1.07323264	1.07513032	1.07703135	1.07893572	1.08084345	1.08275454	1.08466899	1.08658682
259	1.07352667	1.07543224	1.07734118	1.07925349	1.08116918	1.08308826	1.08501074	1.08693661
260	1.07382079	1.07573424	1.07765110	1.07957135	1.08149502	1.08342209	1.08535259	1.08728652
261	1.07411499	1.07603633	1.07796111	1.07988931	1.08182095	1.08375603	1.08569455	1.08763653
262	1.07440926	1.07633851	1.07827121	1.08020736	1.08214697	1.08409006	1.08603662	1.08798666
263	1.07470362	1.07664077	1.07858139	1.08052550	1.08247310	1.08442420	1.08637880	1.08833691
264	1.07499806	1.07694311	1.07889167	1.08084374	1.08279933	1.08475844	1.08672108	1.08868726
265	1.07529258	1.07724554	1.07920204	1.08116207	1.08312565	1.08509278	1.08706347	1.08903773
266	1.07558718	1.07754806	1.07951249	1.08148049	1.08345207	1.08542723	1.08740597	1.08938831
267	1.07588186	1.07785066	1.07982304	1.08179901	1.08377859	1.08576178	1.08774858	1.08973900
268	1.07617663	1.07815334	1.08013367	1.08211762	1.08410521	1.08609643	1.08809129	1.09008981
269	1.07647147	1.07845611	1.08044439	1.08243633	1.08443192	1.08643118	1.08843412	1.09044073
270	1.07676639	1.07875896	1.08075521	1.08275513	1.08475874	1.08676604	1.08877705	1.09079176
271	1.07706140	1.07906190	1.08106611	1.08307402	1.08508565	1.08710101	1.08912009	1.09114291
272	1.07735648	1.07936493	1.08137710	1.08339301	1.08541267	1.08743607	1.08946323	1.09149416
273	1.07765165	1.07966804	1.08168818	1.08371209	1.08573978	1.08777124	1.08980649	1.09184554
274	1.07794690	1.07997123	1.08199935	1.08403127	1.08606699	1.08810651	1.09014985	1.09219702
275	1.07824222	1.08027451	1.08231061	1.08435054	1.08639429	1.08844189	1.09049333	1.09254862
276	1.07853763	1.08057787	1.08262196	1.08466990	1.08672170	1.08877737	1.09083691	1.09290033
277	1.07883312	1.08088132	1.08293340	1.08498936	1.08704920	1.08911295	1.09118059	1.09325215
278	1.07912869	1.08118486	1.08324493	1.08530891	1.08737681	1.08944863	1.09152439	1.09360409
279	1.07942435	1.08148848	1.08355655	1.08562855	1.08770451	1.08978442	1.09186830	1.09395614
280	1.07972008	1.08179219	1.08386826	1.08594829	1.08803231	1.09012031	1.09221231	1.09430830
281	1.08001589	1.08209598	1.08418005	1.08626813	1.08836021	1.09045631	1.09255643	1.09466058
282	1.08031179	1.08239985	1.08449194	1.08658806	1.08868821	1.09079241	1.09290066	1.09501297
283	1.08060776	1.08270381	1.08480392	1.08690808	1.08901631	1.09112861	1.09324500	1.09536548
284	1.08090382	1.08300786	1.08511598	1.08722820	1.08934451	1.09146492	1.09358945	1.09571809
285	1.08119996	1.08331199	1.08542814	1.08754841	1.08967280	1.09180133	1.09393400	1.09607083
286	1.08149618	1.08361621	1.08574039	1.08786871	1.09000120	1.09213784	1.09427867	1.09642367
287	1.08179248	1.08392051	1.08605272	1.08818911	1.09032969	1.09247446	1.09462344	1.09677663
288	1.08208886	1.08422490	1.08636515	1.08850961	1.09065828	1.09281118	1.09496832	1.09712970
289	1.08238532	1.08452938	1.08667767	1.08883019	1.09098697	1.09314801	1.09531331	1.09748289
290	1.08268186	1.08483394	1.08699027	1.08915088	1.09131576	1.09348494	1.09565841	1.09783618
291	1.08297849	1.08513858	1.08730297	1.08947166	1.09164465	1.09382197	1.09600362	1.09818960
292	1.08327520	1.08544331	1.08761575	1.08979253	1.09197364	1.09415911	1.09634893	1.09854312
293	1.08357198	1.08574813	1.08792863	1.09011349	1.09230273	1.09449635	1.09669436	1.09889677
294	1.08386885	1.08605303	1.08824159	1.09043455	1.09263192	1.09483369	1.09703989	1.09925052
295	1.08416580	1.08635802	1.08855465	1.09075571	1.09296120	1.09517114	1.09738553	1.09960439
296	1.08446284	1.08666309	1.08886780	1.09107696	1.09329059	1.09550870	1.09773129	1.09995837
297	1.08475995	1.08696825	1.08918103	1.09139830	1.09362007	1.09584635	1.09807715	1.10031247
298	1.08505714	1.08727349	1.08949436	1.09171974	1.09394966	1.09618411	1.09842312	1.10066668
299	1.08535442	1.08757882	1.08980777	1.09204128	1.09427934	1.09652198	1.09876919	1.10102100
300	1.08565178	1.08788424	1.09012128	1.09236291	1.09460912	1.09685995	1.09911538	1.10137544

Day	10.00%	10.25%	10.50%	10.75%	11.00%	11.25%	11.50%	11.75%
301	1.08594921	1.08818974	1.09043488	1.09268463	1.09493901	1.09719802	1.09946168	1.10172999
302	1.08624674	1.08849533	1.09074856	1.09300645	1.09526899	1.09753620	1.09980808	1.10208466
303	1.08654434	1.08880100	1.09106234	1.09332836	1.09559907	1.09787448	1.10015460	1.10243944
304	1.08684202	1.08910676	1.09137621	1.09365037	1.09592925	1.09821287	1.10050122	1.10279433
305	1.08713979	1.08941261	1.09169017	1.09397247	1.09625953	1.09855136	1.10084796	1.10314934
306	1.08743763	1.08971854	1.09200421	1.09429467	1.09658991	1.09888995	1.10119480	1.10350447
307	1.08773556	1.09002456	1.09231835	1.09461696	1.09692039	1.09922865	1.10154175	1.10385970
308	1.08803357	1.09033066	1.09263258	1.09493935	1.09725097	1.09956745	1.10188881	1.10421506
309	1.08833166	1.09063685	1.09294690	1.09526183	1.09758165	1.09990636	1.10223598	1.10457052
310	1.08862983	1.09094312	1.09326131	1.09558441	1.09791242	1.10024537	1.10258326	1.10492610
311	1.08892809	1.09124948	1.09357581	1.09590708	1.09824330	1.10058449	1.10293065	1.10528180
312	1.08922643	1.09155593	1.09389040	1.09622985	1.09857428	1.10092371	1.10327815	1.10563761
313	1.08952484	1.09186246	1.09420508	1.09655271	1.09890536	1.10126304	1.10362576	1.10599353
314	1.08982334	1.09216908	1.09451985	1.09687566	1.09923653	1.10160247	1.10397348	1.10634957
315	1.09012193	1.09247579	1.09483471	1.09719872	1.09956781	1.10194200	1.10432130	1.10670573
316	1.09042059	1.09278258	1.09514967	1.09752186	1.09989919	1.10228164	1.10466924	1.10706199
317	1.09071933	1.09308945	1.09546471	1.09784511	1.10023066	1.10262139	1.10501729	1.10741838
318	1.09101816	1.09339642	1.09577984	1.09816845	1.10056224	1.10296123	1.10536544	1.10777487
319	1.09131707	1.09370347	1.09609507	1.09849188	1.10089392	1.10330119	1.10571371	1.10813149
320	1.09161606	1.09401060	1.09641038	1.09881541	1.10122569	1.10364125	1.10606208	1.10848821
321	1.09191513	1.09431783	1.09672579	1.09913903	1.10155757	1.10398141	1.10641057	1.10884506
322	1.09221429	1.09462513	1.09704128	1.09946275	1.10188954	1.10432168	1.10675916	1.10920201
323	1.09251353	1.09493253	1.09735687	1.09978656	1.10222162	1.10466205	1.10710787	1.10955908
324	1.09281284	1.09524001	1.09767255	1.10011047	1.10255380	1.10500253	1.10745668	1.10991627
325	1.09311225	1.09554758	1.09798832	1.10043448	1.10288607	1.10534311	1.10780561	1.11027357
326	1.09341173	1.09585523	1.09830418	1.10075858	1.10321845	1.10568380	1.10815464	1.11063099
327	1.09371129	1.09616297	1.09862013	1.10108278	1.10355093	1.10602459	1.10850379	1.11098852
328	1.09401094	1.09647080	1.09893617	1.10140707	1.10388350	1.10636549	1.10885304	1.11134617
329	1.09431067	1.09677871	1.09925230	1.10173145	1.10421618	1.10670649	1.10920241	1.11170393
330	1.09461048	1.09708671	1.09956852	1.10205594	1.10454896	1.10704760	1.10955188	1.11206181
331	1.09491037	1.09739480	1.09988484	1.10238051	1.10488184	1.10738882	1.10990147	1.11241980
332	1.09521035	1.09770297	1.10020124	1.10270519	1.10521481	1.10773013	1.11025116	1.11277791
333	1.09551041	1.09801123	1.10051774	1.10302996	1.10554789	1.10807156	1.11060097	1.11313613
334	1.09581055	1.09831957	1.10083433	1.10335482	1.10588107	1.10841309	1.11095088	1.11349447
335	1.09611077	1.09862801	1.10115101	1.10367978	1.10621435	1.10875472	1.11130091	1.11385292

Day	10.00%	10.25%	10.50%	10.75%	11.00%	11.25%	11.50%	11.75%
336	1.09641107	1.09893652	1.10146778	1.10400484	1.10654773	1.10909646	1.11165104	1.11421149
337	1.09671146	1.09924513	1.10178464	1.10432999	1.10688121	1.10943831	1.11200129	1.11457018
338	1.09701193	1.09955382	1.10210159	1.10465524	1.10721479	1.10978026	1.11235165	1.11492898
339	1.09731248	1.09986260	1.10241863	1.10498058	1.10754847	1.11012231	1.11270211	1.11528789
340	1.09761311	1.10017147	1.10273577	1.10530602	1.10788225	1.11046447	1.11305269	1.11564692
341	1.09791383	1.10048042	1.10305299	1.10563156	1.10821614	1.11080674	1.11340338	1.11600607
342	1.09821463	1.10078946	1.10337031	1.10595719	1.10855012	1.11114911	1.11375418	1.11636533
343	1.09851551	1.10109858	1.10368771	1.10628292	1.10888420	1.11149159	1.11410509	1.11672471
344	1.09881647	1.10140780	1.10400521	1.10660874	1.10921839	1.11183417	1.11445611	1.11708420
345	1.09911752	1.10171710	1.10432280	1.10693466	1.10955267	1.11217686	1.11480724	1.11744381
346	1.09941864	1.10202648	1.10464049	1.10726067	1.10988706	1.11251965	1.11515848	1.11780354
347	1.09971986	1.10233595	1.10495826	1.10758678	1.11022154	1.11286255	1.11550983	1.11816338
348	1.10002115	1.10264551	1.10527612	1.10791299	1.11055613	1.11320556	1.11586129	1.11852334
349	1.10032252	1.10295516	1.10559408	1.10823929	1.11089082	1.11354867	1.11621286	1.11888341
350	1.10062398	1.10326490	1.10591213	1.10856569	1.11122561	1.11389189	1.11656455	1.11924360
351	1.10092552	1.10357472	1.10623027	1.10889219	1.11156050	1.11423521	1.11691634	1.11960390
352	1.10122715	1.10388462	1.10654850	1.10921878	1.11189549	1.11457864	1.11726824	1.11996432
353	1.10152885	1.10419462	1.10686682	1.10954547	1.11223058	1.11492217	1.11762026	1.12032486
354	1.10183064	1.10450470	1.10718523	1.10987225	1.11256577	1.11526581	1.11797239	1.12068551
355	1.10213251	1.10481487	1.10750374	1.11019913	1.11290107	1.11560956	1.11832463	1.12104628
356	1.10243447	1.10512513	1.10782234	1.11052611	1.11323646	1.11595341	1.11867697	1.12140716
357	1.10273650	1.10543547	1.10814102	1.11085318	1.11357196	1.11629737	1.11902943	1.12176817
358	1.10303862	1.10574590	1.10845981	1.11118035	1.11390756	1.11664144	1.11938201	1.12212928
359	1.10334083	1.10605642	1.10877868	1.11150762	1.11424325	1.11698561	1.11973469	1.12249052
360	1.10364311	1.10636702	1.10909764	1.11183498	1.11457905	1.11732988	1.12008748	1.12285187
361	1.10394548	1.10667772	1.10941670	1.11216244	1.11491495	1.11767426	1.12044038	1.12321333
362	1.10424793	1.10698850	1.10973584	1.11248999	1.11525096	1.11801875	1.12079340	1.12357491
363	1.10455046	1.10729936	1.11005508	1.11281764	1.11558706	1.11836335	1.12114653	1.12393661
364	1.10485308	1.10761032	1.11037441	1.11314539	1.11592326	1.11870805	1.12149976	1.12429843
365	1.10515578	1.10792136	1.11069384	1.11347323	1.11625957	1.11905286	1.12185311	1.12466036

Day	12.00%	12.25%	12.50%	12.75%	13.00%	13.25%	13.50%	13.75%
1	1.00032877	1.00033562	1.00034247	1.00034932	1.00035616	1.00036301	1.00036986	1.00037671
2	1.00065764	1.00067135	1.00068505	1.00069875	1.00071246	1.00072616	1.00073986	1.00075357
3	1.00098663	1.00100719	1.00102775	1.00104831	1.00106887	1.00108944	1.00111000	1.00113056
4	1.00131572	1.00134314	1.00137057	1.00139799	1.00142542	1.00145285	1.00148027	1.00150770
5	1.00164492	1.00167921	1.00171350	1.00174780	1.00178209	1.00181639	1.00185068	1.00188498
6	1.00197422	1.00201539	1.00205655	1.00209772	1.00213889	1.00218006	1.00222123	1.00226240
7	1.00230364	1.00235168	1.00239972	1.00244777	1.00249582	1.00254386	1.00259192	1.00263997
8	1.00263317	1.00268809	1.00274301	1.00279794	1.00285287	1.00290780	1.00296274	1.00301768
9	1.00296280	1.00302461	1.00308642	1.00314823	1.00321005	1.00327187	1.00333370	1.00339552
10	1.00329254	1.00336124	1.00342994	1.00349865	1.00356736	1.00363607	1.00370479	1.00377352
11	1.00362239	1.00369798	1.00377358	1.00384918	1.00392479	1.00400041	1.00407603	1.00415165
12	1.00395235	1.00403484	1.00411734	1.00419984	1.00428235	1.00436487	1.00444740	1.00452993
13	1.00428241	1.00437181	1.00446121	1.00455063	1.00464004	1.00472947	1.00481890	1.00490834
14	1.00461259	1.00470889	1.00480521	1.00490153	1.00499786	1.00509420	1.00519055	1.00528691
15	1.00494287	1.00504609	1.00514932	1.00525256	1.00535581	1.00545906	1.00556233	1.00566561
16	1.00527326	1.00538340	1.00549355	1.00560371	1.00571388	1.00582406	1.00593425	1.00604446
17	1.00560377	1.00572082	1.00583790	1.00595498	1.00607208	1.00618919	1.00630631	1.00642345
18	1.00593437	1.00605836	1.00618236	1.00630638	1.00643040	1.00655445	1.00667851	1.00680258
19	1.00626509	1.00639601	1.00652694	1.00665789	1.00678886	1.00691984	1.00705084	1.00718185
20	1.00659592	1.00673377	1.00687164	1.00700953	1.00714744	1.00728537	1.00742331	1.00756127
21	1.00692686	1.00707165	1.00721646	1.00736130	1.00750615	1.00765102	1.00779592	1.00794083
22	1.00725790	1.00740964	1.00756140	1.00771318	1.00786499	1.00801682	1.00816866	1.00832054
23	1.00758905	1.00774774	1.00790646	1.00806519	1.00822395	1.00838274	1.00854155	1.00870038
24	1.00792032	1.00808596	1.00825163	1.00841733	1.00858305	1.00874880	1.00891457	1.00908037
25	1.00825169	1.00842429	1.00859692	1.00876958	1.00894227	1.00911499	1.00928773	1.00946050
26	1.00858317	1.00876273	1.00894233	1.00912196	1.00930162	1.00948131	1.00966103	1.00984078
27	1.00891476	1.00910129	1.00928786	1.00947446	1.00966110	1.00984776	1.01003447	1.01022120
28	1.00924645	1.00943996	1.00963351	1.00982709	1.01002070	1.01021435	1.01040804	1.01060176
29	1.00957826	1.00977875	1.00997927	1.01017983	1.01038043	1.01058107	1.01078175	1.01098247
30	1.00991018	1.01011764	1.01032515	1.01053270	1.01074030	1.01094793	1.01115560	1.01136332
31	1.01024220	1.01045666	1.01067116	1.01088570	1.01110029	1.01131492	1.01152959	1.01174431
32	1.01057434	1.01079578	1.01101728	1.01123882	1.01146040	1.01168204	1.01190372	1.01212545
33	1.01090658	1.01113502	1.01136351	1.01159206	1.01182065	1.01204929	1.01227799	1.01250673
34	1.01123893	1.01147438	1.01170987	1.01194542	1.01218102	1.01241668	1.01265239	1.01288815
35	1.01157139	1.01181384	1.01205635	1.01229891	1.01254153	1.01278420	1.01302693	1.01326972
36	1.01190397	1.01215342	1.01240294	1.01265252	1.01290216	1.01315186	1.01340161	1.01365143
37	1.01223665	1.01249312	1.01274966	1.01300626	1.01326292	1.01351964	1.01377643	1.01403329
38	1.01256944	1.01283293	1.01309649	1.01336011	1.01362381	1.01388757	1.01415139	1.01441528
39	1.01290234	1.01317285	1.01344344	1.01371410	1.01398482	1.01425562	1.01452649	1.01479743
40	1.01323535	1.01351289	1.01379051	1.01406820	1.01434597	1.01462381	1.01490172	1.01517971
41	1.01356846	1.01385304	1.01413770	1.01442243	1.01470724	1.01499213	1.01527710	1.01556214
42	1.01390169	1.01419331	1.01448500	1.01477678	1.01506864	1.01536059	1.01565261	1.01594472
43	1.01423503	1.01453369	1.01483243	1.01513126	1.01543018	1.01572918	1.01602827	1.01632744
44	1.01456848	1.01487418	1.01517998	1.01548586	1.01579184	1.01609790	1.01640406	1.01671030
45	1.01490203	1.01521479	1.01552764	1.01584059	1.01615362	1.01646676	1.01677999	1.01709331
46	1.01523570	1.01555551	1.01587542	1.01619543	1.01651554	1.01683575	1.01715606	1.01747646
47	1.01556948	1.01589635	1.01622333	1.01655041	1.01687759	1.01720488	1.01753226	1.01785976
48	1.01590336	1.01623730	1.01657135	1.01690550	1.01723976	1.01757413	1.01790861	1.01824320
49	1.01623736	1.01657837	1.01691949	1.01726072	1.01760207	1.01794353	1.01828510	1.01862678
50	1.01657146	1.01691955	1.01726775	1.01761607	1.01796450	1.01831306	1.01866172	1.01901051

Day	12.00%	12.25%	12.50%	12.75%	13.00%	13.25%	13.50%	13.75%
51	1.01690568	1.01726084	1.01761613	1.01797154	1.01832707	1.01868272	1.01903849	1.01939438
52	1.01724000	1.01760225	1.01796463	1.01832713	1.01868976	1.01905251	1.01941539	1.01977840
53	1.01757444	1.01794378	1.01831325	1.01868285	1.01905258	1.01942244	1.01979244	1.02016257
54	1.01790898	1.01828541	1.01866198	1.01903869	1.01941553	1.01979251	1.02016962	1.02054687
55	1.01824364	1.01862717	1.01901084	1.01939465	1.01977861	1.02016271	1.02054694	1.02093133
56	1.01857840	1.01896904	1.01935982	1.01975074	1.02014182	1.02053304	1.02092441	1.02131592
57	1.01891328	1.01931102	1.01970891	1.02010696	1.02050516	1.02090351	1.02130201	1.02170067
58	1.01924826	1.01965312	1.02005813	1.02046330	1.02086862	1.02127411	1.02167975	1.02208555
59	1.01958336	1.01999533	1.02040746	1.02081976	1.02123222	1.02164484	1.02205763	1.02247059
60	1.01991856	1.02033766	1.02075692	1.02117635	1.02159595	1.02201572	1.02243565	1.02285576
61	1.02025388	1.02068010	1.02110649	1.02153306	1.02195980	1.02238672	1.02281382	1.02324109
62	1.02058931	1.02102265	1.02145618	1.02188990	1.02232379	1.02275786	1.02319212	1.02362655
63	1.02092484	1.02136533	1.02180600	1.02224686	1.02268790	1.02312914	1.02357056	1.02401217
64	1.02126049	1.02170811	1.02215593	1.02260394	1.02305215	1.02350055	1.02394914	1.02439792
65	1.02159625	1.02205102	1.02250599	1.02296115	1.02341652	1.02387209	1.02432786	1.02478383
66	1.02193211	1.02239403	1.02285616	1.02331849	1.02378103	1.02424377	1.02470672	1.02516988
67	1.02226809	1.02273717	1.02320645	1.02367595	1.02414566	1.02461559	1.02508572	1.02555607
68	1.02260418	1.02308041	1.02355687	1.02403354	1.02451043	1.02498753	1.02546486	1.02594241
69	1.02294038	1.02342378	1.02390740	1.02439125	1.02487532	1.02535962	1.02584414	1.02632889
70	1.02327669	1.02376725	1.02425805	1.02474908	1.02524034	1.02573184	1.02622357	1.02671553
71	1.02361311	1.02411085	1.02460882	1.02510704	1.02560550	1.02610419	1.02660313	1.02710230
72	1.02394964	1.02445455	1.02495972	1.02546513	1.02597078	1.02647668	1.02698283	1.02748922
73	1.02428628	1.02479838	1.02531073	1.02582334	1.02633620	1.02684931	1.02736267	1.02787629
74	1.02462303	1.02514232	1.02566187	1.02618167	1.02670174	1.02722207	1.02774266	1.02826350
75	1.02495989	1.02548637	1.02601312	1.02654013	1.02706742	1.02759496	1.02812278	1.02865086
76	1.02529686	1.02583054	1.02636449	1.02689872	1.02743322	1.02796800	1.02850305	1.02903837
77	1.02563395	1.02617483	1.02671599	1.02725743	1.02779916	1.02834116	1.02888345	1.02942602
78	1.02597114	1.02651923	1.02706760	1.02761627	1.02816522	1.02871446	1.02926400	1.02981382
79	1.02630845	1.02686375	1.02741934	1.02797523	1.02853142	1.02908790	1.02964468	1.03020176
80	1.02664586	1.02720838	1.02777120	1.02833432	1.02889774	1.02946147	1.03002551	1.03058985
81	1.02698339	1.02755313	1.02812317	1.02869353	1.02926420	1.02983518	1.03040648	1.03097809
82	1.02732103	1.02789799	1.02847527	1.02905287	1.02963079	1.03020903	1.03078759	1.03136647
83	1.02765878	1.02824297	1.02882749	1.02941233	1.02999751	1.03058301	1.03116884	1.03175500
84	1.02799664	1.02858806	1.02917982	1.02977192	1.03036435	1.03095712	1.03155023	1.03214367
85	1.02833461	1.02893328	1.02953228	1.03013164	1.03073133	1.03133137	1.03193176	1.03253249
86	1.02867269	1.02927860	1.02988486	1.03049148	1.03109844	1.03170576	1.03231344	1.03292146
87	1.02901089	1.02962405	1.03023756	1.03085144	1.03146568	1.03208029	1.03269525	1.03331058
88	1.02934919	1.02996960	1.03059038	1.03121153	1.03183305	1.03245494	1.03307721	1.03369984
89	1.02968761	1.03031528	1.03094333	1.03157175	1.03220056	1.03282974	1.03345930	1.03408924
90	1.03002614	1.03066107	1.03129639	1.03193210	1.03256819	1.03320467	1.03384154	1.03447880
91	1.03036478	1.03100698	1.03164957	1.03229256	1.03293595	1.03357974	1.03422392	1.03486850
92	1.03070353	1.03135300	1.03200288	1.03265316	1.03330385	1.03395494	1.03460644	1.03525835
93	1.03104239	1.03169914	1.03235630	1.03301388	1.03367187	1.03433028	1.03498910	1.03564834
94	1.03138136	1.03204539	1.03270985	1.03337473	1.03404003	1.03470576	1.03537191	1.03603848
95	1.03172044	1.03239176	1.03306352	1.03373570	1.03440832	1.03508137	1.03575485	1.03642877
96	1.03205964	1.03273825	1.03341731	1.03409680	1.03477674	1.03545712	1.03613794	1.03681921
97	1.03239895	1.03308486	1.03377122	1.03445803	1.03514529	1.03583300	1.03652117	1.03720979
98	1.03273837	1.03343158	1.03412525	1.03481938	1.03551397	1.03620903	1.03690454	1.03760052
99	1.03307790	1.03377841	1.03447940	1.03518086	1.03588278	1.03658518	1.03728805	1.03799140
100	1.03341754	1.03412537	1.03483367	1.03554246	1.03625173	1.03696148	1.03767171	1.03838242

Day	12.00%	12.25%	12.50%	12.75%	13.00%	13.25%	13.50%	13.75%
101	1.03375729	1.03447244	1.03518807	1.03590419	1.03662081	1.03733791	1.03805551	1.03877359
102	1.03409716	1.03481962	1.03554258	1.03626605	1.03699001	1.03771448	1.03843944	1.03916491
103	1.03443713	1.03516692	1.03589722	1.03662803	1.03735935	1.03809118	1.03882352	1.03955638
104	1.03477722	1.03551434	1.03625198	1.03699014	1.03772882	1.03846802	1.03920775	1.03994799
105	1.03511742	1.03586188	1.03660686	1.03735238	1.03809842	1.03884500	1.03959211	1.04033975
106	1.03545774	1.03620953	1.03696187	1.03771474	1.03846816	1.03922212	1.03997662	1.04073166
107	1.03579816	1.03655730	1.03731699	1.03807723	1.03883802	1.03959937	1.04036127	1.04112372
108	1.03613870	1.03690519	1.03767223	1.03843985	1.03920802	1.03997676	1.04074606	1.04151592
109	1.03647935	1.03725319	1.03802760	1.03880259	1.03957815	1.04035428	1.04113099	1.04190827
110	1.03682011	1.03760131	1.03838309	1.03916546	1.03994841	1.04073195	1.04151607	1.04230077
111	1.03716098	1.03794954	1.03873870	1.03952845	1.04031880	1.04110975	1.04190129	1.04269342
112	1.03750196	1.03829790	1.03909443	1.03989158	1.04068933	1.04148768	1.04228665	1.04308622
113	1.03784306	1.03864637	1.03945029	1.04025483	1.04105998	1.04186576	1.04267215	1.04347916
114	1.03818427	1.03899495	1.03980626	1.04061820	1.04143077	1.04224397	1.04305779	1.04387225
115	1.03852559	1.03934366	1.04016236	1.04098171	1.04180169	1.04262232	1.04344358	1.04426549
116	1.03886702	1.03969248	1.04051858	1.04134534	1.04217275	1.04300080	1.04382951	1.04465888
117	1.03920857	1.04004142	1.04087492	1.04170910	1.04254393	1.04337943	1.04421559	1.04505241
118	1.03955023	1.04039047	1.04123139	1.04207298	1.04291525	1.04375819	1.04460181	1.04544610
119	1.03989200	1.04073964	1.04158797	1.04243699	1.04328670	1.04413709	1.04498816	1.04583993
120	1.04023388	1.04108893	1.04194468	1.04280113	1.04365828	1.04451612	1.04537467	1.04623391
121	1.04057587	1.04143834	1.04230151	1.04316540	1.04402999	1.04489530	1.04576131	1.04662804
122	1.04091798	1.04178786	1.04265847	1.04352979	1.04440184	1.04527461	1.04614810	1.04702232
123	1.04126020	1.04213750	1.04301554	1.04389431	1.04477382	1.04565406	1.04653503	1.04741674
124	1.04160253	1.04248726	1.04337274	1.04425896	1.04514593	1.04603364	1.04692211	1.04781132
125	1.04194498	1.04283714	1.04373006	1.04462373	1.04551817	1.04641337	1.04730932	1.04820604
126	1.04228753	1.04318713	1.04408750	1.04498864	1.04589055	1.04679323	1.04769669	1.04860091
127	1.04263020	1.04353724	1.04444506	1.04535367	1.04626306	1.04717323	1.04808419	1.04899594
128	1.04297299	1.04388747	1.04480275	1.04571883	1.04663570	1.04755337	1.04847184	1.04939111
129	1.04331588	1.04423782	1.04516056	1.04608411	1.04700847	1.04793365	1.04885963	1.04978642
130	1.04365889	1.04458828	1.04551849	1.04644952	1.04738138	1.04831406	1.04924756	1.05018189
131	1.04400201	1.04493886	1.04587654	1.04681506	1.04775442	1.04869461	1.04963564	1.05057751
132	1.04434524	1.04528956	1.04623472	1.04718073	1.04812759	1.04907530	1.05002386	1.05097327
133	1.04468859	1.04564037	1.04659302	1.04754653	1.04850090	1.04945613	1.05041223	1.05136919
134	1.04503205	1.04599131	1.04695144	1.04791245	1.04887434	1.04983710	1.05080074	1.05176525
135	1.04537562	1.04634236	1.04730999	1.04827850	1.04924791	1.05021820	1.05118939	1.05216146
136	1.04571931	1.04669353	1.04766866	1.04864468	1.04962161	1.05059945	1.05157818	1.05255783
137	1.04606310	1.04704482	1.04802745	1.04901099	1.04999545	1.05098083	1.05196712	1.05295434
138	1.04640701	1.04739622	1.04838636	1.04937743	1.05036942	1.05136235	1.05235621	1.05335100
139	1.04675104	1.04774775	1.04874540	1.04974399	1.05074353	1.05174401	1.05274544	1.05374781
140	1.04709518	1.04809939	1.04910456	1.05011068	1.05111776	1.05212581	1.05313481	1.05414477
141	1.04743943	1.04845115	1.04946384	1.05047750	1.05149213	1.05250774	1.05352432	1.05454188
142	1.04778379	1.04880302	1.04982324	1.05084445	1.05186664	1.05288982	1.05391398	1.05493914
143	1.04812827	1.04915502	1.05018277	1.05121152	1.05224128	1.05327203	1.05430379	1.05533655
144	1.04847286	1.04950713	1.05054242	1.05157873	1.05261605	1.05365438	1.05469373	1.05573410
145	1.04881756	1.04985937	1.05090220	1.05194606	1.05299095	1.05403687	1.05508383	1.05613181
146	1.04916238	1.05021172	1.05126210	1.05231352	1.05336599	1.05441950	1.05547406	1.05652967
147	1.04950731	1.05056418	1.05162212	1.05268111	1.05374116	1.05480227	1.05586444	1.05692768
148	1.04985235	1.05091677	1.05198226	1.05304883	1.05411647	1.05518518	1.05625497	1.05732584
149	1.05019751	1.05126948	1.05234253	1.05341667	1.05449190	1.05556823	1.05664564	1.05772414
150	1.05054278	1.05162230	1.05270292	1.05378465	1.05486748	1.05595141	1.05703645	1.05812260

Day	12.00%	12.25%	12.50%	12.75%	13.00%	13.25%	13.50%	13.75%
151	1.05088816	1.05197524	1.05306344	1.05415275	1.05524318	1.05633474	1.05742741	1.05852121
152	1.05123366	1.05232830	1.05342407	1.05452098	1.05561902	1.05671820	1.05781851	1.05891997
153	1.05157927	1.05268148	1.05378484	1.05488934	1.05599500	1.05710180	1.05820976	1.05931888
154	1.05192500	1.05303478	1.05414572	1.05525783	1.05637110	1.05748555	1.05860116	1.05971793
155	1.05227083	1.05338819	1.05450673	1.05562645	1.05674735	1.05786943	1.05899269	1.06011714
156	1.05261679	1.05374173	1.05486786	1.05599519	1.05712372	1.05825345	1.05938437	1.06051650
157	1.05296285	1.05409538	1.05522912	1.05636407	1.05750023	1.05863761	1.05977620	1.06091601
158	1.05330903	1.05444915	1.05559050	1.05673307	1.05787688	1.05902191	1.06016817	1.06131567
159	1.05365532	1.05480304	1.05595200	1.05710221	1.05825365	1.05940635	1.06056029	1.06171548
160	1.05400173	1.05515705	1.05631363	1.05747147	1.05863057	1.05979093	1.06095255	1.06211544
161	1.05434825	1.05551118	1.05667538	1.05784086	1.05900761	1.06017565	1.06134496	1.06251556
162	1.05469489	1.05586543	1.05703726	1.05821038	1.05938479	1.06056050	1.06173751	1.06291582
163	1.05504164	1.05621979	1.05739925	1.05858003	1.05976211	1.06094550	1.06213021	1.06331623
164	1.05538850	1.05657428	1.05776138	1.05894980	1.06013956	1.06133064	1.06252305	1.06371680
165	1.05573548	1.05692888	1.05812362	1.05931971	1.06051714	1.06171592	1.06291604	1.06411751
166	1.05608257	1.05728360	1.05848600	1.05968975	1.06089486	1.06210134	1.06330917	1.06451838
167	1.05642977	1.05763845	1.05884849	1.06005991	1.06127271	1.06248689	1.06370245	1.06491939
168	1.05677709	1.05799341	1.05921111	1.06043021	1.06165070	1.06287259	1.06409588	1.06532056
169	1.05712453	1.05834849	1.05957385	1.06080063	1.06202882	1.06325843	1.06448945	1.06572188
170	1.05747207	1.05870369	1.05993672	1.06117119	1.06240708	1.06364440	1.06488316	1.06612335
171	1.05781974	1.05905900	1.06029971	1.06154187	1.06278547	1.06403052	1.06527702	1.06652497
172	1.05816751	1.05941444	1.06066283	1.06191268	1.06316400	1.06441678	1.06567103	1.06692675
173	1.05851540	1.05977000	1.06102607	1.06228362	1.06354266	1.06480318	1.06606518	1.06732867
174	1.05886341	1.06012567	1.06138944	1.06265470	1.06392146	1.06518972	1.06645948	1.06773075
175	1.05921153	1.06048147	1.06175293	1.06302590	1.06430039	1.06557639	1.06685392	1.06813297
176	1.05955976	1.06083738	1.06211654	1.06339723	1.06467945	1.06596321	1.06724851	1.06853535
177	1.05990811	1.06119342	1.06248028	1.06376869	1.06505865	1.06635017	1.06764325	1.06893788
178	1.06025657	1.06154957	1.06284414	1.06414028	1.06543799	1.06673727	1.06803813	1.06934057
179	1.06060515	1.06190585	1.06320813	1.06451200	1.06581746	1.06712451	1.06843316	1.06974340
180	1.06095384	1.06226224	1.06357224	1.06488385	1.06619707	1.06751189	1.06882833	1.07014639
181	1.06130265	1.06261875	1.06393648	1.06525583	1.06657681	1.06789941	1.06922365	1.07054952
182	1.06165157	1.06297538	1.06430084	1.06562794	1.06695668	1.06828708	1.06961912	1.07095281
183	1.06200061	1.06333214	1.06466533	1.06600018	1.06733670	1.06867488	1.07001473	1.07135625
184	1.06234976	1.06368901	1.06502994	1.06637255	1.06771684	1.06906282	1.07041049	1.07175985
185	1.06269902	1.06404600	1.06539467	1.06674505	1.06809713	1.06945091	1.07080639	1.07216359
186	1.06304840	1.06440311	1.06575954	1.06711768	1.06847754	1.06983913	1.07120245	1.07256749
187	1.06339790	1.06476034	1.06612452	1.06749044	1.06885810	1.07022750	1.07159864	1.07297154
188	1.06374751	1.06511769	1.06648963	1.06786333	1.06923879	1.07061601	1.07199499	1.07337574
189	1.06409723	1.06547516	1.06685487	1.06823635	1.06961961	1.07100465	1.07239148	1.07378009
190	1.06444707	1.06583276	1.06722023	1.06860950	1.07000057	1.07139344	1.07278812	1.07418460
191	1.06479703	1.06619047	1.06758572	1.06898278	1.07038167	1.07178237	1.07318490	1.07458926
192	1.06514710	1.06654830	1.06795133	1.06935619	1.07076290	1.07217145	1.07358183	1.07499407
193	1.06549729	1.06690625	1.06831706	1.06972974	1.07114427	1.07256066	1.07397891	1.07539903
194	1.06584759	1.06726432	1.06868293	1.07010341	1.07152577	1.07295001	1.07437614	1.07580415
195	1.06619800	1.06762251	1.06904891	1.07047721	1.07190741	1.07333951	1.07477351	1.07620942
196	1.06654853	1.06798082	1.06941503	1.07085115	1.07228919	1.07372915	1.07517103	1.07661484
197	1.06689918	1.06833925	1.06978126	1.07122521	1.07267110	1.07411892	1.07556869	1.07702041
198	1.06724994	1.06869781	1.07014763	1.07159941	1.07305314	1.07450884	1.07596651	1.07742614
199	1.06760082	1.06905648	1.07051412	1.07197373	1.07343533	1.07489891	1.07636447	1.07783202
200	1.06795181	1.06941527	1.07088073	1.07234819	1.07381765	1.07528911	1.07676258	1.07823805

Day	12.00%	12.25%	12.50%	12.75%	13.00%	13.25%	13.50%	13.75%
201	1.06830292	1.06977419	1.07124747	1.07272278	1.07420010	1.07567945	1.07716083	1.07864424
202	1.06865414	1.07013322	1.07161434	1.07309749	1.07458269	1.07606994	1.07755923	1.07905058
203	1.06900548	1.07049237	1.07198133	1.07347234	1.07496542	1.07646057	1.07795778	1.07945707
204	1.06935693	1.07085165	1.07234845	1.07384732	1.07534829	1.07685134	1.07835648	1.07986371
205	1.06970850	1.07121104	1.07271569	1.07422243	1.07573129	1.07724225	1.07875532	1.08027051
206	1.07006019	1.07157056	1.07308306	1.07459768	1.07611442	1.07763330	1.07915431	1.08067746
207	1.07041199	1.07193020	1.07345055	1.07497305	1.07649770	1.07802450	1.07955345	1.08108457
208	1.07076390	1.07228995	1.07381817	1.07534855	1.07688111	1.07841584	1.07995274	1.08149182
209	1.07111593	1.07264983	1.07418592	1.07572419	1.07726465	1.07880732	1.08035217	1.08189924
210	1.07146808	1.07300983	1.07455379	1.07609996	1.07764834	1.07919894	1.08075176	1.08230680
211	1.07182035	1.07336995	1.07492179	1.07647585	1.07803216	1.07959070	1.08115149	1.08271452
212	1.07217273	1.07373019	1.07528991	1.07685188	1.07841611	1.07998261	1.08155137	1.08312239
213	1.07252522	1.07409055	1.07565816	1.07722804	1.07880021	1.08037466	1.08195139	1.08353042
214	1.07287783	1.07445104	1.07602654	1.07760434	1.07918444	1.08076685	1.08235156	1.08393860
215	1.07323056	1.07481164	1.07639504	1.07798076	1.07956881	1.08115918	1.08275189	1.08434693
216	1.07358340	1.07517236	1.07676367	1.07835731	1.07995331	1.08155166	1.08315236	1.08475542
217	1.07393636	1.07553321	1.07713242	1.07873400	1.08033795	1.08194427	1.08355297	1.08516406
218	1.07428943	1.07589418	1.07750130	1.07911082	1.08072273	1.08233703	1.08395374	1.08557285
219	1.07464263	1.07625526	1.07787031	1.07948777	1.08110764	1.08272994	1.08435465	1.08598180
220	1.07499593	1.07661647	1.07823944	1.07986485	1.08149270	1.08312298	1.08475572	1.08639090
221	1.07534936	1.07697780	1.07860870	1.08024206	1.08187788	1.08351617	1.08515693	1.08680016
222	1.07570290	1.07733925	1.07897809	1.08061941	1.08226321	1.08390950	1.08555829	1.08720957
223	1.07605655	1.07770083	1.07934760	1.08099688	1.08264867	1.08430298	1.08595980	1.08761913
224	1.07641032	1.07806252	1.07971724	1.08137449	1.08303428	1.08469659	1.08636145	1.08802885
225	1.07676421	1.07842434	1.08008701	1.08175223	1.08342001	1.08509035	1.08676326	1.08843873
226	1.07711822	1.07878627	1.08045690	1.08213011	1.08380589	1.08548426	1.08716521	1.08884876
227	1.07747234	1.07914833	1.08082692	1.08250811	1.08419190	1.08587830	1.08756731	1.08925894
228	1.07782658	1.07951051	1.08119707	1.08288625	1.08457805	1.08627249	1.08796956	1.08966928
229	1.07818093	1.07987281	1.08156734	1.08326451	1.08496434	1.08666682	1.08837196	1.09007977
230	1.07853540	1.08023524	1.08193774	1.08364291	1.08535077	1.08706130	1.08877451	1.09049041
231	1.07888999	1.08059778	1.08230827	1.08402145	1.08573733	1.08745592	1.08917721	1.09090122
232	1.07924469	1.08096045	1.08267892	1.08440011	1.08612403	1.08785068	1.08958006	1.09131217
233	1.07959951	1.08132324	1.08304970	1.08477891	1.08651087	1.08824558	1.08998305	1.09172328
234	1.07995445	1.08168615	1.08342061	1.08515784	1.08689785	1.08864063	1.09038620	1.09213455
235	1.08030950	1.08204918	1.08379164	1.08553690	1.08728496	1.08903582	1.09078949	1.09254597
236	1.08066467	1.08241233	1.08416280	1.08591610	1.08767221	1.08943116	1.09119293	1.09295754
237	1.08101996	1.08277561	1.08453409	1.08629542	1.08805960	1.08982663	1.09159652	1.09336927
238	1.08137536	1.08313900	1.08490551	1.08667488	1.08844713	1.09022226	1.09200026	1.09378116
239	1.08173088	1.08350252	1.08527705	1.08705447	1.08883480	1.09061802	1.09240416	1.09419320
240	1.08208652	1.08386616	1.08564872	1.08743420	1.08922260	1.09101393	1.09280820	1.09460540
241	1.08244227	1.08422993	1.08602052	1.08781406	1.08961054	1.09140998	1.09321238	1.09501775
242	1.08279815	1.08459381	1.08639244	1.08819405	1.08999862	1.09180618	1.09361672	1.09543026
243	1.08315413	1.08495782	1.08676450	1.08857417	1.09038684	1.09220252	1.09402121	1.09584292
244	1.08351024	1.08532195	1.08713668	1.08895442	1.09077520	1.09259901	1.09442585	1.09625574
245	1.08386646	1.08568620	1.08750898	1.08933481	1.09116369	1.09299563	1.09483064	1.09666871
246	1.08422280	1.08605058	1.08788142	1.08971533	1.09155233	1.09339241	1.09523557	1.09708184
247	1.08457926	1.08641507	1.08825398	1.09009599	1.09194110	1.09378932	1.09564066	1.09749512
248	1.08493583	1.08677969	1.08862667	1.09047677	1.09233001	1.09418638	1.09604590	1.09790856
249	1.08529252	1.08714443	1.08899949	1.09085769	1.09271906	1.09458359	1.09645129	1.09832216
250	1.08564933	1.08750929	1.08937243	1.09123875	1.09310825	1.09498094	1.09685682	1.09873591

Day	12.00%	12.25%	12.50%	12.75%	13.00%	13.25%	13.50%	13.75%
251	1.08600626	1.08787428	1.08974550	1.09161993	1.09349757	1.09537843	1.09726251	1.09914982
252	1.08636330	1.08823939	1.09011870	1.09200125	1.09388704	1.09577607	1.09766835	1.09956388
253	1.08672046	1.08860462	1.09049203	1.09238270	1.09427664	1.09617385	1.09807433	1.09997810
254	1.08707774	1.08896997	1.09086549	1.09276429	1.09466638	1.09657178	1.09848047	1.10039247
255	1.08743514	1.08933545	1.09123907	1.09314601	1.09505627	1.09696985	1.09888676	1.10080700
256	1.08779265	1.08970105	1.09161279	1.09352786	1.09544629	1.09736806	1.09929319	1.10122169
257	1.08815028	1.09006677	1.09198663	1.09390985	1.09583644	1.09776642	1.09969978	1.10163654
258	1.08850803	1.09043262	1.09236059	1.09429197	1.09622674	1.09816492	1.10010652	1.10205154
259	1.08886589	1.09079858	1.09273469	1.09467422	1.09661718	1.09856357	1.10051341	1.10246669
260	1.08922388	1.09116467	1.09310891	1.09505661	1.09700776	1.09896237	1.10092045	1.10288201
261	1.08958198	1.09153088	1.09348327	1.09543913	1.09739847	1.09936131	1.10132764	1.10329747
262	1.08994020	1.09189722	1.09385775	1.09582178	1.09778932	1.09976039	1.10173498	1.10371310
263	1.09029853	1.09226368	1.09423236	1.09620457	1.09818032	1.10015962	1.10214247	1.10412888
264	1.09065699	1.09263026	1.09460709	1.09658749	1.09857145	1.10055899	1.10255011	1.10454482
265	1.09101556	1.09299697	1.09498196	1.09697054	1.09896272	1.10095851	1.10295790	1.10496092
266	1.09137425	1.09336379	1.09535695	1.09735373	1.09935413	1.10135817	1.10336585	1.10537717
267	1.09173306	1.09373074	1.09573207	1.09773705	1.09974568	1.10175798	1.10377394	1.10579358
268	1.09209198	1.09409782	1.09610732	1.09812051	1.10013738	1.10215793	1.10418219	1.10621014
269	1.09245103	1.09446502	1.09648270	1.09850410	1.10052920	1.10255803	1.10459058	1.10662687
270	1.09281019	1.09483234	1.09685821	1.09888782	1.10092117	1.10295827	1.10499913	1.10704375
271	1.09316947	1.09519978	1.09723385	1.09927168	1.10131328	1.10335866	1.10540783	1.10746078
272	1.09352887	1.09556735	1.09760961	1.09965567	1.10170553	1.10375920	1.10581668	1.10787798
273	1.09388838	1.09593504	1.09798551	1.10003980	1.10209792	1.10415988	1.10622568	1.10829533
274	1.09424802	1.09630285	1.09836153	1.10042406	1.10249045	1.10456070	1.10663483	1.10871284
275	1.09460777	1.09667079	1.09873768	1.10080845	1.10288312	1.10496167	1.10704413	1.10913050
276	1.09496764	1.09703885	1.09911396	1.10119298	1.10327592	1.10536279	1.10745359	1.10954833
277	1.09532763	1.09740703	1.09949037	1.10157765	1.10366887	1.10576405	1.10786319	1.10996631
278	1.09568774	1.09777534	1.09986691	1.10196244	1.10406196	1.10616546	1.10827295	1.11038445
279	1.09604796	1.09814377	1.10024357	1.10234738	1.10445519	1.10656701	1.10868286	1.11080274
280	1.09640831	1.09851233	1.10062037	1.10273244	1.10484855	1.10696871	1.10909292	1.11122119
281	1.09676877	1.09888101	1.10099729	1.10311764	1.10524206	1.10737056	1.10950313	1.11163981
282	1.09712935	1.09924981	1.10137435	1.10350298	1.10563571	1.10777255	1.10991350	1.11205857
283	1.09749005	1.09961873	1.10175153	1.10388845	1.10602950	1.10817468	1.11032401	1.11247750
284	1.09785087	1.09998779	1.10212884	1.10427405	1.10642343	1.10857697	1.11073468	1.11289658
285	1.09821181	1.10035696	1.10250628	1.10465979	1.10681749	1.10897939	1.11114550	1.11331583
286	1.09857286	1.10072626	1.10288386	1.10504567	1.10721170	1.10938197	1.11155647	1.11373523
287	1.09893404	1.10109568	1.10326156	1.10543168	1.10760605	1.10978469	1.11196760	1.11415478
288	1.09929533	1.10146522	1.10363938	1.10581782	1.10800054	1.11018756	1.11237887	1.11457450
289	1.09965675	1.10183489	1.10401734	1.10620410	1.10839517	1.11059057	1.11279030	1.11499437
290	1.10001828	1.10220469	1.10439543	1.10659051	1.10878994	1.11099373	1.11320188	1.11541441
291	1.10037993	1.10257461	1.10477365	1.10697706	1.10918485	1.11139704	1.11361361	1.11583460
292	1.10074169	1.10294465	1.10515200	1.10736375	1.10957991	1.11180049	1.11402550	1.11625494
293	1.10110358	1.10331481	1.10553047	1.10775056	1.10997510	1.11220409	1.11443753	1.11667545
294	1.10146559	1.10368511	1.10590908	1.10813752	1.11037043	1.11260783	1.11484972	1.11709612
295	1.10182771	1.10405552	1.10628781	1.10852461	1.11076591	1.11301172	1.11526206	1.11751694
296	1.10218996	1.10442606	1.10666668	1.10891183	1.11116152	1.11341576	1.11567456	1.11793792
297	1.10255232	1.10479672	1.10704568	1.10929919	1.11155728	1.11381995	1.11608721	1.11835906
298	1.10291481	1.10516751	1.10742480	1.10968669	1.11195318	1.11422428	1.11650001	1.11878036
299	1.10327741	1.10553842	1.10780406	1.11007432	1.11234921	1.11462876	1.11691296	1.11920182
300	1.10364013	1.10590946	1.10818344	1.11046208	1.11274539	1.11503338	1.11732606	1.11962344

Day	12.00%	12.25%	12.50%	12.75%	13.00%	13.25%	13.50%	13.75%
301	1.10400297	1.10628062	1.10856296	1.11084998	1.11314171	1.11543816	1.11773932	1.12004521
302	1.10436593	1.10665191	1.10894260	1.11123802	1.11353818	1.11584308	1.11815273	1.12046715
303	1.10472901	1.10702332	1.10932238	1.11162619	1.11393478	1.11624814	1.11856629	1.12088924
304	1.10509221	1.10739485	1.10970228	1.11201450	1.11433152	1.11665335	1.11898001	1.12131150
305	1.10545553	1.10776651	1.11008232	1.11240294	1.11472841	1.11705872	1.11939388	1.12173391
306	1.10581896	1.10813830	1.11046248	1.11279152	1.11512543	1.11746422	1.11980790	1.12215648
307	1.10618252	1.10851021	1.11084278	1.11318024	1.11552260	1.11786988	1.12022208	1.12257921
308	1.10654620	1.10888224	1.11122320	1.11356909	1.11591991	1.11827568	1.12063641	1.12300210
309	1.10690999	1.10925440	1.11160376	1.11395807	1.11631736	1.11868163	1.12105089	1.12342515
310	1.10727391	1.10962668	1.11198444	1.11434720	1.11671495	1.11908773	1.12146552	1.12384836
311	1.10763794	1.10999909	1.11236526	1.11473645	1.11711269	1.11949397	1.12188031	1.12427172
312	1.10800210	1.11037163	1.11274621	1.11512585	1.11751056	1.11990036	1.12229525	1.12469525
313	1.10836637	1.11074429	1.11312729	1.11551538	1.11790858	1.12030690	1.12271035	1.12511894
314	1.10873077	1.11111707	1.11350849	1.11590505	1.11830674	1.12071359	1.12312560	1.12554278
315	1.10909528	1.11148998	1.11388983	1.11629485	1.11870504	1.12112042	1.12354100	1.12596679
316	1.10945992	1.11186301	1.11427130	1.11668479	1.11910348	1.12152740	1.12395656	1.12639095
317	1.10982467	1.11223617	1.11465290	1.11707486	1.11950207	1.12193453	1.12437227	1.12681528
318	1.11018954	1.11260946	1.11503463	1.11746507	1.11990080	1.12234181	1.12478813	1.12723976
319	1.11055454	1.11298287	1.11541649	1.11785542	1.12029967	1.12274924	1.12520415	1.12766441
320	1.11091965	1.11335640	1.11579848	1.11824590	1.12069868	1.12315681	1.12562032	1.12808921
321	1.11128488	1.11373006	1.11618061	1.11863652	1.12109783	1.12356453	1.12603664	1.12851418
322	1.11165024	1.11410385	1.11656286	1.11902728	1.12149712	1.12397240	1.12645312	1.12893931
323	1.11201571	1.11447776	1.11694524	1.11941817	1.12189656	1.12438042	1.12686976	1.12936459
324	1.11238131	1.11485180	1.11732776	1.11980920	1.12229614	1.12478858	1.12728654	1.12979004
325	1.11274702	1.11522596	1.11771041	1.12020037	1.12269586	1.12519690	1.12770349	1.13021564
326	1.11311286	1.11560025	1.11809318	1.12059167	1.12309573	1.12560536	1.12812058	1.13064141
327	1.11347881	1.11597466	1.11847609	1.12098311	1.12349573	1.12601397	1.12853783	1.13106733
328	1.11384489	1.11634920	1.11885913	1.12137469	1.12389588	1.12642273	1.12895524	1.13149342
329	1.11421108	1.11672387	1.11924230	1.12176640	1.12429617	1.12683163	1.12937280	1.13191967
330	1.11457740	1.11709866	1.11962561	1.12215825	1.12469661	1.12724069	1.12979051	1.13234608
331	1.11494383	1.11747358	1.12000904	1.12255024	1.12509719	1.12764989	1.13020838	1.13277265
332	1.11531039	1.11784862	1.12039260	1.12294236	1.12549791	1.12805925	1.13062640	1.13319938
333	1.11567707	1.11822379	1.12077630	1.12333462	1.12589877	1.12846875	1.13104458	1.13362627
334	1.11604387	1.11859908	1.12116013	1.12372702	1.12629977	1.12887840	1.13146291	1.13405332
335	1.11641078	1.11897450	1.12154409	1.12411955	1.12670092	1.12928819	1.13188139	1.13448053

Day	12.00%	12.25%	12.50%	12.75%	13.00%	13.25%	13.50%	13.75%
336	1.11677782	1.11935005	1.12192818	1.12451223	1.12710221	1.12969814	1.13230003	1.13490790
337	1.11714498	1.11972572	1.12231240	1.12490504	1.12750364	1.13010824	1.13271883	1.13533543
338	1.11751226	1.12010152	1.12269675	1.12529798	1.12790522	1.13051848	1.13313778	1.13576313
339	1.11787967	1.12047744	1.12308124	1.12569107	1.12830694	1.13092888	1.13355689	1.13619099
340	1.11824719	1.12085349	1.12346585	1.12608429	1.12870880	1.13133942	1.13397615	1.13661900
341	1.11861483	1.12122967	1.12385060	1.12647764	1.12911081	1.13175011	1.13439556	1.13704718
342	1.11898259	1.12160597	1.12423548	1.12687114	1.12951296	1.13216095	1.13481513	1.13747552
343	1.11935048	1.12198240	1.12462050	1.12726477	1.12991525	1.13257194	1.13523486	1.13790402
344	1.11971848	1.12235896	1.12500564	1.12765854	1.13031769	1.13298308	1.13565474	1.13833268
345	1.12008661	1.12273564	1.12539092	1.12805245	1.13072027	1.13339437	1.13607478	1.13876151
346	1.12045486	1.12311245	1.12577632	1.12844650	1.13112299	1.13380581	1.13649497	1.13919049
347	1.12082323	1.12348938	1.12616186	1.12884068	1.13152585	1.13421739	1.13691532	1.13961964
348	1.12119172	1.12386645	1.12654753	1.12923500	1.13192886	1.13462913	1.13733582	1.14004895
349	1.12156033	1.12424363	1.12693334	1.12962946	1.13233202	1.13504102	1.13775648	1.14047842
350	1.12192906	1.12462095	1.12731927	1.13002406	1.13273531	1.13545305	1.13817729	1.14090805
351	1.12229791	1.12499839	1.12770534	1.13041879	1.13313875	1.13586524	1.13859826	1.14133785
352	1.12266689	1.12537596	1.12809154	1.13081366	1.13354234	1.13627757	1.13901939	1.14176780
353	1.12303598	1.12575365	1.12847788	1.13120867	1.13394606	1.13669006	1.13944067	1.14219792
354	1.12340520	1.12613147	1.12886434	1.13160382	1.13434993	1.13710269	1.13986211	1.14262820
355	1.12377454	1.12650942	1.12925094	1.13199911	1.13475395	1.13751547	1.14028370	1.14305864
356	1.12414400	1.12688750	1.12963767	1.13239453	1.13515811	1.13792841	1.14070545	1.14348925
357	1.12451358	1.12726570	1.13002453	1.13279010	1.13556241	1.13834149	1.14112735	1.14392001
358	1.12488329	1.12764403	1.13041153	1.13318580	1.13596686	1.13875472	1.14154941	1.14435094
359	1.12525311	1.12802248	1.13079865	1.13358163	1.13637145	1.13916811	1.14197163	1.14478203
360	1.12562306	1.12840107	1.13118591	1.13397761	1.13677618	1.13958164	1.14239400	1.14521329
361	1.12599312	1.12877978	1.13157330	1.13437373	1.13718106	1.13999532	1.14281653	1.14564470
362	1.12636331	1.12915861	1.13196083	1.13476998	1.13758609	1.14040916	1.14323922	1.14607628
363	1.12673362	1.12953758	1.13234849	1.13516637	1.13799125	1.14082314	1.14366206	1.14650802
364	1.12710406	1.12991667	1.13273628	1.13556290	1.13839657	1.14123728	1.14408506	1.14693993
365	1.12747461	1.13029589	1.13312420	1.13595957	1.13880202	1.14165156	1.14450821	1.14737199

Appendix J Continuous compound interest

x	e^x	x	e^x	x	e^x	x	e^x	x	e^x	x	e^x	x	e^x
0.00	1.0000	0.25	1.2840	0.50	1.6487	0.75	2.1170	1.00	2.7183	1.25	3.4903	1.50	4.4817
0.01	1.0101	0.26	1.2969	0.51	1.6653	0.76	2.1383	1.01	2.7456	1.26	3.5254	1.51	4.5267
0.02	1.0202	0.27	1.3100	0.52	1.6820	0.77	2.1598	1.02	2.7732	1.27	3.5609	1.52	4.5722
0.03	1.0305	0.28	1.3231	0.53	1.6989	0.78	2.1815	1.03	2.8011	1.28	3.5966	1.53	4.6182
0.04	1.0408	0.29	1.3364	0.54	1.7160	0.79	2.2034	1.04	2.8292	1.29	3.6328	1.54	4.6646
0.05	1.0513	0.30	1.3499	0.55	1.7333	0.80	2.2255	1.05	2.8577	1.30	3.6693	1.55	4.7115
0.06	1.0618	0.31	1.3634	0.56	1.7507	0.81	2.2479	1.06	2.8864	1.31	3.7062	1.56	4.7588
0.07	1.0725	0.32	1.3771	0.57	1.7683	0.82	2.2705	1.07	2.9154	1.32	3.7434	1.57	4.8066
0.08	1.0833	0.33	1.3910	0.58	1.7860	0.83	2.2933	1.08	2.9447	1.33	3.7810	1.58	4.8550
0.09	1.0942	0.34	1.4049	0.59	1.8040	0.84	2.3164	1.09	2.9743	1.34	3.8190	1.59	4.9037
0.10	1.1052	0.35	1.4191	0.60	1.8221	0.85	2.3396	1.10	3.0042	1.35	3.8574	1.60	4.9530
0.11	1.1163	0.36	1.4333	0.61	1.8404	0.86	2.3632	1.11	3.0344	1.36	3.8962	1.61	5.0028
0.12	1.1275	0.37	1.4477	0.62	1.8589	0.87	2.3869	1.12	3.0649	1.37	3.9354	1.62	5.0531
0.13	1.1388	0.38	1.4623	0.63	1.8776	0.88	2.4109	1.13	3.0957	1.38	3.9749	1.63	5.1039
0.14	1.1503	0.39	1.4770	0.64	1.8965	0.89	2.4351	1.14	3.1268	1.39	4.0149	1.64	5.1552
0.15	1.1618	0.40	1.4918	0.65	1.9155	0.90	2.4596	1.15	3.1582	1.40	4.0552	1.65	5.2070
0.16	1.1735	0.41	1.5068	0.66	1.9348	0.91	2.4843	1.16	3.1899	1.41	4.0960	1.66	5.2593
0.17	1.1853	0.42	1.5220	0.67	1.9542	0.92	2.5093	1.17	3.2220	1.42	4.1371	1.67	5.3122
0.18	1.1972	0.43	1.5373	0.68	1.9739	0.93	2.5345	1.18	3.2544	1.43	4.1787	1.68	5.3656
0.19	1.2092	0.44	1.5527	0.69	1.9937	0.94	2.5600	1.19	3.2871	1.44	4.2207	1.69	5.4195
0.20	1.2214	0.45	1.5683	0.70	2.0138	0.95	2.5857	1.20	3.3201	1.45	4.2631	1.70	5.4739
0.21	1.2337	0.46	1.5841	0.71	2.0340	0.96	2.6117	1.21	3.3535	1.46	4.3060	1.71	5.5290
0.22	1.2461	0.47	1.6000	0.72	2.0544	0.97	2.6379	1.22	3.3872	1.47	4.3492	1.72	5.5845
0.23	1.2586	0.48	1.6161	0.73	2.0751	0.98	2.6645	1.23	3.4212	1.48	4.3929	1.73	5.6407
0.24	1.2712	0.49	1.6323	0.74	2.0959	0.99	2.6912	1.24	3.4556	1.49	4.4371	1.74	5.6973

$x = (r)(t)$

e^x = Factor

x	e^x	x	e^x	x	e^x	x	e^x	x	e^x	x	e^x	x	e^x
1.75	5.7546	2.00	7.3891	2.25	9.4877	2.50	12.182	2.75	15.643	3.00	20.086	4.50	90.017
1.76	5.8124	2.01	7.4633	2.26	9.5831	2.51	12.305	2.76	15.800	3.05	21.115	4.60	99.484
1.77	5.8709	2.02	7.5383	2.27	9.6794	2.52	12.429	2.77	15.959	3.10	22.198	4.70	109.95
1.78	5.9299	2.03	7.6141	2.28	9.7767	2.53	12.554	2.78	16.119	3.15	23.336	4.80	121.51
1.79	5.9895	2.04	7.6906	2.29	9.8749	2.54	12.680	2.79	16.281	3.20	24.533	4.90	134.29
1.80	6.0496	2.05	7.7679	2.30	9.9742	2.55	12.807	2.80	16.445	3.25	25.790	5.00	148.41
1.81	6.1104	2.06	7.8460	2.31	10.074	2.56	12.936	2.81	16.610	3.30	27.113	5.10	164.02
1.82	6.1719	2.07	7.9248	2.32	10.176	2.57	13.066	2.82	16.777	3.35	28.503	5.20	181.27
1.83	6.2339	2.08	8.0045	2.33	10.278	2.58	13.197	2.83	16.945	3.40	29.964	5.30	200.34
1.84	6.2965	2.09	8.0849	2.34	10.381	2.59	13.330	2.84	17.116	3.45	31.500	5.40	221.41
1.85	6.3598	2.10	8.1662	2.35	10.486	2.60	13.464	2.85	17.288	3.50	33.115	5.50	244.69
1.86	6.4237	2.11	8.2482	2.36	10.591	2.61	13.599	2.86	17.462	3.55	34.813	5.60	270.43
1.87	6.4883	2.12	8.3311	2.37	10.697	2.62	13.736	2.87	17.637	3.60	36.598	5.70	298.87
1.88	6.5535	2.13	8.4149	2.38	10.805	2.63	13.874	2.88	17.814	3.65	38.475	5.80	330.30
1.89	6.6194	2.14	8.4994	2.39	10.913	2.64	14.013	2.89	17.993	3.70	40.447	5.90	365.04
1.90	6.6859	2.15	8.5849	2.40	11.023	2.65	14.154	2.90	18.174	3.75	42.521	6.00	403.43
1.91	6.7531	2.16	8.6711	2.41	11.134	2.66	14.296	2.91	18.357	3.80	44.701	6.25	518.01
1.92	6.8210	2.17	8.7583	2.42	11.246	2.67	14.440	2.92	18.541	3.85	46.993	6.50	665.14
1.93	6.8895	2.18	8.8463	2.43	11.359	2.68	14.585	2.93	18.728	3.90	49.402	6.75	854.06
1.94	6.9588	2.19	8.9352	2.44	11.473	2.69	14.732	2.94	18.916	3.95	51.935	7.00	1096.6
1.95	7.0287	2.20	9.0250	2.45	11.588	2.70	14.880	2.95	19.106	4.00	54.598	7.50	1808.0
1.96	7.0993	2.21	9.1157	2.46	11.705	2.71	15.029	2.96	19.298	4.10	60.340	8.00	2981.0
1.97	7.1707	2.22	9.2073	2.47	11.822	2.72	15.180	2.97	19.492	4.20	66.686	8.50	4914.8
1.98	7.2427	2.23	9.2999	2.48	11.941	2.73	15.333	2.98	19.688	4.30	73.700	9.00	8103.1
1.99	7.3155	2.24	9.3933	2.49	12.061	2.74	15.487	2.99	19.886	4.40	81.451	9.50	13360.
												10.00	22026.

Appendix K Annual percentage rate tables for monthly payment plans

Number of Payments	Annual Percentage Rate													
	10.00%	10.25%	10.50%	10.75%	11.00%	11.25%	11.50%	11.75%	12.00%	12.25%	12.50%	12.75%	13.00%	13.25%
	Finance Charge per $100 of Amount Financed													
1	0.83	0.85	0.88	0.90	0.92	0.94	0.96	0.98	1.00	1.02	1.04	1.06	1.08	1.10
2	1.25	1.28	1.31	1.35	1.38	1.41	1.44	1.47	1.50	1.53	1.57	1.60	1.63	1.66
3	1.67	1.71	1.76	1.80	1.84	1.88	1.92	1.96	2.01	2.05	2.09	2.13	2.17	2.22
4	2.09	2.14	2.20	2.25	2.30	2.35	2.41	2.46	2.51	2.57	2.62	2.67	2.72	2.78
5	2.51	2.58	2.64	2.70	2.77	2.83	2.89	2.96	3.02	3.08	3.15	3.21	3.27	3.34
6	2.94	3.01	3.08	3.16	3.23	3.31	3.38	3.45	3.53	3.60	3.68	3.75	3.83	3.90
7	3.36	3.45	3.53	3.62	3.70	3.78	3.87	3.95	4.04	4.12	4.21	4.29	4.38	4.47
8	3.79	3.88	3.98	4.07	4.17	4.26	4.36	4.46	4.55	4.65	4.74	4.84	4.94	5.03
9	4.21	4.32	4.43	4.53	4.64	4.75	4.85	4.96	5.07	5.17	5.28	5.39	5.49	5.60
10	4.64	4.76	4.88	4.99	5.11	5.23	5.35	5.46	5.58	5.70	5.82	5.94	6.05	6.17
11	5.07	5.20	5.33	5.45	5.58	5.71	5.84	5.97	6.10	6.23	6.36	6.49	6.62	6.75
12	5.50	5.64	5.78	5.92	6.06	6.20	6.34	6.48	6.62	6.76	6.90	7.04	7.18	7.32
13	5.93	6.08	6.23	6.38	6.53	6.68	6.84	6.99	7.14	7.29	7.44	7.59	7.75	7.90
14	6.36	6.52	6.69	6.85	7.01	7.17	7.34	7.50	7.66	7.82	7.99	8.15	8.31	8.48
15	6.80	6.97	7.14	7.32	7.49	7.66	7.84	8.01	8.19	8.36	8.53	8.71	8.88	9.06
16	7.23	7.41	7.60	7.78	7.97	8.15	8.34	8.53	8.71	8.90	9.08	9.27	9.46	9.64
17	7.67	7.86	8.06	8.25	8.45	8.65	8.84	9.04	9.24	9.44	9.63	9.83	10.03	10.23
18	8.10	8.31	8.52	8.73	8.93	9.14	9.35	9.56	9.77	9.98	10.19	10.40	10.61	10.82
19	8.54	8.76	8.98	9.20	9.42	9.64	9.86	10.08	10.30	10.52	10.74	10.96	11.18	11.41
20	8.98	9.21	9.44	9.67	9.90	10.13	10.37	10.60	10.83	11.06	11.30	11.53	11.76	12.00
21	9.42	9.66	9.90	10.15	10.39	10.63	10.88	11.12	11.36	11.61	11.85	12.10	12.34	12.59
22	9.86	10.12	10.37	10.62	10.88	11.13	11.39	11.64	11.90	12.16	12.41	12.67	12.93	13.19
23	10.30	10.57	10.84	11.10	11.37	11.63	11.90	12.17	12.44	12.71	12.97	13.24	13.51	13.78
24	10.75	11.02	11.30	11.58	11.86	12.14	12.42	12.70	12.98	13.26	13.54	13.82	14.10	14.38
25	11.19	11.48	11.77	12.06	12.35	12.64	12.93	13.22	13.52	13.81	14.10	14.40	14.69	14.98
26	11.64	11.94	12.24	12.54	12.85	13.15	13.45	13.75	14.06	14.36	14.67	14.97	15.28	15.59
27	12.09	12.40	12.71	13.03	13.34	13.66	13.97	14.29	14.60	14.92	15.24	15.56	15.87	16.19
28	12.53	12.86	13.18	13.51	13.84	14.16	14.49	14.82	15.15	15.48	15.81	16.14	16.47	16.80
29	12.98	13.32	13.66	14.00	14.33	14.67	15.01	15.35	15.70	16.04	16.38	16.72	17.07	17.41
30	13.43	13.78	14.13	14.48	14.83	15.19	15.54	15.89	16.24	16.60	16.95	17.31	17.66	18.02

Number of Payments	**Annual Percentage Rate**													
	10.00%	*10.25%*	*10.50%*	*10.75%*	*11.00%*	*11.25%*	*11.50%*	*11.75%*	*12.00%*	*12.25%*	*12.50%*	*12.75%*	*13.00%*	*13.25%*
	Finance Charge per $100 of Amount Financed													
31	13.89	14.25	14.61	14.97	15.33	15.70	16.06	16.43	16.79	17.16	17.53	17.90	18.27	18.63
32	14.34	14.71	15.09	15.46	15.84	16.21	16.59	16.97	17.35	17.73	18.11	18.49	18.87	19.25
33	14.79	15.18	15.57	15.95	16.34	16.73	17.12	17.51	17.90	18.29	18.69	19.08	19.47	19.87
34	15.25	15.65	16.05	16.44	16.85	17.25	17.65	18.05	18.46	18.86	19.27	19.67	20.08	20.49
35	15.70	16.11	16.53	16.94	17.35	17.77	18.18	18.60	19.01	19.43	19.85	20.27	20.69	21.11
36	16.16	16.58	17.01	17.43	17.86	18.29	18.71	19.14	19.57	20.00	20.43	20.87	21.30	21.73
37	16.62	17.06	17.49	17.93	18.37	18.81	19.25	19.69	20.13	20.58	21.02	21.46	21.91	22.36
38	17.08	17.53	17.98	18.43	18.88	19.33	19.78	20.24	20.69	21.15	21.61	22.07	22.52	22.99
39	17.54	18.00	18.46	18.93	19.39	19.86	20.32	20.79	21.26	21.73	22.20	22.67	23.14	23.61
40	18.00	18.48	18.95	19.43	19.90	20.38	20.86	21.34	21.82	22.30	22.79	23.27	23.76	24.25
41	18.47	18.95	19.44	19.93	20.42	20.91	21.40	21.89	22.39	22.88	23.38	23.88	24.38	24.88
42	18.93	19.43	19.93	20.43	20.93	21.44	21.94	22.45	22.96	23.47	23.98	24.49	25.00	25.51
43	19.40	19.91	20.42	20.94	21.45	21.97	22.49	23.01	23.53	24.05	24.57	25.10	25.62	26.15
44	19.86	20.39	20.91	21.44	21.97	22.50	23.03	23.57	24.10	24.64	25.17	25.71	26.25	26.79
45	20.33	20.87	21.41	21.95	22.49	23.03	23.58	24.12	24.67	25.22	25.77	26.32	26.88	27.43
46	20.80	21.35	21.90	22.46	23.01	23.57	24.13	24.69	25.25	25.81	26.37	26.94	27.51	28.08
47	21.27	21.83	22.40	22.97	23.53	24.10	24.68	25.25	25.82	26.40	26.98	27.56	28.14	28.72
48	21.74	22.32	22.90	23.48	24.06	24.64	25.23	25.81	26.40	26.99	27.58	28.18	28.77	29.37
49	22.21	22.80	23.39	23.99	24.58	25.18	25.78	26.38	26.98	27.59	28.19	28.80	29.41	30.02
50	22.69	23.29	23.89	24.50	25.11	25.72	26.33	26.95	27.56	28.18	28.80	29.42	30.04	30.67
51	23.16	23.78	24.40	25.02	25.64	26.26	26.89	27.52	28.15	28.78	29.41	30.05	30.68	31.32
52	23.64	24.27	24.90	25.53	26.17	26.81	27.45	28.09	28.73	29.38	30.02	30.67	31.32	31.98
53	24.11	24.76	25.40	26.05	26.70	27.35	28.00	28.66	29.32	29.98	30.64	31.30	31.97	32.63
54	24.59	25.25	25.91	26.57	27.23	27.90	28.56	29.23	29.91	30.58	31.25	31.93	32.61	33.29
55	25.07	25.74	26.41	27.09	27.77	28.44	29.13	29.81	30.50	31.18	31.87	32.56	33.26	33.95
56	25.55	26.23	26.92	27.61	28.30	28.99	29.69	30.39	31.09	31.79	32.49	33.20	33.91	34.62
57	26.03	26.73	27.43	28.13	28.84	29.54	30.25	30.97	31.68	32.39	33.11	33.83	34.56	35.28
58	26.51	27.23	27.94	28.66	29.37	30.10	30.82	31.55	32.27	33.00	33.74	34.47	35.21	35.95
59	27.00	27.72	28.45	29.18	29.91	30.65	31.39	32.13	32.87	33.61	34.36	35.11	35.86	36.62
60	27.48	28.22	28.96	29.71	30.45	31.20	31.96	32.71	33.47	34.23	34.99	35.75	36.52	37.29

Number of Payments	Annual Percentage Rate													
	13.50%	*13.75%*	*14.00%*	*14.25%*	*14.50%*	*14.75%*	*15.00%*	*15.25%*	*15.50%*	*15.75%*	*16.00%*	*16.25%*	*16.50%*	*16.75%*
	Finance Charge per $100 of Amount Financed													
1	1.13	1.15	1.17	1.19	1.21	1.23	1.25	1.27	1.29	1.31	1.33	1.35	1.38	1.40
2	1.69	1.72	1.75	1.78	1.82	1.85	1.88	1.91	1.94	1.97	2.00	2.04	2.07	2.10
3	2.26	2.30	2.34	2.38	2.43	2.47	2.51	2.55	2.59	2.64	2.68	2.72	2.76	2.80
4	2.83	2.88	2.93	2.99	3.04	3.09	3.14	3.20	3.25	3.30	3.36	3.41	3.46	3.51
5	3.40	3.46	3.53	3.59	3.65	3.72	3.78	3.84	3.91	3.97	4.04	4.10	4.16	4.23
6	3.97	4.05	4.12	4.20	4.27	4.35	4.42	4.49	4.57	4.64	4.72	4.79	4.87	4.94
7	4.55	4.64	4.72	4.81	4.89	4.98	5.06	5.15	5.23	5.32	5.40	5.49	5.58	5.66
8	5.13	5.22	5.32	5.42	5.51	5.61	5.71	5.80	5.90	6.00	6.09	6.19	6.29	6.38
9	5.71	5.82	5.92	6.03	6.14	6.25	6.35	6.46	6.57	6.68	6.78	6.89	7.00	7.11
10	6.29	6.41	6.53	6.65	6.77	6.88	7.00	7.12	7.24	7.36	7.48	7.60	7.72	7.84
11	6.88	7.01	7.14	7.27	7.40	7.53	7.66	7.79	7.92	8.05	8.18	8.31	8.44	8.57
12	7.46	7.60	7.74	7.89	8.03	8.17	8.31	8.45	8.59	8.74	8.88	9.02	9.16	9.30
13	8.05	8.20	8.36	8.51	8.66	8.81	8.97	9.12	9.27	9.43	9.58	9.73	9.89	10.04
14	8.64	8.81	8.97	9.13	9.30	9.46	9.63	9.79	9.96	10.12	10.29	10.45	10.62	10.78
15	9.23	9.41	9.59	9.76	9.94	10.11	10.29	10.47	10.64	10.82	11.00	11.17	11.35	11.53
16	9.83	10.02	10.20	10.39	10.58	10.77	10.95	11.14	11.33	11.52	11.71	11.90	12.09	12.28
17	10.43	10.63	10.82	11.02	11.22	11.42	11.62	11.82	12.02	12.22	12.42	12.62	12.83	13.03
18	11.03	11.24	11.45	11.66	11.87	12.08	12.29	12.50	12.72	12.93	13.14	13.35	13.57	13.78
19	11.63	11.85	12.07	12.30	12.52	12.74	12.97	13.19	13.41	13.64	13.86	14.09	14.31	14.54
20	12.23	12.46	12.70	12.93	13.17	13.41	13.64	13.88	14.11	14.35	14.59	14.82	15.06	15.30
21	12.84	13.08	13.33	13.58	13.82	14.07	14.32	14.57	14.82	15.06	15.31	15.56	15.81	16.06
22	13.44	13.70	13.96	14.22	14.48	14.74	15.00	15.26	15.52	15.78	16.04	16.30	16.57	16.83
23	14.05	14.32	14.59	14.87	15.14	15.41	15.68	15.96	16.23	16.50	16.78	17.05	17.32	17.60
24	14.66	14.95	15.23	15.51	15.80	16.08	16.37	16.65	16.94	17.22	17.51	17.80	18.09	18.37
25	15.28	15.57	15.87	16.17	16.46	16.76	17.06	17.35	17.65	17.95	18.25	18.55	18.85	19.15
26	15.89	16.20	16.51	16.82	17.13	17.44	17.75	18.06	18.37	18.68	18.99	19.30	19.62	19.93
27	16.51	16.83	17.15	17.47	17.80	18.12	18.44	18.76	19.09	19.41	19.74	20.06	20.39	20.71
28	17.13	17.46	17.80	18.13	18.47	18.80	19.14	19.47	19.81	20.15	20.48	20.82	21.16	21.50
29	17.75	18.10	18.45	18.79	19.14	19.49	19.83	20.18	20.53	20.88	21.23	21.58	21.94	22.29
30	18.38	18.74	19.10	19.45	19.81	20.17	20.54	20.90	21.26	21.62	21.99	22.35	22.72	23.08

Number of Payments	Annual Percentage Rate													
	13.50%	*13.75%*	*14.00%*	*14.25%*	*14.50%*	*14.75%*	*15.00%*	*15.25%*	*15.50%*	*15.75%*	*16.00%*	*16.25%*	*16.50%*	*16.75%*
	Finance Charge per $100 of Amount Financed													
31	19.00	19.38	19.75	20.12	20.49	20.87	21.24	21.61	21.99	22.37	22.74	23.12	23.50	23.88
32	19.63	20.02	20.40	20.79	21.17	21.56	21.95	22.33	22.72	23.11	23.50	23.89	24.28	24.68
33	20.26	20.66	21.06	21.46	21.85	22.25	22.65	23.06	23.46	23.86	24.26	24.67	25.07	25.48
34	20.90	21.31	21.72	22.13	22.54	22.95	23.37	23.78	24.19	24.61	25.03	25.44	25.86	26.28
35	21.53	21.95	22.38	22.80	23.23	23.65	24.08	24.51	24.94	25.36	25.79	26.23	26.66	27.09
36	22.17	22.60	23.04	23.48	23.92	24.35	24.80	25.24	25.68	26.12	26.57	27.01	27.46	27.90
37	22.81	23.25	23.70	24.16	24.61	25.06	25.51	25.97	26.42	26.88	27.34	27.80	28.26	28.72
38	23.45	23.91	24.37	24.84	25.30	25.77	26.24	26.70	27.17	27.64	28.11	28.59	29.06	29.53
39	24.09	24.56	25.04	25.52	26.00	26.48	26.96	27.44	27.92	28.41	28.89	29.38	29.87	30.36
40	24.73	25.22	25.71	26.20	26.70	27.19	27.69	28.18	28.68	29.18	29.68	30.18	30.68	31.18
41	25.38	25.88	26.39	26.89	27.40	27.91	28.41	28.92	29.44	29.95	30.46	30.97	31.49	32.01
42	26.03	26.55	27.06	27.58	28.10	28.62	29.15	29.67	30.19	30.72	31.25	31.78	32.31	32.84
43	26.68	27.21	27.74	28.27	28.81	29.34	29.88	30.42	30.96	31.50	32.04	32.58	33.13	33.67
44	27.33	27.88	28.42	28.97	29.52	30.07	30.62	31.17	31.72	32.28	32.83	33.39	33.95	34.51
45	27.99	28.55	29.11	29.67	30.23	30.79	31.36	31.92	32.49	33.06	33.63	34.20	34.77	35.35
46	28.65	29.22	29.79	30.36	30.94	31.52	32.10	32.68	33.26	33.84	34.43	35.01	35.60	36.19
47	29.31	29.89	30.48	31.07	31.66	32.25	32.84	33.44	34.03	34.63	35.23	35.83	36.43	37.04
48	29.97	30.57	31.17	31.77	32.37	32.98	33.59	34.20	34.81	35.42	36.03	36.65	37.27	37.88
49	30.63	31.24	31.86	32.48	33.09	33.71	34.34	34.96	35.59	36.21	36.84	37.47	38.10	38.74
50	31.29	31.92	32.55	33.18	33.82	34.45	35.09	35.73	36.37	37.01	37.65	38.30	38.94	39.59
51	31.96	32.60	33.25	33.89	34.54	35.19	35.84	36.50	37.15	37.81	38.46	39.12	39.79	40.45
52	32.63	33.29	33.95	34.61	35.27	35.93	36.60	37.27	37.94	38.61	39.28	39.96	40.63	41.31
53	33.30	33.97	34.65	35.32	36.00	36.68	37.36	38.04	38.72	39.41	40.10	40.79	41.48	42.17
54	33.98	34.66	35.35	36.04	36.73	37.42	38.12	38.82	39.52	40.22	40.92	41.63	42.33	43.04
55	34.65	35.35	36.05	36.76	37.46	38.17	38.88	39.60	40.31	41.03	41.74	42.47	43.19	43.91
56	35.33	36.04	36.76	37.48	38.20	38.92	39.65	40.38	41.11	41.84	42.57	43.31	44.05	44.79
57	36.01	36.74	37.47	38.20	38.94	39.68	40.42	41.16	41.91	42.65	43.40	44.15	44.91	45.66
58	36.69	37.43	38.18	38.93	39.68	40.43	41.19	41.95	42.71	43.47	44.23	45.00	45.77	46.54
59	37.37	38.13	38.89	39.66	40.42	41.19	41.96	42.74	43.51	44.29	45.07	45.85	46.64	47.42
60	38.06	38.83	39.61	40.39	41.17	41.95	42.74	43.53	44.32	45.11	45.91	46.71	47.51	48.31

Number of Payments	**Annual Percentage Rate**													
	17.00%	*17.25%*	*17.50%*	*17.75%*	*18.00%*	*18.25%*	*18.50%*	*18.75%*	*19.00%*	*19.25%*	*19.50%*	*19.75%*	*20.00%*	*20.25%*
	Finance Charge per $100 of Amount Financed													
1	1.42	1.44	1.46	1.48	1.50	1.52	1.54	1.56	1.58	1.60	1.63	1.65	1.67	1.69
2	2.13	2.16	2.19	2.22	2.26	2.29	2.32	2.35	2.38	2.41	2.44	2.48	2.51	2.54
3	2.85	2.89	2.93	2.97	3.01	3.06	3.10	3.14	3.18	3.23	3.27	3.31	3.35	3.39
4	3.57	3.62	3.67	3.73	3.78	3.83	3.88	3.94	3.99	4.04	4.10	4.15	4.20	4.25
5	4.29	4.35	4.42	4.48	4.54	4.61	4.67	4.74	4.80	4.86	4.93	4.99	5.06	5.12
6	5.02	5.09	5.17	5.24	5.32	5.39	5.46	5.54	5.61	5.69	5.76	5.84	5.91	5.99
7	5.75	5.83	5.92	6.00	6.09	6.18	6.26	6.35	6.43	6.52	6.60	6.69	6.78	6.86
8	6.48	6.58	6.67	6.77	6.87	6.96	7.06	7.16	7.26	7.35	7.45	7.55	7.64	7.74
9	7.22	7.32	7.43	7.54	7.65	7.76	7.87	7.97	8.08	8.19	8.30	8.41	8.52	8.63
10	7.96	8.08	8.19	8.31	8.43	8.55	8.67	8.79	8.91	9.03	9.15	9.27	9.39	9.51
11	8.70	8.83	8.96	9.09	9.22	9.35	9.49	9.62	9.75	9.88	10.01	10.14	10.28	10.41
12	9.45	9.59	9.73	9.87	10.02	10.16	10.30	10.44	10.59	10.73	10.87	11.02	11.16	11.31
13	10.20	10.35	10.50	10.66	10.81	10.97	11.12	11.28	11.43	11.59	11.74	11.90	12.05	12.21
14	10.95	11.11	11.28	11.45	11.61	11.78	11.95	12.11	12.28	12.45	12.61	12.78	12.95	13.11
15	11.71	11.88	12.06	12.24	12.42	12.59	12.77	12.95	13.13	13.31	13.49	13.67	13.85	14.03
16	12.46	12.65	12.84	13.03	13.22	13.41	13.60	13.80	13.99	14.18	14.37	14.56	14.75	14.94
17	13.23	13.43	13.63	13.83	14.04	14.24	14.44	14.64	14.85	15.05	15.25	15.46	15.66	15.86
18	13.99	14.21	14.42	14.64	14.85	15.07	15.28	15.49	15.71	15.93	16.14	16.36	16.57	16.79
19	14.76	14.99	15.22	15.44	15.67	15.90	16.12	16.35	16.58	16.81	17.03	17.26	17.49	17.72
20	15.54	15.78	16.01	16.25	16.49	16.73	16.97	17.21	17.45	17.69	17.93	18.17	18.41	18.66
21	16.31	16.56	16.81	17.07	17.32	17.57	17.82	18.07	18.33	18.58	18.83	19.09	19.34	19.60
22	17.09	17.36	17.62	17.88	18.15	18.41	18.68	18.94	19.21	19.47	19.74	20.01	20.27	20.54
23	17.88	18.15	18.43	18.70	18.98	19.26	19.54	19.81	20.09	20.37	20.65	20.93	21.21	21.49
24	18.66	18.95	19.24	19.53	19.82	20.11	20.40	20.69	20.98	21.27	21.56	21.86	22.15	22.44
25	19.45	19.75	20.05	20.36	20.66	20.96	21.27	21.57	21.87	22.18	22.48	22.79	23.10	23.40
26	20.24	20.56	20.87	21.19	21.50	21.82	22.14	22.45	22.77	23.09	23.41	23.73	24.04	24.36
27	21.04	21.37	21.69	22.02	22.35	22.68	23.01	23.34	23.67	24.00	24.33	24.67	25.00	25.33
28	21.84	22.18	22.52	22.86	23.20	23.55	23.89	24.23	24.58	24.92	25.27	25.61	25.96	26.30
29	22.64	22.99	23.35	23.70	24.06	24.41	24.77	25.13	25.49	25.84	26.20	26.56	26.92	27.28
30	23.45	23.81	24.18	24.55	24.92	25.29	25.66	26.03	26.40	26.77	27.14	27.52	27.89	28.26

Number of Payments	Annual Percentage Rate													
	17.00%	*17.25%*	*17.50%*	*17.75%*	*18.00%*	*18.25%*	*18.50%*	*18.75%*	*19.00%*	*19.25%*	*19.50%*	*19.75%*	*20.00%*	*20.25%*
	Finance Charge per $100 of Amount Financed													
31	24.26	24.64	25.02	25.40	25.78	26.16	26.55	26.93	27.32	27.70	28.09	28.47	28.86	29.25
32	25.07	25.46	25.86	26.25	26.65	27.04	27.44	27.84	28.24	28.64	29.04	29.44	29.84	30.24
33	25.88	26.29	26.70	27.11	27.52	27.93	28.34	28.75	29.16	29.57	29.99	30.40	30.82	31.23
34	26.70	27.12	27.54	27.97	28.39	28.81	29.24	29.66	30.09	30.52	30.95	31.37	31.80	32.23
35	27.52	27.96	28.39	28.83	29.27	29.71	30.14	30.58	31.02	31.47	31.91	32.35	32.79	33.24
36	28.35	28.80	29.25	29.70	30.15	30.60	31.05	31.51	31.96	32.42	32.87	33.33	33.79	34.25
37	29.18	29.64	30.10	30.57	31.03	31.50	31.97	32.43	32.90	33.37	33.84	34.32	34.79	35.26
38	30.01	30.49	30.96	31.44	31.92	32.40	32.88	33.37	33.85	34.33	34.82	35.30	35.79	36.28
39	30.85	31.34	31.83	32.32	32.81	33.31	33.80	34.30	34.80	35.30	35.80	36.30	36.80	37.30
40	31.68	32.19	32.69	33.20	33.71	34.22	34.73	35.24	35.75	36.26	36.78	37.29	37.81	38.33
41	32.52	33.04	33.56	34.08	34.61	35.13	35.66	36.18	36.71	37.24	37.77	38.30	38.83	39.36
42	33.37	33.90	34.44	34.97	35.51	36.05	36.59	37.13	37.67	38.21	38.76	39.30	39.85	40.40
43	34.22	34.76	35.31	35.86	36.42	36.97	37.52	38.08	38.63	39.19	39.75	40.31	40.87	41.44
44	35.07	35.63	36.19	36.76	37.33	37.89	38.46	39.03	39.60	40.18	40.75	41.33	41.90	42.48
45	35.92	36.50	37.08	37.66	38.24	38.82	39.41	39.99	40.58	41.17	41.75	42.35	42.94	43.53
46	36.78	37.37	37.96	38.56	39.16	39.75	40.35	40.95	41.55	42.16	42.76	43.37	43.98	44.58
47	37.64	38.25	38.86	39.46	40.08	40.69	41.30	41.92	42.54	43.15	43.77	44.40	45.02	45.64
48	38.50	39.13	39.75	40.37	41.00	41.63	42.26	42.89	43.52	44.15	44.79	45.43	46.07	46.71
49	39.37	40.01	40.65	41.29	41.93	42.57	43.22	43.86	44.51	45.16	45.81	46.46	47.12	47.77
50	40.24	40.89	41.55	42.20	42.86	43.52	44.18	44.84	45.50	46.17	46.83	47.50	48.17	48.84
51	41.11	41.78	42.45	43.12	43.79	44.47	45.14	45.82	46.50	47.18	47.86	48.55	49.23	49.92
52	41.99	42.67	43.36	44.04	44.73	45.42	46.11	46.80	47.50	48.20	48.89	49.59	50.30	51.00
53	42.87	43.57	44.27	44.97	45.67	46.38	47.08	47.79	48.50	49.22	49.93	50.65	51.37	52.09
54	43.75	44.47	45.18	45.90	46.62	47.34	48.06	48.79	49.51	50.24	50.97	51.70	52.44	53.17
55	44.64	45.37	46.10	46.83	47.57	48.30	49.04	49.78	50.52	51.27	52.02	52.76	53.52	54.27
56	45.53	46.27	47.02	47.77	48.52	49.27	50.03	50.78	51.54	52.30	53.06	53.83	54.60	55.37
57	46.42	47.18	47.94	48.71	49.47	50.24	51.01	51.79	52.56	53.34	54.12	54.90	55.68	56.47
58	47.32	48.09	48.87	49.65	50.43	51.22	52.00	52.79	53.58	54.38	55.17	55.97	56.77	57.57
59	48.21	49.01	49.80	50.60	51.39	52.20	53.00	53.80	54.61	55.42	56.23	57.05	57.87	58.68
60	49.12	49.92	50.73	51.55	52.36	53.18	54.00	54.82	55.64	56.47	57.30	58.13	58.96	59.80

Number of Payments	Annual Percentage Rate													
	20.50%	*20.75%*	*21.00%*	*21.25%*	*21.50%*	*21.75%*	*22.00%*	*22.25%*	*22.50%*	*22.75%*	*23.00%*	*23.25%*	*23.50%*	*23.75%*
	Finance Charge per $100 of Amount Financed													
1	1.71	1.73	1.75	1.77	1.79	1.81	1.83	1.85	1.88	1.90	1.92	1.94	1.96	1.98
2	2.57	2.60	2.63	2.66	2.70	2.73	2.76	2.79	2.82	2.85	2.88	2.92	2.95	2.98
3	3.44	3.48	3.52	3.56	3.60	3.65	3.69	3.73	3.77	3.82	3.86	3.90	3.94	3.98
4	4.31	4.36	4.41	4.47	4.52	4.57	4.62	4.68	4.73	4.78	4.84	4.89	4.94	5.00
5	5.18	5.25	5.31	5.37	5.44	5.50	5.57	5.63	5.69	5.76	5.82	5.89	5.95	6.02
6	6.06	6.14	6.21	6.29	6.36	6.44	6.51	6.59	6.66	6.74	6.81	6.89	6.96	7.04
7	6.95	7.04	7.12	7.21	7.29	7.38	7.47	7.55	7.64	7.73	7.81	7.90	7.99	8.07
8	7.84	7.94	8.03	8.13	8.23	8.33	8.42	8.52	8.62	8.72	8.82	8.91	9.01	9.11
9	8.73	8.84	8.95	9.06	9.17	9.28	9.39	9.50	9.61	9.72	9.83	9.94	10.04	10.15
10	9.63	9.75	9.88	10.00	10.12	10.24	10.36	10.48	10.60	10.72	10.84	10.96	11.08	11.21
11	10.54	10.67	10.80	10.94	11.07	11.20	11.33	11.47	11.60	11.73	11.86	12.00	12.13	12.26
12	11.45	11.59	11.74	11.88	12.02	12.17	12.31	12.46	12.60	12.75	12.89	13.04	13.18	13.33
13	12.36	12.52	12.67	12.83	12.99	13.14	13.30	13.46	13.61	13.77	13.93	14.08	14.24	14.40
14	13.28	13.45	13.62	13.79	13.95	14.12	14.29	14.46	14.63	14.80	14.97	15.13	15.30	15.47
15	14.21	14.39	14.57	14.75	14.93	15.11	15.29	15.47	15.65	15.83	16.01	16.19	16.37	16.56
16	15.14	15.33	15.52	15.71	15.90	16.10	16.29	16.48	16.68	16.87	17.06	17.26	17.45	17.65
17	16.07	16.27	16.48	16.68	16.89	17.09	17.30	17.50	17.71	17.92	18.12	18.33	18.53	18.74
18	17.01	17.22	17.44	17.66	17.88	18.09	18.31	18.53	18.75	18.97	19.19	19.41	19.62	19.84
19	17.95	18.18	18.41	18.64	18.87	19.10	19.33	19.56	19.79	20.02	20.26	20.49	20.72	20.95
20	18.90	19.14	19.38	19.63	19.87	20.11	20.36	20.60	20.84	21.09	21.33	21.58	21.82	22.07
21	19.85	20.11	20.36	20.62	20.87	21.13	21.38	21.64	21.90	22.16	22.41	22.67	22.93	23.19
22	20.81	21.08	21.34	21.61	21.88	22.15	22.42	22.69	22.96	23.23	23.50	23.77	24.04	24.32
23	21.77	22.05	22.33	22.61	22.90	23.18	23.46	23.74	24.03	24.31	24.60	24.88	25.17	25.45
24	22.74	23.03	23.33	23.62	23.92	24.21	24.51	24.80	25.10	25.40	25.70	25.99	26.29	26.59
25	23.71	24.02	24.32	24.63	24.94	25.25	25.56	25.87	26.18	26.49	26.80	27.11	27.43	27.74
26	24.68	25.01	25.33	25.65	25.97	26.29	26.62	26.94	27.26	27.59	27.91	28.24	28.56	28.89
27	25.67	26.00	26.34	26.67	27.01	27.34	27.68	28.02	28.35	28.69	29.03	29.37	29.71	30.05
28	26.65	27.00	27.35	27.70	28.05	28.40	28.75	29.10	29.45	29.80	30.15	30.51	30.86	31.22
29	27.64	28.00	28.37	28.73	29.09	29.46	29.82	30.19	30.55	30.92	31.28	31.65	32.02	32.39
30	28.64	29.01	29.39	29.77	30.14	30.52	30.90	31.28	31.66	32.04	32.42	32.80	33.18	33.57

Number of Payments	20.50%	20.75%	21.00%	21.25%	21.50%	21.75%	22.00%	22.25%	22.50%	22.75%	23.00%	23.25%	23.50%	23.75%
	Finance Charge per $100 of Amount Financed													
31	29.64	30.03	30.42	30.81	31.20	31.59	31.98	32.38	32.77	33.17	33.56	33.96	34.35	34.75
32	30.64	31.05	31.45	31.85	32.26	32.67	33.07	33.48	33.89	34.30	34.71	35.12	35.53	35.94
33	31.65	32.07	32.49	32.91	33.33	33.75	34.17	34.59	35.01	35.44	35.86	36.29	36.71	37.14
34	32.67	33.10	33.53	33.96	34.40	34.83	35.27	35.71	36.14	36.58	37.02	37.46	37.90	38.34
35	33.68	34.13	34.58	35.03	35.47	35.92	36.37	36.83	37.28	37.73	38.18	38.64	39.09	39.55
36	34.71	35.17	35.63	36.09	36.56	37.02	37.49	37.95	38.42	38.89	39.35	39.82	40.29	40.77
37	35.74	36.21	36.69	37.16	37.64	38.12	38.60	39.08	39.56	40.05	40.53	41.02	41.50	41.99
38	36.77	37.26	37.75	38.24	38.73	39.23	39.72	40.22	40.72	41.21	41.71	42.21	42.71	43.22
39	37.81	38.31	38.82	39.32	39.83	40.34	40.85	41.36	41.87	42.39	42.90	43.42	43.93	44.45
40	38.85	39.37	39.89	40.41	40.93	41.46	41.98	42.51	43.04	43.56	44.09	44.62	45.16	45.69
41	39.89	40.43	40.96	41.50	42.04	42.58	43.12	43.66	44.20	44.75	45.29	45.84	46.39	46.94
42	40.95	41.50	42.05	42.60	43.15	43.71	44.26	44.82	45.38	45.94	46.50	47.06	47.62	48.19
43	42.00	42.57	43.13	43.70	44.27	44.84	45.41	45.98	46.56	47.13	47.71	48.29	48.87	49.45
44	43.06	43.64	44.22	44.81	45.39	45.98	46.56	47.15	47.74	48.33	48.93	49.52	50.11	50.71
45	44.13	44.72	45.32	45.92	46.52	47.12	47.72	48.33	48.93	49.54	50.15	50.76	51.37	51.98
46	45.20	45.81	46.42	47.03	47.65	48.27	48.89	49.51	50.13	50.75	51.38	52.00	52.63	53.26
47	46.27	46.90	47.53	48.16	48.79	49.42	50.06	50.69	51.33	51.97	52.61	53.25	53.89	54.54
48	47.35	47.99	48.64	49.28	49.93	50.58	51.23	51.88	52.54	53.19	53.85	54.51	55.16	55.83
49	48.43	49.09	49.75	50.41	51.08	51.74	52.41	53.08	53.75	54.42	55.09	55.77	56.44	57.12
50	49.52	50.19	50.87	51.55	52.23	52.91	53.59	54.28	54.96	55.65	56.34	57.03	57.73	58.42
51	50.61	51.30	51.99	52.69	53.38	54.08	54.78	55.48	56.19	56.89	57.60	58.30	59.01	59.73
52	51.71	52.41	53.12	53.83	54.55	55.26	55.98	56.69	57.41	58.13	58.86	59.58	60.31	61.04
53	52.81	53.53	54.26	54.98	55.71	56.44	57.18	57.91	58.65	59.38	60.12	60.87	61.61	62.35
54	53.91	54.65	55.39	56.14	56.88	57.63	58.38	59.13	59.88	60.64	61.40	62.16	62.92	63.68
55	55.02	55.78	56.54	57.30	58.06	58.82	59.59	60.36	61.13	61.90	62.67	63.45	64.23	65.01
56	56.14	56.91	57.68	58.46	59.24	60.02	60.80	61.59	62.38	63.17	63.96	64.75	65.54	66.34
57	57.26	58.04	58.84	59.63	60.43	61.22	62.02	62.83	63.63	64.44	65.25	66.06	66.87	67.68
58	58.38	59.18	59.99	60.80	61.62	62.43	63.25	64.07	64.89	65.71	66.54	67.37	68.20	69.03
59	59.51	60.33	61.15	61.98	62.81	63.64	64.48	65.32	66.15	67.00	67.84	68.68	69.53	70.38
60	60.64	61.48	62.32	63.17	64.01	64.86	65.71	66.57	67.42	68.28	69.14	70.01	70.87	71.74

Number of Payments	24.00%	24.25%	24.50%	24.75%	25.00%	25.25%	25.50%	25.75%	26.00%	26.25%	26.50%	26.75%	27.00%	27.25%
	Annual Percentage Rate													
	Finance Charge per $100 of Amount Financed													
1	2.00	2.02	2.04	2.06	2.08	2.10	2.12	2.15	2.17	2.19	2.21	2.23	2.25	2.27
2	3.01	3.04	3.07	3.10	3.14	3.17	3.20	3.23	3.26	3.29	3.32	3.36	3.39	3.42
3	4.03	4.07	4.11	4.15	4.20	4.24	4.28	4.32	4.36	4.41	4.45	4.49	4.53	4.58
4	5.05	5.10	5.16	5.21	5.26	5.32	5.37	5.42	5.47	5.53	5.58	5.63	5.69	5.74
5	6.08	6.14	6.21	6.27	6.34	6.40	6.46	6.53	6.59	6.66	6.72	6.79	6.85	6.91
6	7.12	7.19	7.27	7.34	7.42	7.49	7.57	7.64	7.72	7.79	7.87	7.95	8.02	8.10
7	8.16	8.25	8.33	8.42	8.51	8.59	8.68	8.77	8.85	8.94	9.03	9.11	9.20	9.29
8	9.21	9.31	9.40	9.50	9.60	9.70	9.80	9.90	9.99	10.09	10.19	10.29	10.39	10.49
9	10.26	10.37	10.48	10.59	10.70	10.81	10.92	11.03	11.14	11.25	11.36	11.47	11.58	11.69
10	11.33	11.45	11.57	11.69	11.81	11.93	12.06	12.18	12.30	12.42	12.54	12.67	12.79	12.91
11	12.40	12.53	12.66	12.80	12.93	13.06	13.20	13.33	13.46	13.60	13.73	13.87	14.00	14.13
12	13.47	13.62	13.76	13.91	14.05	14.20	14.34	14.49	14.64	14.78	14.93	15.07	15.22	15.37
13	14.55	14.71	14.87	15.03	15.18	15.34	15.50	15.66	15.82	15.97	16.13	16.29	16.45	16.61
14	15.64	15.81	15.98	16.15	16.32	16.49	16.66	16.83	17.00	17.17	17.35	17.52	17.69	17.86
15	16.74	16.92	17.10	17.28	17.47	17.65	17.83	18.02	18.20	18.38	18.57	18.75	18.93	19.12
16	17.84	18.03	18.23	18.42	18.62	18.81	19.01	19.21	19.40	19.60	19.79	19.99	20.19	20.38
17	18.95	19.16	19.36	19.57	19.78	19.99	20.20	20.40	20.61	20.82	21.03	21.24	21.45	21.66
18	20.06	20.28	20.50	20.72	20.95	21.17	21.39	21.61	21.83	22.05	22.27	22.50	22.72	22.94
19	21.19	21.42	21.65	21.89	22.12	22.35	22.59	22.82	23.06	23.29	23.53	23.76	24.00	24.23
20	22.31	22.56	22.81	23.05	23.30	23.55	23.79	24.04	24.29	24.54	24.79	25.04	25.28	25.53
21	23.45	23.71	23.97	24.23	24.49	24.75	25.01	25.27	25.53	25.79	26.05	26.32	26.58	26.84
22	24.59	24.86	25.13	25.41	25.68	25.96	26.23	26.50	26.78	27.05	27.33	27.61	27.88	28.16
23	25.74	26.02	26.31	26.60	26.88	27.17	27.46	27.75	28.04	28.32	28.61	28.90	29.19	29.48
24	26.89	27.19	27.49	27.79	28.09	28.39	28.69	29.00	29.30	29.60	29.90	30.21	30.51	30.82
25	28.05	28.36	28.68	28.99	29.31	29.62	29.94	30.25	30.57	30.89	31.20	31.52	31.84	32.16
26	29.22	29.55	29.87	30.20	30.53	30.86	31.19	31.52	31.85	32.18	32.51	32.84	33.18	33.51
27	30.39	30.73	31.07	31.42	31.76	32.10	32.45	32.79	33.14	33.48	33.83	34.17	34.52	34.87
28	31.57	31.93	32.28	32.64	33.00	33.35	33.71	34.07	34.43	34.79	35.15	35.51	35.87	36.23
29	32.76	33.13	33.50	33.87	34.24	34.61	34.98	35.36	35.73	36.10	36.48	36.85	37.23	37.61
30	33.95	34.33	34.72	35.10	35.49	35.88	36.26	36.65	37.04	37.43	37.82	38.21	38.60	38.99

Number of Payments	**Annual Percentage Rate**													
	24.00%	*24.25%*	*24.50%*	*24.75%*	*25.00%*	*25.25%*	*25.50%*	*25.75%*	*26.00%*	*26.25%*	*26.50%*	*26.75%*	*27.00%*	*27.25%*
	Finance Charge per $100 of Amount Financed													
31	35.15	35.55	35.95	36.35	36.75	37.15	37.55	37.95	38.36	38.76	39.16	39.57	39.97	40.38
32	36.35	36.77	37.18	37.60	38.01	38.43	38.84	39.26	39.68	40.10	40.52	40.94	41.36	41.78
33	37.57	37.99	38.42	38.85	39.28	39.71	40.14	40.58	41.01	41.44	41.88	42.31	42.75	43.19
34	38.78	39.23	39.67	40.11	40.56	41.01	41.45	41.90	42.35	42.80	43.25	43.70	44.15	44.60
35	40.01	40.47	40.92	41.38	41.84	42.31	42.77	43.23	43.69	44.16	44.62	45.09	45.56	46.02
36	41.24	41.71	42.19	42.66	43.14	43.61	44.09	44.57	45.05	45.53	46.01	46.49	46.97	47.45
37	42.48	42.96	43.45	43.94	44.43	44.93	45.42	45.91	46.41	46.90	47.40	47.90	48.39	48.89
38	43.72	44.22	44.73	45.23	45.74	46.25	46.75	47.26	47.77	48.29	48.80	49.31	49.82	50.34
39	44.97	45.49	46.01	46.53	47.05	47.57	48.10	48.62	49.15	49.68	50.20	50.73	51.26	51.79
40	46.22	46.76	47.29	47.83	48.37	48.91	49.45	49.99	50.53	51.07	51.62	52.16	52.71	53.26
41	47.48	48.04	48.59	49.14	49.69	50.25	50.80	51.36	51.92	52.48	53.04	53.60	54.16	54.73
42	48.75	49.32	49.89	50.46	51.03	51.60	52.17	52.74	53.32	53.89	54.47	55.05	55.63	56.21
43	50.03	50.61	51.19	51.78	52.36	52.95	53.54	54.13	54.72	55.31	55.90	56.50	57.09	57.69
44	51.31	51.91	52.51	53.11	53.71	54.31	54.92	55.52	56.13	56.74	57.35	57.96	58.57	59.19
45	52.59	53.21	53.82	54.44	55.06	55.68	56.30	56.92	57.55	58.17	58.80	59.43	60.06	60.69
46	53.89	54.52	55.15	55.78	56.42	57.05	57.69	58.33	58.97	59.61	60.26	60.90	61.55	62.20
47	55.18	55.83	56.48	57.13	57.78	58.44	59.09	59.75	60.40	61.06	61.72	62.39	63.05	63.71
48	56.49	57.15	57.82	58.49	59.15	59.82	60.50	61.17	61.84	62.52	63.20	63.87	64.56	65.24
49	57.80	58.48	59.16	59.85	60.53	61.22	61.91	62.60	63.29	63.98	64.68	65.37	66.07	66.77
50	59.12	59.81	60.51	61.21	61.92	62.62	63.33	64.03	64.74	65.45	66.16	66.88	67.59	68.31
51	60.44	61.15	61.87	62.59	63.31	64.03	64.75	65.48	66.20	66.93	67.66	68.39	69.12	69.86
52	61.77	62.50	63.23	63.97	64.70	65.44	66.18	66.92	67.67	68.41	69.16	69.91	70.66	71.41
53	63.10	63.85	64.60	65.35	66.11	66.86	67.62	68.38	69.14	69.90	70.67	71.43	72.20	72.97
54	64.44	65.21	65.98	66.75	67.52	68.29	69.07	69.84	70.62	71.40	72.18	72.97	73.75	74.54
55	65.79	66.57	67.36	68.14	68.93	69.72	70.52	71.31	72.11	72.91	73.71	74.51	75.31	76.12
56	67.14	67.94	68.74	69.55	70.36	71.16	71.97	72.79	73.60	74.42	75.24	76.06	76.88	77.70
57	68.50	69.32	70.14	70.96	71.78	72.61	73.44	74.27	75.10	75.94	76.77	77.61	78.45	79.29
58	69.86	70.70	71.54	72.38	73.22	74.06	74.91	75.76	76.61	77.46	78.32	79.17	80.03	80.89
59	71.23	72.09	72.94	73.80	74.66	75.52	76.39	77.25	78.12	78.99	79.87	80.74	81.62	82.50
60	72.61	73.48	74.35	75.23	76.11	76.99	77.87	78.76	79.64	80.53	81.42	82.32	83.21	84.11

Number of Payments	Annual Percentage Rate													
	27.50%	*27.75%*	*28.00%*	*28.25%*	*28.50%*	*28.75%*	*29.00%*	*29.25%*	*29.50%*	*29.75%*	*30.00%*	*30.25%*	*30.50%*	*30.75%*
	Finance Charge per $100 of Amount Financed													
1	2.29	2.31	2.33	2.35	2.37	2.40	2.42	2.44	2.46	2.48	2.50	2.52	2.54	2.56
2	3.45	3.48	3.51	3.54	3.58	3.61	3.64	3.67	3.70	3.73	3.77	3.80	3.83	3.86
3	4.62	4.66	4.70	4.74	4.79	4.83	4.87	4.91	4.96	5.00	5.04	5.08	5.13	5.17
4	5.79	5.85	5.90	5.95	6.01	6.06	6.11	6.17	6.22	6.27	6.33	6.38	6.43	6.49
5	6.98	7.04	7.11	7.17	7.24	7.30	7.37	7.43	7.49	7.56	7.62	7.69	7.75	7.82
6	8.17	8.25	8.32	8.40	8.48	8.55	8.63	8.70	8.78	8.85	8.93	9.01	9.08	9.16
7	9.37	9.46	9.55	9.64	9.72	9.81	9.90	9.98	10.07	10.16	10.25	10.33	10.42	10.51
8	10.58	10.68	10.78	10.88	10.98	11.08	11.18	11.28	11.38	11.47	11.57	11.67	11.77	11.87
9	11.80	11.91	12.03	12.14	12.25	12.36	12.47	12.58	12.69	12.80	12.91	13.02	13.13	13.24
10	13.03	13.15	13.28	13.40	13.52	13.64	13.77	13.89	14.01	14.14	14.26	14.38	14.50	14.63
11	14.27	14.40	14.54	14.67	14.81	14.94	15.08	15.21	15.35	15.48	15.62	15.75	15.89	16.02
12	15.51	15.66	15.81	15.95	16.10	16.25	16.40	16.54	16.69	16.84	16.98	17.13	17.28	17.43
13	16.77	16.93	17.09	17.24	17.40	17.56	17.72	17.88	18.04	18.20	18.36	18.52	18.68	18.84
14	18.03	18.20	18.37	18.54	18.72	18.89	19.06	19.23	19.41	19.58	19.75	19.92	20.10	20.27
15	19.30	19.48	19.67	19.85	20.04	20.22	20.41	20.59	20.78	20.96	21.15	21.34	21.52	21.71
16	20.58	20.78	20.97	21.17	21.37	21.57	21.76	21.96	22.16	22.36	22.56	22.76	22.96	23.16
17	21.87	22.08	22.29	22.50	22.71	22.92	23.13	23.34	23.55	23.77	23.98	24.19	24.40	24.61
18	23.16	23.39	23.61	23.83	24.06	24.28	24.51	24.73	24.96	25.18	25.41	25.63	25.86	26.08
19	24.47	24.71	24.94	25.18	25.42	25.65	25.89	26.13	26.37	26.61	26.85	27.08	27.32	27.56
20	25.78	26.03	26.28	26.53	26.78	27.04	27.29	27.54	27.79	28.04	28.29	28.55	28.80	29.05
21	27.11	27.37	27.63	27.90	28.16	28.43	28.69	28.96	29.22	29.49	29.75	30.02	30.29	30.55
22	28.44	28.71	28.99	29.27	29.55	29.82	30.10	30.38	30.66	30.94	31.22	31.50	31.78	32.07
23	29.77	30.07	30.36	30.65	30.94	31.23	31.53	31.82	32.11	32.41	32.70	33.00	33.29	33.59
24	31.12	31.43	31.73	32.04	32.34	32.65	32.96	33.27	33.57	33.88	34.19	34.50	34.81	35.12
25	32.48	32.80	33.12	33.44	33.76	34.08	34.40	34.72	35.04	35.37	35.69	36.01	36.34	36.66
26	33.84	34.18	34.51	34.84	35.18	35.51	35.85	36.19	36.52	36.86	37.20	37.54	37.88	38.21
27	35.21	35.56	35.91	36.26	36.61	36.96	37.31	37.66	38.01	38.36	38.72	39.07	39.42	39.78
28	36.59	36.96	37.32	37.68	38.05	38.41	38.78	39.15	39.51	39.88	40.25	40.61	40.98	41.35
29	37.98	38.36	38.74	39.12	39.50	39.88	40.26	40.64	41.02	41.40	41.78	42.17	42.55	42.94
30	39.38	39.77	40.17	40.56	40.95	41.35	41.75	42.14	42.54	42.94	43.33	43.73	44.13	44.53

Annual Percentage Rate

Finance Charge per $100 of Amount Financed

Number of Payments	27.50%	27.75%	28.00%	28.25%	28.50%	28.75%	29.00%	29.25%	29.50%	29.75%	30.00%	30.25%	30.50%	30.75%
31	40.79	41.19	41.60	42.01	42.42	42.83	43.24	43.65	44.07	44.48	44.89	45.30	45.72	46.13
32	42.20	42.62	43.05	43.47	43.90	44.32	44.75	45.17	45.60	46.03	46.46	46.89	47.32	47.75
33	43.62	44.06	44.50	44.94	45.38	45.82	46.26	46.70	47.15	47.59	48.04	48.48	48.93	49.37
34	45.05	45.51	45.96	46.42	46.87	47.33	47.79	48.24	48.70	49.16	49.62	50.08	50.55	51.01
35	46.49	46.96	47.43	47.90	48.37	48.85	49.32	49.79	50.27	50.74	51.22	51.70	52.17	52.65
36	47.94	48.42	48.91	49.40	49.88	50.37	50.86	51.35	51.84	52.33	52.83	53.32	53.81	54.31
37	49.39	49.89	50.40	50.90	51.40	51.91	52.41	52.92	53.42	53.93	54.44	54.95	55.46	55.97
38	50.86	51.37	51.89	52.41	52.93	53.45	53.97	54.49	55.02	55.54	56.07	56.59	57.12	57.65
39	52.33	52.86	53.39	53.93	54.46	55.00	55.54	56.08	56.62	57.16	57.70	58.24	58.79	59.33
40	53.81	54.35	54.90	55.46	56.01	56.56	57.12	57.67	58.23	58.79	59.34	59.90	60.47	61.03
41	55.29	55.86	56.42	56.99	57.56	58.13	58.70	59.28	59.85	60.42	61.00	61.57	62.15	62.73
42	56.79	57.37	57.95	58.54	59.12	59.71	60.30	60.89	61.48	62.07	62.66	63.25	63.85	64.44
43	58.29	58.89	59.49	60.09	60.69	61.30	61.90	62.51	63.11	63.72	64.33	64.94	65.56	66.17
44	59.80	60.42	61.03	61.65	62.27	62.89	63.51	64.14	64.76	65.39	66.01	66.64	67.27	67.90
45	61.32	61.95	62.59	63.22	63.86	64.50	65.13	65.77	66.42	67.06	67.70	68.35	69.00	69.64
46	62.84	63.49	64.15	64.80	65.45	66.11	66.76	67.42	68.08	68.74	69.40	70.07	70.73	71.40
47	64.38	65.05	65.71	66.38	67.06	67.73	68.40	69.08	69.75	70.43	71.11	71.79	72.47	73.16
48	65.92	66.60	67.29	67.98	68.67	69.36	70.05	70.74	71.44	72.13	72.83	73.53	74.23	74.93
49	67.47	68.17	68.87	69.58	70.29	70.99	71.70	72.41	73.13	73.84	74.56	75.27	75.99	76.71
50	69.03	69.75	70.47	71.19	71.91	72.64	73.37	74.10	74.83	75.56	76.29	77.02	77.76	78.50
51	70.59	71.33	72.07	72.81	73.55	74.29	75.04	75.78	76.53	77.28	78.03	78.79	79.54	80.30
52	72.16	72.92	73.67	74.43	75.19	75.95	76.72	77.48	78.25	79.02	79.79	80.56	81.33	82.11
53	73.74	74.52	75.29	76.07	76.85	77.62	78.41	79.19	79.97	80.76	81.55	82.34	83.13	83.92
54	75.33	76.12	76.91	77.71	78.50	79.30	80.10	80.90	81.71	82.51	83.32	84.13	84.94	85.75
55	76.92	77.73	78.55	79.36	80.17	80.99	81.81	82.63	83.45	84.27	85.10	85.93	86.75	87.58
56	78.53	79.35	80.18	81.02	81.85	82.68	83.52	84.36	85.20	86.04	86.89	87.73	88.58	89.43
57	80.14	80.98	81.83	82.68	83.53	84.39	85.24	86.10	86.96	87.82	88.68	89.55	90.41	91.28
58	81.75	82.62	83.48	84.35	85.22	86.10	86.97	87.85	88.72	89.60	90.49	91.37	92.26	93.14
59	83.38	84.26	85.15	86.03	86.92	87.81	88.71	89.60	90.50	91.40	92.30	93.20	94.11	95.01
60	85.01	85.91	86.81	87.72	88.63	89.54	90.45	91.37	92.28	93.20	94.12	95.04	95.97	96.89

Number of Payments	Annual Percentage Rate													
	31.00%	31.25%	31.50%	31.75%	32.00%	32.25%	32.50%	32.75%	33.00%	33.25%	33.50%	33.75%	34.00%	34.25%
	Finance Charge per $100 of Amount Financed													
1	2.58	2.60	2.63	2.65	2.67	2.69	2.71	2.73	2.75	2.77	2.79	2.81	2.83	2.85
2	3.89	3.92	3.95	3.99	4.02	4.05	4.08	4.11	4.14	4.18	4.21	4.24	4.27	4.30
3	5.21	5.25	5.30	5.34	5.38	5.42	5.46	5.51	5.55	5.59	5.63	5.68	5.72	5.76
4	6.54	6.59	6.65	6.70	6.75	6.81	6.86	6.91	6.97	7.02	7.08	7.13	7.18	7.24
5	7.88	7.95	8.01	8.08	8.14	8.21	8.27	8.33	8.40	8.46	8.53	8.59	8.66	8.72
6	9.23	9.31	9.39	9.46	9.54	9.61	9.69	9.77	9.84	9.92	9.99	10.07	10.15	10.22
7	10.60	10.68	10.77	10.86	10.95	11.03	11.12	11.21	11.30	11.39	11.47	11.56	11.65	11.74
8	11.97	12.07	12.17	12.27	12.37	12.47	12.57	12.67	12.77	12.87	12.97	13.07	13.17	13.27
9	13.36	13.47	13.58	13.69	13.80	13.91	14.02	14.14	14.25	14.36	14.47	14.58	14.69	14.81
10	14.75	14.87	15.00	15.12	15.24	15.37	15.49	15.62	15.74	15.86	15.99	16.11	16.24	16.36
11	16.16	16.29	16.43	16.56	16.70	16.84	16.97	17.11	17.24	17.38	17.52	17.65	17.79	17.93
12	17.58	17.72	17.87	18.02	18.17	18.32	18.47	18.61	18.76	18.91	19.06	19.21	19.36	19.51
13	19.00	19.16	19.33	19.49	19.65	19.81	19.97	20.13	20.29	20.45	20.62	20.78	20.94	21.10
14	20.44	20.62	20.79	20.96	21.14	21.31	21.49	21.66	21.83	22.01	22.18	22.36	22.53	22.71
15	21.89	22.08	22.27	22.45	22.64	22.83	23.01	23.20	23.39	23.58	23.76	23.95	24.14	24.33
16	23.35	23.55	23.75	23.95	24.15	24.35	24.55	24.75	24.96	25.16	25.36	25.56	25.76	25.96
17	24.83	25.04	25.25	25.47	25.68	25.89	26.11	26.32	26.53	26.75	26.96	27.18	27.39	27.61
18	26.31	26.54	26.76	26.99	27.22	27.44	27.67	27.90	28.13	28.35	28.58	28.81	29.04	29.27
19	27.80	28.04	28.28	28.52	28.76	29.00	29.25	29.49	29.73	29.97	30.21	30.45	30.70	30.94
20	29.31	29.56	29.81	30.07	30.32	30.58	30.83	31.09	31.34	31.60	31.86	32.11	32.37	32.63
21	30.82	31.09	31.36	31.62	31.89	32.16	32.43	32.70	32.97	33.24	33.51	33.78	34.05	34.32
22	32.35	32.63	32.91	33.19	33.48	33.76	34.04	34.33	34.61	34.89	35.18	35.46	35.75	36.04
23	33.88	34.18	34.48	34.77	35.07	35.37	35.66	35.96	36.26	36.56	36.86	37.16	37.46	37.76
24	35.43	35.74	36.05	36.36	36.67	36.99	37.30	37.61	37.92	38.24	38.55	38.87	39.18	39.50
25	36.99	37.31	37.64	37.96	38.29	38.62	38.94	39.27	39.60	39.93	40.26	40.59	40.92	41.25
26	38.55	38.89	39.23	39.58	39.92	40.26	40.60	40.94	41.29	41.63	41.97	42.32	42.66	43.01
27	40.13	40.49	40.84	41.20	41.56	41.91	42.27	42.63	42.99	43.34	43.70	44.06	44.42	44.78
28	41.72	42.09	42.46	42.83	43.20	43.58	43.95	44.32	44.70	45.07	45.45	45.82	46.20	46.57
29	43.32	43.71	44.09	44.48	44.87	45.25	45.64	46.03	46.42	46.81	47.20	47.59	47.98	48.37
30	44.93	45.33	45.73	46.13	46.54	46.94	47.34	47.75	48.15	48.56	48.96	49.37	49.78	50.19

Number of Payments	Annual Percentage Rate													
	31.00%	*31.25%*	*31.50%*	*31.75%*	*32.00%*	*32.25%*	*32.50%*	*32.75%*	*33.00%*	*33.25%*	*33.50%*	*33.75%*	*34.00%*	*34.25%*
	Finance Charge per $100 of Amount Financed													
31	46.55	46.97	47.38	47.80	48.22	48.64	49.06	49.48	49.90	50.32	50.74	51.17	51.59	52.01
32	48.18	48.61	49.05	49.48	49.91	50.35	50.78	51.22	51.66	52.09	52.53	52.97	53.41	53.85
33	49.82	50.27	50.72	51.17	51.62	52.07	52.52	52.97	53.43	53.88	54.33	54.79	55.24	55.70
34	51.47	51.94	52.40	52.87	53.33	53.80	54.27	54.74	55.21	55.68	56.15	56.62	57.09	57.56
35	53.13	53.61	54.09	54.58	55.06	55.54	56.03	56.51	57.00	57.48	57.97	58.46	58.95	59.44
36	54.80	55.30	55.80	56.30	56.80	57.30	57.80	58.30	58.80	59.30	59.81	60.31	60.82	61.33
37	56.49	57.00	57.51	58.03	58.54	59.06	59.58	60.10	60.62	61.14	61.66	62.18	62.70	63.22
38	58.18	58.71	59.24	59.77	60.30	60.84	61.37	61.90	62.44	62.98	63.52	64.06	64.59	65.14
39	59.88	60.42	60.97	61.52	62.07	62.62	63.17	63.72	64.28	64.83	65.39	65.94	66.50	67.06
40	61.59	62.15	62.72	63.28	63.85	64.42	64.99	65.56	66.13	66.70	67.27	67.84	68.42	68.99
41	63.31	63.89	64.47	65.06	65.64	66.22	66.81	67.40	67.99	68.57	69.16	69.76	70.35	70.94
42	65.04	65.64	66.24	66.84	67.44	68.04	68.65	69.25	69.86	70.46	71.07	71.68	72.29	72.90
43	66.78	67.40	68.01	68.63	69.25	69.87	70.49	71.11	71.74	72.36	72.99	73.61	74.24	74.87
44	68.53	69.17	69.80	70.43	71.07	71.71	72.35	72.99	73.63	74.27	74.91	75.56	76.20	76.85
45	70.29	70.94	71.60	72.25	72.90	73.56	74.21	74.87	75.53	76.19	76.85	77.52	78.18	78.84
46	72.06	72.73	73.40	74.07	74.74	75.42	76.09	76.77	77.44	78.12	78.80	79.48	80.17	80.85
47	73.84	74.53	75.22	75.91	76.60	77.29	77.98	78.67	79.37	80.07	80.76	81.46	82.16	82.87
48	75.63	76.34	77.04	77.75	78.46	79.17	79.88	80.59	81.30	82.02	82.74	83.45	84.17	84.89
49	77.43	78.15	78.88	79.60	80.33	81.06	81.79	82.52	83.25	83.98	84.72	85.45	86.19	86.93
50	79.24	79.98	80.72	81.46	82.21	82.96	83.70	84.45	85.20	85.96	86.71	87.47	88.22	88.98
51	81.06	81.81	82.58	83.34	84.10	84.87	85.63	86.40	87.17	87.94	88.71	89.49	90.26	91.04
52	82.88	83.66	84.44	85.22	86.00	86.79	87.57	88.36	89.15	89.94	90.73	91.52	92.32	93.11
53	84.72	85.51	86.31	87.11	87.91	88.72	89.52	90.33	91.13	91.94	92.75	93.57	94.38	95.20
54	86.56	87.38	88.19	89.01	89.83	90.66	91.48	92.30	93.13	93.96	94.79	95.62	96.45	97.29
55	88.42	89.25	90.09	90.92	91.76	92.60	93.45	94.29	95.14	95.99	96.83	97.69	98.54	99.39
56	90.28	91.13	91.99	92.84	93.70	94.56	95.43	96.29	97.15	98.02	98.89	99.76	100.63	101.51
57	92.15	93.02	93.90	94.77	95.65	96.53	97.41	98.30	99.18	100.07	100.96	101.85	102.74	103.63
58	94.03	94.92	95.82	96.71	97.61	98.51	99.41	100.31	101.22	102.12	103.03	103.94	104.85	105.77
59	95.92	96.83	97.75	98.66	99.58	100.50	101.42	102.34	103.26	104.19	105.12	106.05	106.98	107.91
60	97.82	98.75	99.68	100.62	101.56	102.49	103.43	104.38	105.32	106.27	107.21	108.16	109.12	110.07

Number of Payments	Annual Percentage Rate													
	34.50%	*34.75%*	*35.00%*	*35.25%*	*35.50%*	*35.75%*	*36.00%*	*36.25%*	*36.50%*	*36.75%*	*37.00%*	*37.25%*	*37.50%*	*37.75%*
	Finance Charge per $100 of Amount Financed													
1	2.87	2.90	2.92	2.94	2.96	2.98	3.00	3.02	3.04	3.06	3.08	3.10	3.12	3.15
2	4.33	4.36	4.40	4.43	4.46	4.49	4.52	4.55	4.59	4.62	4.65	4.68	4.71	4.74
3	5.80	5.85	5.89	5.93	5.97	6.02	6.06	6.10	6.14	6.19	6.23	6.27	6.31	6.36
4	7.29	7.34	7.40	7.45	7.50	7.56	7.61	7.66	7.72	7.77	7.83	7.88	7.93	7.99
5	8.79	8.85	8.92	8.98	9.05	9.11	9.18	9.24	9.31	9.37	9.44	9.50	9.57	9.63
6	10.30	10.38	10.45	10.53	10.61	10.68	10.76	10.83	10.91	10.99	11.06	11.14	11.22	11.29
7	11.83	11.91	12.00	12.09	12.18	12.27	12.35	12.44	12.53	12.62	12.71	12.80	12.88	12.97
8	13.36	13.46	13.56	13.66	13.76	13.86	13.97	14.07	14.17	14.27	14.37	14.47	14.57	14.67
9	14.92	15.03	15.14	15.25	15.37	15.48	15.59	15.70	15.82	15.93	16.04	16.15	16.27	16.38
10	16.48	16.61	16.73	16.86	16.98	17.11	17.23	17.36	17.48	17.60	17.73	17.85	17.98	18.10
11	18.06	18.20	18.34	18.47	18.61	18.75	18.89	19.02	19.16	19.30	19.43	19.57	19.71	19.85
12	19.66	19.81	19.96	20.11	20.25	20.40	20.55	20.70	20.85	21.00	21.15	21.31	21.46	21.61
13	21.26	21.43	21.59	21.75	21.91	22.08	22.24	22.40	22.56	22.73	22.89	23.05	23.22	23.38
14	22.88	23.06	23.23	23.41	23.59	23.76	23.94	24.11	24.29	24.47	24.64	24.82	25.00	25.17
15	24.52	24.71	24.89	25.08	25.27	25.46	25.65	25.84	26.03	26.22	26.41	26.60	26.79	26.98
16	26.16	26.37	26.57	26.77	26.97	27.17	27.38	27.58	27.78	27.99	28.19	28.39	28.60	28.80
17	27.82	28.04	28.25	28.47	28.69	28.90	29.12	29.34	29.55	29.77	29.99	30.20	30.42	30.64
18	29.50	29.73	29.96	30.19	30.42	30.65	30.88	31.11	31.34	31.57	31.80	32.03	32.26	32.49
19	31.18	31.43	31.67	31.91	32.16	32.40	32.65	32.89	33.14	33.38	33.63	33.87	34.12	34.36
20	32.88	33.14	33.40	33.66	33.91	34.17	34.43	34.69	34.95	35.21	35.47	35.73	35.99	36.25
21	34.60	34.87	35.14	35.41	35.68	35.96	36.23	36.50	36.78	37.05	37.33	37.60	37.88	38.15
22	36.32	36.61	36.89	37.18	37.47	37.76	38.04	38.33	38.62	38.91	39.20	39.49	39.78	40.07
23	38.06	38.36	38.66	38.96	39.27	39.57	39.87	40.18	40.48	40.78	41.09	41.39	41.70	42.00
24	39.81	40.13	40.44	40.76	41.08	41.40	41.71	42.03	42.35	42.67	42.99	43.31	43.63	43.95
25	41.58	41.91	42.24	42.57	42.90	43.24	43.57	43.90	44.24	44.57	44.91	45.24	45.58	45.91
26	43.36	43.70	44.05	44.40	44.74	45.09	45.44	45.79	46.14	46.49	46.84	47.19	47.54	47.89
27	45.15	45.51	45.87	46.23	46.60	46.96	47.32	47.69	48.05	48.42	48.78	49.15	49.52	49.89
28	46.95	47.33	47.70	48.08	48.46	48.84	49.22	49.60	49.98	50.36	50.75	51.13	51.51	51.89
29	48.77	49.16	49.55	49.95	50.34	50.74	51.13	51.53	51.93	52.32	52.72	53.12	53.52	53.92
30	50.60	51.00	51.41	51.82	52.23	52.65	53.06	53.47	53.88	54.30	54.71	55.13	55.54	55.96

Number of Payments	Annual Percentage Rate													
	34.50%	*34.75%*	*35.00%*	*35.25%*	*35.50%*	*35.75%*	*36.00%*	*36.25%*	*36.50%*	*36.75%*	*37.00%*	*37.25%*	*37.50%*	*37.75%*
	Finance Charge per $100 of Amount Financed													
31	52.44	52.86	53.29	53.71	54.14	54.57	55.00	55.43	55.85	56.28	56.72	57.15	57.58	58.01
32	54.29	54.73	55.17	55.62	56.06	56.50	56.95	57.39	57.84	58.29	58.73	59.18	59.63	60.08
33	56.16	56.62	57.07	57.53	57.99	58.45	58.92	59.38	59.84	60.30	60.77	61.23	61.70	62.16
34	58.04	58.51	58.99	59.46	59.94	60.42	60.89	61.37	61.85	62.33	62.81	63.30	63.78	64.26
35	59.93	60.42	60.91	61.40	61.90	62.39	62.89	63.38	63.88	64.38	64.88	65.37	65.87	66.37
36	61.83	62.34	62.85	63.36	63.87	64.38	64.89	65.41	65.92	66.44	66.95	67.47	67.98	68.50
37	63.75	64.27	64.80	65.33	65.85	66.38	66.91	67.44	67.97	68.51	69.04	69.57	70.11	70.64
38	65.68	66.22	66.76	67.31	67.85	68.40	68.95	69.49	70.04	70.59	71.14	71.69	72.25	72.80
39	67.62	68.18	68.74	69.30	69.86	70.43	70.99	71.56	72.12	72.69	73.26	73.83	74.40	74.97
40	69.57	70.15	70.73	71.31	71.89	72.47	73.05	73.63	74.22	74.80	75.39	75.98	76.56	77.15
41	71.53	72.13	72.73	73.32	73.92	74.52	75.12	75.72	76.32	76.93	77.53	78.14	78.74	79.35
42	73.51	74.12	74.74	75.35	75.97	76.59	77.21	77.82	78.44	79.07	79.69	80.31	80.94	81.56
43	75.50	76.13	76.76	77.40	78.03	78.67	79.30	79.94	80.58	81.22	81.86	82.50	83.14	83.79
44	77.50	78.15	78.80	79.45	80.10	80.76	81.41	82.07	82.72	83.38	84.04	84.70	85.36	86.03
45	79.51	80.18	80.85	81.52	82.19	82.86	83.53	84.21	84.88	85.56	86.24	86.92	87.60	88.28
46	81.53	82.22	82.91	83.60	84.28	84.98	85.67	86.36	87.06	87.75	88.45	89.15	89.85	90.55
47	83.57	84.27	84.98	85.69	86.39	87.10	87.81	88.53	89.24	89.95	90.67	91.39	92.11	92.83
48	85.61	86.34	87.06	87.79	88.52	89.24	89.97	90.70	91.44	92.17	92.91	93.64	94.38	95.12
49	87.67	88.41	89.16	89.90	90.65	91.40	92.14	92.89	93.65	94.40	95.15	95.91	96.67	97.42
50	89.74	90.50	91.26	92.03	92.79	93.56	94.33	95.10	95.87	96.64	97.41	98.19	98.96	99.74
51	91.82	92.60	93.38	94.16	94.95	95.74	96.52	97.31	98.10	98.89	99.69	100.48	101.28	102.07
52	93.91	94.71	95.51	96.31	97.12	97.92	98.73	99.54	100.35	101.16	101.97	102.79	103.60	104.42
53	96.01	96.83	97.65	98.47	99.30	100.12	100.95	101.78	102.61	103.44	104.27	105.10	105.94	106.78
54	98.13	98.96	99.80	100.64	101.49	102.33	103.18	104.03	104.88	105.73	106.58	107.43	108.29	109.14
55	100.25	101.11	101.97	102.83	103.69	104.55	105.42	106.29	107.16	108.03	108.90	109.77	110.65	111.53
56	102.38	103.26	104.14	105.02	105.90	106.79	107.67	108.56	109.45	110.34	111.23	112.13	113.02	113.92
57	104.53	105.43	106.32	107.22	108.13	109.03	109.94	110.85	111.75	112.67	113.58	114.49	115.41	116.33
58	106.68	107.60	108.52	109.44	110.36	111.29	112.21	113.14	114.07	115.00	115.93	116.87	117.81	118.74
59	108.85	109.79	110.73	111.67	112.61	113.55	114.50	115.45	116.40	117.35	118.30	119.26	120.22	121.17
60	111.03	111.98	112.94	113.90	114.87	115.83	116.80	117.77	118.74	119.71	120.68	121.66	122.64	123.62

Appendix L Answers to odd-numbered problems and chapter review tests

Chapter 1

Student's self-examination for chapter 1

1. 144,691 **2.** 62,621 **3.** 6,876 **4.** 766 **5.** 1,027,004 **6.** 6,699,615 **7.** 524 **8.** 515 **9.** 64, rem. 5 **10.** 8, rem. 195 **11.** 14,626 **12.** 1,081 **13.** 3,619 **14.** 37 **15.** 1,687 **16.** \$189 **17.** \$34,793 **18.** \$11,483 **19.** \$49 **20.** \$238

Section 1.2

1. 673 **3.** 840 **5.** 8,383,520 **7.** 1,787 **9.** 3,179 **11.** 21,869 **13.** 722 **15.** 5,223 **17.** 714 **19.** 5,523 **21.** 3,079 **23.** 9,275 **25.** \$2,214 **27.** \$243,518 **29.** 4,762 **31.** \$108,500 **33.** \$16,930 **35.** \$68,899 **37.** \$56 **39.** *Horizontal:* bakery, \$2,705; meats, \$4,212; produce, \$3,280; dairy, \$2,032; grocery, \$14,731; *Vertical:* Monday, \$4,346; Tuesday, \$4,623; Wednesday, \$4,255; Thursday, \$4,387; Friday, \$4,962; Saturday, \$4,387; *Total:* \$26,960

Section 1.3

1. 84 **3.** 1,880 **5.** 51,604 **7.** 288,695 **9.** 1,897,101 **11.** 19,503,603 **13.** 17,522,898 **15.** 87, rem. 0 **17.** 14, rem. 0 **19.** 71, rem. 0 **21.** 56, rem. 0 **23.** 754, rem. 0 **25.** 40, rem. 68 **27.** 65, rem. 4 **29.** 95, rem. 12 **31.** 5,461 **33.** \$578 **35.** \$622 **37.** \$42,504 **39.** \$17 **41.** \$30 **43.** \$9,933 **45.** \$27

Chapter 1 review test

1. 82,975 **2.** 52,555 **3.** 172,598 **4.** 2,422,739 **5.** 107,889 **6.** 35,686,952 **7.** 356, rem. 0 **8.** 702, rem. 0 **9.** 568, rem. 44 **10.** 79, rem. 553 **11.** 415 **12.** \$11 **13.** \$184 **14.** \$1,896 **15.** \$454 **16.** \$783 **17.** \$7,608 **18.** *Horizontal:* Beeson, \$23,576; Pruitt, \$22,883; Baker, \$18,635; Rae, \$25,469; Ramirez, \$25,954; *Vertical:* Monday, \$24,460; Tuesday, \$27,640; Wednesday, \$19,117; Thursday, \$16,027; Friday, \$29,273; *Total:* \$116,517

Chapter 2

Student's self-examination for chapter 2

1. 11/15 **2.** 19/20 **3.** 3/14 **4.** 4/5 **5.** $3\frac{1}{3}$ **6.** $4\frac{5}{8}$ **7.** $2\frac{11}{12}$ **8.** $2\frac{8}{13}$ **9.** 4,124.97 **10.** 490.75 **11.** 3.2318 **12.** 2.4 **13.** 13.38 **14.** **(a)** 27.5, **(b)** 27 **15.** **(a)** 4.847, **(b)** 4.85 **16.** 28 **17.** \$11.70 **18.** $5\frac{3}{8}$ bushels **19.** \$5,057.94 **20.** 15 workers retrained

Section 2.2

1. 2/8, 3/12, 4/16 **3.** 9/15, 12/20, 15/25 **5.** 10/12, 15/18, 20/24 **7.** 10/16, 15/24, 20/32 **9.** 10/28, 15/42, 20/56 **11.** 10/60 **13.** 24/60 **15.** 34/60 **17.** 72/90 **19.** 50/90 **21.** 22/90 **23.** equal **25.** unequal **27.** unequal **29.** equal **31.** 6 **33.** 21 **35.** 78 **37.** 1/2 **39.** 3/4 **41.** 2/3 **43.** 19/20 **45.** 7/10 **47.** 1/5 **49.** 2/9 **51.** 3/8 **53.** 1/14, 13/14 **55.** 13/41 **57.** 4/19 **59.** 2/3 **61.** 28/47, 43/47 **63.** 7:1 **65.** **(a)** 3:1; **(b)** 2:1

Section 2.3

1. 10, 7/10 **3.** 12, 7/12 **5.** 35, 29/35 **7.** 16, 15/16 **9.** 69, 35/69 **11.** 11/70 **13.** 21/40 **15.** 17/70 **17.** 13/57 **19.** 1/28 **21.** 23/24 **23.** 71/72 **25.** 31/40 acre **27.** 45/56, 5/168 **29.** 29/35, 6/35 **31.** 53/63, 4/63 **33.** 3/14

Section 2.4

1. 1/6 **3.** $1\frac{2}{3}$ **5.** 2/5 **7.** 4/15 **9.** 3/44 **11.** 1/15 **13.** $1\frac{19}{21}$ **15.** 4/13 **17.** 2 **19.** 45 **21.** 1/2 **23.** 22/5 **25.** 43/8 **27.** 80/11 **29.** $1\frac{5}{9}$ **31.** $2\frac{1}{2}$ **33.** $1\frac{9}{15}$ **35.** $32\frac{1}{2}$ **37.** 8/9 **39.** $24\frac{16}{21}$ **41.** $1\frac{21}{26}$ **43.** 1/2 **45.** $13\frac{17}{24}$ **47.** $11\frac{2}{3}$ **49.** $14\frac{7}{8}$ **51.** 21/32 **53.** 5/24 **55.** 6 **57.** 12 **59.** \$427.50 **61.** 1/4 **63.** $22\frac{1}{2}$ **65.** 20 **67.** 8 **69.** $210\frac{5}{12}$, $26\frac{29}{96}$ **71.** 15,600

Section 2.5

1. 59.7 **3.** 254.3 **5.** 56.64 **7.** 819.081 **9.** 145.598 **11.** 946.39 **13.** 418.746 **15.** 418.63 **17.** 65.9888 **19.** 24.6521 **21.** 334.7205 **23.** 3,686.5214 **25.** 17.8311456 **27.** 31.2 **29.** 21.77 **31.** 84.53 **33.** $87.33 **35.** $3,533.46 **37.** $97.30 **39.** $407.70 **41.** **(a)** 24; **(b)** 23.7; **(c)** 23.71 **43.** **(a)** 217; **(b)** 217.5; **(c)** 217.48 **45.** **(a)** 4,220; **(b)** 4,219.8; **(c)** 4,219.79 **47.** **(a)** 217,500; **(b)** 217,500.0; **(c)** 217,499.98 **49.** **(a)** 23,453; **(b)** 23,452.9; **(c)** 23,452.90 **51.** **(a)** 5,000; **(b)** 4,900; **(c)** 4,872.58 **53.** **(a)** 7,000; **(b)** 7,000; **(c)** 6,975.00 **55.** **(a)** 20,000; **(b)** 19,900; **(c)** 19,942.19 **57.** **(a)** 927,000; **(b)** 927,400; **(c)** 927,399.95 **59.** **(a)** 150,000; **(b)** 149,900; **(c)** 149,891.69 **61.** $74,899.88 **63.** $1,940.37 **65.** $14,847.80 **67.** $1,305,891.72 **69.** $6,526.52 **71.** Total profit = $31,927.35; $42,465.15 more profit **73.** $24,576.04

Chapter 2 review test

1. $1\frac{3}{7}$ **2.** 3/13 **3.** 7/12 **4.** 1/2 **5.** 3/4 **6.** 49/60 **7.** 1 **8.** $1\frac{2}{3}$ **9.** 3 **10.** $2\frac{1}{18}$ **11.** 1/7 **12.** $1\frac{17}{48}$ **13.** 41.40 **14.** 65.16 **15.** 35.30 **16.** 20.48 **17.** 7/8 **18.** $67,545.79 **19.** $543\frac{1}{3}$ **20.** 7

Chapter 3

Sections 3.2 and 3.3

1. 3 **3.** 4 **5.** 4 **7.** 11 **9.** 6 **11.** 20 **13.** 41 **15.** 5 **17.** 5 **19.** 7 **21.** 12 **23.** 11 **25.** 33/5 or $6\frac{3}{5}$ **27.** 10 **29.** 20 **31.** 9/6 or $1\frac{1}{2}$ **33.** 2/3 **35.** 150 **37.** 80/3 or $26\frac{2}{3}$ **39.** 45/28 or $1\frac{17}{28}$ **41.** 9/16 **43.** 15/2 or $7\frac{1}{2}$

Section 3.4

1. 27 **3.** $387.60 **5.** Smith, $2,961; Porter, $2,789 **7.** March, $2,812; February, $1,821 **9.** Television, $7,040; other, $2,200 **11.** Sand, $32\frac{2}{17}$; gravel, $9\frac{15}{17}$ **13.** A, 330,000; B, 110,000 **15.** $16,000 **17.** 65 **19.** 38 **21.** Lowfat, 420 gallons; vitamin D, 1,050 gallons **23.** 19.17 **25.** $54,840

Section 3.5

1. 26 **3.** 42 **5.** 300 **7.** 1 **9.** $z = (y-x)/2$, 3 **11.** $c = 4KR/ab$, 8 **13.** $x = (z+2y)/yz$, 7/6 **15.** $x = (y-yz+z)/z$, $\frac{1}{6}$ **17.** $x = zy + 5y$, 24 **19.** $x = 1/[yz(y+2z)]$, 1/48 **21.** $n = G/p$, 462 **23.** $r = I/Pt$, 0.09 **25.** **(a)** $1.25; **(b)** $1.30; **(c)** $1.40 **27.** **(a)** $6,000; **(b)** $7,000; **(c)** $11,000 **29.** **(a)** $37; **(b)** $61; **(c)** $73 **31.** **(a)** 2,200; **(b)** 2,000; **(c)** 1,800 **33.** **(a)** 33,000; **(b)** 29,250; **(c)** 24,250

Chapter 3 review test

1. **(a)** Conditional; **(b)** Identity; **(c)** Conditional; **(d)** Identity **2.** 4 **3.** 8 **4.** 8 **5.** 250 **6.** 7 **7.** 5 **8.** 20 **9.** 32/15 or $2\frac{2}{15}$ **10.** 28 **11.** 6/17 **12.** 5 **13.** Larger, $13,250; smaller, $11,250 **14.** Men, 86; women, 172 **15.** Last week, $760; this week, $580

Chapter 4

Section 4.2

1. 0.04 **3.** 0.58 **5.** 0.926 **7.** 0.0781 **9.** 0.9242 **11.** 0.145 **13.** 0.0025 **15.** 1.23 **17.** 1.725 **19.** 1% **21.** 53% **23.** 70% **25.** 5.3% **27.** 59.34% **29.** 0.32% **31.** 432% **33.** 724.6% **35.** 702.63% **37.** 3/25 **39.** 7/20 **41.** 1/500 **43.** 1/400 **45.** 11/2500 **47.** 7/800 **49.** 3/500 **51.** 7/400 **53.** 51/50 **55.** 38/25 **57.** 123/125 **59.** 311/200 **61.** 25% **63.** 75% **65.** 45% **67.** 87.5% **69.** 93.75% **71.** $81\frac{9}{11}$% **73.** $26\frac{2}{3}$% **75.** 225%

Section 4.3

1. 18 **3.** 360 **5.** 15% **7.** 4.8 **9.** 600 **11.** 22.5% **13.** 36.48 **15.** 8.5% **17.** 116.67 **19.** 15% **21.** 102.4 **23.** 172.58 **25.** 18.68 **27.** 820 **29.** 9% **31.** 233.18 **33.** $174.96 **35.** 22% **37.** 5% **39.** 5% **41.** $16.71 **43.** 81 **45.** $2.75 **47.** $41.25 **49.** 20% **51.** $1,175 **53.** 112 reconditioned, 8 junked **55.** $160 **57.** 2.4% **59.** 8% **61.** 75% **63.** 43% **65.** 29% **67.** $106.20

Section 4.4

1. 50% increase **3.** 25% increase **5.** 7% increase **7.** 30% increase **9.** 13% decrease **11.** 129 **13.** 174.02 **15.** 192.57 **17.** $101.52 **19.** 175.09 **21.** 15% decrease **23.** 30% increase **25.** 17% increase **27.** 11% increase **29.** 9% decrease **31.** 7% savings **33.** 22% increase **35.** 10% increase **37.** 4% decrease **39.** $172.30 **41.** $2,076.27 **43.** $1,900 **45.** $136.36

Chapter 4 review test

1. **(a)** 0.43; **(b)** 0.195 **2.** **(a)** 73%; **(b)** 2.4% **3.** **(a)** 72; **(b)** 93.6 **4.** **(a)** 60%; **(b)** 28% **5.** 13/20 **6.** **(a)** 35%; **(b)** 0.35 **7.** 350 **8.** 40% **9.** 38% **10.** 60% **11.** 3/5 **12.** 559 **13.** 60 **14.** $9,720 **15.** $1,672 **16.** 35% **17.** $73.44 **18.** 12.5% **19.** 30% **20.** $13.33

Chapter 5

Section 5.2

1. $184, $391 **3.** $235.60, $384.40 **5.** **(a)** $847; **(b)** $909.70 **7.** 22%, 78% **9.** $73, $146 **11.** $1,050 **13.** $917.45

Section 5.3

1. $244.80 **3.** $228.48 **5.** $42.23 **7.** $523.89 **9.** $844.80 **11.** $461.70 **13.** $1,361.11 **15.** **(a)** 64%; **(b)** 85.6%; **(c)** 56.8%; **d.** 43.5% **17.** $6.42 **19.** $30.77 **21.** **(a)** 40%, 15%, 15%; **(b)** 60%, 10%, 10% **23.** Amount column: Extension: $335.60; Trade discounts: $112.43; Net: $223.17 **25.** 20%

Section 5.4

1. $1,001 **3.** $638.77 **5.** $1,105.19 **7.** $1,560.17 **9.** Amount column: Extension: $840; Quantity discount: $126; Net: $714; Total: $742.30

Sections 5.5 and 5.6

1. **(a)** $846.42; **(b)** $872.60 **3.** $917.28 **5.** **(a)** $1,414.55; **(b)** $1,444.33; **(c)** $1,489.00 **7.** $1,792.92; $1,810.25 **9.** $797.77; $806.05 **11.** Amount column: Extensions: $372, $216, $144; Chain discount: $175.68; Net: $556.32; Amount to be remitted: $534.07

Section 5.7

1. **(a)** $458.46; **(b)** $477.56; **(c)** May 31 **3.** **(a)** $549.60; **(b)** $572.50 **5.** $844.50 **7.** **(a)** $824.75; **(b)** $800.01; **(c)** $783.51; **(d)** $791.76 **9.** August 2: $564.27; September 3: $247.61 **11.** Amount column: Extension: $960; Chain discount: $266.88; Total: $700.41. Amount to be remitted: $679.62

Sections 5.8 and 5.9

1. $33.60 **3.** $248.28 **5.** $362.52 **7.** $1,122.00 **9.** $247.93 **11.** $1,217.25 **13.** $39.90 **15.** $96.94 **17.** $177.50 **19.** **(a)** $28.13; **(b)** $29.70 **21.** **(a)** $134.40; **(b)** $137.60 **23.** **(a)** $206.40; **(b)** $234.55 **25.** $675.02 **27.** 25% **29.** $0.98, 28% **31.** $6.68 **33.** $30.16 **35.** $22.86 **37.** $0.93 **39.** $20.89 **41.** $33\frac{1}{3}\%$ **43.** 30% **45.** **(a)** 29%; **(b)** 23% **47.** 32%, $260.03

Sections 5.10 and 5.11

1. 25% **3.** 28% **5.** $148.50 **7.** $9.60 **9.** $18.00 **11.** **(a)** $190.00; **(b)** $162.50 **13.** **(a)** $457.60; **(b)** $384.80 **15.** $231.75 **17.** **(a)** $420; **(b)** $294 **19.** $10.25 profit **21.** $2.01 profit **23.** $71.75 **25.** **(a)** 15%; **(b)** $103.50; **(c)** No, sale will result in profit of $3.60 **27.** $9.60 profit

Section 5.12

1. $1,410 **3.** $522.50 **5.** $494 **7.** $2,304.50 **9.** $1,447.60 **11.** $1,339.50

Section 5.13

1. $46,840 **3.** $80,614.80 **5.** $236,492 **7.** $15,039 **9.** $59,455.20 **11.** $17,590 **13.** 1.6 **15.** 4.2 **17.** 16.7

Chapter 5 review test

1. List price **2.** Overhead **3.** Trade discount **4.** 55% **5.** Markdown **6.** $15 **7.** $32.67 **8.** $590.38 **9.** October 21 **10.** $91.98 **11.** 23% **12.** 29% **13.** $15.90 profit **14.** **(a)** $62.40; **(b)** $62.10 **15.** $34,850 **16.** 4.3

Chapter 6

Section 6.2A

1. $846.15 **3.** $823.08 **5.** $3,692.31 **7.** $1,576.92 **9.** $339.23 **11.** $1,473.33 **13.** $1,235

Section 6.2B

1. $1,358.50 **3.** $1,065.54 **5.** $1,259.19 **7.** $130.60 **9.** 3/4%

11.

Month	Net Sales	Commission	Draw Advance	Draw Deficit Brought Forward	Gross Earnings	Draw Deficit Carried Forward
Jan.	$5,200	$468.00	$107.00	$ 0.00	$575.00	$107.00
Feb.	6,850	616.50	0.00	107.00	575.00	65.50
March	8,450	760.50	0.00	65.50	695.00	0.00

13.

Month	Net Sales	Commission	Draw Advance	Draw Deficit Brought Forward	Gross Earnings	Draw Deficit Carried Forward
April	$ 8,842	$530.52	$19.48	$70.00	$550.00	$89.48
May	11,540	692.40	0.00	89.48	602.92	0.00
June	12,760	765.60	0.00	0.00	765.60	0.00

15. $537.30 **17.** $526.80 **19.** $1,255.41 **21.** $370 **23.** $1,110.20 **25.** $433.94 **27.** $349.33, $379.96, $356.54, $426.40, $381.04

Section 6.2C

1. $228.60 **3.** $479.05 **5.** $60.48 **7.** $260 **9.** $250 **11.** $6.96 **13.** $275.20 **15.** $266 **17.** $216.92 **19.** **(a)** $38.40; **(b)** $45.28

Section 6.3

1. $269.56 **3.** $980.40 **5.** $498.40 **7.** $477.40 **9.** $222.50 **11.** $249.60 **13.** $313.50 **15.** $320.45 **17.** $290.16 **19.** $382.20 **21.** $240.80

Section 6.4

1. $21.00 **3.** $42.00 **5.** $6.00 **7.** $32.00 **9.** $11.00 **11.** $50.00 **13.** (a) $144.42; (b) 25 **15.** $28.73 **17.** $254.50 **19.** $190.48 **21.** March, $848.65; November, $943.25

Section 6.5

1. (a) $58.04; (b) $3,018.08 **3.** (a) $210.28; (b) $7,209.60 **5.** $18,662 **7.** $2,898 **9.** (a) $2,217.78; (b) $1,084.98

Section 6.6

1. $193.79 **3.** $2,804.89 **5.** $699.66 **7.** $2,343.15 **9.** $1,215.29 **11.** Stub no. 87: balance carried forward = $909.21 **13.** Adjusted balance = $381.84 **15.** Adjusted balance = $3,188.31 **17.** Adjusted balance = $2,029.13 **19.** Final check register balance = $536.52; final bank statement balance = $697.85; adjusted balance = $191.34

Chapter 6 review test

1. $1,033.85 **2.** $2,361

3.

Month	Net Sales	Commission	Draw Advance	Draw Deficit Brought Forward	Gross Earnings	Draw Deficit Carried Forward
Jan.	$ 9,422	$ 753.76	$46.24	$ 60.00	$ 800.00	$106.24
Feb.	11,112	888.96	0.00	106.24	800.00	17.28
March	12,748	1,019.84	0.00	17.28	1,002.56	0.00

4. $1,142.80 **5.** $211.60 **6.** $1,076.40 **7.** $185.72 **8.** $16,422 **9.** Adjusted balance = $324.94 **10.** Adjusted balance = $498.64

Chapter 7

Sections 7.2–7.4

1. Sales—$870,000; Total Revenue—$960,900; Operating Expenses—$122,000; Total Expenses—$868,700; Net Income—$92,200.
3. Cost of Goods Sold—$900,000; Salaries—$215,000; Net income—$90,000
5. Net Sales—100.0%; Cost of Sales—83.3%; Depreciation—2.2%; Maintenance—1.4%; Total Cost and Operating Expenses—$391,000, 86.9%; Operating Income—$59,000, 13.1%; Interest Expense—1.0%; Federal Taxes—1.6%; Net Income—$47,300, 10.5%.
7. Sales—91.6%; Rentals—7.5%; Interest—0.9%; Total income—$797,000, 100.0%; Cost of Merchandise—67.8%; Operating Expenses—11.5%; Interest Expenses—0.8%; Taxes—5.8%; Total Expenses—$684,000, 85.8%; Net Income—$113,000, 14.2%.
9. Cash—7.4%; Accounts Receivable—22.4%; Inventory—$230,000, 28.0%; Total Current Assets—57.9%; Land and Equipment—42.1%; Total Assets—$820,000, 100.0%; Accounts Payable—22.0%; Accrued Liabilities—3.2%; Bonds Payable—11.0%; Common Stock—36.6%; Retained Earnings—27.3%; Total Equities—$820,000, 100.0%.
11. Net Sales—$80,000, 21.6%; Cost of Sales—$70,000, 29.2%; Depreciation—$1,800, 29.0%; Maintenance—$400, 8.3%; Total Cost and Operating Expenses—$72,200, 28.8%; Operating Income—$7,800, 6.6%; Interest Expense—$2,000, 16.7%; Federal Taxes—$4,000, 22.2%; Net Income—$1,800, 2.0%.
13. 1990: Total Current Assets—$40,426,000; Total Assets—$40,536,000; Total Current Liabilities—$24,342,000; Total Liabilities—$30,556,000; Total Stockholders' Equity—$9,980,000; Total Liabilities and Stockholders' Equity—$40,536,000.
1989: Total Current Assets—$35,796,000; Total Assets—$35,866,000; Total Current Liabilities—$20,816,000; Total Liabilities—$26,286,000; Total Stockholders' Equity—$9,580,000; Total Liabilities and Stockholders' Equity—$35,866,000.
Increase or Decrease—Amount (top to bottom): ($890,000); 2,600,000; 370,000; 2,550,000; 4,630,000; 40,000; 4,670,000; 1,600,000; 500,000; 624,000; 802,000; 3,526,000; 744,000; 4,270,000; 900,000; (500,000); 400,000; 4,670,000.
Increase or Decrease—Percent (top to bottom): (21.7); 28.6; 4.4; 18.0; 12.9; 57.1; 13.0; 11.3; 22.7; 18.0; 77.1; 16.9; 13.6; 16.2; 10.2; (67.6); 4.2; 13.0.

Percent of Total Assets—1990 (top to bottom): 7.9; 28.9; 21.6; 41.3; 99.7; 0.3; 100.0; 38.7; 6.7; 10.1; 4.5; 60.1; 15.3; 75.4; 24.0; 0.6; 24.6; 100.0.

Percent of Total Assets—1989 (top to bottom): 11.5; 25.4; 23.4; 39.6; 99.8; 0.2; 100.0; 39.3; 6.1; 9.7; 2.9; 58.0; 15.3; 73.3; 24.6; 2.1; 26.7; 100.0.

Section 7.5

1. 2.4:1 **3.** Current ratio = 2.7:1; acid-test ratio = 1.4:1 **5.** Gross profit margin = 41%; operating ratio = 96% **7.** 70% **9.** Stockholder's equity ratio = 60%; debt-equity ratio = 38% **11.** Total current assets = $82,250; total current liabilities = $25,150; land = $19,700; total assets = $184,450; retained earnings = $4,900; net income = $39,000; interest charges = $2,400 **13.** Gross profit margin = 44%; operating ratio = 85% **15.** 31%

Section 7.6

1. Total Available Cash, $63,600; Total Disbursements, $58,660; Excess of Cash, $4,940; Borrowed Funds Needed, $0; Repayment of Borrowed Funds, $0; Interest, $0; Total Financing, $0; Cash Balance, End of Month, $4,940
3. Total Available Cash, $58,600; Total Disbursements, $58,160; Excess of Cash, $440; Borrowed Funds Needed, $1,560; Repayment of Borrowed Funds, $0; Interest, $0; Total Financing, $1,560; Cash Balance, End of Month, $2,000
5. Total Available Cash, $128,400; Total Disbursements, $128,450; Deficiency of Cash, ($50); Borrowed Funds Needed, $15,050; Repayment of Borrowed Funds, $0; Interest, $0; Total Financing, $15,050; Cash Balance, End of Month, $15,000
7. Total Available Cash, $123,600; Total Disbursements, $107,450; Excess of Cash, $16,150; Borrowed Funds Needed, $0; Repayment of Borrowed Funds, $0; Interest, $0; Total Financing, $0; Cash Balance, End of Month, $16,150
9. Total Available Cash, $52,600; Total Disbursements, $56,400; Deficiency of Cash, ($3,800); Borrowed Funds Needed, $6,300; Repayment of Borrowed Funds, $0; Interest, $0; Total Financing, $6,300; Cash Balance, End of Month, $2,500
11. Beginning Cash Balance: $2,500. Receipts: Cash sales, $20,800; Accounts Receivable Collections, $57,000; Total Available Cash, $80,300. Disbursements: Materials Purchased, $7,600; Payroll, $20,000; Rent, $2,100; Other Expenses, $2,520; Equipment Purchase, $0; Total Disbursements, $32,220. Excess of Cash, $48,080. Financing: Borrowed Funds Needed, $0; Repayment of Borrowed Funds ($43,660); Interest, ($350); Total Financing, ($44,010). Cash Balance, End of Month, $4,070
13. Beginning Cash Balance: $1,000. Receipts: Cash sales, $15,000; Accounts Receivable Collections, $13,000; Collection of Notes Receivable, $0; Total Available Cash, $29,000. Disbursements: Manufacturing Expenses, $20,000; Selling and Administrative Expenses, $11,100; Equipment Purchase, $0; Total Disbursements, $31,100. Deficiency of Cash, ($2,100). Financing: Borrowed Funds Needed, $3,100; Repayment of Borrowed Funds, $0; Interest, $0; Total Financing, $3,100. Cash Balance, End of Month, $1,000
15. Cash Sales, $50,000; Total Disbursements, $134,450; Excess of Cash, $13,050; Borrowed Funds Needed, $0; Repayment of Borrowed Funds, $0; Interest, $0; Total Financing, $0; Cash Balance, End of Month, $13,050
17. Beginning Cash Balance: $10,000. Receipts: Cash sales, $63,750; Accounts Receivable Collections, $84,500; Total Available Cash, $158,250. Disbursements: Merchandise Purchases, $84,000; Payroll, $22,950; Utilities, $1,100; Advertising, $14,400; Taxes, $0; Other Expenses, $2,400; Total Disbursements, $124,850; Excess of Cash, $33,400. Financing: Borrowed Funds Needed, $0; Repayment of Borrowed Funds, ($18,300); Interest, ($124); Total Financing, ($18,424). Cash Balance, End of Month, $14,976

Section 7.7

1. $6,920 **3.** First year, $1,850; Third year, $1,776 **5.** First year, $124,930.32; Sixth year, $77,983.10 **7.** First year, $3,166.35; Second year, $4,222.75; Third year, $1,406.95; Fourth year, $703.95 **9.** First year, $643.05; Second year, $1,102.05; Third year, $787.05; Fourth year, $562.05; Fifth year, $401.85; Sixth year, $401.40, Seventh year, $401.85, Eighth year, $200.70 **11.** First year, $3,180; Second year, $4,664; Third year through fifth years, $4,452 **13.** First year, $1,269; Second year, $1,861.20; Third year through fifth years, $1,776.60 **15.** First year, $309,600; Tenth year, $348,300 **17.** First year, $3,744; Eighth year, $4,212 **19.** First year, $25,717.07; Fifth year, $26,841.45; Fourteenth year, $26,841.45

Section 7.8

1. $900 **3.** $2,437.50

5.

Year	Depreciation	Accumulated Depreciation	Book Value
0	—	—	$18,000.00
1	$3,600.00	$ 3,600.00	14,400.00
2	2,880.00	6,480.00	11,520.00
3	2,304.00	8,784.00	9,216.00
4	1,843.20	10,627.20	7,372.80
5	1,474.56	12,101.76	5,898.24
6	1,179.65	13,281.41	4,718.59

7.

Year	Depreciation	Accumulated Depreciation	Book Value
0	—	—	$36,000.00
1	$5,400.00	$ 5,400.00	30,600.00
2	4,590.00	9,990.00	26,010.00
3	3,901.50	13,891.50	22,108.50
4	3,316.28	17,207.78	18,792.22
5	2,818.83	20,026.61	15,973.39
6	2,396.01	22,422.62	13,577.38
7	2,036.61	24,459.23	11,540.77
8	1,731.12	26,190.35	9,809.65

9.

Year	Depreciation	Accumulated Depreciation	Book Value
0	—	—	$16,000.00
1	$3,111.11	$ 3,111.11	12,888.89
2	2,722.22	5,833.33	10,166.67
3	2,333.33	8,166.66	7,833.34
4	1,944.44	10,111.10	5,888.90
5	1,555.56	11,666.66	4,333.34
6	1,166.67	12,833.33	3,166.67
7	777.78	13,611.11	2,388.89
8	388.89	14,000.00	2,000.00

11. (a)

Year	Depreciation	Accumulated Depreciation	Book Value
0	—	—	$10,000
1	$1,200	$1,200	8,800
2	1,200	2,400	7,600
3	1,200	3,600	6,400
4	1,200	4,800	5,200
5	1,200	6,000	4,000

11. (b)

Year	Depreciation	Accumulated Depreciation	Book Value
0	—	—	$10,000.00
1	$1,600.00	$1,600.00	8,400.00
2	1,344.00	2,944.00	7,056.00
3	1,128.96	4,072.96	5,927.04
4	948.33	5,021.29	4,978.71
5	796.59	5,817.88	4,182.12

11. (c)

Year	Depreciation	Accumulated Depreciation	Book Value
0	—	—	$10,000
1	$2,000	$2,000	8,000
2	1,600	3,600	6,400
3	1,200	4,800	5,200
4	800	5,600	4,400
5	400	6,000	4,000

13. Twice the straight-line rate is $\frac{2}{n}$ or $\frac{2}{5} = 40\%$

Year	**Depreciation**	**Accumulated Depreciation**	**Book Value**
0	—	—	$8,000.00
1	$3,200.00	$3,200.00	4,800.00
2	1,920.00	5,120.00	2,880.00
3	1,152.00	6,272.00	1,728.00
4	691.20	6,963.20	1,036.80
5	414.72	7,377.92	622.08

15. $d = \frac{c - s}{n} = \frac{\$15,000 - \$5,000}{8} = \$1,250$

Year	Depreciation	Accumulated Depreciation	Book Value
0	—	—	$15,000
1	$1,250	$ 1,250	13,750
2	1,250	2,500	12,500
3	1,250	3,750	11,250
4	1,250	5,000	10,000
5	1,250	6,250	8,750
6	1,250	7,500	7,500
7	1,250	8,750	6,250
8	1,250	10,000	5,000

17. $d = (c - s) \times r$

Year	Depreciation	Accumulated Depreciation	Book Value
0	—	—	$15,000.00
1	$2,222.22 ($10,000 × 8/36)	$ 2,222.22	12,777.78
2	1,944.44 ($10,000 × 7/36)	4,166.66	10,833.34
3	1,666.67 ($10,000 × 6/36)	5,833.33	9,166.67
4	1,388.89 ($10,000 × 5/36)	7,222.22	7,777.78
5	1,111.11 ($10,000 × 4/36)	8,333.33	6,666.67
6	833.33 ($10,000 × 3/36)	9,166.66	5,833.34
7	555.56 ($10,000 × 2/36)	9,722.22	5,277.78
8	277.78 ($10,000 × 1/36)	10,000.00	5,000.00

19. **(a)** $2,340; **(b)** $2,860 **21.** **(a)** First year, $2,040; Second year, $1,615; **(b)** $12,595

Section 7.9

1. Offices, $1,550; accounting, $4,650; production, $24,800; warehouse, $31,000 **3.** Clothing, $845.25; hardware, $431.25; appliances, $552.00; toys, $224.25; home furnishings, $707.25 **5.** Office supplies, $910.00; furnishings, $625.63; floor coverings, $422.50; office machines, $1,291.88 **7.** Office equipment, $1,513.08; business forms, $302.62; furnishings, $2,005.91; art supplies, $406.37; chemicals, $1,392.03 **9.** Jackson, $1,631.25; Peters, $4,350.00; Adams, $2,718.25 **11.** Barrett, $49,049.60; other partners (each), $9,196.80 **13.** Criswell, $26,428.57; Davis, $66,071.43; Meyer, $92,500.00 **15.** Foster, $5,022.50; Thomas, $5,022.50; Harvey, $2,870.00; Daniels, $1,435.00 **17.** A, $95,435; B, $93,435; C, $63,935; D, $63,935 **19.** **(a)** Kessler, $4,800; Schneider, $7,200; **(b)** Kessler, $3,600; Schneider, $5,400

Chapter 7 review test

1. Accounts receivable = $36,000; total fixed assets = $499,000; total assets = $566,000; total current liabilities = $62,000; total liabilities = $262,000; total equities = $566,000 **2.** 0.8:1 **3.** 54% **4.** 86% **5.** First year, $2,300; second year, $3,496; third year, $3,404 **6.** 1st year, $28,510.00; 2nd year, $45,616.00; 3rd year, $27,369.60; 4th year, $16,421.76; 5th year, $16,421.76; 6th year, $8,210.88 **7.** 40% **8.** $2,125 **9.** $6,000 **10.** Lombardi, $27,720; Berra, $16,280 **11.** Cash Sales, $12,500; Total Disbursements, $30,000; Deficiency of Cash, ($300); Borrowed Funds Needed, $1,800; Repayment of Borrowed Funds, $0; Interest, $0; Total Financing, $1,800; Cash Balance, End of Month, $1,500

Chapter 8

Sections 8.2 and 8.3

1. (**a**) $27.41; (**b**) $27.42 **3.** (**a**) $13.92; (**b**) $3.73 **5.** (**a**) $26.86; (**b**) $27.39 **7.** $0.78 **9.** (**a**) $661.30; (**b**) $29.76 **11.** (**a**) $156.00; (**b**) $2,599.95 **13.** $1,449.42

Section 8.4

1. (**a**) 2.75%; (**b**) $27.50; (**c**) 28 mills **3.** (**a**) 1.96%; (**b**) $19.60; (**c**) 20 mills **5.** (**a**) 2.17%; (**b**) $2.17; (**c**) $21.70; (**d**) 22 mills **7.** (**a**) $4,471.20; (**b**) $3,864.00 **9.** (**a**) $7,115.04; (**b**) $9,331.20 **11.** $650,000 **13.** (**a**) 1.80%; (**b**) 18 mills **15.** $65,000

Section 8.5

1. $24,227 **3.** $47,638 **5.** $50,862 **7.** $27,760 **9.** $23,359 **11.** $19,205 **13.** $5,070.90 **15.** $3,289.02 **17.** $8,964.90 **19.** $12,462.90 **21.** $6,634.70

Chapter 8 review test

1. Excise **2.** Assessed value **3.** Mill **4.** Adjusted gross income **5.** Standard deduction **6.** $4.20 **7.** $48.83 **8.** $3.33 **9.** $83.17 **10.** $9,721.60 **11.** $30,530 **12.** $20,845

Chapter 9

Section 9.2

1. $7,500 **3.** 16% **5.** $7,200 **7.** 11.5% **9.** $2,500.00 **11.** 1/4 year **13.** $120 **15.** $65.63 **17.** $128.13 **19.** $6,000 **21.** 12.5% **23.** 14.5% **25.** $1,884.38 **27.** No, interest would be $715 **29.** $16\frac{2}{3}\%$

Section 9.3

1. 215 **3.** 113 **5.** 156 **7.** 281 **9.** 303 **11.** August 24 **13.** October 16 **15.** May 11 **17.** August 23 **19.** May 11

Section 9.4

1. (**a**) $234.25; (**b**) $237.50 **3.** (**a**) $70.52; (**b**) $71.50 **5.** (**a**) $60.41; (**b**) $61.25 **7.** (**a**) $113.42; (**b**) $115.00 **9.** (**a**) $168.29; (**b**) $170.63 **11.** (**a**) $305.41; (**b**) $309.65 **13.** (**a**) $222.99; (**b**) $226.09 **15.** (**a**) $279.78; (**b**) $283.67 **17.** 9% **19.** 16% **21.** $9\frac{1}{2}\%$ **23.** $15\frac{1}{4}\%$ **25.** $9\frac{1}{4}\%$ **27.** 60 days **29.** 300 days **31.** 150 days **33.** $8,000 **35.** $2,500 **37.** $4,200 **39.** $5,600 **41.** 48.98% **43.** 16.32% **45.** 94.74% **47.** (**a**) $485.00; (**b**) $11.77 **49.** (**a**) $766.85; (**b**) $5.11

Section 9.5

1. $3,300 **3.** $3,714 **5.** $1,694 **7.** $1,857.92 **9.** $2,400 **11.** $1,500 **13.** $2,800 **15.** $3,739.05 **17.** $2,587.50 **19.** $4,112.50 **21.** $2,758.62 **23.** $2,350.06 **25.** $20,000 now **27.** $1,000 now and $700 in six months **29.** 12% **31.** 14 months

Chapter 9 review test

1. $70 **2.** $3,200 **3.** 11.25% **4.** Three months **5.** $23.75 **6.** 165 days **7.** 55.67% **8.** $769.73 **9.** $5,647.06 **10.** $1,000 now and $550 in six months

Chapter 10

Section 10.2

1. $1,500, $3,500 **3.** $394.40, $2,325.60 **5.** $132.19, $2,117.81 **7.** $257.55, $2,617.45 **9.** $737.44, $3,537.56 **11.** $20.58, $1,879.42 **13.** $23.91, $1,326.09 **15.** $58.97, $1,291.03 **17.** $1,875, $5,625 **19.** $1,245.42, $10,754.58 **21.** (**a**) $344.50; (**b**) $9,655.50 **23.** $510.62

Section 10.3

1. 3 **3.** $8\frac{1}{2}\%$ **5.** 11% **7.** $2,700 **9.** $20 **11.** $2,200 **13.** $4,252.50 **15.** $1,067.02 **17.** $6,382.98 **19.** $8\frac{1}{2}\%$ **21.** 12.80%

Section 10.4

1. $3,037.05, $37.05 **3.** $184.17, $655.83 **5.** $2,792.99, $7.01, $127.57 **7.** $3,639.88, $113.32 **9.** $1,568.00, $24.78 **11.** No

Section 10.5

1. 9.52% **3.** 13.53% **5.** 9.99% **7.** 12.68% **9.** 6.90% **11.** 8.47% **13.** 11.89% **15.** 9.30% **17.** 11.28% **19.** Friend **21.** Other sources

Chapter 10 review test

1. (**a**) $67.50; (**b**) $2,632.50 **2.** Discount = $26; proceeds = $1,574 **3.** $3,750 **4.** 9% **5.** $918.33 **6.** $1,684.38 **7.** 12.37% **8.** 11.11% **9.** (**a**) $873; (**b**) $22.61 **10.** $843.87

Chapter 11

Section 11.2

1. $5\frac{1}{2}\%$ **3.** 1% **5.** $6\frac{1}{2}\%$ **7.** $1\frac{1}{4}\%$ **9.** $5\frac{1}{4}\%$ **11.** $332.80 **13.** $434.70 **15.** $172.41 **17.** $275.10 **19.** $96.44 **21.** $883.05 **23.** $2,072.05 **25.** $3,128.04 **27.** 10% compounded annually

Sections 11.3 and 11.4

1. $2,508.80, $508.80 **3.** $771.88, $171.88 **5.** $1,748.93, $148.93 **7.** $30.38 **9.** $435.11 **11.** $485.95 **13.** $413.87 **15.** $23,836.57 **17.** 18 years **19.** 30 months **21.** 10% **23.** 12% **25.** 8% **27.** $39,019.03 **29.** $53,435.67 **31.** $37.89 **33.** $733.50

Section 11.5

1. $3,168.37 **3.** $2,024.91 **5.** $459.84 **7.** $2,446.81 **9.** $730.07 **11.** $1,700 **13.** $9,658.92 **15.** Program B **17.** First proposal

Section 11.6

1. $820.24 **3.** $768.47 **5.** $1,535.34 **7.** $1,564.86 **9.** $843.83 **11.** $510.66 **13.** $2,829.49 **15.** $612.97 **17.** $1,009.52 **19.** $3,175.44 **21.** $976.86 **23.** $1,684.61 **25.** $2,249.42 **27.** 10% compounded semiannually

Section 11.7

1. 10.25% **3.** 12.55% **5.** 16.08% **7.** 9.20% **9.** 10.38% **11.** 11% **13.** 13% **15.** 15%

Chapter 11 review test

1. **(a)** $2\frac{1}{2}\%$; **(b)** 3/4%; **(c)** $6\frac{1}{2}\%$; **(d)** $2\frac{1}{4}\%$ **2.** $1,011.24 **3.** A = $3,600.44; I = $1,000.44 **4.** $20,937.11 **5.** $3\frac{3}{4}$ years **6.** $808.13 **7.** 8.24% **8.** Program B

Chapter 12

Section 12.2

1. $282.79 **3.** $2,072.45 **5.** $2,216.75 **7.** $236.50 **9.** $2,284.44 **11.** $3,655.04

Section 12.5

1. $100.60, $8.20 **3.** $44.10, $7.58 **5.** $59.35, $26.72 **7.** $155.05 **9.** $59.93 **11.** $139.89 **13.** **(a)** May 1; **(b)** March 18, $116.40; March 26, $148.97 **15.** **(a)** December 25; **(b)** November 10, $116.63; November 18, $155.67; November 24, $180.67 **17.** **(a)** October 7; **(b)** August 16, $0.00; August 19, $89.35; August 25, $114.35; September 3, $131.19 **19.** $194.25 **21.** $543.20 **23.** $87.33 **25.** $273.08, $4.23 **27.** $314.41, $5.66 **29.** $228.15, $3.71 **31.** $223.64 **33.** $116.42

Section 12.6

1. **(a)** $117.32; **(b)** $999.46; **(c)** $49.97 **3.** **(a)** $99.24; **(b)** $1,151.42; **(c)** $83.45 **5.** **(a)** $187.28; **(b)** $1,799.54; **(c)** $87.47 **7.** **(a)** $492.34; **(b)** $3,763.94; **(c)** $141.19 **9.** **(a)** $865.17; **(b)** $5,104.62; **(c)** $127.40 **11.** **(a)** $436.25; **(b)** $599.40; **(c)** $88.15 **13.** **(a)** $375.92; **(b)** $438.86; **(c)** $17.68 **15.** **(a)** $952.00; **(b)** $1,392.34; **(c)** $268.16 **17.** **(a)** $882.23; **(b)** $1,117.10; **(c)** $124.15 **19.** **(a)** $2,528.30; **(b)** $3,593.37; **(c)** $701.26 **21.** **(a)** $245.62; **(b)** $2,408.95; **(c)** $104.39

Sections 12.7 and 12.8

1. 15% **3.** 30% **5.** 21.6% **7.** 16.25% **9.** 14.75% **11.** 11.00% **13.** 14.50% **15.** 17.00% **17.** 15.50% **19.** 12.00% **21.** 13.44% **23.** 17.32% **25.** 12.48% **27.** **(a)** 14.75%; **(b)** 15.45%

Section 12.9

1. $21.54 **3.** $0.92 **5.** $6.15 **7.** $23.16 **9.** $12.86 **11.** $8.72 **13.** $11.24 **15.** $299.69

Chapter 12 review test

1. F **2.** F **3.** T **4.** T **5.** T **6.** $435.96 **7.** $235.39 **8.** $4.78 **9.** **(a)** $101.51; **(b)** $741.46; **(c)** $37.64 **10.** **(a)** $24.12; **(b)** $377.38

Chapter 13

Section 13.3

1. $2,389.66 **3.** $7,039.92 **5.** $25,499.88 **7.** $22,905.17 **9.** $398,333.30 **11.** $74,933.70 **13.** $227,338.53 **15.** $181,425.37 **17.** $185,717.87 **19.** $1,689,328.79 **21.** $7,623.42, $14,759.63 **23.** $12,190.17, $33,203.48 **25.** $6,961.50, $14,230.76

Section 13.4

1. $2,401.22 **3.** $25,451.71 **5.** $3,223.16 **7.** $5,412.41 **9.** $43,466.97 **11.** 30 **13.** 360 months or 30 years **15.** 36 months, $1,415.38 **17.** 20 quarterly payments or 5 years, $5,673.18 **19.** $12,894.73, $894.73

Section 13.5

1. \$10,432.23 **3.** \$9,859.49 **5.** \$3,094.11 **7.** \$60,277.17 **9.** \$52,202.39 **11.** 47 **13.** \$18,677.74 **15.** 44 **17.** \$5,167.04

Section 13.6

1. \$7,115.19 **3.** \$8,740.45 **5.** \$9,135.89 **7.** \$9,552.30 **9.** \$23,180.85 **11.** \$9,535.12 **13.** 9 years **15.** (**a**) \$6,569.83; (**b**) \$6,701.23 **17.** \$5,276.98 **19.** \$529,297.78

Section 13.7

1. \$3,229.88 **3.** \$8,620.71 **5.** \$8,854.66 **7.** \$7,276.12 **9.** \$30,181.45 **11.** (**a**) \$50,191.61; (**b**) \$52,952.14 **13.** \$3,644.70 **15.** \$621.75 **17.** \$38,309.50

Chapter 13 review test

1. \$5,596.85 **2.** \$51,015.87 **3.** Annuity Due **4.** 48 months **5.** \$13,033.56 **6.** \$1,125.69 **7.** 21 **8.** \$3,480.96 **9.** \$551,847.82 **10.** \$679.68

Chapter 14

Section 14.2

1. \$2,880.97 **3.** \$2,869.22 **5.** \$388.80

7.

Period	Accumulated Amount	Interest	Payment	Accumulated Amount
1	—	—	\$2,563.22	\$ 2,563.22
2	\$ 2,563.22	\$ 51.26	2,563.22	5,177.70
3	5,177.70	103.55	2,563.22	7,844.47
4	7,844.47	156.89	2,563.22	10,564.58
5	10,564.58	211.29	2,563.22	13,339.09
6	13,339.09	266.78	2,563.22	16,169.09
7	16,169.09	323.38	2,563.22	19,055.69
8	19,055.69	381.11	2,563.22	22,000.02
Total		\$1,494.26		

9.

Period	Accumulated Amount	Interest	Payment	Accumulated Amount
1	—	—	\$1,300.39	\$1,300.39
2	\$1,300.39	\$ 13.00	1,300.39	2,613.78
3	2,613.78	26.14	1,300.39	3,940.31
4	3,940.31	39.40	1,300.39	5,280.10
5	5,280.10	52.80	1,300.39	6,633.29
6	6,633.29	66.33	1,300.39	8,000.01
Total		\$197.67		

11.

Period	Accumulated Amount	Interest	Payment	Accumulated Amount
1	—	—	$6,848.89	$ 6,848.89
2	$ 6,848.89	$ 171.22	6,848.89	13,869.00
3	13,869.00	346.73	6,848.89	21,064.62
4	21,064.62	526.62	6,848.89	28,440.13
5	28,440.13	711.00	6,848.89	36,000.02
Total		$1,755.57		

13.

Period	Accumulated Amount	Interest	Payment	Accumulated Amount
1	—	—	$2,073.72	$ 2,073.72
2	$ 2,073.72	$ 207.37	2,073.72	4,354.81
3	4,354.81	435.48	2,073.72	6,864.01
4	6,864.01	686.40	2,073.72	9,624.13
5	9,624.13	962.41	2,073.72	12,660.26
6	12,660.26	1,266.03	2,073.72	16,000.01

15.

Period	Accumulated Amount	Interest	Payment	Accumulated Amount
1	—	—	$6,694.41	$ 6,694.41
2	$ 6,694.41	$ 167.36	6,694.41	13,556.18
3	13,556.18	338.90	6,694.41	20,589.49
4	20,589.49	514.74	6,694.41	27,798.64
5	27,798.64	694.97	6,694.41	35,188.02
6	35,188.02	879.70	6,694.41	42,762.13
7	42,762.13	1,069.05	6,694.41	50,525.59
8	50,525.59	1,263.14	6,694.41	58,483.14
9	58,483.24	1,462.08	6,694.41	66,639.63
10	66,639.73	1,665.99	6,694.41	75,000.03

17. $25,182.82 **19.** $343.66

Section 14.3

1. $737.16 **3.** $932.45 **5.** $238.50

7.

Period	Amount of Debt	Payment	Interest	Applied to Principal	Remaining Debt
1	$5,250.00	$1,585.08	$420.00	$1,165.08	$4,084.92
2	4,084.92	1,585.08	326.79	1,258.29	2,826.63
3	2,826.63	1,585.08	226.13	1,358.95	1,467.68
4	1,467.68	1,585.08	117.41	1,467.67	0.01

9.

Period	Amount of Debt	Payment	Interest	Applied to Principal	Remaining Debt
1	$3,200.00	$451.07	$88.00	$363.07	$2,836.93
2	2,836.93	451.07	78.02	373.05	2,463.88
3	2,463.88	451.07	67.76	383.31	2,080.57
4	2,080.57	451.07	57.22	393.85	1,686.72
5	1,686.72	451.07	46.38	404.69	1,282.03
6	1,282.03	451.07	35.26	415.81	866.22
7	866.22	451.07	23.82	427.25	438.97
8	438.97	451.07	12.07	439.00	—0.03

11.

Period	Amount of Debt	Payment	Interest	Applied to Principal	Remaining Debt
1	$8,700.00	$760.83	$65.25	$695.58	$8,004.42
2	8,004.42	760.83	60.03	700.80	7,303.62
3	7,303.62	760.83	54.78	706.05	6,597.57
4	6,597.57	760.83	49.48	711.35	5,886.22
5	5,886.22	760.83	44.15	716.68	5,169.54
6	5,169.54	760.83	38.77	722.06	4,447.48
7	4,447.48	760.83	33.36	727.47	3,720.01
8	3,720.01	760.83	27.90	732.93	2,987.08
9	2,987.08	760.83	22.40	738.43	2,248.65
10	2,248.65	760.83	16.86	743.97	1,504.68
11	1,504.68	760.83	11.29	749.54	755.14
12	755.14	760.83	5.66	755.17	—0.03

13.

Period	Amount of Debt	Payment	Interest	Applied to Principal	Remaining Debt
1	$1,500.00	$423.02	$75.00	$348.02	$1,151.98
2	1,151.98	423.02	57.60	365.42	786.56
3	786.56	423.02	39.33	383.69	402.87
4	402.87	423.02	20.14	402.88	—0.01

15.

Period	Amount of Debt	Payment	Interest	Applied to Principal	Remaining Debt
1	$11,000.00	$1,583.59	$357.50	$1,226.09	$9,733.91
2	9,773.91	1,583.59	317.65	1,265.94	8,507.97
3	8,507.97	1,583.59	276.51	1,307.08	7,200.89
4	7,200.89	1,583.59	234.03	1,349.56	5,851.33
5	5,851.33	1,583.59	190.17	1,393.42	4,457.91
6	4,457.91	1,583.59	144.88	1,438.71	3,019.20
7	3,019.20	1,583.59	98.12	1,485.47	1,533.73
8	1,533.73	1,583.59	49.85	1,533.74	—0.01

17. $12,689.06 **19.** $13,404.82 **21.** $627.61 **23.** **(a)** $4,612.57; **(b)** $2,795.38; **(c)** $56,464.36

Chapter 14 review test

1. $5,565.68 **2.** (**a**) $2,907.69; (**b**) $333,692.40 **3.** $1,002.27 **4.** $2,406.36

5.

Period	Amount of Debt	Payment	Interest	Applied to Principal	Remaining Debt
1	$4,700.00	$925.98	$235.00	$690.98	$4,009.02
2	4,009.02	925.98	200.45	725.53	3,283.49
3	3,283.49	925.98	164.17	761.81	2,521.68
4	2,521.68	925.98	126.08	799.90	1,721.78
5	1,721.78	925.98	86.09	839.89	881.89
6	881.89	925.98	44.09	881.89	0.00

6. $2,404.16 **7.** (**a**) $5,723.95; (**b**) $26,062.20; (**c**) $226,062.20 **8.** $3,662.30

Chapter 15

Sections 15.2 and 15.3

1. $0.90 **3.** $45 **5.** $1.25 **7.** $750, $105, $855 **9.** $0.46

Sections 15.4 and 15.5

1. $920.40 **3.** $4,270.41 **5.** $52,050.60 **7.** $1,522.56 **9.** $2,200.55 **11.** $1,276.37 **13.** $14,847.20 **15.** $8,480.52 **17.** $479.29 **19.** $1,491.22 **21.** $772.01 owed **23.** $54.28 received

Section 15.6

1. $2.20 **3.** $2.04 **5.** 15:1 **7.** 14:1 **9.** 2.5% **11.** 8.6% **13.** 6.2%

Sections 15.7–15.9

1. $6,525 **3.** $6,015.04 **5.** $8,104.23 **7.** $8,530 **9.** $2,384.95 **11.** $3,099.59 **13.** $13,482.93 **15.** $16,583.97 **17.** $437.81

Section 15.10

1. 8.9% **3.** 9.3% **5.** 9.1% **7.** 8.9% **9.** 10.1% **11.** 9.8% **13.** 9.9% **15.** 13.7% **17.** NLL

Chapter 15 review test

1. Capital gain **2.** Preferred, common **3.** Price-earnings ratio **4.** Mortgage bond, debenture **5.** Financial risk, interest rates **6.** Round lot **7.** Triple A **8.** $0.64 **9.** $0.45 **10.** $3,850 **11.** $1,674.06 **12.** $2.32 **13.** 5.2% **14.** 10.4% **15.** $5,122.39

Chapter 16

Sections 16.2 and 16.3

1. $504.29 **3.** $476.57 **5.** $1,239.04 **7.** $160.91 **9.** $495.69 **11.** $101.18 **13.** $260.71 **15.** $790.52 **17.** $43.03 **19.** $114.29

Section 16.4

1. $3,099.60 **3.** $1,666.80 **5.** $2,687.50 **7.** $2,332.40 **9.** $2,484 **11.** $3,472.50 **13.** $1,940.25 **15.** $3,529.30 **17.** $99.36 **19.** $1,178.32 **21.** $1,059.24 **23.** $338.44 **25.** $1,790.88 **27.** $252.53 **29.** $1,012.54 **31.** $265.12

Sections 16.5–16.7

1. $14,108.40 **3.** $5,197.50 **5.** $23,433.30 **7.** $30,918.75; life **9.** $25,078; life **11.** $8,174.40; 17 yrs. **13.** $1,153.75 **15.** $188.50 **17.** $401.60 **19.** $945 **21.** $436.25 **23.** $581.10

Sections 16.8 and 16.9

1. $10.50 **3.** $7.70 **5.** Executives, $13.20; supervisors, $9.90; other employees, $6.60 **7.** $8.09 **9.** $3.95 **11.** $36.36

Sections 16.10 and 16.11

1. $32,500 **3.** $45,833.33 **5.** $130,000 **7.** **A:** $138,000; **B:** $69,000 **9.** $1,860 **11.** $859 **13.** $568.62 **15.** $88.80 **17.** $59.50 **19.** $702.80 **21.** $850.73

Sections 16.12 and 16.13

1. $257.40 **3.** $344.10 **5.** $223.85 **7.** $559 **9.** $515.20 **11.** $471.75 **13.** $358.40 **15.** $516.80 **17.** **(a)** $37,575; **(b)** $150,100 **19.** $13,475

Chapter 16 review test

1. Hazard **2.** Insuring agreement **3.** Ordinary life insurance **4.** Participating **5.** Reduced paid-up insurance **6.** Property damage liability **7.** Term insurance, cash value insurance **8.** $72.36 **9.** $198.56 **10.** $93,750 **11.** $301.55

Chapter 17

Section 17.2

1. 5, 9, 14, 15, 19, 21, 27, 33 **3.** 5, 8, 9, 12, 14, 15, 18, 19, 21, 23, 26, 27, 31, 33, 39, 43 **5.** 7, 8, 11, 12, 13, 15, 18, 23, 24, 26, 31, 32, 37, 39, 41, 43 **7.** Frequency: 3, 5, 5, 2, 1

9.

Frequency	Relative Frequency	Percent
4	0.25	25
5	0.3125	31.25
6	0.375	37.5
1	0.0625	6.25
0	0.0	0
16	1.0	

11.

Frequency	Cumulative Frequency
4	4
5	9
6	15
1	16
0	16

13.

Class	Frequency
0–4	1
5–9	4
10–14	3
15–19	2

15.

Frequency	Relative Frequency	Percent
1	0.1	10
4	0.4	40
3	0.3	30
2	0.2	20
10	1.0	

17.

Class	Frequency	Cumulative Frequency
380–399	2	2
400–419	1	3
420–439	3	6
440–459	0	6
460–479	3	9
480–499	1	10
500–519	2	12

19.

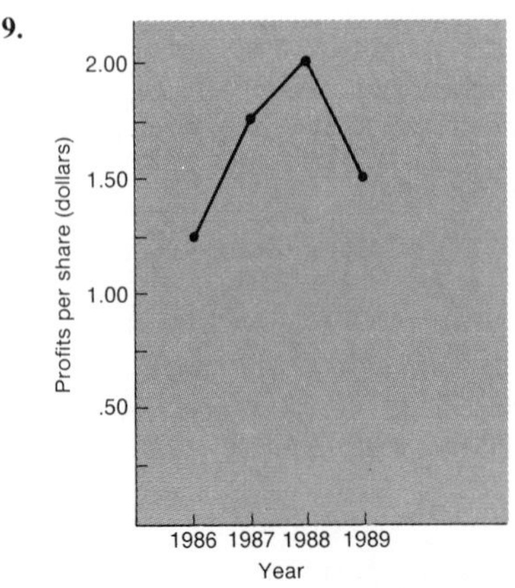

21. $7.50 per unit if 700 units are produced

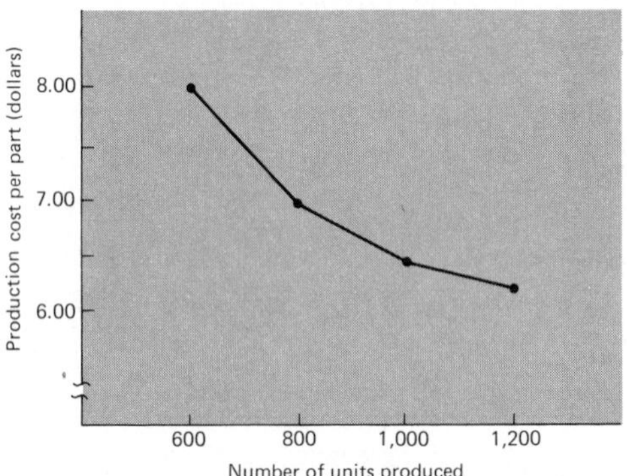

23. (a) 280, (b) 550, (c) 425

25.

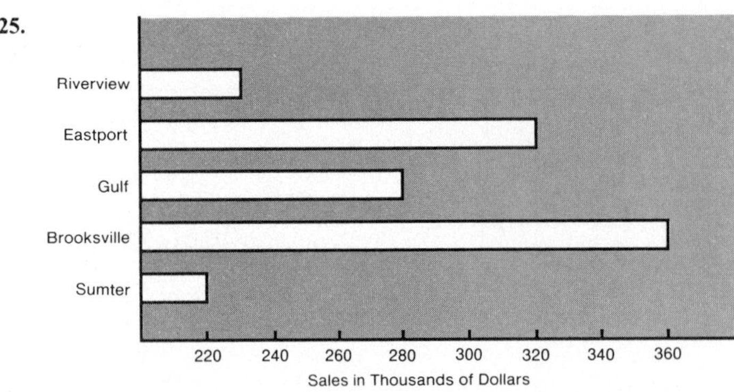

27.

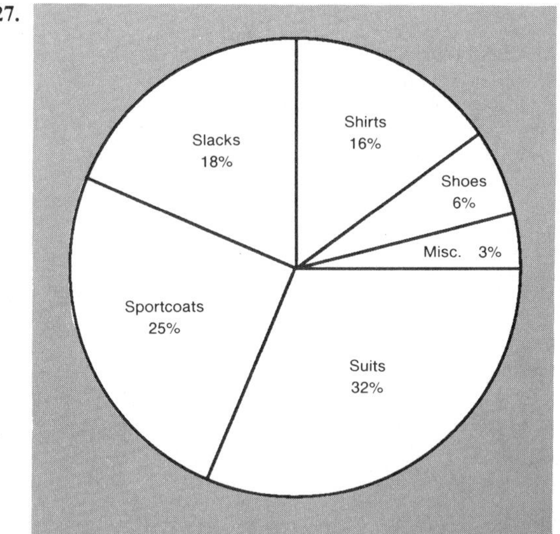

29.

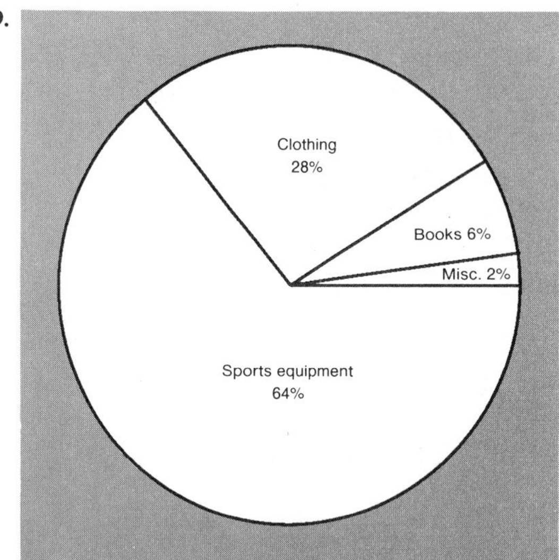

31.

33.

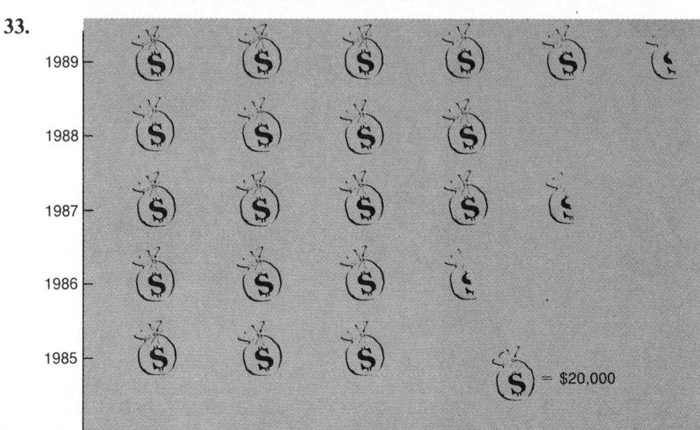

35. Graph C; Graph A—horizontal scale is too spread out; Graph B—vertical scale is too spread out and does not begin at zero **37.** Graph B **39.** Graph C; Graph A—horizontal scale is too compressed; Graph B—horizontal scale is too spread out and does not begin at zero

Section 17.3

1. 14 **3.** 20 **5.** 80 **7.** 332 **9.** 121 **11.** 12.09 **13.** 14 **15.** 14.5 **17.** 12 **19.** 13 **21.** Mean = 12.19; median = 12; mode: bimodal, 12, 14 **23.** $9,460 **25.** $47 **27.** Mean = $448.57; mode = $455

Section 17.4

1.

Class Midpoint (x_i)	f_ix_i
7	7
12	36
17	68
22	88
27	54
	253

Mean = 253/14 = 18.07

3.

Class Midpoint (x_i)	f_ix_i
4.5	9
14.5	43.5
24.5	49
34.5	138
44.5	44.5
	284

Mean = 284/12 = 23.67

5.

Class Midpoint (x_i)	f_ix_i
5	10
16	64
27	162
38	190
49	343
60	180
71	71
	1,020

Mean = 1,020/28 = 36.43

7. 20.5 **9.** 31.5 **11.** Modal class: 20–24; modal value: 22 **13.** Mean = 10.5; median = 11.36; modal class: 11–15 **15.** Mean = $5.37; median = $5.06; modal class: $4.00–$5.99

Section 17.5

1. 7.42 **3.** 3.61 **5.** 2.65 **7.** 2.83 **9.** **(a)** 27 students; **(b)** 38 students **11.** **(a)** 4 boxes; **(b)** 27 boxes

Section 17.6

1. 295 **3.** 225 **5.** **(a)** $117.80; **(b)** $91,217 **7.** 162 **9.** 129 **11.** 128

Chapter 17 review test

1. 0, 2, 3, 3, 4, 7, 7, 8, 8, 8, 8, 10, 10, 11, 12, 13, 14, 16; median = 8 **2.** 8 **3.** 8 **4.** Cumulative frequency: 4, 7, 14, 17, 18 **5.** 15.25 **6.** 15.5 **7.** 10–14 **8.** $\sqrt{10} = 3.16$ **9.** Student A: 100, 100, 100, 100, 0; Student B: 80, 80, 80, 80, 80 **10.** 475 **11.** 161 **12.** 183 **13.** 172

14.

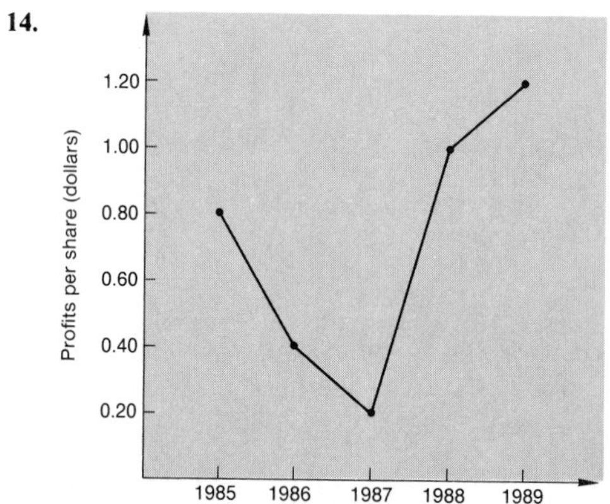

15.

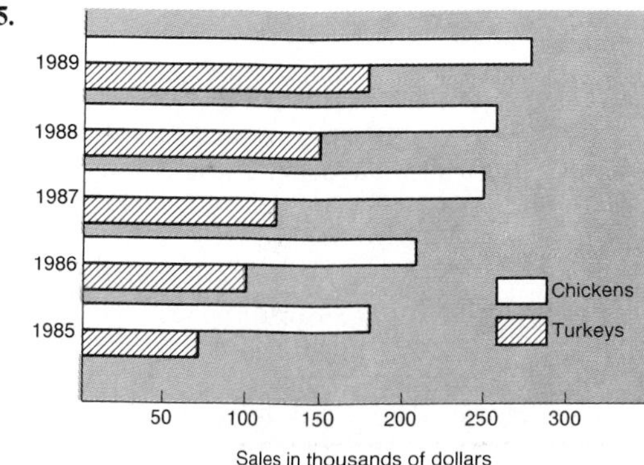

16.

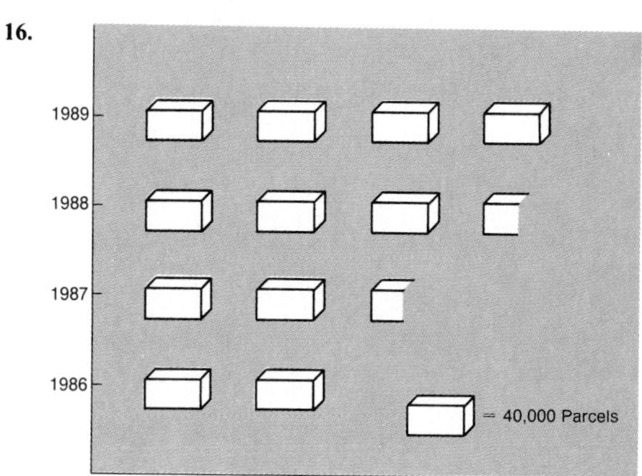

17.

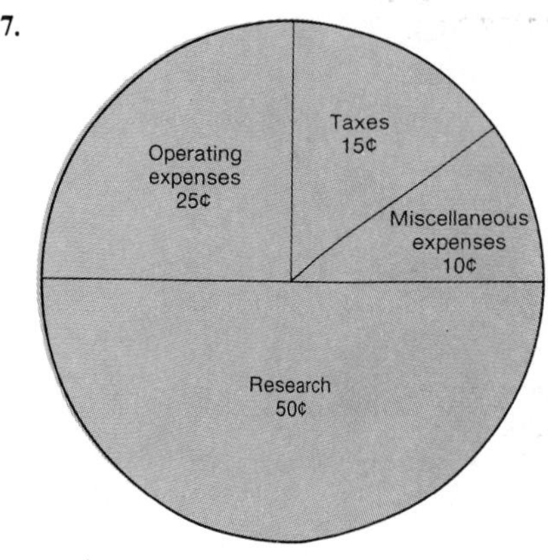

Chapter 18

Section 18.2

1. (**a**) 28,000 m; (**b**) 7.2 dkm **3.** (**a**) 7,210 m; (**b**) 705 cm **5.** (**a**) 15,700 dm; (**b**) 3,221.4 cm **7.** (**a**) 24 cm^2; (**b**) 140,000 ares **9.** 6.21 dkm, 0.621 hm **11.** 3.224 dkm, 322.4 dm **13.** 190,000 m^2, 1,900 ares **15.** (**a**) 7.42 dkm; (**b**) 0.742 hm **17.** (**a**) 20 cm long, 0.7 cm wide, lead is 0.2 cm thick; (**b**) 0.2 m long, 0.007 m wide, lead is 0.002 m thick **19.** $24.30 **21.** $662.64

Section 18.3

1. (**a**) 4,700 liters; (**b**) 27.42 kl **3.** (**a**) 2.71 liters; (**b**) 521 cl **5.** (**a**) 670 g; (**b**) 382.4 hg **7.** (**a**) 7,830 g; (**b**) 412.3 dg **9.** 4.2 dkl, 42,000 ml **11.** 2.7 hl, 27,000 cl **13.** 7,140 dg, 71.4 dkg **15.** Nine bottles **17.** 21 days **19.** 200 hours **21.** (**a**) 340 dkg; (**b**) 34,000 dg **23.** $0.21 **25.** 3,500 kg per hour

Section 18.4

1. 32.81 ft. **3.** 1.77 in. **5.** 4,918.50 yds. **7.** 91.44 m **9.** 1.83 m **11.** 14.35 sq. yds. **13.** 1.54 sq. miles **15.** 108.72 acres **17.** 928.80 cm^2 **19.** 2.76 m^2 **21.** 6.34 quarts **23.** 4.22 gallons **25.** 136.26 liters **27.** 21.82 hl **29.** 20°C **31.** −45°C **33.** −6.7°C **35.** 95°F **37.** 14°F **39.** 46.4°F **41.** $1.16 per liter **43.** 3,306.93 lbs. per hour **45.** $0.26/lb. = $.57/kg; $0.55 per kg is better **47.** 91.54 cubic inches **49.** 200°C

Chapter 18 review test

1. 0.36 hm **2.** 16,000 liters **3.** 67.3 dg **4.** 2.23 dkl **5.** 71,200 cm **6.** 160,000 ares **7.** 267.49 t **8.** 7.2 hl, 72,000 cl **9.** 4,872 dkl, 487,200 dl **10.** 41.02 dkg, 41,020 cg **11.** $1 **12.** 5 **13.** 10°C **14.** 9.84 inches

Index

Boldface page numbers refer to entries within chapter glossaries.